THE OFFICIAL
BIGGEST
PUB
QUIZ
BOOK

Ever!
2

First published in 2001 by
Carlton Books Limited
20 Mortimer Street
London W1T 3JW

Second edition published in 2008

ISBN: 978 1 84732 105 3

Printed and bound in Great Britain

Questions set by The Puzzle House

This book is a compilation of *The Best Pub Quiz Book Ever! 3* and *The
Best Pub Quiz Book Ever! 4.*

THE OFFICIAL

BIGGEST PUB QUIZ BOOK

Ever! 2

SECOND EDITION

CARLTON
BOOKS

Contents

Introduction

Over the past decade snugs and lounges in pubs the length and breadth of the country have become, if not seats of learning at least seats of intellect. Which makes a change from seats of worn leatherette (although these still prevail in some areas). The pub quiz has transformed the bar into an arena of knowledge where beery brethren battle to the final bell. The format is simple: some friends, acquaintances, even complete strangers, will do, a questioner, some paper, a collection of ragged Biros and a surfeit of beer and questions are all that is needed to create the perfect evening's entertainment. Wits are challenged, heads are huddled and patience is tested as teams attempt to outdo each other in their show of trivia retention. At these events you will learn that no fact is too small, no sport star too obscure and no war too insignificant to test the pub crowd's grey matter. In fact, the more obscure and wide-ranging the questions the greater the chance of involving the entire barroom – nothing will gain the pub idiot greater respect than showing that they have the entire cast, storyline and signature tune of "Emergency Ward 10" lodged in their head, except perhaps their switching from slip-ons to lace-ups. So take heart, and a copy of *The Best Pub Quiz Book Ever! 2* to the boozer and have a few warm up sessions and see if you can't organize your own pub quiz. You know it makes sense; it's the only way you'll know all the answers.

The main aim of *The Best Pub Quiz Book Ever! 2* is to entertain, so it is important that you retain a sense of humour and good sportsmanship as you play along, whether you are testing friends at home or setting a quiz for your local hostelry. That aside, you also have to ensure that you are fully in control of your questions and players: remain calm, speak in a steady voice and be constantly unflapped when challenged by any of the more heavily imbibed, as indeed you will be.

If the locals do get testy your best bet is to head for the door while throwing beer nuts in the air to confuse them, though this should happen in only the roughest pubs or on outings with the extended family – in which case you should attempt to rescue your spouse, if you can do so without spilling your drink and it isn't them causing the trouble.

The Best Pub Quiz Book Ever! 2 is divided into three sections of Easy, Medium and Hard questions, which are all subdivided by specialist and pot-luck rounds. The former can be chosen either to help or hinder your players; giving Easy sports questions to the literature fanatics is bound to reveal some interesting answers but it is possibly more challenging to tailor your questions so that the experts receive the brain-wracking Hard questions and the novice the stupefyingly simple Easy questions. Nothing hurts a fanatic more than being beaten on their specialist subject and the division of questions gives you the chance to employ a handicap system. Other handicap systems will also become apparent as you continue as quiz master. The team that wins the Sunday-afternoon quiz will doubtless fail when it comes to Sunday night, although if you want to set a quiz on Friday night you should check pupil dilation first, as on that evening of great relaxation you may find your teams asleep or brawling before calling the whole thing quits and joining them in a drink … or three.

In the interest of further clarification there follows a brief run-down of each section:

Easy

In this primary round the main objective is to keep breathing, these questions are so easy that even the most docile pub idiot could gurgle his way through them in the time it takes to down a pint and still have time left to knock over the stack of pennies on the bar.

Medium

On your toes people, things are getting tricky. By now even the ringers on the out-of-towners' team will be sweating. These questions make for a challenge, but you are bound to get the odd smug bar steward who will fancy his chances, for which you should continue on to section three.

Hard

Ask a full thirty of these questions and only the shrill wail of the pub cat fighting in the yard will be heard, brows will be furrowed, glances exchanged and beer stared into. To set an entire quiz using just these questions is a form of evil so dark-hearted Fu Manchu would blanch.

All that is left to say is good luck with your testing and if you can't keep your spirits up at least try to keep them down.

The Easy Questions

If you think that Louis Armstrong was the first man on the moon or that Uri Geller was the first man in space then you will no doubt struggle through the next few questions terribly. For the rest of us though these are the EASY questions, so called because if the quizzee falters on these they are either three sheets to the wind or far too young to be in the pub – either state rendering them toddling buffoons whose social graces will equal their breadth of knowledge. So beware their flailing arms as you attempt to collect the answers.

These questions are perfect when used in the first round of an open entry quiz as they lull everyone into a false sense of security, although you must ensure that contestants don't shout answers out, which creates a problematic precedent for the later, harder questions. Another way of placing these questions is to dot them about throughout the quiz, thus making sure that on every team everyone should know the answer to at least one question despite their age.

If you are running a league quiz then some of your team members may heap derision on such obvious questions, but don't worry: even the cleverest quiz team member can come a cropper, as was noted in a championship final when a contestant was asked to name the continents. He deliberated before eventually beaming out the answer, "A, E, I, O, U!"

1 Which team did David Beckham play for when he married Victoria?
2 Ashley Cole married a singer from which band?
3 Coleen McLoughlin hails from which city?
4 Nancy Dell'Olio was whose girlfriend during the 2006 World Cup?
5 Which of Victoria and David Beckham's children went to their wedding?
6 Who was Wayne Rooney's fiancée when he was sent off in the World Cup?
7 Suzi Walker was the wife of which goalkeeper?
8 During 2006 Theo Walcott's girlfriend was studying for which exams?
9 What was Cheryl Cole's surname before she married Ashley?
10 What is the first name of Mrs Jamie Redknapp?
11 What does W stand for in WAGS?
12 What nationality is Frank Lampard's other half – French or Spanish?
13 Alex Curran is the mother of Lilly-Ella; which Steven is her dad?
14 What is the nationality of Thierry Henry's wife, French or English?
15 What is the profession of Sven Goran Eriksson's girlfriend Nancy?
16 Cheryl's first No. 1 hit was: "Sound of the" what?
17 Who was stripped of her Miss Great Britain title in 2006?
18 Which Carly was linked to Joe Cole?
19 Is Michael Owen's wife called Chardonnay or Louise?
20 Abbey Clancy was the girlfriend of which striker Peter?
21 Which of the 2006 WAGS was first to have a No. 1 single?
22 Coleen McLoughlin advertised which supermarket?
23 Which German town did the WAGS stay at for the 2006 World Cup?
24 Danielle Lloyd was linked with which former England striker?
25 Melanie Slade's name was linked with which Theo during 2006?
26 Elen Rives is linked to which England player?
27 Was Ms Zucker a fitness trainer or a lawyer?
28 Michaela Henderson-Thynne was linked with which Stewart?
29 Who wrote a fashion book called "That Extra Half Inch"?
30 Abbey Clancy launched a lingerie range with the daughter of which Rolling Stone?

Answers	Nature: Animal World *(see Quiz 2)*

1 (African) elephant. 2 Wolf. 3 Warm blooded. 4 Tooth. 5 Voice box. 6 Alone. 7 Primate. 8 Duck. 9 Dog. 10 Sheep. 11 Sight. 12 Offensive smell. 13 Brown. 14 (South) America. 15 Eye. 16 Hare. 17 Its ears. 18 Alaska. 19 Warm. 20 Carnivorous. 21 Cows. 22 Chimpanzee. 23 Neck. 24 Invertebrates. 25 One. 26 Tail. 27 Polar bear. 28 Milk. 29 Fingerprints. 30 Southern.

1 Which land mammal has the largest ears?
2 Which wild animal is the domesticated dog descended from?
3 Are mammals warm blooded or cold blooded?
4 Which part of the body has a crown and a root?
5 What is another name for the larynx?
6 Do tigers hunt in packs or alone?
7 Which group of animals shares its name with an archbishop?
8 What type of creature is an Aylesbury?
9 What was the first animal to be domesticated?
10 Cheviot and Suffolk are both types of what?
11 Shrews have acute sense of smell and hearing to compensate for which weak sense?
12 The opossum and the skunk are famous for what?
13 What colour is a grizzly bear?
14 The llama is native to which continent?
15 Which part of a human's body has a cornea?
16 A leveret is a young what?
17 What part of a Basset Hound is particularly long?
18 Which northerly US state is famous for the brown bear?
19 Does the moose live in a warm or cold climate?
20 Are crocodiles carnivorous or herbivores?
21 Which farm animals chew the cud?
22 Which primate species is the closest genetic cousin to humanity?
23 Where is a human's jugular vein?
24 Are most animals vertebrates or invertebrates?
25 How many young does a kangaroo usually produce at any one time?
26 What part of the body of a Manx cat is missing which is present on most other cats?
27 Which bear is the largest meat-eating land animal?
28 What do all mammals feed their babies on?
29 Which part of a human includes loops and whorls?
30 In which hemisphere do penguins live in the wild?

Answers	**WAGS** *(see Quiz 1)*

1 Manchester Utd. 2 Girls Aloud. 3 Liverpool. 4 Sven Goran Eriksson. 5 Brooklyn.
6 Coleen McLoughlin. 7 Ian Walker. 8 A levels. 9 Tweedy. 10 Louise. 11 Wives. 12
Spanish. 13 Gerrard. 14 French. 15 Lawyer. 16 Underground. 17 Danielle Lloyd. 18
Carly Zucker. 19 Louise. 20 Peter Crouch. 21 Victoria Beckham. 22 Asda. 23 Baden
Baden. 24 Teddy Sheringham. 25 Theo Walcott. 26 Frank Lampard. 27 Fitness trainer.
28 Stewart Downing. 29 Victoria Beckham. 30 Mick Jagger.

1 What is the surname of cop Maisie played by Pauline Quirke?
2 Michael French left which soap to become a Crime Traveller?
3 In "Murphy's Law", is Murphy named Mick, Pat or Tommy?
4 Which sleuth Jonathan was created by David Renwick?
5 Which early police serial is found at the end of the alphabet?
6 Which Yorkshire police series did Nick Berry leave in 1997?
7 In which county was "Dalziel & Pascoe" originally set?
8 "Dangerfield" deals with what type of police personnel?
9 David Suchet played which Belgian Agatha Christie detective?
10 In which English county does "Wycliffe" take place?
11 Which assistant to Morse was missing from the show in 1998?
12 Michael Gambon played which French detective in the 1990s?
13 How was "The Bill's" DC Lines, played by Kevin Lloyd, better known?
14 Which Glasgow detective was played by Mark McManus?
15 Which Hetty has a sidekick called Geoffrey?
16 What is the surname of detective Jack played by David Jason?
17 Which police station's blues were led by Captain Frank Furillo?
18 What is the first name of Commander Dalgliesh, created by PD James?
19 Which Jimmy starred in "Evita" and played Geordie Spender?
20 Which Victorian sleuth from Baker Street was played by Jeremy Brett?
21 In "Pie in the Sky", which profession did Henry combine with policing?
22 In which northern city was "City Central" set?
23 How is Cordelia Gray's creator Baroness James better known?
24 Which bald TV cop was "Friends" Jennifer Aniston's godfather?
25 In which series might DC Ben Jones be called on to help solve murders?
26 Where did Sonny Crockett aka Don Johnson sort out Vice?
27 Who has played Jack Regan and Morse?
28 In which city was "Cagney & Lacey" set?
29 Which crime buster show shared its name with insects?
30 In which city did Maigret operate?

Answers	Pot Luck 1 *(see Quiz 4)*

1 Drinks. 2 Bread & cheese. 3 Eminen. 4 The Sun. 5 Romantic. 6 Paris. 7 Exempt. 8 Middlesbrough. 9 Pyramids. 10 Sheep. 11 Gates. 12 Christmas. 13 Nile. 14 Dog. 15 Aberfan. 16 Lancashire. 17 Association. 18 Thistle. 19 Cattle. 20 80s. 21 Travel. 22 Wight. 23 Game. 24 Blanchett. 25 Hong Kong. 26 London. 27 Mont Blanc. 28 Pancakes. 29 29th. 30 Beijing.

1 What is usually sold at reduced prices during a happy hour?
2 What are the two main ingredients of a ploughman's lunch?
3 Whose 2005 collection of hits was called "Curtain Call"?
4 Which UK daily newspaper has the shortest name?
5 Dame Barbara Cartland is famous for what type of fiction?
6 In which city is the Louvre Museum?
7 What does the E stand for in the acronym TESSA?
8 Steve McClaren left which soccer club to become England boss?
9 Which surviving tombs were built for the Pharaohs of Egypt?
10 What type of animal was the first successful adult cloning?
11 Which Bill is the world's richest businessman?
12 Twelfth Night marks the end of which festive season?
13 On which river does Cairo stand?
14 What type of animal is a Chihuahua?
15 2006 marked the 40th anniversary of which Welsh mining village disaster?
16 Which county does TV detective Hetty Wainthropp come from?
17 In motoring terms, what does the second A in AA stand for?
18 What is the national emblem of Scotland?
19 What type of animal does BSE affect?
20 In which decade of the 20th century was Prince William born?
21 What sort of tickets would a bucket shop sell?
22 On which Isle is Parkhurst prison?
23 What is hopscotch?
24 Which actress Cate starred in the movie "Charlotte Gray"?
25 Which British colony returned to China in July 1997?
26 In which city did rhyming slang originate?
27 Which alpine peak's name means White Mountain?
28 Which food is traditionally eaten on Shrove Tuesday?
29 If August 31st was a Wednesday what date would August Bank Holiday Monday be in England?
30 In which city is Tiananmen Square?

Answers	TV: Cops & Robbers *(see Quiz 3)*

1 Raine. 2 EastEnders. 3 Tommy. 4 Jonathan Creek. 5 Z Cars. 6 Heartbeat. 7 Yorkshire. 8 Police surgeon. 9 Poirot. 10 Cornwall. 11 Lewis. 12 Maigret. 13 Tosh. 14 Taggart. 15 Wainthropp. 16 Frost. 17 Hill St. Blues. 18 Adam. 19 Nail. 20 Sherlock Holmes. 21 Chef. 22 Manchester. 23 PD James. 24 Kojak (Telly Savalas). 25 Midsomer Murders. 26 Miami. 27 John Thaw. 28 New York. 29 Bugs. 30 Paris.

1 Which movie actress's second marriage was to director Sam Mendes?
2 Raymond Blanc is famous for being what?
3 Which Betty became the House of Commons' first woman Speaker?
4 In 2006 where did Prince William start military training?
5 Which one time husband and wife actors were dubbed Ken and Em?
6 Which trendy homeware store did Terence Conran found in the 60s?
7 Which part of you would you ask Nicky Clarke to cut off?
8 How was Yorkshire-based murderer Peter Sutcliffe better known?
9 Which celebrity daughter was named after the song "Chelsea Morning"?
10 Which ex-Wimbledon champ did Andre Agassi marry?
11 Which 90s PM was in a university pop group called Ugly Rumours?
12 Who is taller, Kylie Minogue or Naomi Campbell?
13 Who launched Virgin Cola and Virgin PEPs ?
14 Which singer Sarah was once Mrs Andrew Lloyd Webber?
15 Which rock star became dad to Alistair at the age of 60 in 2005?
16 Which Monica was intimately associated with Bill Clinton?
17 Was Joan Collins born in the 1920s, 1930s or the 1940s?
18 Which ex-British party leader has the same first names as Bill Clinton?
19 Which model Jerry had a cameo role in "Batman"?
20 Did actress Gwyneth Paltrow call her daughter Apple, Banana or Peach?
21 Which London football club does David Mellor famously support?
22 Which Scot Andrew was the Sunday Times editor from 1983 to 1994?
23 John Prescott became Deputy Leader of which political party?
24 Which Prime Minister had twins called Mark and Carol?
25 The names Saatchi and Saatchi are associated with which industry?
26 Who was the last Beatle to marry twice?
27 What title does the brother of the late Princess Diana have?
28 What type of shops did Tim Waterstone found?
29 Which designer Vivienne is famous for her outrageous clothes?
30 What is the nickname of Royal "nanny" Alexandra Legge-Bourke?

Answers | Pot Luck 2 *(see Quiz 6)*

1 Donkey. 2 Italy. 3 80th. 4 Kirsty Young. 5 Poppy. 6 48. 7 Lah. 8 A calf. 9 China. 10 Frank Sinatra. 11 Chequered. 12 Gareth Gates. 13 C. 14 Bach. 15 Ellen MacArthur. 16 Orange. 17 11. 18 Blue. 19 Dublin. 20 Florence Nightingale. 21 Pumpkin. 22 Bill Haley & the Comets. 23 London. 24 Hans Christian Andersen. 25 The twins. 26 Shropshire. 27 Grapes. 28 Tennis. 29 Sound and noise. 30 Third World.

1 What kind of animal is Eeyore in the children's classic?
2 Which country produces Parmesan cheese?
3 The Queen celebrated which landmark birthday in 2006?
4 Which Kirsty replaced Sue Lawley on "Desert Island Discs"?
5 Which flower is linked with Remembrance Sunday?
6 How many sides are there in a dozen quadrilaterals?
7 Which note follows the musical note "soh"?
8 What name is given to a young elephant?
9 In which country was acupuncture developed?
10 Which singer was known affectionately as "Old Blue Eyes"?
11 Which flag in motor racing signals the end of the race?
12 Whose first album was "What My Heart Wants To Say"?
13 Which vitamin is found in oranges and lemons?
14 Which composer had the forenames Johann Sebastian?
15 In February 2005, who became the fastest female to sail solo around the world?
16 What kind of fruit is a satsuma?
17 How many players are in a hockey team?
18 What colour is the shade of cobalt?
19 The Abbey Theatre is in which Irish city?
20 Which nurse was called "The Lady with the Lamp"?
21 What was Cinderella's coach made from?
22 Who rocked around the clock in 1955?
23 Which zoo is found in Regent's Park?
24 Who wrote "The Ugly Duckling"?
25 What is the Zodiac sign Gemini also called?
26 Shrewsbury is the county town of which county?
27 Which fruit when dried produces raisins?
28 In which sport did Ivan Lendl achieve fame?
29 What is measured in decibels?
30 Underdeveloped countries are said to be which numerical world?

Answers	**Rich & Famous: Names** *(see Quiz 5)*

1 Kate Winslet. 2 Chef/Restaurateur. 3 Boothroyd. 4 Sandhurst. 5 Kenneth Branagh and Emma Thompson. 6 Habitat. 7 Hair. 8 Yorkshire Ripper. 9 Chelsea Clinton. 10 Steffi Graf. 11 Tony Blair. 12 Naomi Campbell. 13 Richard Branson. 14 Brightman. 15 Rod Stewart. 16 Lewinsky. 17 1930s. 18 William Jefferson Hague. 19 Hall. 20 Apple. 21 Chelsea. 22 Neil. 23 Labour. 24 Margaret Thatcher. 25 Advertising. 26 Paul McCartney. 27 Earl Spencer. 28 Bookshops. 29 Westwood. 30 Tiggy.

1 Messrs Docherty, Atkinson and Ferguson have all managed which team?
2 Who was the first football boss to marry one of her former players?
3 Who stood down at Charlton in 2006 after more than ten years as manager?
4 Which Stanley was first winner of the European Footballer of the Year award?
5 Which was the first Rovers side to win the Premiership?
6 Graham Taylor was likened to a turnip after a defeat in which Scandinavian country?
7 Whom did Ruud Gullit replace as manager of Newcastle Utd?
8 In which Asian country did Gary Lineker play club soccer?
9 What colour are the stripes on Newcastle Utd's first choice shirts?
10 Which side moved from Roker Park to the Stadium of Light?
11 Was Alan Shearer sold to Newcastle for £5 million, £15 million or £25 million?
12 In which country was George Best born?
13 What is the nationality of Dennis Bergkamp?
14 Which Premiership keeper fractured his skull in a game in 2006?
15 Which manager took Wigan into the Premiership for the first time?
16 Which Yorkshire side was involved in a plane crash in March 1988?
17 Which Paul was the first black player to captain England?
18 Who was known as El Tel when he managed Barcelona?
19 Who in 1997 became Arsenal's all-time leading goal scorer?
20 How is the Football Association Challenge Cup better known?
21 Which Welshman Ian said living in Italy was like "living in a foreign country"?
22 Which club Charlton were promoted to the Premier League in 1998?
23 Which colour links shirts at Liverpool, Middlesbrough and Southampton?
24 Which Brian managed Notts Forest for 18 years?
25 Gareth Southgate finished his playing career at which club?
26 Which Charlton brother was the first to be knighted?
27 Which Eric was the first overseas PFA Player of the Year winner?
28 Who was dubbed Duncan Disorderly?
29 Paul Le Guen took over as boss of which Scottish giants?
30 Which club did Martin O'Neill manage after Celtic?

1 Vienna is the capital of which European country?
2 What name is given to a young deer?
3 Which fruit when dried produces prunes?
4 Who claimed the F1 motor racing world championship in 2005 and 2006?
5 Which duo won the NTA's Most Popular TV presenters five times at the start of this century?
6 Which musical note follows ray?
7 What do you find in a bunker on a golf course?
8 Who wrote "The Tale of Peter Rabbit"?
9 Winchester is the county town of which county?
10 What is the name of the French National Anthem?
11 Which animal was Androcles very friendly with?
12 Which black wood is used for piano keys?
13 Which island is affectionately called the Emerald Isle?
14 In which sport is the Ryder Cup competed for?
15 What type of creature is Arthur in the CBBC series of the same name?
16 Which animal is linked with the Zodiac sign Taurus?
17 Which town is home to the Bayeux Tapestry?
18 What kind of meat can be silverside and topside?
19 What is the unit of currency in Italy?
20 What is the name of the Queen's youngest son?
21 How many notes are there in an octave?
22 What do you measure with a protractor?
23 The album "Friday's Child" was a No. 1 for which artist?
24 What is it said an ostrich does, if it thinks it is in danger?
25 After a selling price, what do the initials O.N.O. stand for?
26 Which type of soup is a consommé?
27 What colour is magenta?
28 What type of fruit is an Orange Pippin?
29 Which London-based football club are known as "The Hammers"?
30 In which county is Sherwood Forest?

1 The art of self-defence aikido originated in which country?
2 Which Bank Holiday comes immediately before Easter Day?
3 In which country was the 2006 Ryder Cup held?
4 Where might you be entertained by a redcoat?
5 Which reptiles feature in a popular board game?
6 Which is bigger, Disneyland or Disneyworld?
7 What do you play baccarat with?
8 Which leisure park Towers are near Stoke on Trent?
9 In which game is the object to gain checkmate?
10 What is the minimum number of players in a cribbage game?
11 Which quiz board game involves the collection of coloured wedges?
12 Brass rubbing usually takes place in what type of building?
13 Charles and Camilla shared their wedding day with which major sporting event?
14 In which English city could you watch Rovers and City play soccer?
15 Which part of a pub shares its name with an area of a law court?
16 Which End of London is famous for its theatres?
17 Microlighting takes place in what sort of craft?
18 What name is given to the hours that a pub can open to sell alcohol?
19 What type of music is celebrated at the CMA awards?
20 What colour is the L on a normal learner driver's L plate?
21 What sort of accommodation is provided in a B & B?
22 Knitting needs needles, what does crochet need?
23 Which pier is to the north of Blackpool's central pier?
24 What type of castle do young children enjoy jumping up and down on?
25 "The dogs" involves races of which breed?
26 What colour are the segments on a roulette wheel?
27 Which Planet is a celebrity-founded restaurant chain?
28 What colour are Scrabble tiles?
29 Which gambling game's best hand is Royal flush?
30 What colour is the M on the McDonalds logo?

Answers | Pot Luck 4 (see Quiz 10)

1 Green. 2 Fish. 3 Friar Tuck. 4 Bananarama. 5 Leo. 6 Scissor Sisters. 7 Public Limited Company. 8 Switzerland. 9 Bear. 10 Alexandra. 11 April. 12 76. 13 Pancakes. 14 On board ship. 15 A snake. 16 Belgium. 17 Yellow/orange. 18 Apple. 19 George Orwell. 20 Isle of Wight. 21 1960s. 22 Before they're hatched. 23 Holland. 24 Saturday. 25 A pup. 26 Malta. 27 Dark. 28 Eucalyptus leaves. 29 White coffee. 30 The Tower of London.

1 If you mix blue and yellow paint what colour is made?
2 What is usually eaten with Tartare Sauce?
3 Who was Robin Hood's priest?
4 Which 1980s girl group came back in 2005 with "Move In My Direction"?
5 Which sign of the Zodiac is normally shown as a lion?
6 Which Sisters made the album "Ta-Dah"?
7 What do the initials plc stand for after a company name?
8 Berne is the capital of which European country?
9 What type of creature was Baloo in "The Jungle Book"?
10 Which London palace is also called "Ally Pally"?
11 St George's Day is in which month?
12 How many trombones led the big parade according to the song?
13 What are Crêpes Suzettes a type of?
14 Where does a purser usually work?
15 What is a black mamba?
16 Which country does tennis star Kim Clijsters come from – Belgium or Holland?
17 What colour is ochre?
18 What kind of fruit is a russet?
19 Who wrote the novel "Animal Farm"?
20 On which island is Osborne House, home of Queen Victoria?
21 In which decade did Yuri Gagarin become the first man in space?
22 When must you not count your chickens, according to the proverb?
23 Which country makes Gouda cheese?
24 What day of the week is the Jewish Sabbath?
25 What name is given to a young seal?
26 Which island was awarded the George Cross in 1942?
27 Is presenter Carol Vorderman's hair light or dark?
28 What does a koala have for its main source of food?
29 What is cafe au lait?
30 Where are the Crown Jewels kept?

Answers | Hobbies & Leisure 1 *(see Quiz 9)*

1 Japan. 2 Good Friday. 3 Ireland. 4 Holiday camp (Butlin's). 5 Snakes (& ladders).
6 Disneyworld. 7 Cards. 8 Alton Towers. 9 Chess. 10 Two. 11 Trivial Pursuits.
12 Churches. 13 Grand National. 14 Bristol. 15 Bar. 16 West End. 17 Plane. 18
Licensing hours. 19 Country music. 20 Red. 21 Bed & breakfast. 22 Hook. 23 North
pier. 24 Bouncy castle. 25 Greyhounds. 26 Red, black. 27 Hollywood. 28 Cream.
29 Poker. 30 Yellow.

1 Which Spice Girl advertised Milky Bars as a child?
2 Was Billie Piper 10, 15 or 20 when she first went to No. 1?
3 Which Tina sang the title song from "Whistle Down the Wind"?
4 Who put her famous Union Jack dress up for auction?
5 Who had a No. 1 single with "Toxic"?
6 How many girls made up N-Tyce?
7 Janet and La Toyah are from which famous family?
8 What is the first name of the Welsh singer from Catatonia?
9 Whose album "Always and Forever" gives a clue to their name?
10 Which 60s singer's first hit was written by the Rolling Stones?
11 Heather Small found fame with which band?
12 What is the surname of sisters Kylie and Dannii?
13 Who made the big-selling album "J.LO"?
14 Whose third No. 1 was titled "Day & Night"?
15 Where do Scary Spice and Princess Anne's daughter have a stud?
16 Who share their name with an Egyptian queen?
17 Which Aussie soap did Natalie Imbruglia appear in?
18 How many singers make up B*witched?
19 How did the Bangles Walk?
20 Shaznay is in which all-girl band?
21 Which 60s singer hosted "Surprise Surprise"?
22 Which Capstan sang with the B52s and guested with REM?
23 Who was the lead singer for Blondie?
24 Which musical instrument is Vanessa Mae famous for?
25 Which musical star Alicia sang before the 2005 Super Bowl?
26 Alanis Morissette and Celine Dion are from which country?
27 Who sang about "Baboushka" and "Wuthering Heights"?
28 In which decade did Bananarama have their first hit?
29 Miss Nurding dropped her surname and became known as whom?
30 Which singing star married Kevin Federline?

Answers | **Pot Luck 5** *(see Quiz 12)*

1 July. 2 Bull/cow. 3 Cider. 4 Michael Palin. 5 A savoury snack. 6 1969. 7 Venice. 8 Mount Ararat. 9 Forbidden fruit. 10 A will. 11 France. 12 Norwich City. 13 Vincent van Gogh. 14 Aries. 15 Calligraphy. 16 Harley Street. 17 Pinocchio. 18 Tanks. 19 Friday. 20 A bird. 21 David Gray. 22 Cherry. 23 17. 24 September. 25 Devon. 26 Baptism. 27 Cameron. 28 Tottenham Hotspur. 29 Hippopotamus. 30 Colin Firth.

1 St Swithin's Day is in which summer month?
2 Who or what is an Aberdeen Angus?
3 What drink did writer Laurie Lee share with Rosie?
4 Which ex-Python Palin published his diaries in autumn 2006?
5 What are pretzels?
6 Did man first land on the moon in 1966, 1969 or 1972?
7 In which Italian city is St Mark's cathedral?
8 On which Mount is the resting place of Noah's Ark?
9 Which fruit tastes sweetest according to the proverb?
10 What does a testator make, in law?
11 Which country produces Camembert cheese?
12 Which football team is known as "The Canaries"?
13 Which Dutch painter cut off his ear?
14 Which Zodiac sign is normally associated with the ram?
15 What is the study of handwriting called?
16 Which London street is associated with the medical profession?
17 Which wooden puppet was written about by Carlo Collodi?
18 Shermans, Grants and Cromwells are all types of what?
19 Which day of the week is the Muslim Holy Day?
20 What is a quail?
21 Who had a No. 1 album with "A New Day at Midnight"?
22 Which fruit is used to make kirsch?
23 How old should you be to apply for a car driving licence in the UK?
24 In what month is Michaelmas Day?
25 Which county has Exeter as its county town?
26 For which religious ceremony is a font normally used?
27 ROMANCE is an anagram of the surname of which political leader?
28 Michael Carrick joined Man Utd from which other Premiership side?
29 Which animal has a name which means "river horse"?
30 Which Colin starred in the movie "Hope Springs"?

Answers	**Pop Divas** *(see Quiz 11)*

1 Emma (Baby Spice). 2 15. 3 Tina Arena. 4 Geri Halliwell. 5 Britney Spears. 6 Four. 7 Jackson. 8 Nerys. 9 Eternal. 10 Marianne Faithfull. 11 M People. 12 Minogue. 13 Jennifer Lopez. 14 Billie Piper. 15 Tongue. 16 Cleopatra. 17 Home & Away. 18 Four. 19 Like an Egyptian. 20 All Saints. 21 Cilla Black. 22 Kate. 23 Debbie Harry. 24 Violin. 25 Alicia Keys. 26 Canada. 27 Kate Bush. 28 1980s. 29 Louise. 30 Britney Spears.

1 Which early Spielberg blockbuster was about a shark?
2 What was Daniel Craig's first movie as James Bond?
3 In which 1990s musical film did Madonna change costume 85 times?
4 What was the name of the movie based on TV's "The X Files"?
5 Which Julianne played opposite Anthony Hopkins in "Hannibal"?
6 Martin Scorsese made a film about the Gangs Of which city?
7 "The Fellowship of the Ring" was based on which book?
8 Which creatures dominated "Jurassic Park"?
9 What was "Crocodile Dundee's" homeland?
10 "Hook" was based on which children's book?
11 Which lizard-like monster's name is a mix of the Japanese words for gorilla and whale?
12 Who left Kramer in the 1970s movie with Hoffman and Streep?
13 "From Here to Eternity" is set before the Japanese attack on where?
14 "Raging Bull" was about which sport?
15 Which film was an abbreviation of Extra Terrestrial?
16 "The Empire Strikes Back" was a sequel to what?
17 "Raiders of the Lost Ark" was about which Mr Jones?
18 Robin Hood was Prince of what in the 1991 blockbuster?
19 Was "Snow White and the Seven Dwarfs" released before or after World War II?
20 Where was Gary Oldman Lost in the 1998 hit movie?
21 Which Caped Crusader was the subject of one of the top 1980s films?
22 Which watery film succeeded "Waterworld" as the most costly to make?
23 Gene Kelly was An American ... where in the Vincente Minnelli movie?
24 Which star of "Grease" and "Saturday Night Fever" is a qualified pilot?
25 Was "The Sting" a hit in the 1950s, 70s or 90s?
26 Which Disney animal movie was a 1994 blockbuster set in Africa?
27 "Amadeus" told the story of which composer?
28 "Home Alone" shot which child star to fame?
29 Was "Schindler's List" in colour or black and white?
30 Which Kevin played Mariner in "Waterworld"?

Answers	Pot Luck 6 *(see Quiz 14)*

1 Switzerland. 2 Charles. 3 Golden Hind. 4 The Gondoliers. 5 Thrillers. 6 Fleet Street. 7 Suffolk. 8 V-shaped. 9 St Patrick. 10 Pisces. 11 50 Cent. 12 16 years. 13 4. 14 Darren Gough. 15 Reindeer. 16 Golf. 17 Iain Dowie. 18 Rome. 19 Alpha. 20 A dog. 21 France. 22 Lawn. 23 Herbs. 24 Green. 25 Small Island. 26 A newspaper. 27 Eel. 28 Seaweed. 29 The Sound of Music. 30 Dorchester.

1 Which country produces Gruyère cheese?

2 Who was invested as Prince of Wales in 1969?

3 Francis Drake's ship Pelican was renamed what?

4 Which opera by Gilbert and Sullivan is set in Venice?

5 Did John Le Carré write thrillers or romantic fiction?

6 Which London Street was home to several British newspapers?

7 Which county has Ipswich as its county town?

8 What shape are the teeth on pinking shears?

9 Which Saint is commemorated on the 17th of March?

10 Which Zodiac sign is normally associated with two fishes?

11 In March 2005 who had three singles in the same US top five?

12 What is the minimum age for leaving school in England?

13 In snooker, how many points is the brown ball worth?

14 Who was the first cricketer to win TV's "Strictly Come Dancing"?

15 What kind of animals were Cupid, Donner and Blitzen?

16 In which sport would you use a caddie?

17 Which manager moved across London from Crystal Palace to Charlton in 2006?

18 According to the proverb, which Italian city was not built in a day?

19 What is the first letter of the Greek alphabet?

20 What is a Shih-Tzu?

21 Which country does the wine claret come from?

22 In tennis, what does the initial L in LTA stand for?

23 What kind of plants are sage, lovage and basil?

24 Which London park is the name of a colour?

25 Andrea Levy wrote the award-winning novel titled "Small" what?

26 If you bought "Le Figaro" in France what would you be buying?

27 An elver is a young what?

28 What is kelp?

29 Which film featured the Von Trapp Family?

30 What is the county town of Dorset?

Answers	The Movies: Blockbusters (see Quiz 13)

1 Jaws. 2 Casino Royale. 3 Evita. 4 The X Files. 5 Julianne Moore. 6 New York. 7 The Lord of the Rings. 8 Dinosaurs. 9 Australia. 10 Peter Pan. 11 Godzilla. 12 Kramer. 13 Pearl Harbor. 14 Boxing. 15 E.T. 16 Star Wars. 17 Indiana Jones. 18 Thieves. 19 Before. 20 Space. 21 Batman. 22 Titanic. 23 Paris. 24 John Travolta. 25 70s. 26 The Lion King. 27 Mozart. 28 Macaulay Culkin. 29 Black & white. 30 Costner.

1 Did Mourinho join Chelsea in 2000, 2002 or 2004?
2 Which club was Damian Duff sold to in 2006?
3 Mourinho was dubbed the "special" what?
4 Who was skipper of Jose's first Premiership-winning side?
5 Shaun Wright-Phillips was bought from which City club?
6 Which country does Claude Makelele play for?
7 Which midfielder was top scorer in 2005 and 2006?
8 Petr Cech keeps goal for which international Republic?
9 Who went to Arsenal when Ashley Cole came to Chelsea?
10 Mourinho joined Chelsea from which Portuguese club?
11 Who was not signed by Jose – Michael Ballack, Michael Essien or John Terry?
12 Does Crespo play for Argentina or Russia?
13 Joe Cole and Frank Lampard were at which other London club?
14 Carvalho and Ferreira play for which European country?
15 Who bankrolled Chelsea's success?
16 Which Carlo was number-two keeper in 2005 and 2006?
17 Does Andriy Shevchenko play for, Bulgaria or the Ukraine?
18 Was Mourinho born in the 1940s, 1960s or 1970s?
19 Which Claudio was boss before Mourinho?
20 Which English team dumped Chelsea out of 2005's Champions League?
21 Who, in November 2006, beat Chelsea at home for the first time in 19 seasons?
22 Scott Parker moved on to which club?
23 Does Michael Essien play for France or Ghana?
24 When did Chelsea last win the league before 2005 – 1930s or 1950s?
25 Which Chelsea player Wayne has a link to the ground name?
26 Which Liverpool boss was part of the "no handshake" row?
27 Adrian Mutu's contract was cancelled after a scandal involving what?
28 Did Mourinho first win the League Cup or the FA Cup?
29 Arjen Robben plays international soccer with which country?
30 Which Norwegian club held Chelsea to a draw in what became Mourinho's final match?

Answers	Pot Luck 7 *(see Quiz 16)*

1 Tax. 2 Insects. 3 The Boy Scout Movement. 4 Shrove Tuesday. 5 Pink. 6 Sagittarius.
7 Gorillaz. 8 Badger. 9 Hungary. 10 Romeo and Juliet. 11 England. 12 Egypt. 13
Little Acorns. 14 Nazareth. 15 A tutu. 16 The Simpsons. 17 Clouds. 18 In water. 19
Wood. 20 John Cleese. 21 Ontario. 22 Adolf Hitler. 23 Chelsea. 24 Blood. 25 Venice.
26 Silence. 27 Warwickshire. 28 A toad. 29 Gladys Knight. 30 Blonde.

1 What does T stand for in the initials V.A.T.?
2 What does a Venus fly-trap trap?
3 Which movement was founded by Lord Baden-Powell?
4 What day precedes Ash Wednesday?
5 In snooker, is the pink ball or the brown ball of higher value?
6 Which sign of the Zodiac is pictured by an archer?
7 "Dare" was the first No. 1 single for which band?
8 Which animal is often given the name Brock?
9 In which country was the first series of "Robin Hood" with Jonas Armstrong filmed?
10 Which Shakespeare play features the Capulets and Montagues?
11 Which country was called Albion by Greeks and Romans?
12 In which country is the battle site of El Alamein?
13 Great oak trees grow from what, according to the proverb?
14 Which town did Jesus grow up in?
15 What is the name of the dress worn by a ballerina?
16 Which long-running TV series features Marge and Homer?
17 Stratus, Cirrus and Cumulus are all types of what?
18 Where do mosquitoes lay their eggs?
19 What are clogs traditionally made from?
20 Which actor played Basil Fawlty in "Fawlty Towers"?
21 Toronto is the capital of which Canadian province?
22 Who wrote "Mein Kampf"?
23 Which football team plays at Stamford Bridge?
24 What do your arteries carry from your heart?
25 In which northern Italian city is the Doge's Palace?
26 If speech is silver, what is golden according to the proverb?
27 Which county cricket team plays at Edgbaston?
28 What is a natterjack?
29 Which Gladys sang the theme song to the 007 movie "Licence to Kill"?
30 Was Renee Zellwegger a blonde or brunette in "Bridget Jones's Diary"?

Answers | **Mourinho's Chelsea** *(see Quiz 15)*

1 2004. 2 Newcastle United. 3 "The Special One". 4 John Terry. 5 Manchester City. 6 France. 7 Frank Lampard. 8 Czech Republic. 9 William Gallas. 10 Porto. 11 Terry. 12 Argentina. 13 West Ham. 14 Portugal. 15 Roman Abramovich. 16 Carlo Cudicini. 17 Ukraine. 18 1960s. 19 Claudio Ranieri. 20 Liverpool. 21 Tottenham Hotspur. 22 Newcastle United. 23 Ghana. 24 1950s (1955). 25 Wayne Bridge. 26 Rafael Benitez. 27 Drug taking. 28 League Cup. 29 Holland. 30 Rosenborg.

1 Which detective did Dr Watson assist?

2 The cover of Peter Kay's "The Sound of Laughter" is a spoof of which film poster?

3 Mrs Beeton was most famous for writing on what subject?

4 Are Penguin books hardbacks or paperbacks?

5 Was St Trinian's a school for boys or girls?

6 What type of animal is Winnie the Pooh?

7 What relation was Charlotte to Emily and Anne Brontë?

8 Who is Agatha Christie's most famous female detective?

9 What is the name of the book of scripts from "The Catherine Tate Show"?

10 In which building does the murder take place at the start of "The Da Vinci Code"?

11 Who's "Winter Collection" of recipes sold 1.5 million copies in just eight weeks?

12 What sort of Factory is associated with Roald Dahl's Charlie?

13 In which book are there four accounts of Jesus's life called gospels?

14 Which African president's autobiography was called "Long Walk to Freedom"?

15 Who wrote "Cook with Jamie"?

16 What was "Schindler's Ark" renamed when it was made into a film?

17 Where was Douglas Adams' Hitchhiker's Guide to?

18 What type of tales did the Grimm brothers write?

19 What is the nationality of novelist Maeve Binchy?

20 Which novelist Dame Catherine died in 1998?

21 Who wrote "And It's Goodnight from Him..." about himself and his late comedy partner?

22 Who was Ian Fleming's most famous secret agent creation?

23 Whom did Laurie Lee write of Cider with...?

24 Which soccer coach's World Cup Story 1998 caused an outrage over breaches of confidentiality?

25 Which Stephen is famous for horror writing such as "The Shining"?

26 What was Dick Francis's profession before he turned to writing?

27 What was Bram Stoker's most famous monstrous creation?

28 In which century did Charles Dickens live?

29 Which comedian Ben wrote "Gridlock" and "Popcorn"?

30 Which Frederick's first success was "The Day of the Jackal"?

Answers	Pot Luck 8 *(see Quiz 18)*

1 November. 2 The tail. 3 Elvis Presley. 4 An alkali. 5 A small wood. 6 Hamlet. 7 Angels. 8 Conservatives. 9 Afrikaans. 10 Kenya. 11 Willow. 12 Seven. 13 An eyrie. 14 Threadneedle Street. 15 Doncaster. 16 The Osbournes. 17 £1. 18 Ballet. 19 Violet. 20 Adder. 21 Nepal. 22 Agoraphobia. 23 Mercury. 24 Pasta. 25 Spencer. 26 The Hours. 27 Norwich. 28 A news agency. 29 Mars. 30 Bolton.

Quiz 18 | Pot Luck 8 | Answers – page 27 | LEVEL 1

1 In which month is Thanksgiving celebrated in America?
2 Where is the rattle in a rattlesnake?
3 Whose "Are You Lonesome Tonight" was back in the UK charts in 2005?
4 What is the opposite of an acid?
5 What is a spinney?
6 Who said, "To be or not to be, that is the question"?
7 In the Bible, what were seraphim and cherubim?
8 Which political party had Benjamin Disraeli as a leader?
9 Which South African language derives from the Dutch settlers?
10 Which country has Nairobi as its capital?
11 Cricket bats are traditionally made from which wood?
12 How many colours are in the spectrum?
13 What name is given to the home of an eagle?
14 On which Street is the Bank of England?
15 The St Leger is run at which Yorkshire race course?
16 Which real rock family includes Ozzy, Sharon and Kelly?
17 Which coin was first introduced in the UK in 1983?
18 For what type of dancing did Anna Pavlova achieve fame?
19 What colour is an amethyst?
20 What is the only poisonous snake in Britain?
21 Which country is native homeland to the Gurkha troops?
22 Which phobia is the fear of open spaces?
23 Which chemical is also known as quicksilver?
24 Penne, rigatoni and tagliatelle are all types of what?
25 What did the initial "S" stand for in Winston S. Churchill?
26 Did Nicole Kidman win an Oscar for "The Days", "The Hours" or "The Weeks"?
27 Which Norfolk city stands on the River Wensum?
28 What is Reuters?
29 Who was god of war in Roman mythology?
30 Diouf and Anelka played for Liverpool and which other English soccer club?

Answers | **Leisure: Books** *(see Quiz 17)*

1 Sherlock Holmes. 2 The Sound of Music. 3 Cooking. 4 Paperbacks. 5 Girls. 6 Bear. 7 Sister. 8 Miss Marple. 9 Am I Bovvered. 10 Louvre. 11 Delia Smith. 12 Chocolate. 13 Bible. 14 Nelson Mandela. 15 Jamie Oliver. 16 Schindler's List. 17 The Galaxy. 18 Fairy tales. 19 Irish. 20 Cookson. 21 Ronnie Corbett. 22 James Bond. 23 Rosie. 24 Glenn Hoddle. 25 King. 26 Jockey. 27 Dracula. 28 19th. 29 Elton. 30 Forsyth.

1 Mark Spitz won seven Olympic golds at record speeds doing what?
2 Which South American soccer team has won most World Cups?
3 How many seasons did Alan Shearer play for Newcastle – 3, 6 or 10?
4 Lyn Davies broke the British record in which jump event?
5 David Campese was leading try scorer for which country?
6 Which Sally was a world record hurdler and 1992 Olympic champion?
7 Who was made England's youngest ever football coach in 1996?
8 Did Roger Bannister run the first four-minute mile in Oxford or Cambridge?
9 Was Martina Hingis 13, 15 or 17 when she first won Wimbledon doubles?
10 Who was the first Rugby Union player to win 100 England caps?
11 Which Nigel was the first to win both F1 and Indy Car world championships?
12 Which record breaker Sebastian went on to become a Tory MP?
13 Which Tony made the first televised hole in one in Britain?
14 Who won the 100m in Seoul in record time before being disqualified?
15 Which Steve was six times World Snooker Champion in the 1980s?
16 For which former Iron Curtain country did Marita Koch break records?
17 Jerry Rice set a career touchdown record in which sport?
18 How many events were in Daley Thompson's speciality event?
19 Which Pete equalled Borg's five Wimbledon singles wins in 1998?
20 Which Gareth became Wales's youngest ever Rugby captain in 1968?
21 Alain Prost was the first to win the F1 world title for which country?
22 Bob Beaman held which Olympic jump record for over 20 years?
23 Who was Britain's only Men's 100m world record holder between 1983 and 1993?
24 Which David did Graham Gooch overtake to become England's highest-scoring Test player?
25 World record breaker Kip Keino is from which continent?
26 Did Nadia Comaneci first score a perfect Olympic 10 at 14, 18 or 21?
27 Which golfer Jack was first to achieve 15 career professional majors?
28 Colin Jackson was a world record holder in which event?
29 Who was the first player to score 100 goals in the Premiership?
30 Duncan Goodhew held British records in which sport?

---

1 Which snooker star Paul tragically died of cancer in October 2006?
2 Which alcoholic drink contains juniper as a flavour?
3 By what name is the mausoleum at Agra, India normally known?
4 Which dogs are a serious pest in Australia?
5 What would your profession be if you were a member of Equity?
6 Which instruments did Antonio Stradivari produce?
7 Which country is famous for moussaka?
8 In which month is Father's Day in the UK?
9 Pontoon and suspension are both types of which construction?
10 What did the "M" stand for in Louisa M. Alcott's name?
11 Who had the 2005 No. 1 single "Sometimes You Can't Make It on Your Own"?
12 What is a salary paid to a clergyman called?
13 What colour is cochineal?
14 The British Standards Institute uses what mark as a sign of approval?
15 Which American city is served by Kennedy Airport?
16 Which bird has the largest wing span?
17 Which soap is set in the city which hosted the 2002 Commonwealth Games?
18 What kind of drink is Amontillado?
19 What does an early bird catch, according to the proverb?
20 Which Beatle's daughter is a dress designer?
21 Bloomers and baps are both types of what?
22 How many years are there in four and a half decades?
23 Where are your incisors?
24 Who, together with Tim Rice, wrote "Evita"?
25 Where is Lord Nelson buried?
26 On a staircase are the risers flat or vertical?
27 Paddy Kenny was an ever present as which club reached the Premiership?
28 What are the two ingredients of marzipan?
29 Billy Graham is famous for which branch of Christianity?
30 Which black and white bird is usually accused of stealing?

Answers	**Sport: Record Breakers** *(see Quiz 19)*

1 Swimming. 2 Brazil. 3 10 years. 4 Long jump. 5 Australia. 6 Gunnell. 7 Glenn Hoddle. 8 Oxford. 9 15. 10 Jason Leonard. 11 Mansell. 12 Coe. 13 Jacklin. 14 Ben Johnson. 15 Davis. 16 East Germany. 17 American football. 18 Ten. 19 Sampras. 20 Edwards. 21 France. 22 Long jump. 23 Linford Christie. 24 Gower. 25 Africa. 26 14. 27 Jack Nicklaus. 28 Hurdles. 29 Alan Shearer. 30 Swimming.

1 Is 0207 the dialling code for central Manchester or central London?
2 Which mobile phone company shares its name with a fruit?
3 If you dial 1471 whose number are you given?
4 Which four letters preface access to an Internet website?
5 What is the normal size of a floppy disk?
6 NDR is a broadcasting company from which country?
7 What are held in the hands to communicate through semaphore?
8 The fingertips represent which five letters in sign language?
9 112 is an alternative to which number?
10 A modem connects a computer to what?
11 Qantas Airways originated in which country?
12 Which cross-Channel link has its French terminus at Coquelles?
13 Tresco airport links which Isles to the UK?
14 What does a letter c enclosed in a circle stand for?
15 Which country has most Internet users in the world?
16 What does D stand for in IDD?
17 Which character divides the person from the place in an email address?
18 Which type of clock works from shadows?
19 Numbers beginning with 0800 usually cost how much to the caller?
20 On a standard keyboard which letter is to the right of Q?
21 Combinations of which two signs are used in Morse code?
22 What country are PanAm based in?
23 In texting what does TMI stand for?
24 Which number do you ring to contact a BT operator?
25 Which country's airline has the code PK?
26 What is the American version of the British post code?
27 With BT calls when does daytime end Monday to Friday?
28 What does "I" stand for in IT?
29 What is the internet code for the United Kingdom?
30 Ryan Air is a budget airline from which country?

Answers	Pot Luck 10 *(see Quiz 22)*

1 Pastry. 2 Mr Hyde. 3 Jewellery. 4 Red. 5 Loudspeakers. 6 Marriage. 7 Flamingo.
8 Table Mountain. 9 The Rank Organisation. 10 Three. 11 Senorita. 12 Russia. 13
Wolves. 14 Disraeli. 15 Dame Edna Everage. 16 Hong Kong. 17 Church/Cathedral.
18 Agenda. 19 Andrew. 20 Three. 21 Pears. 22 Shrew. 23 The Mayflower. 24
Helen Mirren. 25 Green. 26 Wuthering Heights. 27 Bridgetown. 28 Sultana. 29
Penultimate. 30 Hammer.

1 Choux, puff and short are all types of what?
2 Who was the more unpleasant – Dr Jekyll or Mr Hyde?
3 Generally what is Hatton Gardon in London famous for?
4 What colour is carmine?
5 What are tweeters and woofers?
6 Which ceremony is associated with orange blossom?
7 Which pink bird sleeps on one leg?
8 Which mountain overlooks Cape Town, South Africa?
9 Which British film company used a symbol of a man striking a gong?
10 How many of Will Young's first singles made No. 1?
11 What is the Spanish word for a young or single lady?
12 Where was the news agency Tass based?
13 At which club did Mick McCarthy take over from Glenn Hoddle?
14 Who was the first Jewish Prime Minister in Britain?
15 Comedian Barry Humphries plays which female character?
16 Which colony ceased to be British in June 1997?
17 Where would you be if you were in a transept?
18 What is the list of the subjects to be discussed at a meeting called?
19 Which Prince served in the Falklands War?
20 In the old saying, how many makes a crowd if two are company?
21 Conference and Cornice are types of which fruit?
22 Which animal needs "Taming" in the title of the Shakespeare play?
23 Aboard which ship in 1620 did the Pilgrim Fathers sail to America?
24 Which Helen was a star of the movie "Gosford Park"?
25 What colour is angelica?
26 What connects singer Kate Bush with novelist Emily Brontë?
27 What is the capital of Barbados?
28 What is a wife of a sultan called?
29 What word describes something being next to last?
30 Which British studios were famed for their horror movies of the 1950s, 60s and 70s?

| **Answers** | **Science: Communications** *(see Quiz 21)* |

1 London. 2 Orange. 3 Last person to have called you. 4 http (not all have www).
5 3.5ins. 6 Germany. 7 Flags. 8 Vowels. 9 999. 10 Telephone. 11 Australia.
12 Channel Tunnel. 13 Scilly Isles. 14 Copyright. 15 USA. 16 Dialling. 17 @. 18
Sundial. 19 Nothing. 20 W. 21 Dots & dashes. 22 USA. 23 Too Much Information.
24 100. 25 Pakistan. 26 Zip. 27 6 pm. 28 Information. 29 .uk. 30 Ireland.

1 Which country did Abba come from?
2 Which 70s pop movie with John Travolta was re-released in 1998?
3 Which band did Diana Ross leave at the start of the decade?
4 T Rex was led by which singer?
5 What colour was Debbie Harry's hair which named her band?
6 "Maggie May" provided whom with his first No. 1?
7 Kiki Dee's biggest 70s hit was with whom?
8 Where did Supertramp have Breakfast in 1979?
9 Who was lead singer with the Boomtown Rats?
10 Who cleaned Wimbledon Common and cleaned up in the charts in '74?
11 What went with Peaches in the 70s charts?
12 Who had a posthumous hit with "Way Down"?
13 Song for whom was Elton John's first instrumental hit?
14 Which World Cup football squad did Rod Stewart have a hit with?
15 Which Rollers had two No. 1s in 1975?
16 Who had a single hit from the album "Bat Out of Hell"?
17 Izhar Cohen and Alphabeta won Eurovision for which country?
18 Which brothers included Wayne, Donny and Little Jimmy?
19 Whose first hit was "Wuthering Heights"?
20 Which 70s B side for Queen became a football anthem?
21 Which Abba hit became the name of an Alan Partridge spoof?
22 Which Gary's first hit was as Tubeway Army?
23 Which hostel did the Village People visit in the 70s?
24 How many performers made up The Carpenters?
25 Which soccer side had a hit with "I'm Forever Blowing Bubbles"?
26 "Tubular Bells" is credited with establishing which record label?
27 Which band were "Part of the Union"?
28 Which Bryan founded Roxy Music?
29 Who celebrated his "Ding-A-Ling" in song?
30 Who had the last 70s Xmas No. 1 with "Another Brick in the Wall"?

1 Played in 2005, which team won the first FA Cup Final decided on penalties?
2 Which British sausage is traditionally sold in a coil?
3 What is the luxury hotel and country club called in "The Archers"?
4 Which profession is associated with Savile Row?
5 What colour is the flower of an oil seed rape plant?
6 How many packs of playing cards are needed to play Canasta?
7 Bewick, Black and Whooper are all types of what?
8 Which pop star sang about his blue suede shoes?
9 Which animals live in a holt?
10 For which type of dance was Nijinsky famous?
11 In which country is the Algarve Coast?
12 Which voice is higher - a tenor or a baritone?
13 What colour is the St Andrew's cross on the Scottish flag?
14 Which University is based in Milton Keynes?
15 Who in AD 434 was King of the Huns?
16 Who invented the dot system with which the blind can read by touch?
17 On whose feast day did King Wenceslas look out?
18 Which boy band made the No. 1 album "World of Our Own"?
19 An abacus helps you do what?
20 Which actress sang "A Spoonful of Sugar" in "Mary Poppins"?
21 Which musical does "Climb Every Mountain" come from?
22 The anaconda is native to which continent?
23 How many legs does a spider have?
24 Who wrote the waltz called "The Blue Danube"?
25 Who was the most famous dancing partner of Fred Astaire?
26 What are Gorgonzola, Dolcelatte and Pecorino?
27 On which board game are The Strand, Mayfair and Park Lane?
28 At which Scottish school was Prince Charles educated?
29 What colour is the spot on the Japanese flag?
30 Which Ali is one of the alter egos of Sacha Baron Cohen?

Answers	**Pop: The 70s** (see Quiz 23)

1 Sweden. 2 Grease. 3 The Supremes. 4 Marc Bolan. 5 Blonde. 6 Rod Stewart. 7 Elton John. 8 America. 9 Bob Geldof. 10 The Wombles. 11 Herb. 12 Elvis Presley. 13 Guy. 14 Scottish. 15 Bay City Rollers. 16 Meat Loaf. 17 Israel. 18 Osmond. 19 Kate Bush. 20 We are the Champions. 21 Knowing Me Knowing You. 22 Numan. 23 YMCA. 24 Two. 25 West Ham. 26 Virgin. 27 Strawbs. 28 Ferry. 29 Chuck Berry. 30 Pink Floyd.

1 What is the profession of Geraldine Grainger of Dibley?
2 How do Men Martin Clunes and Neil Morrissey behave in the sitcom?
3 In which country is "Kath & Kim" set?
4 Alphabetically which of the characters in "Friends" comes first?
5 "Whatever Happened to the Likely Lads?" was the sequel to what?
6 Which sitcom classic was about self-sufficiency in Surbiton?
7 How did Hyacinth pronounce "Bucket" in "Keeping Up Appearances"?
8 Which show about Grace Brothers' store had a rerun in 1998?
9 What was the sequel to "Yes Minister"?
10 Which sitcom about the Trotters was originally to be called Readies?
11 Which series featured the character David Brent?
12 Which Penelope alias Audrey was "To the Manor Born"?
13 How many children feature in the sitcom about Bill and Ben Porter?
14 Which Ronnie played Arkwright in "Open All Hours"?
15 Ian McShane starred in which sitcom about a shady antiques dealer?
16 In which historical sitcom did Baldrick first appear?
17 Which show was originally to have been called "Your Bottom"?
18 Which Felicity was the star of "Solo"?
19 In which sitcom did Joanna Lumley play champagne-swilling Patsy?
20 What are the names of the Birds in "Birds of a Feather"?
21 In "Dad's Army", who called Sgt Wilson Uncle Arthur?
22 Frasier was a spin-off from which series based in a Boston bar?
23 Which Craig co-wrote and starred in "The Royle Family"?
24 Which wartime sitcom featured Rene and Edith Artois?
25 Who played Jean, husband of Lionel, in "As Time Goes By"?
26 "Goodnight Sweetheart" is set in the 1940s and which other decade?
27 Which series was based on Butlin's and Pontin's?
28 What was Anton Rodgers' legal job in "May to December"?
29 Which Family is a sitcom with ex-Mrs Merton Caroline Aherne?
30 What is Mrs Victor Meldrew's first name?

Answers	**Pot Luck 12** *(see Quiz 26)*

1 Butterflies. 2 Pork Pie. 3 The Sahara. 4 Horse racing. 5 Wright Brothers. 6 John Ridd. 7 Medicines/Drugs. 8 50 Cent. 9 Fox. 10 Red/green. 11 Asp. 12 Three. 13 Davina McCall. 14 Small pieces of wood. 15 Their wedding. 16 Flower/Shrub. 17 Otter. 18 Flanders. 19 Baloo and Mowgli. 20 Australia. 21 Four. 22 1970s. 23 Italy. 24 Stamps. 25 Blue. 26 Peppermint. 27 Dove. 28 Tom Jones. 29 Soprano. 30 The English Channel.

1 Red Admirals, Fritillaries and Tortoiseshells are all what?
2 Which pie is Melton Mowbray renowned for?
3 Which has more rainfall, the Sahara or Antarctica?
4 Which sport would you see at Chepstow?
5 Which brothers made the first manned powered aero flight in 1903?
6 Who is the main male character in the novel "Lorna Doone"?
7 What was sold by an apothecary?
8 "Get Rich Quick or Die Tryin'" was the breakthrough album for which artist?
9 Which animals live in an earth or lair?
10 Along with white, what colours appear on the Italian flag?
11 Which snake is it said Cleopatra used to poison herself?
12 How many ships came sailing by according to the carol?
13 Who presented the very first series of "Big Brother"?
14 What is chipboard made from?
15 Catherine Zeta Jones and Michael Douglas sued about photos from which event?
16 What is a poinsettia?
17 In the novel what kind of animal was Tarka?
18 Bruges is the capital of which part of Belgium?
19 Which characters sang "The Bare Necessities" in "The Jungle Book"?
20 Which country did keeper Mark Schwarzer play for in soccer's 2006 World Cup?
21 How many wings does a bee have?
22 In which decade did Britain convert to decimal currency?
23 Sardinia is part of which country?
24 What are collected by a philatelist?
25 What colour is the background of the Scottish flag?
26 What flavour is crème de menthe?
27 What type of bird are Ring, Turtle and Collared?
28 Which veteran Welsh pop singer was knighted in the 2006 New Year Honours List?
29 Which is the highest female singing voice?
30 Which sea is called La Manche by the French?

Answers	TV: Sitcoms (see Quiz 25)

1 Vicar. 2 Badly. 3 Australia. 4 Chandler. 5 The Likely Lads. 6 The Good Life. 7 "Bouquet". 8 Are You Being Served? 9 Yes Prime Minister. 10 Only Fools and Horses. 11 The Office. 12 Keith. 13 2 Point 4. 14 Barker. 15 Lovejoy. 16 Blackadder. 17 Bottom. 18 Kendall. 19 Absolutely Fabulous. 20 Sharon & Tracy. 21 Pike. 22 Cheers. 23 Craig Cash. 24 Allo Allo. 25 Judi Dench. 26 1990s. 27 Hi-De-Hi! 28 Solicitor. 29 Royle. 30 Margaret.

1 Which Mr Atkinson created the spoof spy character Johnny English?
2 Sarah Michelle Gellar starred in the movie about which ghost-hunting dog?
3 What was the name of Sacha Baron Cohen's Kazakhstan character?
4 "Addams Family Values" was the follow-up to what?
5 Which west London borough is associated with classic comedies?
6 What age group are the performers in the gangster film "Bugsy Malone"?
7 Which cartoon set in Bedrock starred John Goodman in the human version?
8 What type of Adventure did Bill and Ted have?
9 What sort of farm animal was Babe?
10 Which Tom starred in "Jerry Maguire"?
11 Which Hill in London was the location for a Hugh Grant / Julia Roberts movie?
12 Whose World did Mike Myers and Dana Garvey live in?
13 "A Fish Called" ... what was a John Cleese & Jamie Lee Curtis classic?
14 What was Whoopi Goldberg disguised as in "Sister Act"?
15 Which group sang the theme song for "Four Weddings and a Funeral"?
16 Which Jim was the shy bank clerk in "The Mask"?
17 Forrest Gump said life was like a box of what?
18 Which Julia was the "Pretty Woman" in the film's title?
19 Which British comedy duo were the stars of "The Magnificent Two"?
20 What did Robin Williams in "Mrs Doubtfire" and Dustin Hoffman in "Tootsie" have in common?
21 What unusual handicap did Bernie have as a host in "A Weekend at Bernie's"?
22 Which film of a Book featured "The Bare Necessities"?
23 Which Sid's first Carry On was "Carry On Constable"?
24 To whom did someone say "I Shrunk the Kids" in the film title?
25 Which spinach-loving cartoon character was played by Robin Williams?
26 Which Colin played Mark Darcy in the movie about Bridget Jones?
27 Was Patrick Swayze or Demi Moore the Ghost in the 1990 film?
28 "Look Who's Talking Too" was the sequel to what?
29 Who was the Queen of the Desert in the transvestite comedy?
30 Which Inspector played by Peter Sellers was in "The Pink Panther"?

Answers	Pot Luck 13 (see Quiz 28)

1 Sugababes. 2 Stop bleeding. 3 The King and I. 4 Canada. 5 Sir Cliff Richard.
6 Tower of London. 7 Blue/violet. 8 Suffolk. 9 General Strike. 10 Cricket. 11 Russian. 12 Australia. 13 24. 14 Sturgeon. 15 Heart. 16 White. 17 Man Utd and Real Madrid. 18 Spirit level. 19 Anna Sewell. 20 Maundy money. 21 Kayaks. 22 Oranges. 23 All for one and one for all. 24 Like a Virgin. 25 Windsor. 26 A Sharp. 27 Rolf Harris. 28 Cambridge. 29 Red/white. 30 Men's Marathon.

1 Who had hits in 2005 with "Ugly" and "Push the Button"?
2 What is a tourniquet used for in First Aid?
3 Which musical is based on a book called "Anna and the King of Siam"?
4 The chipmunk is native to America and which other country?
5 Who was pop's first Knight?
6 Where in London is the ceremony of the keys held each night?
7 What colour is indigo?
8 Which East Anglian county is often called "Constable Country"?
9 In 1926 which General crisis happened in England?
10 Which sport links Ted Dexter, Peter May and Ray Illingworth?
11 What was the nationality of composer Rimsky-Korsakov?
12 Budgerigars are native to which country?
13 How many carats in pure gold?
14 Caviar comes traditionally from which fish?
15 What does a cardiologist study?
16 What colour are Aylesbury ducks?
17 Ruud van Nistelrooy and David Beckham were at which two clubs together?
18 What is used to check something is level by a builder?
19 Who wrote the novel "Black Beauty"?
20 What does the Queen give out on the day before Good Friday?
21 What are the sealskin boats used by Eskimos called?
22 What did Nell Gwyn sell when Charles II first saw her?
23 What was the motto of the Three Musketeers?
24 Which Madonna song was performed by Jim Broadbent in "Moulin Rouge"?
25 Which castle is in the royal county of Berkshire?
26 If a musical note is lowered by a flat, what raises it?
27 Who was the first presenter of "Animal Hospital"?
28 In which city is the River Cam?
29 Apart from blue, what other two colours appear on the Dutch flag?
30 What was the final event of the 2004 Athens Olympics?

Answers	**The Movies: Comedies** *(see Quiz 27)*

1 Rowan. 2 Scooby Doo. 3 Borat. 4 The Addams Family. 5 Ealing. 6 Children. 7 The Flintstones. 8 Excellent. 9 Pig. 10 Cruise. 11 Notting Hill. 12 Wayne's. 13 Wanda. 14 Nun. 15 Wet Wet Wet. 16 Carrey. 17 Chocolates. 18 Roberts. 19 Morecambe & Wise. 20 Dressed in drag. 21 Dead. 22 The Jungle Book. 23 James. 24 Honey. 25 Popeye. 26 Colin Firth. 27 Patrick Swayze. 28 Look Who's Talking. 29 Priscilla. 30 Clouseau.

1 Is Holy Island off the east or west coast of England?
2 What is a native of Aberdeen called?
3 Is London's Docklands, north, south, east or west of the city?
4 The Angel of the North was erected next to which major road?
5 Which English gorge takes its name from a nearby village famous for its cheese?
6 Which county has the abbreviation Beds?
7 St Anne's lies to the south of which British seaside resort?
8 Which Royal residence stands by the river Dee?
9 In which country is the UK's highest mountain?
10 What sort of an institution in London is Bart's?
11 On a London Tube map the Central Line is what colour?
12 In which Scottish city did you find the Gorbals?
13 Which motorway links London to Winchester?
14 Which Isle off the south coast of England is a county in its own right?
15 What is Britain's most southerly country?
16 Norwich is the administrative centre of which county?
17 In which city did the National Trust buy the childhood home of Paul McCartney?
18 Which motorway runs almost parallel to the A4?
19 With which profession is London's Harley Street associated?
20 What is Britain's largest international airport?
21 In which county is Land's End?
22 What colour are most London buses?
23 Which motorway goes from Lancashire to Yorkshire east to west?
24 What is the background colour of road signs to tourist sites?
25 In which part of the UK is "Land of My Fathers" a traditional song?
26 Winchester is the adminstrative seat of which county?
27 Aston University is near which Midlands city?
28 Most of the Lake District is in which county?
29 What red flower does Lancs have?
30 In which city is the Barbican Centre?

Answers	**Pot Luck 14** *(see Quiz 30)*

1 Harry Potter. 2 Mozart. 3 A peach. 4 Sark. 5 Brown. 6 He who laughs last. 7 1953. 8 Carpets. 9 Diagonally. 10 Spain. 11 JCB Song. 12 Black/Yellow. 13 A vixen. 14 Cakes. 15 Edmund. 16 Afghanistan. 17 Colour. 18 Isle of Wight. 19 A fish. 20 39. 21 Blackberry. 22 Zambezi. 23 Herring. 24 Marie Antoinette. 25 Spam. 26 Victor Hugo. 27 Puffin. 28 Red, yellow & blue. 29 Four. 30 Italy.

1 Daniel Radcliffe played which famous boy on screen?
2 Who composed the opera "The Marriage of Figaro"?
3 What type of fruit is a nectarine?
4 Which of the four Channel Islands is the smallest?
5 What colour is sepia?
6 Who, according to the proverb, laughs longest?
7 In which year was Everest conquered?
8 Which house furnishing is associated with the town of Kidderminster?
9 How does a bishop move in chess?
10 The drink sangria comes from which European country?
11 What was Nizlopi's Xmas No. 1 single in 2005?
12 What two colours other than red appear on the Belgian flag?
13 What is a female fox called?
14 What is sold in a patisserie?
15 Who is Peter's brother in "The Lion, the Witch and the Wardrobe"?
16 .af is the internet code for which country?
17 What can a chameleon lizard change?
18 The rocks called The Needles are close to which island?
19 What is a barracuda?
20 How many steps were there in the title of the novel by John Buchan?
21 A loganberry is a cross between a raspberry and what?
22 Which river are the Victoria Falls on?
23 Sardines and pilchards are part of which fish family?
24 Which French Queen was executed in the French Revolution?
25 What name was spiced ham given during wartime?
26 Who wrote "The Hunchback of Notre Dame"?
27 Which seabird is associated with Lundy Island?
28 What are the three primary colours in art?
29 How many wings does a moth have?
30 From which country does the football team Juventus come from?

Answers	**Geography: The UK (see Quiz 29)**

1 East. 2 Aberdonian. 3 East. 4 A1. 5 Cheddar. 6 Bedfordshire. 7 Blackpool. 8 Balmoral. 9 Scotland. 10 Hospital. 11 Red. 12 Glasgow. 13 M3. 14 Isle of Wight. 15 England. 16 Norfolk. 17 Liverpool. 18 M4. 19 Medical profession. 20 Heathrow. 21 Cornwall. 22 Red. 23 M62. 24 Brown. 25 Wales. 26 Hampshire. 27 Birmingham. 28 Cumbria. 29 Rose. 30 London.

1 Whom was tennis star Martina Hingis named after?
2 Which lauded soccer star was born Edson Arantes do Nascimento?
3 Which French footballer David advertised L'Oreal hair products?
4 Golfer Ernie Els is from which African country?
5 Which British tennis player was born on Greg Rusedski's first birthday?
6 Jonah Lomu plays for which international side?
7 Athlete Kelly Holmes was formerly a member of which armed service?
8 Which Paula had a hat-trick of London Marathon wins this millennium?
9 Which snooker champ Ray was nicknamed Dracula?
10 What sort of eye accessory does Chris Eubank wear?
11 At which sport was Nokolai Valuev a world champion?
12 Which Monica was stabbed in the back by a fanatical Graf supporter?
13 Was tennis's Michael Chang from Hong Kong or the USA?
14 Which racing driver was first to clock up more than 75 F1 wins?
15 Rahul Dravid captained which international cricket team?
16 Which four-legged, three-times Grand National winner died in 1995?
17 Which Greg rejected a maple leaf for a Union Jack in the 1990s?
18 Who founded the book known as the cricketer's Bible?
19 Rachel Hayhoe Flint is a famous name in which sport?
20 Who was Ben Johnson running for when disqualified in Seoul?
21 Which Princess won the 1971 European Three Day Event?
22 Which David has kept goal for Liverpool, West Ham, Manchester City & Portsmouth?
23 Which temperamental tennis player was dubbed Superbrat?
24 Which Jenny was the first woman to train a Grand National winner?
25 Who was Australia's cricket captain in the 2006 ICC Trophy final?
26 Which boxer's catchphrase was "Know what I mean 'Arry"?
27 Which disappearing horse last won the Derby in 1981?
28 Who founded the Stewart motor racing team?
29 What was cricket umpire Harold Bird's nickname?
30 Who became the first black manager of a Premiership club when he took over at Chelsea in 1996?

Answers | Pot Luck 15 *(see Quiz 32)*

1 Four. 2 Loire. 3 McFly. 4 Cornwall. 5 South-south-east. 6 Thomas Hardy. 7 Slavery.
8 King. 9 Red/White. 10 USA. 11 Seven. 12 Kew. 13 Hadrian's Wall. 14 Purple. 15
Mont Blanc. 16 Venice. 17 June. 18 Malta. 19 Grey. 20 Apple. 21 Queen's Counsel.
22 The Black Death/Bubonic Plague. 23 Cherie Blair. 24 A spring tide. 25 Argentina. 26
Daisy. 27 West Ham. 28 Pigeon racing. 29 Melon. 30 Switzerland.

1 How many wings does a butterfly have?
2 Which river is the longest in France?
3 Who had 2005 hits with "I Wanna Hold You" and "Ultraviolet"?
4 In which county is Bodmin Moor?
5 Which compass point is opposite North-north-west?
6 Which Thomas wrote "The Mayor of Casterbridge"?
7 Which trade was abolished in 1807 in the British Empire?
8 Which chess piece should be protected at all costs?
9 What two colours are on the Austrian flag?
10 In which country was there a North v. South civil war from 1861–65?
11 How many players are in a netball team?
12 Where in Britain are the Royal Botanic Gardens?
13 Which ancient wall crosses England from Wallsend to Solway?
14 What colour is an aubergine?
15 Which mountain is the highest in the Alps?
16 The artist Canaletto was associated with which Italian city?
17 In which month is the Trooping of the Colour?
18 Which island is also called the George Cross Island?
19 Which colour is linked to Sir Ian McKellen's character Gandalf?
20 Cox, Braeburn and Gala are all kinds of which fruit?
21 In legal terms, what do the initials QC stand for?
22 Which disaster struck England in the 1340s?
23 Carole Caplin found fame as adviser to which famous wife?
24 What is the opposite of a neap tide?
25 Which country lies immediately east of Chile?
26 Who was asked to ride "a bicycle made for two" in the song?
27 Jermain Defoe joined Tottenham Hotspur from which other London club?
28 The National Homing Union is involved with which leisure pursuit?
29 What kind of fruit can be cantaloupe?
30 Which country as well as France is Lake Geneva in?

Answers	**Sport: Who's Who? 1** *(see Quiz 31)*

1 Martina Navratilova. 2 Pele. 3 Ginola. 4 South Africa. 5 Tim Henman. 6 New Zealand. 7 Army. 8 Paula Radcliffe. 9 Reardon. 10 Monocle. 11 Boxing. 12 Seles. 13 USA. 14 Michael Schumacher. 15 India. 16 Red Rum. 17 Rusedski. 18 Wisden. 19 Women's cricket. 20 Canada. 21 Anne. 22 David James. 23 John McEnroe. 24 Pitman. 25 Ricky Ponting. 26 Frank Bruno. 27 Shergar. 28 Jackie Stewart. 29 Dickie Bird. 30 Ruud Gullit.

1 Who went straight to No. 1 in 1981 with "Stand and Deliver"?
2 What colour Door gave Shakin' Stevens an 80s hit?
3 Which ex-Beatle had a hit with Stevie Wonder in 1982?
4 Whose album "Thriller" provided several hit singles?
5 Who was KC's backing Band?
6 Which Scot had chart success after Esther Rantzen's "The Big Time"?
7 Which BBC Radio station banned "Relax"?
8 Ravel's "Bolero" charted because of which skaters' Olympic success?
9 Which actor Robert was named in a Bananarama song title ?
10 Which Superstar Rat sang "Love Me Tender"?
11 Which Alison's nickname was Alf?
12 Which Elaine and Barbara topped the charts in 1985?
13 Which Mrs Andrew Lloyd Webber had a hit with "Pie Jesu"?
14 David Bowie and Mick Jagger had a hit after which Concert?
15 Elton John charted with "Nikita" at the same time as Sting had which coincidental hit?
16 Who had hits as part of Visage and Ultravox?
17 Who told you that you were "In the Army Now"?
18 Who fronted Culture Club?
19 Graham McPherson of Madness was known as what?
20 Which Kim reached No. 2 in 1981, 24 years after dad Marty?
21 Which Spanish singer had the UK's first chart topper in Spanish?
22 David Sylvian was part of which Asian-sounding band?
23 Who was the first ventriloquist in the charts with Orville?
24 Who teamed up with Annie Lennox in The Eurythmics?
25 Who was the then oldest man in the charts with "New York New York"?
26 Who joined Cliff Richard for his 80s "Living Doll"?
27 Which TV puppets sang "The Chicken Song"?
28 Which red-haired Royal liked "Lady in Red"?
29 Which future England coach joined Waddle on "Diamond Lights"?
30 Who had a Xmas No. 1 in 1988 after 30 years in the charts?

Answers	**Pot Luck 16** *(see Quiz 34)*

1 Eton. 2 Raymond Briggs. 3 13. 4 Soft fruit. 5 Peter Kay. 6 A soliloquy. 7 Isle of Man. 8 Soccer (Portsmouth v. Man City). 9 Oranges. 10 French. 11 Horse Guards Parade. 12 Drugs. 13 Your Old Kit Bag. 14 Hats. 15 Honey. 16 Five. 17 Distillery. 18 His tools. 19 The Jordan. 20 Needles. 21 Blackbird. 22 Richard I. 23 Whales. 24 American Football. 25 Capricorn. 26 Pears. 27 November. 28 Lisa. 29 Esther Rantzen. 30 Harp.

1 Which school did Prince Harry attend when he was 13?

2 Which cartoonist was the creator of "The Snowman"?

3 How many are there in a baker's dozen?

4 What would you find in a punnet?

5 Who featured on Tony Christie's 2005 smash hit "Amarillo"?

6 What is a Shakespearan speech or scene with only one actor called?

7 Douglas is the capital town of which Isle?

8 Pedro Mendes was knocked out by Ben Thatcher in which sport?

9 The Spanish city of Seville is famous for which fruit?

10 What is the nationality of pianist Richard Clayderman?

11 Where does the Trooping of the Colour take place in London?

12 Pharmacology is the study of what?

13 Where, according to the song, should you pack up your troubles?

14 What is usually kept in a band-box?

15 What is the main ingredient in the drink mead?

16 In music, how many lines are there in a stave?

17 What name is given to the building where whisky is made?

18 According to the proverb, a bad workman always blames what?

19 Jesus Christ was baptised in which river?

20 What are inserted into the body during acupuncture?

21 According to rhyme which bird pecked off the maid's nose?

22 Which King was known as the "Lionheart"?

23 Beluga, Sperm and Blue are all types of what?

24 Which sport is played on a grid iron?

25 Which Zodiac sign is known as the sign of the goat?

26 What is perry made from?

27 In which month is the State Opening of Parliament in England?

28 Who is Bart Simpson's older sister?

29 Which presenter was the star of TV's "That's Esther"?

30 Which musical instrument is a national emblem of Ireland?

Answers	Pop: The 80s (see Quiz 33)

1 Adam and the Ants. 2 Green. 3 Paul McCartney. 4 Michael Jackson. 5 Sunshine Band. 6 Sheena Easton. 7 Radio One. 8 Torvill & Dean. 9 Robert de Niro. 10 Roland. 11 Moyet. 12 Paige, Dickson. 13 Sarah Brightman. 14 Live Aid. 15 Russians. 16 Midge Ure. 17 Status Quo. 18 Boy George. 19 Suggs. 20 Kim Wilde. 21 Julio Iglesias. 22 Japan. 23 Keith Harris. 24 Dave Stewart. 25 Frank Sinatra. 26 The Young Ones. 27 Spitting Image. 28 Duchess of York. 29 Hoddle. 30 Cliff Richard.

1 Which batter mix is an accompaniment to roast beef?
2 Which chef replaced Fern Britton on "Ready Steady Cook"?
3 What colour wine is Beaujolais Nouveau?
4 What colour is the flesh of an avocado?
5 What is the traditional colour for the outside of a stick of rock?
6 Would you eat or drink a Sally Lunn?
7 What type of egg is covered in sausage meat?
8 Scrumpy is a rough form of what?
9 Which mashed vegetable tops a shepherd's pie?
10 Which food has given its name to a road network near Birmingham?
11 Is a Spotted Dick a first course or a pudding?
12 Which fruit is associated with tennis at Wimbledon?
13 Champagne originated in which country?
14 Is a Melton Mowbray pie sweet or savoury?
15 What is a pistachio?
16 What sort of fruit is in a teacake?
17 Which chef Antony appeared in "I'm a Celebrity Get Me Out of Here"?
18 Which is more substantial, afternoon tea or high tea?
19 If you ate al fresco would you be indoors or out of doors?
20 What is the usual shape of a Camembert cheese?
21 Which soft pulpy peas are eaten with fish and chips?
22 What type of food may be served clotted?
23 What would you make in a cafetière?
24 What type of drink is Bristol Cream?
25 Is chowder a soup or a pudding?
26 A "pinta" is usually a pint of what?
27 Should red wine normally be drunk chilled or at room temperature?
28 Is there milk in a cappuccino coffee?
29 Are you more likely to eat a croissant at breakfast or supper?
30 Does celebrity chef Nick Nairn come from England, Scotland or Wales?

1 Which English King was also called "The Confessor"?
2 Don't hum it, but who had a smash European hit with "Axel F"?
3 Which football team play their home games at Goodison Park?
4 PG, 15 and 18 are all classifications for what?
5 Which manufacturer was the first to achieve more than 100 F1 Grand Prix wins?
6 How is US lawyer Hillary Roddam better known?
7 In Cockney rhyming slang, what are your mince pies?
8 According to the proverb, who is soon parted from his money?
9 From which Disney film does Cruella De Vil come from?
10 What is the capital of Iraq?
11 Which letter describes a soft lead pencil?
12 How long is an American president's term of office?
13 The Azores are a part of which European country?
14 Which Michael began his TV chat shows back in 1971?
15 What are the bars on a xylophone made from?
16 What is a mud skipper?
17 What is the second letter of the Greek alphabet?
18 In medicine, what do the initials ENT stand for?
19 With which Italian town is Saint Francis linked?
20 Blanket, back and buttonhole are all types of what?
21 Which Zodiac sign is known as the sign of the crab?
22 Whose life story was called "Stand By Your Man"?
23 Which wire is live in modern three-core electric cable?
24 From which country other than Australia did Anzac troops come from?
25 Who is the patron saint of mountaineers?
26 In which state of the US is the resort of Palm Springs?
27 How many consonants are in the English alphabet?
28 In "Peter Pan" what are the names of Wendy's brothers?
29 The port of Bergen is in which European country?
30 Edwin van der Sar joined Man Utd from which London club?

Answers	Leisure: Food & Drink 1 *(see Quiz 35)*

1 Yorkshire pudding. 2 Ainsley Harriott. 3 Red. 4 Green. 5 Pink. 6 Eat. 7 Scotch egg. 8 Cider. 9 Potato. 10 Spaghetti (junction). 11 Pudding. 12 Strawberries. 13 France. 14 Savoury. 15 Nut. 16 Currants and/or other dried fruit. 17 Antony Worrall Thompson. 18 High tea. 19 Out of doors. 20 Round. 21 Mushy peas. 22 Cream. 23 Coffee. 24 Sherry. 25 Soup. 26 Milk. 27 Room temperature. 28 Yes. 29 Breakfast. 30 Scotland.

1 What type of chef was in the title of Jamie's first TV series?
2 What is Jamie's wife called?
3 In his early TV series how did Jamie travel around London?
4 Which number names the restaurant set up to help under-privileged kids?
5 In which decade of the 20th century did Jamie Oliver first find fame on TV?
6 What were the twizzlers made from in his programme about school dinners?
7 Did Jamie's parents run a pub or work in the theatre?
8 Which Cheeky charity set up by Jamie trains and mentors young people?
9 Which supermarket chain did Jamie advertise in the early 2000s?
10 In which county was Jamie brought up?
11 On which Channel was Jamie's series about school dinners?
12 In which decade of the 20th century was Jamie Oliver born?
13 Who or what are Poppy and Daisy in Jamie's life?
14 What does Jamie's favourite word "pukka" mean?
15 In which county is Jamie's Fifteen restaurant in Newquay?
16 Which Corporation broadcast Jamie's first TV series?
17 Which honour did he receive in the June 2003 Queen's Birthday Honours?
18 How many of Jamie's books had Naked in the title?
19 In "Jamie's Great Escape" which European country did he visit?
20 What was the name of his programme which first criticised school meals?
21 In which famous London Café was he first spotted by a TV producer?
22 In 2006, parents in which county pushed food through the school fence as a protest at Jamie's healthy options?
23 In which city was Jamie's first Fifteen restaurant?
24 What was the occupation of Nora Sands in one of Jamie's TV shows?
25 Which type of oil does Jamie use extensively in his cooking?
26 Was the soundtrack of Jamie's early TV series, rock 'n' roll or classical?
27 In which city were the first "Naked Chef" shows filmed?
28 Which Antonio ran a London restaurant where Jamie did some early training?
29 How many million pounds was added to the school dinner budget after Jamie's campaign, 180, 280 or 380?
30 How many people feature on the cover of "Cook with Jamie"?

Answers	**Pot Luck 18** *(see Quiz 38)*

1 Fishermen. 2 Doctor. 3 Nothing. 4 Siam. 5 H. 6 Scorpio. 7 Bones. 8 Helsinki. 9 Jamie Oliver. 10 You spoil the child. 11 Violin. 12 Lorraine Kelly. 13 Bean. 14 Queen of Sheba. 15 John Prescott. 16 Royal Albert Hall 17 The Shannon. 18 30th November. 19 Double bass. 20 Dr Zhivago. 21 Radio 2. 22 The Mall. 23 Islam. 24 Weather reports. 25 Wiltshire. 26 A thief. 27 Brown. 28 Shakespeare. 29 Knots. 30 A long spoon.

1 What job was done by Peter and Andrew before they were disciples?
2 Ex-MP David Owen previously followed which profession?
3 If you are in your birthday suit, what are you wearing?
4 Thailand was formerly known by what name?
5 Which letter describes a hard leaded pencil?
6 Which Zodiac sign is usually shown as a scorpion?
7 Osteoporosis affects which part of the body?
8 Which city is the most northerly capital in Europe?
9 On TV who was the main character in "Jamie's Kitchen"?
10 According to the proverb, what happens if you spare the rod?
11 Stéphane Grappelli is associated with which musical instrument?
12 Which Scottish presenter is the star of GMTV's "LK Today"?
13 Which vegetable can be dwarf, runner and broad?
14 Which Queen made a visit to Solomon in the Bible?
15 Who was Tony Blair's first Deputy PM?
16 At which London venue did Cream reunite for four nights in May 2005?
17 Which river is the longest in the British Isles?
18 On which date is Saint Andrew's Day?
19 Which is largest – cello, viola or double bass?
20 Which epic film had the theme tune "Somewhere My Love"?
21 Terry Wogan's daily show is on which radio station?
22 Buckingham Palace is at the end of which famous London road?
23 A muezzin is an official of which religion?
24 John Kettley and Sian Davies presented what type of reports on TV?
25 In which county is Salisbury Plain?
26 In Cockney rhyming slang, what is a tea leaf?
27 What colour is the skin of a kiwi fruit?
28 What does "S" stand for in RSC?
29 What can be granny, sheepshank and bowline?
30 What do you need to sup with the devil, according to the proverb?

Answers | **Jamie Oliver (see Quiz 37)**

1 Naked Chef. 2 Jools. 3 Scooter. 4 Fifteen. 5 1990s. 6 Turkey. 7 They ran a pub. 8 Cheeky Chops. 9 Sainsbury's. 10 Essex. 11 Channel 4. 12 1970s. 13 His daughters. 14 Brilliant. 15 Cornwall. 16 BBC. 17 MBE. 18 Three. 19 Italy. 20 Jamie's School Dinners. 21 River Café. 22 South Yorkshire. 23 London. 24 Dinner lady. 25 Olive oil. 26 Rock 'n' roll. 27 London. 28 Antonio Carluccio. 29 280 million. 30 One (himself).

1 Glaucoma affects which part of the body?
2 Which flightless bird lays the world's largest egg?
3 What is a puffball?
4 What happens to a female butterfly after it has laid its eggs?
5 In what type of environment do most crustaceans live?
6 Which natural disaster is measured on the Richter scale?
7 What is the main ingredient of glass?
8 Does a millipede have more, fewer, or exactly 1,000 feet?
9 An ore is a mineral which contains a what?
10 Is the whale shark a mammal like the whale, or a fish like the shark?
11 Which bird is the symbol of the USA?
12 Are butterflies more colourful in warmer or cooler countries?
13 What sort of rock is lava?
14 Which is larger, the dolphin or the porpoise?
15 Which organ of the body has the aorta?
16 How many bones does a slug have?
17 Are worker ants male or female?
18 Altocumulus is a type of what?
19 What is the main source of energy in our ecosystem?
20 Which name for remains of plants and animals which lived on Earth means "dug up"?
21 On which continent is the world's largest glacier?
22 Kelp is a type of what?
23 What order of mammals does the gibbon belong to?
24 What is the staple food of over half of the world's population?
25 Which creatures are larvae and pupae before being adults?
26 Are most bats visible at night or by day?
27 Which part of a jellyfish has stinging cells?
28 Natural rubber is obtained from what?
29 What is the mother of all the bees in a colony called?
30 The giant sequoia is the largest living what?

Answers	Pot Luck 19 *(see Quiz 40)*

1 Confessions. 2 Egg whites. 3 Betjeman. 4 Liquid or gas. 5 Edinburgh. 6 11. 7 Gabriel. 8 Mods. 9 Drei. 10 Winnie The Pooh. 11 Canute. 12 Victor. 13 Bruce Forsyth. 14 Snap-dragon. 15 Sheffield. 16 Quickly. 17 Fountain pen. 18 Italy. 19 Estimated Time of Arrival. 20 Wine. 21 Robbie Fowler. 22 Loch Ness Monster. 23 Seven. 24 The All Blacks. 25 The sparrow. 26 Brazil. 27 James Herriot. 28 Poland. 29 Play. 30 Des O'Connor.

made "On a Dance Floor" according to Madonna's album title?

...gar added to, to make meringues?

3 ...et laureate Sir John died in 1984?

4 What can pass through something if it is porous?

5 In which Scottish city are the Rebus novels set?

6 How many Oscars did "Titanic" win – 6, 11 or 14?

7 In the Bible, which angel foretold the birth of Jesus?

8 What youth group took to wearing parkas?

9 What is the German word for the number three?

10 Which children's favourite bear said he had "very little brain"?

11 Which English king reputedly commanded the sea to retreat?

12 What is the letter "V" if A is Alpha and B is Bravo?

13 Who is famous for saying, "Nice to see you, to see you nice"?

14 What is a popular name for the flower the antirrhinum?

15 Which Yorkshire city were Pulp from?

16 In music what does presto mean?

17 What object was invented by Lewis Waterman in 1884?

18 Tuscany is in which European country?

19 In the world of flying, what do the initials ETA stand for?

20 What is retsina?

21 Which soccer striker Robbie returned to Liverpool in 2006?

22 Which monster first hit the headlines in 1933?

23 How many edges are there around a 20-pence coin?

24 What are the New Zealand rugby union team called?

25 According to the rhyme, who killed Cock Robin?

26 The Samba originated in which South American country?

27 Who wrote "It Shouldn't Happen to a Vet"?

28 The port of Gdansk is in which country?

29 Would you eat, play or sit on a sitar?

30 Which Des presented the 1990s version of "Take Your Pick"?

Answers	**Nature: Living World** *(see Quiz 39)*

1 Eyes. 2 Ostrich. 3 Fungus. 4 It dies. 5 Water. 6 Earthquake. 7 Sand. 8 Fewer. 9 Metal. 10 Fish. 11 Eagle. 12 Warmer. 13 Volcanic rock. 14 Dolphin. 15 Heart. 16 None. 17 Female. 18 Cloud. 19 Sun. 20 Fossil. 21 Antarctica. 22 Seaweed. 23 Primates (also accept apes). 24 Rice. 25 Insects. 26 At night. 27 Tentacles. 28 Rubber Tree. 29 Queen. 30 Tree.

1 Which ex-James Bond has "Scotland Forever" tattooed on his arm?
2 Which Jools starred in "Spiceworld: The Movie"?
3 Which Irish-born 007 starred in "Tomorrow Never Dies"?
4 Which Grease actor danced with Princess Diana at the White House?
5 Which sleuth did Albert Finney play in Agatha Christie's "Murder on the Orient Express"?
6 Which top-selling rapper made his movie debut in "8 Mile"?
7 Who was the star of "Moonwalker" after being in The Jackson Five?
8 Which bespectacled US actor/director directed the musical "Everyone Says I Love You"?
9 What type of hat was Charlie Chaplin most famous for?
10 Who is Emma Forbes' actor/director dad?
11 Who was named after her home town of Winona?
12 Which knighted pop singer wrote the music for "The Lion King"?
13 Hayley Mills is the daughter of which knighted actor?
14 Who separated from husband Bruce Willis in 1998?
15 Which newspaper magnate bought 20th Century-Fox in 1985?
16 Who was Sid played by Gary Oldman in "Sid and Nancy"?
17 What name usually associated with a schoolbag did Woody Allen give his son?
18 Which Welsh actor Sir Anthony bought part of Mount Snowdon in 1998?
19 Which pop star Tina starred in "Mad Max Beyond the Thunderdome"?
20 Which Ms Foster swapped her real first name from Alicia?
21 In rhyming slang what financial term is Gregory Peck?
22 Which child star was Shirley MacLaine named after?
23 Who appeared first at Madame Tussaud's, Harrison Ford or Hugh Grant?
24 Who starred as Steed in the film version of "The Avengers"?
25 Which boxer played himself in "The Greatest"?
26 Film buff Barry Norman is a member of which club with the same name as a Marx brother?
27 Who sang "It's Not Unusual" in "Mars Attacks!"?
28 Which actress appeared on the cover of "The Sound of Music" movie DVD?
29 Judi Dench played which character known by a letter in the Bond movies?
30 "There's Something About Mary" and "Gangs of New York" starred which actress?

Answers	Pot Luck 20 *(see Quiz 42)*

1 John Lennon. 2 Ian Fleming. 3 Cornwall. 4 Skeleton. 5 Oporto. 6 Green. 7 Diamond. 8 Pirates. 9 Deux. 10 August. 11 Wrestling. 12 Intelligence. 13 Draw. 14 Spain. 15 Rice. 16 Indianapolis. 17 Sylvester. 18 Dover. 19 Deer. 20 Light. 21 Blair. 22 42. 23 BBC. 24 Pierce Brosnan. 25 Japan. 26 Horse racing. 27 Orange/Yellow. 28 An elephant. 29 The sea. 30 Par.

1 In December 2005, which pop legend was remembered 25 years after his murder?
2 Who wrote the novel "You Only Live Twice"?
3 Which English county has a border with only one other county?
4 What collective name is given to the structure of bones in the body?
5 The drink port takes its name from which town?
6 What colour is normally associated with ecological groups?
7 What is the hardest substance known to man?
8 Which people are associated with the Jolly Roger flag?
9 What is the French word for the number two?
10 Alphabetically, which is the second of the 12 calendar months?
11 With which sport do we associate a half nelson?
12 In a Steven Spielberg movie if A stood for Artificial what did I stand for?
13 What was the result of the final Ashes Test match of the 2005 series?
14 Which country did the paso doble dance originate in?
15 What type of food can be pilau?
16 In which American city is a 500-mile motor race run annually?
17 Which cartoon cat never manages to catch Tweetie Pie?
18 What is Britain's busiest ferry passenger port?
19 What kind of animal is a hind?
20 What can pass through something if it is translucent?
21 Which Tony first became MP for Sedgefield in 1983?
22 How many sides do seven hexagons have?
23 Was "Crackerjack" shown on BBC or ITV?
24 Who played James Bond in "Die Another Day"?
25 Which country does the drink sake come from?
26 For which sport is Pat Eddery famous?
27 What colour is saffron?
28 In children's books and on TV, what kind of animal is Babar?
29 David Attenborough's "The Blue Planet" was about life in what type of location?
30 What term is used in golf to indicate the stroke rating for each hole?

Answers	The Movies: Who's Who? 1 (see Quiz 41)

1 Sean Connery. 2 Holland. 3 Pierce Brosnan. 4 John Travolta. 5 Poirot. 6 Eminem. 7 Michael Jackson. 8 Woody Allen. 9 Bowler. 10 Bryan Forbes. 11 Winona Ryder. 12 Sir Elton John. 13 Sir John Mills. 14 Demi Moore. 15 Rupert Murdoch. 16 Vicious. 17 Satchel. 18 Hopkins. 19 Turner. 20 Jodie Foster. 21 Cheque. 22 Shirley Temple. 23 Harrison Ford. 24 Ralph Fiennes. 25 Muhammad Ali. 26 Groucho. 27 Tom Jones. 28 Julie Andrews 29 M. 30 Cameron Diaz.

Quiz 43 Hobbies & Leisure 2

Answers – page 54

LEVEL 1

1 What is a bookmaker's licensed premises called?
2 What shape is the target in archery?
3 Where on a dartboard is the bull?
4 Which cubes are necessary for a game of craps?
5 Which direction do you go if you are abseiling?
6 What sort of Park is at Whipsnade?
7 Which locomotive identification hobby shares its name with a controversial 1990s movie?
8 In which game do you aim to call "House!"?
9 Yoga was developed from which nation's religion?
10 Is scuba practised above or below the water's surface?
11 From which part of a vehicle might you sell goods to raise cash?
12 What name is given to a small piece of land rented for growing food?
13 In the UK most Bank Holidays fall on which day of the week?
14 Which commodities would you buy at a PYO centre?
15 What does E stand for in NEC?
16 What colour is the baize on a snooker table?
17 Which word precedes sport to describe killing animals for recreation?
18 What type of weapon is used in fencing?
19 What is the name of a coach trip where few know the destination?
20 If you practised on a pommel horse where would you probably be?
21 The Chamber of Horrors is in which London waxworks museum?
22 Which weekly draw is run by Camelot?
23 Are bonsai trees smaller or larger than average?
24 Which club moved to The Riverside in the 1990s?
25 What sort of establishment is a greasy spoon?
26 Who is a tied house usually tied to?
27 What is the type of billiards played in pubs called?
28 The Summer Bank Holiday takes place in which month in the UK?
29 Which name for an expert in a particular hobby is the same as a padded jacket?
30 What does Y stand for in DIY?

Answers	**Pot Luck 21** *(see Quiz 44)*

1 70s. 2 Tommy Walsh. 3 Cuba. 4 Springfield. 5 Seven. 6 Toboggan. 7 Goliath.
8 On water – it's a boat. 9 Countdown. 10 Elephant. 11 Tower Bridge. 12 Their
gills. 13 Meat. 14 Six. 15 Possession. 16 Green & Yellow. 17 Nephews. 18 Ein.
19 Bride and Prejudice. 20 Catherine Wheel. 21 Victoria. 22 Right Now. 23 Mineral
water. 24 Baldrick. 25 Bergman. 26 650. 27 Rome. 28 Yellow. 29 Moses. 30 Six.

1 Did Britain join the EEC in the 60s, 70s or 80s?
2 Which "Ground Force" presenter was the tallest of the original three?
3 The Rumba originated in which country?
4 Where do the cartoon Simpsons live?
5 How many edges are there around a 50-pence coin?
6 What type of vehicle is seen on the Cresta Run?
7 Which Biblical giant was killed by David?
8 Where would you find a useful junk?
9 Dictionary expert Susie Dent featured regularly on which programme?
10 Which animal does ivory predominantly come from?
11 Which London bridge opens upwards to let tall ships through?
12 Fish breathe through what?
13 What was sold at London's Smithfield market?
14 How many noughts are there in the written number one million?
15 According to the saying, what is "nine points of the law"?
16 What colour is earth in modern three-core electric cables?
17 What relation are Huey, Dewey and Louie to Donald Duck?
18 What is the German word for the number one?
19 What was the name of the Bollywood version of Jane Austen's tale of Mr Darcy?
20 Which firework is named after a saint?
21 Which Queen became Empress of India in 1876?
22 According to the Will Young title when should you "Leave"?
23 Vichy is famous for which drink?
24 Which "Blackadder" character had a fascination for turnips?
25 Which Ingrid was the mother of Isabella Rossellini?
26 How many centimetres are there in six and a half metres?
27 The Vatican City is within which other capital city?
28 What colour is the shade of jonquil?
29 In the Bible, who was found in the bulrushes?
30 How many points does a snowflake have?

Answers	**Hobbies & Leisure 2** *(see Quiz 43)*

1 Betting shop. 2 Circular. 3 Centre. 4 Dice. 5 Downwards. 6 Animal Park. 7 Trainspotting. 8 Bingo. 9 Indian. 10 Below. 11 Car boot. 12 Allotment. 13 Monday. 14 Fruit and vegetables (Pick Your Own). 15 Exhibition. 16 Green. 17 Blood. 18 Sword. 19 Mystery tour. 20 Gym. 21 Madame Tussaud's. 22 The National Lottery. 23 Smaller. 24 Middlesbrough. 25 Cafe. 26 Brewery. 27 Bar billiards. 28 August. 29 Anorak. 30 Yourself.

1 Which ice dance pair have the freedom of the city of Nottingham?
2 In 2006 which Premiership club featured a pair of Bents in attack?
3 What sort of animal takes part in a point-to-point?
4 In snooker what colour ball scores least?
5 In which country did sumo wrestling originate?
6 What was the name of Damon Hill's racing driver father?
7 Mike Tyson was suspended for biting off which part of Evander Holyfield?
8 In which sport did Justin Rose become a pro after the 1998 British Open?
9 In which Channel does the Admiral's Cup take place?
10 Which Scot Stephen won five successive snooker world championships in the 90s?
11 The Winter Olympics held in Nagano took place in which country?
12 In which state is golf's US Masters played?
13 In athletics what is the shortest outdoor track race?
14 What is the national sport of Spain, known as corrida de toros?
15 How often is the Grand National normally run?
16 What would you ride in a velodrome?
17 Which sport has Australian Rules?
18 Which golfer Jack was known as the Golden Bear?
19 How long does the annual motor race at Le Mans last?
20 The "Golden Gloves" championship is in which sport?
21 The Fastnet Race is competed for on what type of surface?
22 Which youngsters run between the ends of the net during a tennis match?
23 How does soccer player Dennis Bergkamp refuse to travel?
24 In which sport do you try to play below par?
25 Which Frankie had seven wins at Ascot at odds of 25,095 to 1?
26 How was Sir Garfield St Auburn Sobers known as a player?
27 Which sport do The Barbarians play?
28 Which game can be lawn or crown green?
29 Which two continents compete for the Ryder Cup?
30 Turin was the centre of which global games in 2006?

| **Answers** | **Pot Luck 22** *(see Quiz 46)* |

1 Greendale. 2 Bruce Forsyth. 3 25. 4 Hutchence. 5 Banned from British racecourses. 6 Travel agents. 7 Liver. 8 Grasshoppers. 9 A letter. 10 Oldest university. 11 Great Britain. 12 Heart. 13 Man City. 14 Peter Gabriel. 15 No. 16 Blue. 17 London and Birmingham. 18 Glasgow. 19 Lancashire. 20 Roxy Music. 21 Hoops. 22 Delilah. 23 Canada. 24 Cook. 25 The Lone Ranger. 26 East. 27 Alan Bennett. 28 16. 29 Aladdin. 30 Guernsey.

1 Where are you if Mrs Goggins serves you in the post office?
2 Whose catchphrase was, "Didn't they do well"?
3 What percentage is half of a half?
4 Which late Michael was lead singer with INXS?
5 What happens if a bookie is "warned off Newmarket Heath"?
6 ABTA is concerned with which group of people?
7 In the body, which organ secretes bile?
8 In Switzerland, which famous soccer club has an insect name?
9 What is returned in Elvis's "Return to Sender"?
10 What will Harvard University always be in America?
11 Which country was the first to use postage stamps?
12 Which part of his anatomy did Tony Bennett leave in San Francisco?
13 At which soccer club did Stuart Pearce follow Kevin Keegan as manager?
14 Which Peter made the album "Solsbury Hill"?
15 Was the great racehorse Red Rum coloured red?
16 Traditionally, what colour is willow pattern?
17 Which two cities in Britain are linked by the Grand Union Canal?
18 Sauciehall Street is in which city?
19 Wasim Akram first played County Cricket for which county?
20 Which group was fronted by Bryan Ferry?
21 What is the distinctive pattern on Dennis the Menace's shirt?
22 In the Bible, who cut off Samson's hair?
23 The province of Manitoba is in which country?
24 Would you expect Antony Worrall Thompson to cook or dance on TV?
25 Which cowboy had a horse named Silver?
26 Is St Andrew's golf course on the east or west coast of Scotland?
27 Who wrote an autobiographical work entitled "Untold Stories"?
28 How many sides would four trapezium have?
29 "The Return of Jafar" was the sequel to which Disney tale from the East?
30 St Peter Port is on which island?

Answers	**Sporting Chance 1** *(see Quiz 45)*

1 Torvill & Dean. 2 Charlton Athletic (Darren & Marcus). 3 Horse. 4 Red. 5 Japan.
6 Graham. 7 Ear. 8 Golf. 9 English Channel. 10 Hendry. 11 Japan. 12 Georgia.
13 100m. 14 Bull fighting. 15 Once a year. 16 Bicycle. 17 Football. 18 Nicklaus.
19 24 hours. 20 Boxing. 21 Water. 22 Ballboys/ballgirls. 23 By air. 24 Golf. 25
Dettori. 26 Gary Sobers. 27 Rugby. 28 Bowls. 29 Europe & America. 30 Winter
Olympics.

1 Who travelled from "Pole to Pole" and "Around the World in 80 Days"?
2 Which "Newsnight" interrogator has the nickname Paxo?
3 Clive James hails from which Commonwealth country?
4 Who was born John Cheese and changed his name by one letter?
5 Would you expect Brendan Cole to cook, dance or sing on TV?
6 Which David and Jonathan hosted the 1998 Election coverage?
7 Which "Gardener's World" presenter wrote a novel "Mr MacGregor"?
8 Which Kate won an OBE for her reporting in Beijing and the Gulf?
9 Which famous part of her did Rachel of "Friends" advertise?
10 Anthony Worrall Thompson replaced Michael Barry on which food magazine show?
11 Which Sir David's catchphrase is "Hello, good evening and welcome"?
12 Who worked with amateur chefs on "Hell's Kitchen"?
13 Which Paula gave interviews on her bed in "The Big Breakfast"?
14 Which Irishman has presented "The Eurovision Song Contest"?
15 Which practical joker Jeremy first hosted "You've Been Framed"?
16 Which "big name" moved her talk show from ITV to BBC in 1998?
17 Is Paul Ross the brother, son or no relation of Jonathan Ross?
18 In 2006, which "Top Gear" presenter suffered a near fatal high-speed crash?
19 Which stock cube did Lynda Bellingham advertise?
20 How were TV cooks Clarissa and Jennifer better known?
21 What is Anthea Turner's TV presenter sister called?
22 Who was the footballing team captain on "They Think It's All Over"?
23 Who is actor Rafe Spall's famous TV dad?
24 Ian McCaskill retired from presenting what in 1998?
25 Which Gloria presented an "Open House" on Channel 5?
26 In "Ground Force" is it Charlie or Tommy who has long red hair?
27 What are the first names of Reeves and Mortimer?
28 Which Judith did Anthea Turner replace on "Wish You were Here"?
29 Which "Match of the Day" presenter took on a Radio 2 show in 1998?
30 Which veteran comic pulled out of "Strictly Come Dancing" for health reasons?

1 Which female star is the most imitated performer on "Stars in Their Eyes"?

2 How many players are on a cricket field during normal play?

3 What fruit comes from the rose?

4 The River Danube flows out into which Sea?

5 Which gas puts the bubbles into bottled fizzy drinks?

6 What gift was forthcoming on the 10th Day of Christmas?

7 The Harlem Globe Trotters are famous in which sport?

8 Who is older, Richard Branson or William Hague?

9 "Supercalifragilisticexpialidocious" comes from which Disney movie?

10 How many noughts are there in the written number ten million?

11 Which month of the year in Britain includes the longest day?

12 Copies of the Bible are left in hotel rooms by which religious organisation?

13 Who wrote the play "A Winter's Tale"?

14 What do the initials M.B.E. stand for?

15 What have you betrayed if you commit treason?

16 Who was swallowed by a whale in the Bible?

17 Andriy Shevchenko left AC Milan to join which club in 2006?

18 Which musician had the nickname "Satchmo"?

19 Which Julie played Jamie Bell's teacher in the movie "Billy Elliot"?

20 What is the children's version of backgammon called?

21 Which Girls band were formed from "Popstars: The Rivals"?

22 Which scientific word deals with the structure of the body?

23 Debra Messing played which character in "Will and Grace"?

24 What does a chronometer measure?

25 Chichester is the county town of which county?

26 Jerez in Spain is famous for which alcoholic drink?

27 In crime what do the initials A.B.H. stand for?

28 In a bull fight, what name is given to the person who kills the bull?

29 Which is the Lower House in British politics?

30 What is the German word for the number five?

---

1 Which pop band did Geri Halliwell leave in spring 1998?
2 What is the married name of Cherie Booth QC?
3 Who was the fiancée of Michael Hutchence at the time of his death?
4 What was Caroline Aherne's showbiz pensioner persona?
5 Which London store did Mohammed Al-Fayed buy in 1985?
6 What is the first name of politician turned author Lord Archer?
7 Who is the man behind the Virgin group?
8 Madonna courted controversy over adoption of a child from which country in 2006?
9 Jennifer Garner had a daughter with which star actor Ben?
10 Which Tory politician did Ffion Jenkins marry?
11 Which rock star did Texan model Jerry Hall marry in 1990?
12 In which country was Ulrika Jonsson born?
13 Which radio DJ has his own company, Ginger Productions?
14 Who left husband Peter Powell for Grant Bovey in 1998?
15 How is former Royal girlfriend Kathleen Stark better known?
16 Who founded the London nightclub Stringfellow's?
17 Which country did Earl Spencer move to in the mid-1990s?
18 Which Royal was Lord Snowdon married to?
19 What was Liz Hurley's infamous Versace dress held together with?
20 Which millionairess cook is a director of Norwich City Football Club?
21 Which chain of cosmetics shops did Anita Roddick found?
22 What was the sporting profession of Jemima Khan's husband?
23 Which singer's "Showgirl" tour resumed in 2006?
24 Which Rolling Stone celebrated his 70th birthday in October 2006?
25 Which celebrity actor Grant's middle name is Mungo?
26 Which nightclub was named after Lady Annabel Goldsmith?
27 What does John Galliano design?
28 Which 60s supermodel helped to revive the fashion fortunes of M & S?
29 Which Foreign Secretary did Gaynor Regan marry in 1998?
30 What is the first name of PR man Mr Clifford?

Answers	Pot Luck 24 *(see Quiz 50)*

1 Athletics. 2 Champion. 3 Dr John Reid. 4 Joseph. 5 Grievous Bodily Harm. 6 Like a lamb. 7 Ron. 8 Five. 9 Caribbean. 10 India. 11 Growing of crops. 12 Mae West. 13 On the shoulder. 14 King Charles. 15 Kenny Chesney. 16 Animal. 17 Boutique. 18 Member of the European Parliament. 19 Grand National. 20 Mg. 21 2000. 22 December. 23 USA. 24 Leather. 25 Five. 26 John Lennon. 27 Democrats & Republicans. 28 Fame Academy. 29 Dix. 30 Harry Corbett.

1 For which sport is Paula Radcliffe famous?
2 In the TV song, who was the "Wonder Horse"?
3 Which doctor became Home Secretary in Tony Blair's government?
4 Which of Jacob's sons had a coat of many colours, in the Bible?
5 In crime what do the initials G.B.H. stand for?
6 According to the saying, how will March go out if it comes in like a lion?
7 Did Rupert Grint play Harry or Ron in the Harry Potter films?
8 After how many years must an election be held in Britain?
9 Jamaica is in which sea?
10 Which country does the musical instrument the sitar come from?
11 Which kind of farming is arable farming?
12 Which famous film star gave her name to a life jacket?
13 Where would you wear an epaulette?
14 Which kind of spaniel was named after a king?
15 Who married Renee Zellwegger in 2005?
16 Is a jellyfish a mineral, vegetable or animal?
17 In the 60s what was Biba?
18 In politics, what do the initials M.E.P. stand for?
19 In 1993, which horse race was made void after a false start?
20 Which two letters form the symbol for the element magnesium?
21 How many centimetres are there in twenty metres?
22 Which month of the year in Britain includes the shortest day?
23 Goalkeeper Tim Howard plays for which country?
24 What is prepared in a tannery?
25 How many lines are there in a limerick?
26 Which member of the Beatles sang "Imagine"?
27 Which are the two main political parties in America?
28 What sort of "Academy" did Cat Deeley co-host?
29 What is the French word for the number ten?
30 Did Harry Corbett, Harry H. Corbett or Ronnie Corbett work with Sooty?

Answers	Celebs *(see Quiz 49)*

1 The Spice Girls. 2 Blair. 3 Paula Yates. 4 Mrs Merton. 5 Harrods. 6 Jeffrey. 7 Richard Branson. 8 Malawi. 9 Ben Affleck. 10 William Hague. 11 Mick Jagger. 12 Sweden. 13 Chris Evans. 14 Anthea Turner. 15 Koo Stark. 16 Peter Stringfellow. 17 South Africa. 18 Princess Margaret. 19 Safety pins. 20 Delia Smith. 21 Body Shop. 22 Cricketer. 23 Kylie Minogue's. 24 Bill Wyman. 25 Hugh Grant. 26 Annabel's. 27 Clothes. 28 Twiggy. 29 Robin Cook. 30 Max.

1 What mighty hero did Prince Adam turn into with the aid of Greyskull castle?
2 Which Stephen narrates "Pocoyo"?
3 What was the follow-up to "How!"?
4 Tom Baker was the longest-serving Doctor in which sci-fi series?
5 Which children's favourite has the number plate PAT 1?
6 Which Linford presented "Record Breakers"?
7 Which Engine's friends were Terence the Tractor and Bertie the Bus?
8 Does Tom or Jerry have the furrier coat?
9 What cuddly creatures are Uncle Bulgaria and Orinoco?
10 What was Worzel Gummidge?
11 Are Smurfs blue or orange?
12 Which Street teaches about letters and numbers?
13 What sort of creature is Pingu?
14 Which family is headed by Homer?
15 What colour is Teletubby Laa Laa?
16 Which Bear was found in a London railway station?
17 What is Popeye's occupation?
18 What sort of creature is Children's BBC's Otis?
19 What is the most number of presenters "Blue Peter" has at once?
20 Matthew Corbett said goodbye to which puppet companion in 1998?
21 What sort of animal was Huckleberry?
22 Who is Maya's twin on the TV show?
23 Who is Dastardly's canine sidekick?
24 "On Your Marks" and "Art Attack" are about what subject?
25 Spot is chiefly what colour?
26 Is "Crush" a game show or a drama?
27 What sort of animal is Garfield?
28 What is Casper?
29 What does Rupert Bear wear on his feet in the 2006 series?
30 Are "Thunderbirds" birds, child actors or puppets?

Quiz 52 | Pot Luck 25 | Answers – page 61 | LEVEL 1

1 Which band were credited with the first cyberspace No. 1 single?
2 What's the greatest number of consecutive calendar months with 31 days?
3 What name is given to the calm area at the centre of a hurricane?
4 Which flower is the symbol of the Labour Party in Britain?
5 Kingston is the capital of which island nation?
6 Michael Ballack joined Chelsea from which German club?
7 Which actress links "Green Wing" and "The Archers"?
8 Complete the Oasis song title "Cigarettes and ....?
9 What is the French word for the number three?
10 Are sponges mineral, vegetable or animal?
11 For which sport is Jean Alesi famous?
12 According to the proverb, there's no smoke without what?
13 Which army bugle call is played to wake up the troops?
14 Which Irish town gives its name to a five-line humorous verse?
15 Who preceded Tony Blair as Labour Party leader?
16 Who is renowned for saying, "I wanna tell you a story"?
17 Which letter of the alphabet is used as a measure of the size of a computer's memory?
18 Which country produces the pine-scented wine called retsina?
19 In 2005 what became the smallest winning margin by England in an Ashes Test?
20 What name is given to a fox's tail?
21 San Salvador is in which country?
22 Which abbreviation means "and so on"?
23 What is a Portuguese Man-o'-War?
24 What do Whipsnade, Chessington and London have in common?
25 What is the English equivalent of the American "faucet"?
26 Alphabetically, which letter is the last of the vowels?
27 Which name links golfers Kite and Watson?
28 Who bowed out of "Blind Date" in 2003?
29 What are we not doing if we send someone to Coventry?
30 How many balls are used in billiards?

Answers | Children's TV (see Quiz 51)

1 He-Man. 2 Stephen Fry. 3 How 2. 4 Doctor Who. 5 Postman Pat. 6 Christie. 7 Thomas the Tank Engine. 8 Tom. 9 Wombles. 10 Scarecrow. 11 Blue. 12 Sesame Street. 13 Penguin. 14 The Simpsons. 15 Yellow. 16 Paddington. 17 Sailor. 18 Aardvark. 19 Four. 20 Sooty. 21 Hound. 22 Miguel. 23 Muttley. 24 Art & crafts. 25 Yellow. 26 Game show. 27 Cat. 28 Ghost. 29 Trainers. 30 Puppets.

1 Tikka is a dish in which country's cookery?
2 A strudel is usually filled with which fruit?
3 What relation is Albert to fellow chef and restaurateur Michel Roux?
4 Which pasta sauce originated in Bologna in Italy?
5 What is a frankfurter?
6 How are eggs usually cooked in the breakfast dish bacon and eggs?
7 What is fromage frais a soft type of?
8 Does an Italian risotto contain rice or pasta?
9 Over what would you normally pour a vinaigrette dressing?
10 Rick Stein's restaurant and cooking specialises in what?
11 What colour wine is a Valpolicella?
12 In which country did Chianti originate?
13 What is the main filling ingredient of a quiche?
14 Is a poppadum crisp or soft?
15 What sort of drink is espresso?
16 Is brioche a type of bread or a fruit?
17 What shape is the pasta used to make lasagne?
18 What is mozzarella?
19 What colour is fudge?
20 Which north of England county is famous for its hotpot?
21 Do you eat or drink a loyal toast?
22 What type of meat is found in a cock-a-leekie soup?
23 In restaurant chains, what type of food would you buy from a Hut?
24 What is the alcoholic ingredient of Gaelic coffee?
25 Which fruit is usually used in marmalade?
26 At what age can you legally drink alcohol in an pub?
27 What does G stand for in G and T?
28 Which country produces more wine – Bulgaria or France?
29 Would you eat or drink schnapps?
30 A Conference is what type of fruit?

Answers	**Pot Luck 26** *(see Quiz 54)*

1 The mice. 2 Sports trophy (golf). 3 American Indians. 4 Questions. 5 Spanish. 6 The Pussycat Dolls. 7 David Schwimmer. 8 Six. 9 Advent. 10 A kimono. 11 Mount Sinai. 12 Johnny Depp. 13 Althorp Park. 14 Quotient. 15 Hiroshima. 16 Tottenham Hotspur. 17 Cook. 18 Germany. 19 Boxing. 20 Neuf. 21 Tiger. 22 Tuxedo. 23 Battle of Hastings. 24 Rabbit. 25 Terry Waite. 26 Yellow. 27 Victory in Europe. 28 168. 29 The eye. 30 Anne Frank.

1 According to the proverb, what plays when the cat's away?
2 Did Harry Vardon give his name to a disease, a sports trophy or a fruit?
3 Which people wore moccasins originally?
4 What does Q mean in FAQ?
5 What is the main spoken language in Mexico?
6 "PCD" was the first album by which girl group?
7 Which "Friends" star was the voice of the neurotic giraffe in "Madagascar"?
8 How many noughts are there in the written number fifty-two million?
9 Which season comes just before Christmas in the Christian calendar?
10 Which long dress is traditionally worn by Japanese women?
11 In the Bible, on which mountain was Moses told the commandments?
12 Who was Captain Jack Sparrow in the movie "Pirates of the Caribbean"?
13 At which Park is Princess Diana buried?
14 What does the Q stand for in IQ?
15 Where was the first atomic bomb dropped on 6 August 1945?
16 White Hart Lane is home to which football club?
17 What does Bill Granger usually do on TV?
18 Hanover, Westphalia and Bavaria are all parts of which country?
19 For which sport is Chris Eubank famous?
20 What is the French word for the number nine?
21 Which animal in the poem by Blake was described as "burning bright"?
22 What do Americans call a dinner jacket?
23 In which battle was King Harold killed?
24 What type of animal can be Dutch, Angora and Chinchilla?
25 Who was a Beirut hostage with John McCarthy and Brian Keenan?
26 What colour was the "itsy bitsy teeny weeny bikini" in the pop song?
27 What do the initials VE stand for in VE Day?
28 How many hours are there in a week?
29 Which part of the body can suffer from an astigmatism?
30 Which Jewish girl kept a diary while hidden in Amsterdam in 1942?

1 Which great screen dancer is on the cover of "Sgt Pepper"?
2 Which wartime classic starred Ingrid Bergman and Humphrey Bogart?
3 Who is Jamie Lee Curtis's actor father?
4 Cary Grant was born in which west country port?
5 Was Rita Hayworth a blonde or a redhead?
6 Was it Bob Hope or Bing Crosby who was born in south London?
7 Which monster was arguably Boris Karloff's most famous role?
8 How was dancer Eugene Curran Kelly better known?
9 Who was the original "Candle in the Wind" dedicated to?
10 Which Anthony starred as the lead character in "Psycho"?
11 Which Sir Alec starred in, and had a share of the profits of, "Star Wars"?
12 Who was taller, Rock Hudson or Mickey Rooney?
13 Which James starred in "Harvey" and "The Philadelphia Story"?
14 Which Italian-born actor is best known for silent movies such as "The Sheikh"?
15 Which Citizen was the subject of Orson Welles' first film?
16 Lauren Bacall was the wife of which Humphrey?
17 Tough guy Frank J. Cooper adopted which first name?
18 Which Joan starred in "Whatever Happened to Baby Jane"?
19 How was Ruth Elizabeth Davis better known?
20 Which Charlie was a founder of the film studio United Artists?
21 Bing Crosby had just finished a round of which game when he died?
22 William Claude Dunkenfield used his first two initials to become who?
23 Jane and Peter are the children of which screen great Henry?
24 Which Katharine enjoyed a long on and off screen relationship with Spencer Tracy?
25 Which Doris enjoyed popularity in films with Rock Hudson?
26 He was born John Uhler Lemmon III but how is he known in films?
27 Who is Michael Douglas's famous actor father?
28 In which German capital was Marlene Dietrich born?
29 Did Clark Gable die during his last film in the 40s, 50s or 60s?
30 Greta Garbo was born in which Scandinavian capital?

Answers	**Pot Luck 27** *(see Quiz 56)*

1 1970s. 2 An ill wind. 3 Harvey Keitel. 4 Beef cattle. 5 Windsor. 6 Runnymede. 7 Washington. 8 Around your waist. 9 Neun. 10 Egypt. 11 J. 12 Jack. 13 Origami. 14 Circus. 15 Dutch. 16 Krypton. 17 Trousers. 18 The teeth. 19 Spain. 20 900. 21 Jennifer Aniston. 22 The Archers. 23 Cavalier. 24 Easter. 25 Pink. 26 France. 27 Arachnophobia. 28 The skin. 29 Horses. 30 80th.

1 Charting again in 2004, in which decade was Abba's "Waterloo" first a hit?
2 What kind of wind blows no good according to the proverb?
3 Which Harvey starred in Quentin Tarantino's "Reservoir Dogs"?
4 What type of animal can be Charolais, Galloway and Simmental?
5 Which is the largest castle in Britain?
6 Where did King John sign the Magna Carta?
7 In which capital is the Capitol Building?
8 Where would you wear a cummerbund?
9 What is the German word for the number nine?
10 Which country had eleven kings called Rameses?
11 What appears most as the initial letter in calendar month names?
12 According to the rhyme, who fixed his head with vinegar and brown paper?
13 What name is given to the Japanese craft of paper folding?
14 Billy Smart and Chipperfields provided what type of entertainment?
15 What was the nationality of diarist Anne Frank?
16 What was the name of Superman's home planet?
17 Who or what are Oxford Bags?
18 What part of your body is covered by orthodontics?
19 Paella is a traditional dish from which country?
20 How many seconds are in a quarter of an hour?
21 Which "Friends" star has advertised L'Oreal?
22 Bridge Farm and Brookfield Farm feature in which long-running soap?
23 What type of person was Laughing in the famous portrait?
24 Which festival follows Lent in the Christian calendar?
25 What colour is the Financial Times?
26 Brittany and Picardy are parts of which country?
27 Which phobia describes the fear of spiders?
28 In medicine, what does a dermatologist specialise in?
29 Suffolk Punch, Shires and Clydesdales are all types of what?
30 David Attenborough celebrated which landmark birthday in 2006?

Answers	The Movies: Greats *(see Quiz 55)*

1 Fred Astaire. 2 Casablanca. 3 Tony Curtis. 4 Bristol. 5 Redhead. 6 Bob Hope. 7 Frankenstein's monster. 8 Gene Kelly. 9 Marilyn Monroe. 10 Perkins. 11 Guinness. 12 Rock Hudson. 13 Stewart. 14 Rudolph Valentino. 15 Citizen Kane. 16 Bogart. 17 Gary. 18 Crawford. 19 Bette Davis. 20 Chaplin. 21 Golf. 22 W.C. Fields. 23 Fonda. 24 Hepburn. 25 Day. 26 Jack Lemmon. 27 Kirk Douglas. 28 Berlin. 29 60s. 30 Stockholm.

1 In which country would you find Jerez?
2 How would you travel if you left for France from a hoverport?
3 In which Sea is the island of Majorca?
4 In which country is Cologne?
5 Does London or Rome have the higher population?
6 The province of Flanders is in which country?
7 Which landlocked country is divided into cantons?
8 In which city would you find the Parthenon?
9 Bohemia is part of which Republic, formerly part of Czechoslovakia?
10 Is Schiphol an airport or a river in the Netherlands?
11 Which island is in the Bay of Naples?
12 Where is the Black Forest?
13 What type of country is Monaco?
14 Andorra lies between France and which other country?
15 In which Sea does Cyprus lie?
16 Belarus and Ukraine were formerly part of which huge republic?
17 What is the English name for the city known to Italians as Venezia?
18 Is Sweden a kingdom or a republic?
19 Vienna lies on which river?
20 Is Ibiza part of the Canaries or the Balearics?
21 In which Circle does about a third of Finland lie?
22 The Hague is the seat of government of which country?
23 Crete and Corfu belong to which country?
24 Which Scandinavian country is opposite Norway and Sweden?
25 Is Europe the second largest or the second smallest continent?
26 Which country marks the most westerly point of mainland Europe?
27 The Iberian Peninsula consists of Portugal and which other country?
28 Which French city is mainland Europe's largest?
29 What are the Balkans, the Apennines and the Pyrenees?
30 Which island is known to the French as Corse?

1 Which Pamela featured in the "Borat" movie?
2 In Bruce Springsteen songs what goes before In The USA and To Run?
3 Which famous cricket commentator died of a heart attack in January 1994?
4 Which Lou wrote and sang "A Perfect Day"?
5 Was Liz Hurley born in the 50s, 60s, or 70s?
6 What does England spinner Ashley Giles often wear on his face when bowling?
7 Which Tory MP earned the name Goldilocks?
8 Which Harry created the character of Frank Doberman?
9 Which insects include drones, queens and workers?
10 Has a violin four, six or eight strings?
11 Which actor Peter played crumple-coated cop Columbo?
12 Fuzzy Zoeller was linked with which sport?
13 Where did Peter Mayle spend a year of his life?
14 In which county was the Plymouth Brethren founded?
15 Athena, Nike and Zeus were all what?
16 The movie "Starter for Ten" is about a student's ambition to be on which TV show?
17 In soccer what is the real first name of the keeper unkindly nicknamed "Calamity" James?
18 Which Derby is run at the Curragh?
19 Who had a best friend with the politically incorrect name of Big Ears?
20 A lateen sail is what shape?
21 Revie, Robson and Taylor have all managed which team?
22 Which valuable things were made by Thomas Sheraton?
23 On TV, Sabrina is the name of the Teenage... what?
24 Which musical instrument does Larry Adler play?
25 Tony Banks was Minister for what in Tony Blair's first Cabinet?
26 What type of crazy cops were created by Mack Sennett?
27 What do XL stand for in Roman numerals?
28 What's the foodie stage name of sizeable singer Marvin Lee Aday?
29 Brady, Macari and Stein have managed which Scottish soccer club?
30 What kind of animal is a fox terrier?

Answers	**Geography: Euro Tour** *(see Quiz 57)*

1 Spain. 2 Hovercraft. 3 Mediterranean. 4 Germany. 5 London. 6 Belgium. 7 Switzerland. 8 Athens. 9 Czech Republic. 10 Airport. 11 Capri. 12 Germany. 13 Principality. 14 Spain. 15 Mediterranean. 16 USSR. 17 Venice. 18 Kingdom. 19 Danube. 20 Balearics. 21 Arctic Circle. 22 Netherlands. 23 Greece. 24 Denmark. 25 Second smallest. 26 Portugal. 27 Spain. 28 Paris. 29 Mountain ranges. 30 Corsica.

1 Where is water stored in a cactus plant?
2 Are most conifers evergreen or deciduous?
3 Ceps and chanterelles are types of what?
4 Flax is grown to produce which fabric?
5 Which drug is obtained from the coca plant?
6 Bamboo is the tallest type of what?
7 Which Mexican drink comes from the agave plant?
8 Is it true or false that laurel has poisonous leaves?
9 The petiole is on which part of a plant?
10 What colour is cuckoo spit?
11 What colour are the flowers on a gorse bush?
12 Which perennial herb can be grown to create lawns?
13 What goes before lavender and holly to make another plant's name?
14 What can be obtained from the cassava plant which would have gone in a typical school dinner pudding?
15 Harebells are usually what colour?
16 Does a polyanthus have a single or several blooms?
17 Which ingredient in tonic water comes from the bark of the cinchona?
18 Which plants would a viticulturist grow?
19 Wild cornflowers are usually what colour?
20 Which paintbrush cleaner is found in the resin of a conifer?
21 Which pear has the most protein?
22 In the garden what would you use secateurs for?
23 Do peanuts grow on trees or low plants?
24 What colour is chlorophyll?
25 In which Gardens is the Princess of Wales Conservatory?
26 Cacti are native to which continent?
27 What would you find in an arboretum?
28 Which fast grower is nicknamed the mile-a-minute vine?
29 Which yellow flower is nicknamed the Lent lily?
30 Which trees carry their seeds in cones?

Answers	Pot Luck 29 *(see Quiz 60)*

1 A will. 2 Four. 3 Corfu. 4 Lion & Unicorn. 5 Zwanzig. 6 Bryan Adams. 7 A cactus.
8 Cheshire. 9 Street-Porter. 10 Australia. 11 World War II. 12 Black. 13 Landscape
Gardening. 14 A size of paper. 15 Edward Woodward. 16 A herb. 17 River Niagara. 18
Snow White. 19 Horse racing. 20 Beef. 21 Purple. 22 Three. 23 Alaska. 24 Wigan. 25
Simple Simon. 26 Luke and Matt Goss. 27 A kind of plum. 28 Celebrity Big Brother. 29
Lizzie. 30 Flattery.

1 If you die intestate you have not made what?
2 What's the least number of Mondays that can occur in July?
3 In which resort did the tragic deaths of the Shepherd children take place in Oct. 2006?
4 Which two animals are featured on the front of a British passport?
5 What is the German word for the number twenty?
6 Who had a No. 1 UK hit with "Everything I Do, I Do It for You"?
7 What is a prickly pear?
8 In which county, beginning with C, is "Goldplated" set?
9 Media person Janet Bull changed her last name to what in her search for "yoof"?
10 Bob Hawke was prime minister of which country?
11 The movie "Enigma" was set during which world conflict?
12 What colour is sable in heraldry?
13 For what was Capability Brown famous?
14 What is foolscap?
15 On TV who played the Equaliser?
16 What kind of plant is marjoram?
17 On which River are the Niagara Falls?
18 Which Disney movie includes the song "Heigh-Ho"?
19 For which sport is Willie Carson famous?
20 Sirloin, Rump and Topside are all joints of which meat?
21 What colour is Tinky Winky in the Teletubbies?
22 How many leaves are on a shamrock?
23 Which American state is the largest in area?
24 When Birmingham were relegated in 2006 Emile Heskey moved to which club?
25 According to the nursery rhyme, who met a pieman going to the fair?
26 Which two brothers made up the group Bros?
27 What is a bullace?
28 On which show did Chantelle Houghton first find fame?
29 A Model T Ford was nicknamed Tin what?
30 According to the proverb, imitation is the sincerest form of what?

Answers	Nature: Plant World *(see Quiz 59)*

1 Stem. 2 Evergreen. 3 Fungi. 4 Linen. 5 Cocaine. 6 Grass. 7 Tequila. 8 True. 9 Leaf stalk. 10 White. 11 Yellow. 12 Camomile. 13 Sea. 14 Tapioca. 15 Blue. 16 Several. 17 Quinine. 18 Vines. 19 Blue. 20 Turpentine. 21 Avocado. 22 Cutting, pruning. 23 Low plants. 24 Green. 25 Kew. 26 America. 27 Trees. 28 Russian Vine. 29 Daffodil. 30 Conifers.

Quiz 61 | Sporting Chance 2 | Answers – page 72

1 What type of sport is eventing?
2 Who celebrated 20 years as boss of the same top soccer club in November 2006?
3 Phidippides was the first runner of which 26-mile race?
4 Which Stephen was the then youngest ever winner of a professional snooker title in 1987?
5 Did Evander Holyfield box at heavyweight or welterweight?
6 Which country did Virginia Leng represent at the Olympic Games?
7 FC Porto play football in which country?
8 At the USA PGA Championships, what game is played?
9 Did Shane Warne first play English county cricket for Essex or Hampshire?
10 At which sport might you see the American Williams sisters play?
11 Does the Le Mans 24-hour race take place in summer or winter?
12 In swimming, is freestyle usually performed on the back or front?
13 Which country won the first 25 America's Cup trophies in yachting?
14 In which sport is there a Foil discipline?
15 How was boxer Rocco Francis Marchegiano better known?
16 Caber tossing is native to which country?
17 In 2006, where did the Cardinals come from who won baseball's World Series?
18 For which national rugby side did Gavin Hastings play?
19 Magic Johnson found fame at which US sport?
20 Which horse race is sometimes called just The National?
21 What was tennis's Billie Jean Moffitt's married name?
22 Which Jackie's record of Grand Prix wins did Alain Prost pass in 1987?
23 Which heavyweight Mike knocked out 15 of his first 25 pro opponents in the first round?
24 Which international rugby venue opened a new South Stand in November 2006?
25 In which sport is a ball hit through a hoop with a mallet?
26 What is Scottish long-distance runner Liz Lynch's married name?
27 What does the first F in FIFA stand for?
28 F1 driver Jacques Villeneuve is from which country?
29 Which winter sport can be alpine or Nordic?
30 Is the Oaks a race for colts or fillies?

Answers	Pot Luck 30 (see Quiz 62)

1 Two. 2 Mean. 3 Lettuce. 4 Five seasons. 5 An even number. 6 Green. 7 Little Britain. 8 The mirror. 9 Half a pound of tuppenny rice. 10 Eight. 11 Westlife. 12 Penny Black. 13 Judas. 14 Half a crown. 15 The Banger Sisters. 16 One. 17 The Alps. 18 Gold. 19 Pepper. 20 Westminster Abbey. 21 A knot. 22 Coffee. 23 Victory. 24 Bread. 25 Green. 26 The harp. 27 Blue. 28 White Star Line. 29 A filament. 30 Queen Victoria.

1. How many people perform a pas de deux in a ballet?
2. If T is time what is M in G.M.T.?
3. Cos and Iceberg are varieties of which salad plant?
4. Did Ruud van Nistelrooy play three, five or seven seasons for Man Utd?
5. What type of number will you always get if you add two odd numbers together?
6. In movies is Shrek blue, green or purple?
7. Which TV series featured the Thai bride Ting Tong?
8. Who told the Queen that Snow White was the "fairest of them all"?
9. What is mixed with half a pound of treacle in "Pop Goes the Weasel"?
10. How many furlongs are there in a mile?
11. Who had a 2003 hit with "Miss You Nights", made famous by Cliff Richard?
12. What was the common name for the first postage stamp?
13. Which biblical character had the second name Iscariot?
14. What was the name for two shillings and sixpence?
15. In which film are Goldie Hawn and Susan Sarandon a pair of 50 something ex-groupies?
16. How many hooks do you use for crochet?
17. The Matterhorn is in which European mountain range?
18. What did Fort Knox originally store?
19. Steak au poivre is steak covered in what?
20. Where did the Queen's Coronation take place?
21. If you asked a Scout to make a sheep-shank, what would he make?
22. What drink is the main export from Brazil?
23. What was the name of Admiral Nelson's ship?
24. Chapatti is a kind of Indian what?
25. What colour is the door of the pub the Rovers Return?
26. Which stringed instrument has the most strings in an orchestra?
27. What colour is connected with the River Danube?
28. Which shipping line did Titanic belong to?
29. What is the name of the glowing curly wire in a light bulb?
30. At the start of the 20th century who was Queen of England?

Answers	Sporting Chance 2 (see Quiz 61)

1 Equestrian. 2 Sir Alex Ferguson. 3 Marathon. 4 Hendry. 5 Heavyweight. 6 Great Britain. 7 Portugal. 8 Golf. 9 Hampshire. 10 Tennis. 11 Summer. 12 Front. 13 USA. 14 Fencing. 15 Rocky Marciano. 16 Scotland. 17 St Louis. 18 Scotland. 19 Basketball. 20 Grand National. 21 King. 22 Stewart. 23 Tyson. 24 Twickenham. 25 Croquet. 26 McColgan. 27 Federation. 28 Canada. 29 Skiing. 30 Fillies.

1 Which "Grease" classic begins "I got chills, they're multiplyin'"?

2 Which Madonna hit contains the words, "Ring, ring ring"?

3 What is the first line of "Nessun Dorma"?

4 What did Tina Turner sing after "Do I love you, my oh my"?

5 What follows the Beatles' "will you still need me, will you still feed me"?

6 Which song begins, "I feel it in my fingers, I feel it in my toes"?

7 In "Candle in the Wind 98" how are England's hills described?

8 How many times is "submarine" sung in the chorus of "Yellow Submarine"?

9 Which hit began "Oh my love, my darlin', I hunger for your touch"?

10 Which song's second line is "and so I face the final curtain"?

11 Which song begins "First I was afraid I was petrified"?

12 In which song did Tammy Wynette complain "Sometime it's hard to be a woman"?

13 Which Slade Xmas hit has the line "Everybody's having fun"?

14 In the "Titanic" song what follows, "Near, far, wherever you are, I believe..."?

15 What follows Bryan Adams' "Everything I do"?

16 Which Dire Straits hit begins "Here comes Johnny"?

17 What follows "Two little boys had two little....."?

18 Which charity hit has the line "Feed the world"?

19 What follows The Spice Girls' "swing it, shake it, move it, make it"?

20 Which Abba hit states "I was defeated you won the war"?

21 What do neighbours become in the original "Neighbours" theme song?

22 What follows "I believe for every drop of rain that falls"?

23 Which football anthem speaks of "Jules Rimet still gleaming"?

24 Which song's second chorus line is "I just called to say I care"?

25 Which Evita song begins, "It won't be easy, you'll think it strange"?

26 What did Boy George sing after singing karma five times?

27 Which "Lion King" song began "From the day we arrive on the planet"?

28 Which Simon & Garfunkel hit begins "When you're weary, feeling small"?

29 Which traditional song has the line, "The pipes, the pipes are calling"?

30 What are the last three words of Queen's "We are the Champions"?

Answers | **Pot Luck 31** *(see Quiz 64)*

1 The Peril. 2 McFly. 3 Mint. 4 Soldier Sailor. 5 Calais. 6 Horse racing. 7 August.
8 Berkshire. 9 Trombone. 10 Tuesday. 11 VAT. 12 Bulb. 13 Yellow. 14 Cricket. 15
Andrew Lloyd Webber. 16 Boxing (heavyweight). 17 Minestrone. 18 Champagne. 19
Little girls. 20 Patience. 21 Melbourne. 22 Silver. 23 Ganges. 24 Tannic/Tannin. 25
Boots. 26 A house. 27 Please. 28 Red. 29 Nose. 30 Sherry.

1 If Dennis is the Menace what is Beryl?
2 Who had a 2004 No. 1 single with "5 Colours in Her Hair"?
3 Which sweet flavoured herb is often used to accompany roast lamb?
4 According to the rhyme, which two characters followed Tinker Tailor?
5 Which French port is closest to Britain?
6 To see which sport could you go to Towcester?
7 Lammas Day is in which month?
8 In which county is the Royal Military Academy at Sandhurst?
9 Which brass instrument has a sliding, adjustable tube?
10 Which day's child is "full of grace" according to the traditional rhyme?
11 Which present-day tax replaced Purchase Tax in 1973?
12 Is a snowdrop grown from a bulb or seed?
13 What colour is Laa Laa in the "Teletubbies"?
14 For which sport is David Gower famous?
15 Who composed the music for "Cats"?
16 Found dead in 2006, Trevor Berbick was a former world champion in which sport?
17 Which soup is made from a variety of vegetables and pasta?
18 What sort of drink is Moet & Chandon?
19 Maurice Chevalier "thanked heaven" for what?
20 Which has smaller cards, an ordinary pack or a patience pack?
21 Which Australian city stands near the mouth of the Yarra river?
22 What colour is argent in heraldry?
23 The city of Calcutta stands on which river?
24 Tea contains which acid?
25 Which High Street chemists shop opened its first store in 1877?
26 What are you probably buying if you are gazumped?
27 What does the Italian "per favore" mean?
28 What colour, together with yellow, is the Spanish flag?
29 The symbol for Comic Relief is a red what?
30 What kind of drink can be Bristol Cream?

Answers | Pop: Karaoke *(see Quiz 63)*

1 You're the One that I Want. 2 Wannabe. 3 Nessun dorma, nessun dorma. 4 River deep mountain high. 5 When I'm sixty-four. 6 Love is All Around. 7 Greenest. 8 Six. 9 Unchained Melody. 10 My Way. 11 I Will Survive. 12 Stand by Your Man. 13 Merry Christmas Everybody. 14 That the heart does go on. 15 I do it for you. 16 Walk of Life. 17 Toys. 18 Do They Know It's Christmas? 19 Who do you think you are?. 20 Waterloo. 21 Good friends. 22 A flower grows. 23 Three Lions. 24 I Just Called to Say I Love You. 25 Don't Cry for Me Argentina. 26 Chameleon. 27 Circle of Life. 28 Bridge Over Troubled Water. 29 Danny Boy. 30 Of the world.

1 Which is the female half of Mulder and Scully?
2 Who first presented "Deal or No Deal" on Channel 4?
3 What is the subject of the Channel 4 show "Hooked"?
4 "Torchwood" is an anagram of which series of which it is a spin-off?
5 What colour is Channel 5's logo?
6 Which Ally is a zany US TV lawyer?
7 What would Peter Cockcroft talk about on TV?
8 Who took over "Gardener's World" from the late Geoff Hamilton?
9 Which Australian co-presents "Animal Hospital"?
10 Maureen Rees found TV fame at what type of School?
11 GMTV is usually seen at what time of day?
12 Which letters does TV's Kavanagh have after his name?
13 What sex is the audience of Chris Tarrant's show "Man O Man"?
14 Which Adrian became a regular presenter of "Match of the Day 2"?
15 Which TV presenter is Johnny Ball's daughter?
16 Which Mary founded the Clean Up TV campaign in 1964?
17 Which female pop quintet launched Channel 5?
18 Does Oz Clarke specialise in food or drink?
19 Which Jerry hosts a controversial talk show?
20 In which work location was the series "The Hello Girls" set?
21 Which Carol took over from Anne Robinson on "Points of View"?
22 What links Terry Wogan, Les Dawson and Lily Savage?
23 Which part of the country is served by Anglia Television?
24 "Ground Force" offered a viewer a makeover in which part of the home?
25 On which day of the week was "Countryfile" broadcast?
26 "It's good to talk" was the ad slogan of which phone company?
27 Who is taller, John Cleese or Ronnie Corbett?
28 Which broadcasting corporation is known as Auntie?
29 How many studio judges are there on "The X Factor"?
30 Who is the human half of Wallace and Gromit?

| **Answers** | **Pot Luck 32** *(see Quiz 66)* |

1 Steve Coppell. 2 The farmer's wife. 3 R.E.M.. 4 Diamonds. 5 Broken. 6 All Saints.
7 1984. 8 Apples. 9 Rutland. 10 Stupid Mistake. 11 Sussex. 12 Hops. 13 Pears.
14 Saviour's Day. 15 Jennifer Lopez. 16 White. 17 He was married. 18 The Doge.
19 Eight. 20 Dance steps. 21 A plant. 22 Richard. 23 Red. 24 Birmingham. 25
Three. 26 Bank of England. 27 Goodwood. 28 Champagne. 29 A bulb. 30 New
York.

1 Which manager took Reading into the Premiership in 2006?
2 According to the nursery rhyme, who cut off the three mice tails?
3 Whose best-of album from 1988–2003 was called "In Time"?
4 What is mined at Kimberley in South Africa?
5 What does a German mean if he says something is "kaput"?
6 Who had a No. 1 UK hit in September 1998 with "Bootie Call"?
7 Which George Orwell novel has a year as its title?
8 Cider is made from which fruit?
9 What was the smallest county in England until 1974?
10 What was in brackets in the title of Gareth Gates's "Anyone of Us"?
11 Chris Adams captained which side to cricket's County Championship?
12 What is dried in Kentish oast houses?
13 Which fruit can be served Belle Helene?
14 Which Day gave Cliff Richard a No. 1 for Christmas 1990?
15 In "Out of Sight" which Jennifer starred along with George Clooney?
16 What colour along with red and blue is the Luxembourg flag?
17 What happened to Solomon Grundy on Wednesday, according to the rhyme?
18 Historically speaking, who was the chief magistrate of Venice?
19 On the Union Jack, how many blue triangles are there?
20 What does a choreographer plan?
21 What is a yucca?
22 In pop music, who is Jagger's long-time writing partner?
23 What colour is Po in the "Teletubbies"?
24 "Crossroads" was set near which major city?
25 How many people are in a boat in a rowing coxed pair race?
26 What is sometimes called the "Old Lady of Threadneedle Street"?
27 Which race meeting is known as "Glorious"?
28 What was invented by Dom Peter Perignon, a French monk?
29 Is a tulip grown from seed or a bulb?
30 Which American city has the Yankees and Mets baseball teams?

---

1 What is the surname of German F1 drivers Ralf and Michael?
2 Which jump event did Carl Lewis specialise in as well as sprinting?
3 Did Man Utd's Gabriel Heinze play for Argentina or Germany in the 2006 World Cup?
4 Is professional badminton an indoor or outdoor game or both?
5 What was the professional name of boxer Joe Louis Barrow?
6 Which much-capped England Rugby star Matt took part in a TV dancing contest?
7 Did Asafa Powell become the world's fastest man at 100m or the London Marathon?
8 At which sport did suspended Irish Olympic gold medal winner Michelle de Bruin compete?
9 Which horned animal name does Leeds' Rugby Super League team have?
10 In which sport might you hit another living thing with a crop?
11 Peter O'Sullevan commentated on which sport?
12 Which Rugby side shares its name with stinging insects?
13 Which red flower is the emblem of the England Rugby Union team?
14 In which country is the golfing venue Valderrama?
15 Which motoring Grand Prix is held at the Hungaroring?
16 What's the highest score in darts from three different doubles?
17 In which country is the oldest football league in the world?
18 Which area of New York has a Globetrotters basketball team?
19 Which Bin was introduced for Rugby League players in 1983?
20 How many disciplines are there in a biathlon?
21 In which Sheffield theatre were the World Snooker Championships first held in 1977?
22 In which country was judo coincidentally added to the Olympic programme?
23 In badminton what were goose feathers used for?
24 What is the usual surface of the lane in ten-pin bowling?
25 Which German Men's Wimbledon champion was born on Billie Jean King's 23rd birthday?
26 Which Lennox of the UK became undisputed world heavyweight champ?
27 On what surface is curling played?
28 Which animal is on top of Rugby's Calcutta Cup?
29 In which sport would you wear a judogi?
30 What type of sporting event was The Rumble in the Jungle?

Answers	**Pot Luck 33** *(see Quiz 68)*

1 Rise & Fall. 2 A hat. 3 Liver. 4 Julie Walters. 5 The Severn Estuary. 6 Music. 7 Swimming. 8 Tower of London. 9 Peter Sellers. 10 1950s. 11 A beetle. 12 Isle of Dogs. 13 Hastings. 14 African. 15 Dudley Moore. 16 Kate Winslet. 17 Antelope. 18 Moscow. 19 Red. 20 The Bill. 21 Saddam Hussein. 22 Two. 23 Vauxhall. 24 A bull. 25 Four. 26 Sheffield. 27 Chippendale. 28 None. 29 Trotters. 30 Australia.

1 Which Craig David hit featured Sting?
2 What is a tam-o'-shanter?
3 Which organ is particularly affected by hepatitis?
4 Who played the title role in the film "Educating Rita"?
5 On which river estuary does Swansea stand?
6 The letters F.R.A.M. mean a Fellow of which Royal Academy?
7 For which sport was Duncan Goodhew famous?
8 The raven is traditionally associated with which Tower?
9 Who played Inspector Clouseau in the original "Pink Panther" films?
10 Was Condoleezza Rice born in the 1950s, 1960s or 1970s?
11 What is a cockchafer?
12 Which animal isle is in the River Thames?
13 Where did a famous battle take place in 1066?
14 Which elephants are the larger - African or Indian?
15 Which English musician and comedian married Tuesday Weld?
16 Who was the female lead in the movie "Enigma"?
17 What kind of mammal is a chamois?
18 In which city is Pushkin Square?
19 Does coq au vin contain red or white wine?
20 Which TV series is set in Sun Hill police station?
21 During the Gulf War, who was the leader of Iraq?
22 How many members of the public join the chefs in "Ready Steady Cook"?
23 Which car maker has the same name as a London bridge?
24 Which animal should you take by the horns, according to the proverb?
25 How many pins are in the back row of a ten-pin bowling triangle?
26 Which city is further North – Bristol or Sheffield?
27 Which of Chippendale, Ming and Wedgwood is not a type of pottery?
28 How much gold is there in a one-pound coin?
29 What are a pig's feet called?
30 Of which country's coast is the world's largest coral reef?

Answers	**Sporting Chance 3** *(see Quiz 67)*

1 Schumacher. 2 Long jump. 3 Argentina. 4 Indoor. 5 Joe Louis. 6 Matt Dawson.
7 100m. 8 Swimming. 9 Rhinos. 10 Equestrianism. 11 Horse racing. 12 Wasps. 13
Rose. 14 Spain. 15 Hungarian. 16 114. 17 England. 18 Harlem. 19 Sin bin. 20
Two. 21 Crucible. 22 Japan. 23 Shuttlecock. 24 Wood. 25 Boris Becker. 26 Lennox
Lewis. 27 Ice. 28 Elephant. 29 Judo. 30 Boxing match.

1 What was the Spice Girls' first film?
2 Who with The Shadows starred in "The Young Ones"?
3 Which movie told of redundant steel workers becoming strippers?
4 "The Bridge on the River Kwai" prisoners are imprisoned by whom?
5 Nick Hornby's "Fever Pitch" is about which game?
6 Which Kenneth directed and starred in "Hamlet"?
7 "The Blue Lamp" preceded which TV series about PC George Dixon?
8 A BAFTA is a British Award for film and what?
9 What nationality was The ... Patient in the 1996 Oscar winner?
10 Which US food expert Loyd is the son-in-law of David Puttnam?
11 Mrs Blake Edwards won an Oscar for "Mary Poppins"; who was she?
12 What is the nationality of Sir Anthony Hopkins?
13 In which part of the UK was "Trainspotting" set?
14 Which one-time British Transport Minister twice won an Oscar?
15 Which Sir Richard directed "Chaplin"?
16 Which 1994 British hit shot Hugh Grant to superstardom?
17 Which Emma wrote the screenplay for "Sense & Sensibility"?
18 Jenny Agutter found fame in which movie about an Edwardian family?
19 Is Helena Bonham Carter a British Prime Minister's or a US President's granddaughter?
20 Elizabeth Taylor was twice married to this Welsh actor; who was he?
21 Who was born Maurice Micklewhite?
22 Which Julie was Oscar nominated in 1998?
23 Which Ewan plays the young Obi Wan Kenobi in Episode I of "Star Wars"?
24 In which film did Tom Conti play Pauline Collins' Greek lover?
25 Which blonde bombshell was born Diana Fluck?
26 Linus Roache's father has played which "Coronation Street" character since the soap began?
27 Who or what was the film "Wilde" with Stephen Fry about?
28 Which former James Bond became a goodwill ambassador for UNICEF?
29 In which part of the UK was Robert Carlyle born?
30 Hot Chocolate's "You Sexy Thing" was the theme for which 1997 film?

Answers | **Pot Luck 34** *(see Quiz 70)*

1 France. 2 Windsor Castle. 3 Yogi Bear. 4 Lime. 5 Badminton. 6 Oysters. 7 Blackburn. 8 Five. 9 Johnny Cash. 10 Coronation. 11 Flock together. 12 Poet. 13 Watford. 14 Javelin. 15 Cornwall. 16 A catamaran. 17 Eeyore. 18 L. S. 19 An apple. 20 Europe, Asia. 21 Elizabeth I. 22 Yachting. 23 Yugoslavia. 24 Goat. 25 Leeds. 26 Peppermint. 27 The humming bird. 28 Cricket. 29 The Kumars. 30 Bottom.

1 The Dauphin was heir to which European throne?
2 Which castle was partly damaged by fire in 1992?
3 Which bear had a friend called Boo Boo?
4 What is another name for a linden tree?
5 Which sport is named after a place which is famous for horse trials?
6 The precious stone, a pearl, can be found in what?
7 Craig Bellamy joined Liverpool from which soccer club?
8 How many senior titles (excluding over-35 events) are contested each Wimbledon?
9 The movie "Walk the Line" was about which singer?
10 At which ceremony is a Monarch given their crown?
11 According to the saying, what do birds of a feather do?
12 Was Ted Hughes a dancer, painter or poet?
13 Elton John is an ex-Chairman of which club back in the Premiership in 2006?
14 For which sport is Tessa Sanderson famous?
15 Prince Charles is Duke of which English county?
16 What is a yacht with two hulls called?
17 Which character from "Winnie The Pooh" lost his tail?
18 What two initials did northern artist Lowry have?
19 What did William Tell shoot from his son's head with a crossbow?
20 Which continents are separated by the Urals?
21 Who was England's Queen when Shakespeare was alive?
22 Cowes on the Isle of Wight is famous for which sport?
23 Which country was formerly ruled by President Tito?
24 Which animal's milk is used to make cheese called Chevre?
25 Which city is further North – Lincoln or Leeds?
26 What flavour is Kendal's most famous cake?
27 Which is the only bird that can fly backwards?
28 What is John Major's favourite sport?
29 Which TV family featured on a No. 1 recording of "Spirit in the Sky"?
30 Which part of your body is a character in Shakespeare's "A Midsummer Night's Dream"?

Answers | The Movies: The Brits *(see Quiz 69)*

1 Spiceworld The Movie. 2 Cliff Richard. 3 The Full Monty. 4 Japanese. 5 Football. 6 Branagh. 7 Dixon of Dock Green. 8 Television. 9 English. 10 Grossman. 11 Julie Andrews. 12 Welsh. 13 Scotland. 14 Glenda Jackson. 15 Attenborough. 16 Four Weddings and a Funeral. 17 Thompson. 18 The Railway Children. 19 British Prime Minister's. 20 Richard Burton. 21 Michael Caine. 22 Christie. 23 McGregor. 24 Shirley Valentine. 25 Diana Dors. 26 Ken Barlow. 27 Oscar Wilde. 28 Roger Moore. 29 Scotland. 30 The Full Monty.

1 What sort of security device is a Chubb?
2 An Entryphone would normally be found at the entrance to what?
3 What in the bedroom would have a TOG rating?
4 What colour is Copydex adhesive?
5 What is the abbreviation for volt?
6 Is pine a soft or hard wood?
7 Which machine tool is used for turning wood?
8 Do weft fibres run across the width or the length of a fabric?
9 What goes between a nut and the surface to protect it?
10 Soldering joins two pieces of what?
11 Cushions, curtains etc. are referred to as what sort of furnishings?
12 Should silk be washed in hot or cool water?
13 Which tool can be band, hand or hack?
14 E numbers refer to additives to what?
15 Is an emery cloth rough or smooth?
16 Which device turns off an appliance when a temperature is reached?
17 A rasp is a type of what?
18 Is Araldite a strong or light glue?
19 In which sort of bank would you deposit waste glass?
20 Canning, bottling and freezing are types of what?
21 What would a bradawl produce in wood?
22 Batik is a type of dyeing on what?
23 What would you normally make in a percolator?
24 Where is the door on a chest freezer?
25 A bedsit usually consists of how many rooms?
26 What type of electrical devices are "white goods"?
27 Is a kilogram less or more than two pounds in weight?
28 What colour does silver turn when it is tarnished?
29 Which wood is darker, mahogany or ash?
30 What does the ply of a yarn refer to?

Answers	**Pot Luck 35** *(see Quiz 72)*

1 George Bush. 2 Sheffield. 3 Dock. 4 North Sea. 5 Angela Lansbury. 6 China.
7 Lines of longitude. 8 Scotland. 9 Australia. 10 Furniture. 11 Buttons. 12 Red
Rum. 13 Daisy. 14 Melinda. 15 Blubber. 16 Red. 17 Bob Dylan. 18 Birds of a
Feather. 19 Chocolate. 20 Roy Rogers. 21 Decathlon. 22 King John. 23 Scotland.
24 Macaulay Culkin. 25 Vodafone. 26 White. 27 At the beginning. 28 Sand. 29
Four. 30 Plane.

1 Who was the last President of the USA elected in the 1980s?
2 Which city is further North – Cardiff or Sheffield?
3 Which plant helps to take away the sting of a stinging nettle?
4 The River Forth flows into which Sea?
5 Which actress plays Jessica Fletcher in "Murder She Wrote"?
6 Which country was ruled by Chairman Mao?
7 What name is given to the imaginary lines drawn from north to south on a map?
8 Where in Britain can you spend paper £1 notes?
9 Which country did Everton's Tim Cahill play for in soccer's 2006 World Cup?
10 Thomas Sheraton was a designer and manufacturer of what?
11 Which came first, zips, velcro or buttons?
12 Which horse named after a drink won the Grand National three times?
13 What was the name of Donald Duck's girlfriend?
14 What is the name of Bill Gates's wife?
15 What is the fat of a whale called?
16 Which is the warmest sea in the world, The Red, Med or Dead?
17 Who wrote the pop anthem "Knockin' on Heaven's Door"?
18 Who or what flock together according to the saying?
19 What is the flavour of a Devil's Food Cake?
20 Which cowboy had a horse called Trigger?
21 For which event is Daley Thompson famous?
22 Which King put his seal on the Magna Carta?
23 Which is nearest to Ireland, England, Scotland or Wales?
24 Who is Kieran Culkin's brother, famed as a movie child star?
25 Which company's name was on the shirts of the 2005 Ashes winners?
26 What colour balls were used at Wimbledon before yellow balls?
27 Where would you expect to hear the prologue in a play?
28 Which of the following will not dissolve in water: salt, sugar or sand?
29 How many teats does a cow have normally?
30 Was the Flying Fortress a plane or a train?

Answers | Leisure: Home & D-I-Y *(see Quiz 71)*

1 Lock. 2 Block of flats. 3 Duvet. 4 White. 5 V. 6 Soft. 7 Lathe. 8 Width. 9 Washer. 10 Metal. 11 Soft furnishings. 12 Cool. 13 Saw. 14 Food. 15 Rough. 16 Thermostat. 17 File. 18 Strong. 19 Bottle bank. 20 Preserving. 21 Hole. 22 Fabric. 23 Coffee. 24 Top. 25 One. 26 Large kitchen appliances, such as freezers and washing machines. 27 More. 28 Black. 29 Mahogany. 30 Its thickness.

1 Which football anthem was co written by Skinner and Baddiel?
2 What is the surname of Oasis brothers Noel and Liam?
3 Whom was "Candle in the Wind" 1997 dedicated to?
4 Which Zoo sang "Spaceman" in 1996?
5 In which drama series did chart toppers Robson & Jerome find fame?
6 Isaac, Taylor and Zac make up which boy band?
7 Who said "Eh Oh" on the their first smash hit?
8 Whose album of "Urban Hymns" hit the top spot?
9 Which 90s band were named after an area of London?
10 "Knockin' on Heaven's Door" was released after which 1996 tragedy?
11 Which single was released by Robson & Jerome and two years later by The Three Tenors?
12 Who was "Older" in the 90s after a long-running battle with Sony?
13 Who were "Back for Good" in 1995 before disbanding?
14 Whose death propelled "Bohemian Rhapsody" back to the charts?
15 Which Peter had a No. 1 with "Flava"?
16 Who had a No. 1 with Nilsson's "Without You"?
17 Who backed Katrina on her 1997 Eurovision winner?
18 Which Damon fronted Blur?
19 Who starred in and sang on the soundtrack of "The Bodyguard"?
20 In September '98 Celine Dion released an album in which language?
21 Which toy provided Aqua with a No. 1?
22 Which country singer John died flying his plane in 1997?
23 Who had a daughter Lourdes Maria in 1996?
24 Which band's name is a US emergency number?
25 Dana International won Eurovision '98 for which Middle East country?
26 Oasis were formed in which UK city?
27 Who had a huge hit with "Drop Dead Gorgeous"?
28 Which Darren appeared in the 90s version of "Summer Holiday"?
29 In which county were Blur formed?
30 "My Heart Will Go On" came from which smash hit film?

Answers | **Pot Luck 36** *(see Quiz 74)*

1 Tasmania. 2 Balsawood. 3 Tennis. 4 The candlestick maker. 5 Up. 6 Roald Dahl. 7 Hindu. 8 St David. 9 USA. 10 1940s. 11 Davy Crockett. 12 Polo. 13 Shoes. 14 South Pacific. 15 George Bush. 16 Sean Hughes. 17 Australia. 18 Jessica. 19 St Ives. 20 Alan Davies. 21 Four. 22 Jacobites. 23 Touché. 24 Rainbow. 25 Avon. 26 Liverpool. 27 Black and yellow. 28 Javelin. 29 One. 30 Chester.

1 Which Australian state is named after its discoverer Abel Tasman?
2 Which very soft wood is popular with model makers?
3 Which sport was played by Gabriela Sabatini?
4 According to the nursery rhyme, who joined the butcher and baker?
5 Do bananas grow pointing up or down?
6 Who wrote "Charlie and the Chocolate Factory"?
7 The River Ganges is sacred to the people of which religion?
8 Which Saint is the patron saint of Wales?
9 Which country was the 1994 football World Cup Final played in?
10 Was Terry Venables born in the 1940s, 1950s or the 1960s?
11 Which American hero wore a hat with a racoon tail hanging from the back?
12 Which sport is played on the largest pitch: cricket, football or polo?
13 What are or were winkle pickers?
14 Which part of an ocean shares its name with a musical?
15 Who was American president immediately before Bill Clinton?
16 Which Sean was was the star of "Sean's Show" on TV?
17 Does Nicole Kidman come from Australia or Austria?
18 What is the middle name of Sarah Parker, famed for "Sex and the City"?
19 Where was the person going, who met a man with seven wives?
20 Which Alan portrayed the character Jonathan Creek?
21 In the neck of a violin how many tuning pegs are there?
22 What were supporters of James II and his Stuart descendants called?
23 What is shouted by people when they make contact in fencing?
24 Which children's TV programme featured Bungle and Zippy?
25 Which English county shares its name with a beauty products range?
26 Man Utd's Alan Smith suffered a serious leg injury against which club early in 2006?
27 What colour is Rupert the Bear's scarf?
28 For which sport was Fatima Whitbread famous?
29 How many players take part in a game of patience at any one time?
30 Which city is further North – Bristol or Chester?

| **Answers** | **Pop: The 90s** *(see Quiz 73)* |

1 Three Lions. 2 Gallagher. 3 Diana, Princess of Wales. 4 Babylon Zoo. 5 Soldier Soldier. 6 Hanson. 7 Teletubbies. 8 The Verve. 9 East 17. 10 Dunblane. 11 You'll Never Walk Alone. 12 George Michael. 13 Take That. 14 Freddie Mercury. 15 Andre. 16 Mariah Carey. 17 The Waves. 18 Albarn. 19 Whitney Houston. 20 French. 21 Barbie. 22 Denver. 23 Madonna. 24 911. 25 Israel. 26 Manchester. 27 Republica. 28 Day. 29 Essex. 30 Titanic.

1 Which former leader went on trial in his own country in October 2005?
2 In which country were the Borgias a powerful family?
3 Benazir Bhutto was Prime Minister of which Muslim state?
4 Which Al was crime boss of Chicago during Prohibition?
5 Which South African shared the Nobel Peace Prize with FW de Klerk in 1993?
6 What was President John F. Kennedy's wife called?
7 Which Australian painter and TV presenter received a CBE in 2006?
8 In which country was Terry Waite imprisoned?
9 Roman Emperor Hadrian gave his name to what in Britain?
10 Which animals did Hannibal use to frighten the Romans?
11 Hirohito was Emperor of which country during WWII?
12 Which Russian word for Caesar was used by Russian monarchs?
13 What was T.E. Lawrence's sobriquet?
14 Which Russian revolutionary took his name from the River Lena?
15 In which century did Columbus discover America?
16 Which 11thC Scottish king was the subject of a Shakespeare play?
17 In which country of the UK was David Livingstone born?
18 Which British admiral Horatio was born in Norfolk?
19 Where is Botany Bay?
20 Which country put the first woman in space?
21 Which journalist John was imprisoned in Beirut with Brian Keenan?
22 What was Argentinean vice president Eva Duarte's married name?
23 Ho Chi Minh founded the Communist Party in which country?
24 Angela Merkel became leader in which country?
25 Which outspoken TV chef received an OBE in the 2006 New Year's Honours?
26 In which country was Joan of Arc born?
27 Where was the tomb of Tutankhamun discovered in 1922?
28 Which famous Indian monument was built by Shah Jahan?
29 Zulu leader Buthelezi became a government minister where?
30 Which nurse is famous for her work during the Crimean War?

Answers	**Pot Luck 37** *(see Quiz 76)*

1 Arsenal. 2 Marzipan. 3 Rural England. 4 Two. 5 22. 6 Putty. 7 Roger Bannister. 8 Ballet. 9 Glasgow. 10 Eleven. 11 Right. 12 A skateboard. 13 Carrot. 14 Gymnasts. 15 Billy Butlin. 16 The sea. 17 A fiddle. 18 Cookery. 19 Canada. 20 19th. 21 Collar bone. 22 Victoria. 23 The service. 24 Forget. 25 Grass. 26 Kill You. 27 Val Kilmer. 28 1990s. 29 The knight. 30 Red and black.

1 Which English team made their first Champions League final appearance in 2006?
2 What name is given to the almond coating often on a Christmas cake?
3 C.P.R.E. is the Council for the Protection of what?
4 How many Bank Holidays are there in May?
5 How many yards are there between the wickets in cricket?
6 What sticky paste usually holds glass in a window?
7 Who was the first person to run a mile in under four minutes?
8 What is performed by the Russian Bolshoi company?
9 Which Scottish city has the biggest population?
10 How many players can a team have on the field in American football?
11 On a UK coin does Elizabeth II face left or right?
12 What has a kicktail and four wheels?
13 Which vegetable, high in vitamin A, is said to be good for the eyes?
14 What kind of athletes perform a flic-flac?
15 Who set up England's biggest chain of holiday camps?
16 Neptune was the god of what?
17 According to the saying, which instrument can you be as fit as?
18 What type of TV programmes are presented by Keith Floyd?
19 Which is biggest – the USA, Germany or Canada?
20 Was basketball developed in the 17th, 18th or 19th century?
21 What is the common name for the clavicle?
22 Africa's biggest lake is named after which British queen?
23 What is the name given to the first hit in a game of tennis?
24 What do elephants never do according to the saying?
25 Bamboo is a very large variety of what?
26 What will too much love do, according to Brian May?
27 In the movies, which Val replaced Michael Keaton as Batman?
28 In which decade was "Hollyoaks" first broadcast?
29 Which chess piece is shaped like a horse's head?
30 What two colours are Dennis the Menace's sweater?

Answers	**People & Places** (see Quiz 75)

1 Saddam Hussein. 2 Italy. 3 Pakistan. 4 Capone. 5 Nelson Mandela. 6 Jackie.
7 Rolf Harris.. 8 Lebanon. 9 Hadrian's Wall. 10 Elephants. 11 Japan. 12 Tsar.
13 Lawrence of Arabia. 14 Lenin. 15 15th century. 16 Macbeth. 17 Scotland. 18
Nelson. 19 Australia. 20 USSR. 21 McCarthy. 22 Peron. 23 Vietnam. 24 Germany.
25 Gordon Ramsay. 26 France. 27 Egypt. 28 Taj Mahal. 29 South Africa. 30
Florence Nightingale

1 On which type of show is Ainsley Harriott most likely to appear?
2 Which Carol was the first presenter of "Changing Rooms"?
3 Which series looks at the love lives of Carrie, Charlotte and Samantha?
4 Which programme is often referred to simply as Corrie?
5 Which Zoe succeeded Gaby Roslin on "The Big Breakfast"?
6 Which impersonator Rory starred in "Who Else"?
7 Patrick Kielty and Fearne Cotton host which "Island"?
8 Do the Royle Family live in London, Manchester or Newcastle?
9 In which country was "Ballykissangel" set?
10 Scriptwriter Carla Lane is famous for campaigning on whose behalf?
11 Who was the BT housewife in the ads as played by Maureen Lipman?
12 In which show did David Jason call Nicholas Lyndhurst a plonker?
13 Which Rik was involved in a quad bike accident in 1998?
14 Which "Have I Got News for You?" star's real name is Paul Martin?
15 Which Helen appeared nude on the cover of Radio Times to celebrate her 50th birthday?
16 Who was the taller in the Peter Cook and Dudley Moore partnership?
17 Which comic Griff has been involved in restoring buildings?
18 Who is Paul O'Grady's blonde, cigarette-smoking alter ego?
19 What was the occupation of Bramwell in the TV series?
20 Was "Dragon's Den" about business plans or wildlife?
21 Who is Reeves' TV comedy partner?
22 In which show would you see the neighbour-from-hell Dorien Green?
23 Which TV cook went on tour on "The Rhodes Show"?
24 What is the first name of "Prime Suspect" writer La Plante?
25 Which morning show did Chris Evans and Gaby Roslin present?
26 Which TV astronomer was born Patrick Caldwell-Moore?
27 The game show "Boys and Girls" was introduced by which Vernon?
28 Who presented "The Full Wax"?
29 Which Victorian drama series has a hospital called The Thrift?
30 Laurence Llewelyn-Bowen is a TV expert on what?

Answers	Pot Luck 38 *(see Quiz 78)*

1 Hovercraft. 2 Three. 3 A mole. 4 Will Smith. 5 Jersey. 6 George Graham. 7 Rats. 8 The Bermuda Triangle. 9 Wheel clamps. 10 Maple. 11 Guinevere. 12 Margaret Thatcher. 13 Hiawatha. 14 A gas. 15 Gareth Gates. 16 Peacocks. 17 Enid Blyton. 18 A harmonica. 19 Debbie McGee. 20 The bully-off. 21 Yellow. 22 Coca-Cola. 23 Golf. 24 Mandolin. 25 Roller skates. 26 Boxing. 27 Squirrel. 28 Brown. 29 Jens Lehmann. 30 The Muppets.

1 In 1959, what kind of vehicle crossed the Channel for the first time?
2 How many minutes are there per round in professional boxing?
3 Which animal built the hill that William III's horse stumbled on?
4 In "Ali", which actor Will played the great Muhammad Ali?
5 Which Channel Isle is famous for very creamy milk?
6 Which soccer boss left Arsenal following "bung" allegations?
7 Which animals do sailors say desert a sinking ship?
8 Which triangle are ships and planes said to disappear in?
9 What were used on illegally parked cars for the first time in 1983?
10 The leaf from which tree is a logo for Air Canada?
11 Who was the legendary King Arthur's wife?
12 Who was the one woman in the late Edward Heath's first cabinet?
13 Which Red Indian married Laughing Water?
14 What does a liquid turn into if it is heated up?
15 Which Gareth was the first runner-up on "Pop Idol"?
16 A muster is a collection of what type of birds?
17 Who wrote about Noddy and Big Ears?
18 What is the proper name for a mouth organ?
19 Who is Paul Daniels' wife?
20 What is the start of a hockey match called?
21 What colour was Bobby Shafto's hair in the nursery rhyme?
22 Which popular drink was invented by Dr John Pemberton?
23 Which sport did Sam Snead play?
24 In book and film, which musical instrument is linked with Captain Corelli?
25 In "Starlight Express" what do the performers wear on their feet?
26 Which sport is featured in the "Rocky" movies?
27 Which animal family do chipmunks belong to?
28 What colour is umber?
29 Which Arsenal keeper was Germany's No. 1 for the 2006 World Cup finals?
30 Which puppet show has two old men called Statler and Waldorf?

Answers	TV Times 2 *(see Quiz 77)*

1 Cookery. 2 Smillie. 3 Sex and the City. 4 Coronation Street. 5 Ball. 6 Bremner. 7 Love Island. 8 Manchester. 9 Ireland. 10 Animals. 11 Beattie. 12 Only Fools and Horses. 13 Mayall. 14 Paul Merton. 15 Mirren. 16 Peter Cook. 17 Griff Rhys Jones. 18 Lily Savage. 19 Doctor. 20 Business plans. 21 Mortimer. 22 Birds of a Feather. 23 Gary Rhodes. 24 Lynda. 25 The Big Breakfast. 26 Patrick Moore. 27 Vernon Kaye. 28 Ruby Wax. 29 Bramwell. 30 Home decorating.

1 Which sport are the Lord's Taverners famous for playing?
2 Which Denise won European gold in the heptathlon in 1988?
3 Which Australian bowler was first to pass 700 Test wickets?
4 Sergey Bubka has set a world record in which field event over 30 times?
5 Which British tennis star reached the Wimbledon semi-finals in 1998?
6 Which summer sport did Kerry Packer revolutionise in the 70s?
7 Did Lance Armstrong dominate the Tour de France or Tour of Italy?
8 Chris Boardman suffered an accident riding what in summer 1998?
9 Which country staged the summer Olympics in 1984 and 1996?
10 Between 1990 and 1998 all Ladies Wimbledon Singles champions were born in which continent?
11 The summer Olympics are held every how many years?
12 In cricket, what must a ball not do to score six runs?
13 Jonathan Edwards specialises in what type of jump?
14 For which international side did Shane Warne play cricket?
15 Which golfer is known as the Great White Shark?
16 Which Martina did Martinez beat in the 1994 Wimbledon final?
17 Which Tour is the world's premier cycling event?
18 Which German tennis player's father Peter was jailed for tax fraud?
19 Sonia O'Sullivan races for which country?
20 How many runners are there in the 400m relay team?
21 Which Jana won Wimbledon in 1998 after her third final?
22 You would do a Fosbury flop in which athletics event?
23 Which cricket club is nicknamed the "Cradle of Cricket"?
24 How many balls an over are there in cricket?
25 Who told a Wimbledon umpire "You cannot be serious!"?
26 Which West Indian cricketer was called Vivian?
27 Who was top National Hunt jockey from 1999–2000 through to 2005?
28 Which Jimmy won Wimbledon doubles with Ilie Nastase?
29 What was the nationality of tennis pin-up Gabriela Sabatini?
30 Which team competes against America in the Ryder Cup?

Answers | **Pot Luck 39** (see Quiz 80)

1 Sunderland. 2 Stirrups. 3 Dogger Bank. 4 Nine. 5 US President. 6 Perception. 7 Scandinavia. 8 One. 9 He was bald. 10 Animated cartoons. 11 A reservoir. 12 A spider. 13 The 1812 Overture. 14 14th February. 15 Tony Blackburn. 16 Victoria. 17 Four. 18 Moses. 19 The Pacific Ocean. 20 Teeth. 21 Elizabeth Hurley. 22 The maiden all forlorn. 23 Arms. 24 Helsinki. 25 Worms. 26 Four. 27 Jade. 28 Four. 29 A collage. 30 Sixpence.

Quiz 80 | Pot Luck 39

1 What was the first soccer club to be managed by Roy Keane?
2 What are the metal loops that you place your feet in when horse riding?
3 Which bank is a dangerous sand bar in the North Sea?
4 How many players are there in a rounders team?
5 Whose official plane is Air Force One?
6 What does the letter P stand for in ESP?
7 Which group of countries did the Vikings come from?
8 How many Popes have been English – one, two or three?
9 What colour was Kojak's hair?
10 What kind of programmes are Hanna and Barbara famous for?
11 What is a man-made lake in which water is stored called?
12 What type of creature is a Black Widow?
13 Which overture has a date in its title and includes cannons and bells?
14 On what date did the St. Valentine's Day Massacre take place?
15 Which Tony won the first "I'm a Celebrity Get Me Out of Here"?
16 Melbourne is the capital of which Australian State?
17 How many walls surround a squash court?
18 In the Bible, who parted the sea?
19 Fiji is in which ocean?
20 Which part of your body has a coating of enamel?
21 In "Austin Powers International Man of Mystery" who was the leading actress?
22 Who milked the cow with the crumpled horn, in the rhyme?
23 Which parts of the Venus de Milo's body are missing?
24 In which city beginning with H was the 2005 World Athletics Championship held?
25 Would a vermicide be used to kill worms or mice?
26 How many presidents' faces are carved into Mount Rushmore?
27 Which green stone was buried by the Chinese with their dead?
28 How many New Testament Gospels are there?
29 What word describes a picture made from sticking scraps on to a background?
30 Which English coin was nicknamed the tanner?

| **Answers** | **Summer Sports** *(see Quiz 79)* |

1 Cricket. 2 Lewis. 3 Shane Warne. 4 Pole vault. 5 Tim Henman. 6 Cricket. 7 Tour de France. 8 Bicycle. 9 USA. 10 Europe. 11 Four. 12 Bounce. 13 Triple jump. 14 Australia. 15 Greg Norman. 16 Navratilova. 17 Tour de France. 18 Steffi Graf. 19 Ireland. 20 Four. 21 Novotna. 22 High jump. 23 Hambledon CC. 24 Six. 25 John McEnroe. 26 Viv Richards. 27 Mark McGwire. 28 Connors. 29 Argentinean. 30 Europe.

1 What force makes the Earth orbit the Sun?
2 What colour is the Great Spot on Jupiter?
3 Is Jupiter larger or smaller than Earth?
4 Which gas is present in the Earth's atmosphere which is not present on any other planet?
5 A solar eclipse occurs when the Moon gets between Earth and what?
6 Which is the seventh planet from the Sun?
7 What is the layer around the Earth called?
8 What is the name given to matter so dense that even light cannot escape its pull?
9 Which planet's name comes nearest the end of the alphabet?
10 Herschel planned to name Uranus after the King; which one?
11 What would you find on a celestial map?
12 Is the science of celestial bodies, astrology or astronomy?
13 Which colour in the rainbow has the shortest name?
14 Which TV programme called space The Final Frontier?
15 Were the first US Shuttle flights in the 1950s, 60s, or 80s?
16 Which show with Reeves & Mortimer shared its name with another term for meteors?
17 What is a group of stars which make a recognisable pattern called?
18 What does "S" stand for in NASA?
19 In which decade was the US's first satellite launched?
20 What is the English name for the lunar sea Mare Tranquillitas?
21 Castor and Pollux are two stars in which constellation?
22 John Young ate which item of fast food in space in 1968?
23 Was Apollo a US or USSR space programme?
24 Prior to being an astronaut was John Glenn in the Air Force or the Marines?
25 How long does it take the Earth to orbit the Sun?
26 Mishka, the 1980 Olympic mascot, was the first of which toy in space?
27 How is Ursa Major better known?
28 How many times did Gagarin orbit the Earth on his first space flight?
29 What travels at 186,272 miles per second?
30 Edward White was the first American to walk where?

Answers	**Pot Luck 40 (see Quiz 82)**

1 Nora Batty. 2 Green. 3 An earthquake. 4 Tennis. 5 Monday. 6 Barber. 7 Robbie Coltrane. 8 A sword. 9 West Ham. 10 Oxford. 11 Boxing Day. 12 Moustache. 13 A bird (falcon). 14 Mo Mowlam. 15 Blue and White. 16 Boyzone. 17 Clint Eastwood. 18 A cherry. 19 Chess. 20 Nuclear. 21 Methane. 22 Jackie Milburn. 23 Cain. 24 Boyzone. 25 Ena Sharples. 26 Annie. 27 Venice. 28 Eight. 29 Eiffel Tower. 30 Strawberry.

1 In "Last of the Summer Wine", which part was played by Kathy Staff?
2 What colour is Dipsy in the "Teletubbies"?
3 An aftershock can sometimes follow what natural disaster?
4 For which sport was Sue Barker famous?
5 Which day's child is "fair of face" according to the traditional rhyme?
6 Which tradesman from Seville is featured in the title of an opera?
7 Which Scottish comic actor Robbie featured in the first Harry Potter movie?
8 In legend, who or what was Excalibur?
9 Which London club did soccer's Ian Wright join from Arsenal?
10 Which university is the oldest in England?
11 St Stephen's Day is generally known by what other name?
12 Did Sacha Baron Cohen's character Borat sport a moustache or a full beard?
13 What is a peregrine?
14 Who was Tony Blair's first Northern Ireland Minister?
15 What are the two main colours of the Argentinean flag?
16 Who had a No. 1 UK hit in September 1998 with "No Matter What"?
17 Which actor links "Play Misty for Me" and "Pale Rider"?
18 What type of fruit is a morello?
19 With which board game are Karpov and Kasparov associated?
20 Sizewell in Suffolk is associated with which form of power?
21 Which gas is the full name for marsh gas?
22 Alan Shearer beat which Newcastle star's goal-scoring record in season 2005–6?
23 In the Bible, who was Adam and Eve's firstborn son?
24 Keith Duffy joined "Coronation Street" from which Irish boy band?
25 Which character in "Coronation Street" was played by Violet Carson?
26 The song "Tomorrow" comes from which musical?
27 In which Italian city is the Rialto Bridge?
28 How many noughts are in the written number one hundred million?
29 What is the most lasting symbol of the French Exhibition of 1889?
30 Royal Sovereign is a type of which soft fruit?

Answers	**Science & Nature: Space** *(see Quiz 81)*

1 Gravity. 2 Red. 3 Larger. 4 Oxygen. 5 The Sun. 6 Uranus. 7 Atmosphere. 8 Black Hole. 9 Venus. 10 George. 11 Stars. 12 Astronomy. 13 Red. 14 Star Trek. 15 80s. 16 Shooting Stars. 17 Constellation. 18 Space. 19 1950s. 20 Sea of Tranquillity. 21 Gemini. 22 Burger. 23 USA. 24 Marines. 25 A year. 26 Teddy bear. 27 Great Bear. 28 Once. 29 Light. 30 Space.

1 Which Oscar winner became a Labour MP?
2 Which actress received an Oscar for "Erin Brokovich"?
3 Which actress Ms Berry won an Oscar for "Monster's Ball"?
4 Which Kevin won Best Director and starred in "Dances with Wolves"?
5 "Braveheart" was set in which country?
6 Who won Best Actor for "The Silence of the Lambs"?
7 Who directed "Schindler's List"?
8 Which British actor Jeremy was a winner with "Reversal of Fortune"?
9 Was it Tom Hanks or Tom Cruise who won in 1993 and again in '94?
10 Sonny's ex-wife won Best Actress in "Moonstruck"; who was she?
11 Which Susan won for "Dead Man Walking"?
12 Which foot is named in the title of the movie with Daniel Day-Lewis?
13 Was Clint Eastwood Best Actor or Best Director for "Unforgiven"?
14 How often are the Oscars presented?
15 Which keyboard instrument gave its name to a film with Holly Hunter?
16 Kathy Bates won with "Misery" based on which Stephen's novel?
17 Which Kate was Oscar-nominated for "Titanic"?
18 Did Madonna receive one, two or no nominations for "Evita"?
19 What was Best Picture when Tom Hanks won Best Actor for "Forrest Gump"?
20 Which Al was Best Actor for "Scent of a Woman"?
21 Which Shirley won an Oscar at the age of five?
22 For which film did James Cameron win a 1997 Oscar?
23 Which British movie about the 1924 Olympics was a 1980s winner?
24 Which Oscar winner based in India holds the record for most extras?
25 Which son of Kirk Douglas won for "Wall Street"?
26 "Platoon" was about which Asian war?
27 Which Ralph was an "English Patient" winner?
28 "Talk to the Animals" came from which movie about a Doctor?
29 For her role in "The Hours" actress Nicole Kidman wore a false what?
30 "Dances with Wolves" was the first film of what type to win Best Picture for 60 years?

| **Answers** | **Pot Luck 41** *(see Quiz 84)* |

1 Lean. 2 Anglesey. 3 A hop, a step and a leap. 4 Gondolas. 5 Canaries. 6 Greece. 7 David Beckham. 8 Spider-Man. 9 Motor racing. 10 Green (the Incredible Hulk). 11 Six. 12 Its age. 13 A flower. 14 A fish. 15 Table tennis. 16 Gordon Ramsay. 17 Universe. 18 A monkey. 19 Hear'Say. 20 Spain. 21 In your bones. 22 Apple trees. 23 The Flintstones. 24 A Christmas Carol. 25 Falkland Islands. 26 White. 27 Ireland. 28 Dick Turpin. 29 Manchester. 30 Six.

1 Which David directed the epic movie "Lawrence of Arabia"?
2 Which island is off the north-western tip of Wales?
3 The triple jump involves a run and then which three movements?
4 Which black boats sail along the canals of Venice?
5 Which bird was taken to work by miners to test for gas?
6 Mount Olympus is in which European country?
7 Who was England's skipper in the 2006 World Cup tournament?
8 Which super hero of comics and movies can spin a web?
9 For which sport was Gilles Villeneuve famous?
10 What colour did Dr Banner become when he got angry?
11 How many legs does a fully grown insect have?
12 What can be discovered by counting the rings in a tree trunk?
13 Who or what is Sweet William?
14 What kind of creature is an anchovy?
15 What game are you playing if you hold a bat in a penholder grip?
16 Which celebrity chef wrote an autobiography entitled "Humble Pie"?
17 Which word collectively describes all the stars and planets?
18 Which has the longer tail, a monkey or ape?
19 Myleene Klass was a member of which TV talent show winners?
20 Which country produces Valencia oranges?
21 Where in your body would you find marrow?
22 Which tree does mistletoe grow on?
23 Who live at 342 Greasepit Terrace, Bedrock?
24 In which Dickens novel does Jacob Marley's ghost appear?
25 Which islands were invaded in 1982 by the Argentineans?
26 What colour are the stars on the American flag?
27 Which country would you visit to kiss the Blarney Stone?
28 Which highwayman had a horse called Black Bess?
29 Was the 2006 Labour Party Conference held in Maidstone, Manchester or Margate?
30 How many strings are there on a Spanish guitar?

Answers | **The Movies: The Oscars 1** *(see Quiz 83)*

1 Glenda Jackson. 2 Julia Roberts. 3 Halle Berry. 4 Costner. 5 Scotland. 6 Anthony Hopkins. 7 Steven Spielberg. 8 Irons. 9 Hanks. 10 Cher. 11 Sarandon. 12 Left Foot. 13 Director. 14 Once a year. 15 The Piano. 16 King. 17 Winslet. 18 None. 19 Forrest Gump. 20 Pacino. 21 Temple. 22 Titanic. 23 Chariots of Fire. 24 Gandhi. 25 Michael. 26 Vietnam. 27 Fiennes. 28 Doolittle. 29 Nose. 30 Western.

1 Which language other than English is an official language of the Channel Islands?
2 In which country did Saddam Hussein's 2005–06 trial take place?
3 You would find Delphi on a map of which country?
4 Which is further North, Clacton or Brighton?
5 Which continent has an Ivory Coast?
6 On which island would you find the Giant's Causeway?
7 If you were on a French autoroute what type of road would you be on?
8 Which Gulf lies between Saudi Arabia and Iran?
9 Lake Superior is on the border of the USA and which other country?
10 Which tiny European landlocked state is a Grand Duchy?
11 Macedonia was formerly a part of which communist republic?
12 Which Himalayan kingdom has been called the world's highest rubbish dump because of waste left behind by climbers?
13 Which Australasian capital shares its name with a Duke and a boot?
14 Which river which flows through Germany is Europe's dirtiest?
15 Where would you be if you saw Nippon on the map?
16 Whose address is often referred to as Number Ten?
17 Which motorway goes past Stoke on Trent?
18 On which continent is the Basque country?
19 The Home Counties surround which city?
20 Malta is to the south of which island to the south of Italy?
21 The Ural Mountains mark the eastern frontier to which continent?
22 How is the London Orbital Motorway better known?
23 Is Moldova in Europe or Africa?
24 Which island republic lies to the north west of the UK?
25 Miami is a port in which US state?
26 Kew Gardens are next to which London river?
27 Which country has Lakes Garda, Maggiore and Como?
28 Is Madagascar an island or is it an African peninsula?
29 In which city is Red Square?
30 Which country's official languages are Hebrew and Arabic?

Answers	**Pot Luck 42** *(see Quiz 86)*

1 Gaz. 2 Rosary. 3 Sewing Machine. 4 University. 5 Herod. 6 Jonathan Ross. 7 Five of a kind. 8 Cat. 9 M. 10 Salmon. 11 Arquette. 12 Finland. 13 Badminton. 14 Walking distance. 15 12. 16 Nigella Lawson. 17 100. 18 The Office. 19 Huit. 20 Notting Hill. 21 Blue. 22 Squirrel. 23 Five. 24 Germany. 25 Golf. 26 Deadly nightshade. 27 The Matrix. 28 Mars. 29 Supper. 30 Blue.

Quiz 86 | Pot Luck 42

Answers – page 95

1 Actor Robert Carlyle led "The Full Monty" as which character?
2 What does a Catholic call the string of beads used when praying?
3 In 1851, what was invented by Isaac Singer?
4 In what type of educational establishment was "Educating Rita" set?
5 In the Bible, which King tried to get the baby Jesus put to death?
6 Which top-earning presenter replaced Barry Norman on BBC's Film programme?
7 What is the highest ranking hand in Poker Dice?
8 In cartoons, what type of animal is Sylvester?
9 Which letter represents 007's boss?
10 Which fish leap up river to get to their spawning grounds?
11 What name did Courteney Cox add to her name after marrying actor David?
12 In which country did saunas originate?
13 A shuttlecock is used in which game?
14 What is measured by a pedometer?
15 How many creatures give their names to Chinese years?
16 Who wrote the best-selling "How to be a Domestic Goddess"?
17 How many decades are there in a millennium?
18 Which comedy was set in the offices of the Wenham Hogg paper merchants?
19 What is the French word for the number eight?
20 In which part of London is there an annual famous carnival?
21 If put in an alkaline solution, what colour does litmus paper become?
22 Which animal lives in a drey?
23 If December 1 is a Tuesday, how many Wednesdays are in the month?
24 Did Beethoven come from Austria, Germany or Holland?
25 For which sport is Sam Torrance famous?
26 Belladonna is also known by which Deadly name?
27 "The Matrix Reloaded" was the first sequel to which movie?
28 The month March is named after which Roman god?
29 Leonardo da Vinci's religious painting featured The Last... what?
30 What colour is connected to neutral in modern three-core electric cable?

Answers	**Geography: On the Map** (see Quiz 85)

1 French. 2 Iraq. 3 Greece. 4 Clacton. 5 Africa. 6 Ireland. 7 Motorway. 8 Persian Gulf. 9 Canada. 10 Luxembourg. 11 Yugoslavia. 12 Nepal. 13 Wellington. 14 Rhine. 15 Japan. 16 Prime Minister. 17 M6. 18 Europe. 19 London. 20 Sicily. 21 Europe. 22 M25. 23 Europe. 24 Iceland. 25 Florida. 26 Thames. 27 Italy. 28 Island. 29 Moscow. 30 Israel.

Quiz 87

1 Which part of the body names a millennium feature on the London skyline?
2 Which sport would you watch at Aintree?
3 Are there more chairs at the start or end of a game of musical chairs?
4 What links a novice's ski slope and a garden centre?
5 What name is given to the promotional scheme to save points for cheaper plane travel?
6 In the year 2005 most Bank Holidays fell on which day of the week?
7 What colour would a Sloane Ranger's wellies be?
8 The initials RSVP come from a request in which language ?
9 What colour are most road signs on UK motorways?
10 In which UK county might you holiday on the Broads?
11 What is the name of the most famous theatre in London's Drury Lane?
12 In which city is the exhibition centre Olympia?
13 What would you hire at Moss Bros?
14 Butlin's was the first type of what?
15 What is the flower-shaped ribbon awarded at gymkhanas called?
16 What is a less formal name for a turf accountant?
17 Which magazine's title is the French word for "she"?
18 On which summer bank holiday is the Notting Hill Carnival held?
19 Which public track can be used for horses but not traffic?
20 On which date in May was May Day traditionally?
21 Does a busker entertain indoors or out of doors?
22 In which month would you celebrate Hogmanay?
23 In golf, what is usually meant by the nineteenth hole?
24 What is a horse chestnut called when it's used in a children's game?
25 Which card game has two forms called auction and contract?
26 What colour uniform do Guides wear?
27 Are seats in the circle of a theatre on the ground or first floor?
28 Where would a shopper be if they went to M&S?
29 If you wore jodhpurs you'd probably be about to do what?
30 On which ground in north west England do you watch Test cricket?

Answers	Pot Luck 43 *(see Quiz 88)*

1 Queen Elizabeth II. 2 Wales. 3 The species. 4 England. 5 Jailhouse Rock. 6 Hair. 7 Cleo Laine. 8 The Teletubbies. 9 Shaken but not stirred. 10 Hadlee. 11 (West) Germany. 12 Raspberry. 13 Oskar. 14 Brazil. 15 Sunday. 16 Scarlet. 17 Isle of Wight. 18 Pet Shop Boys. 19 Dean. 20 Cat. 21 Scotland. 22 Delia (Smith). 23 Skier. 24 Jackson. 25 Salt. 26 Medieval. 27 John Major's son James. 28 Barbie. 29 Gordon Strachan. 30 Rugby Union.

1 Who described 1992 as an "annus horribilis"?

2 In which country would you see the Great and Little Orme?

3 According to Rudyard Kipling the female of what is deadlier than the male?

4 Which country hosted soccer's 1966 World Cup?

5 Which "Jailhouse" song gave Elvis another No. 1 in 2005?

6 What falls out if you have alopecia?

7 Which singer is Mrs Johnny Dankworth?

8 Who live at Home Hill?

9 How does James Bond like his Martini served?

10 Which Richard was the first knighted New Zealand cricketer?

11 Europe's first motorway was built in which country?

12 What rude noise is the English equivalent of a Bronx Cheer?

13 What was Schindler's first name in the film "Schindler's List"?

14 In which South American country was Ayrton Senna born?

15 If January 1 was on a Thursday what day would February 1 be?

16 What colour was The Pimpernel created by Baroness Orczy?

17 Shanklin and Sandown are on which Isle?

18 Which Boys had a No. 1 in the 1980s with "Always On My Mind"?

19 Who was the male half of the Torvill and Dean partnership?

20 What kind of animal was Korky from the Dandy comic?

21 Does Ewan McGregor come from Ireland or Scotland?

22 IDEAL is an anagram of the first name of which famous cook?

23 Is Alberto Tomba a skier, a track athlete or an ice hockey player?

24 Which singer Michael had a No. 1 with "Earth Song"?

25 Sodium chloride is better known as which condiment?

26 Was Brother Cadfael a fictional medieval or Victorian detective?

27 Which Prime Minister's son did Emma Noble become engaged to?

28 Which doll has a boyfriend called Ken?

29 Which Gordon replaced Martin O'Neill as Celtic manager?

30 If Lions are playing Wallabies what sport are you watching?

| **Answers** | **Hobbies & Leisure 3** *(see Quiz 87)* |

1 (London) Eye. 2 Horse racing. 3 Beginning. 4 Nursery. 5 Air miles. 6 Monday.
7 Green. 8 French. 9 Blue. 10 Norfolk. 11 Theatre Royal. 12 London. 13 Formal dress. 14 Holiday camp. 15 Rosette. 16 Bookie. 17 Elle. 18 August Bank Holiday.
19 Bridleway. 20 First. 21 Out of doors. 22 December. 23 The club-house bar. 24 Conker. 25 Bridge. 26 Blue. 27 First floor. 28 Marks & Spencer. 29 Horse riding. 30 Old Trafford.

1 Which day follows TFI on Chris Evans' show?
2 Who was the host of the variety show "Lenny Goes to Town"?
3 Which medical drama takes place in Holby's A & E department?
4 "The Jerry Springer Show" comes from which country?
5 What is the name of Catherine Tate's schoolgirl character?
6 What is presented to the 'victim' at the end of "This is Your Life"?
7 Whose comedy and chat show is called "The Bigger Picture"?
8 Steve Irwin was famous for hunting which creatures?
9 How many rooms are changed in "Changing Rooms"?
10 "Newsround" is aimed at which group of viewers?
11 In which series set in Ireland did barmaid Assumpta meet a sad end?
12 Which near silent walking disaster was created by Rowan Atkinson?
13 Who is Mel Smith's TV comedy partner?
14 Which Geoff gardened at Barnsdale?
15 Which series was dubbed "Barewatch" and "Boobwatch"?
16 Which charity campaign has Pudsey Bear as its mascot?
17 Which Michael's 70s chat show was revived in 1998?
18 In which Practice have doctors Kerruish, Glover and Attwood worked?
19 Which was broadcast later, "Newsnight" or "News at Ten"?
20 Who is the host of GMTV's "Lorraine Live"?
21 What is the profession of TV's Jo Frost?
22 What follows Police, Camera..., in the show about awful drivers?
23 In which city is "The Cosby Show" set?
24 Which drama series where Robson and Jerome found fame is about army life?
25 On which day of the week does the so-called God slot take place?
26 On TV, what is "The Royal"?
27 Which Cilla Black series made dreams come true?
28 Which motor magazine now with Jeremy Clarkson began in 1978?
29 Which "Torchwood" star was a "How Do You Solve a Problem Like Maria?" judge?
30 Which Files feature Mulder and Scully?

1 Which comic did Dan Dare first appear in?
2 Golfer Ian Woosnam comes from which country?
3 Which song links Rolf Harris and Led Zeppelin?
4 Which inventor Michael appeared on a £20 note?
5 Gouache is a type of what?
6 The notorious Klaus Barbie was the Butcher of where in France?
7 Which county do the Arctic Monkeys come from?
8 What shape is something if it is campanulate?
9 Was "Cutting It" set in a butcher's, a hair salon or a hospital?
10 Which Robin was the spoof film "Men in Tights" about?
11 Which word can go in front of BISCUIT, CLOSET and COLOUR?
12 As which character was "Coronation Street" actor Bruce Jones the neighbour from hell?
13 Which ticking instrument keeps perfect time for a musician?
14 Was the Automobile Association founded before or after World War I?
15 Which nation came back to international rugby in 1993?
16 Which is bigger, A3 or A4 paper?
17 Which band featured Noddy Holder and Dave Hill?
18 The mesosphere and the stratosphere are layers of what?
19 With which country are Walloons associated?
20 What links a chocolate bar, a planet and a god of war?
21 "Aliens" and "Alien Evolution" were sequels to which movie?
22 In which part of the body are the smallest bones?
23 In Greek legend, who had a bad hair day with snakes on her head?
24 Gubby Allen was linked with which sport?
25 What was the first name of Wacky Racer Mr Dastardly?
26 Was Chris Tarrant born in the 1940s or the 1960s?
27 Operation Overlord was the codename for the 1944 Allied invasion of where?
28 Who took a "Careless Whisper" to No. 1 in the 1980s?
29 Which country do golfers Nick Price and Mark McNulty come from?
30 Which Lisa presented the show "You've Been Framed"?

1 Who sang a "Barcelona" duet with Freddy Mercury?
2 Which composer wrote the "Four Seasons"?
3 Which branch of performing is Michael Flatley famous for?
4 In which country was the Halle Orchestra founded?
5 Which dancer Wayne toured in 1998 to mark his 50th birthday?
6 Who composed the incidental music for Ibsen's play "Peer Gynt"?
7 Which writers of comic opera are referred to as G&S?
8 Which playwright was known as the Bard of Avon?
9 Billy Smart was associated with what type of entertainment?
10 In which country is an eisteddfod held?
11 Which Circle is a professional association of conjurors?
12 Which charity gala with many different performers is held in November and attended by the Royal Family?
13 Which Lord Andrew wrote the musical "Whistle Down the Wind"?
14 In Rodgers and Hammerstein who wrote the music?
15 In which country was the Bolshoi Ballet founded?
16 Which famous Paul wrote the oratorio "Ecce Cor Meum"?
17 Which London theatre shared its name with a half human, half fish mythical creature?
18 At what time of year would you go and watch a nativity play?
19 Which Monty Python-based musical opened in the UK in the autumn of 2006?
20 The Last Night of the Proms takes place in which month?
21 A person playing a pantomime dame is usually which sex?
22 What type of singing made Maria Callas famous?
23 What was the surname of US musical composers George and Ira?
24 What is the final concert at the Promenade Concerts called?
25 Two out of the Three Tenors are which nationality?
26 Which Sir Noel wrote and starred in his plays and musicals?
27 What is the first name of Scarborough-based playwright Ayckbourn?
28 Opera singer Lesley Garrett is from which county?
29 Do you stand or sit for the Hallelujah Chorus from "The Messiah"?
30 In panto how do you respond to "Oh yes it is!"?

Answers	**Pot Luck 45** *(see Quiz 92)*

1 50 Cent. 2 Arsenal. 3 Bill Wyman. 4 H.G. 5 Felicity. 6 Pub. 7 Pottery. 8 Long-haired. 9 James Bond. 10 Goldie Hawn. 11 Wok. 12 The Archers. 13 Beef. 14 Horse. 15 Spoons. 16 Hello. 17 Nigel. 18 King Edward. 19 Crawford. 20 Arkansas. 21 Canada. 22 Etna. 23 Smoking. 24 Deer. 25 Outside. 26 Two (South Australia & New South Wales). 27 Moonlight Serenade. 28 New Testament. 29 Jeroboam. 30 Bronx.

1 Which rapper works with G-Unit?
2 England soccer star Ashley Cole began his career at which London club?
3 Who is older, Bill Wyman or the Prince of Wales?
4 What are the two initials of early 20th Century sci-fi writer Wells?
5 Which Kendall starred in the sitcom "Solo"?
6 Craig Cash's "Early Doors" was set in what type of establishment?
7 What did Clarice Cliff make?
8 Is an Afghan hound short-haired or long-haired?
9 Which secret agent was created by Ian Fleming?
10 Kate Hudson is the daughter of which actress Goldie?
11 What is a round-bottomed Chinese cooking pan called?
12 In which radio series is there a pub called The Bull?
13 What sort of meat is usually in a hamburger?
14 What type of animal is a palomino?
15 What is Uri Geller famous for bending?
16 Would you say Bonjour to a French person when you say hello or goodbye?
17 Violinist Kennedy chose to drop which first name professionally?
18 Which monarch gave his name to a type of potato?
19 Which Michael created the Phantom in Lloyd Webber's musical?
20 Is Bill Clinton's home state Arkansas or Arizona?
21 In which country is Hudson Bay?
22 Which Sicilian mountain is Europe's highest volcano?
23 ASH is a pressure group against what?
24 Which animal might be fallow or red?
25 Would you find a gazebo inside or outside your home?
26 How many Australian states have South in their names?
27 Was Glenn Miller's theme tune "Moonlight Sonata" or "Moonlight Serenade"?
28 Is the book of Jude in the Old or New Testament?
29 Which is larger, a magnum of champagne or a Jeroboam?
30 Which tough area of New York gives its name to a gin, vermouth and orange cocktail?

Answers	Leisure: Performing Arts *(see Quiz 91)*

1 Monserrat Caballe. **2** Vivaldi. **3** Dance. **4** UK. **5** Sleep. **6** Edvard Grieg. **7** Gilbert & Sullivan. **8** William Shakespeare. **9** Circus. **10** Wales. **11** Magic Circle. **12** Royal Variety Show. **13** Lloyd Webber. **14** Rodgers. **15** Russia. **16** Paul McCartney. **17** Mermaid. **18** Christmas. **19** Spamalot. **20** September. **21** Male. **22** Opera. **23** Gershwin. **24** Last Night of the Proms. **25** Spanish. **26** Coward. **27** Alan. **28** Yorkshire. **29** Stand. **30** "Oh no it isn't!".

1 How often is the World Cup held?
2 Did Jimmy Greaves ever play in a World Cup Final?
3 Who won the last World Cup of the 20th century?
4 What colour shirts were England wearing when they won in 1966?
5 Who became known sarcastically as The Hand of God?
6 Who was sent off in France 98 and fled to Posh Spice in New York?
7 Which side from Great Britain did not make France 98?
8 Which 1966 World Cup veteran resigned as Eire manager in 1995?
9 Which British side did Brazil play in the first match of France 98?
10 Which European country hosted the 2006 tournament?
11 Which country did Louis Saha play for in the 2006 World Cup?
12 Who were beaten finalists in the last World Cup of the 20th century?
13 In France 98 which Caribbean side were called the Reggae Boys?
14 Who was axed from the England side in '98 after reports of kebab binges?
15 Which former Man Utd keeper played in the 2006 Final?
16 Which German boss Jurgen resigned after the 2006 tournament?
17 In France 98 whom did Suker play for?
18 Who was the only Englishman to lift the World Cup before 2000?
19 Which central American country was the first to host the World Cup twice, in 1986?
20 Which ex-World Cup manager's autobiography is "An Englishman Abroad"?
21 What colour are Brazil's shirts?
22 Who were the only non-Europeans to win the World Cup in the 90s?
23 Who was England's youngest player in France 98?
24 What colour-coded hair was seen on the Nigerian team in France 98?
25 Which Gary was top scorer in the 1986 World Cup?
26 In which month did France 98 finish?
27 Which Scandinavian side was third in the 1994 US tournament?
28 Which South American side knocked England out of France 98?
29 In which city did France 98 begin and end?
30 Which country did Blackburn's Lucas Neill play for in the 2006 World Cup?

Answers	Pot Luck 46 *(see Quiz 94)*

1 Lancashire. 2 L.B. 3 Kent. 4 Rum. 5 Locum. 6 Argentina. 7 Dog. 8 Northamptonshire. 9 DH Lawrence. 10 Apple. 11 Germany. 12 Italy. 13 Alan Titchmarsh. 14 Gunnell. 15 Ernie Wise. 16 China. 17 Westlife. 18 Potter. 19 Holly. 20 Colin Farrell. 21 Cuckoo. 22 Tenor. 23 Bit. 24 Addams. 25 Chris de Burgh. 26 Tennis. 27 Alice (in Wonderland). 28 Sleeve. 29 Celine Dion. 30 Perambulator.

1 Mike Atherton played for which county cricket club?

2 Which were the initials of US President Johnson?

3 In which county is Ashford International station?

4 Does a Pina Colada contain rum or gin?

5 Which word for a duty doctor is a Latin name for place holder?

6 Which country's Rugby Union side are the Pumas?

7 Is a Dandie Dinmont, a dog, a cat or a horse?

8 In which county is the stately home of Althorp?

9 Which controversial author used the initials for his first names David Herbert?

10 What sort of fruit flavour does Calvados have?

11 In which country were BMWs first made?

12 St Francis of Assisi is patron saint of which country?

13 Which Alan presented the TV programme "How to be a Gardener"?

14 Which Sally was British women's team captain in the 1996 Olympics?

15 Which late comedian was the one with "short, fat hairy legs"?

16 Which country was once called Cathay?

17 Which boy band had a No. 1 with their version of Billy Joel's "Uptown Girl"?

18 Which Dennis created "The Singing Detective"?

19 Which Buddy did Alvin Stardust sing about?

20 Which Irishman Colin starred in the movie "Phone Booth"?

21 Which bird lays its eggs in the nests of other birds?

22 Was the singer Mario Lanza a bass, baritone or tenor?

23 What name is given to the part of the bridle in a horse's mouth?

24 Wednesday and Pugsley are part of which family?

25 Christopher Davidson found fame as a singer as which Chris?

26 Maria Bueno was famous for which sport?

27 In fiction, which girl swam in a pool of her own tears?

28 A raglan forms which part of a garment?

29 Who had a huge 1995 hit with "Think Twice"?

30 Pram is an abbreviation of which word?

1 Which Yasser founded the PLO?
2 Which Kennedy announced he was running for President in 1960?
3 Nikita Krushchev was head of state of which Union?
4 In which Italian city were the 1960 summer Olympics held?
5 Whose Lover was the subject of a court case in book form?
6 The USSR sent its first man where in April 1960?
7 Which Russian dancer Rudolph defected to the West?
8 Across which former European capital was a Wall built?
9 Which drug taken by pregnant mothers caused abnormalities in babies?
10 Which Harold became Labour leader in 1963?
11 Of where did Neil Armstrong say, "The surface is like fine powder"?
12 What were mailbags containing over £1 million stolen from?
13 Caroline was the name of Britain's first offshore pirate what?
14 Which British WWII leader died in 1965?
15 What sort of champion was Arkle?
16 Which communist country had its famous Red Guards?
17 Which knighted soccer star retired aged 50?
18 Who launched the Queen Elizabeth II – QE2 – on Clydebank?
19 Which model Jean was called The Shrimp?
20 Which homeless charity was set up after TV's "Cathy Come Home"?
21 What product was banned from TV advertising on health grounds?
22 Which Rolling Stone singer was best man at David Bailey's wedding?
23 Which notorious East End gangland twins were jailed for murder?
24 Which rock star married Patricia Beaulieu?
25 Which capital was said to Swing in the 60s?
26 Which Martin famously gave his "I have a dream" speech?
27 If Mods rode scooters, who rode motorbikes?
28 LBJ was President of which country?
29 How were Ian Brady and Myra Hindley known?
30 Which actress Marilyn was found dead in her bungalow near Hollywood?

1 Which John married actress Sheila Hancock?
2 Which pre-decimal coin had the value of two shillings?
3 Which group revived a previous hit in the 90s with the help of Roy "Chubby" Brown?
4 Which TV presenter's shows have had Toothbrush and Breakfast in their titles?
5 Were the Olympic Games last held in Russia in 1960, 1980 or 1988?
6 Who is Popeye's rival?
7 Was Sir Walter Scott Scottish?
8 Which English soccer side was managed by the late Bob Paisley?
9 What is the main language in Brazil?
10 Which Macaulay starred in the cartoon and live action film "The Pagemaster"?
11 Which is greater in distance, a mile or a kilometre?
12 Which MP Harriet was axed in Tony Blair's first Cabinet reshuffle?
13 Who had a 2005 No. 1 single with "I'll be OK"?
14 How many red cards are there in a standard pack of cards?
15 Ray Davies was writer and singer with which band?
16 Adonis, Apollo and Poseidon were all what?
17 Tara and Willow featured in which occult-based series?
18 Which dog is larger – a borzoi or a corgi?
19 The Micra was made by which car company?
20 "Crossroads" was set near which major city?
21 A vixen is the female of which animal?
22 Which alphabet is used by Muscovites?
23 What links the names Chamberlain, Heath and Wilson?
24 Which jockey Bob fought back from cancer to win the Grand National?
25 Who is Simply Red's lead singer?
26 Which was the first antibiotic to be discovered?
27 Which Welsh actress won an Oscar for her role in "Chicago"?
28 For which sport is Sunningdale famous?
29 A Muscovy is what type of bird?
30 Which musical Paul got involved with frogs and Rupert Bear?

Answers	Past Times: The 60s *(see Quiz 95)*

1 Arafat. 2 John. 3 Soviet. 4 Rome. 5 Lady Chatterley's. 6 Space. 7 Nureyev. 8 Berlin. 9 Thalidomide. 10 Wilson. 11 The Moon. 12 Train. 13 Radio station. 14 Churchill. 15 Horse. 16 China. 17 Sir Stanley Matthews. 18 Queen Elizabeth II. 19 Jean Shrimpton. 20 Shelter. 21 Cigarettes. 22 Mick Jagger. 23 Kray twins. 24 Elvis Presley. 25 London. 26 Luther King. 27 Rockers. 28 USA. 29 Moors murderers. 30 Monroe.

1 Which actor was nicknamed "Bogey"?

2 Which actor Marlon was paid $18 million for nine minutes in "Superman" in 1978?

3 Which western star John first acted as Duke Morrison?

4 Which Samuel starred as a gangster in "Pulp Fiction"?

5 Which Bruce starred in "The Jackal"?

6 Which Kiwi won an Oscar for his role in "Gladiator"?

7 Tough guy Robert de Niro sang about New York in which film?

8 Which lager did "Crocodile Dundee" star Paul Hogan advertise?

9 Which Vietnam veteran Oliver directed "Platoon"?

10 Which star of "The Godfather" bought an island called Tetiaroa?

11 Which Martin was assigned to assassinate Brando in "Apocalypse Now"?

12 What did George C. Scott refuse to do about his Oscar for "Patton"?

13 Gene Hackman played cop Popeye Doyle in which classic thriller?

14 Ray Liotta played a member of which criminal organisation in "Goodfellas"?

15 Which Bruce was the psychiatrist in "The Sixth Sense"?

16 Was Charles Bronson one of ten or fifteen children?

17 Is Bruce Willis a cop or a soldier in the "Die Hard" movies?

18 Which hell raiser Oliver released a single "Lonely for a Girl" in 1965?

19 Lee Marvin headed a Dirty cast of how many in the 1967 movie?

20 Which singer who died in 1998 was the tough guy captain in "Von Ryan's Express"?

21 How many gunfighters were hired in The Magnificent film of 1960?

22 On what vehicle did Steve McQueen try to flee in "The Great Escape"?

23 Which Sylvester starred in "Judge Dredd"?

24 What is the first name of "Reservoir Dogs" director Tarantino?

25 Which tough guy Arnold has appeared on a postage stamp of Mali?

26 Which Mel starred in the "Lethal Weapon" series of films?

27 Which bare-headed actor was in "The Magnificent Seven" and "The King and I"?

28 Which Clint got the part in "Dirty Harry" when Sinatra pulled out?

29 Which James Bond has an actor son called Jason?

30 Was "The Untouchables" with Kevin Costner set in the 20s, 40s or 60s?

Answers	**Pot Luck 48** *(see Quiz 98)*

1 Tennis. 2 Heart. 3 Chris Tarrant. 4 Australia. 5 Frog. 6 Dingle. 7 Rot away. 8 Five. 9 Ten. 10 Aberdeen. 11 Boyzone. 12 Belgium. 13 Black Bess. 14 Purdy. 15 Eric Clapton. 16 Marylebone. 17 Bahamas. 18 The Taming of the Shrew. 19 Margaret Thatcher. 20 Hidden Agenda. 21 Violin. 22 Cornwall. 23 English. 24 British Prime Minister. 25 Susannah. 26 Vingt. 27 Aircraft. 28 Wizzard. 29 Blue. 30 France.

1 For which sport is Billie-Jean King famous?
2 According to the proverb, absence makes which organ grow fonder?
3 Who hosted ITV's "Who Wants to be a Millionaire"?
4 In which country is Ayer's Rock?
5 Which species of creature includes the most poisonous animal in the world?
6 Which soap family included Lisa, Marlon and Shadrach?
7 If something is biodegradable, what will it do?
8 How many noughts are in the written number two hundred thousand?
9 Every how many years is a National Census taken in Britain?
10 Where are you if you visit the Granite City?
11 Which group had a No. 1 album in 1998 with "Where We Belong"?
12 In which country is the town of Spa?
13 What was the name of Dick Turpin's horse?
14 In the "New Avengers", which character was played by Joanna Lumley?
15 Which guitarist is nicknamed "Slowhand"?
16 In cricket, what does the initial M stand for in MCC?
17 Nassau is the capital of which group of islands?
18 In which Shakespeare play does Kate marry Petruchio?
19 Who was Tory leader immediately before John Major?
20 What sort of "Agenda" was a 2003 hit for Craig David?
21 Which musical instrument does Tasmin Little play?
22 Which English county boasts the longest coastline?
23 What nationality was Bridget in "Bridget Jones's Diary"?
24 Eden, Heath and Macdonald have all held which important position?
25 Who is Trinny's partner giving advice on "What Not to Wear"?
26 What is the French word for the number twenty?
27 What are DC-10s and 747s?
28 "See My Baby Jive" was a 70s No. 1 for which magic-sounding group?
29 What colour is azure in heraldry?
30 Which country is immediately south of Belgium?

Answers | **The Movies: Tough Guys** (*see Quiz 97*)

1 Humphrey Bogart. 2 Brando. 3 John Wayne. 4 Jackson. 5 Willis. 6 Russell Crowe. 7 New York, New York. 8 Fosters. 9 Stone. 10 Marlon Brando. 11 Sheen. 12 Accept it. 13 French Connection. 14 Mafia. 15 Bruce Willis. 16 Fifteen. 17 Cop. 18 Reed. 19 Dozen. 20 Frank Sinatra. 21 Seven. 22 Motorcycle. 23 Stallone. 24 Quentin. 25 Schwarzenegger. 26 Gibson. 27 Yul Brynner. 28 Eastwood. 29 Sean Connery. 30 20s.

1 In which country did black activist Steve Biko die in 1977?
2 Which US President was brought down by the Watergate scandal?
3 What did a policeman use to hide a streaker's embarrassment in a famous incident at Twickenham in 1974?
4 Which London-born comic Charlie was knighted?
5 Which tree population was decimated by a Dutch disease?
6 Did Skytrain provide cut price tickets by air or rail?
7 Who succeeded John Paul I as Pope?
8 The New English version of which Book was published in 1970?
9 Which Czech tennis star Martina defected to the West?
10 In which country did Pol Pot conduct a reign of terror?
11 Which Sebastian was a record-breaking middle-distance runner?
12 Which father of twins was the husband of the British PM?
13 Which princess was sportswoman of the year in 1971?
14 The Queen celebrated how many years on the throne in her Jubilee?
15 Which Lord disappeared after his nanny was murdered?
16 Who beat four male candidates to become Tory leader in 1975?
17 Which war ended with the fall of Saigon in 1975?
18 Which country's athletes were murdered at the 1972 Olympics?
19 John Curry won Olympic gold on what surface?
20 In which county did a Ripper carry out horrific murders?
21 Which Lord and Royal uncle was murdered off Ireland?
22 Which Mother won a Nobel Peace Prize?
23 Charles de Gaulle died after being president of which country?
24 Were Sunderland in the first or second division when they won the FA Cup in 1973?
25 Where was the monarchy restored after the death of Franco?
26 In 1971 the first British soldier was killed in which British province?
27 Evonne Goolagong from which country won Wimbledon in 1971?
28 Which Chris was Jimmy Connors' fiancée when he first won Wimbledon?
29 Which James succeeded Harold Wilson as Prime Minister?
30 David Steel became leader of which political party in 1976?

Answers	Pot Luck 49 *(see Quiz 100)*

1 Orange. 2 Jennifer Saunders. 3 Madonna. 4 London & Birmingham. 5 Unchained Melody. 6 Goldcrest. 7 18. 8 Martin. 9 Cricket. 10 1940s. 11 Enya. 12 Red Indian tribes. 13 Take That. 14 White. 15 Four. 16 Mind. 17 Alfred Hitchcock. 18 Five. 19 Charles Dickens. 20 Hutch. 21 Accrington Stanley. 22 Northumberland. 23 MW. 24 Green. 25 A king. 26 Yorkshire. 27 Food. 28 Angostura Bitters. 29 Jennifer Aniston. 30 Queensland.

1 In international soccer, what is the main colour of Holland's shirts?
2 Who is older – Ruby Wax or Jennifer Saunders?
3 "Into the Groove" gave a first UK No. 1 for which singer?
4 Which two cities were linked by the M1 when it first opened?
5 Which song was a British No. 1 for Jimmy Young, the Righteous Brothers, Robson & Jerome and Gareth Gates?
6 What is Britain's smallest songbird?
7 How many sides are there in a pair of nonagons?
8 Which George was the main producer of The Beatles' hits?
9 EW Swanton wrote about which sport?
10 Was Joanna Lumley born in the 1940s, 50s or 60s?
11 How is Eithne Ni Bhraonain better known in the music world?
12 Mohawk, Seminole and Sioux are all names of what?
13 Which star group was Jason Orange a member of?
14 Is Riesling a red or white wine?
15 How many Teletubbies are there?
16 Russell Crowe starred in the movie "A Beautiful" what?
17 Who links the films "Rebecca", "Psycho" and "Vertigo"?
18 What's the most number of Sundays that could occur in December?
19 Which author created the reclusive character Miss Havisham?
20 On TV, did David Soul play Starsky or Hutch?
21 Which founder members of the Football League returned to the League in 2006?
22 What is England's most north easterly county?
23 Is Radio 5 Live broadcast on MW or FM?
24 What colour is verdigris which appears on copper or brass?
25 Who is killed if regicide is committed?
26 Ridings used to divide which county?
27 Is Robert Carrier linked with food, theatre or sport?
28 Pink gin is gin flavoured with what?
29 Who played the character Rachel in "Friends"?
30 Brisbane is the capital of which Australian state?

Answers	**Past Times: The 70s** *(see Quiz 99)*

1 South Africa. 2 Nixon. 3 His helmet. 4 Chaplin. 5 Elm. 6 Air. 7 John Paul II. 8 Bible. 9 Navratilova. 10 Cambodia. 11 Coe. 12 Denis Thatcher. 13 Anne. 14 25. 15 Lucan. 16 Margaret Thatcher. 17 Vietnam. 18 Israel. 19 Ice. 20 Yorkshire. 21 Mountbatten. 22 Teresa. 23 France. 24 Second. 25 Spain. 26 Northern Ireland. 27 Australia. 28 Evert. 29 Callaghan. 30 Liberal.

1 Which corporation developed the iPod?
2 What type of company can be found in Silicon Glen in Scotland?
3 In a car, what might be disc or drum?
4 Was the first modern cassette made in the 1940s, 60s or 70s?
5 Which type of transport has rubber skirts?
6 A rotor propels what type of aircraft?
7 Did early TV have 405 or 625 lines?
8 The Manhattan Project in the early 1940s was developing what?
9 Which substance, found to be dangerous, is called "woolly rock"?
10 What is the lowest number on the Beaufort Scale?
11 Apples and Apricots were what in the technological world?
12 Is coal obtained from decayed animal or plant matter?
13 What produces bubbles in the making of champagne?
14 Is the empennage of a plane at the front or the tail?
15 William Morris, Lord Nuffield was the first UK manufacturer of mass-produced what?
16 What does "P" stand for in DTP?
17 Which British bridge became the world's longest when completed in 1980?
18 What ill-fated personal transport was invented by Sir Clive Sinclair?
19 Which letter is farthest left on a computer keyboard?
20 Which country is the world's largest exporter of grain?
21 Which metal is used in thermometers?
22 Which colour identifies an ordinary diesel pump at a service station?
23 Nylon took its name from which two cities?
24 What device is indicated by a circle inside a square in clothing labels?
25 Which boom is produced by breaking the sound barrier?
26 C-Curity was the first type of which fastener?
27 What does "C" stand for in ASCII?
28 What sort of factory did Joseph Rowntree found?
29 What does a pluviometer measure?
30 Bournville was established for the workers of which company?

Answers	**Pot Luck 50** *(see Quiz 102)*

1 No. 2 Simon & Garfunkel. 3 Claustrophobia. 4 Palm Sunday. 5 Sunday. 6 September. 7 Fossils. 8 Bambi. 9 Bob Hope. 10 Harry Houdini. 11 York. 12 Esther Rantzen. 13 Iron. 14 Pratchett. 15 Warwickshire. 16 American football. 17 Bank. 18 Scotland. 19 Red Dwarf. 20 Eyre. 21 Dvorak. 22 Cafe. 23 The Half Blood Prince. 24 Ireland. 25 Paris. 26 The Archies. 27 Party. 28 Drew. 29 Independent. 30 Will Young.

1 Had Theo Walcott played in the Premiership before his 2006 World Cup call-up?
2 Which duo had hits with "Mrs Robinson" and "America"?
3 What is the fear of enclosed spaces called?
4 Which Sunday comes before Easter Day?
5 On TV, which night featured a show from the London Palladium?
6 Alphabetically, which is the last of the calendar months?
7 What would a palaeontologist study?
8 Which Disney creature nickname was given to Tony Blair?
9 Which veteran comic Bob celebrated his 100th birthday on 29th May 2003?
10 When Eric Weiss escaped from his name he was known as who?
11 Which race course hosts the Ebor Handicap?
12 Which female presenter fronted the long-running "That's Life"?
13 Which metal has the chemical symbol Fe?
14 Which Terry writes the best-selling sci-fi "Discworld" novels?
15 Which English county did Brian Lara first play for?
16 What's the sport if the Chicago Bears take on the Miami Dolphins?
17 What does a contestant call in "The Weakest Link" to keep the accumulated cash?
18 In which country did golf originate?
19 Holly the computer appeared on which TV sci-fi comedy?
20 Which is Australia's largest lake?
21 Who composed the "New World Symphony"?
22 In "Coronation Sreet" was Roy's Rolls the name of a cafe or a car hire?
23 Which Harry Potter novel was the first with the word Blood in the title?
24 Vocalist Enya hails from which country?
25 In which city was the movie "Moulin Rouge" set?
26 "Sugar Sugar" was a one-off No. 1 for which group?
27 Which word can go in after BIRTHDAY, HEN, LABOUR and STAG?
28 Which Barrymore was in "E.T." and "Batman Forever"?
29 What does the I stand for in ITV?
30 Who had a No. 1 album with "Friday's Child"?

Answers	Science: Technology *(see Quiz 101)*

1 Apple. 2 Computer firms. 3 Brakes. 4 1960s. 5 Hovercraft. 6 Helicopter. 7 405.
8 Atomic bomb. 9 Asbestos. 10 0. 11 Computers. 12 Plant. 13 Carbon dioxide.
14 Tail. 15 Cars. 16 Publishing. 17 Humber. 18 C5. 19 Q. 20 USA. 21 Mercury.
22 Black. 23 New York, London. 24 Tumble drier. 25 Sonic boom. 26 Zip. 27 Code.
28 Cocoa. 29 Rainfall. 30 Cadbury's.

1 Who was head of the family in "Till Death Us Do Part"?
2 Which house was Revisited in the classic 1980s drama?
3 Where was the BBC's 1992 ill-fated soap set?
4 On which weekend evening was "Jim'll Fix It" broadcast?
5 In "Tenko" the women were imprisoned by whom?
6 What was Lovejoy's occupation?
7 Which series was about a Mobile Army Surgical Hospital in Korea?
8 Which Michael played the hapless Frank Spencer?
9 What was unusual about Hopkirk in the Randall and Hopkirk agency?
10 What institution was "Please Sir" set in?
11 What was the rank of Phil Silvers' "Bilko"?
12 Who were the US TV equivalent of The Beatles?
13 Which Leonard Rossiter sitcom sounds like a problem with old houses?
14 How was Arthur Fonzerelli known in "Happy Days"?
15 Which animals did Barbara Woodhouse work with?
16 Who was June in "Terry and June"?
17 What sort of animal was Grizzly Adams?
18 What was Torquay's most famous hotel run by Basil and Sybil?
19 "Jewel in the Crown" was set in wartime where?
20 In which county was "All Creatures Great and Small" set?
21 What sort of performers were in Spitting Image?
22 Which father of Paula Yates presented "Stars on Sunday"?
23 What was the profession of Albert Steptoe and son Harold?
24 Which hero was "Riding through the glen, With his band of Men"?
25 Which classic sci-fi series began in the 23rd century?
26 In which country was "Van der Valk" set?
27 What sort of statesman was Alan B'Stard?
28 Which Eric played Hattie Jacques' brother?
29 Was it Mork or Mindy who came from the planet Ork?
30 What sort of Men were Bill and Ben?

Answers	**Past Times: The 80s** *(see Quiz 104)*

1 Margaret Thatcher. 2 London. 3 Eggs. 4 Johnson. 5 North Sea. 6 King's Cross. 7 Neil Kinnock. 8 Duchess of Windsor. 9 Zeebrugge. 10 Philippines. 11 South Africa. 12 Prince Andrew. 13 Runner. 14 Wembley. 15 Morecambe. 16 Parkinson. 17 Bradford. 18 Liberal Democrats. 19 In space. 20 Greenham. 21 Harrods. 22 Bjorn Borg. 23 Car accident. 24 Dallas. 25 Falklands. 26 Tyson. 27 Champion. 28 Reagan. 29 New York. 30 Kindergarten.

1 Which serving British PM survived an assassination attempt?
2 In which city did the SAS storm the Iranian embassy?
3 Edwina Currie resigned over what type of farm food?
4 Which Ben was disqualified from the Seoul Olympics for drug taking?
5 In which Sea did the oil rig Piper Alpha catch fire?
6 Which north London Tube station was gutted by fire in 1987?
7 Who was Labour leader when Thatcher had her third election victory?
8 Which late Duchess's jewels were auctioned for over £30 million?
9 The Herald of Free Enterprise sank off which Belgian port?
10 President Marcos was ousted in a rebellion in which island country?
11 Desmond Tutu became an Archbishop in which country?
12 Who was the second of the Queen's sons to marry in the 80s?
13 Was Zola Budd a swimmer, a runner or a gymnast?
14 At which UK stadium was the Live Aid concert held?
15 Which Eric, half of a classic comedy duo, died in 1984?
16 Which Tory minister Cecil resigned in a scandal in 1983?
17 In which Yorkshire city's football ground was there a fatal fire in '85?
18 What is the full name of the Lib Dems, formed in 1989?
19 Sally Ride became the USA's first woman where?
20 At which Common was there a camp against cruise missiles?
21 Outside which London store did a bomb explode in December 1983?
22 Which Swedish tennis star retired age 26?
23 In what type of accident was Princess Grace of Monaco killed?
24 Which soap asked the audience asked "Who shot JR?"
25 Which war in the south Atlantic was Britain involved in?
26 Which Mike became the youngest heavyweight boxing champion?
27 Which Bob rode Aldaniti to a Grand National win in 1981?
28 Which US president was the victim of an assassination attempt?
29 In which city was Beatle John Lennon murdered?
30 Where was Lady Diana Spencer working when photographed in a seemingly see-through skirt?

Answers | **TV Gold** (see Quiz 103)

1 Alf Garnett. 2 Brideshead. 3 Spain. 4 Saturday. 5 Japanese. 6 Antiques dealer. 7 M*A*S*H. 8 Crawford. 9 He was a ghost. 10 School. 11 Sergeant. 12 The Monkees. 13 Rising Damp. 14 The Fonz/Fonzie. 15 Dogs. 16 June Whitfield. 17 Human. 18 Fawlty Towers. 19 India. 20 Yorkshire. 21 Puppets. 22 Jess Yates. 23 Rag & bone merchants. 24 Robin Hood. 25 Star Trek. 26 Holland. 27 New Statesman. 28 Sykes. 29 Mork. 30 Flowerpot men.

1 Whose album "True Blue" was No. 1 in 28 countries?
2 What was The Spice Girls' first No. 1?
3 Whose charity hit included "Something About the Way You Look Tonight"?
4 Which of Madonna's two hits from "Evita" got higher in the charts?
5 Which Frank Sinatra hit has spent most weeks in the UK charts?
6 In which decade did the UK singles charts begin?
7 Who as well as The Troggs charted with "Love is All Around"?
8 Which wartime song charted with Robson & Jerome's "Unchained Melody"?
9 Which father and daughter had a No. 1 with "Somethin' Stupid"?
10 "I Bet You Look Good on the Dancefloor" was a 2005 No. 1 for which band?
11 Which soccer side charted with "Come On You Reds"?
12 Whose "Release Me" spent a record number of weeks in the charts?
13 Was Celine Dion's "Power of Love" the same as Jennifer Rush's or Frankie Goes to Hollywood's?
14 Who was the first all-female band to have three consecutive No. 1s?
15 Who was singing "All The Way" in the 2005 charts?
16 Was Gareth Gates aged 17, 20 or 27 when he first had a No. 1 single?
17 Which musical did Boyzone's No. 1 "No Matter What" come from?
18 Who is the most successful Australian female to have been in the UK singles charts?
19 Billboard is a list of best-selling records where?
20 "Stickwitu" was the second No. 1 for which girl group?
21 Which family were at No. 1 with "Do the Bartman"?
22 Which Scandinavian country do chart toppers Aqua come from?
23 Who accompanied Vic Reeves on his No. 1 hit "Dizzy"?
24 Whose '96 No. 1s were "Firestarter" and "Breathe"?
25 Which Boys' first No. 1 was "West End Girls"?
26 Which Boys had the 2005 hits "Incomplete" and "Just Want You to Know"?
27 Which solo Briton Cliff has spent most weeks in the UK singles charts?
28 Which female solo star has spent most weeks in the British charts?
29 "Love Me for a Reason" charted for The Osmonds and which band?
30 Who wrote the series "Crocodile Shoes" and its chart songs?

Answers | **Who was Who?** (see Quiz 106)

1 Bill Clinton. 2 Arthur Miller. 3 Louis Pasteur. 4 Nobel. 5 Three. 6 Guy Fawkes. 7 Henry Ford. 8 Second World War. 9 India. 10 Oil. 11 Glenys Kinnock. 12 Charles. 13 Che Guevara. 14 Queen Victoria. 15 Pankhurst. 16 Saddam Hussein. 17 One. 18 American. 19 W.G.Grace. 20 56. 21 Buster Keaton. 22 Mandela. 23 Mao Zedong. 24 Groucho. 25 Mary. 26 Miller. 27 Mussolini. 28 Italian. 29 John Kerry. 30 John F. Kennedy.

1 Who became US President in 1992 when Governor of Arkansas?
2 Which playwright Arthur, an ex- of Marilyn Monroe, died in 2005?
3 Which scientist gave his name to the process of pasteurisation?
4 Who left $9 million to give prizes in five different fields?
5 Did Tony Blair have one, three or five children when he became Prime Minister?
6 Who lit the fuse for the 1605 Gunpowder Plot?
7 Was it John Ford or Henry Ford who manufactured cars?
8 During which war did Anne Frank write her diary?
9 Indira Gandhi was Prime Minister of which country?
10 John Paul Getty made his millions from which commodity?
11 Who was Labour leader Neil Kinnock's wife who became an MEP?
12 Who was the first 20th-century Prince of Wales to be divorced?
13 How was Argentinean Ernesto Guevara de la Serna better known?
14 William Gladstone was Prime Minister under which monarch?
15 What was suffragette leader Emmeline Goulden's married name?
16 Who became President of Iraq in 1979?
17 How many English kings have been called Stephen?
18 What was the nationality of the Duchess of Windsor?
19 Which legendary cricketer had the first names William Gilbert?
20 How old was Hitler when he died, 46, 56 or 66?
21 By which name was silent movie star Joseph Keaton better known?
22 Which Nelson was the first black President of South Africa?
23 Which Chinese leader instigated the Great Leap Forward in 1958?
24 Which Marx brother had a moustache, cigar and funny walk?
25 According to the Bible who was the mother of Jesus?
26 Which trombonist Glenn became a famous bandleader?
27 Who was Italian dictator between 1926 and 1943?
28 What was the nationality of inventor Marconi?
29 Whom did George W. Bush defeat standing as President for the second term?
30 Who was the youngest US President to die in office?

Answers	Pop: Charts (see Quiz 105)

1 Madonna. 2 Wannabe. 3 Elton John. 4 Don't Cry for Me Argentina. 5 My Way.
6 1950s. 7 Wet Wet Wet. 8 The White Cliffs of Dover. 9 Frank & Nancy Sinatra.
10 Arctic Monkeys. 11 Manchester United. 12 Engelbert Humperdinck. 13 Jennifer Rush's. 14 Spice Girls. 15 Craig David. 16 17 years. 17 Whistle Down the Wind. 18 Kylie Minogue. 19 USA. 20 The Pussycat Dolls. 21 The Simpsons. 22 Denmark. 23 The Wonder Stuff. 24 Prodigy. 25 Pet Shop. 26 Backstreet Boys. 27 Richard. 28 Madonna. 29 Boyzone. 30 Jimmy Nail.

1 Sir Paul McCartney was awarded the freedom of which city?
2 Which legendary band released "The Wall"?
3 Which soul star Ray has the nickname The Genius?
4 Which Shirley was dubbed the Tigress from Tiger Bay?
5 Supermodel Rachel Hunter married which superstar Rod?
6 Which ex-Police singer founded the Rainforest Foundation in 1988?
7 Who does not use her surname Ciccone?
8 Which brother completed the Gibb trio with Maurice and Robin?
9 "Hung Up" gave a 12th No. 1 single for which superstar?
10 Which rock superstar was Lisa Marie Presley's second husband?
11 Which female sang on Westlife's "When You Tell Me that You Love Me"?
12 In 2005 which Robbie Wiliams song was voted best in 25 years of BRIT awards?
13 Which drummer's solo album "No Jacket Required" was a best-seller?
14 Which Rolling Stone did not normally play an instrument on stage?
15 Which group was heard on the soundtrack of "Saturday Night Fever"?
16 Whose hits range from "The Laughing Gnome" to "Space Oddity"?
17 Who sang "You Don't Bring Me Flowers" with Barbra Streisand?
18 Which Queen of Soul sang the best version of "Nessun Dorma" according to Pavarotti?
19 Which band would you find The Edge and Bono in?
20 Who lived in a mansion called Graceland?
21 Which boys liked "California Girls"?
22 Whose "Streets of Philadelphia" was his highest hit at the time in 1994?
23 Which Stevie dropped the tag Little and had hits well into adulthood?
24 Which Tina recorded Bond theme "Goldeneye"?
25 Which superstar founded the Rocket record label?
26 All Lionel Richie's early hits were on which record label?
27 Which Scottish football fan has the first names Roderick David?
28 Which Roy charted with "Crying" with kd lang four years after his death?
29 Which Barbra did actor James Brolin marry in 1998?
30 Which Barry's song "Copacabana" became a musical?

Answers | **Leisure: The Media** (see Quiz 108)

1 World Service. 2 Piers Morgan. 3 Horse racing. 4 Radio Times. 5 Classic FM. 6 Radio 4. 7 London. 8 Sunday Sport. 9 Five. 10 Manchester. 11 Gossip column. 12 Musical. 13 Men. 14 Rebekah Wade. 15 Top shelf. 16 Financial Times. 17 Mail on Sunday. 18 Sunday. 19 BBC. 20 Hello! 21 Murdoch. 22 Three. 23 Milkshake! 24 Private Eye. 25 Daily Express. 26 England & Scotland. 27 Doctor. 28 Weekly. 29 Ricky Gervais. 30 Frost.

1 Which BBC radio and TV service broadcasts abroad?
2 Which ex-newspaper editor Piers became a star presenter on American TV?
3 The Sporting Life devotes itself to which sport?
4 Which radio and TV listings magazine is published by the BBC?
5 Which independent radio station specialises in classical music?
6 Is "The Archers" on Radio 1 or Radio 4?
7 Where does Capital Radio broadcast to?
8 What is the Sunday version of Daily Sport called?
9 Which BBC Radio station has Live after its number?
10 In which north of England city is Granada TV based?
11 What sort of column tells of stories and rumours about celebrities?
12 What does M stand for in the pop paper NME?
13 Is GQ for men or women?
14 Which Rebekah was the first female to edit "The Sun" newspaper?
15 On which shelf would someone buy an "adult" magazine?
16 What does FT stand for in the name of the financial daily newspaper?
17 What is the Daily Mail's Sunday paper called?
18 On which day of the week is the News of the World published?
19 Which corporation is known as Auntie?
20 Which magazine about celebs is based on the Spanish mag Hola!?
21 Which Rupert founded Sky Television?
22 Which page in a newspaper is famous for its nude photos?
23 Which frothy beverage shares the name of a children's morning TV show on Five?
24 Which satirical magazine shares its name with the nickname for a detective?
25 Rupert Bear is linked with which newspaper?
26 Border TV serves the borders of which two countries?
27 What professional person would read The Lancet?
28 How often does the magazine Take A Break appear?
29 Which comic Ricky was a pioneer in podcasting?
30 Which Sir David co-founded LWT and TV-am?

Answers	Geography: World Tour 1 *(see Quiz 111)*

1 Nile. 2 Pope. 3 West. 4 Afghanistan. 5 Bombay. 6 Abominable. 7 Australia. 8 Southern. 9 India. 10 Peru. 11 Caribbean. 12 Zimbabwe. 13 Suez. 14 Coast. 15 Pacific. 16 South Africa. 17 Abraham Lincoln. 18 Arizona. 19 Australia. 20 Sahara. 21 Monarchy. 22 Africa. 23 Danube. 24 Atlantic. 25 Iran. 26 Arctic Circle. 27 Southern. 28 Hungary. 29 China. 30 Canada.

1 Who is Julian Lennon's stepmother?
2 Which pop wife has Liam and a shamrock tattooed on her ankle?
3 Which George did not make a record for five years because of a dispute with Sony?
4 Which female released an album declaring she was "No Angel"?
5 Which Elaine changed her surname from Bickerstaff and went on to star in many West End musicals?
6 Which Stevie led the campaign to commemorate Martin Luther King's birthday in the US?
7 How is Katherine Dawn Lang better known?
8 Bernie Taupin collaborated with which performer for over 20 years?
9 Which Boys were famous for their surfing sound?
10 Whose real name is Charles Edward Anderson Berry?
11 In what type of tragic accident did John Denver meet his death?
12 Which composer of Boyzone's "No Matter What" appeared with them on "Top of the Pops"?
13 Andrew Ridgeley was the less famous half of which group?
14 Which band always comes last alphabetically?
15 Who was "Born to Do It" according to his No. 1 selling album?
16 The Spice Girls recorded their early hits on which label?
17 PJ and Duncan were also known as who?
18 Which soul star did Bryan Ferry name his son Otis after?
19 What are the first names of the Everly Brothers?
20 Was Bryan Adams born in Canada or the USA?
21 Who was left-handed, Lennon or McCartney?
22 Which ex-husband of Cher died in a skiing accident ?
23 Bjork hails from which country?
24 Who made the album "Let's Talk About Love"?
25 Which band released the album "Hail to the Thief"?
26 "That's My Goal" was a first No. 1 single for which Shayne?
27 Which Mark co-founded Dire Straits?
28 What name links Ant and Faith?
29 Which hit by D:Ream was used in the 1997 Labour election campaign?
30 Who changed his name to a symbol?

1 Which famous actress Koo was romantically linked to Prince Andrew?
2 What relation was Prince Philip to Princess Margaret?
3 What did the Princess of Wales sell at auction in 1997?
4 What is the Princess Royal's real first name?
5 Who played the Queen in a 2006 film about the death of Princess Diana?
6 What is the title of the wife of Prince Michael of Kent?
7 Which Princess was prevented from marrying divorced Peter Townsend in the 1950s?
8 On which programme did Princess Diana say her marriage had been "a bit crowded"?
9 Prince Harry followed Prince William to which school in 1998?
10 Which dietary illness did Princess Diana allegedly suffer from?
11 Who is the mother of Princesses Beatrice and Eugenie?
12 Which son of Prince Charles has red hair?
13 Who is older, Prince Andrew or Prince Edward?
14 Which Royal is always referred to as Her Majesty?
15 Which Royal yacht was decommissioned in 1997?
16 Is Princess Anne's daughter a Princess, or a Miss?
17 Where is the Queen's holiday home north of the border?
18 What is the first name of Princes William and Harry's step sister?
19 At which time of year does the Queen always make a TV broadcast?
20 What did Elton John sing at Princess Diana's funeral?
21 Which wife of Prince Rainier of Monaco was an Oscar winner?
22 Was Charles and Camilla's first overseas tour together to Russia or USA?
23 In which Abbey did Prince Andrew and Sarah Ferguson marry?
24 Prince Albert succeeded to which throne in 2005?
25 Which profession is shared by Lords Snowdon and Lichfield?
26 In which city was Princess Diana tragically killed?
27 Which castle was reopened in 1998 after being damaged by fire?
28 Who was the last British monarch of the 19th century?
29 Before his marriage was Prince Philip in the army or the navy?
30 Which Princess was married to Captain Mark Phillips?

Answers	Pop: Superstars *(see Quiz 107)*

1 Liverpool. 2 Pink Floyd. 3 Charles. 4 Bassey. 5 Stewart. 6 Sting. 7 Madonna. 8 Barry. 9 Madonna. 10 Michael Jackson. 11 Diana Ross. 12 Angels. 13 Phil Collins. 14 Mick Jagger. 15 Bee Gees. 16 David Bowie. 17 Neil Diamond. 18 Aretha Franklin. 19 U2. 20 Elvis Presley. 21 Beach Boys. 22 Bruce Springsteen. 23 Wonder. 24 Turner. 25 Elton John. 26 Motown. 27 Rod Stewart. 28 Orbison. 29 Streisand. 30 Manilow.

1 Which long river has White and Blue tributaries?
2 Which religious leader is head of state of the Vatican?
3 Is Perth on the west or east coast of Australia?
4 Which country was the centre of operations for the Taliban?
5 Does Bombay or Tokyo have the higher population?
6 What sort of Snowman is another name for the Himalayan yeti?
7 What is the world's smallest, flattest and driest continent?
8 Is Argentina in the northern or southern half of South America?
9 Pakistan and Bangladesh both border which country?
10 Which country's name is an anagram of PURE?
11 The West Indies lie in which Sea?
12 Zambia is a neighbour of which country which also begins with Z?
13 Which Egyptian canal links the Red Sea and the Mediterranean?
14 Is Ghana on the African coast or wholly inland?
15 Which ocean is the world's deepest?
16 In which country is the homeland of KwaZulu?
17 Who is commemorated at Washington's Lincoln Memorial?
18 Which US state has the zipcode (postcode) AZ?
19 New South Wales is in which country?
20 Which African desert is the world's largest?
21 Is Swaziland a monarchy or a republic?
22 Mount Kilimanjaro is the highest point of which continent?
23 Which river runs through Belgrade, Budapest and Vienna?
24 Which ocean lies to the east of South America?
25 Which Islamic Republic used to be called Persia?
26 Two thirds of Greenland lies in which Circle?
27 Is Namibia in northern or southern Africa?
28 In which country in Europe could you spend a forint?
29 Which People's Republic has the world's largest population?
30 Alberta is a province of which country?

Answers	**Pop: Who's Who?** *(see Quiz 109)*

1 Yoko Ono. 2 Patsy Kensit. 3 Michael. 4 Dido. 5 Paige. 6 Wonder. 7 kd lang. 8
Elton John. 9 Beach Boys. 10 Chuck Berry. 11 Plane crash. 12 Andrew Lloyd Webber.
13 Wham! 14 ZZ Top. 15 Craig David. 16 Virgin. 17 Ant & Dec. 18 Otis Redding.
19 Don & Phil. 20 Canada. 21 McCartney. 22 Sonny. 23 Iceland. 24 Celine Dion. 25
Radiohead. 26 Shayne Wardr. 27 Knopfler. 28 Adam. 29 Things Can Only Get Better.
30 Prince.

1 Which of Durham, Kent and Suffolk is part of East Anglia?
2 What would a Venezuelan do with a Bolivar?
3 Who played Rachel in "Friends"?
4 What does the B stand for in LBW in cricket?
5 Which Spice Girl wore a dress with a Union Jack flag pattern?
6 Which word can be a worker's eating place or a cutlery set?
7 What was President George W Bush's father's first name?
8 Which caped hero flew his way round the city of Metropolis?
9 Which fruit goes in the pudding named after opera diva Nellie Melba?
10 What is a pomegranate?
11 Which was built first – the Eiffel Tower or the Empire State Building?
12 What comes after New South in the name of an Australian state?
13 Which has the most sides – a hexagon, a pentagon or a quadrilateral?
14 Capricorn, Libra, Phoenix – which of these is not a sign of the zodiac?
15 How many faces would a dozen dice have in total?
16 What shape is in the middle of the Japanese flag?
17 In e mail what does the e stand for?
18 What was the name of the bear that belonged to Christopher Robin?
19 In athletics, how many events have taken place when half a decathlon is completed?
20 What is coffee produced from?
21 Where did turkeys originally come from?
22 Who might display, on a British road, a sign worth fifty in Roman numerals?
23 What name is given to buying goods via the Internet?
24 When texting, the word YOU is usually shown by which letter?
25 Which numbers feature in the ads using 1970s-style mustachioed runners?
26 Houston is in which US state?
27 On which continent is the Panama Canal?
28 Which brothers made the first controlled powered flight?
29 Which Mark has managed Blackburn and Wales at soccer?
30 In history the "Marie Celeste" was a type of what?

Answers	**People: Stars (see Quiz 114)**

1 Dance. 2 Elton John. 3 Lennon. 4 Ireland. 5 Scotland. 6 Joely. 7 Reese. 8 Laine. 9 Five. 10 Henshall. 11 Martine. 12 Snooker. 13 Sir Bobby. 14 Wade. 15 Red. 16 Iceland. 17 Jensen. 18 Blanchett. 19 Harry. 20 Honor. 21 Liverpool. 22 Slim. 23 Cruise. 24 Carol. 25 Charlie Dimmock. 26 Sarong. 27 Yorkshire. 28 Bean. 29 Terry. 30 Zinedine Zidane.

Answers – page 125

1 Jane Collins was lined up to be the fourth bride of which "Eastenders" Ian?

2 On which Channel did "Family Affairs" debut?

3 Which northern soap was the most successful of the 1990s?

4 Which former landlady of the Queen Vic returned to the Square in 2001 after "living in America"?

5 In "Coronation Street" in September 2001 who did Fred marry?

6 Where did Bianca go when she left Albert Square?

7 In "Emmerdale" what responsible job does Angie Reynolds have?

8 Which Ron shot a suspected burglar in the summer of 2001?

9 Which "Straw Dogs" actress Susan joined the Albert Square cast as Terry's love interest?

10 Who was Phil Mitchell's brother as played by Ross Kemp?

11 Who did Mike Baldwin marry after he was divorced from Alma?

12 Which family did Lisa Riley belong to when she starred in "Emmerdale"?

13 Who did Ian Beale marry after his disastrous ceremony with Mel?

14 In "Corrie" what colour did the Battersbys add to the end of their name?

15 In which soap did film actress Anna Friel make her name?

16 Who is Barry Evans' dad in "EastEnders", sharing his name with an ex-Liverpool FC boss?

17 Who were the "Coronation Street" "family from hell", which included Toyah and Janice?

18 Where is "Hollyoaks" set?

19 Which "Coronation Street" character died of cancer in 2001?

20 Which actress Sheila came to Albert Square as Steve Owen's mum?

21 Which soap ran a campaign to free the Weatherfield One?

22 Who did Curly marry after Raquel left him?

23 Which soap features the Lamberts and the Kings?

24 What colour was Rita Sullivan's famous hair?

25 What was the name of the "EastEnders" character played by Martine McCutcheon?

26 Which soap introduced an extra Friday-night instalment in 2001?

27 In "Coronation Street", what was Ashley and Maxine's surname?

28 Who is the evil member of the "EastEnders" Cotton family?

29 Which Midlands soap returned to ITV in 2001?

30 Which teen soap features the Hunters and the Morgans?

Answers	**Pot Luck 53** *(see Quiz 117)*

1 New Zealand. 2 Vietnam. 3 English. 4 Sweetcorn. 5 Mick McCarthy. 6 Penguins. 7 Pistol. 8 East. 9 Pierce Brosnan. 10 Cricket. 11 Computer. 12 Madonna. 13 Europe. 14 Nests. 15 Invention. 16 (South) America. 17 Air. 18 Rake. 19 Flags. 20 1992. 21 Autobahn. 22 Vegetative state. 23 Yellow. 24 Fluid ounces. 25 Apples. 26 180. 27 Egg. 28 Throat. 29 General Pinochet. 30 Easter.

1 Michael Flatley was dubbed Lord of the what?
2 Which megastar sang his own song at Princess Diana's funeral?
3 After which Beatle did Liam Gallagher name his son with Patsy Kensit?
4 From where does ex-"Ballykissangel" star Dervla Kirwan hail?
5 In which part of the UK did Madonna marry Guy Ritchie?
6 Which blonde actress Richardson split with Jamie Theakston in 2001?
7 Which Ms Witherspoon starred in "Walk the Line"?
8 Which Cleo is Mrs John Dankworth?
9 How many members of Hear'Say were there?
10 Which Ruthie starred in the musical "Peggy Sue Got Married"?
11 Which Ms McCutcheon played Eliza Doolittle on the London stage?
12 Ronnie O'Sullivan is a star in which sport?
13 Who is Jack Charlton's famous younger brother?
14 Which former tennis star Virginia had a father who was a clergyman?
15 When she was a Spice Girl, Geri Halliwell had what colour hair?
16 Bjork has an emblem from which country on her shoulder?
17 Which DJ David had the name "Kid"?
18 Which actress Cate portrayed Katharine Hepburn in "The Aviator"?
19 Which singer Connick adds Junior to his name?
20 Which Ms Blackman, an ex-Bond girl, has a brown belt in judo?
21 Sir Paul McCartney received the freedom of which city, his childhood home?
22 What does Fatboy Norman Cook add to his name for DJ purposes?
23 Which Tom split with wife Nicole Kidman in 2001?
24 Which first name is shared by TV stars Smillie and Vorderman?
25 Who is the female gardener on "Ground Force"?
26 David Beckham famously wore what normally female garment?
27 Opera star Lesley Garrett hails from which northern county?
28 Which zany Mr is Rowan Atkinson's most famous creation?
29 Who is broadcaster Alan Wogan's famous dad?
30 Which French footballer got his marching orders in the 2006 World Cup Final?

Answers	Pot Luck 51 (see Quiz 112)

1 Suffolk. 2 Spend it. 3 Jennifer Aniston. 4 Before. 5 Geri. 6 Canteen. 7 George. 8 Superman. 9 Peach. 10 A fruit. 11 Eiffel Tower. 12 Wales. 13 Hexagon. 14 Phoenix. 15 72. 16 Circle. 17 Electronic. 18 Winnie the Pooh. 19 Five. 20 Beans. 21 North America. 22 A learner driver – L. 23 Shopping on line. 24 U. 25 118 118. 26 Texas. 27 America. 28 Wright. 29 Hughes. 30 Boat/ship.

1 Which equestrian champion was 2006 BBC Sports Personality of the Year?
2 Which zodiac sign of Gemini, Pisces and Taurus represents a human shape?
3 Which Sharon starred in "Basic Instinct" and "Total Recall"?
4 How is a sound produced from a euphonium?
5 What colour is the magic linked with a wicked witch?
6 If you multiply the length of rectangle by the width what do you get?
7 A penny farthing was an early type of bike, but how many farthings made up the value of a penny farthing?
8 What is a nun's head dress called?
9 Which girl band featuring the Appleton girls got back together in 2006?
10 Manx, Marmalade and Tabby are all types of what?
11 In the saying, many what will make light work?
12 Following the gruesome nursery rhyme recipe, how many blackbirds would be baked in two pies?
13 Which fruit of grapes, pears and plums is bought by the bunch?
14 What form of transport is the French TGV?
15 Tortillas are originally from which country?
16 When did Yeovil first play in the Football League – 1973, 1983 or 2003?
17 What was the number of the first Apollo mission to land on the Moon?
18 The Dalai Lama is the spiritual leader of which country?
19 Around which part of your body would you tie a cummerbund?
20 What did the Romans keep in a catacomb?
21 Which object appears on the Canadian flag?
22 What happens to the rows of letters when reading down an eye-test chart?
23 Pevez Musharraf was president of which country?
24 Which of Funny, Grumpy and Happy is not one of Snow White's seven dwarfs?
25 What did David Bowie call his first child?
26 If the first of a month is a Thursday, what day will the eighth be?
27 Cassata is a type of which food?
28 In "The Wombles", which Great Uncle shares his name with a country?
29 Which side of a ship is starboard?
30 Which colour is usually used to show the sea on a map?

Answers | TV: Soaps *(see Quiz 113)*

1 Ian Beale. 2 5. 3 Coronation Street. 4 Sharon. 5 Eve. 6 Manchester. 7 Police officer. 8 Dixon. 9 George. 10 Grant. 11 Linda. 12 Dingles. 13 Laura. 14 Brown. 15 Brookside. 16 Roy. 17 Battersby. 18 Chester. 19 Alma. 20 Hancock. 21 Coronation Street. 22 Emma. 23 Emmerdale. 24 Red. 25 Tiffany. 26 Coronation Street. 27 Peacock. 28 Nick. 29 Crossroads. 30 Hollyoaks.

1 Which Ian captained Europe to Ryder Cup success in 2006?
2 How many events did Denise Lewis compete in to win her heptathlon Olympic gold?
3 Against which country did England play the first ever Test Match in cricket?
4 Mike Powell beat Bob Beamon's long-standing record in which event?
5 Allan Border made a record number of runs for which international cricketing side?
6 How long does Le Mans's most famous motor race last?
7 In which Greek city were the first modern Olympics held?
8 In which decade did Roger Bannister run his first sub-four-minute mile?
9 Which Czech-born Martina won her ninth Wimbledon singles title in 1990?
10 Gymnast Nadia Comaneci was the first person ever to score what out of 10 at the Olympic Games?
11 In 1988 tennis was re-introduced at which four-yearly sporting event?
12 What colour shirts were England wearing when they won the 1966 World Cup?
13 Eleven athletes from which country were killed at the 1972 Munich Olympics?
14 In which decade did Jesse Owens win four gold medals at the Berlin Olympics?
15 Charismatic gymnast Olga Korbut represented which country?
16 In which city were the 1980 Olympics, boycotted by the Americans?
17 Which cricketer Geoffrey made his hundredth 100 in a 1977 Test Match?
18 Which racehorse was taken from his box in an Irish stud in 1983 and was never seen again?
19 Which German Boris won Wimbledon in 1985?
20 Who, with Jayne Torvill, was awarded a full set of perfect Olympic sixes for ice dancing in 1984?
21 Which Steve was Sebastian Coe's main British rival in middle-distance running in 1980?
22 What was the nickname of James Douglas who beat Mike Tyson in 1990?
23 Who hit six sixes in an over in 1968?
24 Which Manchester side won the European Cup in 1968?
25 Which Second Division team beat Leeds United in the 1973 FA Cup final?
26 What is the nationality of Ballesteros who won the British Open in 1984?
27 How many times did Red Rum win the Grand National?
28 Which England footballer was famous for his tears at Italia 90?
29 Which Briton won gold in the triple jump in the 2001 World Championships?
30 Which English player was sent off against Argentina in the 1998 World Cup?

Answers | **New Millennium Movies** *(see Quiz 118)*

1 Diary. 2 Cage. 3 Travolta. 4 Pearl Harbor. 5 Ballet. 6 Egypt. 7 Cruz. 8 China. 9 Cruise. 10 Green. 11 Chocolate. 12 Hannibal. 13 Gibson. 14 Harry Potter. 15 Caine. 16 Animation. 17 Desert Island. 18 Croft. 19 Finney. 20 Matt Dillon. 21 Kate Winslet. 22 X. 23 Satellite dish. 24 Low Lifes. 25 Gladiator. 26 St Bernard dog. 27 Ring. 28 Storm. 29 Toy Story 2. 30 Ralph.

1 Maoris were the first settlers in which country?
2 "The Deer Hunter" has which war as its subject matter?
3 What is the main language of North America's two main countries?
4 Which vegetable is produced from the plant maize?
5 Which Mick has managed the Republic of Ireland, Sunderland and Wolves?
6 The animated movie "Happy Feet" is about what kind of creatures?
7 Which weapon is used in Pete Sampras's nickname?
8 Mozambique is on which coast of Africa?
9 Who starred as 007 in "The World is Not Enough"?
10 Which sport is covered by the "Wisden Almanac"?
11 William Henry Gates III became seriously rich through which industry?
12 Which superstar did film producer Guy Ritchie marry in 2000?
13 Which continent is the most crowded and the smallest?
14 Which word describes homes for birds as well as sets of tables?
15 Frank Zappa was leader of the group The Mothers of what – Convention, Intention or Invention?
16 In which continent is the Amazon rainforest?
17 A hovercraft moves along on a cushion of what?
18 Which one of the following tools is pronged – hoe, spade or rake?
19 What does a person hold in their hand when practising semaphore?
20 Which of the following was a leap year –1991, 1992, 1994?
21 What is the German word for a motorway?
22 In medical terms PVS stands for persistent what?
23 What colour does the skin become if someone suffers from jaundice?
24 What does the abbreviation "fl oz" stand for?
25 Which fruit is mainly used when making a strudel?
26 How many degrees are there in a right-angled triangle?
27 What is the main ingredient of mayonnaise other than oil?
28 Laryngitis affects which part of your body?
29 Which former Chilean leader died in December 2006?
30 Lent comes before which Christian festival?

1 What did Bridget Jones write?
2 Which Nicolas starred in "Captain Corelli's Mandolin"?
3 Which John was the counter-terrorist in "Swordfish"?
4 Which 2001 movie was about a Japanese bombing 60 years before?
5 Billy Elliot trained to be what type of dancer?
6 Where is "The Mummy Returns" set?
7 Which Penelope played opposite Johnny Depp in "Blow"?
8 Where was "Crouching Tiger, Hidden Dragon" produced?
9 Which Tom teamed up – both on and off the screen – with Penelope Cruz in the movie "Vanilla Sky"?
10 What colour is Shrek?
11 What type of shop does Juliette Binoche open in "Chocolat"?
12 What was the sequel to "Silence of the Lambs" called?
13 Which Mel read Helen Hunt's thoughts in "What Women Want"?
14 Warner Brothers made a series of movies about which boy wizard?
15 Which Michael co-starred with Sandra Bullock in "Miss Congeniality"?
16 What type of movie was "The Emperor's New Groove"?
17 Where is Tom Hanks trying to survive in "Castaway"?
18 Which Lara was a character in "Tomb Raider"?
19 Which Albert co-starred with Julia Roberts in "Erin Brokovich"?
20 Which Matt starred in "Crash"?
21 Which star of "Titanic" also starred in "Quills"?
22 In which TV "Files" did "Evolution"'s David Duchovny find fame?
23 What is "The Dish" in the title of the movie with Sam Neill?
24 What went with "High Heels" in the movie title?
25 Which Roman epic starred Russell Crowe?
26 Which animal is the hero of "Beethoven's 3rd"?
27 What completes the title – "Fellowship of the ____"?
28 What was "Perfect" in the 2000 movie with George Clooney?
29 What was the sequel to "Toy Story" called?
30 Which Fiennes starred in "The End of the Affair"?

Answers	Memorable Sporting Moments (see Quiz 116)

1 Ian Woosnam. 2 Seven. 3 Australia. 4 Long jump. 5 Australia. 6 24 hours. 7 Athens. 8 1950s. 9 Navratilova. 10 10. 11 Olympics. 12 Red. 13 Israel. 14 1930s. 15 USSR (Soviet Union). 16 Moscow. 17 Boycott. 18 Shergar. 19 Becker. 20 Christopher Dean. 21 Ovett. 22 Buster. 23 Gary (Garfield) Sobers. 24 United. 25 Sunderland. 26 Spanish. 27 Three. 28 Paul Gascoigne. 29 Jonathan Edwards. 30 David Beckham.

1 Duplo is a younger version of which favourite toy?
2 What is the name of Mrs Addams in "The Addams Family"?
3 What is a large gathering of Boy Scouts called?
4 What colour car does the Pink Panther drive in his cartoon show?
5 Which politically incorrect adjective is applied to Thomas the Tank Engine's Controller?
6 What's the difference between the highest single dart treble and the lowest single dart treble?
7 What shape is a tambourine?
8 Who has had hits with "Down 4 U" and "Only U"?
9 What is a Barbie's usual hair colour?
10 Which country hosted the last soccer World Cup played in the 20th century?
11 In computing what does O mean in OS?
12 In which Greek city is the Acropolis situated?
13 Chile is on which coast of South America?
14 The edelweiss is a native flower to which mountains?
15 The kiwi fruit is also known as which gooseberry?
16 What did Jodhpur in India give its name to?
17 In which decade of the last century did the Channel Tunnel open to the public?
18 Lebanon is situated at the eastern end of which Sea?
19 A warning of which computer bug was given prior to the start of the year 2000?
20 Which US state is known as the Sunshine State?
21 What are the least number of points needed to win a single game in tennis?
22 Terracotta is made by baking what?
23 What is the abbreviation used for metre?
24 What type of "Sleep" was a classic Bacall and Bogart movie?
25 Which Frenchman gave his name to an item worn by ballet dancers?
26 In 2004, Piers Morgan resigned as editor of which British daily paper?
27 Charlie Chaplin found fame in America but where was he born?
28 Which word means clever and can also be a stinging pain?
29 Which 19th-century American President was murdered in a theatre?
30 Which Kelly got double gold in the 2004 Olympics in Greece?

Answers	**Pot Luck 55** *(see Quiz 121)*

1 Argentina. 2 CJ. 3 Washington DC. 4 Children. 5 Long. 6 Watford. 7 Morocco. 8 Plane. 9 Two. 10 Tail. 11 Water. 12 Gown. 13 Peas. 14 Margaret. 15 Monsoon. 16 Raspberry. 17 West Ham. 18 Your family. 19 Polly. 20 Hungary. 21 Top. 22 Cricket. 23 Ritual suicide. 24 Chicago. 25 Wine. 26 India. 27 Radioactivity. 28 Bamber Gascoigne. 29 Cribbage. 30 Tiger.

Answers – page 132

1 Is Aberdeen to the north or south of Glasgow?

2 Prestwick and Gatwick are both what?

3 The Dales are mainly in which county?

4 On which Devon moor is there a famous prison?

5 Denbighshire is in the north of which country?

6 Who is London's Downing Street's most famous resident?

7 What is the capital of Scotland's Dumfries and Galloway region?

8 Which of Eastbourne, Esher and Eccles is on the coast?

9 In London, Richmond is on which river?

10 In which county is Rutland Water?

11 Where in the UK is Armagh?

12 Dorchester is the county town of which county?

13 Salford is part of which city?

14 Who has their HQ at Scotland Yard?

15 Sherwood Forest is associated with which historical hero?

16 Which food item is associated with London's Smithfield market?

17 Durham is in which part of England?

18 What is Eton's most famous institution?

19 Who has a home at Sandringham?

20 What is the highest mountain in Snowdonia National Park?

21 Which S in central London is an area associated with clubs and nightlife?

22 In which county is Stansted airport?

23 The resort of Aberystwyth is on which coast of Britain?

24 Dudley in the West Midlands is near which major city?

25 Ealing is an area of which city?

26 What is the Savoy in London as well as a theatre?

27 Prince William chose to go to St Andrews university in which part of the UK?

28 What is Salisbury's most famous building?

29 Who are trained at Sandhurst?

30 Who would you be watching if you went to the JJB Stadium?

Answers | **21st Century Music (see Quiz 122)**

1 Ireland. 2 The Beatles. 3 Builder. 4 7. 5 None. 6 Manic. 7 Gallagher. 8 American. 9 Scream. 10 Piper. 11 Olympics. 12 David. 13 Carey. 14 Williams. 15 Mel G. 16 Country. 17 Oasis. 18 Church. 19 "Black". 20 Children in Need. 21 Big Brother. 22 Atomic Kitten. 23 Louise. 24 Britney Spears. 25 Five. 26 Texas. 27 Tom. 28 Hear'say. 29 Corr. 30 Eminem.

Quiz 121 | Pot Luck 55

Answers – page 129

1 The football team Boca Juniors play in which country?
2 Which initials did Pamela Anderson have in her "Baywatch" role?
3 In which city was Pete Sampras born?
4 UNICEF is an organisation caring for which people?
5 Which jump record was held by Bob Beamon for over 20 years?
6 Did Adrian Boothroyd first manage Watford, Wigan or WBA in the Premiership?
7 Where did athlete Said Aouita come from?
8 In what type of transport did Charles Lindbergh make history?
9 How many people were on the poster for the 1990s movie "Titanic"?
10 Where does a scorpion have its sting?
11 What is most of the Earth's surface covered by?
12 Which word is a type of frock and also an academic robe?
13 Which vegetable goes after The Black Eyed to name a top-selling hip-hop group?
14 What was Mrs Victor Meldrew's first name?
15 What's the weather word linked to an "Absolutely Fabulous" character's surname?
16 Glen Cova and Malling Jewel are types of which fruit?
17 Which football team did TV terror Alf Garnett support?
18 Who do you favour if you are a nepotist?
19 What was the name of the hotel chambermaid in "Fawlty Towers"?
20 Which country beginning with a H joined the European Union in 2004?
21 Q is on which row on a British/US keyboard?
22 In which sport can there be a night watchman?
23 In Japan, what is Hara-Kiri?
24 "ER" is set in which city?
25 Oz Clarke is a TV expert on what?
26 In the 1980s there was a catastrophic chemical accident at Bhopal in which country?
27 What is detected by a Geiger counter?
28 Who was the first presenter of TV quiz show "University Challenge"?
29 In which card game do you peg for cards making 15?
30 Which of scarlet, swine and tiger, is not a type of fever?

Answers	**Pot Luck 54** *(see Quiz 119)*

1 Lego. 2 Morticia. 3 Jamboree. 4 Pink. 5 Fat. 6 57. 7 Round. 8 Ashanti. 9 Blonde. 10 France. 11 Operating. 12 Athens. 13 West. 14 Alps. 15 Chinese. 16 Riding trousers (breeches/britches). 17 1990s. 18 Mediterranean 19 Millennium bug. 20 Florida. 21 Four. 22 Clay. 23 M (m). 24 Big. 25 Leotard. 26 Daily Mirror. 27 England. 28 Smart. 29 Abraham Lincoln. 30 Kelly Holmes.

1 Which country does Ronan Keating come from?
2 The 2006 album "Love" featured which iconic 1960s band?
3 What was the occupation of chart topper Bob?
4 Which number follows S Club in the band's title?
5 How many boys are there in Destiny's Child?
6 How are the Street Preachers described?
7 What is the surname of the two brothers in Oasis?
8 Which "Pie" did Madonna sing about?
9 What did Geri Halliwell say to do "If You Want to Run Faster"?
10 What was Billie's surname when she first topped the charts?
11 Which sporting event did Kylie Minogue close in 2000?
12 Which Craig had a hit with "Fill Me In"?
13 Which Mariah had a hit with Westlife in 2000?
14 Which Robbie was a "Rock DJ"?
15 What was Mel B called during her brief first marriage?
16 What type of music is LeAnn Rimes famous for?
17 "Stop the Clocks" was a compilation of songs from which band?
18 Which teenage Charlotte wowed audiences on both side of the Atlantic?
19 What type of "Coffee" was a chart topper for All Saints?
20 "Never Had a Dream Come True" was the theme song to which children's TV charity?
21 Craig Phillips charted after winning on which Big TV show?
22 Who charted with The Bangles' "Eternal Flame"?
23 Who was "2 Faced" in 2000?
24 Whose third UK No 1 was "Oops I Did It Again"?
25 How many members of Westlife are there?
26 Which band named after a US state were "In Demand" in 2000?
27 Which Jones was a "Sex Bomb" with the Stereophonics in 2000?
28 Which band were formed from the "Popstars" TV show?
29 What is the surname of all the Corrs?
30 How is controversial rapper Marshall Mathers better known?

Answers	**UK Tour** (see Quiz 120)

1 North. 2 Airports. 3 Yorkshire. 4 Dartmoor. 5 Wales. 6 The Prime Minister. 7 Dumfries. 8 Eastbourne. 9 Thames. 10 Rutland. 11 Northern Ireland. 12 Dorset. 13 Manchester. 14 Metropolitan Police. 15 Robin Hood. 16 Meat. 17 North east. 18 School/College. 19 The Queen. 20 Snowdon. 21 Soho. 22 Essex. 23 West. 24 Birmingham. 25 London. 26 Hotel. 27 Scotland. 28 Cathedral. 29 Soldiers. 30 Wigan Athletic.

1 In which sport can Canaries take on Owls?
2 How many colours are there on the German flag?
3 In a limerick which line does the third line rhyme with?
4 Which three initials was the 1960s' US President Johnson known by?
5 Which solo singer sang "Baby One More Time" in 1999?
6 What sort of creature is a shrike?
7 Edmund Hillary became the first man to climb which mountain?
8 Charles Holley became known as which entertainer Buddy?
9 Which word describes sailors as well as medicinal minerals?
10 What was Beijing called immediately before adopting the name Beijing?
11 In which US state is the resort of Orlando?
12 What was the occupation of the hero of the movie "Raging Bull"?
13 What covers most of the Antarctic?
14 Skater Kurt Browning comes from which country?
15 What term is given to a human being's complete set of genes?
16 TE Lawrence became known as Lawrence of where?
17 Carl Lewis found fame running and in which other athletics event?
18 What colour was Marilyn Monroe's hair in most of her movies?
19 Which country does Monaco border?
20 Which way do the stripes on the American flag run?
21 Which country was first to have ten kings all called Rameses?
22 A tsunami is another name for what?
23 Which Kate released the album "Aerial" in 2005, her first in 12 years?
24 Who were the beaten finalists of the 2006 FIFA World Cup?
25 Ellen MacArthur became known for her solo what?
26 What did a sundial used to tell?
27 Which of pink, purple or red is a primary colour?
28 The Wolf Cubs evolved as a junior branch of which organisation?
29 Yasser Arafat led which organisation known by its initials?
30 What was the horse made out of that was delivered to the ancient city of Troy?

Answers | TV: Stars (see Quiz 125)

1 Yorath. 2 Aspel. 3 Ainsley Harriott. 4 Rolf Harris. 5 The Simpsons. 6 Alistair McGowan. 7 Gloria Hunniford. 8 Chris Tarrant. 9 Sue Barker. 10 Frost. 11 Penguin. 12 Titchmarsh. 13 G. 14 McDonald. 15 Doctor/surgeon. 16 Robin Hood. 17 Vaughan. 18 Davidson. 19 Cilla Black. 20 Rantzen. 21 Lorraine Kelly. 22 History. 23 Cook. 24 Graham Norton. 25 Parkinson. 26 Thaw. 27 David. 28 Smillie. 29 Jeremy. 30 Schofield.

1 What sort of creature is an aardvark?
2 What colour are a daisy's petals?
3 Which of the following dogs is the biggest: Pekinese, Labrador or St Bernard?
4 The dove is a member of which bird family?
5 What is the largest and most powerful land mammal?
6 What sort of feet do antelopes have?
7 A caribou is a type of what?
8 What is a rhododendron?
9 What is a Scots pine?
10 The lynx belongs to which family?
11 What do herbivores eat?
12 Where is a horse's muzzle?
13 How many nostrils does a dog have?
14 In the animal world what is an adder?
15 What colour are rhubarb stalks?
16 In the very early part of which season do snowdrops appear?
17 Which big cat has a mane?
18 What is an antirrhinum?
19 Mushrooms and puffballs are what types of living things?
20 Which of cacti, root vegetables or water lilies can survive in the desert?
21 In plants, pollination is the transfer of what?
22 Where do wetland plants grow?
23 What do carnivorous plants eat?
24 What colour are natural sponges?
25 How many tentacles does a starfish have?
26 Which animal can be field or harvest?
27 Where would an insect have its antenna?
28 In animals what is another name for the backbone?
29 Which is the heaviest of chimpanzee, gorilla or man?
30 Where are a deer's antlers?

| **Answers** | **Pot Luck 57** *(see Quiz 126)* |

1 Depp. 2 Australia. 3 USA. 4 Spirits. 5 Suffolk. 6 Wales. 7 Square. 8 Canada. 9 Two. 10 Ear. 11 American Football. 12 Bulls. 13 India. 14 St Francis. 15 14. 16 Thinking Day. 17 Telescope. 18 Scarface. 19 Globe. 20 Abbey. 21 Lines of longitude. 22 Water. 23 Vacuum cleaner. 24 1950s. 25 His manager. 26 Photocopier. 27 Cake. 28 Tenor. 29 Latin. 30 Songs.

1 How was sports commentator Gabby Logan known before her marriage?
2 Which Michael replaced Hugh Scully on the "Antiques Roadshow"?
3 Which chef replaced Fern Britton on "Ready Steady Cook"?
4 Which Australian presents "Animal Hospital"?
5 In which series are Marge and Homer the stars?
6 Who starred in his own show impersonating stars and made a "Big Impression"?
7 Which Irish presenter hosts "Open House" daily on Channel 5?
8 Who hosts the UK version of "Who Wants to be A Millionaire"?
9 Who was the first female presenter of "A Question of Sport"?
10 David Jason starred in the detective series "A Touch of what"?
11 Which animal is the star of "Pingu"?
12 Which Alan succeeded Geoff Hamilton on "Gardener's World"?
13 Which Ali is the alter ego of Sacha Baron Cohen?
14 Which singer Jane found fame on "The Cruise"?
15 What was George Clooney's profession in ER?
16 Jonas Armstrong played which hero Robin?
17 Which Johnny moved from "The Big Breakfast" to the BBC in 2001?
18 Which Jim presented "The Generation Game"?
19 Which Liverpool singer presented "Moment of Truth"?
20 Who is the Esther of "That's Esther"?
21 Which Scottish presenter is the star of GMTV's "LK Today"?
22 Does David Starkey present shows on health, history or house plants?
23 What would you expect Antony Worrall Thompson to do on TV?
24 Who was the star of "So Graham Norton"?
25 Which Michael began his chat shows back in 1971?
26 Which John has played Morse and Kavanagh?
27 Which Attenborough presented "The Blue Planet" about life beneath the sea?
28 Which Carol presented "Changing Rooms"?
29 What is the first name of "Newsnight" interrogators Vine and Paxman?
30 Which Phillip, star of "Dr Doolittle", presented "National Lottery Winning Lines"?

Answers	**Pot Luck 56** *(see Quiz 123)*

1 Soccer. 2 Three. 3 The fourth. 4 LBJ. 5 Britney Spears. 6 Bird. 7 Mount Everest. 8 Holly. 9 Salts. 10 Peking. 11 Florida. 12 Boxer. 13 Ice. 14 Canada. 15 Human genome. 16 Arabia. 17 Long jump. 18 Blonde. 19 France. 20 Horizontally. 21 Egypt. 22 Tidal wave. 23 Kate Bush. 24 France. 25 Sailing. 26 Time. 27 Red. 28 Boy Scouts. 29 PLO. 30 Wood.

1 Which actor Johnny was in "Sleepy Hollow", "Edward Scissorhands" and "Fear and Loathing in Las Vegas"?

2 Which of Australia, the UK and the USA does not have a large city called Birmingham?

3 The Sears Tower became the tallest skyscraper in which country?

4 Which word means ghosts and also means strong drinks?

5 In which county is Ipswich, the scene of grisly murders at the end of 2006?

6 The Stereophonics come from which part of the UK?

7 Which shape name is given to the area in which Nelson's Column stands?

8 The Great Lakes border the USA along with which other country?

9 How many people usually play a game of chess?

10 Which part of the body can go before the words ache and muff?

11 Jerry Rice and Emmitt Smith are both connected with which sport?

12 In rugby league are Bradford the Bears, the Braves or the Bulls?

13 Mahatma Gandhi was a leader in which country?

14 Which Saint founded the Franciscan order of monks?

15 How many letters are there in the English alphabet between E and T?

16 What kind of Day do Scouts and Guides call the anniversary of their founder's birth?

17 Which instrument did Galileo invent as an aid to study the stars?

18 What was Al Capone's nickname, after he was injured in a knife fight?

19 What name is given to a world map presented in spherical form?

20 Queen Elizabeth II was crowned in what type of building?

21 Which type of lines on a map run north to south?

22 What does a coracle travel on?

23 William Hoover first marketed which household appliance?

24 In which decade did the Mini car first appear on British roads?

25 In the 1990s Macaulay Culkin sacked his dad from which job?

26 Invented as the xerox machine what is this device usually known as today?

27 French Queen Marie Antoinette famously said, "Let them eat" what?

28 Is operatic singer Andrea Bocelli a tenor or a base?

29 Which language was spoken by the ancient Romans?

30 Irving Berlin was famous for writing what?

Answers	**Plants & Animals** (see Quiz 124)

1 Mammal. 2 White. 3 St Bernard. 4 Pigeon. 5 Elephant. 6 Hooves. 7 Reindeer. 8 Plant. 9 Tree. 10 Cat. 11 Plants. 12 Head. 13 Two. 14 Snake. 15 Pink. 16 Spring. 17 Lion. 18 Plant. 19 Fungus. 20 Cacti. 21 Pollen. 22 In water. 23 Insects. 24 Yellow. 25 Five. 26 Mouse. 27 Head. 28 Spine. 29 Gorilla. 30 Head.

1 Which sport did Joe Davis play in addition to billiards?
2 Jack Dempsey was a heavyweight what?
3 Which Ramsey took England to be World Cup champions?
4 Which Steve was knighted after the 2000 Olympics?
5 By which name was IVA Richards known?
6 Which country does tennis's Pete Sampras come from?
7 In which decade of the 20th century did Ayrton Senna meet his untimely death?
8 Which club has a commemorative gate in memory of Bill Shankly?
9 In which position did soccer legend Lev Yashin play?
10 Mark Spitz won his seven gold medals in 1972 doing what?
11 Which motor racing star became Sir Jackie in the new millennium?
12 Brian Lara played international cricket for which country?
13 Athlete Frederick Carleton Lewis was better known by which first name?
14 Aussie cricketer Dennis Lillee was a specialist what?
15 Gary Lineker has which Churchillian middle name?
16 In addition to his sporting skill John McEnroe was also famous for what?
17 Diego Maradona led which side to World Cup victory in 1986?
18 Sir Stanley Matthews played for which famous seaside resort town?
19 Which Bobby captained England's World Cup soccer winning side?
20 Which Mr Moss was a successful motor racing legend of the 1950s?
21 Which boxer modestly announced "I am the greatest!", and went on to prove it?
22 Which 1990s football international is nicknamed Gazza?
23 Which US tennis star with 13 Grand Slams to his credit lost to Leighton Hewitt in the 2001 US Open?
24 Which Coe became an adviser to the then Tory Party leader William Hague?
25 In which gambling city did Evander Holyfield become world boxing champion in 1997?
26 In which decade was Arnold Palmer most successful in competition?
27 For which country did Jonah Lomu win his rugby caps?
28 Which British boxer did Mike Tyson beat to become champion in 1996?
29 Whom did Denis Law play international football for?
30 Which childlike first name did baseball's George Herman Ruth have?

Answers	The Movies: Heroes & Heroines *(see Quiz 129)*

1 Hugh. 2 John. 3 Madness. 4 Grace. 5 Horror. 6 Hamlet. 7 Steel. 8 Forrest. 9 Dr Evil. 10 Cruise. 11 Sundance. 12 Pierce Brosnan. 13 Catwoman. 14 Robin Hood. 15 Doctor. 16 India. 17 Starling. 18 The Mafia. 19 Soldier. 20 Pan. 21 Mel Gibson. 22 Kennedy. 23 Astronauts. 24 Harry. 25 Romeo. 26 Schindler. 27 Irons. 28 Toy Story. 29 Mason "The Line" Dixon. 30 Wayne.

1 In which quiz show are individual contestants dismissed with Ms Robinson saying "Goodbye"?
2 Where would a spade, a club and a diamond be kept together?
3 King Hussein was ruler of which Middle East country?
4 In which country was John Lennon shot?
5 Which legendary king held court at Camelot?
6 How many letters are not vowels in the word queen?
7 Which trio split in 2005 after having a No 1 with "Thunderbirds"?
8 Standing down as an MP in 2005, Michael Portillo was in which party?
9 Oxford bags were a type of which item of clothing?
10 What can be a musical sound or a short letter?
11 In place-names what can precede England, Hampshire and York?
12 What name is given to the part of a parachute jump before the parachute opens?
13 Shrove Tuesday – or Pancake Day – is celebrated in which month?
14 Caviar is a great food delicacy but what is it?
15 Northern Territory is a "state" in which country in the southern hemisphere?
16 A rhombus is a shape with how many sides?
17 Which word meaning talk is the name of a bird?
18 How many letters are there in the English alphabet before Y?
19 In Monopoly what do you pass, collecting £200, when you complete one circuit of the board and start another?
20 What is the name of the special mark on precious metals to denote their purity?
21 A kilogram is just over how many pounds in imperial weight?
22 Are Leeds Metropolitan and Manchester Metropolitan stations or universities?
23 How many minutes are there in half a day?
24 Dermatitis is the inflammation of what part of the body?
25 In communications, what does P stand for in the initials ISP?
26 Gibraltar is separated from which European country by the Neutral Zone?
27 What sort of transport is a clipper?
28 Which of dog, fish and rat is not a Chinese year?
29 Which Martin became manager of Spurs in November 2004?
30 Is an area around a city designated not to be built on known as a green belt, a life belt or an urban belt?

Answers	Music Charts (see Quiz 130)

1 The Builder. 2 Simpsons. 3 Bohemian. 4 Blue. 5 Mariah Carey. 6 Green. 7 50s. 8 In a Bottle. 9 Rush. 10 Boyzone. 11 Rap. 12 Stop. 13 Eminem. 14 Billie. 15 Ronan Keating. 16 911. 17 The Dance Floor. 18 Prodigy. 19 Mel B. 20 1990s. 21 Kylie Minogue. 22 Millennium Prayer. 23 And the Beast. 24 R. 25 Marmalade. 26 Diana Ross. 27 Billie. 28 Spice Girls. 29 1997. 30 Victoria Beckham.

1 Which Grant played the cad in "Bridget Jones's Diary"?

2 What was Jim Belushi's ill-fated elder brother called?

3 What did King George suffer from in the Nigel Hawthorne and Helen Mirren movie?

4 Which Jones starred in "A View to a Kill" in 1985?

5 What type of movies made Boris Karloff famous?

6 Which Prince of Denmark is the hero of Shakespeare's most filmed play?

7 In which industry had the heroes of "The Full Monty", based in Sheffield, worked?

8 Which "Gump" was the hero of a 1994 movie?

9 Which evil doctor was the enemy of Austin Powers?

10 Which Tom starred in "A Few Good Men"?

11 Which Kid was Butch Cassidy's sidekick?

12 Which James Bond actor got married in the summer of 2001?

13 What sort of woman did Michelle Pfeiffer play in "Batman Returns"?

14 Which heroic outlaw was "Prince of Thieves" on the big screen?

15 What was the title of Doolittle who could talk to the animals?

16 "Gandhi" was about a hero of which country?

17 What was the bird-related last name of the agent played by Jodie Foster in "The Silence of the Lambs"?

18 "The Godfather" was the head of which organisation?

19 What was the occupation of Private Ryan in Spielberg's movie?

20 Which Peter was the hero of "Hook" based on the children's story by JM Barrie?

21 Which actor starred in the "Lethal Weapon" movies and "Braveheart"?

22 What was the surname of the subject of "JFK"?

23 "Apollo 13" was about a group of what type of people?

24 Who was the hero who "Met Sally" in the movie with Billy Crystal and Meg Ryan?

25 Leonardo DiCaprio starred in a 1996 movie about which character "and Juliet"?

26 Which hero had a List in a Spielberg movie?

27 Which Jeremy starred in "Reversal of Fortune"?

28 In which "Story" was Woody a hero?

29 Who did 54-year-old Rocky Balboa come out of retirement to fight?

30 Which John landed a best actor Oscar for "True Grit"?

Answers	**Sporting Legends** *(see Quiz 127)*

1 Snooker. 2 Boxer. 3 (Sir) Alf. 4 Redgrave. 5 Viv. 6 USA. 7 1990s. 8 Liverpool FC. 9 Goalkeeper. 10 Swimming. 11 Stewart. 12 West Indies. 13 Carl. 14 Fast bowler. 15 Winston. 16 His temper. 17 Argentina. 18 Blackpool. 19 Moore. 20 Stirling. 21 Cassius Clay/Muhammad Ali. 22 Paul Gascoigne. 23 Pete Sampras. 24 Sebastian. 25 Las Vegas. 26 1960s. 27 New Zealand. 28 Frank Bruno. 29 Scotland. 30 Babe.

Quiz 130 | Music Charts

1 Which Bob went to No 1 with "Can We Fix It?"?
2 Which family had a hit with "Do the Bartman"?
3 Which "Rhapsody" was a chart topper for Queen?
4 What colour was the name of the boy band who had a No 1 with Elton John?
5 Which female singer went straight to No 1 in the US with "Fantasy"?
6 Which actor Robson had a string of hits in 1995 with Jerome Flynn?
7 In which age group was Cher when she hit No 1 with "Believe"?
8 Where was the "Genie" in the 1999 hit of Christine Aguilera?
9 Which Jennifer sang "The Power of Love" in 1985?
10 Which band's singles include "No Matter What" and "Words"?
11 What type of single was Puff Daddy's "I'll be Missing You"?
12 Which Spice Girls hit put a stop to a run of No 1s?
13 Which controversial rapper's No 1s include "The Real Slim Shady" and "Stan"?
14 Which British teenager's second No 1 was "Girlfriend"?
15 Which Irish group member had a solo No 1 with "Life is a Rollercoaster"?
16 Which US emergency phone number hit No 1 with "A Little Bit More"?
17 The Arctic Monkeys' first No 1 was "I Bet You Look Good on" what?
18 Which band's singles include "Firestarter" and "Breathe"?
19 Which Spice Girl did Missy Misdemeanour Elliott record "I Want You Back" with?
20 In which decade did Wet Wet Wet have their huge No 1 hit "Love is All Around"?
21 Which Australian singer/actress is the most successful ex-soap star in the British pop charts?
22 Which "Prayer" was a millennium chart topper for Cliff Richard?
23 What went with "Beauty" in the title of Celine Dion's first UK chart success?
24 Which Kelly charted with "I Believe I Can Fly"?
25 Which "Lady" was a 1998 chart hit for All Saints?
26 Which ex-member of the Supremes has charted with Marvin Gaye and Lionel Richie?
27 Which future Mrs Evans charted with "Because We Want To"?
28 Whose follow-up to their first No 1 was "Say You'll be There"?
29 In which year did Elton John have the best-ever-selling single?
30 Who was "Not Such an Innocent Girl" in 2001?

1 Which shredded vegetable goes into sauerkraut?
2 What does the P stand for in the education initials PTA?
3 In 1997 Hong Kong was returned to the rule of which country?
4 Which number puzzle featured in a series of best-selling books in 2005?
5 Which US grunge band shares a name with the Buddhist state of bliss?
6 In film which Doctor could talk to the animals?
7 Which of these celebs has not guested on "Friends" – Duchess of York, George Clooney or Prince Charles?
8 Out of his six wives, how many did Henry VIII have beheaded?
9 Which tennis player's name was given to a 2001 computer virus?
10 Which Scotsman gave his name to a type of raincoat?
11 Which Mel voiced Rooster in "Chicken Run"?
12 Which word is a type of trousers and also means to breathe rapidly?
13 Who or what is a great bustard?
14 Who was the blonde in the movie "Some Like It Hot"?
15 The late politician Dr Marjorie Mowlam was known by which short first name?
16 What is the shape of a pie chart?
17 Which was the second country to send a man into space?
18 What colour is platinum?
19 The caribou is another name for what?
20 If a number is squared what is it multiplied by?
21 The collapse of a star leads to the formation of what type of a hole?
22 Which bone is the longest bone in the human body?
23 What does U stand for in VDU?
24 Southampton left The Dell to go to which stadium?
25 Hr is the abbreviation for what?
26 What type of creature is a mandrill?
27 If you possessed a Canaletto would you own a painting, a small barge or a tin of stuffed olives?
28 What is a fox's tail known as?
29 What did the Russians call their first spacemen?
30 In which decade did Steve Redgrave win his first Olympic gold?

| **Answers** | **Pot Luck 60** *(see Quiz 133)* |

1 Bank. 2 Golf. 3 Emma Bunton. 4 Five. 5 Careers. 6 Linford Christie. 7 1980s. 8 Dylan. 9 Yasser Arafat. 10 Two. 11 Kingfisher. 12 Bird. 13 In water. 14 Stripes. 15 Bulb. 16 Private Frazer. 17 Y. 18 Fish and chips. 19 Books. 20 Salmon. 21 Fawlty Towers. 22 West Ham United. 23 Gold. 24 West. 25 Yuppies. 26 France. 27 Tyres. 28 None. 29 Teaching. 30 March.

1 What is Lucy Henman's tennis-playing husband called?
2 What is the Prince of Wales's first name?
3 Which Chris did Billie Piper marry?
4 Who was the first British PM of the new millennium?
5 What is Chelsea Clinton's dad called?
6 What would you ask Anna Ryder Richardson to design?
7 Which Ms Boothroyd was the first lady Speaker of the House of Commons?
8 What is Christine Hamilton's ex-MP husband called?
9 Which Gordon was Tony Blair's first Chancellor of the Exchequer?
10 Which of Paul McCartney's daughters is a dress designer?
11 Which 1960s model took over a morning TV show in September 2001?
12 Which Max acts as publicist to the famous?
13 What is the first name of ex-athlete and William Hague adviser Lord Coe?
14 From which part of the UK does Eamonn Holmes come?
15 Novelist Baroness James is known with which initials?
16 In 2006 Lord Stevens produced a report on the death of which Princess?
17 Under which female name is Paul O'Grady widely known?
18 What is the surname of TV brother celebs David and Jonathan?
19 What is the name of Dame Norma Major's husband?
20 Which Roger was the long-time singer with The Who?
21 Which former runner led Britain's Olympic bid for 2012?
22 Which Miss MacArthur sailed around the world on her own?
23 Vidal Sassoon is famous in which beauty industry?
24 Which country is Ruby Wax from?
25 Who is Tessa Dahl's famous model daughter?
26 Who was Julian Lennon's famous dad?
27 What are the initials of Harry Potter creator Rowling?
28 What is the first name of MEP Glenys Kinnock's husband?
29 Martin Bell is famous for wearing what colour suit?
30 What is Leo Blair's mum called?

Answers	**20th Century News** (see Quiz 134)

1 William Hague. 2 Cuba. 3 Wales. 4 France. 5 USSR/Soviet Union. 6 Clothes. 7 Austria. 8 Edward VIII. 9 Somme. 10 Soviet Union. 11 Three. 12 Russian. 13 Scotland. 14 France. 15 WWII. 16 Women. 17 China. 18 Major. 19 1990s. 20 Nellie. 21 Glenn. 22 Iran. 23 Italy. 24 East. 25 Wembley. 26 Mineworkers. 27 Neil. 28 Three. 29 Drink driving. 30 Brighton.

1 Robert Barclay founded what type of business?
2 For which sport is Jim Furyk famous?
3 Which Emma went from the Spice Girls to "Strictly Come Dancing"?
4 How many people were there in the original line-up of Hear'Say?
5 Which word means vocations and also means moves wildly?
6 Which Briton is the oldest 100m Olympic winner of the 20th century?
7 In which decade of the 20th century was Britney Spears born?
8 What did Michael Douglas and Catherine Zeta Jones call their baby son?
9 Which leader of the Palestine independence movement was buried in November 2004?
10 How many kidneys do humans normally have?
11 What was the name of the boat in which Ellen MacArthur sailed around the world?
12 The now extinct dodo was what type of creature?
13 Where does a hippopotamus spend most of its life?
14 What type of pattern is on a raccoon's tail?
15 What does a hyacinth grow from?
16 In "Dad's Army" which character often declared, "We're doomed"?
17 When texting, the word WHY is usually shown by which letter?
18 What type of food is associated with Harry Ramsden's?
19 What do you fear if you have bibliophobia?
20 A smolt or smelt is a young of which creature?
21 Manuel the waiter appeared in which classic comedy series?
22 Which soccer club has a stand dedicated to the late Bobby Moore?
23 What were the 19th-century Forty Niners searching for?
24 Which is not the name of a sea – Black Sea, North Sea or West Sea?
25 In the 1980s, young upwardly mobile persons became known as what?
26 In which country would you watch Nantes play a home soccer match?
27 What was manufactured by the business set up by Harvey Firestone?
28 How many English kings known as Henry came after Henry VIII?
29 What was Ken Barlow's main career throughout his many years as a "Coronation Street" character?
30 Which month was named after Mars, the god of war?

1 Who was Conservative party leader on 31 December 1999?

2 Fidel Castro took power on which island?

3 The tragedy of Aberfan took place in which part of the UK?

4 Charles de Gaulle was President of which European country?

5 Where did the Red Army come from?

6 Yves St Laurent found fame designing what?

7 Oskar Schindler, whose story was told in a Spielberg movie, was from which country?

8 Which former English king did Wallis Simpson marry?

9 Which S is an area of France where there was massive loss of life in WWI?

10 How was the USSR also known?

11 How many children did Tony Blair have when he became Prime Minister?

12 Lenin was a key figure in which revolution?

13 In which country did a Pan Am jumbo jet explode over Lockerbie in 1988?

14 François Mitterrand was a Socialist head of state in which country?

15 The Battle of El Alamein was during which war?

16 The suffragettes campaigned for votes for whom?

17 Mao Tse Tung led the Long March in which country?

18 Which John succeeded Margaret Thatcher as Prime Minister?

19 In which decade of the 20th century did Nelson Mandela become South African president?

20 What was the first name of famous opera star Melba?

21 Which bandleader Miller disappeared over the English Channel during WWII?

22 In 1979 the Shah was deposed in which country?

23 Mussolini led which country in WWII?

24 After WWII, Germany was divided into West Germany and Communist what?

25 Where was the FA Cup Final held during the 1990s?

26 Particularly in the news in the 1980s, the NUM was the National Union of what?

27 Martin Bell beat which Hamilton to take the constituency of Tatton in the 1997 General Election?

28 How many UK Prime Ministers were there in the 1990s?

29 Arsenal soccer player Tony Adams was jailed for what offence?

30 In which seaside location did an IRA bomb explode at a Tory Party Conference in 1984?

Answers | Famous Names *(see Quiz 132)*

1 Tim. 2 Charles. 3 Evans. 4 Blair. 5 Bill. 6 Your house. 7 Betty. 8 Neil. 9 Brown.
10 Stella. 11 Twiggy. 12 Clifford. 13 Sebastian. 14 Northern Ireland. 15 PD.
16 Princess Diana. 17 Lily Savage. 18 Dimbleby. 19 John. 20 Roger Daltrey. 21
Sebastian Coe. 22 Ellen. 23 Hairdressing. 24 USA. 25 Sophie. 26 John. 27 JK. 28
Neil. 29 White. 30 Cherie.

1 Does the B in ASBO stand for bad, behaviour, bully?
2 According to the Manic Street Preachers who were "The Masses Against"?
3 Who carries out their profession routinely wearing a tutu?
4 The UAE stands for which United Emirates?
5 Which word describes both a paragraph and a corridor?
6 What sort of Hat was the title of an elegant Fred Astaire movie?
7 A praying mantis is a type of what?
8 What is the name for a German from Hamburg?
9 The perambulator was an early type of what?
10 In which town is Harvey's Bitter brewed?
11 Which English queen's head was on the first postage stamp?
12 It's no official secret – which Stella became head of MI5?
13 Which character did Joanna Lumley play in "The New Avengers"?
14 In the ancient world what type of Gardens were created at Babylon?
15 Which item can be carriage, grandmother, alarm or digital?
16 In which US state is Miami?
17 Who, in Holland, is known as Zinter Klaus?
18 Ferrari cars were originally manufactured in which country?
19 Which word for a dissolving substance also means financially in the black?
20 Which girl goes with Educating in the title of a play by Willy Russell?
21 In which year was the 60th anniversary of VE Day?
22 Anna Edson Taylor became the first person to travel Niagara Falls in what?
23 What is the traditional colour of the headwear known as a fez?
24 Which fabric is made by worms?
25 What title does the vampire have in the story "Dracula"?
26 How many angles do 12 separate triangles contain in total?
27 On a compass, which direction is directly opposite to Northeast?
28 What does the middle letter stand for as used in HRH?
29 What sort of busters featured in a Sigourney Weaver movie – Blockbusters, Dambusters or Ghostbusters?
30 What did PM Tony Blair call his son, born in 2000?

Answers	Pot Luck 62 (see Quiz 137)

1 Watergate. 2 Wide. 3 11. 4 Japan. 5 Music. 6 Aeronautics. 7 Henry. 8 Golf. 9 Marathon. 10 Temperature. 11 Atlantic. 12 Rink. 13 Three. 14 Bridge. 15 Little John. 16 Scrooge. 17 Nine. 18 Diameter. 19 Cameron Diaz. 20 January. 21 New Orleans. 22 Three. 23 Green. 24 Newcastle. 25 Earl of Sandwich. 26 Wear it on the head. 27 USA. 28 Ash Wednesday. 29 First. 30 Green fingers.

1 In which country was "Father Ted" set?
2 How many Friends are there in the series of the same name?
3 Which Steve's alter ego is Alan Partridge?
4 Which two Js featured in the title of Jennifer Saunders' 2006 WI comedy?
5 Which Caroline created Mrs Merton?
6 Who played Sir Humphrey in "Yes Minister"?
7 Which Hancock hosted "They Think It's All Over"?
8 How many teams competed in "Have I Got News for You"?
9 Which animal follows "Drop the Dead" in the show about a newsroom?
10 What is the name of Harry Enfield's revolting teenager?
11 Mrs Bucket had which floral first name?
12 Where is the series "Chambers" set?
13 Which McBeal was a series with Calista Flockhart?
14 What's the main colour in the wardrobe of "Little Britain" character Vicky Pollard?
15 How many main characters were there in "Men Behaving Badly"?
16 What happened to Victor in the final episode of "One Foot in the Grave"?
17 Which US sitcom's cast included Michael Richards and Jerry Seinfeld?
18 Where did the late comedian Dave Allen come from?
19 In which city was "The Liver Birds" set?
20 Which "Two" stars with the same first name began a long-running comedy series in the 1970s?
21 Which June has starred in comedies from "Terry & June" to "Ab Fab"?
22 In "Are You Being Served"? which department along with ladies' fashions was shown?
23 In which series did the late Compo appear?
24 Which Frank was the star character in "Some Mothers Do 'Ave 'Em"?
25 Dawn French was the "Vicar" of where?
26 Which Irish presenter introduces programme of "Auntie's Bloomers", featuring funny and embarrassing outtakes?
27 What was the name of Mrs Wayne Slob played by Kathy Burke?
28 "Two Point" how many children were in the popular sitcom?
29 Which "Ladies" were the subject of a series with Victoria Wood?
30 What colour is Lily Savage's hair?

Answers	**Football** *(see Quiz 138)*

1 Football. 2 Blackburn. 3 Gary Lineker. 4 Northern Ireland. 5 Italy. 6 Southampton. 7 Burley. 8 Gerard Houllier. 9 Mohammed Al Fayed. 10 Petr Cech. 11 Watford. 12 Royle. 13 Sky. 14 1930s. 15 France. 16 Manchester Utd. 17 Shilton. 18 Munich. 19 European Champions Cup. 20 Rapid. 21 1994. 22 Liverpool. 23 Ginola. 24 Air. 25 Middlesbrough. 26 Milan. 27 World Cup. 28 Arsenal. 29 David Beckham. 30 Arsenal.

1 Which building was burgled by aides of President Nixon in 1972?
2 In Internet abbreviations, what does the middle w in www stand for?
3 What is the next prime number after 7?
4 Honda cars were originally manufactured in which country?
5 Napster was developed for downloading what?
6 What does the first A stand for in NASA?
7 Which is the first name to have been used by eight kings of England?
8 Businessman Samuel Ryder initiated a cup that is still contested in which sport?
9 Which name for a long race comes from a battle in the years BC?
10 What do Fahrenheit and Celsius measure?
11 The "Titanic" sank while travelling across which ocean?
12 What is the name for an ice hockey pitch?
13 How many colours appear on the Australian flag?
14 Cantilever, railway, suspension and toll can all go before which word?
15 Who was the tallest person in Robin Hood's gang of merry men?
16 What was the last name of the miser in "A Christmas Carol" by Charles Dickens?
17 In the English alphabet, how many letters are there before J?
18 What is the line across the middle of a circle called?
19 Who played opposite Leonardo DiCaprio in "The Gangs of New York"?
20 The Roman God Janus gives his name to which calendar month?
21 In the traditional song, is the "House of the Rising Sun" in Newcastle, New Orleans or New York?
22 How many angles does an equilateral triangle contain?
23 Which colour links Kermit and Shrek?
24 Shay Given and Scott Parker were together at which Premiership club?
25 Was it the Earl of Burger, the Earl of Pancake or the Earl of Sandwich who gave his name to a popular type of food?
26 What would you do with a deerstalker?
27 Which of these three countries has got the biggest population – USA, Sweden or Greece?
28 What is the special day that follows Shrove Tuesday?
29 In which course is gazpacho usually served?
30 If you are good at growing plants you are said to have what?

Answers | **Pot Luck 61** *(see Quiz 135)*

1 Behaviour. 2 The Classes. 3 Ballet dancer. 4 Arab. 5 Passage. 6 Top. 7 Insect. 8 Hamburger. 9 Baby buggy. 10 Lewes. 11 Victoria. 12 Rimington. 13 Purdey. 14 Hanging. 15 Clock. 16 Florida. 17 Santa Claus. 18 Italy. 19 Solvent. 20 Rita. 21 2005. 22 A barrel. 23 Red. 24 Silk. 25 Count. 26 36. 27 Southwest. 28 Royal. 29 Ghostbusters. 30 Leo.

Answers – page 146

1 What does the second F stand for in FIFA?
2 Which Lancashire club received a record-breaking £15 million when Alan Shearer went to Newcastle?
3 Who is second only to Bobby Charlton as England's greatest goalscorer?
4 Pat Jennings won 119 full international caps for which British side?
5 Which team won the 2006 World Cup?
6 Which club did Glenn Hoddle leave when he rejoined Spurs in 2001?
7 Which manager George led Ipswich Town back to the Premiership in the year 2000?
8 Who was the first Frenchman to manage Liverpool?
9 Which entrepreneur was chairman of Fulham when they went into the Premiership?
10 In 2006, which goalkeeper fractured his skull playing at Reading?
11 Which side did Vialli take on after leaving Chelsea?
12 Which Joe left Manchester City immediately before Keegan took over?
13 Coventry City are nicknamed which shade of blue?
14 In which decade did the World Cup begin?
15 Who did Platini play international football for?
16 Which British football club is the richest in the world?
17 Which Peter is England's most capped goalkeeper?
18 Which major German side has Bayern before its name?
19 How was the UEFA Champions League formerly known?
20 Which quick sounding word precedes Vienna's name?
21 When was the previous World Cup before 1998?
22 Michael Owen was attached to which club when he scored for England in the World Cup in France 1998?
23 Which David then of Spurs was Footballer of the Year in 1999?
24 Dennis Bergkamp refuses to use which form of travel?
25 Which side plays at the Riverside Stadium?
26 AC and Inter are from which Italian city famous for its fashion?
27 The Jules Rimet trophy was the prize for which tournament?
28 Robert Pires left which London club in 2006?
29 Who captained England in their 2001 5–1 win over Germany?
30 Alphabetically which team is first in the Premiership?

Answers	TV: Comedy *(see Quiz 136)*

1 Ireland. 2 Six. 3 Coogan. 4 Jam & Jerusalem. 5 Aherne. 6 Nigel Hawthorne. 7 Nick. 8 Two. 9 Donkey. 10 Kevin. 11 Hyacinth. 12 Legal practice. 13 Ally. 14 Pink. 15 Four. 16 Died. 17 Seinfeld. 18 Ireland. 19 Liverpool. 20 Ronnies. 21 Whitfield. 22 Menswear. 23 Last of the Summer Wine. 24 Spencer. 25 Dibley. 26 Terry Wogan. 27 Waynetta. 28 4. 29 Dinner Ladies. 30 Blonde.

1 Which of these inventions was developed last – lightbulb, motor car or television?
2 How many sides do 13 rectangles have?
3 What sort of beans are used in the manufacture of chocolate?
4 Which band made the albums "Garbage" and "Beautiful Garbage"?
5 Was the great plague of the 14th century known as The Black Death, The Cold Death or The Creeping Death?
6 What is John McEnroe's middle name?
7 What is the favourite food of Popeye?
8 What was spaceman Yuri Gagarin's home town renamed after his death?
9 The "News of the World" is the top-selling paper on which day of the week?
10 With which item of clothing is the name Levi Strauss linked?
11 Who set up a communications system that used dots and dashes?
12 The first atom bomb was dropped on the city Hiroshima, in which country?
13 Mark Spitz won seven gold medals at one Olympic Games doing what?
14 Which Labour MP and former Foreign Secretary Robin died in 2005?
15 Which of Cantonese, German and Spanish is a major language that is spoken in South America?
16 What was the wife of a tsar called?
17 Where does a nun usually live?
18 What is the name of Fred Flintstone's pet?
19 If a number is not an odd number what is it?
20 Which comedian Jack's surname sounds like a letter of the alphabet?
21 How many women in total travelled to the Moon throughout the 20th century?
22 What is the name of the stick used in croquet to strike the ball?
23 Does goalkeeper Tim Howard play for Australia, Austria or the USA?
24 Richard I of England was known as which Heart – Braveheart, Brokenheart or Lionheart?
25 Puri is a bread that originally came from which country?
26 What name is given to a bank of sand near the coastline?
27 A squirrel can be grey and which other colour?
28 What actually gets trapped in a Venus Fly Trap?
29 "Saving All My Love for You" was the first No 1 for which female singer?
30 What is a baked Alaska's outer layer made from?

Answers	Pot Luck 64 *(see Quiz 141)*

1 California. 2 Maggie. 3 Ghost. 4 Brazil. 5 Biography. 6 Andy Murray. 7 Baker. 8 Gomez. 9 Musical instrument. 10 White. 11 Hawk. 12 Will Young. 13 Boat. 14 White. 15 29th February. 16 Play. 17 Bolivia. 18 Walkman. 19 February/March. 20 Coral. 21 Rope. 22 Eight. 23 Belgium. 24 Alice. 25 Wood. 26 Johnny. 27 London. 28 Moscow. 29 King Kong. 30 Medical treatment.

1 Which Dustin links "Finding Neverland" and "Meet the Fockers"?
2 Which Ford played Han Solo in the original "Star Wars" movie?
3 What is the surname of Susan, star of "Dead Man Walking"?
4 Who played Bridget in "Bridget Jones's Diary"?
5 Which Tom was the voice of Woody in the original "Toy Story"?
6 Which Woody had a son called Satchel Farrow?
7 Which star of "Mary Poppins" has written children's stories under the name Julie Edwards?
8 Which actress Kate announced a split from her husband Jim Threapleton in September 2001?
9 Which Kim married Alec Baldwin?
10 Annette Bening is the first wife of which Hollywood playboy actor director?
11 In which decade was Helena Bonham Carter born?
12 Which actor Richard was once married to supermodel Cindy Crawford?
13 Which Mel starred in "What Women Want"?
14 In which city of Northern Ireland was Kenneth Branagh born?
15 In film journalism, what sort of column did Hedda Hopper write?
16 Which Annette fell for Michael Douglas in "The American President"?
17 Which Tom married TV star Roseanne?
18 Which Liam played Alfred Kinsey in the movie "Kinsey"?
19 Which fantasy creature did Daryl Hannah play in "Splash"?
20 Which singer/actress played a music diva in "The Bodyguard"?
21 Which James Bond producer Cubby shares his name with a vegetable?
22 On which continent was Richard E Grant born?
23 Which Patsy who starred in "The Great Gatsby" was once Mrs Liam Gallagher?
24 Which family includes actors Davis, Patricia, Rosanna and Alexis?
25 What is the name of the actress daughter of John Drew Barrymore?
26 Which Kate is the daughter of Goldie Hawn?
27 "The Crying Game"'s director Neil Jordan hails from where?
28 What was silent star Joseph Keaton's nickname?
29 Tobey Maguire played which web-weaving super hero?
30 Which Jeff did Geena Davis marry?

Answers	Euro Tour *(see Quiz 142)*

1 Dublin. 2 Danish. 3 Dunkirk. 4 Dublin. 5 Greece. 6 Mediterranean. 7 Winter sports. 8 Rome. 9 Portugal. 10 Italy. 11 France. 12 Czechoslovakia. 13 Paris. 14 Switzerland. 15 Mountains. 16 West. 17 Spain. 18 Car. 19 Limerick. 20 Munich. 21 France. 22 Lisbon. 23 Brussels. 24 Berlin. 25 Spain. 26 France. 27 Hungary. 28 Ireland. 29 Arctic. 30 North.

Quiz 141 | Pot Luck 64

Answers – page 149

LEVEL 1

1 Los Angeles is in which US state?
2 Who is Bart Simpson's youngest sister?
3 A banshee is a type of what?
4 Which is the largest country in South America?
5 What category of book describes the life of another real person?
6 In 2005, which Andy became the youngest male Brit to qualify for the US tennis Open?
7 In fiction, Sherlock Holmes lived in a street named after which type of worker?
8 Who is head of the family in the fiendishly funny "Addams Family"?
9 What is a clavichord?
10 What colour is the Taj Mahal?
11 Which bird is part of the name for a native American Indian's war axe?
12 Which Will produced the 2005 big-selling album "Keep On"?
13 In transport terms a smack is a small type of what?
14 What colour was Tin Tin's dog called Snowy?
15 When were you born if your birthdate occurs only once in four years?
16 In the saying, what will the mice do when the cat's away?
17 Which country along with Brazil in South America begins with a B?
18 What was the first personal stereo called?
19 The zodiac sign Pisces covers which two months?
20 What is the Great Barrier Reef made out of?
21 What is a lasso usually made from?
22 How many kings are there in two packs of playing cards?
23 In which country can you visit the Francorchamps race track?
24 Alice, Elizabeth, Mary and Victoria – which of these has never been the name of a queen of England?
25 What was a totem pole usually made from?
26 What is the name of presenter Zoe Ball's dad?
27 In which city can you visit the Tate Modern and Tate Britain?
28 Which city does a Muscovite come from?
29 Which King returned in 2005 in a big-budget movie?
30 Is acupuncture a form of bicycle tyre repairing, medical treatment or recycling of waste material?

Answers	**Pot Luck 63** *(see Quiz 139)*

1 Television. **2** 52. **3** Cocoa beans. **4** Garbage. **5** The Black Death. **6** Patrick. **7** Spinach. **8** Gagarin. **9** Sunday. **10** Jeans. **11** Morse. **12** Japan. **13** Swimming. **14** Robin Cook. **15** Spanish. **16** Tsarina. **17** Convent. **18** Dino. **19** Even. **20** Dee. **21** None. **22** Mallet. **23** USA. **24** Lionheart. **25** India. **26** Dune. **27** Red. **28** Insects. **29** Whitney Houston. **30** Meringue.

1 In which Irish city is the Abbey Theatre?
2 What is the official language of Denmark?
3 What do the British call what the French call Dunkerque?
4 Dun Laoghaire is the port for which Irish city?
5 Rhodes is an island belonging to which country?
6 The Riviera is on the French/Italian coast on which sea?
7 St Moritz is famous for what type of sports?
8 St Peter's Basilica is in which Italian city?
9 Faro, or the Algarve, is in which country?
10 Rimini is a resort of the Adriatic in which country?
11 The Seine reaches the sea from which country?
12 Slovakia was formerly part of which country?
13 In which French city is the university called the Sorbonne?
14 Which European country is made up of cantons?
15 What are the Alps?
16 County Sligo is on which coast of Ireland?
17 Catalonia, Andalusia and Valencia are parts of which country?
18 The French town of Le Mans hosts what type of race?
19 Which Irish county has given its name to a comic rhyme?
20 Which German city is known locally as München?
21 In which country was the Academie Française founded?
22 Which city do the Portuguese call Lisboa?
23 Which city is also known locally as Bruxelles?
24 Which city replaced Bonn as Germany's capital?
25 Where would you spend pesetas?
26 In which country are baguettes and brioches traditional breads?
27 Which country beginning with H is to the east of Austria?
28 The Shannon is which country's chief river?
29 Lapland is nearest to which ocean?
30 In which part of Europe is the Baltic Sea?

Answers	**The Movies: Who's Who? 2** *(see Quiz 140)*

1 Dustin Hoffman. 2 Harrison. 3 Sarandon. 4 Renee Zellweger. 5 Hanks. 6 Allen.
7 Julie Andrews. 8 Winslet. 9 Basinger. 10 Warren Beatty. 11 1960s. 12 Gere.
13 Gibson. 14 Belfast. 15 Gossip. 16 Bening. 17 Arnold. 18 Liam Neeson. 19
Mermaid. 20 Whitney Houston. 21 Broccoli. 22 Africa. 23 Kensit. 24 Arquette. 25
Drew Barrymore. 26 Hudson. 27 Ireland. 28 Buster. 29 Spiderman. 30 Goldblum.

1 The "New York Herald" and the "Washington Post" are types of what?
2 Which letter along with H appears on pencils?
3 According to the legend, which weapon did William Tell use to shoot an apple off his son's head?
4 In a calendar year which is the first month to have exactly 30 days?
5 California is on which coast of the USA?
6 Which Arsenal keeper was Germany's No 1 for the 2006 World Cup?
7 Which West European country beginning with an S is landlocked?
8 Ford cars were originally made in which country?
9 Which word links a chess piece and an ancient soldier?
10 Pisa's famous leaning tower was built to house what?
11 CS Lewis wrote about "The Lion, the Witch and the" what?
12 Hermit and spider are types of what?
13 In which city was John Lennon murdered?
14 Who did France beat in the final of the 1998 FIFA World Cup?
15 How many pairs of ribs does a human have?
16 The game of boules comes from which country?
17 Which gas is believed to be encouraging global warming?
18 Which soul singer Luther died at the age of 54 in 2005?
19 Which word names a conductor's stick and also a small French loaf?
20 What items by Georgia O'Keefe fetch record prices at auctions?
21 What is the second highest mountain in the world called?
22 Which John returned to prominence in the movie "Pulp Fiction"?
23 Which female went to "The Edge of Reason" in a 2004 movie?
24 What do people usually do with a Stradivarius?
25 Which TV show was responsible for the the catchphrase "Pass"?
26 What colour describes the extra-time goal to decide certain football matches?
27 Which item of swimwear is named after an atoll in the Pacific?
28 In the human skeleton, is the fibula below or above the patella?
29 In which street would you have been wise to avoid the premises of a barber named Sweeney Todd?
30 In "Bewitched" which part of her body did Samantha move to cast a spell?

Answers | **Pot Luck 66** *(see Quiz 145)*

1 Buffalo. 2 Pole vault. 3 Pacific. 4 Roald Dahl. 5 Never. 6 Ice. 7 Louis Pasteur. 8 Smith. 9 Mexico. 10 Cos. 11 French. 12 Beavis. 13 Moses. 14 Mozart. 15 Johnny Depp. 16 Justine Henin-Hardenne. 17 52. 18 Oasis. 19 An earthquake. 20 Africa. 21 Motor town. 22 Nobel Prize. 23 Sun. 24 Knife. 25 Beautiful. 26 A will. 27 Clubs. 28 Liverpool. 29 White. 30 Television.

1 Who was Simon's singing partner?
2 By which first name is Roderick David Stewart known?
3 Who has the surname Ciccone?
4 Freddie Mercury led which regal-sounding band?
5 Which superstar singer Barbra starred in the hit movie "Meet the Fockers"?
6 Which Elton John song was reworked and dedicated to Princess Diana?
7 What was the Spice Girls' first album called?
8 Which Elvis hit of 2005 has the line, "You ain't a never caught a rabbit"?
9 Which band's singles include "Country House" and "Beetlebum"?
10 Who made the album "Best of Bob Marley"?
11 Whose "Come On Over" album is a top-selling country album in the US?
12 Which ex-Take That member won a Brit Award for "She's the One" in 2000?
13 Whose hits include "Jesus to a Child" and "Outside"?
14 Which band has had the most gold albums of any band in the UK?
15 Which grandfather was a "Sex Bomb" in 2000?
16 In 2000 U2 received the keys to which city?
17 Which Beatle announced his engagement in 2001?
18 Which band's singles include "Common People" and "Disco 2000"?
19 Which band did Sting front?
20 Which late blue-eyed superstar had the first names Francis Albert?
21 Which "Jagged Little" album was a huge hit for Alanis Morissette?
22 Bjorn Again are a tribute band to which superstars?
23 Which Irish band made the album "By Request"?
24 Which Diana fronted The Supremes?
25 Eric Clapton had a transatlantic hit with "I Shot" who?
26 Who was in the news after the break-up of his marriage to Heather Mills?
27 Which George's early solo single was "Careless Whisper"?
28 Which band's singles include "Australia" and "A Design for Life"?
29 Who had hit albums "True Blue" and "Erotica"?
30 Who had huge hits with "Sacrifice" and "Rocket Man"?

| **Answers** | Technology (see Quiz 146) |

1 Calculator. 2 Wikipedia. 3 Cars. 4 Nanjing Automobile Company. 5 Sky. 6 Sewing machine. 7 Sun. 8 1970s. 9 1960s. 10 Two. 11 Water. 12 Read. 13 Fax. 14 Car. 15 Camera. 16 Apple Macintosh. 17 Personal. 18 Internet. 19 Stars. 20 Menu. 21 Bar code. 22 Temperature. 23 Camera. 24 Lap top. 25 Ipod. 26 Hearing. 27 Voice mail. 28 1980s. 29 IBM. 30 Hypertext.

Quiz 145 | Pot Luck 66

Answers – page 153

1 What went before Bill in the Wild West's William Cody's name?
2 Sergey Bubka broke over 30 world records in which event?
3 What is the largest of the Earth's oceans?
4 Who wrote "The BFG" and "Revolting Rhymes"?
5 How many times did Queen Elizabeth I marry?
6 On which sporting surface did Wayne Gretzky find fame?
7 Which scientist pioneered the pasteurisation process to purify milk?
8 In the UK and the USA what is the most common surname for people?
9 The Aztecs came from which part of the world?
10 Which word names a Greek Island and a lettuce?
11 Other than English, which language is spoken in Canada?
12 Who went with Butthead in the TV series?
13 In the Bible which infant was hidden in bulrushes for his own safety?
14 Which famous composer had the first names Wolfgang Amadeus?
15 Which Johnny was in the movies "Chocolat" and "Charlie and the Chocolate Factory"?
16 Which Justine was the first Belgian to win a tennis Grand Slam tournament?
17 How many fortnights are there in two years?
18 Which band's album title advised "Don't Believe the Truth"?
19 The Richter scale measures the strength of what?
20 On which continent is the world's largest desert?
21 Detroit's nickname is Motown – what does Motown stand for?
22 Masters Trophy, Nobel Prize and Oscar – which of these awards links with science?
23 Earth takes 365 days to travel round what?
24 What type of weapon is a kukri?
25 What kind of "Day" gave U2 a No 1 hit?
26 What does a testator make?
27 In whist, which trumps usually follow on after Hearts in descending order?
28 The late David Sheppard was Bishop of which city from 1975 to 1997?
29 What colour are the stars on the American flag?
30 Paper, soap and television – which of these items could not have been found in a house in 1901?

Answers | Pot Luck 65 (see Quiz 143)

1 Newspaper. 2 B. 3 Crossbow. 4 April. 5 West. 6 Jens Lehmann. 7 Switzerland. 8 USA. 9 Knight. 10 Bells. 11 Wardrobe. 12 Crab. 13 New York. 14 Brazil. 15 Twelve. 16 France. 17 Carbon dioxide. 18 Vandross. 19 Baton. 20 Paintings. 21 K2. 22 Travolta. 23 Bridget Jones. 24 Play it. 25 Mastermind. 26 Golden goal. 27 Bikini. 28 Below it. 29 Fleet Street. 30 Her nose.

1 An abacus was an early type of what?
2 Which W is the most visited on-line encyclopaedia?
3 What did engineer Louis Renault manufacture?
4 Which car manufacturer built the first Chinese-made MG?
5 Which of the following is a UK satellite TV company – Sky, Sun, Mars?
6 Which needlework machine did Isaac Singer invent?
7 What provides solar power?
8 In which decade did Apple computers first appear?
9 In which decade did man first land on the Moon?
10 A stereo music system has a minimum of how many speakers?
11 An aqueduct was constructed to carry what?
12 In CD-ROM what does the letter R stand for?
13 What is the more common name for a facsimile telegraphy machine?
14 The Ford Model T was an early model of what form of transport?
15 Which of these inventions was developed first – the camera, the modem or satellite television?
16 What make is a computer which has an apple symbol on it?
17 What does P refer to in PCs?
18 Which system of communication developed from ARPANET?
19 Astronomy is the study of what?
20 What's the name for the selection bar at the top of a computer monitor?
21 What kind of code is scanned at a supermarket?
22 What does a thermostat control?
23 Polaroid is a type of what?
24 What name is given to a portable computer?
25 Nano and Shuffle were second-generation versions of which portable media device?
26 Audio refers to which of the senses?
27 Which mail is a type of telephone answering machine?
28 In which decade were PCs invented?
29 Which company manufactured the first generally available PC?
30 What does H stand for in HTTP?

Answers	**Music Superstars** *(see Quiz 144)*

1 Garfunkel. 2 Rod. 3 Madonna. 4 Queen. 5 Streisand. 6 Candle in the Wind. 7 Spice. 8 Hound Dog. 9 Blur. 10 Bob Marley. 11 Shania Twain. 12 Robbie Williams. 13 George Michael. 14 Queen. 15 Tom Jones. 16 Dublin. 17 Paul McCartney. 18 Pulp. 19 Police. 20 Sinatra. 21 Pill. 22 Abba. 23 Boyzone. 24 Ross. 25 The Sheriff. 26 Sir Paul McCartney. 27 George Michael. 28 Manic Street Preachers. 29 Madonna. 30 Elton John.

Quiz 147 | Pot Luck 67

Answers – page 159

1 Which L is a country on the south-eastern frontier of Belgium?
2 Which was developed last – space flight, television or the telephone?
3 Born in Yugoslavia, Monica Seles eventually played for which country?
4 The movie "Vera Drake" was set in which European capital city?
5 Which sauce is eaten with turkey at Thanksgiving in the USA?
6 Which word names a mobile home and also a line of camels?
7 Which young blonde is a "Vampire Slayer" on TV?
8 How is Uluru also known?
9 Which sport is governed by FIFA?
10 In which war-torn country is the city of Baghdad?
11 What was the first name of the Queen of Scots, beheaded in 1587?
12 What breed of dog was film and TV star Lassie?
13 Which anniversary of the Gunpowder Plot was celebrated in 2005?
14 What main colour goes with white on the flag of Argentina?
15 Carragher and Kewell were together in which club soccer side?
16 Cleopatra's Needle now standing in London came from which country?
17 How many letters appear in the English alphabet before Q?
18 If Albert is the dad and Harold is the son what is the famous TV sitcom?
19 Brass was originally made from copper and which other metal?
20 The star sign Gemini is represented as what?
21 What is the French word meaning yellow?
22 How many straight lines are needed to make a plus sign?
23 Who won the first FA Cup Final played in Cardiff?
24 The coast of Belgium is on which Sea?
25 What is the colour of the cheapest property on a Monopoly board?
26 The most common pub name in the UK is the Red what – Giraffe, Lion or Elephant?
27 Which place name can go before Triangle and shorts?
28 Which initials are linked with genetic fingerprinting?
29 Diwali is an important feast in which religion?
30 How many individual squares are there on a chess board?

Answers	**Quiz & Game Shows** (see Quiz 149)

1 No limit. 2 Anne Robinson. 3 Two. 4 Ulrika Jonsson. 5 Celebrity Ready Steady Cook. 6 The Generation Game. 7 Schofield. 8 John Parrott. 9 Channel Four. 10 Keith. 11 Tennis player. 12 Unlucky. 13 Mortimer. 14 The Price is Right. 15 Your Cards. 16 Telephone. 17 Leather. 18 Gladiators. 19 Cilla's. 20 Trophy. 21 Noel Edmonds. 22 Countdown. 23 Smillie. 24 O'Connor. 25 Dustbin. 26 University Challenge. 27 Woman. 28 They Think It's All Over. 29 Glass. 30 Chris Tarrant.

1 Mario Andretti found fame in which sport?

2 Which sisters fought out the US Open tennis final in 2001?

3 By which first name was cricketer Sir Garfield Sobers known?

4 Who was England's youngest player in the 2006 World Cup tournament squad?

5 Decathlete Dean Macey competes in how many events?

6 How was athlete James Cleveland Owens better known?

7 Clive Lloyd captained which international cricket side?

8 Which young golfer was "Sports Illustrated"'s sportsman of the year In 1996?

9 Which sport did Michael Jordan play professionally for more than 12 years?

10 Which Phil won the US Masters in 2004 and again in 2006?

11 Whom did the late Don Bradman play international cricket for?

12 Which country does racing driver Riccardo Patrese come from?

13 How did golfer Payne Stewart meet his tragic death in 1999?

14 What type of sporting competitor was Lammtarra?

15 Which Mr Fallon is a top money-winning jockey?

16 Which national side did rugby's Rob Andrew play for?

17 Czech-born Martina Hingis represents which country?

18 In which sport did Shaquille O'Neal make his name – and a fortune?

19 In which sport did Australian Dawn Fraser find fame?

20 World record holder Zola Budd originally came from which country?

21 What is the first name of South African rugby star Pienaar?

22 Novelist Dick Francis had a successful career as what type of sportsman?

23 Which Champion rode the Grand National winner Aldaniti in 1981?

24 Jockey Lester Piggott served a prison sentence for what evasion?

25 Will Carling captained which national rugby side?

26 Franz Klammer and Jean-Claude Killy are famous names in which winter sport?

27 What is the first name of Finnish F1 driver Hakkinen?

28 Graham Gooch is from which English county?

29 Which Caribbean island did Merlene Ottey compete for?

30 Maurice Greene sprints for which country?

Answers	Pot Luck 68 *(see Quiz 150)*

1 Pretty Woman. 2 Wall. 3 I. 4 Rome. 5 Robert. 6 Writing. 7 India. 8 Osama Bin Laden. 9 America. 10 Lockerbie. 11 Round. 12 Four. 13 Emperor. 14 Silver. 15 March. 16 Madison. 17 Katherine Jenkins. 18 Destiny's Child. 19 Waterfall. 20 16.45. 21 Red. 22 Green. 23 Mount Everest. 24 Japan. 25 Africa. 26 Braille. 27 Pear. 28 In the sea. 29 Temple. 30 Alan Pardew.

1 How long does the contestant have to answer the question in "Who Wants to be a Millionaire?"?
2 Who asked the questions in the US version of "The Weakest Link"?
3 How many teams take part in one episode of "University Challenge"?
4 Which Swedish-born personality first presented "Dog Eat Dog"?
5 What is "Ready Steady Cook" with famous stars providing the ingredients called?
6 Lea Kristensen helped Jim Davidson on which Saturday-night family show?
7 Which Phillip hosted "National Lottery: Winning Lines"?
8 Which snooker player led a team opposite Ally McCoist on "A Question of Sport"?
9 On which Channel was the afternoon show "Number One" shown?
10 Which actress Penelope presented a later series of "What's My Line?"?
11 Annabel Croft was what type of sportswoman before taking part in the 1980s "Treasure Hunt"?
12 In "Strike It Rich", was a hotspot lucky or unlucky?
13 If Vic was Reeves who was Bob in "Shooting Stars"?
14 On which show did Leslie Crowther invite contestants to "come on down"?
15 What did Bruce Forsyth invite contestants to "Play Right"?
16 Which means of communication replaced postal votes on "Opportunity Knocks"?
17 What was the chair covering made from on the original "Mastermind"?
18 Which show shared its name with Roman fighters?
19 Whose "Moment of Truth" was a family quiz show?
20 What was the prize in "The Krypton Factor"?
21 Which Noel fronted "Deal or No Deal"?
22 In which long-running show did a Des take over from a Des?
23 Which future TV star Carol was a hostess on "Wheel of Fortune"?
24 Which Des presented the 1990s "Take Your Pick"?
25 What receptacle was the booby prize on "3-2-1"?
26 Which student show has the phrase, "Your starter for 10"?
27 Was the first "Who Wants to be a Millionaire?" millionaire, a man or a woman?
28 Which sports quiz always ends with the end of the famous sporting quote, "It is now"?
29 What was the trophy usually made from on "Mastermind"?
30 Which Saturday-night prime-time quizman Chris split from his wife in 2006?

Answers	Pot Luck 67 *(see Quiz 147)*

1 Luxembourg. 2 Space flight. 3 USA. 4 London. 5 Cranberry. 6 Caravan. 7 Buffy. 8 Ayers Rock. 9 Football. 10 Iraq. 11 Mary. 12 Collie. 13 400th. 14 Light blue. 15 Liverpool. 16 Egypt. 17 16. 18 Steptoe & Son. 19 Zinc. 20 Twins. 21 Jaune. 22 Two. 23 Liverpool. 24 North. 25 Brown. 26 Lion. 27 Bermuda. 28 DNA. 29 Hindu. 30 64.

1 For which movie with "Woman" in the title was Julia Roberts nominated for an Oscar?
2 What would a mural be painted on?
3 Which of these is not the name of a note in music – E, G or I?
4 Nero was the Emperor of which ancient empire when its main city was destroyed?
5 What was the first name of Boy Scouts founder Baden-Powell?
6 Lazlo Biro's most famous invention was used for what?
7 Mother Teresa was particularly noted for her work with the poor of which country?
8 Who founded Al Qaeda in the late 1980s?
9 Did the Grunge movement begin in Australia or America?
10 In the 1980s, over 250 died after a terrorist bomb exploded a plane over which town in Scotland?
11 Christopher Columbus became convinced that the Earth was what shape?
12 In Spanish, what is the number quatro?
13 What is the name of the largest species of penguin?
14 In heraldry, what is argent?
15 In which month is St David's Day?
16 Which of Madison, Maryland or Montana is not a state of the USA?
17 "Second Nature" was which singer's second album?
18 Who had a hit single with "Independent Woman"?
19 The Angel, in Venezuela, is the world's highest what?
20 In digits, what time is quarter to five in the afternoon on a 24-hour clock?
21 What is the top colour on a rainbow?
22 What colour goes before land to name the world's largest island?
23 What is named after George Everest who was a Surveyor General of India?
24 The Sony company originally developed in which country?
25 Nigeria is the largest country in which continent?
26 Who gave his name to a reading system designed for people who are visually impaired?
27 Which of the following is not a citrus fruit – lemon, lime or pear?
28 "The Blue Planet" was a TV documentary series about life where?
29 A pagoda is a type of what?
30 Which boss Alan took West Ham to their first FA Cup final this century?

Answers	**Sport: Who's Who? 2** *(see Quiz 148)*

1 Motor racing. 2 Venus and Serena Williams. 3 Gary. 4 Theo Walcott. 5 Ten. 6 Jesse. 7 West Indies. 8 Tiger Woods. 9 Basketball. 10 Phil Mickelson. 11 Australia. 12 Italy. 13 His Lear Jet suffered decompression, killing all on board, and later crashed. 14 Horse. 15 Kieren. 16 England. 17 Switzerland. 18 Basketball. 19 Swimming. 20 South Africa. 21 Francois. 22 Jockey. 23 Bob. 24 Tax. 25 England. 26 Skiing. 27 Mika. 28 Essex. 29 Jamaica. 30 USA.

1 Which ex-soccer manager of Nottm Forest died aged 69 in September 2004?
2 The Good Friday Agreement was drawn up to help solve problems in which part of the UK?
3 In which decade did Queen Elizabeth II come to the throne?
4 In which month of 2005 was London first bombed?
5 Which island has a political party called Sinn Fein?
6 Which Princess did the future Lord Snowdon marry in 1960?
7 How was the trades union Solidarnosc known in English?
8 Which Maxwell disappeared off his yacht in 1991 before news about misappropriation of pension funds?
9 Marilyn Monroe is thought to have died due to an overdose of what?
10 Which Louis was killed by an IRA bomb in 1979?
11 BSE was also called mad what disease?
12 Which African country entertained only rebel cricket tours because its policy on apartheid meant no official tours could be made?
13 Ken Russell was a controversial name in which area of the arts?
14 Which Act affecting foxes and hares came into force in February 2005?
15 Which tax, also called community charge, was the cause of riots in the 1990s?
16 1990's round-the-world yacht "Maiden" had a crew made up entirely of who or what?
17 Sir Ranulph Fiennes hit the headlines in what capacity?
18 In the 1970s the Americans withdrew troops from which V?
19 Which country has had most experience of spaceflight?
20 The campaign to ban which weapons was supported by Princess Diana?
21 Which O in Northern Ireland was the scene of a horrific bomb in 1998?
22 Which Royal ship ceased service at the end of the 1990s?
23 Apartheid was most well known in which African country?
24 Which television dolls virtually walked off the shelves in a 1990s Christmas buying frenzy?
25 Which sculpture of the North was erected near Gateshead?
26 Which meat did the government ban from being eaten on the bone during the crisis concerning BSE?
27 Princess Anne's daughter Zara hit the headlines with a pierced what?
28 In which decade did Edmund Hillary climb Everest?
29 Salman Rushdie hit the headlines with a controversial what?
30 How many goals did France score when they beat Brazil to win the World Cup?

Answers	Gardening *(see Quiz 153)*

1 Yellow. 2 Wood. 3 Monty Don. 4 Leaves. 5 Artichokes. 6 Over plants. 7 Bulbs. 8 Cut. 9 Cooking. 10 Lawnmower. 11 Compost. 12 Beans. 13 Hedge. 14 Holly. 15 Lavender. 16 Brownish/black. 17 One. 18 Small. 19 Roses. 20 Rockery. 21 Blue. 22 Sweet. 23 Cones. 24 Greenhouse. 25 Apples. 26 William. 27 Mowing. 28 Bulbs. 29 Blue. 30 Elderberries.

1 Tony Blair visited the Faisal mosque in which country in November 2006?
2 Which Niall took over as Sunderland chairman and manager?
3 Who is in the title with the Owl in Edward Lear's poem?
4 What went with Hide in the title of a 2005 Robert de Niro movie?
5 How many people are involved in a fencing match?
6 Which British PM during the 1970s "winter of discontent" died in 2005?
7 What are the sides of a stage called?
8 In music, the lines on which notes are written go in which direction?
9 Which people used C, D, L and M in their counting system?
10 John Glenn became the first person over 70 to do what?
11 What is the first name of Ms Hill who sang with the Fugees?
12 Which Texan gave his name to a tall hat – was it Homburg, Stetson or Tengallon?
13 A Bruxellois is a person coming from which city?
14 Marmite yeast extract is rich in which vitamin?
15 Which of these three spoons is the largest – a coffeespoon, a dessertspoon or a tablespoon?
16 What is the piece of the mushroom above the stalk called?
17 What were the pyramids made out of?
18 In the past, Kampuchea was known by which of these names: Cambodia, Sri Lanka or Thailand?
19 Which common kitchen item can also be a type of drum?
20 Which girl band made a movie called "Honest"?
21 Jonathan Edwards won an Olympic gold medal in which event?
22 What job did Peter and Andrew do before becoming disciples of Jesus?
23 Geometry is a branch of which subject?
24 Coal, diamonds, leather – which of these three items is not mined from underground?
25 What is the first of the three letters that invites you to turn over a piece of paper?
26 How many spaces are contained in a frame for noughts and crosses?
27 On a camera, what opens and closes to allow light in?
28 Is a kayak a type of currency, a hairy animal or a sailing craft?
29 Whose first No 1 hit was "Because We Want to"?
30 In the nursery rhyme "Hey Diddle Diddle", who did a runner with the dish?

Answers	**Music Who's Who?** (see Quiz 154)

1 Duran Duran. 2 Andrew Lloyd Webber. 3 Madonna. 4 Michael Jackson. 5 Ireland. 6 Suede. 7 Enrique. 8 U2. 9 Michael. 10 Robbie Williams. 11 Lopez. 12 Phil. 13 Noel. 14 Spice Girls. 15 Britney Spears. 16 Eternal. 17 Kylie Minogue. 18 Adams. 19 Take That. 20 Eva. 21 US. 22 Barbie. 23 Canada. 24 Martin. 25 Sonny. 26 Kitten. 27 Five. 28 Eminem. 29 Stephen. 30 Sinatra.

1 What is the most common colour for a daffodil?
2 What is decking usually made from?
3 Which Monty took over on BBC's "Gardener's World"?
4 What is a plant's foliage?
5 Which vegetables can be globe or Jerusalem?
6 Where does a cloche go?
7 What are tulips grown from?
8 What do secateurs do?
9 What are culinary herbs used for?
10 Which piece of garden equipment can be hover or rotary?
11 Which heap provides fertiliser for the garden?
12 Which vegetables can be French or broad?
13 If you grew a box in your garden what would it be?
14 Which prickly green shrub with red berries is a Christmas decoration?
15 Which purple aromatic plant takes its name from the Latin Lavo, meaning I wash?
16 What colour is peat?
17 How many wheels does a wheelbarrow usually have?
18 What is significant about bonsai plants?
19 Hybrid tea and floribunda are types of what?
20 Which part of the garden has decorative stones?
21 What is the most common colour of a cornflower?
22 Which Peas are decorative flowers?
23 What do conifers produce?
24 Which house is used for rearing delicate plants?
25 What sort of fruit do you grow if you grow Cox's Orange Pippin and Bramley?
26 Which princely name follows Sweet in a cottage garden plant?
27 Which word describes cutting a lawn?
28 What do lilies grow from?
29 What is the most common colour for a delphinium?
30 Which fruits follow elderflowers?

1 Which 1980s band led by Simon Le Bon were back in the top five in 2004?

2 Who is Timothy Miles Bindon Rice's most famous musical collaborator?

3 Who won the MTV Best Video for "Ray of Light"?

4 Who recorded the album "Thriller"?

5 Where do The Corrs come from?

6 Which band's singles include "Trash" and "Stay Together"?

7 Which Iglesias made the albums "Bailamos" and "Cosas El Amor"?

8 Which Irish band made the album "The Joshua Tree"?

9 Which Jackson has had the most platinum albums in the UK?

10 Which ex-Take That member won a Brit Award for "Angel" in 1999?

11 Which Jennifer's name was linked to that of rapper Puff Daddy?

12 Which Collins, formerly of Genesis, won awards for his songs for the movie "Tarzan"?

13 Who is the oldest Gallagher brother?

14 Which band's singles include "2 Become 1" and "Too Much"?

15 Which teen queen charted with "Born to Make You Happy"?

16 Louise, aka Mrs Jamie Redknapp, belonged to which all-girl band?

17 Which Aussie songstress got to No 1 on both sides of the Atlantic with "Spinning Around"?

18 What was Victoria Beckham's maiden name?

19 Which band's singles included "Relight My Fire" and "Back for Good"?

20 Which Cassidy had a posthumous hit with "Over the Rainbow"?

21 Do Destiny's Child come from the UK or the US?

22 Which toy "Girl" was a hit for Aqua?

23 Which country does Celine Dion come from?

24 Which Ricky had the top-selling album "Vuelve" in 1999?

25 Who was Cher's singing partner on her very first UK hit?

26 Which Atomic band had a hit with "Eternal Flame"?

27 How many members of Boyzone are there?

28 Which rapper recorded the albums "Encore" and "The Eminem Show"?

29 What is the first name of songwriter Sondheim?

30 Which Frank was 70 when he had a single in the top ten?

1 The Appleton girls were in which pop band?
2 What were the initials of foodmaker Mr Heinz?
3 Who were the beaten finalists in the 2002 FIFA World Cup?
4 Orly airport is in which country?
5 VSO stands for what type of charitable service overseas?
6 Who did Thumbelina marry?
7 What is the dog called in a Punch and Judy show?
8 In Enid Blyton's stories, what colour is Noddy's hat?
9 When texting, what does a letter l, a number 8 and a letter r stand for?
10 Queen Nefertiti ruled in which country?
11 In song, Nancy Sinatra had boots that were made for doing what?
12 In which country would you watch Real Sociedad play a home soccer match?
13 Joey Barton and Richard Dunn were together at which Premiership club?
14 In military diplomacy SALT involves what kind of limitation talks – Secret Arms, Specialist Arms or Strategic Arms?
15 What did a spinet make?
16 What is the occupation of Phil, David and Tony Archer in the radio soap?
17 What type of map indicates areas of high and low ground?
18 What is the pattern on a bumblebee?
19 The port of Plymouth is in England and which other country?
20 Is Terry Wogan's radio show in the morning or the evening?
21 Which is the last month in a calendar year to have exactly 30 days?
22 In the signs of the zodiac, Pisces represents which creature?
23 What can be a sheet of paper or part of a plant?
24 How is the famous French lady Jeanne d'Arc known in English?
25 Which animal's "eyes" did Percy Shaw invent to help motorists?
26 Thomas Barnardo set up homes for what type of people?
27 Which word completes the Shania Twain album title "Come On ____"?
28 What shaped puzzle did Mr Rubik invent?
29 Does the letter P in OPEC stand for – petroleum, plastic or price?
30 In which country is the musical "Cabaret" set?

Answers	**Pot Luck 71** *(see Quiz 157)*

1 Geoff Ogilvy. 2 None. 3 Patrick Moore. 4 Friendly. 5 Germany. 6 Leaves (vegetation). 7 Blood. 8 On land. 9 Nocturnal. 10 Change colour. 11 Vacuum cleaner. 12 The X Files. 13 Calorie. 14 Abacus. 15 Russia. 16 Yellow. 17 Japan. 18 Ballet. 19 Ginger. 20 Thomas. 21 Silver. 22 Drew Barrymore. 23 Little. 24 Fat. 25 USA. 26 China. 27 Second. 28 Kingdom. 29 Metals. 30 Steam.

1 Which bird's name goes between "Where" and "Dare" in the Richard Burton/Clint Eastwood film?

2 Which director Alfred's first Hollywood movie was "Rebecca"?

3 In which country is "The Sound of Music" set?

4 Which TV canine star was originally a male called Pal?

5 Where did Tarzan live?

6 On which night of the week was there "Night Fever"?

7 What went after "White" in the seasonal song from the movie "Holiday Inn"?

8 In which decade was "Gone with the Wind" made?

9 How many "Commandments" were in the title of the 1950s classic?

10 Which 1940s classic had the Ugly Sisters among its characters?

11 In how many days did David Niven travel "Around the World" in 1956?

12 Where was "An American" in the 1950s movie?

13 The action for "Bridge on the River Kwai" was set in which war?

14 Which musical movie was based on Dickens' "Oliver Twist"?

15 Which "High" time of day was an award-winning movie with Gary Cooper?

16 Where was Gene Kelly "Singin'" in 1952?

17 Which Walt directed the first eight Oscar-winning animation films?

18 What sort of animal was Bugs?

19 Who was the hero of "Goldfinger"?

20 What were the first movies with speech called?

21 What was the first name of movie star Ms Swanson?

22 "All Quiet" on which "Front" was a classic of the 1930s?

23 Which "Man" was a post-war thriller set in Vienna?

24 John Wayne was famous for playing what type of character?

25 Which future US President starred in "Stallion Road" in the 1940s?

26 Which convenient initials did the grumpy actor Fields have?

27 What type of "Encounter" did Celia Johnson and Trevor Howard have?

28 What was the name of the "Citizen" in the all-time classic with Orson Welles?

29 What colour Brick Road was followed in "The Wizard of Oz"?

30 "Born Free" was about which African cats?

Answers | Celebs *(see Quiz 158)*

1 Alex Curran. 2 Andrew Lloyd Webber. 3 Sophie. 4 Red. 5 Frankie. 6 Feltz. 7 Emma Bunton. 8 Jules. 9 Madonna. 10 Nigella. 11 Cooking. 12 Wogan. 13 Wales. 14 Turner. 15 Butler. 16 Windsor. 17 Vet. 18 Jonathan. 19 Brad Pitt. 20 Scotland. 21 David. 22 Swansea. 23 Harrison. 24 Cricketer. 25 Michael. 26 Hervey. 27 Clarissa. 28 Hurley. 29 Luciano Pavarotti. 30 Pete Doherty.

1 Which Geoff won golf's US Open in 2006?
2 How many teeth do most human babies have at birth?
3 Which Patrick has presented TV's "The Sky at Night" for 50 years?
4 In comic books and movies what word describes Casper the ghost?
5 Supermodel Claudia Schiffer comes from which country?
6 A giraffe's diet consists mainly of what?
7 What contains red and white corpuscles?
8 Where did George Stephenson's Rocket travel – on land, on sea or in space?
9 A creature that is more active at night is said to be what?
10 What does a chameleon do to disguise itself?
11 What kind of machine did William Hoover develop?
12 Which TV series had the line "The truth is out there"?
13 Which of these terms is a measure of energy in food, calorie, fat, cholesterol?
14 Which ancient counting device uses beads and string?
15 Anna Kournikova is originally from which country?
16 What colour is Nintendo's Pikachu?
17 The first Disneyland in Asia was built in which country?
18 An entrechat and a glissade appear in what type of dancing?
19 Who made up the original Spice Girls along with Baby, Posh, Sporty and Scary?
20 The Rev. Awdry wrote about which Tank Engine?
21 Which precious metal is associated with the Lone Ranger?
22 How is movie star Andrew Blyth Barrymore better known?
23 What did Stevie Wonder have before his name when he was a young performer?
24 What does a camel keep stored in its hump?
25 What is Britney Spears' home country?
26 Life-size figures in terracotta of an army were found in which country?
27 Did World War I begin in the first, second or third decade of the 20th century?
28 A king rules a kingdom but what does a queen rule?
29 An alloy is a combination of two different what?
30 What powered James Watt's engine built in 1777?

| **Answers** | **Pot Luck 70** *(see Quiz 155)* |

1 All Saints. 2 HJ. 3 Germany. 4 France. 5 Voluntary. 6 Prince Cornelius. 7 Toby. 8 Blue. 9 Later. 10 Egypt. 11 Walking. 12 Spain. 13 Man City. 14 Strategic Arms. 15 Music. 16 Farmers. 17 Relief map. 18 Stripes. 19 America. 20 Morning. 21 November. 22 Fish. 23 Leaf. 24 Joan of Arc. 25 Cat's. 26 Children. 27 Over. 28 Cube. 29 Petroleum. 30 Germany.

1 Which Ms Curran is the other half of footballer Steve Gerrard?
2 Sarah Brightman was married to which big theatre name?
3 Which Ms Dahl is famous in the modelling world?
4 What colour is Charlie Dimmock's hair?
5 How is Lanfranco Dettori better known?
6 Which Vanessa was in the celebrity "Big Brother" House?
7 Who was the first ex-Spice Girl to appear on "Strictly Come Dancing"?
8 What is Jamie Oliver's wife called?
9 Guy Ritchie married which US megastar In 2000?
10 Which Lawson was dubbed "a domestic goddess"?
11 What were the Two Fat Ladies famous for on TV?
12 Which Radio 2 star Terry's autobiography was called "Is It Me"?
13 From which part of the UK does Catherine Zeta Jones hail?
14 What is the surname of TV sister celebs Anthea and Wendy?
15 What was the position of the ex-employee of Princess Diana who was arrested for theft of some of her property?
16 Which Barbara went from "Carry On" films to "EastEnders"?
17 Trude Mostue found TV fame in which profession?
18 Who is Paul Ross's famous younger brother?
19 Angelica Jolie linked up with which actor Brad?
20 The name of which country does Sean Connery have tattooed on his arm?
21 Which Mellor was dubbed the Minister of Fun?
22 Prince Charles received the freedom of which city, which has a link with his title?
23 Which Ford split with wife Melissa Mathison in 2001?
24 Jemima Khan married what type of sportsman in Imran Khan?
25 Which actor is ex-beauty queen Shakira Caine married to?
26 What is the surname of tabloid celeb Lady Victoria?
27 What is the first name of Ms Dickson Wright, famous for her cooking and country pursuits?
28 Which Elizabeth ceased to be the main face of Estee Lauder in 2001?
29 Who was the heaviest of the Three Tenors?
30 Which Pete is the frontman of Babyshambles?

| **Answers** | **The Movies: Golden Oldies** *(see Quiz 156)* |

1 Eagles. 2 Hitchcock. 3 Austria. 4 Lassie. 5 Jungle. 6 Saturday. 7 Christmas. 8 1930s. 9 Ten. 10 Cinderella. 11 80. 12 Paris. 13 WWII. 14 Oliver!. 15 Noon. 16 In the Rain. 17 Disney. 18 Bunny. 19 James Bond. 20 Talkies. 21 Gloria. 22 Western. 23 Third Man. 24 Cowboy. 25 Ronald Reagan. 26 WC. 27 Brief. 28 Kane. 29 Yellow. 30 Lions.

Quiz 159 | Pot Luck 72

Answers – page 171

LEVEL 1

1 Which sprinter Michael won 200m and 400m gold at the Atlanta Olympics?
2 Which group included two girls with the same name but differentiated by letters of the alphabet?
3 Which W is a jacket that has no sleeves?
4 Which form of transport is Christopher Cockerell famous for developing?
5 What is the name for the place where coins manufactured?
6 Who was Gilbert's partner in writing comic operas?
7 What do you do if you dawdle – do you idle, do you run or do you rinse your mouth out?
8 In rhyme, what precedes "paddywack, give the dog a bone"?
9 Kissing the Blarney Stone is supposed to gift you the power to do what?
10 What is the usual colour of healthy parsley?
11 Which type of puzzle requires a grid to be filled in so that every row, every column and every 3 x 3 box contains the numbers 1 to 9?
12 What sort of pit do athletes jump into during a triple jump?
13 "Revenge of the Sith" was one of which series of movies?
14 Which swimming stroke is named after an insect?
15 Which ex-England football captain was a manager at Middlesbrough and WBA?
16 Which fabric is made from flax?
17 Korea is divided into how many countries?
18 Algeria is in which part of Africa?
19 Which classical composer had the names George Frederick?
20 According to the TV programme title "Sabrina is the Teenage" what – Doctor, Vampire or Witch?
21 In the "Shrek" movies did Eddie Murphy voice Cat, Donkey or Elephant?
22 In which Disney classic movie does Jiminy Cricket appear?
23 Which of these musical instruments does not use a reed when being played – clarinet, guitar or oboe?
24 Lourdes Maria was the first daughter of which pop superstar?
25 In the wartime song what do you pack up in your old kit bag?
26 Which of black, purple and yellow is a primary colour?
27 In fiction, what did Oliver Twist ask for after he had eaten all his food in the workhouse?
28 Attila was a leader of which tribe of which group of people?
29 Which B is the second largest city in Spain?
30 In which country is the musical "Evita" set?

Answers	**Pot Luck 73 (see Quiz 161)**

1 Iraq. 2 Jet engine. 3 First Lady. 4 Isaac. 5 Uma Thurman. 6 Ryder. 7 Egyptians. 8 Pins & needles. 9 Dance. 10 Dark blue. 11 Two. 12 Nappy. 13 Portugal. 14 Romans. 15 It boils. 16 Software. 17 Comet. 18 Countess. 19 Travellers. 20 Ten. 21 Jack. 22 Under the sea. 23 Yarn. 24 Guillotine. 25 2000. 26 General Custer. 27 Face. 28 Iced. 29 Blue. 30 Andre.

1 Who is Tracey's sister in "Birds of a Feather"?
2 Which series set in a prison shared its name with a breakfast food?
3 Who was Tom's wife in "The Good Life"?
4 What is British TV's longest-running children's show?
5 Which BBC show ended its Saturday-night run in 2001 when Premiership football moved to ITV?
6 On which night of the week is "Songs of Praise" usually shown?
7 Which "Team" included Mr T?
8 Which series with John Cleese was set in a hotel in Torquay?
9 Who was Inspector Morse's sidekick?
10 What was the occupation of Perry Mason?
11 Sergeant Wilson and Captain Mainwaring were in which "Army"?
12 In Morecambe & Wise, what was Morecambe's first name?
13 What was the nickname of Simon Templar, first played by Roger Moore?
14 Which "Challenge" was first presented by Bamber Gascoigne and later by Jeremy Paxman?
15 Which "Cars" were an early police drama?
16 Which "Doctor" first appeared in the 1960s in a phone box?
17 Which "Roundabout" became a children's classic?
18 Which type of workplace gave Ricky Gervais his first hit series?
19 "Jeux Sans Frontières" was also called "It's a" what?
20 Which Prime Minister's father-in-law was in "Till Death Us Do Part"?
21 Which weapon was used in the game show "The Golden Shot"?
22 Where did singer Val Doonican hail from?
23 Which puppet bear had friends called Sweep and Soo?
24 Which show was associated with a "Flying Circus"?
25 Who presented "The Generation Game" back in the 1970s?
26 What was the favourite item of footwear of Compo as played by the late Bill Owen?
27 Barry Norman began the first of many review programmes on which subject in 1972?
28 John Craven pioneered a "Newsround" programme for whom?
29 What colour was the chair in "Mastermind"?
30 Which Ricky appeared in "The Royle Family"?

Answers	Science & the Natural World *(see Quiz 162)*

1 Heel. 2 Cows/cattle. 3 Bee. 4 Temperature. 5 Tropical. 6 Orange/yellow. 7 Cold-blooded. 8 Rib cage. 9 Red. 10 Eating. 11 Asia. 12 Mouth. 13 Slime. 14 Your voice. 15 Back. 16 Needles. 17 Cat. 18 Spider. 19 Africa. 20 Blood. 21 Man. 22 Snake. 23 Sheep. 24 Plus. 25 Red. 26 Pink. 27 Australia. 28 Ice. 29 Mistletoe. 30 Mercury.

1 In which country is the war-scarred city of Basra?
2 What sort of engine was invented by Frank Whittle?
3 Which unofficial title is given to the wife of a US President?
4 What was the first name of scientist Newton?
5 Which actress Uma featured in the "Kill Bill" movies?
6 Which Winona links the movies "Little Women", "The Crucible" and "Alien: Resurrection"?
7 Isis and Osiris were gods of which ancient people?
8 Which sewing items can also be a sharp pain?
9 A palais glide is a type of what?
10 On a Monopoly board, what colour is the most expensive property?
11 How many players are on court in a game of tennis singles?
12 What do the British call what the Americans call a diaper?
13 Deco, Figo and Pauleta played soccer for which country?
14 Queen Boudicca led a revolt against which people?
15 What happens to water at 100 degrees centigrade?
16 What's the name for the instructions or programs used in computers?
17 Astronomer Edmond Halley gave his name to what?
18 What is the wife of an Earl called?
19 St Christopher is the patron saint of which group of people?
20 How many sides does a decagon have?
21 Which name can go before the words frost and knife?
22 Which part of the Earth was Jacques Cousteau famous for exploring?
23 What can be either a piece of thread or a long story?
24 Which device from the French Revolution is now used to trim paper?
25 What was the first leap year beginning with the numbers 20?
26 Which General made his "last stand" at the Battle of the Little Big Horn?
27 Where on her body would a Muslim woman wear a yashmak?
28 Is a sorbet served hot, iced or warm?
29 What colour blood are you said to have if you have a noble family?
30 Which Peter had No 1s with "Flava" and "I Feel You"?

1 Which part of the body is associated with Achilles?

2 Dairy farming is usually associated with the rearing of which animals?

3 A drone is a type of which insect?

4 What does the Kelvin scale measure?

5 In what sort of climate do rainforests appear?

6 What colour is amber?

7 What charachteristic of reptiles is also a phrase used to describe a callous act?

8 What is the framework of ribs called?

9 What colour is a robin's breast?

10 Anorexia nervosa is what type of disorder?

11 Which continent grows the most rice?

12 Saliva is produced in which part of the body?

13 What sort of trail does a slug leave behind?

14 If you have laryngitis what may you lose?

15 Lumbago causes pain in which part of the body?

16 What is inserted in the body in acupuncture?

17 The Florida cougar is a member of which family?

18 Which eight-legged creature do many people have a phobia about?

19 On which continent are most elephants found?

20 What do arteries in the body carry?

21 Chimpanzee, gorilla and man – present company excepted – which is the most intelligent?

22 What is a black mamba?

23 Cats, dogs and sheep – which of these animals are sheared?

24 Which contains more lines a plus or a minus sign?

25 Mars is called what colour planet?

26 What colour are a flamingo's feathers?

27 Koalas are natives to which country?

28 If water freezes what does it become?

29 Which plant increases in popularity at Christmas when you kiss under it?

30 Which metal is used in thermometers?

Answers	TV: Classics *(see Quiz 160)*

1 Sharon. 2 Porridge. 3 Barbara. 4 Blue Peter. 5 Match of the Day. 6 Sunday. 7 A Team. 8 Fawlty Towers. 9 Lewis. 10 Lawyer (barrister). 11 Dad's Army. 12 Eric. 13 The Saint. 14 University. 15 Z Cars. 16 Who. 17 Magic. 18 Office. 19 Knockout. 20 Tony Blair's. 21 Crossbow. 22 Ireland. 23 Sooty. 24 Monty Python. 25 Bruce Forsyth. 26 Wellies. 27 Films. 28 Children. 29 Black. 30 Ricky Tomlinson.

1 Which Oscar-winner was a "Beauty", with Annette Bening and Kevin Spacey?
2 In which country was Warren Beatty's political thriller "Reds" set?
3 Which Juliette won Best Supporting Actress for "The English Patient"?
4 Where was Nicolas Cage "Leaving" in his 1995 winner?
5 Which Julia won for "Erin Brokovich"?
6 Which Ben shared a screenplay Oscar with Matt Damon for "Good Will Hunting"?
7 Which Jennifer did Oscar-nominee Brad Pitt marry?
8 Which English Oscar-winner Emma has a sister called Sophie?
9 In which US city was "The Godfather" set?
10 How old was Jessica Tandy when she won an Oscar for "Driving Miss Daisy", in her 50s, 60s, 70s or 80s?
11 Which English Julie, a 1960s winner, was nominated for "Afterglow" in the 1990s?
12 In which film venue were the first Oscars presented?
13 Which fighter was the subject of the 2001 winner with Russell Crowe?
14 Which blonde American cried all the way through her acceptance speech for "Shakespeare in Love"?
15 What was the nationality of the main character in "Braveheart"?
16 Which Hilary won Best Supporting Actress for "Boys Don't Cry"?
17 Which language was "La vita e bella in"?
18 Which was the highest-grossing Oscar-winner of the 1990s?
19 "Amadeus" was an Oscar-winner about which composer?
20 "Dances with" which animals was the third-best Oscar-winning earner of the 1990s?
21 Which mythical creature follows "Crouching Tiger, Hidden _____" in the movie title?
22 Which United studio had 13 winning films by the end of the millennium?
23 Which 1990s winner has "English" in the title?
24 In which decade was "Cabaret" a winner?
25 What sort of Games was "Chariots of Fire" about?
26 Which John won for "True Grit"?
27 Which Susan played a nun in "Dead Man Walking"?
28 How many Oscars had Julia Roberts won before "Erin Brokovich"?
29 Which Fonda won for "On Golden Pond"?
30 What type of "Foot" won for Daniel Day Lewis?

Answers	**Geography: World Tour 2** *(see Quiz 165)*

1 Virgin. 2 Switzerland. 3 Texas. 4 Salt. 5 South America. 6 New York. 7 Eskimo. 8 Rockies. 9 Africa. 10 Delhi. 11 Russian. 12 Amazon river. 13 Rhodesia. 14 Oil. 15 America. 16 Europe. 17 Africa. 18 South Africa. 19 New York. 20 Canal. 21 Canaries. 22 Long. 23 Cars. 24 Louisiana. 25 Australia. 26 Northwest. 27 Canada. 28 Cote d'Ivoire. 29 Sydney. 30 Africa.

1 "Lonely" was the first No 1 single for which rapper beginning with an A?
2 Standing down as an MP in 2005, Dr Jack Cunningham was in which party?
3 A skull and what else appeared on the Jolly Roger flag?
4 A bird's feather was used to make what type of old-fashioned pen?
5 Which country in South America is also the name of a nut?
6 What are you said to tread if you act on stage?
7 In mythology, Neptune is the god of what?
8 What type of vegetable would a vampire not eat In a vegetarian restaurant?
9 How many days are there in April and May together?
10 Which part of the egg is used to make meringues?
11 What does a somnambulist do while asleep?
12 Paul Robinson was at which club during the 2006 World Cup?
13 Who or what were druids in Ancient Britain?
14 In song, who looked out on the Feast of Stephen?
15 What is needed for a game of whist?
16 If something is there to mislead it is said to be a red type of which fish?
17 Who were the first people to settle in New Zealand?
18 What was the nationality of the thinker Archimedes?
19 Which continent has the greatest number of people?
20 What does the first C stand for in CCTV?
21 What sort of fingers does a person have who is always dropping things called?
22 How many angles are contained in a pentagon?
23 Which of the following colours is not a type of rice – black, brown or white?
24 What is the maximum number of people who can sit in a rickshaw?
25 Ratatouille is made from what type of food?
26 What does a kilowatt measure?
27 Which Jack, who died in 2001, starred in "The Odd Couple"?
28 In which season is the festival of the Passover?
29 Which popular small car was invented by Alec Issigonis?
30 Who landed on the Moon along with Neil Armstrong?

Answers	Pot Luck 75 *(see Quiz 166)*

1 Gromit. 2 Net. 3 Music. 4 Shilpa Shetty. 5 Sax. 6 University. 7 Snake. 8 The ear.
9 Bucks. 10 Palace. 11 Baseball. 12 Female. 13 Hundred Acre Wood. 14 Friends.
15 Ice hockey. 16 SEGA. 17 Haddock. 18 Virtual. 19 California. 20 Can. 21
Japan. 22 The Great. 23 Four. 24 JK Rowling. 25 1990 World Cup. 26 Billboard. 27
Ronaldo. 28 Three. 29 50. 30 UK.

1 Which islands share their name with Richard Branson's airline?
2 Which country beginning with S borders the east of France?
3 Dallas is in which US oil state?
4 What does the Dead Sea taste of?
5 Ecuador is on which continent?
6 In which US city is the Empire State Building?
7 What is another name for Inuit?
8 What is the nickname for the Rocky Mountains?
9 Algeria is to the north of which continent?
10 Which city comprises Old Delhi and New Delhi?
11 What is the official language of Russia?
12 In Spanish it's Rio de las Amazonas, what is it in English?
13 What name did Zimbabwe have in the 1960s?
14 Saudi Arabia is famous for producing which fuel?
15 The Sioux are a native tribe of which continent?
16 Scandinavia is in which continent?
17 Which continent is the next largest after Asia?
18 Soweto is a suburb of Johannesburg in which country?
19 In which harbour is the Statue of Liberty?
20 What type of waterway is at Suez?
21 Gran Canaria is in which islands?
22 What describes the famous Beach resort in California where the "Queen Mary" was brought?
23 Los Angeles suffers from a severe smog problem due to a high percentage of which vehicles?
24 Which is the only US state to begin with L?
25 Aborigines are from which Commonwealth country?
26 In which part of the USA is Alaska?
27 Quebec is a French-speaking part of which country?
28 Which of the following used to be called the Ivory Coast – Cote d'Ivoire, Gold Coast or Rhodesia?
29 What is Australia's largest city?
30 On which continent is Swahili spoken?

Answers	**The Movies: The Oscars 2** *(see Quiz 163)*

1 American. 2 Russia/Soviet Union. 3 Binoche. 4 Las Vegas. 5 Roberts. 6 Affleck.
7 Aniston. 8 Thompson. 9 New York. 10 80s. 11 Christie. 12 Hollywood.
13 Gladiator. 14 Gwyneth Paltrow. 15 Scottish. 16 Swank. 17 Italian. 18 Titanic.
19 Mozart. 20 Wolves. 21 Dragon. 22 Artists. 23 The English Patient. 24 1970s.
25 Olympics. 26 Wayne. 27 Sarandon. 28 None. 29 Henry. 30 My Left Foot.

1 Who is the four-legged hero in the movie "The Wrong Trousers"?
2 What is at the end of a stick in lacrosse?
3 What does the letter M stand for in MTV?
4 Which Bollywood actress won "Celebrity Big Brother" in 2007?
5 What was the surname of the inventor of the saxophone?
6 What type of institution in America was named after John Harvard?
7 Which of these has least legs – bird, kangaroo or snake?
8 Where in the body is the smallest bone?
9 Which word names male rabbits and American money?
10 Which type of building did Louis XIV have built at Versailles?
11 Which sport did Hank Aaron play?
12 In pop music is Anastacia female, male or a group?
13 Which Wood is Winnie the Pooh's home?
14 Which TV series includes the characters Phoebe and Chandler?
15 What is the fastest team game in the world?
16 The Dreamcast video game console was developed by which computer company?
17 Which fishy-sounding Captain is in the Tintin stories?
18 What does V stand for in VR?
19 In 2003 Arnold Schwarzenegger became governor of which US state?
20 Which word names a metal container and also means is able to?
21 In which country was the first CD made?
22 What name was given to the English King Alfred – The Awful, The Great or The Lionheart?
23 How many beats to the bar are there in basic rock music?
24 The character Albus Dumbledore was created by which writer?
25 The Three Tenors first sang at which sporting event?
26 What are the US pop charts called – Billboard, Groundhog or Skateboard?
27 Which R was top scorer in the 2002 FIFA World Cup?
28 In a knock-out competition how many games are left – excluding replays or third-place playoffs – after all the quarter finals are completed?
29 About how many countries are there altogether in Europe – 15, 50 or 100?
30 Which country was the first in the world to have a TV service?

Answers | **Pot Luck 74 (see Quiz 164)**

1 Akon. 2 Labour. 3 Cross bones. 4 Quill pen. 5 Brazil. 6 The boards. 7 Sea. 8 Garlic. 9 61. 10 White. 11 Walk. 12 Spurs. 13 Priests. 14 Good King Wenceslas. 15 Pack of cards. 16 Herring. 17 The Maoris. 18 Greek. 19 Asia. 20 Closed. 21 Butterfingers. 22 Five. 23 Black. 24 Two. 25 Vegetables. 26 Electrical power. 27 Lemmon. 28 Spring. 29 Mini. 30 Buzz Aldrin.

1 Which is the title of an opera – "The Crying Dutchman", "The Flying Ditchman" or "The Flying Dutchman"?

2 Which composer had the first names Johann Sebastian?

3 Edward Elgar was from which country?

4 What sort of music is "Tosca"?

5 How do you get a sound out of a saxophone?

6 What are the surnames of the Three Tenors?

7 Charlotte Church came from which part of the UK?

8 Which insect follows "Madame" in the title of an opera?

9 Which opera star Andrea had top-selling albums "Romanza" and "Sogno"?

10 In which city is La Scala Opera House?

11 In which venue in London do the Proms take place?

12 Which tenor Russell had a brain tumour removed in 2006?

13 Placido Domingo is particularly famous for which type of music?

14 How many performers are there in a string quartet?

15 In which country is the Sydney Opera House?

16 Which is the highest female voice?

17 What is the first name of conductor Rattle?

18 What was the name of opera singer Callas?

19 What was the nationality of Tchaikovsky?

20 What do you do to a tambourine to get a noise out of it?

21 Where do you hold a flute to play it?

22 Which is the largest of these instruments – violin, viola or double bass?

23 Which musical instrument did Sax invent?

24 Which musical instrument did Yehudi Menuhin play?

25 In which Garden is London's Royal Opera House?

26 Which overture with cannon and bell effects has a date for its title?

27 What night of the week is the Last Night of the Proms?

28 Which country does Kiri Te Kanawa come from?

29 Which is the lowest male voice?

30 "Riverdance" was based on classic, traditional dance from which country?

Answers	21st Century News (see Quiz 169)

1 September. 2 Poisoned. 3 Labour. 4 London. 5 Conservative. 6 Hussein. 7 John Paul II. 8 Gordon Brown. 9 Rail. 10 Foot & mouth. 11 Swedish. 12 Internet. 13 Farepack. 14 Ships. 15 Alistair. 16 Three. 17 Concorde. 18 Sydney. 19 Asylum. 20 Straw. 21 Venus Williams. 22 Doctor/GP. 23 June. 24 Russia. 25 Labour. 26 Bridget Jones. 27 Florida. 28 Ann. 29 David Cameron. 30 2005.

Answers – page 180

1 Who won a Bafta for her film portrayal of Queen Elizabeth II?

2 From which country does goulash originate?

3 What can be odd, even or whole?

4 Apart from being a TV programme, what is a Blue Peter?

5 Which country starting with an S did England play in the World Cup 2006?

6 In which US state is Walt Disney World?

7 "Just do it" was featured in ads for which company products?

8 Which Peter had a hit with "Mysterious Girl" In 1996 and 2004?

9 What is a flexible diving board called?

10 The Taliban were a guerrilla group operating in which country?

11 Both World War I and World War II began in which continent?

12 What is French for ten?

13 A clutch is a collection of what?

14 The Beaufort scale identifies different speeds of what?

15 Is "Woman's Hour" on Radio 1, 2, 3 or 4?

16 In the movie title who is described as "International Man of Mystery"?

17 What are the minimum number of notes needed to produce a chord?

18 Which part of a car did John Dunlop invent?

19 In its nickname Chicago is known as what type of city?

20 What type of animal was the first to travel in space?

21 In which country was the first Marathon race run?

22 Josiah Wedgwood found fame making what?

23 What was the first name of the character Dr Lecter in "The Silence of the Lambs"?

24 The emu comes from which country?

25 Tibia and fibula are names of of what?

26 Which English county is part of Superman's secret alias?

27 What is the playing area called in a basketball match?

28 What is Bart Simpson's full first name – is it Bartram, Bartholomew or Stobart?

29 What does Costa Blanca actually mean?

30 In a pack of cards what is the Queen of Spades often known as?

Quiz 169 21st Century News

Answers – page 177

LEVEL 1

1 In which month in 2001 was the World Trade Center in New York destroyed by a terrorist attack?
2 In 2006, was the ex-Russian spy Alexander Litvinenko knifed, poisoned or shot?
3 David Blunkett became Home Secretary for which party?
4 In which city did the ill-fated Millennium Dome open?
5 Jailed peer Lord Archer was Deputy Chairman of which political party?
6 Which Saddam led Iraq into the 21st century?
7 Which Pope died in April 2005?
8 Which Chancellor gave the first Budget of the new millennium?
9 What sort of crash at Hatfield caused travel problems for many months?
10 Tony Blair postponed the 2001 General Election because of which farming disaster?
11 What nationality was the full-time England soccer manager who succeeded Kevin Keegan?
12 How did the Kilshaws adopt baby twin girls?
13 Which major Christmas savings club collapsed in 2006?
14 Cammell Laird, which called in the receivers in 2001, manufactured what?
15 Which Campbell was Tony Blair's press secretary?
16 How many children did Madonna have when she married Guy Ritchie?
17 Which supersonic aircraft was grounded in 2000 after crashing outside Paris?
18 Where were the 2000 Olympic Games held?
19 Which seekers were apprehended in the Channel Tunnel?
20 Which Jack replaced Robin Cook as Foreign Secretary?
21 Which sister of Serena won the first two Ladies' Singles Championships of the 21st century at Wimbledon?
22 What was the profession of convicted mass murderer Harold Shipman?
23 In which month did the 2001 UK General Election take place?
24 Vladimir Putin became head of state of which country?
25 Standing down as an MP in 2005, Tony Banks was in which party?
26 Whose film "Diary" broke all box office records when it opened in 2001?
27 Results in which sunshine state held the result of the US Presidential election?
28 Which Shadow Home Secretary Widdecombe published a novel?
29 In 2006 which David took a cycle ride to Westminster, as the chauffeur-driven car followed?
30 In which year did Prince Charles marry Camilla Parker Bowles – 2000, 2003 or 2005?

| **Answers** | **Classical Music** *(see Quiz 167)* |

1 The Flying Dutchman. 2 Bach. 3 England. 4 Opera. 5 Blow it. 6 Carreras, Domingo, Pavarotti. 7 Wales. 8 Butterfly. 9 Bocelli. 10 Milan. 11 Albert Hall. 12 Russell Watson. 13 Opera. 14 Four. 15 Australia. 16 Soprano. 17 Simon. 18 Maria. 19 Russian. 20 Shake it. 21 To the side. 22 Double bass. 23 Saxophone. 24 Violin. 25 Covent Garden. 26 1812. 27 Saturday. 28 New Zealand. 29 Bass. 30 Ireland.

1 Which Chris is the lead vocalist for Coldplay?
2 John F Kennedy became President of the USA in which decade?
3 How many days are there in June and July together?
4 What gruesome adjective was given to Mary I?
5 What is the date that is two days after Saint Patrick's day?
6 Which Orlando was Legolas Greenleaf in the "Lord of the Rings" films?
7 If a lady is a soprano what does she do?
8 What is named after the Duke of Wellington – a type of boot, a metal helmet or a breed of dog?
9 What is popcorn made from?
10 A right-angled triangle contains one angle that must be how many degrees?
11 Which creature has a name that means idle and lazy?
12 Which sci-fi movie was Harrison Ford's first film?
13 Miguel Indurain was a record-breaker on what sort of vehicle?
14 Where on a horse are its withers?
15 In 1989 which country's students protested in Tianenmen Square?
16 Which of these is not a member of the cat family – panther, tiger or zebra?
17 What is the first name of President George W Bush's wife?
18 What was the name of the Russian Tsar who founded St Petersburg?
19 Captain James Cook became famous for doing what – cooking, exploring or swimming underwater?
20 Which cartoon young hero did Belgian Hergé create?
21 What was the last name of the fairy tale collecting brothers Jacob and Wilhelm?
22 Charles Goodyear developed what important item for cars?
23 Which animal is included in the nickname of Jack Nicklaus?
24 Which record company was founded by Richard Branson?
25 What type of markings does a cheetah have?
26 Which keeper Jerzy was Liverpool's hero in the 2005 Champions League final?
27 Which land contained a Yellow Brick Road?
28 Explorer Francis Drake had a ship called "The Golden" what?
29 Which environmentally friendly shop did Anita Roddick found?
30 A diplodocus was a type of what – a counting frame, a dinosaur or a steam bath from Roman times?

Answers	**Pot Luck 76** *(see Quiz 168)*

1 Helen Mirren. 2 Hungary. 3 A number. 4 Flag. 5 Sweden. 6 Florida. 7 Nike.
8 Peter Andre. 9 Springboard. 10 Afghanistan. 11 Europe. 12 Dix. 13 Eggs. 14 Wind. 15 Radio 4. 16 Austin Powers. 17 Two. 18 Tyres. 19 Windy. 20 Dog. 21 Greece. 22 Pottery. 23 Hannibal. 24 Australia. 25 Bones. 26 Kent. 27 Court. 28 Bartholomew. 29 White Coast. 30 The Black Lady.

1 Judith Keppel was the first million-pound winner of what?
2 What is the Duke of Edinburgh's first name?
3 Which Al Fayed bought Harrods?
4 What is the first name of Lady Archer, wife of the disgraced peer?
5 Which blonde Ball had a baby called Woody?
6 Which Robbie's name was linked with Geri Halliwell?
7 Raymond Blanc is a rich and famous what?
8 Which train service is Richard Branson most associated with?
9 Which Ms Campbell was a supermodel in the 1990s and 2000s?
10 Which Whitney filed for divorce from Bobby Brown in 2006?
11 What is the Countess of Wessex's first name?
12 What is Prince Michael of Kent's wife called?
13 Which Ms Kidd was one of the faces of the Nineties?
14 What is the nickname of Ms Legge Bourke, former "nanny" to Princes William and Harry?
15 Which Peter had to resign from the Cabinet because of the purchase of a house in Notting Hill?
16 Which TV cook Smith has her own on-line service?
17 Which Palmer-Tomkinson has been dubbed the It Girl?
18 What is the first name of Princess Beatrice's mother?
19 Which Catherine did Michael Douglas marry?
20 Which TV interviewer is Lady Carina Frost's husband?
21 Was Nell McAndrew's boy named Devon, Durham or Essex?
22 Ex-King Constantine was King of which European country?
23 Which William led the Conservative Party to defeat in the 2001 election?
24 Who is Prince William's younger brother?
25 Which 007 Roger had a father who was a policeman?
26 Cake-maker and actress Jane Asher has what colour hair?
27 What is the first name of tennis star and product endorser Ms Sharapova?
28 Which was the first of the Williams sisters to win the Wimbledon singles title?
29 Who is Jermaine Jackson's more famous younger brother?
30 Which Elton collected a Disney Legends award in 2006?

Answers	**TV: Greats** *(see Quiz 173)*

1 Attenborough. 2 Thaw. 3 Monk. 4 Keeping Up Appearances. 5 Coltrane. 6 Yorkshire. 7 Square. 8 The Good Life. 9 Three. 10 David Frost. 11 Friends. 12 Dog. 13 French. 14 Flowerpot men. 15 Sybil. 16 ER. 17 Afternoon. 18 Porridge. 19 Doctor. 20 Red. 21 Tell a story. 22 Four. 23 Police. 24 New York. 25 Two. 26 Barker. 27 Perrin. 28 Dibley. 29 Charles. 30 Barrister (lawyer).

Answers – page 184

1 Ronaldinho played for which 2006 Champions League final winners?
2 How many kings are there on a chessboard at the start of a game?
3 How many do you score in darts with all three arrows in double top?
4 Which Pole was explorer Amundsen the first to reach?
5 What is the name for plant and animal remains preserved in rock?
6 Which Robert who died in 2006 directed the movie "Gosford Park"?
7 Would you expect an animator to collect beer mats, make cartoon movies or search for jewels?
8 What is the nationality of most Popes?
9 Sally Ride was the first American woman to travel where?
10 What was the surname of Wild West outlaw brothers Frank and Jesse?
11 What was the name of Pierre Curie's scientist wife?
12 Terrell Davis is famous for which sport?
13 How many different vowels are there in the word relieved?
14 How does twenty past six pm appear on a 24-hour clock?
15 What is the Paris's underground railway system called?
16 Which imaginary line goes across the middle of Africa?
17 Which term is used to describe developing countries?
18 What is the sparsely populated region of Australia called?
19 What do you collect if you are a philatelist?
20 In which country is the Ganges a sacred river?
21 Papyrus was an early form of what everyday item?
22 In "Peter Pan", how many hands does Captain Hook have?
23 WHO is the world what organisation?
24 What do you do if you take part in a mazurka?
25 Actors and actresses join which trade union?
26 Which former England soccer boss has also managed Ipswich, Porto, Barcelona and Newcastle?
27 What are dried to make prunes?
28 In the 1960s, "The Shrimp" was the nickname given to a famous what?
29 Channel 4 broadcast a biopic about which Royal in November 2005?
30 How many rings are linked in the symbol for the Olympic Games?

| **Answers** | **Pot Luck 79** *(see Quiz 174)* |

1 Pie. 2 (South) Yorkshire. 3 Arctic. 4 Walk. 5 Madeleine Albright. 6 Green. 7 Poles. 8 Eating in binges. 9 Panther. 10 East. 11 Giraffe. 12 Herd. 13 Wane. 14 Dan Maskell. 15 Home page. 16 Two. 17 Japan. 18 Monkey. 19 Atlantic. 20 Star Wars. 21 Coach. 22 Pasta. 23 A pole. 24 Earthquakes. 25 Kentucky. 26 Whales. 27 Novelist. 28 Pacific. 29 Green. 30 Lopez.

1 Which David with a famous brother investigated "The Private Life of Plants"?

2 Which John played Kavanagh QC?

3 What was the profession of Cadfael?

4 In which series might Hyacinth have tried to impress Emmet?

5 Which Robbie found fame as Cracker?

6 The classic "All Creatures Great and Small" was set in which county?

7 What shape was the medallion on a "Jim'll Fix It" badge?

8 Which 1970s sitcom was set in The Avenue, Surbiton?

9 How many Goodies were there?

10 Who fronted "The Frost Report"?

11 Which Channel 4 modern classic featured six New York chums?

12 What was the most famous pet in "Frasier"?

13 Who is the brunette in "French & Saunders"?

14 What type of Men were Bill and Ben?

15 What was the name of Mrs Basil Fawlty?

16 How is the drama set in a US Emergency Room better known?

17 At what time of day was "Emmerdale Farm" first screened?

18 "Going Straight" was the sequel to which hugely popular Ronnie Barker sitcom?

19 In the original "Heartbeat" what was the profession of Nick's wife?

20 What colour was Inspector Morse's Jaguar?

21 What did stars do on "Jackanory"?

22 How many candles are asked for in the classic "Two Ronnies" shop sketch?

23 "Juliet Bravo" was a popular series about someone in which profession?

24 In which city did Kojak work?

25 How many males shared a flat in "Men Behaving Badly"?

26 Which Ronnie played Arkwright in "Open All Hours"?

27 Which Reginald was played by the late Leonard Rossiter?

28 Alice was married by a female Vicar in which village?

29 Which Prince was interviewed by Jonathan Dimbleby in "The Private Man, the Public Role"?

30 What was the profession of TV great Horace Rumpole?

Answers	**Rich & Famous** *(see Quiz 171)*

1 Who Wants to be a Millionaire? 2 Philip. 3 Mohammed. 4 Mary. 5 Zoe. 6 Williams. 7 Chef. 8 Virgin. 9 Naomi. 10 Whitney Houston. 11 Sophie. 12 Princess Michael. 13 Jodie. 14 Tiggy. 15 Mandelson. 16 Delia. 17 Tara. 18 Sarah. 19 Zeta Jones. 20 David. 21 Devon. 22 Greece. 23 Hague. 24 Harry. 25 Moore. 26 Red. 27 Maria. 28 Venus. 29 Michael. 30 Elton John.

1 What sort of chart presents data seen as slices of a circle – a cake chart, a flow chart or a pie chart?
2 In which county was "The Full Monty" set?
3 The Inuit live around which ocean?
4 Aleksey Leonov was the first man to do what in space?
5 Which Madeleine was the first woman US Secretary of State?
6 What colour is a banana before it is ripe to eat?
7 What are the ends of a magnet called?
8 A bulimia sufferer has an urge to do what?
9 What name is given to a leopard that is coloured black?
10 Lake Tanganyika is in which part of Africa – east, north or south?
11 Which of these creatures has its head furthest from the ground – giraffe, gorilla or rhinoceros?
12 What is the term for a group of elephants?
13 The Moon is said to wax and what else?
14 Which late Dan was the BBC's voice of tennis from the 1950s to the 1990s?
15 What is the introductory page of a web site known as?
16 Excluding borders, how many different colours appear on a chess board playing area?
17 In which country were the Winter Olympics held when they were staged in Nagano?
18 A howler is what type of creature?
19 At the beginning of the last century, Marconi sent radio signals across which ocean?
20 Which "Star" movie was the biggest box office success of the 1970s?
21 In the pantomime "Cinderella", what is the pumpkin turned into?
22 Are Conchiglie and Rigatoni types of cheese, types of pasta or famous soccer strikers once of Juventus?
23 What is used to propel a punt?
24 What does a seismologist study?
25 In which state is the Derby, which is part of the USA's thoroughbred Triple Crown, run?
26 Which mammals will expire when stranded on dry land?
27 Was Iris Murdoch, the subject of the movie "Iris", an actress, nurse or novelist?
28 In which ocean is the US state of Hawaii?
29 In board games, what colour is the Reverend in Cluedo?
30 Which Jennifer did a voiceover in "Antz"?

| **Answers** | **Pot Luck 78** *(see Quiz 172)* |

1 Barcelona. 2 Two. 3 120. 4 North Pole. 5 Fossils. 6 Robert Altman. 7 Make cartoons. 8 Italian. 9 Space. 10 James. 11 Marie. 12 American Football. 13 Two. 14 18.20. 15 Metro. 16 Equator. 17 Third World. 18 Outback. 19 Stamps. 20 India. 21 Paper. 22 One. 23 World Health. 24 Dance. 25 Equity. 26 Bobby Robson. 27 Plums. 28 Model. 29 Princess Margaret. 30 Five.

1   Which Denise won Heptathlon gold in Sydney?
2   How was record-breaking baseball star Henry Louis Aaron better known?
3   Who scored the goal which took England into the 2002 World Cup Finals?
4   Which Jack was the first golfer to win six US Masters titles?
5   Peter Shilton played a record number of soccer matches in which position?
6   In which country was tennis star Greg Ruzedski born?
7   Maurice Greene was part of the gold-medal-winning 4x100m. relay team in Sydney for which nation?
8   The Chicago Cubs and Chicago White Sox are cross-city rivals in which sport?
9   In which country was England's 5–1 win over Germany in 2001?
10 What type of golfers compete for the Solheim Cup?
11 Which country has won soccer's World Cup more than any other?
12 Which American has won the Men's Singles at Wimbledon more than any other man?
13 Merlene Ottey has won 14 World Championship medals in what sport?
14 How is Eldrick Woods better known?
15 Which soccer side won the FA Cup, the Premier League and the European Champions League in 1999?
16 Which Martina is Wimbledon's most successful Ladies' Champion?
17 What did Ed Moses jump over to win world records between 1977 and 1987?
18 How many were in the boat in which Steve Redgrave won his fifth Olympic gold?
19 In 2006 which Frenchman Robert played his last game for Arsenal?
20 Joe Montana and Dan Marino were high-profile stars of which sport in the 1980s and 1990s?
21 Which Chris won the French Open tennis title seven times?
22 Which driver Alain was dubbed "The Professor of the Track"?
23 Was Krisztina Egerszegi cold or wet when she won her five Olympic gold medals?
24 In which decade was the first Rugby League World Cup held?
25 In what colour shirts do India play floodlit cricket matches?
26 Where did the US women's basketball team win Olympic gold immediately after Atlanta?
27 In June 2000, which young American won golf's US Open by 15 strokes?
28 What colour was the ball in the 1966 World Cup?
29 Dawn Fraser won four Olympic gold medals for which Olympic host?
30 The 2006 Ryder Cup was staged at the K Club, in which country?

Answers	Movie Memories (see Quiz 177)

1 Arthur. 2 Eastwood. 3 Meg Ryan. 4 Deer. 5 Marilyn Monroe. 6 Grace Kelly. 7 US. 8 Henry VIII. 9 Harrison. 10 Notting Hill. 11 Mrs Robinson. 12 Rosanna. 13 Cat. 14 Ballet. 15 Streetcar. 16 Ghostbusters. 17 Psycho. 18 Disney. 19 Newman. 20 Purple. 21 Shut. 22 Lemmon. 23 Andrews. 24 Ewan. 25 Notting Hill. 26 Paris. 27 Powers. 28 Hairdresser. 29 Natalie Wood. 30 Star Wars.

1 Which country's capital is on the Potomac river?
2 In Italy what is mascarpone?
3 Which Glenn took over from Graeme Souness as Newcastle boss in 2006?
4 Where would you go to visit the Sea of Tranquillity?
5 To get past a portcullis would you go over it, through it or under it?
6 What was the first name of brilliant physicist Einstein?
7 In which of these countries is there not a place called Halifax – Canada, Austria or England?
8 Which creature may be Golden or Bald?
9 What sort of Detective was Ace Ventura?
10 Which colour can be linked with admiral, card and flag?
11 Which spirit was mixed with water to make grog?
12 When texting, how is the word text usually written?
13 Which English city has given its name to a bun and a wheelchair?
14 How old was Marlon Brando when he died in 2004 – 60, 70 or 80?
15 Cape Horn is at the southern tip of which continent?
16 Mandarin is a form of which world language?
17 What was the first No 1 hit on both sides of the Atlantic for the Spice Girls?
18 The English king Alfred was said to have burnt what?
19 What is the most eaten food in Asia?
20 Who went straight to No 1 in the US with "Fantasy"?
21 Which soccer star advertised Brylcreem then had his head shaved?
22 How many years are involved if a silver celebration is two years away?
23 Which part of his own body did painter Van Gogh cut off?
24 Gottlieb Daimler gave his name to what type of transport?
25 Who wrote the children's story "Matilda"?
26 Writer JM Barrie was the central character in which movie?
27 Bill Gates was head of which computer company?
28 What kind of creatures inhabited the Lake in Tchaikovsky's ballet music?
29 Which 1990s champion was named after tennis great Martina Navratilova?
30 Leonardo DiCaprio starred in "The Man in the Iron" what?

Answers | Pot Luck 81 *(see Quiz 178)*

1 Venice. 2 Blow it. 3 X. 4 Spain. 5 Moss. 6 Emergency. 7 Red. 8 Monte Carlo. 9 521. 10 Australia. 11 Shark. 12 Space. 13 Israel. 14 Skiing. 15 Round. 16 Music. 17 Dried fruit. 18 Horse. 19 Cathy Freeman. 20 Peter Jackson. 21 New Zealand. 22 Who's there?. 23 Hay Fever. 24 Mad. 25 Playing cards. 26 Running. 27 Furniture. 28 Golf. 29 Heart. 30 Washington.

1. "Arthur 2: On the Rocks" was the sequel to what?
2. Which Clint appeared in "Coogan's Bluff"?
3. Which actress fakes an orgasm at a diner in "When Harry Met Sally"?
4. Which "Hunter" had the Vietnam war as its subject matter?
5. Who was the famous blonde in "Bus Stop"?
6. Which future movie princess starred in "High Noon"?
7. Which country's Cavalry is John Ford's "Rio Grande" about?
8. "Carry On Henry" was a Carry On spoof about which English King?
9. Which Ford was "The Fugitive" on the big screen?
10. Which part of London, famous for its carnival, shares its name with a Hugh Grant movie?
11. How does Dustin Hoffman always address Mrs Robinson in "The Graduate"?
12. Which Arquette starred in "Pulp Fiction"?
13. What animal goes before "Ballou" in the movie title?
14. What type of shoes were the "Red Shoes"?
15. What was named "Desire" in the movie with Marlon Brando?
16. What sort of busters were the subject of a movie with Dan Aykroyd?
17. In which movie did Janet Leigh play Marion Crane?
18. Which studio made "The Lion King"?
19. Which Paul starred opposite real wife Joanne Woodward in "Mr & Mrs Bridge"?
20. "The Color" was what in the 1985 Steven Spielberg movie?
21. How were "Eyes Wide" in Stanley Kubrick's final movie?
22. Which Jack, who died in 2001, starred in "Missing"?
23. Which Julie starred in two of the top five box office musical successes of the 1960s?
24. Which McGregor played the young Obi-Wan Kenobi in "The Phantom Menace"?
25. Which Hill was trailed as "an equal not a sequel" to "Four Weddings and a Funeral"?
26. Where was Marlon Brando's "Last Tango" in the 1970s?
27. Which Austin was played by Mike Myers?
28. What was Warren Beatty's job in "Shampoo"?
29. Which actress was on the poster for "West Side Story"?
30. Which sci-fi movie was the biggest box office success of the 1970s?

---

1 In which watery city is the Bridge of Sighs?
2 How would you get a note out of a bassoon?
3 Which letter is a Roman numerals and used in grading movies for viewing suitability?
4 The island of Majorca belongs to which country?
5 Which model Kate became the face of L'Oreal in 1998?
6 In a hospital what does E stand for in ER?
7 In the movies what colour is Superman's cape?
8 Which part of Monaco is famous for its car rally?
9 How many weeks are there in ten years?
10 The Murray is the main river of which country?
11 What sort of creature was the villain in the blockbuster movie "Jaws"?
12 Helen Sharman was the first female from the UK to go where?
13 In which country is there a Parliament called the Knesset?
14 Franz Klammer found fame in which sport?
15 What shape is a bagel?
16 In which branch of the creative arts did Stravinsky find fame?
17 What is mincemeat made from?
18 A mustang is a wild what?
19 Which famous Australian lit the Olympic torch in Sydney?
20 Which Peter directed the "Lord of the Rings" series of movies?
21 Which of these countries is the furthest south – India, Japan or New Zealand?
22 What is always the second line of a "Knock knock" joke?
23 People suffer when the pollen count is high if they have which fever?
24 In "Alice in Wonderland" which word is used to describe The Hatter?
25 What is needed for a game of canasta?
26 How did Maurice Greene win gold at Sydney 2000?
27 Thomas Chippendale was famous for making what?
28 Paul Azinger is linked to which sport?
29 In 1967 Christiaan Barnard performed the first transplant of what?
30 Which American city was named after the country's first President?

Answers | **Pot Luck 80** *(see Quiz 176)*

1 USA. 2 Cheese. 3 Glenn Roeder. 4 The moon. 5 Under it. 6 Albert. 7 Austria. 8 Eagle. 9 Pet. 10 Red. 11 Rum. 12 txt. 13 Bath. 14 80. 15 America. 16 Chinese. 17 Wannabe. 18 Cakes. 19 Rice. 20 Mariah Carey. 21 David Beckham. 22 23. 23 Ear. 24 Car. 25 Roald Dahl. 26 Finding Neverland. 27 Microsoft. 28 Swans. 29 Martina Hingis. 30 Mask.

1 What is an anchovy?
2 What would you find in the middle of a damson?
3 Darjeeling is a type of what?
4 Guinness was first made in which Irish city?
5 What is endive?
6 What would you do with a claret?
7 Saffron tinges food what colour?
8 Which vegetable shares its name with a fruit drink?
9 Which village in Leicestershire gives its name to a classic British blue cheese?
10 All citrus fruits are rich in which vitamin?
11 The island of Madeira shares its name with a cake and also what?
12 What colour is root ginger?
13 What are the tops of asparagus called?
14 Which of the following are not types of tomatoes – plum, orange, cherry?
15 What is rocket?
16 What is the most common fuel for a barbecue?
17 Sirloin is which meat?
18 What ingredient is balsamic?
19 What is the most common colour of an aubergine's skin?
20 Which food item is sold at London's Billingsgate market?
21 How is white wine usually served?
22 Mangetout and sugar snaps are types of what?
23 What is feta?
24 If coffee is drunk without milk or cream how is it described?
25 Which Earl gave his name to a type of mild tea?
26 Ciabatta bread originated in which country?
27 What sort of wine is chardonnay?
28 A shallot is a type of what?
29 What shape is the pasta used to make lasagne?
30 Seville is famous for which fruit used to make marmalade?

Answers	Sea Life *(see Quiz 181)*

1 Fish. 2 Skate. 3 Blue whale. 4 Shell. 5 Calf. 6 Sharks. 7 Lobster. 8 Portuguese. 9 Eight. 10 In the sea. 11 None. 12 Osprey. 13 Gills. 14 Herring. 15 10. 16 In the sea. 17 Whale. 18 Milk. 19 97%. 20 Poor. 21 Blubber. 22 Oxygen. 23 Cod. 24 White. 25 12%. 26 Sturgeon. 27 Shark. 28 Gold. 29 Blowhole. 30 Lobster.

1 Which group of people first developed central heating?
2 Which Margaret became Foreign Secretary of the UK?
3 Which country does supermodel Kate Moss come from?
4 In the movie "Beethoven" what sort of animal saves the day?
5 If the first of a month is a Tuesday what day will the tenth be?
6 In a building what can be made from thatch, slates or tiles?
7 Which country in the world has the most computers?
8 How did Marion Jones first win gold at Sydney 2000?
9 In the theatre who stands in for an actor or actress?
10 Which branch of science was Einstein famous for?
11 What colour was Queen Elizabeth I's hair?
12 Which James Bond actor was born on the same day as first man on the moon Neil Armstrong?
13 How many pieces of bread are used to make a club sandwich?
14 What name is given to an extra file sent with an e mail?
15 Who wrote the children's book "Charlotte's Web"?
16 In grammar what sort of word describes another word?
17 What does Giorgio Armani design?
18 Roger Bannister was the first man to run a mile in less than how many minutes?
19 Which bird can go before the words holed and toed?
20 Which Colin played the title role in Oliver Stone's movie "Alexander"?
21 In which month of the year is Father's Day in the UK?
22 The novel "Watership Down" is about a colony of what?
23 What is the lead ballerina in a company called?
24 How many people play in a game of backgammon?
25 What is fi short for in hi-fi?
26 Where are the highest notes on a piano keyboard – to the far left, the far right, or in the middle?
27 What is the the name of the toy dinosaur in "Toy Story"?
28 Mark Antony was in love with which famous queen?
29 What is the currency of Belgium?
30 Which Hilton heiress is named after a European capital city?

Answers | **Pot Luck 83** *(see Quiz 182)*

1 Drum. 2 2006. 3 Emma Thompson. 4 3. 5 Jan/Feb. 6 Polo. 7 Soup/Vegetables.
8 E. 9 Gym. 10 Ursula. 11 Weight. 12 A drop of golden sun. 13 Squares/checks.
14 Boy. 15 100. 16 Paris. 17 Lyrics for operas. 18 Dogs. 19 Face. 20 Ararat. 21
None. 22 White. 23 At. 24 Beetle. 25 Orbit. 26 Press ganging. 27 Nell McAndrew.
28 Gaggle. 29 Aubergine. 30 Morrissey.

Quiz 181 Sea Life

Answers – page 189

1 The whale shark is the largest what?
2 Which fish shares its name with a sports boot?
3 What is the name of the heaviest mammal which lives in the sea?
4 A mollusc's body is covered in what?
5 What is a baby whale called?
6 Great white and hammerhead are types of what?
7 Which one of these creature has pincers – dolphin, lobster or seal?
8 Which nationality Man o' War is a sea creature?
9 The word octo means an octopus has how many tentacles?
10 Where would you find plankton?
11 How many legs does a seahorse have?
12 Which of these is not a fish – cod, osprey or perch?
13 A fish breathes through what?
14 A sardine is a young what?
15 How many tentacles does a squid have?
16 Where does a marine creature live?
17 Blue, fin and humpback are all types of what?
18 What do marine mammals feed their babies on?
19 Approximately how much of the Earth's water is in the oceans – 67%, 87% or 97%?
20 Which term best describes the eyesight of a whale – excellent, outstanding or poor?
21 What is the name for a whale's layer of fat?
22 What do fish absorb through their gills?
23 Which fish was at the centre of the so-called fishing Wars involving Great Britain and Iceland?
24 What colour fur does a baby grey seal have?
25 How much of an iceberg is visible on or above the surface of the sea – 12%, 50% or 90%?
26 Caviar is the name given to which fish's eggs, seen by many as a great delicacy?
27 Nurse and tiger are both types of what?
28 Which of the following is not a type of whale – Blue, Gold or White?
29 Which hole helps a dolphin to breathe?
30 Which of the following is the crayfish related to – lobster, sardine or whale?

Answers	Leisure: Food & Drink 3 (see Quiz 179)

1 Fish. 2 Stone. 3 Tea. 4 Dublin. 5 Salad plant. 6 Drink it. 7 Yellow. 8 Squash.
9 Stilton. 10 C. 11 A wine. 12 Brown. 13 Spears. 14 Orange. 15 Salad leaf.
16 Charcoal. 17 Beef. 18 Vinegar. 19 Purple. 20 Fish. 21 Chilled. 22 Peas. 23
Cheese. 24 Black. 25 Grey. 26 Italy. 27 White. 28 Onion. 29 Rectangular. 30
Oranges.

Quiz 182 Pot Luck 83

Answers – page 190

1 On which instrument might a roll be played?
2 When was the Ryder Cup first played at an Irish course?
3 Which Emma starred in, and wrote the screenplay for "Nanny McPhee"?
4 Which number on a dartboard is furthest from the ceiling?
5 The zodiac sign of Aquarius covers which two months?
6 Which sport is also a type of shirt collar?
7 What is usually served from a tureen?
8 On a keyboard which letter is directly below 3 and 4?
9 Where would you be if you were on a pommel horse?
10 What was the first name of Bond girl actress Andress?
11 A kilogram is a measure of what?
12 According to the song "Do-Ray-Mi", ray is a drop of what?
13 What is the pattern on gingham material?
14 Which word went before George in the name of the Culture Club lead singer?
15 Cent before a word relates to which number?
16 Near which city did Concorde crash on takeoff in 2000?
17 What does a librettist write?
18 What would you be displaying if you took part in Crufts?
19 In a suit of armour which parts of the body did the visor protect?
20 Noah's Ark was believed to have struck land at which Mount?
21 How many months of the year begin with a letter T?
22 What colour is the inside of a coconut?
23 How is @ pronounced in an e mail address?
24 A scarab, an Egyptian good luck charm, was shaped like which creature?
25 What is the term for a satellite's path round the Earth?
26 What name was given to the practice of kidnapping people to join the navy?
27 How is model Tracey Jane McAndrew better known?
28 What is a group of geese called?
29 Eggplant is another name for what?
30 Which Neil is the voice of Bob the Builder?

Answers	**Pot Luck 82** (see Quiz 180)

1 Romans. 2 Margaret Beckett. 3 England. 4 St Bernard dog. 5 Thursday. 6 Roof. 7 USA. 8 Running. 9 Understudy. 10 Physics. 11 Red. 12 Sean Connery. 13 Three. 14 Attachment. 15 EB White. 16 Adjective. 17 Clothes. 18 Four. 19 Pigeon. 20 Colin Farrell. 21 June. 22 Rabbits. 23 Prima ballerina. 24 Two. 25 Fidelity. 26 Far right. 27 Rex. 28 Cleopatra. 29 Franc. 30 Paris.

1 Which group gazed at "Waterloo Sunset"?

2 Which Elvis hit was about a letter without a reply?

3 The Dakotas were not from Dakota; which UK city did they hail from?

4 Elvis's "Wooden Heart" was based on a folk song from which country?

5 Which Gerry & The Pacemakers No 1 became a football anthem?

6 What went with "Needles" in the title of a Searchers hit?

7 How many Beatles were there when they had their very first No 1?

8 Which word followed "Do Wah Diddy" in the title of a Manfred Mann hit?

9 What type of alpine singing featured on Frank Ifield's "I Remember You"?

10 Was Peter Noone 16, 26 or 36 when he fronted Herman's Hermits?

11 Who could get "No Satisfaction" in 1965?

12 Which musical instrument was played by most of The Shadows?

13 How many people were there in Dave Clark's band?

14 Which famous daughter sang "These Boots are Made for Walkin'"?

15 Which US west coast city was the subject of several hippy songs of the mid-1960s?

16 Who wrote Roy Orbison's recording of "Only the Lonely"?

17 What did the Beatles sing they "Want to Hold" in the title of 1964 No 1 single?

18 Which Boys had "Good Vibrations" in 1966?

19 Which Cliff Richard hit became a standard song for celebratory occasions?

20 How many Everly Brothers were there?

21 What sort of "Children" did Billy J Kramer sing about?

22 Which Beatles song about a certain type of writer was released shortly after their last live concert?

23 How many Tops were there?

24 According to Eddie Cochran, how many "Steps to Heaven" were there?

25 What was "My Old Man" according to Lonnie Donegan in 1960?

26 On which fruity label was The Beatles' "Hey Jude" released?

27 Which "bandits" backed Johnny Kidd?

28 Who went to No 1 with "I Heard It Through the Grapevine" in 1969?

29 Which Liverpool lady went to No 1 with "Anyone Who Had a Heart"?

30 What sort of "Women" gave the Rolling Stones their eighth No 1?

Answers | Late Greats (see Quiz 185)

1 Barbara. 2 Yates. 3 Esther Rantzen. 4 Sammy. 5 London. 6 Wilde. 7 Sport. 8 Motor cycle. 9 London. 10 Spy. 11 Blyton. 12 Victoria. 13 Hailsham. 14 Shaving accessories. 15 Adam. 16 Charles. 17 Film. 18 Germany. 19 Jane. 20 France. 21 Richard. 22 The Galaxy. 23 Linda. 24 Albert. 25 Children. 26 Clothes. 27 Cello. 28 Paul. 29 Fables. 30 John F Kennedy.

1 "Setting Sun" and "Block Rockin' Beats" were No 1s for which Brothers?
2 In Australia what is a jumbuck?
3 In "The Magic Roundabout" what kind of creature was Dougal?
4 What colour are triple-word squares in Scrabble?
5 What person would be a member of RIBA?
6 Which day of the year is described as Ash?
7 In "Oliver!" which character sings "As Long as He Needs Me"?
8 Who in 2005 became Arsenal's leading league scorer of all time?
9 What used to be sold by an apothecary?
10 Early Giant, Figaro and Nantes are types of which vegetable?
11 How many black cards are there in a standard pack of playing cards?
12 In printing, what are uppercase letters?
13 In which country is Zurich?
14 In the Bible which book follows directly after Genesis?
15 What is mulligatawny – an Irish port, a small owl or a type of soup?
16 What do you withdraw from an ATM?
17 Which French royal family share their name with a biscuit?
18 In the past in a hospital what was ether used for?
19 Is a kumquat a fruit or a vegetable?
20 Aloha means hello and goodbye on which island?
21 Which number upside down looks like an E on a calculator's LCD?
22 What is the term for an empty space from which air is removed?
23 Which word links a seaside confection and stone?
24 Were Luddites machine wreckers or prison reformers?
25 Which Disney fantasy film and stage show featured the song "Be Our Guest"?
26 What do the numbers on one standard die/dice total?
27 In medicine what is the term for the exchange of blood?
28 The feet of zebras take what form?
29 If Christmas Day was a Wednesday on what day would the following New Year's Day fall?
30 Foods do not brown in what type of oven?

1 What was the first name of prolific novelist Ms Cartland?
2 Who was the ex-Mrs Geldof Paula?
3 Desmond Wilcox was the husband of which chat show hostess and TV presenter?
4 Which entertainer Davis added Junior to his name?
5 In which British capital city did Lord Olivier have a theatre named after him?
6 Which playwright Oscar is on the cover of The Beatles' "Sgt Pepper" album?
7 Which type of TV show did Helen Rollason present?
8 What type of transport did Jennifer Paterson use in her TV cookery series?
9 In which city was Jill Dando murdered?
10 Kim Philby found notoriety as a what?
11 Which Enid wrote the Noddy books?
12 Which Queen said, "We are not amused"?
13 Which Lord sat in Parliament as Quintin Hogg?
14 King Camp Gillette pioneered which grooming aid?
15 According to Jewish and Christian teaching, who was the very first person?
16 Which Darwin set out his theory of evolution?
17 For which branch of the arts was James Dean famous?
18 In which country was actress Marlene Dietrich born?
19 What was the first name of novelist Miss Austen?
20 In which country did Princess Diana tragically die?
21 What was the first name of the late broadcaster Dimbleby, father of David and Jonathan?
22 The late Douglas Adams wrote about "The Hitch Hiker's Guide" to where?
23 What was the name of Lady McCartney, wife of Sir Paul, who died from breast cancer?
24 Who was Queen Victoria's consort?
25 Roald Dahl mainly wrote stories for whom?
26 Christian Dior was famous for designing what?
27 Jacqueline Du Pré, whose story was told in the movie "Hilary and Jackie", played which musical instrument?
28 Which actor Eddington found fame in "The Good Life" and "Yes Minister"?
29 What did Aesop write?
30 Which assassinated leader of the USA was the first Catholic to be elected as President?

Answers	Sounds of the 60s *(see Quiz 183)*

1 The Kinks. 2 Return to Sender. 3 Liverpool. 4 Germany. 5 You'll Never Walk Alone. 6 Pins. 7 Four. 8 Diddy. 9 Yodelling. 10 16. 11 Rolling Stones. 12 Guitar. 13 Five. 14 Nancy Sinatra. 15 San Francisco. 16 Roy Orbison. 17 Your Hand. 18 Beach Boys. 19 Congratulations. 20 Two. 21 Little. 22 Paperback Writer. 23 Four. 24 Three. 25 Dustman. 26 Apple. 27 The Pirates. 28 Marvin Gaye. 29 Cilla Black. 30 Honky Tonk.

1 How many Days were in the title of Craig David's 2000 No 1?
2 Which sportsman said quite seriously, "You cannot be serious"?
3 In Monopoly what makes a set with Mayfair?
4 What does pre mean when it goes before a word?
5 What is the ball hit through in croquet?
6 Which female songwriter/singer won a Grammy Song of the Year for "Fallin'"?
7 Which word can refer to a sporting fixture or a type of meat?
8 Which of these creatures is not in the same family as humans – chimpanzee, gorilla or horse?
9 Where do numbers most usually appear on a computer keyboard?
10 What colour is the nose of a polar bear?
11 Which is the furthest from the ground in the human body – the fibula, the patella or the skull?
12 How many leaves does a clover plant usually have?
13 Which Liverpool manager collapsed at a soccer match in October 2001?
14 Who on TV said, "I've started so I'll finish"?
15 Which creatures are kept in an apiary?
16 Which song by The Beatles mentions Father Mackenzie?
17 In which country would you watch Galatasaray play a home soccer match?
18 Horseshoes resemble which letter of the alphabet?
19 Which "Sound of Music" flower was a hit?
20 In which month is the Jewish feast of Hannukah?
21 The Lincoln Center is in which US city?
22 What do Internet users derisively call postal mail?
23 Bob Dylan's music is particularly associated with which decade of the last century?
24 What type of body does the ancient monument the Sphinx have?
25 Johannesburg is noted for the cutting of which gems?
26 Modulator-Demodulator is usually shortened to which five-letter word?
27 Who wrote the lyrics for "Candle in the Wind"?
28 Which of these countries does not spend dollars – Australia, New Zealand or South Africa?
29 Which city-state within Rome is the centre of the Roman Catholic Church?
30 Which Alan stopped playing soccer in 2006 and became a BBC pundit?

Answers	Pot Luck 84 (see Quiz 184)

1 Chemical Brothers. 2 A sheep. 3 Dog. 4 Red. 5 Architect. 6 Wednesday. 7 Nancy.
8 Thierry Henry. 9 Medicine. 10 Carrot. 11 26. 12 Capitals. 13 Switzerland. 14
Exodus. 15 Soup. 16 Money. 17 Bourbon. 18 Anaesthetic. 19 Fruit. 20 Hawaii.
21 3. 22 Vacuum. 23 Rock. 24 Machine wreckers. 25 Beauty and the Beast. 26 21.
27 Transfusion. 28 Hooves. 29 Wednesday. 30 Microwave.

Answers – page 199

1 Which Spice Girl presented "This is My Moment"?
2 Which group were formed after "Popstars"?
3 What sort of events take place according to the title of the series set in Midsomer Parva?
4 Which "Little Britain" star played Toad in TV's "The Wind in the Willows"?
5 Which series featured Sylvia "Bodybag" Hollamby?
6 What is the first name of the builder on "Ground Force"?
7 Which Denis presented the long-running TV show "It'll be Alright on the Night"?
8 Which chef replaced Loyd Grossman on "Masterchef"?
9 Which Anne presents "The Weakest Link"?
10 Who hosts a "Supermarket Sweep" on daytime TV?
11 Which chocolate makers first sponsored "Coronation Street" in 1996?
12 At what time of day is GMTV broadcast?
13 Which Steve created the comical Portuguese superstar Tony Ferrino?
14 How many people compete against each other in "Countdown"?
15 Which sitcom was set on Craggy Island?
16 What type of "Rescue" does Wendy Turner Webster host?
17 How is "Breakfast" described on Channel 4?
18 Who or what is CBBC aimed at?
19 "TOTP 2" is a rerun of which TV show?
20 What type of Feet were in the title of the series with James Nesbitt and Helen Baxendale?
21 "This is 5" was the first programme shown on which channel?
22 "London's Burning" was about life in which emergency service?
23 On which day of the week was the children's morning show "Live & Kicking" shown?
24 What was ITV1's Saturday-night show about the Premiership called?
25 In which show might tubby toast appear?
26 If Alistair McGowan impersonated David Beckham whom did Ronni Ancona "do"?
27 Whom can you "ask" on "Who Wants to be a Millionaire?"?
28 Did Channel 4 start in the 1960s or 1980s?
29 Which Tory MP Boris has hosted "Have I Got News for You"?
30 What is the first name of the older psychiatrist Dr Crane?

Answers | **Sports Mixed Bag** *(see Quiz 189)*

1 Ben Foster. 2 Round. 3 Tennis. 4 Yearly. 5 Golfers. 6 Motor racing. 7 South Korea. 8 Wrestling. 9 Cricket. 10 Winter. 11 Japan. 12 Horse racing. 13 Eagles. 14 Cambridge. 15 Bobsleigh. 16 Horse. 17 France. 18 10. 19 Birdie. 20 Curved. 21 1970s. 22 Plastic. 23 Racket. 24 Four. 25 Circular. 26 Throw it. 27 Four. 28 Every four years. 29 Liverpool. 30 10,000 Guineas.

1 What is a sudden rush of snow down a mountain known as?
2 In which part of London was the Millennium Dome built?
3 On a plane or a boat a galley is a type of what?
4 Who draws the Doonesbury cartoon strip?
5 What sort of weather occurs in a monsoon?
6 Which groups are linked together through Interpol?
7 Myanmar is a modern name for which country?
8 What is pulped to make paper?
9 What does I stand for in the communications initials ISP?
10 Whose hits this century include "Amazing" and "Flawless"?
11 The society for magicians is called the Magic what?
12 How many miles are there in a marathon to the nearest mile?
13 The Suez Canal joins which continent to Asia?
14 James Beattie and Phil Neville were in which Premiership side together?
15 How was the ancient king Alexander described?
16 War-torn Falluja is situated in which country?
17 If food is cooked au gratin what ingredient does it contain?
18 What colour is pure gold?
19 If a five shows on the top of a die/dice, what number is on the bottom?
20 Glenn Close acted in a movie about "101" dogs of which breed?
21 Which H is Britain's largest international airport?
22 Which material is used to make things in origami?
23 Who is Venus Williams' tennis player sister?
24 What is a person from Tangier called?
25 Who was the US President on 31 December 1999?
26 What did Madonna call her second child?
27 What is the currency of Canada?
28 What was the name of the explosive invented by Alfred Nobel?
29 Chris Boardman was involved in which type of racing?
30 Which of the following is not the name of a real Sea – Blue Sea, Red Sea or Yellow Sea?

Answers	**Pot Luck 87** *(see Quiz 190)*

1 Cornflakes. 2 Pacific. 3 Dish. 4 Cricket. 5 France. 6 Great Lakes. 7 Lindsay Davenport. 8 Heptathlon. 9 Finland. 10 Pavement. 11 Violin. 12 660. 13 Water. 14 Chess. 15 America. 16 Cartoons. 17 Happy. 18 Famine. 19 Two. 20 Police officers. 21 Estonia. 22 Fencing. 23 10. 24 Brass. 25 Thames. 26 50s. 27 Nine. 28 George W Bush. 29 Eye. 30 Whirlpool bath.

1 Which Watford goalkeeper made his England debut against Spain in February 2007?
2 What shape is a dartboard?
3 In which sport do players compete for the Davis Cup?
4 How often is the Epsom Derby held?
5 Which sportsmen compete for the Ryder Cup?
6 Formula 1 usually refers to which sport?
7 The Seoul Olympics were in which country?
8 Sumo is a type of what?
9 Which sport is played at Lord's?
10 Which season other than summer has an Olympic Games?
11 Which country has won most Olympic gold medals for judo?
12 The Prix de L'Arc de Triomphe is one of Europe's biggest events in which sport?
13 Which birds of prey did Sheffield's Rugby League club add to its name?
14 Who do Oxford compete against in the university boat race?
15 What do you travel in if you compete in a two-man bob event?
16 What type of racing takes place at Ascot?
17 Boules is similar to bowls and originated in which country?
18 How many pins are there in bowling in a bowling alley?
19 Which B is one under par in golf?
20 What shape is a hockey stick?
21 In which decade was Tiger Woods born?
22 What is a table tennis ball made from?
23 What do you use to hit the shuttlecock in badminton?
24 In tennis how many events make up the Grand Slam?
25 If you throw the discus, competitively, what shape is the area you throw it from?
26 If you "put" a shot what do you actually do with it?
27 How many legs or sections are there in an Olympic relay race?
28 How frequently are the Paralympics held?
29 The racecourse at Aintree is near which northern city?
30 Which of the following is not a major horse race in Britain – 1,000 Guineas, 2,000 Guineas, 10,000 Guineas?

Answers	TV: Trivia *(see Quiz 187)*

1 Mel B. 2 Hear'Say. 3 Murders. 4 Matt Lucas. 5 Bad Girls. 6 Jonny. 7 Denis Norden. 8 Gary Rhodes. 9 Robinson. 10 Dale Winton. 11 Cadbury's. 12 Morning. 13 Coogan. 14 Two. 15 Father Ted. 16 Pet. 17 Big. 18 Children. 19 Top of the Pops. 20 Cold. 21 Channel 5. 22 Fire brigade. 23 Saturday. 24 The Premiership. 25 Teletubbies. 26 Victoria Beckham. 27 The audience. 28 1980s. 29 Boris Johnson. 30 Frasier.

1 WK Kellogg created which present-day breakfast favourite in the 19th century?
2 The name of which ocean means peace?
3 Which kitchen item is linked to receiving satellite television?
4 Which sport has wooden uprights that are 22 yards apart?
5 Which country did Renault cars originally come from?
6 Lakes Michigan, Erie, Ontario, Huron and Superior are known as what?
7 Which Lindsay staged a tennis comeback to end 2004 as World No 1?
8 Denise Lewis won gold at the 2000 Olympics in which event?
9 Which country has the Finnmark as its currency?
10 What do the British call what the Americans call a sidewalk?
11 Which musical instrument is associated with Vanessa Mae?
12 How many minutes are there in exactly 11 hours?
13 What does a cactus store up inside it?
14 Gary Kasparov was famous for playing which game?
15 The explorer Amerigo Vespucci gave his name to which continent?
16 What did Barbera work with Hanna to create?
17 Which of Snow White's Seven Dwarfs begins with a H?
18 The charity Oxfam was founded to help relieve which world problem?
19 How many members of Oasis were brothers?
20 Which group of law enforcers was set up by Robert Peel?
21 Which of these countries is not included in Scandinavia – Denmark, Estonia or Norway?
22 In which sport is there a foil discipline?
23 How many letters remain in the English alphabet after P?
24 Trumpets and cornets belong to which section of instruments?
25 Vauxhall Bridge, Tower Bridge and Waterloo Bridge all cross which river?
26 Blondie's Debbie Harry was in which decade of her life when "Maria" topped the UK charts?
27 In sayings, how many lives is a cat meant to have?
28 Who was sworn in as US President for a second term in office in 2005?
29 Which part of the body refers to the centre of a storm?
30 What water feature did Roy Jacuzzi invent?

Answers | **Pot Luck 86** *(see Quiz 188)*

1 Avalanche. 2 Greenwich. 3 Kitchen. 4 Garry Trudeau. 5 Rain. 6 Police forces. 7 Burma. 8 Wood. 9 Internet. 10 George Michael. 11 Circle. 12 26. 13 Africa. 14 Everton. 15 The Great. 16 Iraq. 17 Cheese. 18 Yellow. 19 Two. 20 Dalmatians. 21 Heathrow. 22 Paper. 23 Serena. 24 Tangerine. 25 Bill Clinton. 26 Rocco. 27 Dollar. 28 Dynamite. 29 Bicycle. 30 Blue Sea.

1 What is the largest planet in our Solar System?
2 In space, what is Mir?
3 What's the name of the explosion that began Universe?
4 A constellation is a group of what?
5 To make a rainbow what weather conditions are needed?
6 In a storm what can be forked or sheet?
7 If the Moon looks like an illuminated circle what is it called?
8 What is a moving sheet of ice called?
9 In which country is the tropical rain forest of Amazonia?
10 Which layer above Antarctica has a hole in it?
11 Which of these is a danger to the environment – heavy rain, acid rain, drizzly rain?
12 The term fauna refers to what?
13 Which ocean is the deepest?
14 Which M is the largest lake in the USA?
15 What type of natural phenomenon is K2?
16 Which is the most valuable metal – gold, platinum or silver?
17 A monsoon is a wind which brings what along with it?
18 Which river is the longest – Amazon, Mississippi or Nile?
19 What is a meteorite made from?
20 In which southern hemisphere country is Ayers Rock?
21 Which Sea is the lowest point on Earth?
22 Reservoirs are man made to hold what?
23 Europe's longest river the Volga flows in which country?
24 Which of these regions has the most glaciers – Antarctica, Asia or Europe?
25 The water in rivers is provided by either melting snow or what?
26 Cumulus and Nimbostratus are types of what?
27 Which is the world's largest desert?
28 Which "effect" is associated with global warming?
29 What colour is linked to caring for nature and the environment?
30 The Yangtze, Congo and Mekong are all types of what?

Answers	Newsworthy (see Quiz 193)

1 European. 2 USA. 3 Republican. 4 Edinburgh. 5 DH. 6 John Major. 7 BSE.
8 1940s. 9 Wall. 10 1980s. 11 National Lottery. 12 Prescott. 13 White. 14
Scottish. 15 Italian. 16 Eton College. 17 Cool. 18 Foot and mouth. 19 Portillo.
20 Livingstone. 21 Nanny. 22 £2. 23 George Osborne. 24 Michael Richards. 25
Channel 4. 26 Heath. 27 Ireland. 28 Clinton. 29 Peace. 30 Her children.

1 In which country was Martina Hingis born?

2 Scotsman Mr Macintosh invented what type of fabric – easy clean, see through or waterproof?

3 Which ocean surrounds the North Pole – the Arctic Ocean, the Atlantic Ocean or the Indian Ocean?

4 Where can you purchase two items and still have bought lots?

5 WMDs stands for weapons of mass what?

6 Which invention was developed last – CD, fax or photocopier?

7 Geronimo was a warrior involved in the fight against which government?

8 Which missile did David use to slay Goliath?

9 Which actor John famously danced with Princess Diana at the White House?

10 Is a valise a type of dance, a holdall or a sunken plain?

11 Which Iain lasted only just over half a year as Charlton soccer boss in 2006?

12 Which ball is heaviest among these sports – table tennis, tennis, volleyball?

13 In which card game do you shout out if two cards match?

14 Who played Maximus in "Gladiator"?

15 Which doll is Ken's girlfriend?

16 Which Catherine appeared in the "Zorro" movies of 1998 and 2005?

17 "Simba's Pride" was a sequel to which movie?

18 Daniel Fahrenheit created a device to measure what?

19 Which company launched the Playstation?

20 What colour is a female pheasant?

21 Which of these will not dissolve in water – salt, sand or sugar?

22 How was Louis XIV of France known?

23 What did a troubadour do?

24 What number appears top left on a standard pocket calculator?

25 A fritillary is a type of what?

26 Aromatherapy treats people using what?

27 In 2001, which Corporation was involved in the largest bankruptcy in the US?

28 Which American hero died at the Alamo?

29 Standing down as an MP in 2005, Paul Boateng was in which party?

30 Who definitely said, "I never said 'You dirty rat'."?

Answers | Pot Luck 89 *(see Quiz 194)*

1 5. 2 Piano. 3 Geri Halliwell. 4 Networking. 5 Celtic. 6 Down. 7 Ike. 8 17.
9 Red. 10 December. 11 White. 12 Carnivore. 13 Bat. 14 Chimpanzees. 15
Furniture polish. 16 Space Shuttle. 17 Pink. 18 Murder. 19 Happy Feet. 20
Makelele. 21 Double bass. 22 Rainbow. 23 Mercury. 24 Hover. 25 Eye. 26 Letter o.
27 Julia Roberts. 28 American Football. 29 Asia. 30 Rollercoaster.

Quiz 193 | Newsworthy

1 What does the first E stand for in EEC?
2 Dwight D Eisenhower was President of which country?
3 Which of the following is a major US political party – Christian Democrat, Republican, Socialist?
4 Where is the HQ of the Scottish parliament?
5 What were the initials of controversial novelist Lawrence?
6 Which former British Prime Minister became a guardian to Princes William and Harry after their mother's death?
7 CJD was the human form of which disease?
8 In which decade was the first atomic bomb dropped on Hiroshima?
9 What was built across Berlin to stop East Germans escaping to the west?
10 In which decade was the disease AIDS identified?
11 Which money-making draw did Camelot control – Football Pools, National Lottery or Premium Bonds?
12 Which John was Tony Blair's first Deputy Prime Minister?
13 What colour is the background of the flag of the Red Cross?
14 What does the S stand for in the British political party the SNP?
15 What nationality were all the Popes between 1522 and 1978?
16 Which school near Windsor did Princes William and Harry attend?
17 How was trendy Britain – Britannia – dubbed in the media in the 1990s?
18 Which animal disease closed down vast rural areas of the UK in 2001?
19 Which Michael was William Hague's last shadow Chancellor of the Exchequer?
20 Which Ken became the first popularly elected London Mayor?
21 In what capacity was Louise Woodward employed when a baby died in her care?
22 Which value coin was introduced in Britain 1998?
23 Which George became Shadow Chancellor under David Cameron?
24 Which actor Michael of "Seinfeld" fame was in a 2006 racist comment storm?
25 Which TV Channel won the right to broadcast Test cricket after the BBC lost out in the bidding battle?
26 Which former Prime Minister Edward left Parliament in 2001?
27 Bertie Ahern and Albert Reynolds were Prime Ministers of where?
28 Which 1990s US President had the first names William Jefferson?
29 Which Nobel Prize did Nelson Mandela win?
30 Whom did Princess Diana leave most of her money to?

Answers	The Universe (see Quiz 191)

1 Jupiter. 2 Space station. 3 Big Bang. 4 Stars. 5 Sun and rain. 6 Lightning. 7 Full moon. 8 Glacier. 9 Brazil. 10 Ozone layer. 11 Acid rain. 12 Animals. 13 Pacific. 14 Michigan. 15 Mountain. 16 Gold. 17 Rain. 18 Nile. 19 Rock. 20 Australia. 21 Dead Sea. 22 Water. 23 Russia. 24 Antarctica. 25 Rain. 26 Cloud. 27 Sahara. 28 Greenhouse. 29 Green. 30 River.

1 On a calculator's LCD display which number resembles letter S?
2 Which instrument can be upright or a baby grand?
3 Who had her first solo top ten hit in 1999 with "Look at Me"?
4 Which word describes linking computers together?
5 Which was the first Scottish club that Chris Sutton played for?
6 Which direction do you travel when abseiling?
7 What was the nickname of US President Dwight Eisenhower?
8 If you have displayed 35 cards in a game of patience, how many are left to play?
9 What was the colour in the nickname of flying ace Manfred von Richthofen?
10 In the southern hemisphere, Christmas is in which month?
11 What is the main colour of the White House in Washington?
12 Someone whose diet consists exclusively of meat is known as a what?
13 What is the only mammal that can fly?
14 Who are the most intelligent creatures after humans – chimpanzees, elephants or horses?
15 What is beeswax chiefly used for?
16 What was the name of the first reusable spacecraft?
17 What colour is cooked salmon?
18 What sort of crime has been committed in the game Cluedo?
19 In which movie did Nicole Kidman provide the voice for the character Norma Jean?
20 Which Frenchman Claude played the holding midfield role for Chelsea FC?
21 Which is the largest member of the violin family – the cello, the double bass, or the violin?
22 Which word completes the song title, "Somewhere Over the_____"?
23 Which planet is nearest to the Sun?
24 What does a kestrel do while looking for its prey?
25 Where on the body might a cataract appear?
26 When texting, which letter is left out of the word how?
27 Which actress links the movies "Erin Brokovich", "Runaway Bride" and "My Best Friend's Wedding"?
28 The Dallas Cowboys and Washington Redskins play which sport?
29 The giant panda is native to which continent?
30 In his No 1 hit, Ronan Keating thought "Life" was like which fairground ride?

Answers | **Pot Luck 88** (see Quiz 192)

1 Czechoslovakia. 2 Waterproof. 3 Arctic. 4 Auction. 5 Destruction. 6 CD. 7 American. 8 Stone (rock/pebble). 9 Travolta. 10 Holdall. 11 Iain Dowie. 12 Volleyball. 13 Snap. 14 Russell Crowe. 15 Barbie. 16 Catherine Zeta-Jones. 17 The Lion King. 18 Temperature. 19 Sony. 20 Brown. 21 Sand. 22 The Sun King. 23 Sing. 24 7. 25 Butterfly. 26 Perfumed oil. 27 Enron. 28 Davy Crockett. 29 Labour. 30 James Cagney.

1 Who is the father of Fraser Heston who played baby Moses in his dad's famous movie?

2 In most of her films what colour was Rita Hayworth's hair?

3 Which Sean played Harrison Ford's father in "Indiana Jones and the Last Crusade"?

4 Which Roy had a horse called Trigger?

5 In which country was Brigitte Bardot born?

6 What is the first name of Bridget Fonda's famous aunt?

7 Which Moore starred in "Indecent Proposal"?

8 How was Roscoe Arbuckle better known?

9 What type of movies was Lucille Ball famous for?

10 Where was Ingrid Bergman born?

11 Which comedy star Charlie did Paulette Goddard marry?

12 Who was famous for Goldwynisms such as, "A verbal contract isn't worth the paper it's written on"'?

13 Which Alec played Obi-wan Kenobi in the original "Star Wars"?

14 Which Hepburn starred in "My Fair Lady"?

15 Which Fred's autobiography was called "Steps in Time"?

16 Which actor Tom turned to directing with "That Thing You Do"?

17 Rex Harrison was Oscar-nominated for which ruling part in "Cleopatra"?

18 What condition led directly to Rock Hudson's death?

19 What did Yul Brynner notably shave to play the King in "The King and I"?

20 Which series of comedy films was Bob Hope famous for?

21 Which part of the UK is Anthony Hopkins from?

22 Which actor had the first names Humphrey DeForest?

23 How was Greta Louisa Gustaffson better known?

24 Who sang "Somewhere Over the Rainbow" in "The Wizard of Oz"?

25 Who did Richard Burton marry after the release of "Cleopatra"?

26 What is Samuel Jackson's middle initial?

27 Who married Carole Lombard while making "Gone with the Wind"?

28 Which "blue-eyed" singer did Ava Gardner marry?

29 What is the surname of actors and directors Walter, John and Anjelica?

30 Who wrote "Lauren Bacall by Myself"?

Answers	**Sport: The 50s** *(see Quiz 197)*

1 Billiards and snooker. 2 Roger Bannister. 3 Australian. 4 Golf. 5 Moss. 6 Brazil. 7 Grand National. 8 Marciano. 9 Australia. 10 American. 11 Jake. 12 Tennis. 13 Boxing. 14 Helsinki. 15 Czech. 16 Matthews. 17 Knighthood. 18 Derby. 19 The Commonwealth Games. 20 Jim. 21 Manchester United. 22 Munich. 23 Derek. 24 Wimbledon. 25 Billy Wright. 26 Sweden. 27 Cricket. 28 The Marathon. 29 Floodlights. 30 Footballers.

1 Which Irish group were "Breathless" at making No 1 in the year 2000?
2 England keepers David Seaman and Richard Wright were together at which club in September 2001?
3 Which ocean is to the east of South Africa?
4 What part of the body goes after Winged to name golf's 2006 US Open venue?
5 Under which nationality did Navratilova play her final Wimbledon?
6 If an animal has not been sighted for 50 years it is described as what?
7 What kind of game is bridge?
8 Which country beginning with an E joined the European Union in 2004?
9 Which dance was connected with Marlon Brando and Paris?
10 A natural sponge is what colour?
11 What is the sport of Riddick Bowe and Buster Douglas?
12 Which insect carries the disease malaria?
13 In which decade did Wet Wet Wet have their first hit?
14 Which Sir George masterminded the Beatles album "Love"?
15 What is the first word sung in the popular carol "Away in a Manger"?
16 Which is the fastest speed – a gale, a hurricane or a storm?
17 Which country is directly west of southern Spain?
18 In which decade of last century was Thierry Henry born?
19 Suffragettes campaigned so that women had the right to do what?
20 Ornithophobia is a fear of what?
21 Which former US President died in June 2004?
22 Which bird shares its name with a famous nurse?
23 The disease tuberculosis is often abbreviated to which initials?
24 Which letter is the symbol of the euro currency?
25 What colour is a female blackbird?
26 The Marquis of Queensberry established rules relating to what?
27 How many noughts appear when one million is written in figures?
28 How does a venomous snake kill things?
29 A wishbone resembles letter of the alphabet?
30 What is the name of the system that enables humans to breathe?

Answers | **Famous Firsts** (see Quiz 198)

1 Fernando Alonso. 2 Zip fastener. 3 Neil Armstrong. 4 Chelsea. 5 Israel. 6 United States. 7 Space. 8 Psycho. 9 Heart transplant. 10 Severiano Ballesteros. 11 1980s. 12 Lindbergh. 13 Glenda Jackson. 14 Ashe. 15 Al Jolson. 16 Sheep. 17 Soccer World Cup. 18 Fleming. 19 Roald Amundsen. 20 Spice Girls. 21 Sunday. 22 Rev. Ian Paisley and Gerry Adams. 23 Climbing Everest. 24 Edward VIII. 25 My Way. 26 Hovercraft. 27 Alan Shearer. 28 Elvis Presley. 29 Brazil. 30 USSR.

1 Which two table sports was Joe Davis famous for?
2 Which athlete was the first to run a mile in under four minutes?
3 What nationality were tennis stars Lew Hoad and Ken Rosewall?
4 In which sport did Ben Hogan win the British Championship?
5 Which driver Stirling won his first Grand Prix in 1955?
6 Which South American country gave a soccer debut to Pele?
7 In which steeplechase did Devon Loch fall when victory was in sight?
8 Which boxer Rocky retired undefeated in 1956?
9 In which country south of the Equator were the 1956 Olympics held?
10 What was the nationality of boxer Sugar Ray Robinson?
11 What was the first name of boxer La Motta known as the "Bronx Bull"?
12 Which sport did Maureen "Little Mo" Connolly play?
13 In which sport was Freddie Mills a star during the decade?
14 The opening of the 1952 Olympics was in which Finnish city?
15 What was the nationality of athlete Emil Zatopek?
16 Mortensen and which other Stanley helped Blackpool win the FA Cup?
17 Which honour did Gordon Richards receive shortly before his first Derby win?
18 Which race was Lester Piggott the youngest ever winner of in June 1954?
19 What are The Empire and Commonwealth Games known as today?
20 What was the first name of Yorkshire-born Surrey off spinner Laker?
21 Which football team were known as "The Busby Babes"?
22 Where in Germany were this team involved in an air crash in 1958?
23 What was the first name of world mile record holder Ibbotson?
24 In 1957 Althea Gibson became the first black champion at which tennis tournament?
25 Which soccer player received his 100th England cap in April 1959?
26 Heavyweight boxer Ingemar Johansson came from which country?
27 Len Hutton became the first professional to captain which England team?
28 Jim Peters was the first person to run which race in less than 2 hours 20 minutes?
29 What was used for the first time in a Wembley international in 1955?
30 Which sportsmen asked for extra fees for televised matches in 1956?

1 Who was Spain's first ever F1 World Champion?
2 C-Curity was the name of the first of what type of fastener?
3 Who was the first man to set foot on the moon?
4 Ruud Gullit became the Premiership's first black manager at which club?
5 Golda Meir was the first female Prime Minister of which country?
6 In which country did the Grunge movement first begin?
7 Helen Sharman was the first British woman to go where?
8 The Bates Motel first appeared in which film?
9 Christiaan Barnard carried out which medical first?
10 Who was the first Spanish golfer to win the British Open?
11 In which decade did the first wheel clamps arrive in Britain?
12 Which Charles first flew non-stop across the Atlantic?
13 Who was the first of Tony Blair's MPs to have won a film Oscar?
14 In 1975, who became the first black Men's Singles champion at Wimbledon?
15 Who starred in the first talkie movie?
16 The first successful cloning of an adult took place with what type of animal?
17 Which major sporting contest first took place in 1930?
18 Which Alexander discovered the first antibiotic?
19 Who was the leader of the first successful expedition to the South Pole?
20 Which chart-topping girls were the first group seen on Channel 5?
21 In January 1974 British professional soccer was played for the first time on which day?
22 Which two Northern Ireland politicians reached an historic accord in March 2007?
23 Which famous first is claimed by Hillary and Tenzing?
24 Which Edward was the first British monarch to abdicate last century?
25 Which Frank Sinatra single was first to spend 100 weeks in the UK charts?
26 Which type of transport was designed by Christopher Cockerell in the 1950s?
27 Who was the first soccer player to score 100 Premiership goals?
28 "A Little Less Conversation" was this century's first No 1 hit for which late, great star?
29 Which country tops the world list in producing coffee?
30 Which country was the first to send a woman into space?

Answers	Pot Luck 90 *(see Quiz 196)*

1 Corrs. 2 Arsenal. 3 Indian. 4 Foot. 5 American. 6 Extinct. 7 Card game. 8 Estonia. 9 Tango. 10 Yellow. 11 Boxing. 12 Mosquito. 13 1980s. 14 Martin. 15 Away. 16 Hurricane. 17 Portugal. 18 1970s. 19 Vote. 20 Birds. 21 Ronald Reagan. 22 Nightingale. 23 TB. 24 E. 25 Brown. 26 Boxing. 27 Six. 28 Poisoning. 29 Y. 30 Respiratory system.

1 What type of festival has become associated with Reading?
2 In which country is an Eisteddfod celebrated?
3 What is the season leading up to Christmas known as?
4 Which Scottish city hosts what is claimed to be the world's largest arts festival?
5 Yom Kippur is the Day of what?
6 Which Hall is the centre for the BBC Proms?
7 Which religion celebrates the festival of Passover?
8 Since the 1940s, Cannes has hosted what type of Festival?
9 The Buddhist festival of Parinirvana is also known as which Day?
10 The celebrated Spalding Flower Festival takes place in which county?
11 The ninth month in the Islamic calendar is a fasting period known as what?
12 Which C is the Essex venue for the annual rock and pop Festival?
13 The Golden Gate Prize is awarded at which Californian film festival?
14 Which flower features in the Royal British Legion's Festival of Remembrance?
15 Does Rosh Hashanah celebrate the beginning or end of the Jewish New Year?
16 Which music festival is staged at Pilton near Shepton Mallet?
17 Does the Edinburgh Fringe Festival take place in summer or winter?
18 Holi is the Hindu festival marking the coming of which season?
19 The G & S Festival at Buxton celebrates which Victorian writers of comic opera?
20 Is Thanksgiving Day in the USA in February or November?
21 Did the Woodstock festival take place in the 1950s, 1960s or 1980s?
22 What does the festival of Diwali celebrate?
23 The Aldeburgh Festival takes place in which Eastern county of England?
24 The 1951 Festival of Britain saw the opening of the Festival Hall in which city?
25 In Christianity, what is the name for the period of six weeks before Easter?
26 The Lantern Festival in Japan celebrates the harvesting of which crop?
27 Is Henry Wood linked to a flower festival, folk festival or musical concerts?
28 Which religion celebrates the festival of Hanukkah?
29 How many minutes' silence are observed in the Festival of Remembrance?
30 In the USA, which bird is traditionally eaten at Thanksgiving?

1 Which comic David hosted TV's 2006 special "My Life with James Bond"?

2 Which Meryl starred in the movie "The Devil Wears Prada"?

3 What's the lowest total you can get from any single row in a 9 x 9 Sudoku box?

4 Which boy band made the No 1 album "Face to Face"?

5 Michael Owen and Titus Bramble were at which Premiership club together?

6 Which British rock band had the late Syd Barrett among its founders?

7 Which MP Clare has represented the Birmingham constituency of Ladywood?

8 Is the pub frequented by the Archers called The Bull, The Cow or The Dog?

9 Which M is the cheese used on top of pizzas?

10 Which Brad gets a name check in Shania Twain's "That Don't Impress Me Much"?

11 How many angles are there in a trapezium?

12 Which sport does Mike Weir play professionally?

13 Who canoodled with Sam the cowman in "The Archers"?

14 How many correct answers will win a million on "Who Wants to be a Millionaire?"?

15 Which two words are repeated in WYSIWYG?

16 Renee Zellweger and Ewan Mcgregor were in the romance "Down with" what?

17 Which club has had Bobby Robson and Jose Mourinho among its managers?

18 "The Green Green Grass" was a spin-off from which favourite TV show?

19 In what year was the Act of Union signed between Scotland and England?

20 Which London Premiership soccer club had Mohammed Al Fayed as chairman?

21 What type of natural disaster devastated Pakistan in October 2005?

22 Pop star Billie married in May 2001 in which US city?

23 The WI became what type of Girls in the movie where they bared all for charity?

24 What is the name of the Gloucestershire home of Prince Charles?

25 In 2005 Charlotte Church released an album called "Tissues and" what?

26 Which vegetable in recent years has been linked with the word "couch"?

27 "Boys Don't Cry" won the best Supporting Actress for which Hilary?

28 William Hartnell was the first person to play which TV Doctor?

29 By what name is cricketer Mudhsuden Singh Panesar better known?

30 Was David Beckham's first son named after an area in Madrid or New York?

Answers	**20th Century Who's Who?** *(see Quiz 202)*

1 Andy Warhol. 2 Marinus van der Lubbe. 3 Jonathan Aitken. 4 Brian Epstein. 5 Gorbachev. 6 Margaret Thatcher. 7 Princess Diana. 8 Victoria. 9 Jean Shrimpton. 10 Juan Carlos. 11 Shaw. 12 Tutankhamun. 13 Jimmy Carter. 14 Gordon Brown. 15 Mother Theresa. 16 Ken Livingstone. 17 Jim Henson. 18 Alex Ferguson. 19 Sutch. 20 Paul McCartney. 21 Martin Luther King. 22 Agnetha. 23 Dior. 24 India. 25 Albert Einstein. 26 John Paul I. 27 Elvis Presley. 28 Yuri Gagarin. 29 Marilyn Monroe. 30 Elizabeth II.

1 Which is the main river of Dublin?
2 Which village with a shrine is found in Co. Mayo?
3 What sort of building was the focal point of the Easter Rising?
4 Which river is famous for Tara, home of the Kings of Ireland?
5 Which ocean does Cork border?
6 Which river flows through Belfast?
7 Blarney Castle is in which county?
8 Which shellfish does Dublin give its name to?
9 How many Irish counties are bigger than Co. Cork?
10 What is Ireland's biggest Lough?
11 Which famous 9th-century book is in Trinity College?
12 Which M is the county where Trim Castle is situated?
13 Which C is the river on which Galway stands?
14 Which city of Co. Londonderry is on the river Foyle?
15 Which leader has a home in Phoenix Park?
16 Which freshwater food fish is Lough Conn famous for?
17 Grafton Street is most famous for what?
18 What are the most famous mountains of County Down?
19 Donegal is famous for which fabric?
20 Is Larne to the north or south of Belfast?
21 Which Merseyside city is Dublin linked to by ferry?
22 Are the Aran Islands in the Atlantic or the Irish Sea?
23 Which K is Ireland's only inland city?
24 In which city is Crumlin Road gaol?
25 Which E is the county town of Fermanagh?
26 Armagh, the Orchard County, is known for which fruit?
27 Which is Dublin's main thoroughfare?
28 Which river S has a tidal estuary in Limerick?
29 In which Dublin street is St Patrick's Cathedral?
30 Is Dromore Castle in the north or south of Ireland?

Answers	Festivals (see Quiz 199)

1 Rock festival. 2 Wales. 3 Advent. 4 Edinburgh. 5 Atonement. 6 Albert Hall. 7 Judaism. 8 Film Festival. 9 Nirvana Day. 10 Lincolnshire. 11 Ramadan. 12 Chelmsford. 13 San Franciscan. 14 Poppy. 15 Beginning. 16 Glastonbury. 17 Summer. 18 Spring. 19 Gilbert & Sullivan. 20 November. 21 1960s. 22 Light. 23 Suffolk. 24 London. 25 Lent. 26 Rice 27 Musical concerts. 28 Judaism. 29 Two minutes. 30 Turkey.

1 Who thought that everyone would be famous for 15 minutes?
2 Who was said to have started the fire in the Reichstag in 1933?
3 Which ex-cabinet minister Jonathan was jailed for 18 months in 1999?
4 Who was manager of The Beatles?
5 Which Russian introduced policies of glasnost?
6 Who became the first woman to lead a British political party?
7 Whose dresses raised £2 million for charity in a June 1997 auction?
8 Which British monarch died in 1901?
9 Which 1960s model was known as "The Shrimp"?
10 Who became king of Spain in the 1970s after General Franco's death?
11 Which GB wrote the play "Pygmalion" that was adapted into "My Fair Lady"?
12 Whose ancient tomb was discovered in Egypt in 1922?
13 Who was the ex-peanut farmer who became US President?
14 Who delivered Labour's first budget of the 1990s?
15 Who was awarded a Nobel Peace Prize for her work with the poor in India?
16 Which Ken was leader of the GLC?
17 Who was the man who created "The Muppets"?
18 Which Scot became Man Utd manager in 1986?
19 Which Screaming Lord stood unsuccessfully in many parliamentary elections?
20 Which pop star in the news in 2006 married Linda Eastman in the 1960s?
21 Who declared he had "a dream" where all Americans would live as equals?
22 Who teamed up with Benny, Bjorn and Anni-Frid to form Abba?
23 Which Christian unveiled the New Look of the late 1940s?
24 Mahatma Gandhi led the non-violent struggle for which country to break free from Britain?
25 Who formulated the theory of relativity early in the century?
26 Who did Pope John Paul II succeed as Pope?
27 Fans visited Graceland to pay homage to which rock legend?
28 Which Yuri made the first human journey into space?
29 Which blonde icon made her name in "Gentlemen Prefer Blondes"?
30 Who was the second Queen of England in the 20th century?

Answers	**Pot Luck 91** *(see Quiz 200)*

1 David Walliams. 2 Meryl Streep. 3 6 (1,2,3). 4 Westlife. 5 Newcastle. 6 Pink Floyd. 7 Short. 8 Bull. 9 Mozzarella. 10 Brad Pitt. 11 Four. 12 Golf. 13 Ruth Archer. 14 15 questions. 15 What you. 16 Love. 17 Porto. 18 Only Fools and Horses. 19 1707. 20 Fulham. 21 Earthquake. 22 Las Vegas. 23 Calendar Girls. 24 Highgrove. 25 Issues. 26 Potato. 27 Hilary Swank. 28 Dr Who. 29 Monty Panesar. 30 New York.

1 Which ground did Arsenal play at when Wenger joined the club?
2 Which Dutch star played throughout Wenger's first ten years in charge?
3 Which country does Freddy Ljunberg represent?
4 Sol Campbell joined the Gunners from which London rivals?
5 Which Ian, now a TV presenter, was top scorer in Wenger's first season?
6 In 2006, which England left back made a much publicised move to Chelsea?
7 The first FA Cup final success was against which NE club?
8 Who were the opponents in Arsenal's first Champions League final in 2006?
9 Which Nigerian striker moved on to WBA then Portsmouth?
10 Which England keeper was the regular No 1 when Wenger joined the club?
11 Which legendary French striker scored the final league goal at Highbury?
12 Which London-born centre half was skipper in Wenger's early seasons?
13 Which club was young Theo Walcott signed from?
14 Which Utd were beaten in the 2005 FA Cup final penalty shoot-out?
15 Gilberto Silva joined after winning the World Cup with which country?
16 Which position did Lee Dixon play?
17 Cygan, Keown and Upson all played which position?
18 Which side managed by Gordon Strachan were beaten in an FA Cup Final?
19 Which Frenchman Nicolas, later of Liverpool, Man City and Bolton, was signed?
20 England's Richard Wright played which position?
21 Which country did Sylvain Wiltord play for?
22 Wenger's second FA Cup triumph was against which London side?
23 Which Patrick had left Arsenal before playing in 2006's World Cup Final?
24 Which keeper was sent off in the 2006 Champions League final?
25 With which West Ham manager did Wenger have a touchline feud in 2006?
26 Which long-serving midfielder Ray moved to Middlesbrough?
27 Fabregas and Reyes both came from which country?
28 How many times did Arsenal lose in winning the 2003–04 Premiership?
29 Which Arsenal star was in his home city Paris for 2006's Champions League final?
30 Who did Wenger succeed as manager – Howe, Pleat or Rioch?

Answers	Sport: The 90s (see Quiz 207)

1 Three. 2 Motherwell. 3 Japan. 4 Bayern Munich. 5 Nasser Hussain. 6 Williams. 7 Winter Olympics. 8 Blackburn Rovers. 9 Rugby World Cup. 10 Australia. 11 Newcastle. 12 Dallas. 13 Lawrence Dallaglio. 14 Andre Agassi. 15 Spurs. 16 Mark James. 17 David Beckham. 18 Tour de France. 19 Bruce Grobbelaar. 20 Leicester Tigers. 21 India. 22 Nick Faldo. 23 Sweden. 24 Leeds. 25 Michael Atherton. 26 Holland. 27 Tiger Woods. 28 Brian Lara. 29 Dennis Bergkamp. 30 Ponytail.

1 Which supermarket used the "Taste the Difference" banner on its foods?
2 What was Take That's first No 1 single of this century?
3 Leaving their mark on America this century, who or what were Katrina and Rita?
4 In December 2005 who sparred with Tony Blair as new leader of the Opposition?
5 Since deregulation all directory enquiry service numbers begin with which three digits?
6 In November 2006, which Andy left the post as head coach of England's rugby team?
7 How is excellent usually abbreviated when texting?
8 Who was sent off playing soccer for England in 1998 and again in 2005?
9 Visiting the UK in November 2006, the "Emma Maersk" was the biggest what in the world?
10 Which "King of Skiffle" Lonnie died in November 2002?
11 Which Agatha wrote the long-running play "The Mousetrap"?
12 Which Zara held European and World equestrian titles at the same time?
13 What does the letter E stand for in the acronym NICE?
14 Who featured on Britney's single "Me Against the Music"?
15 Which season names the Bay provided the location for "Home and Away"?
16 Standing down as an MP in 2005, Tam Dalyell was in which party?
17 What was "For Rent" in the title of Dido's hit album?
18 Prince Rainier III ruled for over 50 years in which place?
19 Puri is a bread that originally came from which country – India or Italy?
20 Which 2005 TV series was about British land bordering the sea?
21 Which Buffalo side lost three Super Bowl finals in a row in the 1990s?
22 Which word completes the title of the farce "No Sex Please We're _____"?
23 Which "Corrie" couple remarried the week Charles and Camilla married?
24 Who presented the first UK government budget of this century?
25 What completes the book title, "Harry Potter and the Chamber of ____"?
26 In which month was New York's World Trade Center destroyed by terrorists?
27 On "Who Wants to be a Millionaire?" how do you contact a friend?
28 Is the name of Tony Blair's eldest child Dylan, Euan or Tory?
29 Which Hal was Burt Bacharach's long-time writing partner?
30 Who was Liberal Democrat leader immediately before Charles Kennedy?

Answers	Leaders *(see Quiz 206)*

1 Australia. 2 Libya. 3 John Major. 4 Marcos. 5 Margaret Thatcher. 6 Fidel Castro.
7 Iron Curtain. 8 Tutankhamen. 9 Ethiopia. 10 Saddam Hussein. 11 Bill Clinton.
12 Pol Pot. 13 1960s. 14 African. 15 Tony Blair. 16 Franco. 17 Italy. 18 Israel.
19 Poland. 20 Chris Patten. 21 Mussolini. 22 Salman Rushdie. 23 Clinton. 24
Tsar. 25 Denis. 26 House of Commons. 27 Boris Yeltsin. 28 Arthur Scargill. 29
Poland. 30 Uganda.

1 Who directed Kenneth Branagh in "Mary Shelley's Frankenstein"?
2 Who, according to the movie, fathered Rosemary's Baby?
3 In which Dracula movie did Anthony Hopkins play Professor van Helsing?
4 What was the sequel to "Scream" called?
5 Who wrote the screenplay of William Peter Blatty's "The Exorcist"?
6 What was the first name of Dracula actor Lugosi?
7 What sort of "Man" was Claude Rains in 1933?
8 Which Stephen's first novel "Carrie" became a hit movie?
9 Who was Transylvania's most famous vampire?
10 Which Tom played a vampire with Brad Pitt in "The Vampire Chronicles"?
11 Which creepy crawlies are the subject of "Arachnophobia"?
12 Which Stanley made "The Shining" featuring Jack Nicholson?
13 What part did Boris Karloff play in the pre-World War II "Frankenstein"?
14 Which 1978 movie shares its name with the spooky 31st October?
15 Which Sissy played the title role in "Carrie"?
16 On which Street was the Nightmare in the 1980s movie series?
17 Was "The Exorcist " first released in the 1950s or 1970s?
18 Which Egyptian terror featured in the Rachel Weisz movies?
19 What was Frankenstein's first name in the Kenneth Branagh version?
20 In which English city was the American Werewolf in the 1981 movie?
21 Which Hitchcock movie featured feathered attackers?
22 Which Anthony directed and starred in "Psycho 3" in 1986?
23 Which British actor won an Oscar for "The Silence of the Lambs"?
24 Which Michelle co-starred with Jack Nicholson in "Wolf"?
25 Which British studios were famous for their horror movies?
26 Which PM's name completes the title "The _____ Witch Project"?
27 Edward Woodward played Sergeant Neil Howie in which cult movie?
28 Sam Raimi directed "The Evil" what?
29 In which US state was there a "Chain Saw Massacre"?
30 Which Vincent was the star of "The House of Wax"?

1 Bob Hawke and Paul Keating were Prime Ministers of which country?
2 In which country did Gadaffi seize power in the 1960s?
3 Who was British Prime Minister at the time of the 1990s Gulf War?
4 What was the last name of Ferdinand and Imelda, leaders of the Philippines?
5 Who was Prime Minister of the UK throughout the 1980s?
6 Who failed to appear for his 80th birthday celebrations in Cuba, 2006?
7 How did Winston Churchill describe the East and West divide in Europe?
8 Which Egyptian pharaoh of the 18ᵗʰ dynasty succeeded Akhnaton?
9 Haile Selassie ruled in which country?
10 Which deposed leader of Iraq was captured by US troops in 2003?
11 Which 1990s leader said, "I did not have sexual relations with that woman"?
12 Who was the leader of the brutal Khmer Rouge government?
13 Was Nelson Mandela sent to prison in South Africa in the 1960s or 1980s?
14 What did the letter A stand for in Mandela's ANC?
15 Who became Britain's youngest Prime Minister of the 20th century?
16 Which General's death led to the restoration of the monarchy in Spain?
17 In the 1990s Silvio Berlusconi won the general election in which country?
18 David Ben-Gurion was the first Prime Minister of which new state?
19 Lech Walesa led the conflict against the government in which country?
20 Which Chris was the last British governor of Hong Kong?
21 Who was known as Il Duce ?
22 Ayatollah Khomeini ordered a death threat on which UK-based writer?
23 Which US President had a daughter named Chelsea?
24 Nicholas II was the last person to hold which title in Russia?
25 What was the name of Margaret Thatcher's late husband?
26 Betty Boothroyd was the first female Speaker in which House?
27 Which Boris succeeded Mikhail Gorbachev?
28 Which Arthur was miners' leader in the 1980s?
29 Which eastern country did Pope John Paul II come from?
30 Idi Amin became president of which country?

| **Answers** | Pot Luck 92 *(see Quiz 204)* |

1 Sainsbury's. 2 Patience. 3 Hurricanes. 4 David Cameron. 5 118. 6 Andy Robinson. 7 xlnt. 8 David Beckham. 9 Ship. 10 Lonnie Donegan. 11 Agatha Christie. 12 Zara Phillips. 13 Excellence. 14 Madonna. 15 Summer Bay. 16 Labour. 17 Life. 18 Monaco. 19 India. 20 Coast. 21 Buffalo Bills. 22 British. 23 Ken and Deirdre. 24 Gordon Brown. 25 Secrets. 26 September. 27 Phone. 28 Euan. 29 Hal David. 30 Paddy Ashdown.

1 How many goals were scored in the 1998 World Cup Final?
2 Which football team won the Scottish Cup in 1991?
3 Which far eastern country hosted the 1998 Winter Olympics?
4 Who did Man Utd defeat in the 1999 European Champions Cup Final?
5 Which Nasser captained England's cricket team?
6 Which team dropped Damon Hill the season he became world champion?
7 Albertville and Lillehammer were the two 90s venues for which event?
8 Which was the first team not called United to win the Premiership?
9 Which best-on-the-planet trophy did Francois Pienaar collect in 1995?
10 Which team inflicted West Indies' first home Test series defeat in over 20 years?
11 Which NE team were FA Cup beaten finalists in two consecutive seasons?
12 Where do the Super Bowl-winning Cowboys come from?
13 Which England skipper resigned after allegations about taking cocaine?
14 Which man managed victory in all the tennis Grand Slam titles?
15 Teddy Sheringham joined Man Utd from which London club?
16 Which Mark was captain of the European Ryder Cup team?
17 Which soccer star advertised Adidas and Brylcreem?
18 What did Miguel Indurain win each year from 1991 to 1995?
19 Which Liverpool goalkeeper was charged with match fixing?
20 Which rugby club did Martin Johnson play for?
21 Ganguly and Tendulkar played cricket for which country?
22 Which golfer Nick split from his coach David Leadbetter in 1998?
23 Defeat by which country prompted the Graham Taylor turnip jibes?
24 Which Rugby League team became known as Rhinos?
25 Which England cricketer was accused of ball tampering in a Test?
26 Ronald Coeman was a star international with which country?
27 In 1997, which young golfer recorded the lowest ever US Masters total?
28 Which Brian was a captain of the West Indian cricket team?
29 Which Arsenal and Holland star earned the nickname "The Iceman"?
30 Roberto Baggio was known as The Divine what?

1 The holiday island of Ibiza belongs to which country?
2 Which European country popular with Brits has the rivers Guadiana and Tagos?
3 In which ocean is Fiji?
4 Is Tasmania to the north or south of Australia?
5 Majorca is part of which island group?
6 In which country is Vigo airport?
7 What is the principal seaside resort of the North Norfolk coast?
8 What name is given to America's most westerly time zone?
9 On which European island is the beach of Mazzaro?
10 The resort of Kuta is on which island – Bali or Malta?
11 What colour flag is awarded to quality beaches in Europe?
12 On which island is North Front airport?
13 The Californian coast fronts which ocean?
14 Which island are you on if you visit Mellieha?
15 In Australia, which state is commonly called the "Sunshine State"?
16 Tenerife is part of which island group?
17 In which country is the much-visited Saumur Castle?
18 The Isle of Tiree is part of which country?
19 In which country is Luxor airport?
20 Did "Captain Corelli's Mandolin" feature a Greek island or an Italian one?
21 What is another name for Tonga?
22 Which famous surfing beach is on the outskirts of Sydney?
23 Ludwig II built a fairytale style castle situated in which European country?
24 What is the largest city of Hawaii?
25 Which Italian island has a famous Blue Grotto?
26 The beautiful city of Florence stands on which river?
27 What is the oldest and largest city in Australia?
28 Salina Bay is on which island?
29 In which country would you find the capital city of Ankara?
30 Which US state are you visiting if you are in Miami?

1 Which Brit was first ranked in the top 100 tennis stars in 2005?
2 Who was the female lead of the film "Dreamgirls"?
3 Actress Eva Green was the leading lady in which Bond film?
4 Which rugby league side were voted Team of the Year at the 2006 BBC awards?
5 Which pop charity concert took place at the same time as 2005's G8 summit?
6 Tilda Swinton was which Witch in 2005's "The Lion, the Witch and the Wardrobe"?
7 Who had a 2004 No 1 single with "Obviously" – McFly or Oasis?
8 Was the movie "Million Dollar Baby" about boxing or baseball?
9 Which country was invaded by the United States and Britain in March 2003?
10 What did Dionicio Ceron win in London in 1994, 1995 and 1996?
11 David Suchet was famed for playing for which character Hercule?
12 What was Ian Huntley's job when he carried out the Soham murders?
13 What does a BACS system transfer – blood, footballers or money?
14 Martha Huber was killed in which series with Housewives in the title?
15 Is the letter M on the top, middle or bottom row of letters on a keyboard?
16 Martina Navratilova won most of her doubles trophies with which partner Pam?
17 In advertising what is the last name of the brothers Charles and Maurice?
18 "Waterloo" was the first hit for which group who became the subject of a musical?
19 Which Michael starred with Sandra Bullock in the film "Miss Congeniality"?
20 Which name links singers Grace, Howard, Norah and Tom?
21 Robbie Williams made a 2005 album about what sort of "Care"?
22 Stamp duty is normally paid on the sale of what – houses or stamps?
23 Which Ian played Mel Hutchwright in "Coronation Street"?
24 What letter is next to the right of the "Y" on a Qwerty keyboard?
25 Was Cruz Beckham born in England, Scotland or Spain?
26 What did David Walliams swim to raise money for charity in 2006?
27 Was the hero of the Mel Gibson's "Braveheart" English, Scottish or Welsh?
28 Which writer Jaqueline was children's laureate in 2005?
29 Did Nelson Mandela become S. African president in the 1960s, 1970s or 1990s?
30 David Beckham announced he would leave Real Madrid and play in which country?

Answers | Pot Luck 94 *(see Quiz 211)*

1 Numbers. 2 50 Cent. 3 Johnny Depp. 4 Bernhard Langer. 5 Ian McKellen. 6 Iraq.
7 Petula Clark. 8 Oak. 9 Sender. 10 Sistine Chapel. 11 Lancashire. 12 China. 13
Angel. 14 James. 15 Ireland. 16 Britney Spears. 17 Sean Connery. 18 Cucumber.
19 Madonna. 20 Robert. 21 Oxford. 22 Christopher Eccleston. 23 1990s. 24
Guy Ritchie. 25 Dublin. 26 Thomas. 27 Max Clifford. 28 Steffi Graf. 29 Five. 30
Norah Jones.

1 Which Sheila, widow of John Thaw, starred in the 2006 revival of "Cabaret"?
2 Which movie Mary played by Julie Andrews came to the London stage?
3 What is the full name of the musical known as "Les Mis"?
4 A man-eating what was the subject of "Little Shop of Horrors"?
5 Was the musical "Cats" based on poems or paintings?
6 Which John of "Torchwood" appeared on the musical stage with Elaine Paige?
7 "How Do You Solve a Problem Like Maria" was a TV contest linked to which musical?
8 Which knighted superstar wrote the music for "Billy Elliot"?
9 In which musical about women in jail does "Cell Block Tango" appear?
10 In which musical does Frank N Furter appear?
11 Which show does "I Don't Know How to Love Him" come from?
12 In "Starlight Express" what do the performers wear on their feet?
13 Which Alan wrote the words for "My Fair Lady" and "Camelot"?
14 From which musical does the song "One" come?
15 Which "Boulevard" is the title of a musical?
16 Lloyd Webber's musical "The Woman in White" is based on whose novel?
17 Which musical is about a cub called Simba?
18 "Spamalot" was based on which cult TV show?
19 The story of "Evita" takes place in which country?
20 What sort of Dancing hit the stage nearly 20 years after Patrick Swayze's film?
21 "Wicked" was based on which classic story immortalised by Judy Garland?
22 "The Producers" is set in which city famous for its Broadway theatres?
23 "Dancing in the Streets" is based on which Detroit record label?
24 Which theatre, famed for "Mamma Mia", has a name linked to Prince Charles?
25 Which name links with Porgy in a 2006 Trevor Nunn revival?
26 In "Phantom of the Opera", in which French city is the Opera?
27 Is "Mack and Mabel" about silent movies or 1930s Berlin?
28 Was the West End musical, "The Woman in Black" or "The Woman in White"?
29 In Frank Loesser's classic what links with Guys?
30 "We Will Rock You" was based on the music of which regal-sounding band?

Answers	**Holiday Destinations** *(see Quiz 208)*

1 Spain. 2 Portugal. 3 Pacific. 4 South. 5 Balearics. 6 Spain. 7 Cromer. 8 Pacific. 9 Sicily. 10 Bali. 11 Blue. 12 Gibraltar. 13 Pacific. 14 Malta. 15 Queensland. 16 Canaries. 17 France. 18 Scotland. 19 Egypt. 20 Greek. 21 Friendly Islands. 22 Bondi beach. 23 Germany. 24 Honolulu. 25 Capri. 26 River Arno. 27 Sydney. 28 Malta. 29 Turkey. 30 Florida.

1 What does the solver have to write into the grid in a kakuro puzzle?
2 Who took "P.I.M.P." into the 2003 charts?
3 The movie "The Brave" was the directorial debut of which actor Johnny?
4 Which German was Europe's captain in the 2004 Ryder Cup?
5 Which Ian has played Gandalf the Grey in film and Widow Twankey on stage?
6 Which country with Q as the last letter has four letters in its name?
7 Who went "Downtown" in the charts in the 1960s and the 1980s?
8 The leaves of which tree feature as the symbol of the National Trust?
9 Where does bounced e mail return to?
10 Which famous building is used for the election of a pope?
11 England cricket skippers Atherton and Flintoff played for which county?
12 In the 2004 Olympics, which country won the most gold medals after the US?
13 Whom did Jane Asher play in the short-lived revival of "Crossroads"?
14 Which one of Thomas the Tank Engine's friends is somewhat vain?
15 In which country beginning with I were Victoria and David Beckham married?
16 Whose second album was called "Oops I Did It Again"?
17 Who was the first non-Englishman to play the role of James Bond?
18 Is a Tokyo Slicer a cucumber, an oriental sword or a word game?
19 Which American sang about "American Life" and "American Pie"?
20 Does the R in R Kelly's name stand for Robert, Roy or Rupert?
21 Where is the Radcliffe Camera?
22 Who first played Dr Who in the 2005 revival of the show?
23 Did the Channel Tunnel open to the public in the 1970s, 1990s or in 2000?
24 Which Guy directed the 2005 movie "Revolver"?
25 The Abbey Theatre is in which Irish city?
26 Which Tank Engine celebrated its 60th anniversary in 2005?
27 Which Max's memoirs were called "Read All About It"?
28 Which tennis player married Andre Agassi early this century?
29 How many "Desperate Housewives" featured in the original series?
30 Ravi Shankar is the father of which album-topping Norah?

Quiz 212 | Double Take

Answers – page 224

LEVEL 1

1 Which word can mean to hinder and can be a basket of food?
2 Which word for an aquatic bird can also be an order to take cover?
3 Which word for a money container also means to pucker the lips?
4 Which word for stripes can also mean rock groups?
5 Which word for a female's garment also means to tend a wound?
6 Which word for lazy is the surname of Eric of "Monty Python" fame?
7 Which word can be a chess piece or a cleric?
8 Which word meaning to laze around describes a quantity of bread?
9 Which word for a main performer can also mean a heavenly body?
10 Which fish shares a name with a place for a bird to rest?
11 Which word names a shrub as well as a stiff bristled brush?
12 Which word for financially in the black can also be a dissolving substance?
13 Which flat fish shares a name with part of the foot?
14 Which word describes where someone lives as well as a speech?
15 Which word can mean to drill and to be tiresome and dull?
16 Which word can be a dish or it can mean to send down a delivery in cricket?
17 Which word for a pointed weapon is also part of an asparagus?
18 Which word is a measurement for horses and a dealing of playing cards?
19 Which British Prime Minister of the 1970s also means a large open space?
20 Which word describes a piece of hair or a barrier on a canal?
21 Which word for oars also means to walk through water?
22 Which word for illumination can also mean not heavy?
23 Which borough of London shares a name with the cry of a dog?
24 Which word for grumbling also is the quarry on the Glorious Twelfth?
25 Which name of a bird also means to gulp?
26 Which word for something found on a beach can also be part of an egg?
27 Which word links a chess piece and an ancient soldier?
28 Which word for lightly cooked meat also means infrequent?
29 Which word can be the flow of electricity or mean up to date?
30 Which word for a corpse can also mean fullness of flavour?

Answers | **Tiger Woods** *(see Quiz 214)*

1 Hoylake. **2** Erin Nordegren. **3** Tom Lehman. **4** California. **5** Earl. **6** US Masters. **7** None. **8** Eldrick. **9** Caddie. **10** Pebble Beach. **11** Jack Nicklaus. **12** St Andrews. **13** Singh. **14** Elin. **15** His father. **16** Roger Federer. **17** Hawaii. **18** Nike. **19** 15 strokes. **20** September. **21** 21 years. **22** Augusta. **23** US Masters. **24** Gary Player. **25** None. **26** Walter Hagen. **27** The Open. **28** US Masters. **29** 2006. **30** US Masters 2006.

1 Prince William graduated from which Scottish university in 2005?
2 Which album by The Beatles was released in 2006?
3 Who is the most well-known employee of cartoon character Mr Burns?
4 In which Australian city is the WACA cricket ground?
5 Which John wrote the book "Mission Song"?
6 Which singer Bob became a Tory Party's adviser on global warming in Nov. 2005?
7 Sam Walton founded which US-based chain of stores?
8 A bruschetta is fried or toasted what?
9 What is the first name of supermodel Ms MacPherson, dubbed "The Body"?
10 Queens is the largest borough in which famous American city?
11 Which David had a No 1 album with "Life in Slow Motion"?
12 Which Colin featured with Al Pacino in the movie "The Recruit"?
13 In "Cats" which showstopper does Grizabella remember to sing?
14 A millennium best seller, what is added to champagne to make Bucks Fizz?
15 In which city is the Dome of the Rock?
16 Which Keanu played the lead in "The Matrix" series of movies?
17 If IC stands for Inter-Continental what does M stand for in ICBM?
18 Pippa and Patrick lived next door to which elderly sitcom couple?
19 Which movie actress links "Gangs of New York" and "In Her Shoes"?
20 A sufferer from alopecia is likely to lose what?
21 Who or what are James M Cox and Norman Manley International?
22 In which programme did Desmond Lynam replace Richard Whiteley?
23 The term alter ego originated from which language?
24 Which Katie is better known as Jordan?
25 In a Sudoku what is usually fitted back into the frame?
26 Max and Dr Russell worked as what in "Inspector Morse"?
27 How is a footpath indicated on a modern map?
28 Who was the Labour Party's youngest ever leader of the 20th century?
29 In Roman Polanski's movie "Oliver Twist" which Ben was Fagin?
30 Who sold No. 32 Smith Square in February 2007?

Answers – page 222

1 At which course did Tiger win the Open in 2006?
2 To whom did Tiger Woods get married in October 2004?
3 Which Tom was Tiger's captain in the US 2006 Ryder Cup team?
4 Which C is the state in which he was born?
5 Was his father called Earl, Elton or Ethan?
6 What was the first major he won back in 1997?
7 How many players before him had won four consecutive majors?
8 What is Tiger's actual first name?
9 What role did Steve Williams play in the Open in 2006?
10 At which Beach did he run away with the 2000 US open?
11 Before Tiger, which Jack was the youngest player to win a career grand slam?
12 At which Scottish course did Tiger first win the Open?
13 Which Vijay from Fiji won the US Masters to stop Tiger winning all four majors in a year?
14 What is his wife's name?
15 Tiger dedicated his 2006 Open win to the memory of which person?
16 Which tennis player pipped Tiger as BBC Overseas Personality in 2006?
17 The 2006 PGA Grand Slam of Golf was played at Poipu Beach in where?
18 Tiger deals with which sportswear company with four letters, the first one N?
19 Was Tiger's new record in the 2000 US Open a winning margin of 10, 15 or 19?
20 In which month did Tiger play in the 2006 Ryder Cup – May or September?
21 Was Tiger 19, 21 or 24 when he became the youngest US Masters winner?
22 Which A was the venue for his US Masters triumph of 1997?
23 Which major of 2001 gave him his fourth consecutive major?
24 Who is the only Gary to share Tiger's feat of winning all four majors?
25 How many majors did he win in 2003 and 2004?
26 Tiger's eleventh major took him level with which great player Walter of the 1920s?
27 After winning which major in 2006 did he break down and weep at the 18th?
28 Tiger established the lowest ever winning total in which of the majors?
29 In which year did Tiger complete his hat trick of British Open titles?
30 What was the last event that Tiger played when his father was alive?

Answers	**Double Take** *(see Quiz 212)*

1 Hamper. 2 Duck. 3 Purse. 4 Bands. 5 Dress. 6 Idle. 7 Bishop. 8 Loaf. 9 Star. 10 Perch. 11 Broom. 12 Solvent. 13 Sole. 14 Address. 15 Bore. 16 Bowl. 17 Spear. 18 Hand. 19 Heath. 20 Lock. 21 Paddles. 22 Light. 23 Barking. 24 Grouse. 25 Swallow. 26 Shell. 27 Knight. 28 Rare. 29 Current. 30 Body.

Quiz 215 | Pot Luck 96

1 Which Helen won the Emmy for Best Actress at the 2006 TV Awards?
2 In which decade was Sven Goran Eriksson born?
3 What was Grace's surname in the comedy "Will and Grace"?
4 In which French city did unrest begin on the streets in October 2005?
5 UK soap "Hollyoaks" featured a map of which place in its opening credits?
6 Which Bob introduced "Shooting Stars" along with Vic Reeves?
7 What letter is used for numbers relating to food additives – A, E or X?
8 Who was the first man to claim 13 tennis Grand Slam titles?
9 Is good behaviour on the net known as netiquette or nice-loading?
10 Which lady won gold in the Sydney Olympics in the 100m, 200m and 4 x 4 relay?
11 Which Terry of the Monthy Python team made the movie "The Brothers Grimm"?
12 How many goals did Wayne Rooney score in the 2006 World Cup in Germany?
13 Which band did Morrissey leave to go solo – The Browns or The Smiths?
14 Which Stephen was the first Irishmam to win the Tour de France?
15 Which one-time pop princess was Dr Who's assistant in the 2005 series?
16 Who did Victoria Adams marry in 1999?
17 What is the nationality of golfer Vijay Singh?
18 In May 2000 what sort of virus was the Love Bug?
19 Who in 2000 became the first golfer to hold all majors at the same time?
20 Who was the father of Uday and Qusay Hussein?
21 Which Prime Minister was a witness at the Hutton Inquiry?
22 Which Ozzy had his first No 1 in the UK single charts with "Changes"?
23 Who did Man Utd defeat in the 1999 European Champions Cup Final?
24 The Dead Sea is in Israel and which other country begining with a J?
25 Which ex-boxer appeared at the opening ceremony of the 1996 Olympics?
26 What completes the book title, "Harry Potter and the Goblet of ____"?
27 Was Wet Wet Wet's "Love Is All Around" a huge hit in the 1960s or the 1990s?
28 Which actor Tom's first movie as director was "That Thing You Do"?
29 What is the name of currency of Malaysia?
30 Sabrina the Teenage Witch had a pet what called Salem?

Answers | Pot Luck 95 (see Quiz 213)

1 St Andrews. 2 Love. 3 Homer Simpson. 4 Perth. 5 John Le Carré. 6 Bob Geldof. 7 Wal Mart. 8 Bread. 9 Elle. 10 New York. 11 David Gray. 12 Firth. 13 Memory. 14 Orange juice. 15 Jerusalem. 16 Reeves. 17 Missile. 18 The Meldrews. 19 Cameron Diaz. 20 Hair. 21 Airports. 22 Countdown. 23 Latin. 24 Katie Price. 25 Numbers. 26 Pathologists. 27 A dotted line. 28 Tony Blair. 29 Ben Kingsley. 30 The Conservative Party.

Quiz 216 Irish Americans | Answers – page 228 | **LEVEL 1**

1 Which actress Grace who became a Princess had ancestors in Newport?
2 Which Kennedy became US President?
3 Which tennis player John Patrick was dubbed "Superbrat"?
4 John Ford (born Sean Aloysius O'Feeney), directed what type of movies?
5 Did Ed Sullivan have a famous chat show on TV or radio?
6 Which dancer Gene starred in the movie "Singin' in the Rain"??
7 What was the first name of silent movie actor Keaton?
8 By which first name was singer/actor Harry Crosby better known?
9 Did F Scott Fitzgerald write novels or TV scripts?
10 What was the first name of actor Peck?
11 Did Henry Ford manufacture cars or boats?
12 Eugene O'Neill was the father-in-law of which comedy film star Charlie?
13 Was John F Kennedy's father called Joseph or Bobby?
14 Did William Randolph Hearst find fame in newspapers or shipping?
15 Was Joseph McCarthy in US politics in the 19th or 20th century?
16 Which US President married Nancy?
17 Did John F Kennedy Jr die in a plane or car crash?
18 Grace Kelly became Princess Grace of where?
19 Which comic Kops did Mack Sennet establish?
20 Which Big John starred in John Ford's famous film "The Quiet Man"?
21 Which Davy died at the Battle of the Alamo?
22 How was William Frederick Cody better known?
23 Which James won an Oscar for "Yankee Doodle Dandy"?
24 Which John won the Men's US Open four times between 1979 and 1984?
25 Frank McCourt's book became the film titled "Angela's" what?
26 Which Daniel explored the Wilderness Road?
27 Which Prince did Grace Kelly marry?
28 Was John McCormack famed for painting, singing or writing?
29 Ronald Reagan was Governor of which state before becoming President?
30 What was Gene Kelly's real first name?

Answers	**Dinosaurs of Rock** (see Quiz 218)

1 Bill Wyman. 2 Freddie Mercury. 3 Pink Floyd. 4 Rod Stewart. 5 Drums. 6 Status Quo. 7 Carlos Santana. 8 Black Sabbath. 9 Mick Jagger. 10 ZZ Top. 11 Ziggy Stardust. 12 The Who. 13 Moon. 14 The Rolling Stones. 15 Status Quo. 16 Rod Stewart. 17 Deep Purple. 18 Eric Clapton. 19 Syd Barrett. 20 Keith Richards. 21 Ozzy Ozbourne. 22 Roger Daltrey. 23 Dancing. 24 Coronation Street. 25 Queen. 26 Cream. 27 Rod Stewart. 28 The Who. 29 Three. 30 Arnold Layne.

1 What type of creature was Lassie?
2 Which series had "Strictly" added to its title in the 21stC version?
3 Which current BBC current affairs programme began in 1953?
4 Ladies and gentlemen! Which programme re-created Old Time Music Hall?
5 Which TV puppet appeared with his creator Harry Corbett?
6 Which much-knocked talent show began its 20-year run in 1956?
7 Which series about astronomy started with Patrick Moore?
8 Which programme surprised its "victims" with a big red book?
9 Which children's series used the phrase, "Here's one we made earlier"?
10 Which BBC sports programme began in 1958?
11 Which long-running series from 1956 looked at the week's press?
12 Gerald Campion played which overweight pupil of Greyfriars school?
13 Which Tony had a Half Hour show?
14 What was the number of the Emergency Ward in the hospital drama?
15 Who played the title role in "I Love Lucy"?
16 What major TV event happened as Grace Archer died on radio?
17 What piece of furniture were you invited to sit in to watch some Theatre?
18 Desmond Morris presented which natural history programme?
19 What type of entertainer was David Nixon?
20 Where was PC George Dixon's "patch"?
21 What were the names of the Flowerpot Men?
22 Which London theatre staged a Sunday-night variety show?
23 Which bandleader's catchphrase was "Wakey Wakey!"?
24 Whose coronation was televised in 1953?
25 What could ITV include with its programmes that BBC could not?
26 Cliff Michelmore presented which nightly information programme?
27 What was the first name of eminent broadcaster of the 1950s Mr Dimbleby?
28 In which show did a celebrity panel try to guess someone's occupation?
29 In which "Game" did a group of National Service soldiers appear?
30 "Laramie" and "Maverick" were what types of series?

Answers	Pot Luck 97 *(see Quiz 219)*

1 Doctor Who. 2 Mads Mikkelsen. 3 Me. 4 Cardiff and Edinburgh. 5 Robin Cook.
6 Martin Clunes. 7 Cliff Richard. 8 The Fast Show. 9 New England Patriots. 10 Phil
Collins. 11 Nanny. 12 Lance Armstrong. 13 Gibb. 14 Martin. 15 Robert Lindsay.
16 Nigella Lawson. 17 Thanks. 18 Nelly. 19 Cheers. 20 Millennium Stadium. 21
Springfield. 22 Oslo. 23 Tam Dalyell. 24 Border. 25 Paul Gascoigne. 26 Kristin
Davis. 27 Venus Williams. 28 Liam Neeson. 29 Hungary. 30 Think.

1 Which Rolling Stone celebrated his 70th birthday in 2006?
2 Who was the late great first vocalist with Queen?
3 Which Pink band re-formed to perform at the 2005 Live 8 concert?
4 Which rocker Rod released "The Great American Songbook" albums?
5 Which musical instrument does Charlie Watts play?
6 Which band has Francis Rossi fronted since the late 1960s?
7 Which Carlos was in his 50s as his band first made the Top Ten with "Smooth"?
8 Ozzy Ozbourne made his name fronting which Black band?
9 Which singer became Sir Mick in 2002?
10 Which US band chose a name to get them last in alphabetical lists?
11 Which Ziggy did Bowie take back in the album charts in 2004?
12 Who recorded "Then and Now! – 1964–2004"?
13 Pink Floyd's "Dark Side of the" what album spent 28 years on the US charts?
14 Which rock veterans embarked on the Forty Licks tour in 2003?
15 Which band are still "Rockin' All Over the World"?
16 Who asked "Da Ya Think I'm Sexy" over a quarter of a century ago?
17 Ian Gillan sang with which Purple heavy rock band?
18 Which guitarist earned the nickname "Slowhand"?
19 Which Syd lived a reclusive life from the late 1960s until his death in 2006?
20 Who has been Mick Jagger's main songwriting partner for over 40 years?
21 "Changes" was a 2003 No 1 single for which veteran with daughter Kelly?
22 Which Roger is the long-time vocalist with The Who?
23 What were Jagger and Bowie doing "In the Street" back in 1985?
24 Members of Status Quo dropped in to which TV soap in 2005?
25 John Deacon and Roger Taylor play in which record-breaking band?
26 Which 1960s trio featuring Ginger Baker played reunion gigs in 2005?
27 Which Mr Stewart was the first solo Brit to top the US album charts this century?
28 Which band sang about "My Generation" over forty years ago?
29 Status Quo claimed that their songs are based on how many chords?
30 Which "Arnold" got a 2006 makeover by David Gilmour and Bowie?

Answers	Irish Americans *(see Quiz 216)*

1 Kelly. 2 John. 3 McEnroe. 4 Westerns. 5 TV. 6 Kelly. 7 Buster. 8 Bing.
9 Novels. 10 Gregory. 11 Cars. 12 Chaplin. 13 Joseph. 14 Newspapers. 15
20th. 16 Reagan. 17 Plane. 18 Monaco. 19 Keystone Kops. 20 John Wayne. 21
Crockett. 22 Buffalo Bill. 23 Cagney. 24 John McEnroe. 25 Ashes. 26 Boone. 27
Rainier III of Monaco. 28 Singing. 29 California. 30 Eugene.

1 Which BBC TV series featured murderous robot Santas?
2 Which actor Mads plays the villain in the 2006 movie "Casino Royale"?
3 What completes the Norah Jones album title "Come Away with __"?
4 Which two cities outside France staged matches in the 2007 Rugby World Cup?
5 Which politician Robin resigned as Leader of the House in 2003?
6 Which Martin played Dr Martin Ellingham on TV?
7 Who had an Xmas hit with "Santa's List", 55 years after his first hit?
8 Which show had the "suits you sir!" catchphrase?
9 Which Patriots won the Super Bowl in 2002 and 2004?
10 "Face Value" was the first solo No 1 album for which long-established singer?
11 On film and in the West End, what was Mary Poppins' job?
12 Which US cyclist was the first to win the Tour de France six successive times?
13 What is the surname of musical brother Barry, Robin and the late Maurice?
14 In "EastEnders", what was the name of Pauline Fowler's younger son?
15 Which actor Robert played Tony Blair in TV's "A Very Social Secretary"?
16 Who wrote "How to Eat "and "How to be a Domestic Goddess"?
17 Thx usually stands for what in a text message?
18 What is the first name of singer Ms Furtado?
19 In which series did Kirstie Alley play Rebecca Howe?
20 Wales played Argentina at Rugby in the inaugural match at which stadium?
21 What was founded by Jebediah Springfield in "The Simpsons"?
22 Which European capital begins and ends with the letter O?
23 Which Tam became Father of the House after the 2001 General Election?
24 Which Allan made a record number of runs for the Aussies at cricket?
25 Which controversial footballer Paul married Sheryl Failes?
26 Which Kirstin played Charlotte York in "Sex and the City"?
27 Which tennis champion had a first name the same as a planet?
28 Which Liam voiced Aslan the lion in the 2005 Narnia film?
29 Which European country has the internet code .hur?
30 Blur's 2003 album was named about what kind of "Tank"?

Answers	TV: The 50s *(see Quiz 217)*

1 A dog. 2 Come Dancing. 3 Panorama. 4 The Good Old Days. 5 Sooty. 6 Opportunity Knocks. 7 The Sky at Night. 8 This is Your Life. 9 Blue Peter. 10 Grandstand. 11 What the Papers Say. 12 Billy Bunter. 13 Hancock. 14 10. 15 Lucille Ball. 16 First night of ITV. 17 Armchair. 18 Zoo Time. 19 Magician. 20 Dock Green. 21 Bill and Ben. 22 Palladium. 23 Billy Cotton. 24 Queen Elizabeth II. 25 Advertisements. 26 Tonight. 27 Richard. 28 What's My Line?. 29 Army. 30 Westerns.

1 What is the highest even number used in a 9 x 9 Sudoku frame?
2 A4 paper is 210 by how many millimetres?
3 What is the fifth Book of the Old Testament?
4 How old was Tony Blair when he became Prime Minister – 33, 43 or 53?
5 How many days make up the celebrations of Chinese New Year?
6 How many Weddings went with a Funeral in the Hugh Grant movie?
7 What is a stitch in time meant to save?
8 Which jailhouse song was Elvis's first No 1 on both sides of the Atlantic?
9 Andy Wharhol thought that everyone would be famous for how many minutes?
10 How many different topics are there in a game of Trivial Pursuits?
11 Which number goes with "Dollar Baby" in an Oscar-winning movie title?
12 How many days are there in the last six months of the year?
13 How many dwarfs did Snow White meet?
14 Which number is represented as M in Roman numerals?
15 Which Shakespeare play has Twelfth in the title?
16 How many winks describe a nap or short sleep?
17 Roger Bannister was the first man to run a mile in how many minutes?
18 How many gold rings are there in the song "The Twelve Days of Christmas"?
19 How many men are on a dead man's chest in the pirate song?
20 Which number appears in the name of Bono's band?
21 How many hills of Rome are there?
22 Which animal is said to have nine lives?
23 How many were in the group where Georgina wanted to be known as George?
24 Which number looks like an S when read upside down on a calculator?
25 What is 4 cubed?
26 What were the "Forty niners" searching for in California?
27 Which sense is intuition or clairvoyance?
28 What bingo number is the politically incorrect two fat ladies?
29 Which number names the motorway that links Manchester and Leeds?
30 What would the Americans call the 6th of May in numbers?

Answers	**Healthy Eating** *(see Quiz 224)*

1 Jamie Oliver. 2 Cottage cheese. 3 Five. 4 Green. 5 Without. 6 Calcium. 7 Oats.
8 Blender. 9 Steaming. 10 Lettuce. 11 Chickpea. 12 Italy. 13 High. 14 Orange.
15 Sugars. 16 Saturated. 17 Fibre. 18 0%. 19 Poached. 20 Middle. 21 Turkey
Twizzlers. 22 Vitamin A. 23 Red. 24 Iron. 25 Vitamin C. 26 Seeds. 27 Orange.
28 Carbohydrate. 29 Skimmed. 30 Red.

1 How many squares are there in total in a Sudoku grid based on nine numbers?

2 Who had a 2005 No 1 single with "I'll be OK"?

3 What does w/e usually stand for when texting?

4 Which Mr Jacobs is famed for designer handbags?

5 What type of charge did the V&A Museum get rid of in 2001?

6 "Ah, Mr Bond"...how many best actor Oscars did Sean Connery win for that role?

7 What type of friend gave British teenager Billie her second No 1?

8 Is Prince William's second name Andrew, Arthur or Ashley?

9 Dying in November 2005, which horse was a three times winner of the Gold Cup?

10 Michael Ancram was chairman of which political party?

11 Which Jennifer was the star of the movie "Maid in Manhattan"?

12 Craig Phillips hit the pop charts after winning which "Big" TV show?

13 Fitness trainer Carlos Leon was the father of which singer's child?

14 In which sport can Tampa Bay Lightning take on Calgary Flames?

15 Jim and Annie Hacker were characters in which TV series?

16 What's the name of the first Builder to have a No 1 hit single?

17 Which TV soap featured the character Mrs Mangel?

18 In which month was St Patrick's Day in the new millennium year?

19 What colour goes with Simply to name the group who recorded "Stars"?

20 In 1995 which Jacques became president of the European Commission?

21 Which Tess co-hosted "Strictly Come Dancing" with Bruce Forsyth?

22 Which singer Celine recorded the album "A New Day Has Come"?

23 The city of Lincoln gave its name to a shade of what colour?

24 Which actor links "Quills" and an Oscar-winning performance in "Shine"?

25 Which leader has more daughters – George W Bush or Tony Blair?

26 Which Brit band had a hit with the album "This is Hardcore"?

27 Which actress Angelina became a Goodwill Ambassador to the UN?

28 Which Engine had friends called Terence the Tractor and Bertie the Bus?

29 Is County Sligo is on the east or west coast of Ireland?

30 Which novel featured the character Wendy Darling?

1 In which month do the Wimbledon tennis championships begin?
2 How many days of rain are said to follow if it rains on St Swithin's Day?
3 The song "Summer Nights" comes from which musical?
4 The summer solstice is celebrated at which ancient site on Salisbury Plain?
5 Fruit and what are the two main ingredients of a summer pudding?
6 Which V is a starsign for summer months?
7 What is the first name of sultry disco diva Ms Summer?
8 Which US state is called the Sunshine State?
9 Shakespeare wrote the play "A Midsummer Night's" what?
10 In which month is Midsummer Day in the Northern Hemisphere?
11 Which Lovin' Sixties band sang about "Summer in the City"?
12 Which Michael led England to their 2005 summer success in the Ashes?
13 In which city were the summer Olympics of 2000 held?
14 Which Tom starred in the movie "Born on the Fourth of July"?
15 If you were born on 4th July what would your star sign be?
16 Which US state is nicknamed the Sunflower State?
17 Which George wrote the song "Summertime (and the livin' is easy)"?
18 The long hot days between 3rd July and 11th August are known as what days?
19 Eddie Cochran sang "there ain't no cure for the Summertime" what?
20 Which L is a star sign for summer?
21 Which film and stage musical is about taking a bus to Europe for a vacation?
22 In 2005, which worldwide concerts were held to raise awareness of African poverty?
23 Which Prince has a summer birthday in June?
24 What is the least number of days there can be in a calendar month in summer?
25 Which Mungo sang the feel-good, chart-topper "In the Summertime"?
26 St Swithin's Day is the 15th of which month?
27 In which month would you go to watch Trooping the Colour?
28 Which Irish family group had a 2004 hit with "Summer Sunshine"?
29 Which Aussie bowler took his 600th Test wicket in 2005 in England?
30 In which month is Independence Day celebrated in America?

| **Answers** | **Number Crunching** (see Quiz 220) |

1 8. 2 297mm. 3 Deuteronomy. 4 43. 5 15 days. 6 Four. 7 Nine. 8 Jailhouse Rock. 9 15 minutes. 10 Six. 11 Million. 12 184 days. 13 Seven Dwarfs. 14 Thousand. 15 Twelfth Night. 16 Forty. 17 Four. 18 Five. 19 15. 20 2. 21 Seven. 22 Cat. 23 Five (Famous). 24 Number 5. 25 64. 26 Gold. 27 Sixth. 28 88. 29 62. 30 5/6.

1 Which legendary Hungarian soccer star passed away aged 79 in November 2006?
2 Which Jamie fronted Sainsbury's Try Something New campaign?
3 Which group reunited in 2006 had 1990s No 1 hits with "Babe" and "Pray"?
4 What type of flu was confirmed in Turkey in October 2005?
5 Which club did Jose Mourinho leave when he came to Chelsea?
6 Standing down as an MP in 2005, Sir Brian Mawhinney was in which party?
7 Jude Law played Lord Alfred Douglas in a movie about which Irish writer?
8 Krotons and Voords have all done battle with which fictional TV traveller?
9 Which great golfer first won the US Amateur Championship in 1994?
10 Which Jimmy was the first male tennis player to win 100 tournaments?
11 Which profession is represented by the union NAS/UWT?
12 On TV, were Bird and Fortune known as the Long Johns or the Wrong Johns?
13 Which Kate was Prince William's girlfriend when he graduated from university?
14 Are Glen Cova and Joy types of perfume, raspberry or rose?
15 In which decade of the 20th century was Bruce Forsyth born?
16 Does the word chassis originate from French, Latin or Russian?
17 Who were the beaten finalists in soccer's Euro 2004?
18 Which Marion was the first female to win five track and field medals at a single Olympics?
19 Is Idaho known as the Gem State or the Gopher State?
20 What colour were the shorts of the home team in Germany 2006 World Cup?
21 Which supermodel Naomi featured in the movie "Miami Rapture"?
22 In TV's "Will and Grace", which Karen was Grace's assistant?
23 Was 142, 911 or 999 the band who had a 1999 No 1 with "A Little Bit More"?
24 Which Northern soccer side did the late John Peel support?
25 In music ENO stands for English National what?
26 Which Elijah made his name by playing Frodo Baggins?
27 Are the trendy animated kids known as Bratz male or female?
28 How many boys were in the original line-up of Destiny's Child?
29 What was the profession of the late Fred Elliott in "Corrie"?
30 In the 2005 Ashes, which Paul of England played in only the final Test match?

Answers	Pot Luck 98 *(see Quiz 221)*

1 81. 2 McFly. 3 Whatever. 4 Marc Jacobs. 5 Entrance charge. 6 None. 7 Girlfriend. 8 Arthur. 9 Best Mate. 10 Conservatives. 11 Lopez. 12 Big Brother. 13 Madonna. 14 Ice Hockey. 15 Yes (Prime) Minister. 16 Bob. 17 Neighbours. 18 March. 19 Red. 20 Jacques Santer. 21 Tess Daly. 22 Celine Dion. 23 Green. 24 Geoffrey Rush. 25 George W Bush. 26 Pulp. 27 Angelina Jolie. 28 Thomas the Tank Engine. 29 West. 30 Peter Pan.

1 Which celeb chef was credited with removing "Turkey Twizzlers" from school menus?
2 Which has most fat, cream cheese or cottage cheese?
3 How many portions of fruit and vegetables a day are recommended?
4 What colour are the bottle tops on semi-skimmed milk?
5 Which has the lower fat content, chicken with skin or chicken without?
6 Which helps to maintain strong bones and teeth, calcium or carbohydrate?
7 Which porridge ingredient helps keep cholesterol levels down?
8 Which B is a piece of equipment used to make a smoothie?
9 Which is the healthier way to cook green vegetables, boiling or steaming?
10 Which salad ingredient can be Iceberg or Little Gem?
11 Which "pea" is an ingredient of houmous or falafels?
12 Mozzarella is a low-fat cheese originally from which country?
13 By eating too much salt do you run the risk of high or low blood pressure?
14 Beta-carotene is responsible for which colour in carrots and sweet potatoes?
15 Glucose and sucrose are types of what?
16 Which is less healthy, saturated or non-saturated fat?
17 Which anagram of brief is an important food element?
18 How much fat is there in watermelon and cucumber, 0% or 50%?
19 Which has a lower fat content, poached eggs or fried eggs?
20 Is it healthier to eat a high-protein meal in the middle of the day or right at the end?
21 Which processed food product did Jamie Oliver campaign to get removed from school menus?
22 Is milk high in Vitamin A or Vitamin C?
23 What colour is the rind on Edam cheese?
24 Which nutrient, the name of a metal, ensures healthy blood and prevents anaemia?
25 Which Vitamin in fruit and vegetables is destroyed by over-cooking?
26 Sunflower, linseed, sesame and pumpkin are all types of what?
27 Which is usually larger, a satsuma or an orange?
28 Carb is an abbreviation of which food term?
29 Which has less fat, skimmed milk or Channel Islands milk?
30 What colour is the salad ingredient radicchio?

1 Which two numbers are missing from a Sudoku line if they total 16?
2 What's the name of the penguin who wants to be a tap dancer in "Happy Feet"?
3 Which boy band made the No 1 album "Turnaround"?
4 Which leader David made a much-photoed 2006 trip to a Norwegian glacier?
5 Which Manhattan store is reckoned to be the world's largest deprtment store?
6 In finance, what does the letter F stand for in IMF?
7 What complete's the Craig David hit title – "Rise and ____"?
8 Alphabetically which word appears first in the acronym WYSIWYG?
9 In the 1990s, which world heavyweight boxing champion was jailed?
10 The character Vesper Lynd appeared in which 2006 blockbuster movie?
11 Which Sue was the first female presenter of "Desert Island Discs"?
12 Tony Blair was MP for which constituency when he first became PM?
13 What is the profession of Raymond Blanc?
14 What completes the book title, "Harry Potter and the Order of the ____"?
15 In which decade was the Brazilian Grand Prix first held?
16 TV's "Heartbreak High" was set in which Australian city?
17 "Eyes Wide Shut" was the final movie directed by which Stanley?
18 Which veteran rock band visited Les Battersby's birthday in "Coronation Street"?
19 Which is the only symbol in the Chinese calendar without legs?
20 What was Billie's surname the first time that she topped the singles charts?
21 Who wrote the play "The Entertainer"?
22 Which Iain was followed as Tory leader by Michael Howard?
23 What is the oldest inn in England?
24 Which Keira played Elizabeth Bennet in the 2005 film of "Pride and Prejudice"?
25 In IVF treatment what does the V stand for?
26 In which country was François Mitterrand a Socialist head of state?
27 In sport, how often is the Super Bowl contested?
28 Which Dale first hosted a "Supermarket Sweep" on daytime TV?
29 Who took "Millennium Prayer" to the top of the charts?
30 Which team went through the 2003–04 Premiership without losing a game?

Answers	**Pot Luck 99** *(see Quiz 223)*

1 Ferenc Puskas. 2 Jamie Oliver. 3 Take That. 4 Bird flu. 5 Porto. 6 Conservative. 7 Oscar Wilde. 8 Dr Who. 9 Tiger Woods. 10 Jimmy Connors. 11 Teaching. 12 Long Johns. 13 Kate Middleton. 14 Raspberry. 15 1920s. 16 French. 17 Portugal. 18 Marion Jones. 19 Gem State. 20 Black. 21 Campbell. 22 Karen Walker. 23 911. 24 Liverpool. 25 Opera. 26 Elijah Wood. 27 Female. 28 None. 29 Butcher. 30 Paul Collingwood.

1 Which Paddy led the Liberal Democrats?
2 FW De Klerk was President of which country?
3 Which Hussein ruled Iraq during the Gulf War?
4 What were the initials of the US footballer Simpson accused of murdering his wife?
5 Which Gerry was a president of Sinn Fein in 2000?
6 Dr Spock made news in a book about looking after whom or what?
7 In July 2006 which political leader advised people to "hug a hoodie"?
8 Which name was shared by Steel and Owen of the Liberal/Social Democrat Alliance?
9 Which former Chancellor of the Exchequer is the father of TV cook Nigella Lawson?
10 Ferdinand and Imelda Marcos led which country beginning with P?
11 Which Patricia has been health secretary this century?
12 What is the first name of Zimbabwe's President Mugabe?
13 What was the name of Nelson Mandela's wife during the years he was in jail?
14 William Hague was a government minister in which country before leading his party?
15 Benazir Bhutto was Prime Minister of which Asian country?
16 Which Keenan was freed from Beirut after being held hostage for nearly four years?
17 Alex Salmond led which Nationalist Party?
18 In the period 1981–2001, which two US Presidents have had the same surname?
19 Who is Elisabeth Murdoch's media mogul father?
20 In the 1980s who became the USA's oldest President?
21 What was the surname of suffragettes Emmeline, Sylvia and Christabel?
22 Who was the youngest British Prime Minister of the 20th century?
23 Who celebrated fifty years as a monarch in 2002?
24 Which Miss Lewinsky had the so-called "inappropriate relationship" with Bill Clinton?
25 Which Kray died in 2001 after being released from prison after suffering from cancer?
26 Which McGuinness became Northern Ireland's Education Minister after the Good Friday agreement?
27 David Trimble became First Minister in which country of the UK?
28 Which Joseph led the Communist Party in the USSR for over 30 years?
29 Which Arthur led the 1980s miners' strike?
30 Deng Xiaoping was leader of which country?

| **Answers** | **Pirates** *(see Quiz 230)* |

1 Walking the plank. 2 Samuel Bellamy. 3 A skeleton's skull. 4 Radio stations. 5 Robert Louis Stevenson. 6 The Caribbean. 7 Atlantic. 8 Salem. 9 17th. 10 Black Bart or Barty. 11 William. 12 Irish. 13 Black. 14 His left hand. 15 Off North Africa. 16 Red Beard. 17 Penzance. 18 Marco Pantani. 19 Baseball. 20 Blackbeard. 21 One that has been illegally produced or reproduced. 22 Bandit. 23 Revenge. 24 Johnny Kidd. 25 New England, USA. 26 Blackbeard. 27 Privateer or corsair. 28 Jack Sparrow. 29 Jolly. 30 South Africa.

1 Which former US President died in December 2006 at the age of 93?
2 Which position did Tony Blair have in the Shadow Cabinet before he became leader of the Labour Party?
3 Barbara Castle became Baroness Castle of which town which was her constituency?
4 Nicolae Ceausescu led which country until 1989?
5 What did Gandhi's title Mahatma mean?
6 Who was George W Bush's first Attorney General?
7 What is the first name of Mrs Al Gore, wife of the former Vice President?
8 Who was Iain Duncan Smith's first Shadow Chancellor?
9 Roy Jenkins became Baron Jenkins of where?
10 How old was Steven Jobs when he developed the first Apple computer?
11 Who was the youngest Kennedy brother, son of ex-Ambassador Joseph Kennedy?
12 Who was the 1st Earl of Stockton?
13 Who left for the Soviet Union with Guy Burgess and Donald Maclean?
14 Richard Beeching is best remembered for his closure of what?
15 Which leader of a Northern Ireland-based party has the first names Ian Richard Kyle?
16 What did John Prescott train to be immediately after leaving school?
17 Which Simon suffered horrendous injuries in the Falklands War?
18 Gitta Sereny caused controversy over her book about which child murderer?
19 Jane Couch became the first woman in Britain to be given a licence to do what?
20 The new British Library was opened near which station?
21 Which Diane won a court case to have the child of her deceased husband using his frozen sperm?
22 Who was in The Sun's 1998 photo headed "Is this the most dangerous man in Britain?"
23 How was Aneurin Bevan familiarly known?
24 Which Eileen was Glenn Hoddle's faith healer during France 98?
25 Which veteran film director left "Celebrity Big Brother" after rowing with Jade Goody?
26 Who is mum to Jayden James Federline?
27 Which Welsh Secretary Ron had a "moment of madness" on Clapham Common?
28 Which world leader has twin daughters called Barbara and Jenna?
29 Who was the first player to make 500 Premiership appearances?
30 George W Bush was Governor of which state before he became President?

Answers	The Last Round (see Quiz 231)

1 Spice Girls. 2 Tim Henman. 3 The cheetah. 4 David Cameron. 5 The Booker Prize. 6 Botany. 7 The artist J.M.W. Turner. 8 Toucan. 9 London. 10 Heir/Air. 11 The Great Wall of China. 12 26 December. 13 Paris Hilton. 14 Channel Four. 15 New Road, Worcester. 16 Liverpool and AC Milan. 17 Cutty Sark. 18 John Cleland. 19 Berlin. 20 Practically perfect in every way. 21 Size Zero. 22 Pink Panther. 23 Northern Rock. 24 Cent. 25 Turkey. 26 Luciano Pavarotti. 27 Katrina. 28 Zara Phillips. 29 Jonny Wilkinson. 30 Albania.

1 How is Shrove Tuesday better known as around the world?
2 "The Feast of Stephen" from "Good King Wenceslas" is celebrated on what day?
3 What is the four-week period before Christmas called?
4 In Islam what is the month of fasting during daylight hours called?
5 Which Saint's day is 30 November?
6 The Feast of All Hallows is celebrated on which day?
7 How many English Bank Holidays are there each year between 1 June and Christmas Day?
8 On which religious holiday do children go egg-hunting?
9 Which Bank Holiday falls closest to Whitsun?
10 Which Bank Holiday was designated most recently?
11 In America, what is celebrated on 4 July?
12 If Christmas Day falls on a Sunday, what day is the following New Year's Day?
13 In which city was the St Valentine's Day Massacre involving Al Capone?
14 What eight-day festival do Jews celebrate around Easter?
15 What follows British Summer Time?
16 What event was Guy Fawkes trying to disrupt on 5 November 1605?
17 What is the term for the spring and autumn days with equal light and darkness?
18 Which month has two of Britain's patron saints' days?
19 On which day of the week are British General Elections held?
20 What period precedes Easter for Catholics?
21 When does France celebrate Bastille Day?
22 At what time is there a minute's silence on Remembrance Sunday?
23 What day follows Shrove Tuesday?
24 In which month is St George's Day?
25 In which month is the day with the most hours of daylight?
26 Who sang the original No. 1 hit "White Christmas"?
27 On which day of the week do large shops and stores have limited opening hours?
28 When is Twelfth Night?
29 Which federal holiday in the United States falls on the third Monday of January each year?
30 Which Saint's Day is celebrated on 23 April in England?

Answers	**Who's Who?** *(see Quiz 226)*

1 Ashdown. 2 South Africa. 3 Saddam. 4 OJ. 5 Adams. 6 Babies/young children. 7 David Cameron. 8 David. 9 Nigel Lawson. 10 Philippines. 11 Patricia Hewitt. 12 Robert. 13 Winnie. 14 Wales. 15 Pakistan. 16 Brian. 17 Scottish. 18 Bush. 19 Rupert. 20 Ronald Reagan. 21 Pankhurst. 22 Tony Blair. 23 Queen Elizabeth II. 24 Monica. 25 Reggie. 26 Martin. 27 Northern Ireland. 28 Stalin. 29 Scargill. 30 China.

1 Which former Liverpool midfielder left Bolton Wanderers in October 2007?
2 Which former England coach was a Premiership manager in August 2007?
3 Which former Welsh international was sacked by Fulham in spring 2007?
4 Who was Sunderland's manager when they won promotion in 2006–07?
5 Who succeeded Steve McClaren as Middlesbrough manager?
6 What nationality is the man who succeeded Jose Mourinho at Chelsea?
7 Who has managed the most games in the Premiership?
8 How many English-born managers have won the Premiership title?
9 Who was Crewe Alexandra manager from 1983 to 2007?
10 Which Dutchman was a Premiership manager at the start of 2006–07?
11 Which Spanish club sacked their coach after winning La Liga in 2007?
12 Who did Chris Hutchings succeed as manager of Wigan Athletic in 2007?
13 Who managed Charlton Athletic between Iain Dowie and Alan Curbishley?
14 How did Rafa Benitez change his appearance for the 2007–08 season?
15 Which Premiership manager went through a whole league season undefeated?
16 Which League Two club has Lawrie Sanchez and Martin O'Neill as ex bosses?
17 Which country did Blackburn boss Mark Hughes represent and manage?
18 How many times has Steve Bruce won promotion with Birmingham City?
19 Which Premiership manager retired as a player, aged 28, in 1983?
20 Which club did Harry Redknapp manage between his two spells at Portsmouth?
21 Which club did David Moyes leave to take charge at Everton?
22 Who took over as Real Sociedad coach after being sacked as Fulham manager?
23 Who became Derby County manager in 2006?
24 Which former England international became full-time Under-21s coach in 2007?
25 For how many matches was Peter Taylor in charge of the full England squad?
26 Which Rangers manager was sacked in January 2007?
27 Which Scottish club did Sir Alex Ferguson manage to European glory in 1983?
28 Which manager was sacked after winning the Serie B championship with Juventus in 2007?
29 At which club was Kenny Dalglish a Premiership winning manager?
30 Who was the last England international to be manager of Fulham?

1 What bloodless execution did pirates carry out while at sea?
2 Which pirate was captain of the "Whydah"?
3 On a pirate flag, what was normally the top image?
4 What types of pirates were Caroline and London in the 1960s?
5 Who wrote the famous pirate novel "Treasure Island"?
6 From where do Disney's Pirates come from in their 2000s movie series?
7 In which ocean did Blackbeard roam in the early 18th century?
8 In which witch-hunting town is the Pirate Museum of New England?
9 In which century did Henry Morgan sail the seas?
10 How was pirate Bartholomew Roberts better known?
11 What was Captain Kidd's first name?
12 What was the nationality of Anne Bonny, who sailed with Calico Jack?
13 What colour was the normal background of a pirate flag?
14 What was the pirate skipper in "Peter Pan" missing?
15 Where is the Barbary Coast, once patrolled by the Barbary Pirates?
16 What is the English translation of the name pirate Barbarossa, Khair ad Din?
17 Where were the Pirates from in the Gilbert & Sullivan opera?
18 Which Italian winner of the 1998 Tour de France was nicknamed "Il Pirata"?
19 The Pittsburgh Pirates play which American sport?
20 What was the nickname of Edward Teach?
21 What is a pirate copy of a tape or disc?
22 What is a land-based pirate called?
23 On which ship was Mary Read captured off Jamaica?
24 Who had a backing group called The Pirates?
25 Off which coast did the "Whydah" sink in 1717?
26 Which famous pirate died in a battle with Lt Robert Maynard in 1718?
27 What was a pirate called if commissioned by a government to capture bounties?
28 Who did pirate does Johnny Depp play in the Disney trilogy?
29 What adjective goes with "Roger", Captain Hook's ship?
30 The Orlando Pirates are a top football team in which country?

Answers	Holidays & Notable Days (see Quiz 228)

1 Mardi Gras. 2 26 December. 3 Advent. 4 Ramadan. 5 Andrew. 6 1 November. 7 One. 8 Easter Sunday. 9 Late May Bank Holiday. 10 May Day. 11 Independence Day. 12 Sunday. 13 Chicago. 14 Passover. 15 Greenwich Mean Time. 16 The Opening of Parliament. 17 Equinox. 18 March. 19 Thursdays. 20 Lent. 21 14 July. 22 11.00 a.m. 23 Ash Wednesday. 24 April. 25 June. 26 Bing Crosby. 27 Sundays. 28 6 January. 29 Martin Luther King Day. 30 George.

1 Which re-forming girl group did Victoria Beckham rejoin?
2 Who retired after winning a Davis Cup tennis tie at Wimbledon in September 2007?
3 Which cat is recognised as the fast land-based mammal on the planet?
4 Who was leader of the opposition when Gordon Brown became Prime Minister?
5 Anne Enright's "The Gathering" won which prestigious fiction award in 2007?
6 What is the study of plants?
7 Who is the Turner Prize awarded in honour of?
8 Which bird was synonymous with advertising for the drink Guinness?
9 In which city did the "Gherkin" become part of the early 21st-century landscape?
10 Which homonyms could be the eldest of the next generation or what we breathe?
11 What is the only man-made structure visible from space?
12 What was the date of the horrific Tsunami in 2004 that killed around 230,000 people in South Asia?
13 Who was sent to a California jail in June 2007 for an alcohol-related driving offence?
14 Which British TV channel celebrated its 25th anniversary in November 2007?
15 Which English county cricket ground was flooded out in the summer of 2007?
16 Which two clubs met in the 2005 and 2007 Champions League finals?
17 Which famous tea clipper was damaged in a fire at Greenwich in May 2007?
18 Who wrote the novel "Fanny Hill"?
19 In which city did Jesse Owens win four gold medals in 1936?
20 How does Mary Poppins measure up?
21 What sized models have been banned from catwalks in 2007?
22 Inspector Clouseau was the main character in which series of movies?
23 Which British money-lender needed Government support in September 2007?
24 What is the sub-division of Euro called?
25 Ankara is the capital of which country?
26 Which member of the Three Tenors died in the summer of 2007?
27 What was the name of the Hurricane that destroyed New Orleans in 2005?
28 Which member of the Royal Family was the 2006 BBC Sports Personality of the Year?
29 Who scored all of England's points in their 2007 Rugby World Cup win over Australia?
30 Which country had Enver Hoxha as its leader throughout the 1970s?

Answers	**Football Managers** *(see Quiz 229)*

1 Sammy Lee. 2 Sven-Goran Eriksson. 3 Chris Coleman. 4 Roy Keane. 5 Gareth Southgate. 6 Israeli. 7 Sir Alex Ferguson. 8 None. 9 Dario Gradi. 10 Martin Jol. 11 Real Madrid. 12 Paul Jewell. 13 Les Reed. 14 He grew a goatee beard. 15 Arsene Wenger. 16 Wycombe Wanderers. 17 Wales. 18 Twice. 19 Steve Coppell. 20 Southampton. 21 Preston North End. 22 Chris Coleman. 23 Billy Davies. 24 Stuart Pearce. 25 One. 26 Paul Le Guen. 27 Aberdeen. 28 Didier Deschamps. 29 Blackburn Rovers. 30 Kevin Keegan.

The Medium Questions

This next selection of questions is getting a little more like it. For an open entry quiz then you should have a high percentage of medium level questions – don't try to break people's spirits with the hard ones just make sure that people play to their ability.

Like all questions this level of question can be classed as either easy or impossible depending on whether you know the answer or not and although common knowledge is used as the basis for these questions there is a sting in the tail of quite a few. Also, if you have a serious drinking squad playing then they can more or less say goodbye to the winner's medals, but that isn't to say they will feel any worse about it.

Specialists are the people to watch out as those with a good knowledge of a particular subject will doubtless do well in these rounds so a liberal sprinkling of pot-luck questions are needed to flummox them.

1 Stamp duty is normally paid on the sale of what?
2 In which country is Aceh province, scene of the 2004 tsunami?
3 What does a BACS system transfer?
4 Who wears a chasuble?
5 Who or what is your doppelganger?
6 Emphysema affects which part of the body?
7 Which term for school or university is from the Latin meaning "bounteous mother"?
8 Which salts are hydrated magnesium sulphate?
9 What was the last No. 1 single made by Steps?
10 What did Plaid Cymru add to its name in 1998?
11 Which punctuation mark would an American call a period?
12 For which film did George Clooney win Best Supporting Actor in 2006?
13 Where were the Elgin marbles from originally?
14 Which song starts, "Friday night and the lights are low"?
15 According to legend, what will happen to Gibraltar's ape population if the British leave?
16 Is BST before or behind GMT?
17 Which country does Man Utd's Nemanja Vidic represent?
18 How many valves does a bugle have?
19 What name is given to the compulsive eating disorder?
20 What is a Blenheim Orange?
21 Which childhood disease is also called varicella?
22 What do citronella candles smell of?
23 Which part of the anatomy shares its name with a punctuation mark?
24 Which tax did council tax immediately replace?
25 Which English archbishop signs his name Ebor?
26 Which saint was born in Lourdes?
27 Which proposal for a single currency shares its name with a bird?
28 Where is the auditory canal?
29 Where is a fresco painted?
30 How long must a person have had to be dead to qualify for a blue plaque?

Answers	**Sport: Cricket** *(see Quiz 2)*

1 Brisbane. 2 Chris Read. 3 Tony Lewis. 4 Trevor McDonald. 5 Terrence. 6 Kapil Dev. 7 Somerset. 8 Denis Compton. 9 Shakoor Rana. 10 Dennis Lillee. 11 Michael Atherton. 12 The Oval. 13 Graham Alan Gooch. 14 Langer & Hayden. 15 Headingley. 16 Muthiah Muralitharan. 17 William Gilbert. 18 David Gower. 19 Northants. 20 Lancashire. 21 Sunglasses. 22 Sunil Gavaskar. 23 Hansie Cronje. 24 Don Bradman. 25 Graeme Hick. 26 Imran Khan. 27 Antigua. 28 The Times. 29 Sri Lanka. 30 Left.

1 Where was the first Test played in the 2006–7 Ashes?
2 Who was Geraint Jones's main rival as keeper in the 2006–7 Ashes?
3 Which former test cricketer became President of the MCC in 1998?
4 Which newsreader has written biographies of Viv Richards and Clive Lloyd?
5 What is Ian Botham's middle name?
6 Which Indian was the second bowler to reach 400 Test wickets?
7 Which English county did Viv Richards play for?
8 Which cricketer was the first British sportsman to appear in a major advertising campaign?
9 Which umpire did Gatting publicly argue with in Faisalabad?
10 Which Australian was the first man to take 300 wickets in Test cricket?
11 Who played in the most tests as England captain?
12 Which is the most southerly of the six regular English Test grounds?
13 Which cricketer's initials are GAG?
14 In Aussie opening partnerships, who are Justin and Matthew?
15 At which ground did England beat South Africa to clinch the 1998 series?
16 David Lloyd was reprimanded for criticising which Sri Lankan bowler in 1998?
17 What were WG Grace's first two names?
18 Whose record did Graham Gooch pass when he became England's leading run scorer?
19 Which county does Monty Panesar play for?
20 Who won the 1998 Nat West Trophy?
21 In 1996 Darren Gough became the first England bowler to bowl wearing what?
22 Which Indian cricketer scored 10,122 runs in 125 matches between 1971 and 1987?
23 Who captained the South Africans on their 1998 England tour?
24 Which cricketer's bat was auctioned for £23,000 in 1997?
25 Which Rhodesian became Zimbabwe's youngest professional at the age of 17 in 1985?
26 Who captained Pakistan in the 1992 World Cup victory?
27 On which island did Brian Lara make his record-breaking 375?
28 In which newspaper was it announced that English cricket had died, leading to competition for the Ashes?
29 In which country is Khettarama Stadium?
30 Which hand does David Gower write with?

Answers | Pot Luck 1 *(see Quiz 1)*

1 House. 2 Indonesia. 3 Money. 4 Priest. 5 Double. 6 Lungs. 7 Alma Mater. 8 Epsom salts. 9 Stomp. 10 the Party of Wales. 11 Full stop. 12 Syriana. 13 Greece. 14 Dancing Queen. 15 It will die out. 16 Before. 17 Serbia & Montenegro. 18 None. 19 Bulimia. 20 Apple. 21 Chicken pox. 22 Lemons. 23 Colon. 24 Community Charge or Poll Tax. 25 York. 26 Bernadette. 27 EMU. 28 In the ear. 29 On a wall. 30 20 years.

1 Which "EastEnders" funeral took place at Christmas 2005?
2 Why does a glow worm glow?
3 Which comedy actor swam the Channel for Sports Relief in 2006?
4 Who had hits with "Caught in a Moment" and "In The Middle"?
5 Cambodian leader Saloth Sar was better known by what name?
6 How many holes are most major golf tournaments played over?
7 In the song, what colour rose is linked with Texas?
8 Tokai wine comes from which country?
9 In which month did Samuel Pepys begin his famous diary?
10 Whom was Lord Lucan said to have murdered?
11 Mont Blanc stands in France as well as which other country?
12 William Wilkins designed which London gallery?
13 Which city has an American football team called the Cowboys?
14 Which is the world's oldest surviving republic?
15 Which Latin words did HM the Queen use to describe the year 1992?
16 Which cave is the most famous on the Scottish Isle of Staffa?
17 Cars with the international vehicle registration SF come from where?
18 Number 22 in bingo is represented by a pair of little what?
19 What is the core of an ear of maize called?
20 What was the title of the Eurovision winner for Bucks Fizz?
21 How many did Arsenal score to win the first FA Cup Final decided on penalties?
22 Which country's stamps show the word "Hellas"?
23 Who were the subject of the Cat and Mouse Act of 1913?
24 How many points are scored for a motor racing Grand Prix win?
25 What is the largest structure ever made by living creatures?
26 Papworth Hospital is in which county?
27 Who said, "Float like a butterfly, sting like a bee"?
28 Which magazine was first published in the 1840s and last in the 1990s?
29 Which road is crossed by the horses during the Grand National?
30 Which religious ceremony comes from the Greek word for "to dip"?

Answers	**The Movies: All Action** *(see Quiz 4)*

1 Goldeneye. 2 Platoon. 3 Jeremy Irons. 4 Ridley Scott. 5 Charles Bronson. 6 Jim Carrey. 7 Best Director. 8 Wesley Snipes. 9 Live and Let Die. 10 Faye Dunaway. 11 Donald Pleasence. 12 Die Hard with a Vengeance. 13 Harrison Ford. 14 Marseilles. 15 Apollo 13. 16 Bruce Willis. 17 Popeye Doyle. 18 James Caan. 19 Irish. 20 Brad Pitt. 21 Lost in Space. 22 Phil Collins. 23 Cabbie. 24 Paul & Linda McCartney. 25 JFK. 26 Sean Bean. 27 Jeremy Irons. 28 Arnold Schwarzenegger. 29 New York. 30 Leonardo DiCaprio.

1 Which Bond film shares its name with Ian Fleming's Jamaican home?
2 What was the third of Oliver Stone's films about Vietnam?
3 Which English Oscar winner was the villain in "Die Hard III"?
4 Which Brit directed "Black Hawk Down" and "Hannibal"?
5 Who played Bernardo in "The Magnificent Seven" and Danny Velinski in "The Great Escape"?
6 Who was The Riddler in "Batman Forever"?
7 Which Oscar did Kevin Costner win for "Dances with Wolves"?
8 Who played the defrosted super-villain in "Demolition Man"?
9 What was Roger Moore's first Bond film in 1973?
10 Who had her first major starring role in "Bonnie & Clyde"?
11 Who plays the President in "Escape from New York"?
12 Which was the third Die Hard film?
13 Who played Indiana Jones?
14 Where was "French Connection II" set?
15 Astronaut Jim Lovell was portrayed by Tom Hanks in which film?
16 Who heads the crew which saves the world in "Armageddon"?
17 Whom did Gene Hackman play in "The French Connection"?
18 Who played Sonny Corleone in "The Godfather" and its sequel?
19 What nationality cop did Sean Connery play in "The Untouchables"?
20 Who co-starred with Morgan Freeman in "Seven"?
21 Which 1998 film of a 60s cult TV series starred Gary Oldman and William Hurt?
22 Who played the train robber of the title role in "Buster"?
23 What was Mel Gibson's job in the 1997 thriller "Conspiracy Theory"?
24 Which husband and wife were Oscar nominated for the song from "Live and Let Die"?
25 Which Oliver Stone movie with Kevin Costner was about events prior to Kennedy's assassination?
26 Which Yorkshireman played the IRA terrorist in "Patriot Games"?
27 Which British 90s Oscar winner featured in "The Man in the Iron Mask"?
28 Who was the construction worker who had flashbacks in "Total Recall"?
29 Where does the action of "Godzilla" take place?
30 Who played two roles in the 90s version of "The Man in the Iron Mask"?

Answers	Pot Luck 2 *(see Quiz 3)*

1 Nana Moon. 2 To attract mates. 3 David Walliams. 4 Sugababes. 5 Pol Pot. 6 72. 7 Yellow. 8 Hungary. 9 January. 10 Sandra Rivett. 11 Italy. 12 The National Gallery. 13 Dallas. 14 San Marino. 15 Annus horribilis. 16 Fingal's cave. 17 Finland. 18 Two little ducks. 19 A corncob. 20 Making Your Mind Up. 21 5 (in 2005). 22 Greece. 23 Suffragettes. 24 10. 25 The Great Barrier Reef. 26 Cambridgeshire. 27 Muhammad Ali. 28 Punch. 29 Melling Road. 30 Baptism.

1 Which Nigel went from "EastEnders" to the West End in "Guys and Dolls"?
2 Who was voted Beard of the Year 2006?
3 Spy-writer David J. Cornwell writes under which name?
4 What is the unit of measurement for the brightness of stars?
5 Which "-ology" is the study of birds' eggs?
6 Which Dire Straits album included "Money for Nothing"?
7 Who were Janet, Pam, Barbara, Jack, Peter, George and Colin?
8 In which country would you be to visit Agadir?
9 What name is given to a bell tower not attached to a church?
10 Van Pelt is the surname of which "Peanuts" character?
11 What is the best hand in a game of poker?
12 The Virgin record label was launched by which instrumental album?
13 Was Madonna's "Confessions on a Dance Floor" a No. 1 album in 5, 15 or 25 countries?
14 In the official conker rules, how many strikes per turn are allowed?
15 Which country celebrated its bicentenary in 1988?
16 What word commonly describes a spasm of the diaphragm?
17 Daniel Carroll found theatrical fame under which name?
18 In pop music, who looked into his father's eyes?
19 Who lit the funeral pyre of Mrs Indira Gandhi?
20 What was the name of Sports Relief's 2006 equine celebrity show?
21 Which comedian plays the role of Brian Potter in "Phoenix Nights"?
22 John Sentamu was Bishop of where, before becoming Archbishop of York?
23 Switzerland's Mont Cervin is better known by what name?
24 Who wrote the novel "Where Eagles Dare"?
25 Which England cricket captain had the middle name Dylan?
26 What do the initials CND stand for?
27 What is the collective name for a group of frogs?
28 Who was the first act to have seven consecutive US No. 1 singles?
29 Eton school is in which county?
30 Which country was first to host Summer and Winter Olympics in the same year?

Answers	Leisure: Food & Drink 1 *(see Quiz 6)*

1 Fish. 2 Kirschwasser. 3 Gin. 4 Sugar. 5 November. 6 Curry powder. 7 Greece. 8 Halal. 9 20. 10 Kiwi fruit. 11 Gelatine. 12 Marty Wilde. 13 Mrs Beeton. 14 Nut. 15 Coca Cola. 16 Guinness Red. 17 Clarified butter. 18 Carrot. 19 Bloody Mary. 20 Manchester United. 21 Nouvelle cuisine. 22 Aluminium. 23 Bergamot. 24 Rhodes to Home. 25 Black. 26 Tana. 27 Poisonous raw. 28 Mushroom. 29 Cherry. 30 Milk.

1 What type of food is gravadlax?
2 Which type of brandy is made from cherries?
3 Which spirit is Pimm's No. 1 based on?
4 Aspartame is an alternative to what when added to food?
5 In which month does Beaujolais Nouveau arrive?
6 Which powder includes turmeric, fenugreek, chillies and cumin?
7 Which country produces more than 70% of the world's olive oil?
8 What name is given to food prepared according to Muslim law?
9 How many standard wine bottles make up a Nebuchadnezzar?
10 Which fruit is also called the Chinese gooseberry?
11 Agar agar is a vegetarian alternative to what?
12 Which 50s pop star's name is cockney rhyming slang for mild?
13 How is cook Isabella Mary Mayson better known?
14 What sort of food is a macadamia?
15 Atlanta is the headquarters of which drinks company?
16 In 2006 Guinness announced they were to launch which colour variety?
17 What is ghee?
18 Caraway is related to which family of vegetables?
19 Which queen's nickname is the name of a cocktail?
20 Which football team does Gary Rhodes support?
21 Which term coined in the 70s describes food which does not have rich sauces?
22 What are most beer and soft drinks cans made from?
23 Which flavour is traditionally used in Earl Grey tea?
24 What was Gary Rhodes' range of convenience foods called?
25 What colour are fully ripened olives?
26 What is TV chef Gordon Ramsay's wife called?
27 Why do cashew nuts have to be roasted to be eaten?
28 What is a morel?
29 What is a morello?
30 Which drink did Bob Geldof advertise?

Answers	**Pot Luck 3** (see Quiz 5)

1 Nigel Harman. 2 Monty Panesar. 3 John Le Carré. 4 Magnitude. 5 Oology. 6 Brothers in Arms. 7 The Secret Seven. 8 Morocco. 9 A campanile. 10 Lucy. 11 Royal flush. 12 Tubular Bells. 13 25. 14 Three. 15 Australia. 16 Hiccough. 17 Danny La Rue. 18 Eric Clapton. 19 Rajiv Gandhi. 20 Only Fools On Horses. 21 Peter Kay. 22 Birmingham. 23 The Matterhorn. 24 Alistair MacLean. 25 Bob Willis. 26 Campaign for Nuclear Disarmament. 27 An army (or colony). 28 Whitney Houston. 29 Berkshire. 30 France.

1 The illness pertussis is more commonly called what?
2 Who spent longer as Middlesbrough manager – Bryan Robson or Steve McClaren?
3 Which rock is the largest monolith in the world?
4 Which Spanish team were the first winners of the European Cup?
5 What type of animal can be Texel and Romney Marsh?
6 Where would you hurt if you were kicked on the tarsus?
7 The Bee Gees were born on which island?
8 What action does a dromophobic fear?
9 In which country is the world's second highest mountain, K2?
10 What nationality is Salman Rushdie?
11 Who made the top ten albums with "Then and Now – 1964–2004"??
12 Which tanker went down on the Seven Stones reef off Land's End?
13 Which large forest is the nearest to London's Liverpool Street Station?
14 Which hit by Judy Collins entered the UK charts on eight occasions?
15 Who played Lord Longford in the 2006 drama about his life?
16 In which decade did Constantinople become Istanbul?
17 How many bridesmaids attended Princess Diana?
18 Which poet gave his name to a Cape to the south of Brisbane?
19 Which Russian town produced deformed sheep after a 90s disaster?
20 What is Paul McCartney's first name?
21 Which drug took its name from the Greek god of dreams?
22 Which is the largest borough in the city of New York?
23 Which doll's name gave Aqua a No. 1 hit?
24 In 2005, why did Richard Griffiths ask a member of the audience to leave a West End show?
25 What is examined using an otoscope?
26 What is measured on the Mercalli Scale?
27 Along with Doric and Ionic, what is the third Greek order of architecture?
28 What is lowered by a Beta Blocker?
29 How many pieces does each backgammon player use?
30 A Blue Orpington is a type of what?

Answers	**Nature: Animal World** *(see Quiz 8)*

1 Suffocation. 2 Sett. 3 Velvet. 4 Black. 5 Dachshund. 6 It cannot bark. 7 Afrikaans. 8 Mauritius. 9 Antelope. 10 Snow leopard. 11 Fight. 12 Squirrel. 13 One. 14 Cattle. 15 Hearing. 16 32. 17 Fawn. 18 Hooves. 19 Blood of birds and mammals. 20 Sheep. 21 Pink. 22 White. 23 Japan. 24 Caribou. 25 Lemurs. 26 White / cream. 27 V shape. 28 Elk. 29 Sand. 30 Border collie.

1 How do the anaconda's victims die?
2 What is the badger's system of burrows called?
3 What is the skin on a deer's antlers called?
4 What colour face does a Suffolk sheep have?
5 Which small breed of dog has a German name meaning badger dog?
6 What is unusual about the sound of the dingo?
7 Aardvark means "earth pig" in which African language?
8 On which island was the dodo formerly found?
9 What is an impala?
10 What type of leopard is another name for the ounce?
11 Pit bull terriers were bred to do what?
12 To which family does the prairie dog belong?
13 Does the Indian rhinoceros have one or two horns?
14 Bovine Spongiform Encephalitis is a fatal disease of which animals?
15 Tinnitus affects which of the senses?
16 How many teeth do human adults have?
17 What is the most common colour of a Great Dane?
18 What does an ungulate animal have?
19 What do vampire bats feed on?
20 Lanolin is a by product of which domestic animal?
21 If a mammal has albinism what colour are its eyes?
22 What colour are dalmatians when they are born?
23 The tosa is a dog native to which country?
24 What is the reindeer of North America called?
25 Which group of primates are found only on Madagascar?
26 What colour is the coat of a samoyed?
27 What shaped mark does an adder have on its head?
28 What is another name for the wapiti?
29 What do alligators lay their eggs in?
30 Which dog do shepherds now most commonly use for herding sheep?

Answers	**Pot Luck 4** *(see Quiz 7)*

1 Whooping cough. 2 Bryan Robson. 3 Ayers Rock. 4 Real Madrid. 5 Sheep. 6 Ankle. 7 Isle of Man. 8 Crossing the road. 9 Pakistan. 10 British. 11 The Who. 12 Torrey Canyon. 13 Epping Forest. 14 Amazing Grace. 15 Jim Broadbent. 16 1930s. 17 Five. 18 Byron. 19 Chernobyl. 20 James. 21 Morphine. 22 Queens. 23 Barbie. 24 Her mobile phone kept ringing. 25 Ear. 26 Earthquakes. 27 Corinthian. 28 Blood pressure. 29 15. 30 Chicken.

1 In which US state is Death Valley?
2 Which Sea does the River Jordan flow into?
3 Who was Speaker of the House after Bernard Weatherill?
4 What was the first Craig David hit to feature the word "Love" in the title?
5 Which BBC magazine was launched in 1929?
6 What did Captain Cook call the Islands of Tonga?
7 Which celebrity was murdered in 1980 outside New York's Dakota Building?
8 Who played Lennie Godber in the TV series "Porridge"?
9 Which naval base is situated in Hampshire?
10 Who featured on The Pussycat Dolls' No. 1 "Don't Cha"?
11 What is Marc Bolan's son's Christian name?
12 Which war is the first for which there are photographic records?
13 Writer Mary Westmacott is better known by what name?
14 Who or what was a ducat?
15 Which day is the last quarter day in a calendar year in England?
16 Which actor links "The Charmer" with "Dangerfield"?
17 In the Bible, who was Jacob's youngest son?
18 What was suffragette Mrs Pankhurst's Christian name?
19 In which sport is the Plunkett Shield competed for?
20 Which animal has breeds called Roscommon, Kerry Hill, Ryedale?
21 Which two countries was the Cod War of the 1970s between?
22 What colour are Rupert Bear's trousers?
23 Caboc, Dunlop and Morven are cheeses from which country?
24 Which animal can be red, arctic, bat-eared and fennec?
25 Newman Noggs appears in which Charles Dickens novel?
26 What name is given to the base of your spine?
27 Whom did Sandy Powell ask "Can You Hear Me, ..?"
28 Which actress links the films "Ghostbusters" and "Alien"?
29 Perth is the capital of which state?
30 Which word describes both a blunt sword and a very thin sheet of metal?

Answers | **Geography: The UK** *(see Quiz 10)*

1 Brighton. 2 Melinda Messenger. 3 South Kensington. 4 Stoke Mandeville. 5 Suffolk. 6 Severn Tunnel. 7 Newgate. 8 Canary Wharf (Isle of Dogs). 9 Salopian. 10 Army exercises. 11 Essex & Suffolk. 12 Bristol. 13 M6. 14 Glastonbury. 15 Big Ben. 16 Blackpool. 17 Windscale. 18 Horses. 19 Clyde. 20 Nottingham. 21 Wiltshire. 22 Edinburgh. 23 Petticoat Lane. 24 Papworth. 25 Hyde Park. 26 Aberdeen. 27 Bath. 28 Straits of Dover. 29 Castle. 30 Bristol.

1 Which seaside resort has Lanes and a nudist beach?
2 Which Page Three blonde is Swindon's most famous export?
3 In which part of London is the Natural History Museum?
4 Where is the National Spinal Injuries Unit?
5 In which county is Sizewell nuclear power station?
6 What is Britain's longest tunnel?
7 The Old Bailey is on the site of which former prison?
8 Where in London would a Canary sit on Dogs?
9 What is a native of Shropshire called?
10 What is Salisbury Plain primarily used for?
11 In which two counties is Constable Country?
12 Where is the Clifton Suspension Bridge?
13 Spaghetti Junction is on which road?
14 Which Somerset town is said to be the burial place of King Arthur?
15 Which bell was named after Benjamin Hall?
16 Which pleasure beach was the UK's top tourist attraction in 2005?
17 What was the former name of Sellafield?
18 Which animals are kept in the Royal Mews near Buckingham Palace?
19 Holy Loch is an inlet of which river?
20 Which city has an annual Goose Fair?
21 In which English county is Europe's largest stone circle?
22 Which castle is at the west end of the Royal Mile?
23 How is the Sunday market in London's Middlesex Street better known?
24 Which Cambridgeshire hospital is famous for its transplant surgery?
25 Speaker's Corner is on the corner of what?
26 Where is the administrative headquarters of the Grampian region?
27 Which city has a famous Royal Crescent?
28 The Goodwin Sands are at the entrance to which straits?
29 What type of historic structures can be found at Framlingham, Orford and Windsor?
30 Where is Temple Meads railway station?

Answers	Pot Luck 5 *(see Quiz 9)*

1 California. 2 Dead Sea. 3 Betty Boothroyd. 4 World Filled with Love. 5 The Listener. 6 The Friendly Islands. 7 John Lennon. 8 Richard Beckinsale. 9 Gosport. 10 Busta Rhymes. 11 Roland Bolan. 12 Crimean. 13 Agatha Christie. 14 A coin. 15 Christmas Day. 16 Nigel Havers. 17 Benjamin. 18 Emmeline. 19 Cricket. 20 Sheep. 21 Iceland and Britain. 22 Yellow check. 23 Scotland. 24 Fox. 25 Nicholas Nickleby. 26 Coccyx. 27 Mother. 28 Sigourney Weaver. 29 Western Australia. 30 Foil.

1 How many other months have the same number of days as January?
2 December, January and February have the maximum of how many days?
3 In the carol "In the bleak midwinter...," what is the second line?
4 Prince Albert buying one in 1841 helped popularise which Xmas item?
5 In Islam Hajj Day is in which month?
6 Which word is used to mean flying away for the winter, as with many birds?
7 What name is given to the strike-filled winter of 1978–79?
8 In which winter month is Martin Luther Day?
9 Where in Italy were the 2006 Winter Olympics held?
10 December came where in sequence in the Roman calendar?
11 Thinking Day is celebrated in February by which female movement?
12 Which winter sport uses skates, stones and brooms?
13 What are the winter months in the southern hemisphere?
14 In which winter month was Elvis Presley's birthday?
15 What do frogs and bats do during the winter?
16 To ten years, when did Charles Dickens write "A Christmas Carol"?
17 Which winter month is named after the god of doorways and beginnings?
18 What is hit by sticks in ice hockey?
19 Who wrote "Winter" from the musical work "The Four Seasons"?
20 Which David Jason TV character's name is a personification of winter?
21 In the Christian calendar what are the four weeks before Christmas called?
22 In which Scandinavian country is December called joulukuu, meaning month of Christmas?
23 Whose birthday is celebrated on Burns Night?
24 In January 1901 oil was first discovered in which US state?
25 What is the French word for winter?
26 December begins in which star sign?
27 Waitangi Day is celebrated in February in which country?
28 In which country is Pearl Harbor Day celebrated?
29 December always begins with the same day as which autumnal month?
30 Which winter month's birthstone is the amethyst?

Answers	**Pot Luck 6** (see Quiz 12)

1 Yellowstone National Park. 2 International Monetary Fund. 3 Volcanic gases. 4 Lentils. 5 Sheffield. 6 Barry Manilow. 7 Dean Kiely. 8 Hattie Jacques. 9 A will. 10 Thanksgiving. 11 Black. 12 The Wailers. 13 Fish soup. 14 National Exhibition Centre. 15 Boy George. 16 21. 17 Versailles. 18 30 minutes. 19 Scotland. 20 Belshazzar. 21 White rum. 22 Thunder & lightning. 23 Mick Hucknall. 24 The Andes. 25 The Derby. 26 An unborn baby. 27 Prunella Scales. 28 The peacock. 29 The Baltic. 30 Frogmore.

1 In which US National Park is the Old Faithful geyser?
2 What do the initials IMF stand for?
3 What is emitted from a fumarole?
4 What is the main ingredient in dhal, the Indian dish?
5 In which city is Bramall Lane?
6 Westlife had a No. 1 with "Mandy", but who had the original hit?
7 Who was in goal for the "great escape" run-in for Portsmouth 2006?
8 How is Josephina Jacques known in Carry On films?
9 To what would a codicil be added?
10 Which American annual celebration was first marked during 1789?
11 The first Girl Guides had to wear what colour stockings?
12 Which band claimed fifty per cent of Bob Marley's estate?
13 Cullen Skink is what kind of soup?
14 What does NEC stand for around Birmingham?
15 Who left Bow Wow Wow to form Culture Club?
16 What is the maximum score in blackjack?
17 Which building in France has a famous Hall of Mirrors?
18 Does one revolution of the London Eye take around 15, 30 or 70 minutes?
19 Which country did Arsenal keeper Bob Wilson play for?
20 In the Bible, which character saw the first writing on the wall?
21 A Daiquiri is made from fruit juice and which alcoholic drink?
22 Astraphobia is the fear of which meteorological event?
23 Which male pop superstar once played with the Frantic Elevators?
24 Machu Picchu is in which mountain range?
25 What is the English equivalent of the Melbourne Cup?
26 What is surrounded by amniotic fluid?
27 Who links "Fawlty Towers" and "After Henry"?
28 Which bird is India's national symbol?
29 Which sea is the least salty in the world?
30 Where was the Duke of Windsor buried in 1972?

Answers	**Winter Quiz** (see Quiz 11)

1 Six. 2 91 days. 3 Frosty wind made moan. 4 Tree. 5 January. 6 Migration. 7 Winter of discontent. 8 January. 9 Torino. 10 Tenth month. 11 Girl Guides. 12 Curling. 13 June, July, August. 14 January. 15 Hibernate. 16 1834. 17 January. 18 Puck. 19 Vivaldi. 20 Jack Frost. 21 Advent. 22 Finland. 23 Poet Robbie Burns. 24 Texas. 25 Hiver. 26 Sagittarius. 27 New Zealand. 28 USA. 29 September. 30 February.

1 Which No. 1 hit for the Archies was in the charts for twenty six weeks?
2 Which Park was a hit for the Small Faces in 1967?
3 Who was singing about "Sheila" in 1962 and "Dizzy" in 1969?
4 Which 60s hit for Kitty Lester was an 80s hit for Alison Moyet?
5 When did the Shirelles want to know "Will You Still Love Me..."?
6 Which crime busting organisation gave the Shadows a 1961 hit?
7 What was Petula Clark's first No. 1 UK hit in 1961?
8 Which three numbers gave Len Barry his No. 3 hit in 1965?
9 Who had consecutive hits with "Daydream" and "Summer in the City"?
10 What was over for the Seekers in their 1965 UK No. 1 hit?
11 Charting again for Elvis in 2005, what was the name of "His Latest Flame"?
12 What were Emile Ford and the Checkmates Counting in 1960?
13 What was the Searchers' first No. 1?
14 What was on the other side of Shirley Bassey's "Reach for the Stars"?
15 Whose first Top Ten hit was 5-4-3-2-1 in 1964?
16 Which country was in the title of a '63 hit by Matt Monro?
17 Who recorded the original of the song used in "Four Weddings and a Funeral"?
18 What Girl was Neil Sedaka singing about in 1961?
19 The song "Starry Eyed" was a No. 1 on 1 January 1960 for which Michael?
20 Which words of exclamation were a 1960 No. 4 hit for Peter Sellers?
21 Which "Opportunity Knocks" star had a hit with "Those were the Days"?
22 What did The Move say they could hear grow in a 1967 hit title?
23 Which 60s hit for Kenny Lynch was a No. 1 for Robson and Jerome in 1995?
24 Who were "Glad All Over" in their No. 1 hit from 1963?
25 What was "skipped" in the lyrics of "Whiter Shade of Pale"?
26 What type of Feelings did Tom Jones have in his 1967 hit?
27 Which Group had consecutive No. 1s with "Keep On Running" and "Somebody Help Me"?
28 To which religious building were the Dixie Cups going in 1964?
29 Which weather sounding group had hits with "Robot" and "Globetrotter"?
30 Known by another name, Yusuf had his first Top Ten hit with which 60s song?

Answers	**Pot Luck 7** *(see Quiz 14)*

1 1950s. 2 The Undertones. 3 The Hobbit. 4 Jeanette MacDonald. 5 Excalibur. 6 Woody Allen. 7 Colchester. 8 Uncle Mac. 9 You walk. 10 Ariel Sharon. 11 Roy Wood. 12 Brookside. 13 Arthur Lucan. 14 Eric Idle. 15 Hairy. 16 My Love (2000). 17 George III. 18 A dog. 19 Alex Ferguson. 20 Red Square, Moscow. 21 Private Fraser. 22 Schools. 23 Sheep & goats. 24 Mumps. 25 Shirley Williams. 26 A bolt or quarrel. 27 Amsterdam. 28 Shirley Temple. 29 Pig. 30 George VI.

Quiz 14 | Pot Luck 7

Answers – page 255

1 In which decade did Lester Piggott first win the Derby?
2 Who had hits with "My Perfect Cousin" and "Jimmy Jimmy"?
3 Which folklore fantasy tale is subtitled "There and Back Again"?
4 Who was Nelson Eddy's singing partner in many musical films?
5 Which famous sword is sometimes called Caliburn?
6 Which famous film director has a son called Satchel?
7 Which is further North, Chelmsford or Colchester?
8 Children's broadcaster Derek McCulloch was known on the radio as whom?
9 What is your mode of transport if you go by Walker's Bus?
10 Which Israeli leader suffered a severe stroke in January 2006?
11 Which Wizzard star formed ELO in 1971?
12 In which TV soap was Trevor Jordache buried under the patio?
13 Who played Old Mother Riley in films and on stage?
14 Which member of the Monty Python team was born on the same day as John Major?
15 What does the word piliferous mean?
16 What was the first Westlife No. 1 to feature the word "Love" in the title?
17 Which King George bought Buckingham Palace?
18 What kind of animal is a Schnauzer?
19 Which soccer boss was the first to win the English double twice?
20 In which famous Square is St Basil's cathedral?
21 In the series "Dad's Army" which soldier's daytime job was an undertaker?
22 Chris Woodhead and Mike Tomlinson have both been Chief Inspectors of what?
23 Which animals are attacked by a disease called Scrapie?
24 Which childhood disease affects the parotid salivary gland?
25 Which female MP was one of the founder members of the SDP?
26 What can be fired by a crossbow?
27 In which city was Anne Frank when she wrote her diary?
28 Which actress played lead in the films "Dimples" and "Curly Top"?
29 Lard is mainly produced from which animal?
30 Which king was the last Emperor of India?

Answers	**Pop Music: The 60s** *(see Quiz 13)*

1 Sugar Sugar. 2 Itchycoo Park. 3 Tommy Roe. 4 Love Letters. 5 Tomorrow. 6 FBI. 7 Sailor. 8 1-2-3. 9 Lovin' Spoonful. 10 The Carnival is Over. 11 Marie. 12 Teardrops. 13 Sweets for My Sweet. 14 Climb Ev'ry Mountain. 15 Manfred Mann. 16 Russia. 17 Troggs. 18 Calendar Girl. 19 Holliday. 20 Goodness Gracious Me. 21 Mary Hopkin. 22 The Grass. 23 Up on the Roof. 24 Dave Clark Five. 25 The Light Fandango. 26 Funny Familiar Forgotten. 27 Spencer Davis. 28 Chapel of Love. 29 Tornadoes. 30 Matthew and Son (Cat Stevens).

1 Who succeeded Ossie Ardiles as Spurs manager?
2 Which football team plays its home matches at Love Street?
3 Which English international played for three Italian clubs before moving to Arsenal?
4 Who was fined £20,000 for making a video on how to foul players?
5 Whose 1996 penalty miss prompted Des Lynam to say "You can come out from behind your sofas now"?
6 Who was PFA Young Player of the Year in '95 and '96?
7 Who left Tottenham immediately before George Graham took over?
8 Which football manager is singer Louise's father-in-law?
9 Which club side was Alan Ball playing for during the 1966 World Cup?
10 What is Glenn Hoddle in the cockney rhyming slang dictionary?
11 Which was the first Lancashire side Kenny Dalglish managed?
12 How is Mrs Paul Peschilsolido better known?
13 Wayne Rooney was doubtful for Germany 2006 after an injury sustained in which match?
14 Who was Man Utd manager immediately prior to Alex Ferguson?
15 Which team did Arsenal beat in the 2006 Champions League semi-finals?
16 Who was the first UK manager to walk out on a contract and work abroad?
17 Who has managed Internazionale of Milan and Blackburn Rovers?
18 Which 1980s FA Cup winners came nearest the start of the alphabet?
19 Who was Blackburn's top scorer in 2005–06, his only season at the club?
20 Who stayed longer as Newcastle boss – Sir Bobby Robson or Graeme Souness?
21 Who became Everton's record signing in June 2006?
22 Who was made Northern Ireland manager in February 1998?
23 Which England player was seen on the town wearing a sarong prior to France 98?
24 Who should Scotland have been playing when they arrived for a World Cup qualifier with no opposition?
25 Which ex-international managed Burnley in the 1997–98 season?
26 Whom did Jack Charlton play all his League football with?
27 George Graham was accused of taking a "bung" in the transfer of which player?
28 Whom did David O'Leary take over from as Aston Villa boss?
29 In which season did evergreen Ryan Giggs make his Man Utd league debut?
30 Which team beat Middlesbrough in the 2006 UEFA Cup Final?

Answers	Pot Luck 8 *(see Quiz 16)*

1 Docklands. 2 Clare Short. 3 David Bowie. 4 Everglades. 5 A waterhole. 6 21.
7 Asia Minor. 8 Will Carling. 9 Loose rocks. 10 Jude Law. 11 Dysentery. 12 Trilby.
13 Corinth Canal. 14 London. 15 Elizabeth Bennet. 16 Football match. 17 Bhopal.
18 Hudson Bay. 19 155. 20 Stevie Wonder. 21 Borussia Dortmund. 22 Agnes
Baden-Powell. 23 1990. 24 Stereophonics. 25 Dodecanese. 26 Clay. 27 Vogue. 28
September 15th. 29 1972. 30 The Queen was pregnant.

1 Canary Wharf is in which London development?
2 Which lady resigned as a Labour MP in 2006 vowing to remain as an independent?
3 Which superstar was a former member of the group the King Bees?
4 Which Florida national park has a highway called Alligator Alley?
5 What do Australians mean when they talk about a billabong?
6 How old was Billy the Kid when he died?
7 What was the former name of Turkey?
8 Julia Smith became the wife of which famous sportsman?
9 What on a mountainside is scree?
10 Who was Kate Winslet's co star in "All the King's Men"?
11 What killed Sir Francis Drake?
12 What type of hat took its name from a novel by George DuMaurier?
13 The Aegean Sea is linked to the Ionian Sea by which canal?
14 Florence Nightingale was given the Freedom of which city in 1908?
15 Who is the heroine in Jane Austen's "Pride and Prejudice"?
16 What game started the 1969 war between El Salvador and Honduras?
17 In the 80s two thousand people were killed by a gas leak in which Indian town?
18 Which Bay is the largest in the world?
19 What is the highest break in snooker with the advantage of a free black ball?
20 Which blind music star ran for Mayor of Detroit in 1989?
21 Tomas Rosicky joined Arsenal from which club?
22 Who was responsible for setting up the Girl Guides movement?
23 In what year was Nelson Mandela released from prison?
24 Which band's album title reasoned "You Gotta Go There To Come Back"?
25 Rhodes is the largest of which group of islands?
26 What is a sumo wrestling ring made from?
27 The film "Dick Tracy" was promoted by which Madonna single?
28 The Battle of Britain is remembered on which date?
29 Which year did John Lennon perform his final live concert?
30 The 1959 Royal Variety Performance was cancelled for what reason?

---

1 Which Ponchielli piece features in "Fantasia"?
2 Which US-born Australian was the voice of John Smith in "Pocahontas"?
3 In which year was the Best Animated Feature Oscar first awarded?
4 What was the sequel to "Aladdin" called?
5 What colour are Mickey Mouse's gloves?
6 Perdita and Pongo are what type of animals?
7 How many Oscars, in total, was Disney given for "Snow White and the Seven Dwarfs"?
8 Which 1991 animated film was later a musical in London and the US?
9 Who is the best-known rabbit in "Bambi"?
10 Featuring Elton John songs, what was the highest-grossing animation movie of the 1990s?
11 Which of the Gabor sisters was a voice in "The Aristocats"?
12 Who created Tom and Jerry at MGM in the 40s?
13 What did Dumbo do immediately before his ears grew so big?
14 Which film of a fairy tale features the song "Bibbidy Bobbidy Boo"?
15 Which part did Kathleen Turner voice in "Who Framed Roger Rabbit?"?
16 Which Disney film was the first with a synchronised soundtrack?
17 "Colours of the Wind" was a hit song from which movie?
18 Which film with an animated sequence featured Angela Lansbury using her magic powers against the Nazis?
19 Who sings "He's a tramp" in "Lady and the Tramp"?
20 Where did Kim Basinger star as a sexy animated doodle, Holly, brought over to the real world?
21 Who sang in "Aladdin" after making her name in "Miss Saigon"?
22 Which 1990 film was about pizza-loving, sewer dwelling reptiles?
23 Which was the first film to feature, appropriately enough, computer-animated sequences?
24 What type of orphaned creature featured in "The Land Before Time"?
25 Which was the first animated film in the 90s which Tim Rice won an Oscar for?
26 Which dancer commissioned Hanna and Barbera to do an animation sequence in "Anchors Aweigh" in 1945?
27 Which Tchaikovsky ballet piece features in "Fantasia"?
28 In which film does Shere Khan appear?
29 Which characters made their debut in "Puss Gets the Boot" in 1940?
30 Who was the voice of Stuart in "Stuart Little 2"?

1 Cars with the international vehicle registration C come from where?
2 The Paul Getty Museum is in which American state?
3 What is the American equivalent of an English bilberry?
4 What is added to Galliano to make a Harvey Wallbanger?
5 Which country is nearest to where the Titanic was found?
6 An average man has twenty square feet of what about his person?
7 In which country were the last summer Olympics of the 20th century in Europe?
8 In which decade was Cassius Clay – later Muhammad Ali – born?
9 From which tree family is the basket-making osier a member?
10 Which sport other than rugby is played for the Currie Cup?
11 In which country is the Great Sandy Desert?
12 Who had "Sticky Moments on Tour"?
13 The Cheviot hills run along the boundary between which countries?
14 Which seeds are in the sweet, Halva?
15 What note does an orchestra tune to?
16 What featured on McFly's No. 1 single with "All About You"?
17 Which Shakespeare play was banned during George III's time of madness?
18 Before being used as a name for US soldiers, what did "GI" stand for?
19 What is the flowery name of the daughter of Jennifer Garner and Ben Affleck?
20 Which gas is produced by adding water to calcium carbide?
21 Which berries are used in a Cumberland sauce?
22 What is a wadi?
23 In which country is the Potomac River?
24 Which element has the highest melting point?
25 Which Adrian Mole creator wrote "Queen Camilla"?
26 Which part of a tree gives Angostura Bitters its taste?
27 What is the metric word for a million?
28 What is the southern American stew of rice and okra called?
29 Which famous pop guitarist performed with the Notting Hillbillies?
30 George Galloway was in which party for the 2005 Parliamentary election?

Answers	**Movies: Animation** *(see Quiz 17)*

1 Dance of the Hours. 2 Mel Gibson. 3 2002. 4 The Return of Jafar. 5 White. 6 Dalmatians. 7 Eight. 8 Beauty and the Beast. 9 Thumper. 10 The Lion King. 11 Eva. 12 Hanna & Barbera. 13 He sneezed. 14 Cinderella. 15 Jessica Rabbit. 16 Steamboat Willie. 17 Pocahontas. 18 Bedknobs & Broomsticks. 19 Peggy Lee. 20 Cool World. 21 Lea Salonga. 22 Teenage Mutant Ninja Turtles. 23 Tron. 24 Dinosaur. 25 Aladdin. 26 Gene Kelly. 27 Nutcracker Suite. 28 Jungle Book. 29 Tom & Jerry. 30 Michael J. Fox.

1 Where according to the Bible is the site of the final battle between nations which will end the world?

2 In which Dickens novel did Uriah Heep appear?

3 "Old Possum's Book of Practical Cats" is composed of what?

4 To £5,000 how much do you receive for winning the Booker Prize?

5 In which book did John Braine introduce Joe Lampton?

6 What type of book is the OED?

7 What is the subject of Desmond Morris's "The Naked Ape"?

8 What type of books did Patricia Highsmith write?

9 Which detective first appeared in "A Study in Scarlet" in 1887?

10 The sequel to "Peter Pan" was called "Peter Pan in" what?

11 Which Gothic horror story has the alternative title "The Modern Prometheus"?

12 For what types of book is Samuel Pepys famous for?

13 Who wrote "The Female Eunuch" in 1970?

14 In which county were Jane Austen and Charles Dickens born?

15 Which former politician narrated the diaries of his dog Buster?

16 In "Charlie and the Chocolate Factory", what is Charlie's surname?

17 Which ex-jockey wrote a book of short stories called "Field of Thirteen"?

18 Whose horror stories include "Carrie" and "The Shining"?

19 Which "Sex & the City" star wrote the teen advice book "Being a Girl"?

20 Who wrote "Das Kapital"?

21 What was the name of the Original Conjuring Cat in "Old Possum's Book of Practical Cats"?

22 Which writer and politician bought poet Rupert Brooke's house?

23 Which fictional barrister was created by John Mortimer?

24 Whose first novel, "A Woman of Substance" became a best-seller?

25 The "Dummies" advice books are coloured black and what other main colour?

26 "The Day of the Jackal" is about an assassination plot on whom?

27 For which Salman Rushdie book did the Ayatollah impose a fatwa?

28 Who wrote "It's All Over Now" after her brief marriage to Bill Wyman?

29 To five years, how old was Mary Wesley when her first best-seller was published?

30 Award-winning novelist Ben Okri hails from which country?

Answers	**Pot Luck 10** *(see Quiz 20)*

1 Cross Fell, Cumbria. 2 Agatha Christie. 3 27. 4 Henry Cooper. 5 Their Mum. 6 Hyde Park. 7 Spurs. 8 Phone cards. 9 Steve Davis. 10 Graeme Hick. 11 Sullivan. 12 Tottenham Hotspur. 13 20th. 14 Nevada. 15 Five. 16 Pavlova. 17 Volga. 18 Asparagus. 19 Clint Eastwood. 20 Mack Sennett. 21 Michael Henchard. 22 The alphabet. 23 Ronald Reagan. 24 Montreux. 25 Rhodes. 26 Katherine Jenkins. 27 Mr Men. 28 Lily. 29 Tea. 30 1960s.

1 What is the highest point of the Pennines?
2 2006 marked the 30th anniversary of the death of which crime writer?
3 How many years was Nelson Mandela held in prison?
4 Which British boxer was the first to win three Lonsdale belts outright?
5 Who, according to a NOP survey in 1998, do young men call most on their mobile phones?
6 In which London park is Rotten Row?
7 Defender Stephen Carr joined Newcastle from which club?
8 What will a green phone kiosk only take for payment?
9 Which snooker star was nicknamed "Interesting" by "Spitting Image"?
10 In 1988 who scored 405 not out at Taunton?
11 Who died first, Gilbert or Sullivan?
12 Which was the first London football club to win a European title?
13 In which century did Joan of Arc become a saint?
14 Which American state is called the "Gambling State"?
15 Did John Glenn's first spaceflight last five, ten or 24 hours?
16 Which dessert is named after a famous ballerina?
17 Which river flows from northern Moscow to the Caspian Sea?
18 A Bruxelloise sauce is flavoured with which vegetable?
19 Who was the leading actor in "Play Misty for Me" with Jessica Walker?
20 Who created the Keystone Kops?
21 Who was the Mayor of Casterbridge in the Thomas Hardy novel?
22 What does an alphabetarian study?
23 Who became US President in the year John Lennon died in New York?
24 In which Swiss resort are the Golden Rose TV accolades awarded?
25 Which island is the largest of the Dodecanese group?
26 Which singer's third album was called "Living the Dream"?
27 What characters were created by Roger Hargreaves?
28 To which flower family does garlic belong?
29 Which drink can be green, black and oolong?
30 In which decade was the first American Superbowl?

Answers	Leisure: Books 1 *(see Quiz 19)*

1 Armageddon. **2** David Copperfield. **3** Poems. **4** £20,000. **5** Room at the Top. **6** Dictionary. **7** Man. **8** Crime fiction. **9** Sherlock Holmes. **10** Scarlet. **11** Frankenstein. **12** Diary. **13** Germaine Greer. **14** Hampshire. **15** Roy Hattersley. **16** Buckett. **17** Dick Francis. **18** Stephen King. **19** Kim Cattrall. **20** Karl Marx. **21** Mr Mistoffelees. **22** Jeffrey Archer. **23** Rumpole. **24** Barbara Taylor Bradford. **25** Yellow. **26** Charles de Gaulle. **27** The Satanic Verses. **28** Mandy Smith. **29** 70. **30** Nigeria.

1 What colour is the flesh of a cantaloupe melon?
2 Simnel cake was traditionally eaten on which Sunday?
3 What is the fishy ingredient in Scotch woodcock?
4 What is a champignon?
5 Which spirit is Russia famous for producing?
6 What alcoholic drink is made in Hakushu, Yoichi and Yamazaki?
7 What is added to pasta to make it green?
8 Which drink is grown in the Douro basin and exported from Oporto?
9 Which cooking pot boils food at a higher temperature than boiling point?
10 What is another name for dietary fibre?
11 Which sauce/salad shares its name with Latin big-band music?
12 Where did satsumas originate?
13 What are cornichons?
14 Puerto Rico and Jamaica are the main producers of which spirit?
15 What colour is cayenne pepper?
16 What type of pastry is used to make a steak and kidney pudding?
17 Which drink is served in a schooner?
18 What is a Laxton's Superb?
19 Which seafood, usually fried in breadcrumbs, is the Italian name for shrimps?
20 Tofu and TVP come from which bean?
21 Tartrazine colours food which colour?
22 What is added to whisky to make a whisky mac?
23 Where would you buy a pint of Shires?
24 What colour is Double Gloucester cheese?
25 Which Mexican drink is distilled from the agave plant?
26 Which black, gourmet fungus is a native of France's Perigord region?
27 Which expensive vinegar is aged in wooden barrels?
28 Which grain is whisky made from?
29 What is red wine made with that white wine is not?
30 Vermouth is wine flavoured with what?

Answers	Kylie *(see Quiz 22)*

1 Spinning Around. 2 The Magic Roundabout. 3 Showgirl. 4 Melbourne. 5 You.
6 Fever. 7 Parlophone. 8 Love at First Sight. 9 Gemini. 10 Little Eva. 11 Dancing
Queen. 12 Mushroom. 13 Breathe. 14 In Your Eyes. 15 Glastonbury. 16 Spinning
Around. 17 Green Fairy. 18 Red Blooded Woman (2004). 19 Kylie. 20 Deconstruction.
21 Princess. 22 Can't Get You Out of My Head. 23 Body Language. 24 Lingerie. 25
Jason Donovan. 26 Body Language. 27 1960s. 28 13. 29 Kath & Kim. 30 Kylie.

1 Which was Kylie's first UK No. 1 of the new millennium?

2 Kylie voiced Florence in which 2006 movie?

3 Which tour was postponed when Kylie was diagnosed with cancer?

4 Which city does Kylie come from?

5 Which word completes her hits, "I Believe In ..." and "Giving ... Up"?

6 In 2001 which release returned her to No. 1 in the album charts?

7 Kylie moved to which UK label that launched The Beatles?

8 What was Kylie's first single to contain the word "Love"?

9 What is Kylie's star sign?

10 Who had the original hit with "The Loco-Motion"?

11 Which Abba classic did Kylie cover when closing the Sydney Olympics?

12 Which fungus-linked word names her early Australian recording label?

13 Which Kylie hit has the same title as a 2005 hit by Erasure?

14 Which charted first, "Chocolate" or "In Your Eyes"?

15 Which major British festival did Kylie pull out of in 2005?

16 Which No. 1 was promoted with a video showing Kylie in gold hot pants?

17 She played what colour of fairy in the movie "Moulin Rouge"?

18 What was Kylie's first Top Ten single with a colour in the title?

19 "On a Night Like This" was the first hit single on which she used which billing?

20 Which label handled Kylie's records in the UK for most of the 1990s?

21 What word completes her children's book, "The Showgirl..."?

22 What was Kylie's first million-seller single in the UK?

23 What kind of "Language" featured in the title of Kylie's 2003 hit album?

24 Love Kylie was the name of a range of what?

25 Kylie's first hit duet was with which artist?

26 Both "Chocolate" and "Slow" featured on which album?

27 In which decade of the twentieth century was Kylie born?

28 Kylie started off with how many consecutive Top Ten hits – 3, 9 or 13?

29 In which TV series did she play a cameo as Epponnee Rae?

30 What was the one-word title of Kylie's first album?

Answers	Leisure: Food & Drink 2 *(see Quiz 21)*

1 Orange. 2 Mothering Sunday. 3 Anchovies. 4 Mushroom. 5 Vodka. 6 Japanese Whisky. 7 Spinach. 8 Port. 9 Pressure cooker. 10 Roughage. 11 Salsa. 12 Japan. 13 Gherkins (pickled cucumbers). 14 Rum. 15 Red. 16 Suet pastry. 17 Sherry. 18 Apple. 19 Scampi. 20 Soya. 21 Yellow. 22 Ginger wine. 23 Ambridge. 24 Orange-red. 25 Tequila. 26 Truffle. 27 Balsamic. 28 Malted barley. 29 Skins of the grape. 30 Bitter herbs.

1 Who supposedly brought about the downfall of Barings Bank?
2 Which country was the first to legalise abortion?
3 Which Eurovision-winning group formed the Polar Music Company?
4 Luis Saha joined Man Utd from which club?
5 Mount Elbert is the highest peak in which American mountain range?
6 Adam and Eve were the main characters in which work by John Milton?
7 The movie "Cinderella Man" is about which boxer?
8 Whose murder conviction was overturned after 45 years in 1998?
9 Which famous riding school is in Austria?
10 What colour traditionally is an Indian wedding sari?
11 Which county first won the Benson and Hedges Cricket Cup twice?
12 Which Copenhagen statue is a memorial to Hans Christian Andersen?
13 Which Derbyshire town is famous for the church with a crooked spire?
14 The Parthenon in Athens was built as a temple to whom?
15 Which actress links Jackie in "Footballers' Wives" and Nikki in "The Bill"?
16 Which glands produce white blood cells?
17 What sort of creature is a guillemot?
18 What was the first film Bogart and Bacall starred in together?
19 Which role did Billie Piper play in "Dr Who"?
20 Which girl's name gave the Damned their only top ten hit?
21 Which chess piece can only move diagonally?
22 Which female's Living Proof farewell tour ended in April 2005?
23 William "Fatty" Foulkes played which sport?
24 Which oil company was founded by John D. Rockefeller?
25 At which Southwark inn did Chaucer's Canterbury Pilgrims meet?
26 Joseph Marie Jacquard is most remembered for which invention?
27 Before Winston Churchill went bald, what colour was his hair?
28 The word micro is what fraction in the metric system?
29 Which county included WG Grace as a team member?
30 Which musical instrument was first developed by Bartolomeo Cristofori?

Answers | Past Law & Order *(see Quiz 24)*

1 Haiti. 2 Bluebeard. 3 20th (1941). 4 Ruth Ellis. 5 Dr Crippen. 6 Philip Lawrence. 7 Official Secrets Act. 8 Lester Piggott. 9 Slavery. 10 Director of Public Prosecutions. 11 Cape Town. 12 St Valentine's Day. 13 Nick Leeson. 14 Michael Howard. 15 Iceland. 16 Back to Basics. 17 Treason. 18 Colditz. 19 Ethiopia didn't have electricity. 20 Cromwell Street. 21 Richard I. 22 Jack Straw. 23 Louise Woodward. 24 Road rage attack. 25 Robert Maxwell. 26 Peter Sutcliffe. 27 The Butcher of Lyon. 28 The Ritz. 29 Monster. 30 The Clintons.

Quiz 24 | Past Law & Order

Answers – page 265

1 Which country had the private security force the Tontons Macoutes?
2 What was the nickname of mass murderer Gilles de Rais who killed six of his seven wives?
3 In which century was the last execution at the Tower of London?
4 Which woman was hanged in 1955 for murdering David Blakely?
5 Cora was the wife of which doctor who murdered her?
6 In the 1990s which London head teacher was killed outside his school?
7 Which Act bans the disclosure of confidential items from government sources by its employees?
8 Which world-famous jockey was jailed in 1987 for tax evasion?
9 What did abolitionism seek to abolish?
10 What is the DPP, a post created in 1985?
11 Robben Island was a prison near which city?
12 Which Day saw seven of Bugs Moran's gang murdered by members of Al Capone's, disguised as policemen?
13 Whose crime was recounted in the film "Rogue Trader"?
14 Which one-time Home Secretary led his party in the 2005 general election?
15 The Althing is the parliament of which country?
16 Which phrase used by John Major in 1993 was used as a slogan to return to traditional British values?
17 In 1965 capital punishment was abolished except for which crime?
18 How was the prison camp Oflag IVC near Leipzig better known?
19 In what way was Ethiopian Emperor Menelik III thwarted in bringing the electric chair to his country?
20 What was the Gloucester street where Rose & Frederick West lived?
21 Robin Hood is said to have lived in Sherwood Forest during the reign of which king?
22 Which Home Secretary took his son to the police after allegations of drug selling?
23 Which British nanny's US trial was televised after a baby died in her care?
24 Why was the death of Stephen Cameron in 1996 a tragic first?
25 Who fell from the Lady Ghislaine leaving debts behind him?
26 What is the real name of the criminal dubbed The Yorkshire Ripper?
27 What was the nickname of Nazi war criminal Klaus Barbie?
28 Jonathan Aitken's court case centred on a stay in which Paris hotel?
29 Which 2004 movie starred Charlize Theron playing a real-life serial killer?
30 In the US whose involvement in the Whitewater affair had lengthy repercussions?

Answers	Pot Luck 11 *(see Quiz 23)*

1 Nick Leeson. 2 Iceland. 3 Abba. 4 Fulham. 5 The Rockies. 6 Paradise Lost.
7 James J. Braddock. 8 Derek Bentley. 9 The Spanish Riding School. 10 Scarlet.
11 Leicestershire. 12 The Little Mermaid. 13 Chesterfield. 14 Athena. 15 Gillian
Taylforth. 16 Lymph glands. 17 Bird. 18 To Have and Have Not. 19 Rose Tyler. 20
Eloise. 21 The Bishop. 22 Cher. 23 Football. 24 Standard Oil. 25 The Tabard Inn.
26 The Jacquard loom. 27 Red. 28 A millionth. 29 Gloucestershire. 30 The piano.

1 What nationality was the spy Mata Hari?
2 The Dickens work Edwin Drood is different for what reason?
3 Which Australian soap star had the biggest-selling UK single in 1988?
4 What were the Boston Tea Party protesters against?
5 What is a Wessex Saddleback?
6 Who succeeded Gerhard Schroeder as German Chancellor?
7 Lyncanthropy involves men changing into what?
8 Which city's American football team is known as the Vikings?
9 Queen Wilhelmina who died in 1962 was Queen of which country?
10 The pop band America were formed in which country?
11 In curling how many shots at the target is each player allowed?
12 What was Janet Street-Porter's beastly last name before marriage?
13 Which Band Aid No. 1 hit was written by Midge Ure and Bob Geldof?
14 Which late singer became the third biggest-selling singles act of 2005?
15 Which American symbol was famously painted by Jasper Johns?
16 In fencing how many hits must a male fencer score for a win?
17 In gin rummy how many cards are dealt per player?
18 What nationality was the inventor of the Geiger counter?
19 Before it moved to Wales on which London hill was the Royal Mint?
20 In which century was the first circumnavigation of the earth?
21 Which is further South, Cardiff or Oxford?
22 Which river rises in the Black Forest?
23 Which road vehicle takes its name from the Hindu God Jagganath?
24 In which South American country is the condor sacred?
25 The first modern Olympics were held in which city?
26 Whom did Michael Sheen play in "Fantabulosa"?
27 What have you on your mouth if you suffer from herpes labialis?
28 Prince Edward resigned from which part of the military in 1987?
29 Mike Burden is the sidekick to which TV detective?
30 It ended in 2006, but in which city was the first ever "Top of the Pops" recorded?

Answers	**Communications** *(see Quiz 26)*

1 Stansted. 2 Leeds. 3 Philips. 4 Decibel. 5 Seattle. 6 Telephone handset. 7 Trans Siberian. 8 Paris. 9 999 service. 10 Nothing. 11 Service. 12 Acoustics. 13 The Speaking Clock. 14 You Got M@il. 15 Video Cassette Recorder. 16 USA. 17 FBI's. 18 Derbyshire. 19 A12. 20 ADA. 21 Dundee. 22 Grand Canal. 23 Alaska. 24 A. 25 M62. 26 Some insects. 27 8. 28 Moscow. 29 Madam Mayor. 30 Channel Tunnel.

1 What is Britain's third largest airport?
2 Which northern city has the dialling code 0113?
3 Which company launched the CD-i in 1992?
4 dB is the symbol for what?
5 Where in America was the on-line bookstore Amazon first based?
6 An acoustic coupler allows computer data to be transmitted through what?
7 Which railway links European Russia with the Pacific?
8 Which city linked up with London by phone in 1891?
9 Which vital communications link began in July 1937?
10 How much is the maximum charge for postage in Andorra?
11 What does S stand for in ISP?
12 What is the science of sound and its transmission called?
13 What is another name for Timeline?
14 Which Tom Hanks movie had an email symbol in its title?
15 What is a VCR?
16 Which country has the most telephone subscribers?
17 On whose website did Leslie Ibsen Rogge appear, leading to his arrest?
18 In which county is East Midlands airport?
19 Which A road links London with East Anglia?
20 Which computer language was named after Ada Augusta Byron?
21 Which is the nearest city to the Tay road bridge?
22 Which waterway does Venice's Rialto bridge span?
23 Which state is the northern terminus of the Pan American highway?
24 In France all motorways begin with which letter?
25 Which motorway links Hull and Leeds?
26 Which living creatures can you send through the post?
27 How many bits are there in a byte?
28 In which city is the TASS news agency based?
29 How would you verbally address a Mayor who is a woman?
30 Which tunnel goes from Cheriton to Sangatte?

Answers	**Pot Luck 12** *(see Quiz 25)*

1 Dutch. 2 It is not finished. 3 Kylie Minogue. 4 Tea taxes. 5 Pig. 6 Angela Merkel.
7 Wolves. 8 Minnesota. 9 Holland. 10 England. 11 2. 12 Bull. 13 Do They Know
It's Christmas. 14 Elvis Presley. 15 The stars & stripes. 16 Five. 17 10. 18 German.
19 Tower Hill. 20 16th. 21 Cardiff. 22 Danube. 23 Juggernaut. 24 Peru. 25
Athens. 26 Kenneth Williams. 27 Cold Sores. 28 The Marines. 29 Reg Wexford. 30
Manchester.

1 Who had a No. 1 UK hit with "The Reflex"?
2 In English what is the only anagram of the word ENGLISH?
3 Which rules are American football played to?
4 In which South African city was the 1995 Rugby Union World Cup Final?
5 Which musical was based on the play "Pygmalion"?
6 If you suffer from bulimia, what do you have a compulsive urge to do?
7 Which striker Paul rejoined Man City in 2006?
8 Which triangular-shaped Indian pastry contains meat or vegetables?
9 Which part of Spain is named after its many castles?
10 The range of the pH scale is zero to what?
11 Which everyday objects can be decorated with the King's Pattern?
12 Stage performer Boy Bruce the Mighty Atom became known as who?
13 Which Russian word means "speaking aloud"?
14 Which Top Ten "ride" was taken by the group Roxette?
15 What is the name of the world's largest Gulf?
16 At which UK oil depot was there a massive fire in December 2005?
17 Ouzo is what flavour?
18 What does a trishaw driver do with his legs?
19 Which hospital did TV Doctor Kildare work at?
20 Which is the slowest swimming stroke?
21 What is the best-selling single of all time?
22 What does E stand for in "E-numbers"?
23 In Peter Pan which part of Peter was kept in a drawer?
24 What word links an ice cream holder and a brass instrument?
25 Who performed "Sgt Pepper" to open Live 8 with Paul McCartney?
26 In which Dickensian drama did Gillian Anderson play Lady Dedlock?
27 What is the epicarp of an orange?
28 Who was George W. Bush's first Secretary of State?
29 Which three Time Travel films were directed by Robert Zemeckis?
30 Which European country has the only active volcanoes in Europe?

Answers	**Pop Music: The 70s** *(see Quiz 28)*

1 Love Me for a Reason. 2 Pigeon. 3 Cher. 4 Eddie Holman. 5 Dawn. 6 Ray Stevens. 7 Heart. 8 Squeeze. 9 January. 10 The Kinks. 11 10538. 12 Matthews Southern Comfort. 13 Leo Sayer. 14 Your Song. 15 The Floral Dance. 16 Minnie Riperton. 17 Sweet Sensation. 18 Paul Simon. 19 Nathan Jones. 20 B A Robertson. 21 Rainbow. 22 New York. 23 Samantha. 24 Summer Nights. 25 The Commodores. 26 Rivers of Babylon. 27 Midnight. 28 In the Summertime. 29 Donna Summer. 30 Eye Level.

1 Which 70s hit by the Osmonds gave Boyzone a hit in '94?
2 Which Lieutenant's only UK No. 1 hit was "Mouldy Old Dough"?
3 Who sang that she was "born in the wagon of a travelling show"?
4 "(Hey There) Lonely Girl" was the only UK hit for which vocalist?
5 Tony Orlando sang in which group that had a girl's name?
6 The craze for streaking gave a No. 1 to which Ray?
7 Which part of the body was mentioned in the title of a Blondie hit?
8 Who were "Up The Junction" in 1979?
9 Which month links Pilot and part of a song title for Barbara Dickson?
10 Whose hits from 1970 include "Victoria" and "Apeman"?
11 What was the number of ELO's Overture in their first hit?
12 The No. 1 UK hit "Woodstock" was a one-hit wonder for which group?
13 Who had a No. 1 single in 2006, but first charted with "The Show Must Go On"?
14 Which Elton John 70s hit with a two-word title returned to the Top Ten in 2002?
15 What links Terry Wogan and the Brighouse and Rastrick Brass Band?
16 "Loving You" was a high-pitched No. 2 UK hit for which female singer?
17 Which group had a No. 1 UK hit with "Sad Sweet Dreamer"?
18 Who wanted to be taken to the Mardi Gras?
19 Which 1971 Supremes hit was later a hit for Bananarama?
20 Who had hits with "Bang Bang" and "Knocked It Off" in 1979?
21 The 1979 No. 6 hit "Since You've Been Gone" was a hit for whom?
22 Which US city was named twice in a Gerard Kenny hit from 1978?
23 Whom did Cliff Richard say Hello to when he said Goodbye to Sam?
24 In which song do the chorus beg, "Tell me more, tell me more!"?
25 Which group had hits in the 70s with "Easy", "Still" and "Sail On"?
26 What was on the other side of Boney M's "Brown Girl in the Ring"?
27 What time was Gladys Knight's train leaving for Georgia?
28 Which Mungo Jerry hit was used in an anti drink-drive campaign?
29 Which disco-style singer had the word Love in the title of four of her first five Top Ten hits?
30 Which No. 1 from 1972 was the theme for the Van Der Valk series?

Answers | **Pot Luck 13** *(see Quiz 27)*

1 Duran Duran. 2 Shingle. 3 The Harvard rules. 4 Johannesburg. 5 My Fair Lady. 6 Eat. 7 Paul Dickov. 8 Samosa. 9 Castile. 10 Fourteen. 11 Cutlery. 12 Bruce Forsyth. 13 Glasnost. 14 Joyride. 15 Gulf of Mexico. 16 Buncefield. 17 Aniseed. 18 Pedal. 19 Blair Hospital. 20 Breast stroke. 21 Candle in the Wind (1997). 22 European. 23 His shadow. 24 Cornet. 25 U2. 26 Bleak House. 27 The peel. 28 Colin Powell. 29 Back to the Future. 30 Italy.

Quiz 29 Pot Luck 14

Answers – page 272

LEVEL 2

1 If a bridge player has a Yarborough, what is the top scoring card?
2 Which "Strictly Come Dancing" judge has the longest name?
3 In the Grand National, how many times did Red Rum run?
4 Which was the first railway terminus in London?
5 Which term is used when a mortgage is more than the value of a house?
6 Whose hits include "Slave to Love" and "This is Tomorrow"?
7 What is a Clouded Yellow?
8 How was Agatha Miller better known?
9 El Paso is in which American state?
10 Which road leads from Westminster to Blackfriars along the north bank of the Thames?
11 The first player to score 100 Premier League goals played for which club?
12 In which board game is FIDE the governing body?
13 A BBC estimate said half the population had watched which live event in 2005?
14 In which year did TV soap "EastEnders" first appear?
15 What is the Mirror of Diana, located in Northern Italy?
16 Beta Vulgaris is the Latin name for which crop?
17 Which film featured the Joe Cocker hit "Up Where We Belong"?
18 Who wrote the opera from which Here Comes the Bride is taken?
19 Lime Street Station is in which English city?
20 Cars with the international vehicle registration IS come from where?
21 Which magazine, established in 1922, claims to be the most widely read in the world?
22 What happened to Ken Barlow's second wife in "Coronation Street"?
23 What type of fruit is a Laxton Superb?
24 Who plays grandma Kumar at No. 42?
25 A sericulturist breeds which creatures?
26 Robbie Elliott and Nobby Solano have both had two spells at which soccer club?
27 What term describes the fineness of yarns?
28 Where do mice live who are proverbially poor?
29 Joseph Grimaldi achieved everlasting fame as what?
30 Who made history in 1982 by going to an Anglican service in Canterbury Cathedral?

Answers	**World Football** *(see Quiz 30)*

1 Japan. 2 Lazio. 3 Ruud Gullit. 4 Gary Lineker. 5 Australia. 6 Croatia. 7 Barcelona. 8 Prague. 9 Graham Poll. 10 Mario Zagallo. 11 Benfica. 12 Germany. 13 Davor Suker. 14 Argentina. 15 Roger Milla. 16 Uruguay. 17 Gerard Houllier. 18 Edson Arrentes do Nascimento. 19 Italy. 20 Switzerland. 21 Emmanuel Petit. 22 Ronaldo's. 23 Zinedine Zidane. 24 Dennis Bergkamp. 25 Matthias Sammer. 26 St Denis. 27 Dunga. 28 Stanley Matthews. 29 Marco Materazzi. 30 Alexi Lalas.

1 In which country is the club Grampus Eight?

2 Which Italian team did Gazza play for?

3 Who was Dutch captain when they won the European Championship in 1988?

4 Who was leading scorer in the 1986 World Cup finals?

5 Which international side did Venables manage after England?

6 Who won the third-place final in the 1998 World Cup?

7 Which side did Cruyff move to from Ajax in 1973?

8 Dukla and Sparta are from which European city?

9 In a 2006 game, which British ref. showed three yellow cards to the same player?

10 Which Brazilian football coach was sacked after France '98?

11 Which Portuguese side did Graeme Souness manage?

12 Which country ran a full-page "thank you" ad in The Times after Euro 96?

13 Who won the Golden Boot in the 1998 World Cup?

14 Cesar Menotti managed which victorious World Cup side?

15 Who is the oldest player ever to score in the World Cup finals?

16 Penarol is a club side in which country?

17 Which Frenchman moved to Liverpool when Ronnie Moran retired?

18 What is Pele's full name?

19 Who, with England and Holland, was eliminated from France 98 on penalties?

20 Which country does Arsenal's Philippe Senderos represent?

21 Who scored the last goal in France 98?

22 Whose much-seen girlfriend in France 98 was Suzana Werner?

23 Who received the Golden Ball as outstanding player of the 2006 World Cup?

24 Which overseas star won most Premiership Player of the Month awards in 1997–98?

25 Which German won European Player of the Year in 1996?

26 In which stadium was the opening match of France 98?

27 Who captained Brazil in the 1998 World Cup Finals?

28 Who was the first European Footballer of the Year?

29 Who scored Italy's open play goal in the 2006 World Cup Final?

30 Which US star of the 1994 World Cup became the first American player to take part in Italy's Serie A?

Answers | Pot Luck 14 *(see Quiz 29)*

1 Nine. 2 Craig Revel Horwood. 3 Five. 4 Euston Station. 5 Negative equity. 6 Bryan Ferry's. 7 A Butterfly. 8 Agatha Christie. 9 Texas. 10 The Embankment. 11 Blackburn (Alan Shearer). 12 Chess. 13 Live 8 concert. 14 1985. 15 A lake. 16 Sugar beet. 17 An Officer and a Gentleman. 18 Wagner. 19 Liverpool. 20 Iceland. 21 Reader's Digest. 22 She committed suicide. 23 An apple. 24 Meera Syal. 25 Silkworms. 26 Newcastle United. 27 Denier. 28 Church. 29 A clown. 30 The Pope.

1 In 2005 Mahmoud Abbas triumphed in which elections?
2 Which Man Utd player signed in 2005 had played for Ajax and Juventus?
3 Which group had a No. 1 UK hit in 1992 with Ebenezer Goode?
4 In which sport were Jack Broughton and James Figg champions?
5 Which Aldous Huxley novel is set in the seventh century AF?
6 Which instrument was Jose Feliciano famous for playing?
7 Which Queen was played in films by Jean Simmons and Bette Davis?
8 US talent show "You're the One that I Want" chooses performers for which musical?
9 Which musical instruments represent Peter in "Peter and the Wolf"?
10 Who presented "Restoration Village" on TV?
11 A glaive was what kind of weapon?
12 In which century was the first Indianapolis 500 first held?
13 In which country do soldiers wear skirts called fustanella?
14 What can be done if an object is scissile?
15 Which film studios were founded by Harry, Sam, Albert and Jack?
16 Which word can describe a listening device, an illness and an insect?
17 Which famous actress starred in "Courage of Lassie" and "Lassie Come Home"?
18 Who was older when he died, Benny Hill or Richard Burton?
19 TV presenter Alison Holloway became which comic Jim's third wife?
20 What type of fruit is a jargonelle?
21 Which part of the head is studied by a phrenologist?
22 Whose ancestral home is Woburn Abbey?
23 Who wrote the poem "Four Quartets"?
24 Which children's game is played on the fingers with looped string?
25 Jane Harris and Nel Mangel appeared in which soap?
26 Brassica Rapa is the Latin name for which vegetable?
27 Which band's hits include "Infinite Dreams" and "Holy Smoke"?
28 Which two letters are in the internet code for Malta?
29 Excess bile pigment in the bloodstream causes which illness?
30 Whom was Dennis Bergkamp named after?

Answers | **Blockbusters** *(see Quiz 32)*

1 Five. 2 Chocolate. 3 The Robe. 4 Francis Ford Coppola. 5 Normandy. 6 M*A*S*H. 7 Hearst. 8 Crocodile Dundee. 9 James Caviezel. 10 Midnight Cowboy. 11 Dan Aykroyd. 12 The English Patient. 13 Vito Corleone. 14 Pierce Brosnan. 15 Ron Kovic. 16 Gone with the Wind. 17 Wall Street. 18 Braveheart. 19 Dune. 20 John Huston. 21 Terminator II. 22 Austrian. 23 All About Eve. 24 1930s. 25 Goldblum. 26 Jim Carrey. 27 Carrie Fisher. 28 Celine Dion. 29 The Last Samurai. 30 Cop.

1 How many crew members were there in the Nostromo in "Alien"?
2 What type of sauce was used in the shower scene in "Psycho"?
3 Which 1953 film was the first made in Cinemascope?
4 Who directed "The Godfather" and all its sequels?
5 "Saving Private Ryan" dealt with events in which part of France?
6 Which anti-war comedy did Robert Altman direct?
7 Which newspaper magnate was said to be the model for Orson Welles' Citizen Kane?
8 Which 80s film was the most profitable in Australian history?
9 Who played Christ in Mel Gibson's "The Passion of the Christ"?
10 What was John Schlesinger's first US film, made in 1969 with Dustin Hoffman and Jon Voight?
11 Who starred in, and co-wrote "Ghostbusters"?
12 Which film starred Juliette Binoche and Kristin Scott Thomas?
13 What was the name of Marlon Brando's character in "The Godfather"?
14 Which James Bond actor starred in "Dante's Peak"?
15 What was the name of Tom Cruise's character in "Born on the Fourth of July"?
16 In which classic did Olivia de Havilland play Melanie Wilkes?
17 In which film did Michael Douglas say "Greed is good"?
18 What was Mel Gibson's first film as actor, director and producer?
19 Which David Lynch space epic was based on the work of Frank Herbert?
20 Who was directing "The African Queen" when his daughter Anjelica was born?
21 Which sequel had the subtitle "Judgement Day"?
22 What is Schindler's nationality in "Schindler's List"?
23 What was the last film before Titanic to win 14 Oscar nominations?
24 In which decade was "Gone with the Wind" made?
25 Which Jeff was the mathematician in "Jurassic Park"?
26 Who became a human cartoon in "The Mask"?
27 Who played Princess Leia in the "Star Wars Trilogy"?
28 Who sang the theme song for "Titanic"?
29 In which movie did Tom Hanks play Captain Nathan Algren?
30 What was Michael Douglas' profession in "Basic Instinct"?

1 Which TV cop was christened Ilynea Lydia Mironoff?
2 In which crime drama did Tim Pigott-Smith play DCI Vickers?
3 Which show features DCI Michael Jardine?
4 What was Paul Nicholls' first major series after leaving "EastEnders"?
5 Who was Don Johnson's character in "Miami Vice"?
6 What was the name of law enforcer Michael Knight's computer buddy?
7 Which series featured Shell who gave birth to Ronan Beckham?
8 Which series featured the Wentworth Detention Centre?
9 Who played the TV "Avengers" role played by Uma Thurman on the big screen?
10 Which member of the Ruth Rendell Mysteries cast also scripted some of the shows?
11 In which series did the character Charlie Barlow first find fame?
12 Which "Blue Peter" presenter played Dangerfield's son in the police surgeon series?
13 In which 90s series did Neil Pearson star as Det. Sup. Tony Clark?
14 In which police station was Frank Farillo the chief?
15 What was Fitz's full name in "Cracker"?
16 Peter Falk played which offbeat TV cop?
17 Which real crime series was based on the German "File XY Unsolved"?
18 In which series did Rowan Atkinson appear as a police officer?
19 Who was the British half of "Dempsey and Makepeace"?
20 Which long-running show increased the length of episodes in 1998 to one hour in a bid to improve ratings?
21 Stacey Keach played which detective from Mickey Spillane's novels?
22 "The Body in the Library" was the first in an 80s series about which sleuth?
23 Which series began with an Armchair Theatre production "Regan"?
24 Loretta Swit from "M*A*S*H" was replaced by Sharon Gless in which US series?
25 Who played barrister Kavanagh in the TV series?
26 Which detective was based at Denton police station?
27 How long did the "Morse" episodes usually last?
28 In which series did Samantha Janus star as Isobel de Pauli?
29 In which series did Charlie Hungerford appear?
30 Which series was based on the Constable novels by Nicholas Rea?

Answers	**Pot Luck 16** (see Quiz 34)

1 Hamlet. 2 Central Park Zoo, New York. 3 Take That. 4 Surrey. 5 Elizabeth I. 6 Tommy Steele. 7 Tutti Frutti. 8 A boat. 9 Rockall. 10 Portillo. 11 Fox. 12 Rudyard Kipling. 13 Van Gogh. 14 Trams. 15 George I. 16 Johnny Dankworth. 17 Chaka Khan. 18 Peter Davison. 19 Vertigo tour. 20 Michel Platini. 21 Scurvy. 22 Time. 23 Glucose. 24 Sheridan. 25 Texas. 26 Best Supporting Actress. 27 July, August. 28 Fairy tales. 29 Epiglottis. 30 Much.

1 In which Shakespeare play does a ghost walk on the battlements?
2 In "Madagascar" where do the animals escape from?
3 Which group had No. 1 hits with "Babe" and "Pray" in 1993?
4 Charterhouse Public School is found in which county?
5 Miranda Richardson played whom in the second "Blackadder" series?
6 Whose autobiography was called "Bermondsey Boy"?
7 Which 1987 TV series featured the ageing rock band The Majestics?
8 What is a gallivat?
9 Which British island is 230 miles West of the Hebrides in the Atlantic?
10 Which Michael lost his Enfield seat in the 1997 general election?
11 A skulk is the collective name for a group of which animal?
12 Who wrote "How the Leopard Got His Spots"?
13 Who painted the picture called "Irises"?
14 On which forms of transport would you find knifeboards?
15 Handel's "Water Music" was composed for which English King?
16 Who is Cleo Laine's bandleader husband?
17 Who had UK hits with "Ain't Nobody" and "I'm Every Woman"?
18 Georgia Moffett is the daughter of which ex-"Dr Who"?
19 What was the name of U2's 2005 tour of America?
20 From 1983–85 which Frenchman was European Footballer of the Year?
21 What disease are you suffering if you are scorbutic?
22 Dr Steve Hawking wrote the best-selling a brief history of what?
23 What is the other name for grape-sugar?
24 Who wrote the play "The School for Scandal"?
25 Which band made the hit albums "White on Blonde" and "The Hush"?
26 The film "The Piano" received Oscars for Best Actress and Best what?
27 In a single calendar year which two consecutive months total most days?
28 What did Charles Perrault collect?
29 Which flap of cartilage prevents food from entering your windpipe?
30 Which member of Robin Hood's gang was the son of a miller?

1 What are the three Baltic states?
2 In which country does the Douro reach the Atlantic?
3 What is the capital of Catalonia?
4 What is Northern Ireland's chief non-edible agricultural product?
5 What do the Germans call Bavaria?
6 Which European capital stands on the river Liffey?
7 What is the Eiffel Tower made from?
8 How is the Danish region of Jylland known in English?
9 In which forest does the Danube rise?
10 Which was the first country to legalise voluntary euthanasia?
11 What covers most of Finland?
12 In which country is the world's highest dam?
13 What is the capital of the Ukraine?
14 What is a remarkable feature of the caves at Lascaux in SW France?
15 What is Europe's highest capital city?
16 Where is France's Tomb of the Unknown Soldier?
17 Which area of the Rhone delta is famous for its nature reserve?
18 In which country would you find Kerkyra?
19 What are the two official European languages of Luxembourg?
20 The Magyars are the largest ethnic group of which country?
21 Where is Castilian an official language?
22 Abruzzi is a mountainous region of which country?
23 Which is the largest of the Balearic Islands?
24 On which island was the Mafia founded?
25 What is the UK's chief Atlantic port?
26 Tallinn is the capital of which Baltic state?
27 What is the main religion of Albania?
28 In which country would you meet Walloons?
29 In which country was the Millau Viaduct built?
30 Which country has Larisa and Volos amongst its chief towns?

1 Tony Christie tried to find it, but in which US State is Amarillo?
2 Whose hits include "Victims" and "Church of the Poison Mind"?
3 What is Rupert Murdoch's first name?
4 On CBeebies who is Charlie's younger sister?
5 In a calendar year what is the second quarter day in England?
6 Which robber on the run was in the film "The Great Rock and Roll Swindle"?
7 Who was older when he died, John Lennon or Elvis Presley?
8 Which fashion designer opened a shop in 1957 called Bazaar?
9 In which sport would you find a movement called a Salchow?
10 What is the name of the detective in "Pie in the Sky"?
11 What material does a topiarist work with?
12 Which actor was Rita's tutor in the film "Educating Rita"?
13 Which Saint has 15th July as his Feast Day?
14 Which two musical notes do not have flats on black keys?
15 Striker James Beattie made his league debut with which club?
16 Sabina Park is most famous for which sport?
17 Which animal can be described as vulpine?
18 "Atom Heart.....", what was the first Pink Floyd album to top the UK charts?
19 Where are Union Mills and Onchan Head in the British Isles?
20 Author HW Fowler produced a book in 1926 as a guide to what?
21 How many minutes are there in a day?
22 Who had a hit on the telephone in 1972 with "Sylvia's Mother"?
23 Moving through rooms to solve a murder involves which board game?
24 What can be 84cm, 91cm or 106cm in height in sport ?
25 The towns of Anaconda and Moscow are in which US State?
26 Which TV series features Dr Caroline Todd?
27 The university sited in Uxbridge is named after which engineer?
28 Which Melanie has been the partner of Antonio Banderas?
29 Which creatures mainly belong to the arachnidae family?
30 Who had hits with "Senza Una Donna" and "Come Back and Stay"?

Answers	**Euro Tour** *(see Quiz 35)*

1 Estonia, Latvia and Lithuania. 2 Portugal. 3 Barcelona. 4 Flax. 5 Bayern.
6 Dublin. 7 Iron. 8 Jutland. 9 Black Forest. 10 Netherlands. 11 Trees. 12
Switzerland. 13 Kiev. 14 Cave paintings. 15 Madrid. 16 Under L'Arc de Triomphe.
17 Camargue. 18 Greece. 19 French & German. 20 Hungary. 21 Spain. 22 Italy.
23 Majorca. 24 Sicily. 25 Liverpool. 26 Estonia. 27 Muslim. 28 Belgium. 29
France. 30 Greece.

1 The Sealed Knot Society re-enacts what?
2 Which racecourse has a famous Royal Enclosure?
3 What is the Quorn in Leicestershire?
4 What colour are hotels in Monopoly?
5 Where is the National Motor Museum?
6 What is the maximum number of pieces on a chessboard at any one time?
7 Sam Wanamaker founded which London theatre?
8 In which month do the French celebrate Bastille Day?
9 If you played outdoor hockey in the US what would it be called?
10 In which opera is the song "Summertime"?
11 Where in London did Laura Ashley open her first shop?
12 What is the world's biggest-selling copyrighted game?
13 Which organisation is the largest private landowner in Britain?
14 How high is a netball post?
15 If you have a credit card what is an APR?
16 Where did karaoke singing originate?
17 Who opened a bistro called Le Petit Blanc in 1984?
18 David Mercer, Chris Bailey and John Barrett have commentated on which sport?
19 Where was the first Virgin record shop?
20 During which months was the museum to Diana, Princess of Wales open at Althorp in 1998?
21 What might a numismatist collect along with coins?
22 Which day at Royal Ascot is Ladies' Day?
23 Who founded a theme park called Dollywood?
24 Bronco busting and steer wrestling take place at what type of event?
25 Which form of tennis is played on a smaller court, usually by children?
26 In which US state did skateboarding begin as an alternative to surfing?
27 What does the D stand for in NODA?
28 Which game is played at Hurlingham?
29 In slalom skiing what must you turn between?
30 What would be your hobby if you used slip?

Answers | Pot Luck 18 (see Quiz 38)

1 A bear. 2 Graham Hill. 3 The Booker Prize. 4 Reet Petite. 5 A fish. 6 Cat Stevens. 7 Spring. 8 Roots Hall. 9 Both beheaded. 10 Rattlesnakes. 11 Woman's Hour. 12 The Comet. 13 Saxophone. 14 Steve Fossett. 15 Eliza Doolittle. 16 Land. 17 A farrow. 18 Abel Magwitch. 19 Michael Crichton. 20 32. 21 Regent's Park. 22 Turn at different speeds. 23 Gross Domestic Product. 24 Africa. 25 Friday. 26 Manitoba. 27 A bat. 28 Sporting Lisbon. 29 1960s. 30 Lady Day.

1 Which animal can be described as ursine?

2 Who was older when he died, Graham Hill or James Hunt?

3 Which prize for fiction was instigated in 1969?

4 Which Jackie Wilson hit was No. 1 nearly thirty years after it was made?

5 A tarpon is a type of what?

6 In the pop charts in 2004, how was Yusuf Islam known when last in the charts?

7 If something is vernal, what is it connected with?

8 Where do Southend United football club play their home games?

9 How did both James I's mother and son die?

10 The sidewinder belongs to which group of snakes?

11 Which Radio 4 programme celebrated its 60th birthday in October 2006?

12 Which was the first commercial jet aircraft in the world?

13 Jazz musician John Coltrane played which instrument?

14 In March 2005, who became the first person to fly a plane solo, non-stop around the globe without refuelling?

15 Which part was played by Audrey Hepburn in the film "My Fair Lady"?

16 Wapentakes, hundreds and hides were all areas of what?

17 What is the collective name for a litter of piglets?

18 Who gave Pip his wealth in "Great Expectations"?

19 Who wrote the novel "Jurassic Park"?

20 How many squares have pieces on them at the start of a chess game?

21 In which London park are The Holme, The Broad Walk and Winfield House?

22 What does the differential on a car allow the driving wheels to do?

23 The abbreviation GDP stands for what?

24 The Gulf of Sidra is located off the coast of which continent?

25 Which day of the week is named after the Norse Goddess Freya?

26 Winnipeg is the capital of which Canadian province?

27 What type of creature is a flying fox?

28 Cristiano Ronaldo joined Man Utd from which club?

29 In which decade was the Guinness Book of Records first published?

30 In a calendar year what is the first quarter day in England?

| **Answers** | Hobbies & Leisure 1 *(see Quiz 37)* |

1 Battles of the English Civil War. 2 Ascot. 3 Hunt. 4 Red. 5 Beaulieu. 6 32. 7 Shakespeare's Globe. 8 July. 9 Field hockey. 10 Porgy and Bess. 11 Kensington. 12 Monopoly. 13 National Trust. 14 10 feet (3.05m). 15 Annual Percentage Rate. 16 Japan. 17 Raymond Blanc. 18 Tennis. 19 Oxford Street. 20 July and August. 21 Medals. 22 Second day. 23 Dolly Parton. 24 Rodeo. 25 Short tennis. 26 California. 27 Dramatic. 28 Polo. 29 Flags. 30 Pottery.

1 Which US President's father was a former Ambassador in the UK?

2 Edith Cresson was which country's PM from 1991–92?

3 The Downing Street Declaration in 1993 involved the Prime Ministers of which two countries?

4 Which family died at Ekaterinburg in 1918?

5 Which school provided the UK with 19 Prime Ministers before 2000?

6 In which war did British soldiers first wear balaclava helmets?

7 Which mountaineer was the first person since Scott to reach the South Pole overland, in 1958?

8 The "Bomb Plot" of 1944 failed to assassinate whom?

9 What was the minimum age for joining the UK Home Guard in WWII?

10 Which former US President was a distant relative of Princess Diana?

11 Who was the first woman President of Ireland?

12 In which US state did Martin Luther King lead the 1955 bus boycott?

13 Who lost power in Germany in 1998 after 16 years?

14 Who became Secretary General of the UN in 1997?

15 Who was Bonnie Prince Charlie disguised as when he escaped to France with Flora MacDonald?

16 Who defected to the USSR with Guy Burgess in 1951?

17 Carlos Menem became President of which country in 1989?

18 Who was the first Governor General of India, until 1948?

19 What was the alliance between the Germans and the Italians in World War II called?

20 Where in the East End of London did Jack the Ripper operate?

21 As a double agent, Mata Hari was executed by whom?

22 Mrs Meir was the first woman PM in which country?

23 Who was the USA's first Roman Catholic President?

24 Which country has had Jospin and Raffarin as Prime Ministers?

25 Which Panamanian leader was nicknamed Pineapple Face?

26 Which Pass did Hannibal use to cross the Alps?

27 Who became President of Ireland in 1997?

28 In which Vietnamese village were 109 civilians massacred by US troops in 1968?

29 Who was the first woman US Secretary of State?

30 TV's "Murphy's Law" is set in which city?

Answers	Pot Luck 19 *(see Quiz 40)*

1 One square mile. 2 Slaves. 3 Stocks & share prices. 4 Fleet Air Arm. 5 Father of the House. 6 70. 7 Park Lane. 8 Moses. 9 Cunard. 10 Corgi. 11 Kent and Sussex. 12 Red. 13 RAF. 14 Tigris. 15 48. 16 Ageism. 17 Charlotte Church. 18 Railway carriage. 19 High blood pressure. 20 Wheel clamp. 21 Vice Squad. 22 Motherwell. 23 The soul. 24 JRR Tolkien. 25 A cough. 26 Westminster Cathedral. 27 Orange. 28 Siouxsie and the Banshees. 29 Extinction. 30 Simon Amstell.

1 What is the area of the City of London?
2 What is the last word of Rule Britannia?
3 What does the Footsie show?
4 Which branch of the Royal Navy is concerned with aviation?
5 What name is given to the MP who has served in the House of Commons the longest?
6 A driving licence is issued until the driver reaches what age?
7 In which Lane is London's Dorchester Hotel?
8 In the Old Testament Aaron was the elder brother of which prophet?
9 Which shipping company operated the Queen Mary and the Queen Elizabeth?
10 Which dog's name comes from the Welsh for dwarf dog?
11 In which two English counties are the Cinque Ports?
12 What colour coats do Chelsea Pensioners wear in the summer?
13 Cranwell trains cadets for which of the armed forces?
14 Which river flows through Baghdad?
15 How many kilometres per hour is 30 miles an hour?
16 What is discrimination against the elderly called?
17 Which former child singing star presented a late-night chat show on Channel 4 in 2006?
18 In what type of vehicle was the 1918 World War armistice signed?
19 What is another name for hypertension?
20 What is another name for a Denver boot?
21 Which police department deals with illegal gambling and pornography?
22 James McFadden joined Everton from which club?
23 In religious terms what does absolution purify?
24 Who wrote the fantasy novel "The Silmarillion"?
25 Which condition will an antitussive help alleviate?
26 What is the principal Roman Catholic church in England?
27 What colour is a disabled driver's badge?
28 Who had hits with "Dear Prudence" and "Hong Kong Gardens"?
29 The permanent disappearance of a species is described by which word?
30 Which Simon replaced Mark Lamarr as host of "Never Mind the Buzzcocks"?

Answers	**People & Places** *(see Quiz 39)*

1 Kennedy. 2 France. 3 UK & Ireland. 4 The Romanovs. 5 Eton. 6 Crimean War. 7 Edmund Hillary. 8 Hitler. 9 17. 10 Ronald Reagan. 11 Mary Robinson. 12 Alabama. 13 Helmut Kohl. 14 Kofi Annan. 15 Flora's maid. 16 Donald Maclean. 17 Argentina. 18 Lord Mountbatten. 19 Axis. 20 Whitechapel. 21 The French. 22 Israel. 23 John F. Kennedy. 24 France. 25 Noriega. 26 Little St Bernard. 27 Mary McAleese. 28 My Lai. 29 Madeleine Albright. 30 Dublin.

1 Which hit was No. 2 for Rick Astley and No. 4 for Nat King Cole in '87?
2 What was the first Top Ten hit for Tanita Tikaram?
3 What were "shattered" in the 1987 No. 5 hit for Johnny Hates Jazz?
4 Who joined Kenny Rogers on "We've Got Tonight"?
5 Which Jimmy Nail hit was a cover of a Rose Royce hit?
6 New Edition got to No. 1 in '83 with which Girl?
7 Who were spun around by their No. 1 "You Spin Me Round (like a record)"?
8 Which group had Top Ten hits with "Breakout" and "Surrender"?
9 Whose first UK No. 1 hit was "West End Girls"?
10 What was KC and the Sunshine Band's only UK No. 1 in the 80s?
11 Which twins had hits with "Love on Your Side" and "Doctor Doctor"?
12 Which town got The Specials to No. 1 in 1981?
13 What followed "Ooh La La La" in the 1982 hit for Kool and the Gang?
14 The name of which Asian country gave Kim Wilde an 80s hit?
15 Having left the Jam, Paul Weller charted regularly with which band?
16 Where did Lipps Inc. take us to in their No. 2 from 1980?
17 Which antipodean title was a No. 1 for Men at Work in 1983?
18 The song "Intuition" was the only UK Top Ten single for which duo?
19 Mental As Anything had a No. 3 with "Live It Up" from which film?
20 Who joined Julio Inglesias on his No. 5 success "My Love"?
21 Which animal was sleeping on the No. 1 hit by Tight Fit?
22 Which '87 Billy Idol hit was a cover of an earlier Tommy James hit?
23 What was Simply Red's first Top Ten UK hit?
24 Which Del Shannon hit became an 80s hit for Icehouse?
25 How many No. 1 singles did The Bee Gees have throughout the 1980s?
26 What in 1986 was Spandau Ballet's last UK Top Ten hit?
27 Who joined Fun Boy Three on "It Ain't What You Do" in 1982?
28 Which day links a No. 2 by the Bangles with a No. 3 by New Order?
29 Who had No. 1 singles working with Queen and then Mick Jagger?
30 Whose first Top Ten hit was "Harvest for the World" in 1988?

Answers | Pot Luck 20 *(see Quiz 42)*

1 Whiskey. 2 Amanda Barrie. 3 The Pope. 4 Tuberculosis. 5 On the bridge. 6 Cabaret. 7 JD Fortune. 8 Fennel. 9 Deep Purple. 10 Monkey bread. 11 A prison. 12 Kate Moss. 13 Ewan McGregor. 14 Harold Wilson. 15 Number game. 16 French. 17 Trees. 18 The Sex Pistols. 19 Gardner. 20 In water. 21 A dog. 22 Harry. 23 Denmark and Norway. 24 Grace Kelly. 25 Animals. 26 Edinburgh. 27 Ecuador. 28 George Gershwin. 29 Conciliation. 30 Que Sera Sera.

1 Which drink did American Indians call Firewater in the Wild West ?
2 Which former Corrie actress played Beverley Tull in "Bad Girls"?
3 Who sends encyclical letters?
4 The White Death was a name for which former common disease?
5 According to the song, where does everyone dance in Avignon?
6 Which musical and movie is based on the writing of Christopher Isherwood?
7 Who was the first permanent replacement for Michael Hutchence in INXS?
8 Which leaves taste of aniseed?
9 Which group had a Top Ten hit with "Black Knight"?
10 What is the fruit of a baobab tree called?
11 What was a bridewell?
12 Which model's childhood nickname was "Mosschops"?
13 Who is the voice of Rodney Copperbottom in "Robots"?
14 "A week is a long time in politics" was said by which politician?
15 Who or what is Futoshiki?
16 What is the official language of the Ivory Coast?
17 What are pruned in coppicing?
18 Which group featured in "The Great Rock 'n' Roll Swindle"?
19 Which Ava was one of Frank Sinatra's wives?
20 If a plant is a hydrophyte where does it live?
21 A papillon is a type of what?
22 What was Bing Crosby's first name?
23 Which two countries are separated by the Skagerrak?
24 Which royal film star appeared in "Dial M for Murder"?
25 What does the Blue Cross Charity, founded in 1897, provide aid to?
26 In which Scottish city are Salisbury Crags?
27 Which South American country has the sucre as the unit of currency?
28 Who composed the music for the musical "Strike Up the Band"?
29 What does the C stand for in ACAS?
30 Which song was sung in three different films by Doris Day?

1 Which American was UK champion jockey in 1984, 1985 and 1987?

2 In which month does the Cheltenham Festival take place?

3 Which two races make up the autumn double?

4 How long is the Derby?

5 How many times did Willie Carson win the Derby?

6 Which late Cabinet Minister had been the Glasgow Herald's racing tipster?

7 Who had nine Derby wins and was champion jockey 11 times?

8 Which British racehorse owner sold Vernons Pools in 1988?

9 Who was Champion Jockey a record 26 times between 1925 and 1953?

10 Which Light was a Derby winner for Kieren Fallon?

11 Which Classic was the first to be run on a Sunday in England?

12 In 1995 which horse won the Derby, the King George VI and the Prix de l'Arc de Triomphe?

13 Alex Greaves was the first female jockey in which race?

14 Where is Valentine's Brook?

15 At which racecourse is the Steward's Cup competed for annually?

16 Who was riding Devon Loch when it so nearly won the National?

17 What is Frankie Dettori's real first name?

18 Which Jim was rider for Best Mate's Cheltenham Gold Cup triple triumphs?

19 Which horse won the Cheltenham Gold Cup in 1964, '65 and '66?

20 Who was the UK's first overseas champion jockey after Steve Cauthen?

21 Where is Tattenham Corner?

22 What is the highest jump in the Grand National?

23 Where did Walter Swinburn sustain severe injuries in February 1997?

24 Who won the Grand National in 1993?

25 Which auctioneers were founded in London in 1766 but now have annual sales in Newmarket?

26 Which racecourse is near Bognor Regis?

27 What was unusual about the status of Mr Frisk's winning rider in the 1990 National?

28 How old are horses who run in nursery stakes?

29 In which month is Royal Ascot?

30 What colour was in the name of 2001 Grand National winner Marauder?

Answers | TV: Sitcoms *(see Quiz 44)*

1 Dermot. 2 Gareth Blackstock. 3 Only Fools and Horses. 4 Drop the Dead Donkey. 5 Richard Wilson. 6 Jean Alexander. 7 Seinfeld. 8 A wheelchair. 9 Till Death Us Do Part. 10 Fawlty Towers. 11 Porridge. 12 Annie. 13 Cockerel. 14 Thelma. 15 Napoleon. 16 Bubble. 17 After Henry. 18 Are You Being Served?. 19 Gary Sparrow. 20 As Time Goes By. 21 Barker. 22 Cher. 23 They were witches. 24 Baldrick. 25 Allo Allo. 26 Green. 27 Christopher Biggins. 28 Geraldine Grainger. 29 Bottom. 30 Gordon.

1 What was the name of Harry Enfield's character in "Men Behaving Badly"?

2 What was the name of the Chef in "Chef!"?

3 What was the most successful sitcom of the 1980s?

4 Which series took place at the Globelink News Office?

5 Which sit com star worked in a hospital laboratory before becoming an actor?

6 Which former soap star plays Auntie Wainwright in "Last of the Summer Wine"?

7 Which US sitcom, which had 180 episodes, finished in May 1998?

8 In "Phoenix Nights" Peter Kay's character used what for mobility?

9 "All in the Family" was a US spin-off from which UK sitcom?

10 Where would you find guests Major Gowen, Miss Tibbs and Miss Gatsby?

11 "Going Straight" was the sequel to what?

12 What was the name of Jim Hacker's wife in "Yes Minister"?

13 In "The Good Life", who or what was Lenin?

14 In "The Likely Lads", whom did Bob marry?

15 In "Dad's Army" what did the air raid warden always call Mainwaring?

16 Who was Edina's PA in "Absolutely Fabulous"?

17 Which series with Prunella Scales as Sarah France had three years on radio before transferring to TV?

18 "Grace and Favour" was a sequel to which sitcom?

19 What is the name of the time traveller in "Goodnight Sweetheart"?

20 Which show's theme song begins, "You must remember this..."?

21 Which Ronnie's famous roles have included Arkwright and Fletcher?

22 Which star of "Mermaids" made a guest appearance on "Will & Grace"?

23 What was strange about Samantha Stephens and her mother Endora?

24 Who was Blackadder's servant?

25 Which sitcom was a send-up of "Secret Army"?

26 What was Dorien's surname in "Birds of a Feather"?

27 Who was the effeminate Lukewarm in "Porridge"?

28 What was the Vicar of Dibley's name?

29 In which series did Richie and Eddie first appear?

30 What was Brittas's first name in "The Brittas Empire"?

Answers	**Sport: Horse Racing** *(see Quiz 43)*

1 Steve Cauthen. 2 March. 3 Cesarewitch and the Cambridgeshire. 4 A mile and a half. 5 Four. 6 Robin Cook. 7 Lester Piggott. 8 Robert Sangster. 9 Gordon Richards. 10 North Light. 11 1,000 Guineas. 12 Lammtarra. 13 The Derby. 14 Aintree. 15 Goodwood. 16 Dick Francis. 17 Lanfranco. 18 Jim Cullohy. 19 Arkle. 20 Frankie Dettori. 21 Epsom. 22 The Chair. 23 Hong Kong. 24 No one, it was abandoned. 25 Tattersall's. 26 Fontwell Park. 27 Amateur. 28 Two. 29 June. 30 Red Marauder.

1 If you nictitate at someone, what do you do?
2 Who offered Demi Moore a million dollars in "Indecent Proposal"?
3 Monument Valley is in which American state?
4 Which island off the north Devon coast is named after the Norse for puffin?
5 Who had 2005 hits with "Devil" and "Superman"?
6 On 14 April 1912, what occurred off Newfoundland?
7 Which "Strictly Come Dancing" star kept goal for both Man Utd and City?
8 Which instrument was played by David in the Bible?
9 Who is taller, Madonna or Dawn French?
10 Which organisation was founded in 1953 by Reverend Chad Varah?
11 In corned beef what are the corns?
12 Which people used knotted cords called quipu for calculation?
13 Which character was played by Maggie Smith in "Sister Act"?
14 Who wrote the novel "Journey to the Centre of the Earth"?
15 At which school was Thomas Arnold a famous headmaster?
16 Which "Cagney & Lacey" star appeared in the TV thriller "The State Within"?
17 How many squadrons make up a wing in the Royal Air Force?
18 Who followed U Thant as Secretary General of the United Nations?
19 Which high street chain was founded in 1961 by Selim Zilkha?
20 What does the book Glass's Guide contain?
21 What does B stand for in ASBO?
22 Who directed the epic action movie "Gladiator"?
23 What is an aspen?
24 The Battle of Pinkie of 1547 was fought in which country?
25 What nationality was Amy Johnson?
26 Which animal has the longest pregnancy?
27 Anything above scale 12 on the Beaufort Scale would describe what?
28 Which group were made up of Cass, Michelle, John and Denny?
29 Cars with the international vehicle registration PA come from where?
30 Whom did Shylock want to take his pound of flesh from?

Answers	**Musical Movies** *(see Quiz 46)*

1 Amos Hart. 2 Ursula Andress. 3 Cyd Charisse. 4 Maurice Chevalier. 5 The Philadelphia Story. 6 Martin Scorsese. 7 Dirty Dancing. 8 Whitney Houston. 9 Richard E. Grant. 10 Master of ceremonies. 11 Antonio Banderas. 12 The Nightmate Before Christmas. 13 Rex Harrison. 14 Moulin Rouge. 15 Marlon Brando. 16 Yul Brynner. 17 Baron Georg Von Trapp. 18 Freddie Eynsford-Hill. 19 Saturday Night Fever. 20 Autry. 21 1950s. 22 Albert Finney. 23 South Pacific. 24 Chim Chim Cheree. 25 Help! 26 Fiddler on the Roof. 27 Jonathan Pryce. 28 Sammy Davis Jr. 29 Cabaret. 30 Monroe.

1 Which Chicago character calls himself Mr Cellophane?

2 Which Bond girl starred with Elvis Presley in "Fun in Acapulco"?

3 Who danced with Gene Kelly in the Broadway Ballet section of "Singin' in the Rain"?

4 Who sang "Thank Heaven for Little Girls" in "Gigi"?

5 "High Society" was a musical version of which classic?

6 Which controversial figure directed the musical "New York, New York"?

7 Josef Brown starred in the West End stage premiere of which hit movie?

8 Who sang most of the soundtrack of "The Bodyguard"?

9 Who had a managerial role in "Spiceworld"?

10 Joel Grey won an Oscar for which role in the 1970s classic "Cabaret"?

11 Who played Che in the film version of "Evita"?

12 Which Tim Burton film featured a hostile takeover of present delivery at Christmas?

13 Who played the Doctor in the musical film version of "Doctor Doolittle"?

14 "Children of the Revolution" and "The Red Room" are songs featured in which film?

15 Which tough guy actor played Sky Masterson in "Guys and Dolls"?

16 Which star of "The King and I" was born in Russia?

17 Whom does Julie Andrews's character marry in "The Sound of Music"?

18 Which character sings "On the Street Where You Live" in "My Fair Lady"?

19 Which 1970s film became a stage musical in London in 1998?

20 Which Gene was the singing cowboy?

21 In which decade does the action of "Grease" take place?

22 Which English actor played the millionaire benefactor in "Annie"?

23 In which musical does Nurse Nellie Forbush appear?

24 Which of the many songs in "Mary Poppins" won the Oscar?

25 What was The Beatles' second film?

26 Which musical is the tale of a Jewish milkman in pre-revolutionary Russia?

27 Who played Eva's husband in "Evita"?

28 Who led "The Rhythm of Life" sequence in Sweet Charity?

29 Which 1970s musical film was set in pre-war Berlin?

30 Which Marylin sang "Diamonds are a Girl's Best Friend"?

---

1 What is a pickled gherkin made from?
2 Which keeper was a winner in the first FA Cup Final decided on penalties?
3 What is the name of Britney Spears' second son?
4 Pooh Bah appears in which Gilbert and Sullivan operetta?
5 Which Classic race is run over the longest distance?
6 Who was the brother of Flopsy, Mopsy and Cottontail?
7 What form did the head of the Sphinx take?
8 Which voice in singing is pitched between a tenor and a soprano?
9 Which birds collect in a covey?
10 Which now deposed leader led Iraq into the 1990s Gulf War?
11 Titian is what colour?
12 What part did Madonna play in the film "Shanghai Surprise"?
13 What does the M stand for in MIRAS?
14 Which almost eradicated disease was called Phthisis?
15 "The Moonstone" by Wilkie Collins is about a jewel from which country?
16 In which country is Lake Bala the largest natural lake?
17 Which "Pop Idol" sang at the Queen's Jubilee celebrations?
18 The US state of Maryland was named after the wife of which King?
19 What type of bars join places of equal atmospheric pressure on a chart?
20 Which tennis star was sued by Judy Nelson for palimony?
21 Who played Mark Antony opposite Liz Taylor in the film "Cleopatra"?
22 Which veteran presented "Old Dogs, New Tricks" with Lynn Faulds Wood?
23 Which European city hosted the 2004 summer Olympics?
24 What is the first name of PD James' detective Dalgleish?
25 Which part did Dustin Hoffman play in the film "Hook"?
26 What was the title of the 1994 East 17 Christmas No. 1 UK hit?
27 Who was British PM directly before Edward Heath?
28 Which Open win was Nick Faldo's first?
29 What can be solo boxing, a lush mineral or a round timber?
30 Which part did Gene Hackman play in the "Superman" films?

| **Answers** | **Living World** *(see Quiz 48)* |

1 Tidal wave. 2 On the skin. 3 CJD. 4 Worm. 5 Haematology. 6 Hermaphrodite. 7 Falcon. 8 Ear. 9 Marine snail. 10 Knee. 11 Pigeons. 12 Anaemia. 13 Orange. 14 Fungus. 15 Skin. 16 Abdomen. 17 Shoulder blade. 18 Fish. 19 Short-sighted. 20 12. 21 Idi Amin. 22 Acne. 23 The kiss of life. 24 Tuberculosis. 25 Base of the brain. 26 Achilles tendon. 27 Liver. 28 Green. 29 Kidney. 30 Herring.

1 Tsunami is another name for what type of wave?

2 Where would a melanoma appear?

3 Which disease in humans has been linked to the cattle disease BSE?

4 What sort of creature is a fluke?

5 Which branch of medicine is concerned with disorders of the blood?

6 What name is given to an organism which is both male and female?

7 What sort of bird is a Merlin?

8 Which part of the body might suffer from labyrinthitis?

9 What sort of creature is an abalone?

10 Where is a bird's patella?

11 Which racing creatures live in lofts?

12 What condition is caused by a shortage of haemoglobin?

13 What colour are the spots on a plaice?

14 What is a puffball?

15 Which part of the body does scabies affect?

16 Which digestive organ lies below the thorax in invertebrates?

17 Where is a human's scapula?

18 What do most sharks live on?

19 If a person has myopia what problem does he or she have?

20 How many pairs of ribs does a human have?

21 Which putative monarch was portrayed in the film "The Last King of Scotland"?

22 Which skin disorder is caused by inflammation of the sebaceous glands?

23 What is the popular name for mouth-to-mouth resuscitation?

24 A BCG is a vaccination against which disease?

25 Where is the pituitary gland?

26 Which tendon pins the calf muscle to the heel bone?

27 Hepatic refers to which organ of the body?

28 What colour head does a male mallard usually have?

29 The adrenal gland is above which organ?

30 The pilchard is a member of which fish family?

1 Was Craig David aged 18, 22 or 25 when he first had a No. 1 single?
2 The city of Philadelphia was founded by which religious group?
3 Where would you normally play shovel-board?
4 Which is further North, Blackburn or Blackpool?
5 Which husband of Demi Moore starred in "The Guardian"?
6 Which motor racing team is named after the sacred flower in India?
7 Donald McGill was particularly associated with what seaside art form?
8 Who wrote "Willie Wonka and the Chocolate Factory"?
9 Who narrates "Treasure Island" other than Jim Hawkins?
10 What is the New Zealand National Day called?
11 Paul Merson made his league debut with which club?
12 Which ship sent the first S.O.S.?
13 Which actress penned the autobiography "The Two of Us"?
14 Who wrote "The God Delusion"?
15 Which flower is on the badge of the Boy Scouts?
16 Which former Lebanese hostage wrote a book with Jill Morrell?
17 Maddy Magellan is the partner of which fictional detective?
18 Which Marlon Brando film is based on Conrad's "Heart of Darkness"?
19 In which group of islands is Panay?
20 Sandra Kim became the youngest winner of which contest?
21 The Sierra Nevada mountains are in which American state?
22 Who played Edward in TV's "Edward and Mrs Simpson"?
23 STASHING is an anagram of which famous battle?
24 The TV series "Rebus" was based on the novels of which writer?
25 Whose hits include "Kayleigh" and "Lavender"?
26 Was the Sopwith Camel designed by Sopwith or Camel?
27 Where in the UK is Compton Bay?
28 From 2003 to 2006 which Andy was at Blackburn, Fulham, Man City and Portsmouth?
29 Which word links a pastime, a small horse and a small falcon?
30 Which daily food includes the protein casein?

Answers	**Famous Celebs** (see Quiz 50)

1 Mohammed Al-Fayed. 2 Longleat. 3 Sarah. 4 Oprah Winfrey. 5 Alan Clark. 6 Antonia de Sancha. 7 Edwina Currie. 8 Countess Spencer. 9 Holloway Prison. 10 Beatrice. 11 Texas. 12 Michael Heseltine. 13 Everton. 14 Jemima Khan. 15 Max Clifford. 16 Loos. 17 Sir Cameron Mackintosh. 18 Demi Moore. 19 David Bailey. 20 Elizabeth Hurley. 21 Diana, Princess of Wales. 22 Lord Snowdon. 23 Spencer. 24 Peter Stringfellow. 25 French. 26 Vivienne Westwood. 27 Chef. 28 George Galloway. 29 Geri Halliwell. 30 Martine McCutcheon.

1 Who owns The Ritz in Paris?
2 Which stately home and safari park belongs to the Marquis of Bath?
3 What were two out of Andrew Lloyd-Webber's three wives called?
4 On which US chat show did Madonna first discuss the adoption of a baby from Malawi?
5 Which Tory MP philanderer said "Only domestic servants apologise" after his Diaries were published?
6 The story of whose affair with David Mellor broke in 1992?
7 Which outspoken ex-MP shares her birthday with Margaret Thatcher?
8 What was the previous title of Raine, Comtesse de Chambrun?
9 Where did Geri Halliwell have a meeting behind closed doors to launch 1998 Breast Cancer Awareness Week?
10 What is the name of the daughter of Paul McCartney and Heather Mills?
11 Jerry Hall is from which US state?
12 Whose heart attack in Venice prevented him from pursuing the Tory leadership?
13 Theatre impresario Bill Kenwright is a director of which soccer club?
14 Which late billionaire's daughter has a son called Sulaiman?
15 Which PR man acted for Mandy Allwood and Bienvenida Buck?
16 Lady Lucinda Lambton is an expert on which convenient necessity?
17 Which knighted impresario had a record six West End musicals running in 1996?
18 Which Hollywood star actress is Rumer Willis's mum?
19 Which photographer discovered Jean Shrimpton in the 60s?
20 Who became the face of Estee Lauder in the mid-1990s?
21 Who was Mrs Frances Shand Kydd's youngest daughter?
22 How was Anthony Armstrong-Jones known after his royal marriage?
23 Which future Earl did model Victoria Lockwood marry in 1990?
24 Which Sheffield-born nightclub owner's most famous club is named after him?
25 What is the nationality of designer Catherine Walker?
26 Which outrageous designer was once the partner of Sex Pistols' manager Malcolm McLaren?
27 In which profession did Marco Pierre White find fame?
28 Dr Amineh Abu-Zayyad married which Respect MP?
29 Which singing celeb's autobiography was called "Just for the Record"?
30 Which ex "EastEnders" star was a bridesmaid to Liza Minnelli in 2002?

Answers	**Pot Luck 23** (see Quiz 49)

1 18. 2 The Quakers. 3 On a ship's deck. 4 Blackpool. 5 Ashton Kutcher. 6 Lotus. 7 Postcards. 8 Roald Dahl. 9 Dr Livesey. 10 Waitangi Day. 11 Arsenal. 12 Titanic. 13 Sheila Hancock. 14 Richard Dawkins. 15 Fleur de Lis. 16 John McCarthy. 17 Jonathan Creek. 18 Apocalypse Now. 19 Philippines. 20 Eurovision Song Contest. 21 California. 22 Edward Fox. 23 Hastings. 24 Ian Rankin. 25 Marillion. 26 Sopwith. 27 Isle of Wight. 28 Andy Cole. 29 A hobby. 30 Milk.

1 Which England player was likened to Mary Poppins by a director of his own club?
2 What would you do with a saxhorn?
3 Who was singer Lorna Luft's famous actress mother?
4 "What Will the Neighbours Say?" was the second album from which group?
5 Which cartoon character is in the class with bully Nelson Muntz?
6 Who said, "4–5 isn't a football result, it's an ice hockey match"?
7 Which is the largest and oldest Australian city?
8 Whose autobiography was called "Mustn't Grumble"?
9 How is the wife of a Knight addressed?
10 Light, Home and Third used to be what?
11 What name is given to a person who eats no food of animal origin?
12 Who wrote the song "Moon River"?
13 Who led the Scottish troops at Bannockburn?
14 Which Palace is the official home of the French president?
15 What is a water moccasin?
16 In which group of islands are St Martin's, St Mary's and Tresco?
17 Which people made an idol in the form of a Golden Calf in the Bible?
18 Which actor starred in the film "North by Northwest"?
19 Which city is called the City of Brotherly Love?
20 In which sport were John Louis and Barry Briggs associated?
21 Whose biography was called "Neither Shaken nor Stirred"?
22 Which famous Falls are on the Zambezi river?
23 What kind of flower can be a goldilocks?
24 Philippa Braithwaite married which star of "Doc Martin" and "Losing It"?
25 If you are a member of the Q Guild, what is your profession?
26 Which creature's name can go in front of crab, plant, wasp and monkey?
27 How many cards are in a tarot pack?
28 In "Trading Places" who traded places with Dan Aykroyd?
29 Diluted acetic acid is the correct name for which foodstuff?
30 Whose hits include "The Bitch is Back" and "Kiss the Bride"?

Answers	Leisure 2 *(see Quiz 52)*

1 Role Playing. 2 Boules. 3 May. 4 British Museum. 5 22. 6 Sumo wrestling. 7 Lawn tennis. 8 Their hands. 9 Yin and Yang. 10 York. 11 Weightlifting. 12 Bonsai. 13 Plastic shuttlecocks. 14 Scotland. 15 Windsurfing. 16 Lego. 17 Horse racing, cards. 18 Michael Caine. 19 Phillip Schofield. 20 Rose. 21 Normandy. 22 One. 23 AA. 24 China. 25 MCC. 26 Hamley's Regent Street, London. 27 In its ear. 28 Ever After. 29 Swimming. 30 Four.

1 What imaginative type of Game is known by the initials RPG?
2 Which French game's name is the French word for balls?
3 In which month is Spring Bank Holiday?
4 Which London Museum was the most visited in 2005?
5 How many balls are needed to play a game of snooker?
6 What is the national sport of Japan?
7 What is lawn tennis called when played on shale or clay?
8 In volleyball what do players hit the ball with?
9 What is the Chinese for "dark" and "light" believed to maintain equilibrium?
10 Where is the Jorvik Viking Museum?
11 In which sport would you snatch and jerk?
12 The name of which type of tree cultivation comes from the Japanese for "bowl cultivation"?
13 Which major change was introduced in badminton in 1949?
14 In which country is the oldest angling club in the world?
15 What is another name for boardsailing?
16 Which toy was invented by Danes Ole and Godtfred Christiansen?
17 If you were at or playing Newmarket which leisure pursuits would you be following?
18 Which cockney actor was a part owner of Langan's Brasserie?
19 Who played Dr Doolittle when it first appeared on the London stage?
20 Bourbon and Gallica are types of what?
21 In which French region is the annual apple festival at Orne?
22 If you received cotton, how many wedding anniversaries would you be celebrating?
23 Which UK motoring association describes itself as the fourth emergency service?
24 Which is the largest country where membership of the Scouts is not allowed?
25 Which club founded in 1787 voted to allow women members in 1998?
26 Where is the world's oldest toyshop?
27 Where does a Steiff teddy bear have its tag of authenticity?
28 What was the 1998 movie based on Cinderella, and starring Drew Barrymore called?
29 If you joined the Wasps in Wigan what sport would you compete in?
30 How many tournaments make up the Grand Slam in golf?

Answers	Pot Luck 24 *(see Quiz 51)*

1 Alan Shearer. 2 Play it. 3 Judy Garland. 4 Girls Aloud. 5 Bart Simpson. 6 Jose Mourinho (about Spurs v. Arsenal). 7 Sydney. 8 Terry Wogan. 9 Lady. 10 Radio channels. 11 A vegan. 12 Henry Mancini. 13 Robert the Bruce. 14 Elysée. 15 Snake. 16 Scilly Isles. 17 The Israelites. 18 Cary Grant. 19 Philadelphia. 20 Speedway. 21 Sean Connery. 22 Victoria Falls. 23 A buttercup. 24 Martin Clunes. 25 A Butcher. 26 Spider. 27 78. 28 Eddie Murphy. 29 Vinegar. 30 Elton John.

1 Which club joined the Football League in 1978 and made the Premiership in 2005?

2 Dove Cottage was home of which poet?

3 Which Pole was first reached in 1909?

4 Which Day replaced Empire Day in 1958?

5 Alfred the Great ruled which Kingdom?

6 Estoril is a resort north east of which major city?

7 Which No. 1 for Norman Greenbaum was reworked by Gareth Gates?

8 Who was the founder lead singer with Led Zeppelin in 1968?

9 Freddie Powell found fame as which crazy comic?

10 Which British surgeon was a pioneer in improving surgery hygiene?

11 Who was the female lead in "Singing in the Rain"?

12 Which common garden flower has the name Dianthus barbatus?

13 Where were the Spode pottery works established in the 1760s?

14 Cars with the international vehicle registration BG come from where?

15 Which Club included Mr Winkle and Mr Tupman as members?

16 Never Say Die was the first Derby winner for which famous jockey?

17 In which area of England is "Wire in the Blood" set?

18 Which castle is the largest in Britain?

19 Edwin Hubble was concerned with which branch of science?

20 Which part did Albert Finney play in the 1974 film "Murder on the Orient Express"?

21 Sir Alfred Munnings is famous for painting which animals?

22 Comic character Dan Dare was known as the pilot of what?

23 Colonel Thomas Blood tried to steal what in 1671?

24 In a famous 1990s case, Robert Hoskins was convicted of stalking which star?

25 What sort of creature was a brawn?

26 If you suffered a myocardial infarction, what would have happened?

27 Who partnered Annie Lennox in the Eurythmics?

28 The Peace River is in which country?

29 In 1957, in which US state were there race riots at Little Rock?

30 Who won a best supporting actor Oscar for a role in "Million Dollar Baby"?

Answers | Pop Music: The 90s *(see Quiz 54)*

1 I Believe. 2 Too Much. 3 Sting & Bryan Adams. 4 Saturday. 5 Gabrielle. 6 Boombastic. 7 Colchester. 8 Back to Black. 9 Without You. 10 Would I Lie to You. 11 Germany. 12 The Bodyguard. 13 Prodigy. 14 Fairground. 15 Boyz II Men. 16 Looking Up. 17 I Wonder Why. 18 Spice Girls. 19 Cecilia. 20 Peter Andre. 21 Too Young to Die. 22 Ebeneezer Goode. 23 James Brown. 24 Kylie Minogue. 25 Think Twice. 26 Shiny Happy People. 27 Doop. 28 Beverley Craven. 29 The Real Thing. 30 Lady Marmalade.

1 What was the other side of Robson and Jerome's "Up on the Roof"?
2 Which Spice Girl hit came first – "Goodbye" or "Too Much"?
3 Which two singers joined Rod Stewart on the 1994 hit "All for Love"?
4 What night links Whigfield, Alexander O'Neal and Omar?
5 Who featured on East 17's No. 2 "If You Ever" in 1996?
6 Which 1995 hit gave Shaggy his second No. 1?
7 Blur were formed in which East Anglian town?
8 What is the title of Amy Winehouse's second album?
9 Which song title links No. 1s for Mariah Carey and Nilsson?
10 Which title links the Eurythmics to a 1992 No. 1 for Charles and Eddy?
11 Which country did pop/dance act Sash! come from?
12 Which film featured the song that was Whitney Houston's fourth UK No. 1?
13 Which dance/rock act was fronted by Keith Flint?
14 What was Simply Red's first UK No. 1 in 1995?
15 Who partnered Mariah Carey on "One Sweet Day"?
16 What was "EastEnders'" Michelle Gayle's first hit?
17 What was Curtis Stigers' first UK Top Ten success?
18 Which group held the Christmas single and album top spots in 1996?
19 Which female name was a No. 4 hit for Suggs in 1996?
20 Whose first two UK No. 1s were "Flava" and "I Feel You"?
21 What was Jamiroquai's first UK Top Ten hit?
22 Which song title gave The Shamen their only No. 1 in 1992?
23 Who was the self-styled "Hardest Working Man in Show Business?"
24 "Better the Devil You Know" was a hit for Sonia and which soap star?
25 What was the first UK No. 1 for Celine Dion?
26 What kind of people did R.E.M. take to No. 6 in 1991?
27 What was the one-hit wonder of the Dutch duo Doop?
28 Whose highest chart position was No. 3 in 1991 with "Promise Me"?
29 Which Tony Di Bart No. 1 hit from 1994 is the name of a group?
30 Which All Saints No. 1 was a cover of a 70s hit for Labelle?

Answers | **Pot Luck 25** *(see Quiz 53)*

1 Wigan. 2 William Wordsworth. 3 North. 4 Commonwealth Day. 5 Wessex. 6 Lisbon. 7 Spirit in the Sky. 8 Robert Plant. 9 Freddie Starr. 10 Joseph Lister. 11 Debbie Reynolds. 12 Sweet William. 13 Stoke. 14 Bulgaria. 15 Pickwick Club. 16 Lester Piggott. 17 North east. 18 Windsor. 19 Astronomy. 20 Hercule Poirot. 21 Horses. 22 The Future. 23 Crown Jewels. 24 Madonna. 25 A wild pig. 26 A heart attack. 27 Dave Stewart. 28 Canada. 29 Arkansas. 30 Morgan Freeman.

1 Which soap features the unlikely named character Mercedes McQueen?
2 What was "Coronation Street" originally going to be called?
3 What was the name of Joan Collins' character in "Dynasty"?
4 The Hart family appeared in which daily soap?
5 Which ex-husband of Joan Collins appeared on "EastEnders"?
6 Who played mechanic Chris in "Coronation Street" and left to pursue a pop career?
7 Which "Corrie" star produced a fitness video called "Rapid Results"?
8 In "Coronation Street", what is Spider's real name?
9 In which soap were Shane and Angel an item?
10 How did Kathy Glover's husband die in "Emmerdale"?
11 In "Coronation Street" what was Fiona's baby called?
12 Where did Kathy Mitchell go when she left Albert Square?
13 Which badboy Billy was played by David Crellin?
14 Whom did Dannii Minogue play in "Home & Away"?
15 Which Kemp joined Ross Kemp on the "EastEnders" cast?
16 In "Corrie" which of the Battersby girls is Janice's daughter?
17 Which Kim disappeared from "Emmerdale" and was thought to have been murdered?
18 Which soap did "Silent Witness" star Amanda Burton appear in?
19 Which TV company first produced "Emmerdale Farm"?
20 Which role did Norman Bowler play in "Emmerdale"?
21 Which ex-"Corrie" actress toured in the controversial play "The Blue Room"?
22 Which member of Emmerdale's Dingle family went on to present "You've Been Framed"?
23 Who was buried under the patio in "Brookside"?
24 Emmerdale's Sheree Murphy is married to which famous footballer?
25 Whose son in "Corrie" was once played by his real son Linus?
26 Where did Mavis go when she left The Street?
27 Which one-time boy band member played Ciaran in "Corrie"?
28 "Damon & Debbie" was a short-lived spin-off from which soap?
29 Who links narrating "The Wombles" and playing Wally in a soap?
30 Which soap had a bar called the Waterhole?

Answers	Pot Luck 26 *(see Quiz 56)*

Answers | Pot Luck 26 *(see Quiz 56)*

1 Sunderland. 2 Lucille. 3 Fencing. 4 Freddie Mercury. 5 John Major. 6 Sam the piano player. 7 Noel Coward. 8 James Dyson. 9 Simple Minds. 10 Dr Who. 11 Beatrix Potter. 12 10,800. 13 Timmy. 14 Bricklaying. 15 I'm into Something Good. 16 India. 17 Begging. 18 Agatha Christie. 19 Aberdeen. 20 Whitechapel. 21 Hitler. 22 Saturday Live. 23 Peak District. 24 Table Tennis. 25 Denise Robertson. 26 Vulture. 27 Australia. 28 Dr Jonathan Sacks. 29 Ben Kingsley. 30 Ray Reardon.

1 Alan Shearer's league career finished with a game against which team?
2 Which Kenny Rogers hit starts, "On a bar in Toledo..."
3 In which sport is there a piste other than skiing?
4 Which member of Queen would have been 60 in September 2006?
5 Which Chancellor of the Exchequer introduced TESSA?
6 Which character was played by Dooley Wilson in "Casablanca"?
7 Who wrote the play "Private Lives"?
8 Who invented the bagless vacuum cleaner?
9 Whose hits include "Waterfront" and "Alive and Kicking"?
10 Voords, Krotons and Autons have all appeared on which TV series?
11 Which children's writer's real name was Mrs Heelis?
12 How many seconds are there in three hours?
13 What was the dog called in the Famous Five books?
14 If you were using Dutch or Diaper Bonds what would you be doing?
15 What was Herman's Hermits' only No. 1 UK hit?
16 In which country was Salman Rushdie born?
17 What are you doing if you are mendicanting?
18 Who wrote the novel "Murder in Mesopotamia" in 1936?
19 Which team from outside Glasgow won the Scottish FA Cup three times from 1982–84?
20 In Monopoly, what is the next property after the Old Kent Road?
21 Whose mountain retreat was at Berchtesgaden?
22 Which programme replaced "Home Truths" on Radio 4?
23 Which was the first British National Park?
24 Fred Perry was World Champion in 1929 in which sport?
25 Which TV agony aunt's autobiography was "Agony? Don't Get Me Going"?
26 The condor belongs to which family of birds?
27 In which country is Arnhem Land?
28 In 2006, who was the Chief Rabbi??
29 Which actor was Gandhi in the 1982 film?
30 Who was first to win four World Snooker Championships in a row?

Answers | TV: Soaps *(see Quiz 55)*

1 Hollyoaks. 2 Florizel Street. 3 Alexis Carrington. 4 Family Affairs. 5 Anthony Newley. 6 Matthew Marsden. 7 Beverley Callard. 8 Geoffrey. 9 Home and Away. 10 In a fire. 11 Morgan. 12 South Africa. 13 Billy Hopwood. 14 Emma. 15 Martin. 16 Toyah. 17 Tate. 18 Brookside. 19 Yorkshire TV. 20 Frank Tate. 21 Tracy Shaw. 22 Mandy. 23 Trevor Jordache. 24 Harry Kewell. 25 William Roache's. 26 Lake District. 27 Keith Duffy. 28 Brookside. 29 Bernard Cribbins. 30 Neighbours.

1 What does TT stand for in the Isle of Man races?
2 Who first had a record-breaking car and a boat called Bluebird?
3 Who was the youngest F1 world champion before Fernando Alonso?
4 Which team did Jim Clark spend all his racing career with?
5 How many people are in the car in drag racing?
6 Which Belgian cyclist was known as "The Cannibal"?
7 How many times did Stirling Moss win the world championship?
8 In which country was the first organised car race?
9 Speedway's world champion Tony Rickardsson comes from which country?
10 By 1993 which French driver had won 51 Grand Prix from 199 starts?
11 Which ex-world champion was killed at the San Marino Grand Prix in 1993?
12 Which motor racing Park is east of Chester?
13 What type of racing is known in the US as Demolition Derbies?
14 How frequently does the Tour de France take place?
15 Who was the first man to be world champion on two and four wheels?
16 What relation was Emerson to Christian Fittipaldi?
17 Which Japanese team won its first F1 Grand Prix in 1967?
18 Who was the first man to win a Grand Prix in a car he designed?
19 Which non-French city was the first to start the Tour de France this century?
20 In 1994 who was the first Austrian to win the German Grand Prix since Niki Lauda?
21 Which Briton was the first world driver's champion to win Le Mans, in 1972?
22 In which country did the first mountain bike world championship take place?
23 Which Briton did Alain Prost overtake for a record number of Grand Prix wins?
24 Which was the first manufacturer to have over 100 Grand Prix wins?
25 Which famous British car won the Monte Carlo rally in 1967?
26 Who was the first Briton to wear the Tour de France yellow jersey after Tommy Simpson?
27 Who was the first British F1 Champion after James Hunt?
28 Who was the first driver to be sacked by Benetton twice?
29 Who was the first Frenchman to win the World Grand Prix title in '85?
30 Where is the home of the French Grand Prix?

| **Answers** | **Pot Luck 27** *(see Quiz 58)* |

1 Suspicious Minds. 2 I'm with Stupid. 3 Karl Marx. 4 An insect. 5 Skull. 6 Woody Guthrie. 7 Winston Graham. 8 A clock. 9 Russia. 10 Belfast. 11 Bruce Lee. 12 David Lloyd. 13 Flies. 14 First signatory. 15 Michaelmas Day. 16 A dress. 17 Volcanic eruption. 18 Oak. 19 Goldfinger. 20 Desert-dweller. 21 Remington. 22 Augustus. 23 Rod. 24 Bob Hoskins. 25 Steve Coogan. 26 David Seaman. 27 Messengers. 28 Una Stubbs. 29 Tomato. 30 Neneh Cherry.

1 Which Gareth Gates hit contains the words, "We're caught in a trap"?
2 In which series did Mark Benton play a tramp called Sheldon?
3 Who produced the Communist Manifesto with Friedrich Engels?
4 What is a firebrat?
5 Where are your fontanelles?
6 Which American protest singer is linked to the "dustbowl ballads"?
7 Who wrote the stories subsequently televised as "Poldark"?
8 In which time device would you find an escapement?
9 The port of Archangel is in which country?
10 The Titanic was launched in which city?
11 Film star Lee Yuen Kam achieved fame as which kung fu expert?
12 Which former tennis player sold Hull City in 1998?
13 Which dirty insects are members of the Diptera family?
14 John Hancock was first to do what at the American Declaration of Independence?
15 In a calendar year what is the third quarter day in England?
16 What is a dirndl?
17 What, in 1902, destroyed the Martinique village of St Pierre?
18 Cork is produced mainly from which species of tree?
19 In which Bond film does the character "Oddjob" appear?
20 What does the word 'Bedouin' mean?
21 Which family made typewriters and invented the breech-loading rifle?
22 Who was the first Roman Emperor?
23 Which word can be a unit of measure, a stick or a fishing implement?
24 Which actor played a black prostitute's minder in the film "Mona Lisa"?
25 Which comedian wrote and performed in "Saxondale"?
26 Who was England's first-choice keeper in the 2002 World Cup?
27 Is St Gabriel the patron saint of messengers, millers or musicians?
28 Which actress played the daughter of Alf Garnett?
29 A love apple is an archaic term for what?
30 Whose hits include "Manchild" and "Buffalo Stance"?

Answers	**Sport: Hot Wheels** *(see Quiz 57)*

1 Tourist Trophy. 2 Malcolm Campbell. 3 Emerson Fittipaldi. 4 Lotus. 5 One. 6 Eddie Merckx. 7 Never. 8 France. 9 Sweden. 10 Alain Prost. 11 Ayrton Senna. 12 Oulton Park. 13 Stock car racing. 14 Annually. 15 John Surtees. 16 Uncle. 17 Honda. 18 Jack Brabham. 19 London. 20 Gerhard Berger. 21 Graham Hill. 22 France. 23 Jackie Stewart. 24 Ferrari. 25 Mini. 26 Chris Boardman. 27 Nigel Mansell. 28 Johnny Herbert. 29 Alain Prost. 30 Magny Cours.

1 Which actor/director started the trend for spaghetti westerns?
2 What was the nationality of Meryl Streep's character in "A Cry in the Dark"?
3 Who was shunned by Hollywood in the 1940s when she left her husband for Roberto Rossellini?
4 Which poet's name was the middle name of James Dean?
5 Who was Hollywood's first black superstar?
6 Which famous dancer played a straight role in "On the Beach"?
7 Which Burt appeared in "Bean – The Ultimate Disaster Movie"?
8 On the set of which film did the Richard Burton/Elizabeth Taylor affair begin?
9 What is the first name of Julia Roberts' character in "Closer"?
10 Who received her first Oscar nomination for "Silkwood"?
11 Whose roles vary from Cruella de Vil on film to Norma Desmond on stage?
12 How old was Macaulay Culkin when he was first married?
13 Which married superstars starred in "The Big Sleep" in 1946?
14 Which comedian co-founded United Artists in 1919?
15 Dietrich appeared in the German "The Blue Angel"; who appeared in the US version?
16 Which actor's last film was "The Misfits" in 1960?
17 Who was voted No. 1 pin-up by US soldiers in WWII?
18 How many parts did Alec Guinness play in "Kind Hearts and Coronets"?
19 What is the profession of Nicole Kidman's father?
20 In which country did Charlie Chaplin spend the final years of his life?
21 Who was Truman in "The Truman Show"?
22 Which superstar did Tony Curtis parody in "Some Like It Hot"?
23 Who portrayed Frankie Dunn in a sport-related movie?
24 Who is the physician in the 1990s remake of "Doctor Doolittle"?
25 How many Road films did Crosby, Hope and Lamour make?
26 Who was the psychotic cabbie in Scorsese's "Taxi Driver"?
27 Who announced her retirement when she married Ted Turner in 1991?
28 Who was Jodie Foster's character in "The Silence of the Lambs"?
29 Who directed "The Horse Whisperer"?
30 Who played Margo Channing in "All About Eve"?

Answers | Pot Luck 28 *(see Quiz 60)*

1 Three. 2 A Helicopter. 3 MI5. 4 M People. 5 Labrador. 6 Gabrielle. 7 The Old Curiosity Shop. 8 Greece. 9 On the seabed. 10 Kent. 11 Shoes. 12 Melvyn Hayes. 13 Sistine. 14 Music of Black Origin. 15 Bismarck. 16 Le Mans. 17 Sap. 18 Peru. 19 The World War. 20 Pregnant. 21 Jackie Rae. 22 Aston Villa. 23 Bits and pieces. 24 Guildford. 25 Isle of Wight. 26 The Lion King. 27 Nkima. 28 Pearl Harbor. 29 Commissioner Dreyfus. 30 Whitewater.

1 How many times did Joe Frazier fight Muhammad Ali?
2 What was designed and made in a viable form by Sikorsky in 1941?
3 The TV series "Spooks" is about which organisation?
4 Who had hits with "One Night in Heaven" and "Moving On Up"?
5 Which "dog like" peninsula formed Canada's tenth province in 1949?
6 What was Coco Chanel's Christian name?
7 Quilp appears in a book about what kind of Shop?
8 In which European country are the Pindus Mountains?
9 If a creature is demersal, where does it live?
10 In which county was the first Youth Custody Centre set up in 1908?
11 Espadrilles are a type of what?
12 Who played the part of "Gloria" in "It Ain't Half Hot, Mum"?
13 Michelangelo painted the ceiling of which famous Chapel?
14 In the music world what does MOBO mean?
15 Who was called the "Iron Chancellor"?
16 Where is motor racing's Grand Prix d'Endurance staged?
17 If a creature is succivorous what does it feed on?
18 The source of the Amazon is in which South American country?
19 Al Capone said he was accused of every death except the casualty list of what?
20 If something or someone is gravid what does it mean?
21 Who was the first presenter of the TV series "The Golden Shot"?
22 At which club did Gareth Southgate play most league games?
23 What does "Chop Suey" literally mean?
24 In which city is the University of Surrey?
25 Carisbrooke Castle is on which Isle?
26 In which Disney film is a young lion called Simba?
27 What was the name of Tarzan's monkey friend in the Tarzan stories?
28 Which 2001 film was about real-life events in the Pacific 60 years ago?
29 Which part was played by Herbert Lom in the Pink Panther films?
30 The Clintons were implicated in which 1990s US property scandal?

Answers	Movie Superstars (see Quiz 59)

1 Clint Eastwood. 2 Australian. 3 Ingrid Bergman. 4 Byron. 5 Sidney Poitier. 6 Fred Astaire. 7 Reynolds. 8 Cleopatra. 9 Anna. 10 Cher. 11 Glenn Close. 12 17. 13 Lauren Bacall and Humphrey Bogart. 14 Charlie Chaplin. 15 Dietrich. 16 Clark Gable. 17 Betty Grable. 18 Eight. 19 Psychologist. 20 Switzerland. 21 Jim Carrey. 22 Cary Grant. 23 Clint Eastwood. 24 Eddie Murphy. 25 Seven. 26 Robert de Niro. 27 Jane Fonda. 28 Clarice Starling. 29 Robert Redford. 30 Bette Davis.

1 Which South American city has a famous Copacabana beach?
2 The Bass Strait divides which two islands?
3 Which Middle East capital is known locally as El Qahira?
4 Where is the official country home of US Presidents?
5 Whose Vineyard is an island off Cape Cod?
6 Where was Checkpoint Charlie?
7 Which US state has a 'pan handle' separating the Atlantic from the Gulf of Mexico?
8 In which two countries is the Dead Sea?
9 The site of ancient Babylon is now in which country?
10 On which river is the Aswan Dam?
11 The Trump International Hotel & Tower was built where in the USA?
12 The Fens were formerly a bay of which Sea?
13 What is Japan's highest peak?
14 To which country do the Galapagos Islands belong?
15 Aconcagua is an extinct volcano in which mountain range?
16 Where in California is the lowest point of the western hemisphere?
17 In which London Square is the US Embassy?
18 Ellis Island is in which harbour?
19 Which city is known to Afrikaners as Kaapstad?
20 On which Sea is the Gaza Strip?
21 What are the three divisions of Glamorgan?
22 Which river cuts through the Grand Canyon?
23 Where in India are Anjuna beach and Morjim beach?
24 Which continents are separated by the Dardanelles?
25 Which US state capital means "sheltered bay" in Hawaiian?
26 Hampstead is part of which London borough?
27 Which country owns the southernmost part of South America?
28 Where is the seat of the UN International Court of Justice?
29 The Golan Heights are on the border of which two countries?
30 Which is the saltiest of the main oceans?

Answers	Pot Luck 29 (see Quiz 62)

1 West Side Story. 2 Tom and Jerry. 3 Love. 4 John Hunt. 5 Backstreet Boys. 6 The Real Thing. 7 Rugby League. 8 Potato famine. 9 Language sounds. 10 Joe Louis. 11 Tom Cruise. 12 Robert Mugabe. 13 Calcium. 14 40. 15 Honeysuckle. 16 Shoe. 17 Clerestory. 18 Nine. 19 Rock Hudson. 20 Fred Astaire. 21 Trampolining. 22 Niagara Falls. 23 Bournemouth. 24 Ole Gunnar Solskjaer. 25 Mariah Carey. 26 A Nelson. 27 Britain. 28 Freddie Laker. 29 Cameron Diaz. 30 15th.

1 The song "America" comes from which musical?
2 Which cartoon duo starred in the Oscar-winning film "Quiet Please"?
3 Kate Bush had an album called The Hounds Of ... what?
4 In 1953 who was leader of the British expedition which conquered Everest?
5 Which group had a huge hit with "Millennium"?
6 Who had a UK Top Ten hit with "Can You Feel the Force"?
7 Which sport was founded in Britain on 28 August 1895?
8 Black Forty Seven in Ireland in the 19th century related to what?
9 What is phonetics the study of?
10 Who was World Heavyweight boxing champion in WWII?
11 Which actor links "Risky Business", "Cocktail" and "Top Gun"?
12 Who was the first president of Zimbabwe?
13 Which element is found in shells, bones and teeth?
14 How old are you if you are a quadragenarian?
15 Which flower is also called the Woodbine?
16 Which item of clothing features on the poster for the movie "The Devil Wears Prada"?
17 A row of windows in the upper wall of a church is known by what name?
18 What is the most times a day of the week can occur in two months?
19 Who was older when he died, Humphrey Bogart or Rock Hudson?
20 Who starred opposite Judy Garland in the film "Easter Parade"?
21 In which sport are there moves called Triffus, Rudolf and Miller?
22 The Horseshoe and American combine to form which famous falls?
23 Which is further West, Bognor or Bournemouth?
24 Who completed ten seasons at Old Trafford in 2006 after playing for Molde?
25 Who has had hits with "Hero" and "Anytime You Need a Friend"?
26 What name is given to a score of 111 in cricket?
27 In Orwell's 1984 what is called Airstrip One?
28 Whose cheap transatlantic air service in 1977 was called "Skytrain"?
29 Who was the third of "Charlie's Angels" with Drew Barrymore and Lucy Liu?
30 In which century was the Battle of Agincourt?

Answers | On the Map (see Quiz 61)

1 Rio de Janeiro. 2 Australia & Tasmania. 3 Cairo. 4 Camp David. 5 Martha's Vineyard. 6 Between East and West Berlin. 7 Florida. 8 Israel & Jordan. 9 Iraq. 10 Nile. 11 Chicago. 12 North Sea. 13 Mount Fujiyama. 14 Ecuador. 15 Andes. 16 Death Valley. 17 Grosvenor. 18 New York. 19 Cape Town. 20 Mediterranean. 21 Mid, South, West. 22 Colorado. 23 Goa. 24 Europe & Asia. 25 Honolulu. 26 Camden. 27 Chile. 28 The Hague. 29 Israel & Syria. 30 Atlantic.

1 Which cereal can survive in the widest range of climatic conditions?
2 The hellebore is known as what type of rose?
3 What colour are edelweiss flowers?
4 Which plant is St Patrick said to have used to illustrate the Holy Trinity?
5 Succulents live in areas lacking in what?
6 How many points does a sycamore leaf have?
7 What is the ornamental shaping of trees and shrubs called?
8 What is an alternative name for the narcotic and analgesic aconite?
9 What colour are laburnum flowers?
10 What is another name for a yam?
11 What shape are flowers which include the name campanula?
12 What is a frond on a plant?
13 Which climbing plant is also called hedera helix?
14 Agronomy is the study of what?
15 What is a Sturmer?
16 Which fruit is called "earth berry" in German from where the plant grows?
17 What is another name for belladonna?
18 What is the effect on the nervous system of taking hemlock?
19 Are the male, female or either hop plants used to make beer?
20 What is the most common plant grown in Assam in India?
21 Aspen is what type of tree?
22 Which flowering plant is named after the sixteenth-century German botanist Leonhart Fuchs?
23 The ground powder form turmeric dyes food which colour?
24 The pineapple plant is native to which continent?
25 What is the purpose of a plant's petals?
26 Which type of pesticide is used to kill weeds?
27 What colour are the leaves of a poinsettia?
28 What name is given to the wild yellow iris?
29 Which plant is famous for having a "clock"?
30 What colour are borage flowers?

1 Which former First Lady was nicknamed "The Smiling Mamba"?
2 Who had hits with "Joanna" and "Celebration"?
3 Where would you see a facula?
4 Who played the title character in "The Life and Death of Peter Sellers"?
5 Which country has a unit of currency called the Leone?
6 The seaside town of Westward Ho is in which county?
7 Oloroso is a type of which drink?
8 Back in the charts in 2005, in what year was Bananarama's first hit?
9 Which Wonder of the World statue was at Olympia?
10 In which century did William Caxton establish the first English printing press?
11 Cocoa is prepared from the seeds of which tree?
12 Who joined John Torode as a judge on "Celebrity Masterchef"?
13 What is driven by a mahout?
14 What does the cooking expression al dente mean?
15 Which Oliver was Lord Protector of Britain?
16 Which label is distinguished as fashion designed by Armani?
17 Which celeb's childhood nickname was Liver Lips?
18 Who would use a jacquard?
19 In "The Wizard of Oz", which animal was seeking courage?
20 Who captained the US Ryder Cup team in 1997?
21 Who was the Bond girl in "Die Another Day"?
22 Pumpkin Pie is the traditional dessert on which special American day?
23 Who played Eleanor Bramwell in the TV series of the same name?
24 Who painted "The Starry Night"?
25 Which word can be a swan, a horse, a bread roll and a basket?
26 What was Diana Ross's first solo No. 1 in the UK?
27 What are progeny?
28 Who had hits with "I Can't Dance" and "Invisible Touch"?
29 In which part of East London was David Beckham born?
30 If you heard a John Gabel Entertainer, what would be playing?

Answers	Nature: Plant World *(see Quiz 63)*

1 Barley. 2 Christmas rose. 3 White. 4 Shamrock. 5 Water. 6 Five. 7 Topiary.
8 Monkshood. 9 Yellow. 10 Sweet potato. 11 Bell-shaped. 12 Leaf. 13 Ivy. 14 Crops and soils. 15 Apple. 16 Strawberry. 17 Deadly nightshade. 18 Paralysis. 19 Female. 20 Tea. 21 Poplar. 22 Fuchsia. 23 Yellow. 24 South America. 25 Attract pollinators. 26 Herbicide. 27 Red. 28 Flag. 29 Dandelion. 30 Blue.

1 Germany's Red Army Faction was popularly called what after its two founders?
2 The Equal Opportunities Commission was set up to implement which act?
3 Who became US Vice President after Spiro Agnew resigned?
4 Where did the Gang of Four seize power in 1976?
5 Which natural disaster did Guatemala City suffer in 1976?
6 In the Vietnam War who or what was Agent Orange?
7 Who was Nixon's White House Chief of Staff at the height of the Watergate scandal?
8 On which Pennsylvania Island was there a nuclear leak in 1979?
9 In 1978 Mujaheddin resistance began in which country?
10 Who made a precocious speech aged 16 at the 1977 Tory Party conference?
11 Who opened her first Body Shop in 1976?
12 Where was Obote replaced by Amin in 1971?
13 The Pahlavi Dynasty was overthrown by the Islamic revolution in which country?
14 Which Argentine leader died in 1974 and was succeeded by his third wife?
15 Which woman MP did Jack Straw replace as MP for Blackburn?
16 In films, which actor played the comic book character with an S on his chest?
17 Which dictator was deposed in Cambodia in 1979?
18 Which "King" died in 1977 aged 42?
19 What was Harare called until the end of the 1970s?
20 What was inside US incendiary bombs during the Vietnam War?
21 Which title did Quintin Hogg take when made Lord Chancellor in '70?
22 SALT negotiations took place between which two countries?
23 Which future Labour leader became Trade & Industry Secretary in '78?
24 Who first charted in the 1970s and had a 2005 No. 1 with "Ghetto Gospel"?
25 In which country was a monarchy restored in 1975?
26 The Sandinistas overthrew which government in 1979?
27 Who succeeded Heath as Tory leader?
28 Sapporo was the centre of the 1972 winter Olympics in which country?
29 Which country did the USSR invade in 1979?
30 In which department was Thatcher a Minister before leading the Party?

| **Answers** | TV: TV Times 1 *(see Quiz 66)* |

1 Anne Charleston. 2 Nephew. 3 Warrior. 4 Miss America. 5 New Faces. 6 Helicopters. 7 Kel. 8 Grant Bovey. 9 Elton John. 10 Ulrika Jonsson. 11 Assumpta. 12 Michael Jackson. 13 Shoplifting. 14 Snowball Merriman. 15 Basildon. 16 Trevor McDonald. 17 Bingo. 18 Jennifer Patterson. 19 Tony Slattery. 20 Torvill & Dean. 21 Delia Smith. 22 Televangelism. 23 Girls Aloud. 24 Sian Lloyd. 25 Sam Malone. 26 The Bee Gees. 27 Les Dennis. 28 Ricki Lake. 29 John Virgo. 30 On a bed.

1 Which actress moved from Madge in "Neighbours" to Millie in "Emmerdale"?

2 What relation is "ER"'s George Clooney to US singer Rosemary?

3 Which Gladiator was jailed in 1998 for corruption?

4 Superwoman Lynda Carter held which beauty queen title?

5 On which TV show was Jim Davidson "discovered"?

6 Outside TV what type of transport business does Noel Edmonds run?

7 What is the name of Kath's husband in Australian comedy "Kath & Kim"?

8 In the celeb boxing's "The Fight", Ricky Gervais took on which Grant?

9 The TV profile "Tantrums and Tiaras" was about which pop superstar?

10 Which TV presenter's relationship with Stan Collymore ended violently in Paris during the 1998 World Cup?

11 Who was the first landlady of Fitzgerald's in "Ballykissangel"?

12 Martin Bashir's 2003 UK TV interview led to involvement in a court trial of which celeb?

13 What was Richard Madeley arrested for in 1990?

14 Which character did Nicole Faraday play in "Bad Girls"?

15 In which town was Essex girl Denise Van Outen born?

16 Which "News at Ten" presenter had the first British TV interview with Nelson Mandela after his release?

17 Which game was "Bob's Full House" based on?

18 Which TV cook wears a diamond-studded crash helmet?

19 Who presented the C5 medical quiz show "Tibs and Fibs"?

20 Who were the first couple to be BBC Sports Personality of the Year?

21 Which cook founded Sainsbury's The Magazine with her husband?

22 In the US Jim Bakker and Jimmy Swaggart are famous for what type of show?

23 Which girl band won the first "Popstars: The Rivals"?

24 Which weather girl went to the same university as Glenys Kinnock?

25 Which character did Ted Danson play in "Cheers"?

26 Which pop group walked out on Clive Anderson on his "All Talk" show?

27 Which comedian's marriage foundered after he appeared in "Celebrity Big Brother"?

28 Which talk show hostess appeared in the film "Hairspray" with Divine?

29 Who was the resident snooker player on "Big Break"?

30 Where did Paula Yates conduct her "Big Breakfast" interviews?

1 Mica Paris and who replaced Trinny & Susannah on "What not to Wear"?
2 Which famous survey started in 1086?
3 From which musical does the song "One" come?
4 Ronald Reagan was in which political party?
5 Which Stephen directed the movie "Billy Elliot"?
6 In the Bible, what was the prophet Elijah carried up to heaven in?
7 What nationality was Casanova?
8 What was Al Jolson's most famous line?
9 If a substance is oleaginous what does it mainly contain?
10 Which General led the junta in the 1982 seizure of the Falklands?
11 Which famous Castle is on the River Dee?
12 What did the Owl and the Pussycat dine on?
13 Vera Welch sang under what name?
14 What was presenter Gabby Logan's surname before she married?
15 Which outlandish musician's real name was Simon Ritchie?
16 Which handicapped physicist has appeared in adverts for BT?
17 Who is buried at the Arc de Triomphe?
18 During exercise which acid builds up in the muscles?
19 Which Kevin has played for WBA, Sunderland, Everton and Wigan?
20 Which singer had a backing group called the Checkmates?
21 What is added to egg yolks and vanilla to make advocaat?
22 Who played "Blanco" in the TV series "Porridge"?
23 What nationality was Rachmaninov the composer?
24 What is xerography?
25 Which 1956 hit links The Platters with a 1987 Freddie Mercury hit?
26 Which Dutch town is particularly famous for its blue pottery?
27 Where would you find an apse?
28 What was abolished on 18 December 1969 in Britain?
29 Which tycoon started the newspaper called Today?
30 Who was the first golfer to lose play-offs in all four majors?

| **Answers** | **Pop Music: Albums** *(see Quiz 68)* |

1 Chris Rea. 2 Chicago XIII. 3 Eternal. 4 George Michael. 5 News of the World. 6 The Revolution. 7 Pet Shop Boys. 8 Frank Sinatra. 9 OK Computer. 10 Sting. 11 No Parlez. 12 River Deep – Mountain High. 13 Wannabe. 14 Definitely/Maybe. 15 Pulp. 16 Alanis Morisette. 17 Be Here Now. 18 Blue. 19 Physical. 20 Slippery When Wet. 21 The Rolling Stones. 22 Sex. 23 Nigel Kennedy. 24 Gasoline Alley. 25 Goat. 26 The Wall. 27 Enya. 28 Waterloo. 29 Ten. 30 Diva.

1 Who released the album "Auberge"?
2 What was the thirteenth album released by Chicago?
3 Which group's debut album, "Always & Forever", shadowed their name?
4 Whose debut solo album was called "Faith"?
5 Which Queen album shares its name with a newspaper?
6 On the 80s album "Purple Rain" who backed Prince?
7 Which duo released albums called "Introspective" and "Very"?
8 Which US superstar has had over 70 chart albums in his career?
9 What was Radiohead's first album to make No. 1 in the British charts?
10 Who guested with Dire Straits on the "Money For Nothing" track?
11 Which phrase with a French flavour was the title of Paul Young's debut album?
12 What was the title of Ike and Tina Turner's only album?
13 What is the first track on "Spice"?
14 A picture of Burt Bacharach appeared on the cover of which best-selling 90s album?
15 Whose debut album was called "Different Class"?
16 "Supposed Former Infatuation Junkie" was whose follow-up to a 30 million-selling album?
17 Which Oasis album came out first – "Be Here Now" or "The Masterplan"?
18 On the Beautiful South's 1996 album what is the "Colour"?
19 Which Olivia Newton-John 1981 album could describe some exercise?
20 Which Bon Jovi album was best kept dry?
21 What was the title of the first album released by The Rolling Stones?
22 What were Madonna's book and 1992 album called?
23 Which musician took Vivaldi's "The Four Seasons" into the charts?
24 Rod Stewart's first album was called after which alley?
25 What animal is on the cover of the Beach Boys' album "Pet Sounds"?
26 Which construction has given its name to a Pink Floyd album?
27 Which Irish singer got to No. 1 with "Shepherd Moons"?
28 Which battle was the title of the first Abba album?
29 How many Good Reasons had Jason Donovan on his first No. 1?
30 Which Annie Lennox album topped the charts in 1993?

1 Who formed the famous dance troupe the Bluebell Girls?
2 Whose CDs include "Seven Year Itch" and "Stickin' to My Guns"?
3 What would you do with a futon?
4 Which play is performed every ten years at Oberammagau?
5 Which wood was mainly used by Thomas Chippendale?
6 In which London area is The Royal Hospital?
7 In Nov. 2006, a Cardiff get together was organised for people with which surname?
8 Bruce Willis destroyed a plane with his cigarette lighter in which film?
9 What does a blue flag at a beach mean?
10 Which carbohydrate causes jam to gel?
11 If a dog is suffering from "hard pad" what form of disease has it got?
12 What is a hawser?
13 In "The Amazing Mrs Pritchard" what did Mrs P become?
14 Theophobia is a fear of what?
15 In which French town was Joan of Arc burnt at the stake?
16 What was the name of cowboy Tom Mix's horse ?
17 The quail is the smallest member of which bird species?
18 What is the singular of axes in mathematics?
19 Which actress's real name was Maria Magdalena von Losch?
20 Which port is the most easterly in Britain?
21 What is the common weather in a pluvial region?
22 Which Polynesian word means prohibited or forbidden?
23 What colour is the egg of a kingfisher?
24 The Dodecanese Islands are in which sea?
25 What nationality was Secretary General of the UN Boutros Boutros Ghali?
26 In board games, what colour is the Reverend in Cluedo?
27 Whose hits include "Sunny Afternoon" and "Tired of Waiting for You"?
28 What is on top of the Mona Lisa's left hand?
29 What do Americans call Perspex?
30 In which girl group did Amelle Berrabah replace Mutya Buena?

Answers | Leisure 3 *(see Quiz 70)*

1 Deep sea diving. 2 Stamps. 3 Green. 4 Circular. 5 Yoga. 6 Cribbage. 7 Admiral's Cup. 8 Lacrosse. 9 Gare Du Nord. 10 RSPB. 11 Pottery. 12 Star Wars. 13 13 tricks by one team. 14 Hurling (or hurley). 15 Synchronised swimming. 16 Cadbury, Fry, Rowntree. 17 The Netherlands. 18 Tennis. 19 Pizza Express. 20 Golf Club. 21 Women's Institute. 22 World Wildlife Fund. 23 Whipsnade. 24 Tintin. 25 Dark green. 26 Hammer. 27 Wrestling. 28 Isle of Wight. 29 Paris. 30 Leicester.

1 After what sort of activity might you suffer from the bends?
2 What would you buy from Stanley Gibbons?
3 What colour are houses in Monopoly?
4 What shape is a sumo wrestling ring?
5 Which Hindu system of philosophy is used as a means of exercise and meditation in the west?
6 In which game do you score "one for his knob"?
7 The Fastnet race is part of the contest for which Cup?
8 Which game's name comes from a piece of its equipment looking like a bishop's crosier?
9 At which station do you arrive in Paris if you have travelled from the UK by Eurostar?
10 The YOC is the junior branch of which organisation?
11 If you were a collector of Clarice Cliff what would you collect?
12 A Monopoly game based on which Sci-fi film was released in 1997?
13 What is a grand slam in Bridge?
14 Camogie is the women's equivalent of which sport?
15 What sort of swimming takes place with musical accompaniment?
16 Which three Quaker families made most of Britain's chocolate?
17 In which country is De Efteling Theme Park?
18 Which sport is played at London's Queen's Club?
19 Which pizza restaurant was the first of a chain founded in London?
20 What sort of club is the Royal and Ancient?
21 Which organisation's anthem is "Jerusalem"?
22 What was the Worldwide Fund for Nature formerly called?
23 Which open-air zoo is near Dunstable in Bedfordshire?
24 Which boy reporter was created by Belgian artist Herge?
25 What colour carrier bag do you get when you shop at Laura Ashley?
26 In athletics, what is attached to a chain and a handle and thrown?
27 Which sport has Greco-Roman and Freestyle, as two distinct styles?
28 The annual Round the Isle race goes round which Isle?
29 La Defence and Les Halles are Christmas markets in which city?
30 Where were Walker's Crisps first made?

Answers	**Pot Luck 32** *(see Quiz 69)*

1 Margaret Kelly. 2 Etta James. 3 Sleep on it. 4 The Passion Play. 5 Mahogany. 6 Chelsea. 7 Jones. 8 Die Hard 2. 9 Clean & pollution free. 10 Pectin. 11 Distemper. 12 A rope. 13 Prime Minister. 14 God. 15 Rouen. 16 Tony. 17 Partridge. 18 Axis. 19 Marlene Dietrich. 20 Lowestoft. 21 Rain. 22 Taboo. 23 White. 24 Aegean Sea. 25 Egyptian. 26 Green. 27 The Kinks. 28 Her right hand. 29 Plexiglass. 30 Sugababes.

1 What describes descending a sheer face by sliding down a rope?
2 Donna Reed replaced Barbara Bel Geddes in which TV series?
3 Who won TV's "How Do You Solve a Problem Like Maria?"
4 Which animal is feared by a hippophobe?
5 Whose hits include "Wide Boy" and "Wouldn't It be Good"?
6 The novel "Shirley" was written by which of the Bronte sisters?
7 In which London building does the Lutine Bell hang?
8 Which is further South, Folkestone or Southampton?
9 Which American sportsman was said to be earning more than the US president in 1925?
10 Which famous bear came from Peru?
11 What did the S stand for in Charlie Chaplin's middle name?
12 Nuno Valente joined Everton from which club?
13 What is a passepied?
14 Which species can be Fairy, Black-footed and Crested?
15 Which game uses flattened iron rings thrown at a hob?
16 What was the title of Captain Sensible's No. 1 UK hit in 1982?
17 Which mammals will expire when stranded on dry land?
18 In which movie did Ewan McGregor sing Elton John's "Your Song"?
19 What is tansy?
20 Which island is in the Bay of Naples?
21 In which series did Amanda Mealing play Connie Beauchamp?
22 Cyril Mead became known as which comic?
23 In the order of accession to the British throne who is the first female?
24 In which London Square is the American Embassy?
25 What is a taipan?
26 Is Coventry North or South of Leicester?
27 Which English King was the last to die in battle?
28 Who was older when he died, Peter Sellers or Tony Hancock?
29 What is the smallest administrative unit in the Church of England?
30 In "Pride and Prejudice" whom does Elizabeth Bennet finally marry?

Answers | **Record Breakers** *(see Quiz 72)*

1 Donald Budge. 2 Kapil Dev. 3 Stefan Edberg. 4 Chris Evert. 5 Nick Faldo. 6 Paula Radcliffe. 7 Billie Jean King. 8 Skiing. 9 Gabriela Sabatini. 10 Brian Lara. 11 Seven. 12 Ian Woosnam. 13 Steve Ovett's. 14 Karen Pickering. 15 Michael. 16 Frankie Fredericks. 17 Sandy Lyle. 18 Sugar Ray Leonard. 19 US Masters. 20 James Wattana. 21 Freestyle & butterfly. 22 Ian Rush. 23 Mike Powell. 24 Seve Ballesteros. 25 Johnny Haynes. 26 Ed Moses. 27 Geoff Capes. 28 McColgan. 29 Ipswich. 30 Graham Hill.

1 Which American was the first to win the Men's Singles Grand Slam?
2 Who in 1979 became the youngest player to complete the double of 1,000 runs and 100 wickets?
3 Which Swede, in 1987, was the first man for 40 years to win a match at Wimbledon without losing a game?
4 Who was the first woman tennis player to win $1 million?
5 Who was the first Briton after 1950 to win the British Open golf three years in succession?
6 Which lady claimed three fastest winning times in the London Marathon?
7 Which woman won 20 Wimbledon titles between 1961 and 1979?
8 Franz Klammer was a record breaker in which sport?
9 Which woman became the youngest Wimbledon semi-finalist for 99 years in 1986?
10 Who broke the world record for an individual innings of 501 in 1994?
11 How many world records did Mark Spitz break when he won his seven gold medals?
12 Who, in 1987, was the first British golfer to win the World Match-Play Championship?
13 Whose 1500m world record did Steve Cram break in 1985?
14 Who was the first British woman swimmer to win a world title?
15 Who is the elder of the motor racing Schumacher's – Michael or Ralf?
16 Which Namibian was the first to break the 200m indoors 20-second barrier?
17 Who was the first British winner of the US Masters in 1988?
18 In 1988 who became the first boxer to win world titles at five official weights?
19 What was the first major to be claimed by Tiger Woods?
20 Who was the first Thai snooker player to win a major tournament?
21 In 1972 Mark Spitz broke Olympic records doing which two strokes?
22 Who holds the record for most goals scored in FA Cup Finals?
23 Who broke Bob Beaman's long jump record set at the 1968 Olympics?
24 Who was the then youngest ever winner of the US Masters in 1980?
25 Who was the first British soccer player to earn £100 per week?
26 Which US hurdler was undefeated in 122 races?
27 Which British shot putter was world No. 1 in 1975?
28 Which Liz won the fastest ever debut marathon when she won in New York in 1991?
29 Which Town did Man Utd beat by a record nine goals in 1995?
30 Who in 1968 became the oldest Briton to win a Grand Prix?

Answers | Pot Luck 33 *(see Quiz 71)*

1 Abseiling. 2 Dallas. 3 Connie Fisher. 4 Horses. 5 Nik Kershaw. 6 Charlotte. 7 Lloyds of London. 8 Southampton. 9 Babe Ruth. 10 Paddington. 11 Spencer. 12 Porto. 13 A dance. 14 Penguins. 15 Quoits. 16 Happy Talk. 17 Whales. 18 Moulin Rouge. 19 A herb. 20 Capri. 21 Holby City. 22 Syd Little. 23 Princess Beatrice. 24 Grosvenor Square. 25 A snake. 26 South. 27 Richard III. 28 Peter Sellers. 29 A Parish. 30 Mr Darcy.

1 Where is fibrin found in your body?
2 What is the vegetable common to the Indian dishes of Aloo Gobi and Aloo Palak?
3 Which group had hits including "Homely Girl" and "Kingston Town"?
4 The word "ketchup" comes which language?
5 Who presented "The Secret Life of the Manic Depressive"?
6 Who first took the much-covered song "Light My Fire" to No. 1?
7 With 7 goals, Lua-Lua was top scorer for which Premiership side?
8 Woburn Abbey is the home of which family?
9 What is a durian?
10 Which film starred John Cleese as an under-pressure headmaster?
11 The composer Bela Bartok came from which country?
12 What can be an animal enclosure or a unit of weight?
13 What does the abbreviation BHP stand for?
14 Which poetic names lend themselves to an expression for a devoted, elderly couple?
15 How does a judge hear a case when it is heard In Camera?
16 From 1968 to 1970 which actor was Mr Universe?
17 What does the word 'biscuit' literally mean?
18 The Lent Lily is sometimes used as another name for which flower?
19 What is a Tree Ear?
20 What was Little Lord Fauntleroy's name?
21 Toad of Toad Hall was a dramatised version of which Kenneth Grahame tale?
22 Which sport is Clare Francis famous for?
23 In the film "Look Who's Talking" whose voice was the baby's thoughts?
24 Which tree usually provides the wood for the Highland Games caber?
25 Whose hits include "Wishing Well" and "All Right Now"?
26 What colour is the tongue of a giraffe?
27 Which sport featured in the movie "A League of Their Own"?
28 Californian, Yellow Horned and Opium are all types of which flower?
29 Where is the Sea of Vapours?
30 What is the wading bird the bittern's cry called?

Answers | **The Oscars** *(see Quiz 74)*

1 Morgan Freeman. **2** Casablanca. **3** The Deer Hunter. **4** Christy Brown. **5** Henry Fonda. **6** As Good as It Gets. **7** Philadelphia. **8** Marlee Matlin. **9** James Cameron. **10** Philadelphia, Forrest Gump. **11** Gary Cooper. **12** Butler. **13** 1930s. **14** Woody Allen. **15** The Godfather. **16** Dustin Hoffman. **17** Frank Sinatra. **18** Schindler's List. **19** She never spoke. **20** Walter & John Huston. **21** Meryl Streep. **22** Bette Davis. **23** Jessica Tandy. **24** Eight (all of them). **25** Kathy Bates. **26** Oscar. **27** Vivien Leigh. **28** Anthony Minghella. **29** Tatum O'Neal. **30** Helena Bonham-Carter.

1 Who played Eddie to claim a Best Supporting Actor Oscar in a boxing movie?
2 Which World War II film would have been called Dar el-Beida had it been titled in the local language?
3 Which Michael Cimino film about Vietnam won five Oscars in the 70s?
4 Whom did Daniel-Day Lewis portray in "My Left Foot"?
5 Which veteran won an Oscar in 1981 two years after his daughter?
6 For which movie did Helen Hunt win in 1997?
7 For which film did Tom Hanks win playing a lawyer dying from AIDS?
8 Who overcame deafness to win for "Children of a Lesser God"?
9 Who won the Best Director award for "Titanic"?
10 For which films did Tom Hanks win in successive years?
11 Who won the Best Actor Oscar for "High Noon"?
12 What type of worker did John Gielgud play when he won his Oscar for "Arthur"?
13 In which decade did Katharine Hepburn win her first Oscar?
14 Who won three Oscars for "Annie Hall"?
15 For which film did Brando win his second Oscar?
16 Who won his first best actor Oscar for "Kramer vs. Kramer"?
17 Which singer won an Oscar for "From Here to Eternity"?
18 For which film did Steven Spielberg win his first award?
19 What was unusual about Holly Hunter's performance in "The Piano"?
20 Which father and son actor and director won for "The Treasure of the Sierra Madre"?
21 In the year "Gandhi" won almost everything who was Best Actress for "Sophie's Choice"?
22 Who won Oscars for "Dangerous", "Jezebel" and "All About Eve"?
23 Who won as Dan Aykroyd's mother in "Driving Miss Daisy"?
24 How many times between 1990 and 1997 did Best Picture and Best Director Oscars go to the same film?
25 Who played the psychotic nurse in "Misery" and won Best Actress?
26 What did Anthony Hopkins win first, a knighthood or an Oscar?
27 Who won for her role as Blanch in "A Streetcar Named Desire"?
28 Who won Best Director for "The English Patient?"
29 Who won for her first film "Paper Moon"?
30 Which actress was nominated for "The Wings of the Dove"?

1 What are Spode, Bow and Chelsea all types of?
2 Whick rock star teamed up with Sir Patrick Moore and Phil Lintott to write a book on astronomy?
3 Which Italian area produces Chianti?
4 Which scale measures the level of alkalinity and acidity?
5 TV's "Death of a President" was about the fictional assassination of which world leader?
6 Where will you return to if you throw a coin into the Trevi Fountain?
7 What in your body are affected by phlebitis?
8 Who was caretaker manager of Spurs after the departure of Glenn Hoddle in 2003?
9 Whose hits include "Again" and "That's the Way Love Goes"?
10 Which TV character lived on Scatterbrook Farm?
11 Which High Street travel agents devised the holiday package tour?
12 In finance what is a PEP?
13 How did Curtis Jackson, born 1976, become known in the music world?
14 What does the Greek odeon mean?
15 If you were using a tambour, what needlecraft would you be doing?
16 What is the currency of Greece?
17 Which actor co-starred with Juliette Binoche in "Breaking & Entering"?
18 In which century was cockfighting banned?
19 Which supermarket chain paid for the new National Gallery wing opened in 1991?
20 Cars with the international vehicle registration ET come from where?
21 Who started the Habitat chain of shops in 1964?
22 Who is smaller, Janet Street Porter or Naomi Campbell?
23 Edmonton is the capital of which Canadian province?
24 Who played Shirley Valentine in the film?
25 What is the white of an egg called as an alternative to albumen?
26 Which 007 actor was also TV's Remington Steele?
27 The Ashanti tribe live in which African country?
28 Which lady took over as Secretary of State for Education from David Blunkett?
29 What is held annually in London in Ranelagh Gardens?
30 Where was tennis star Monica Seles playing when she was stabbed?

Answers	Famous Names *(see Quiz 76)*

1 Gianni Versace. 2 Pierre Cardin. 3 Queen Mother. 4 Ffion. 5 Getty. 6 Madonna. 7 Elizabeth. 8 Kevin Pietersen. 9 Mao Zedong. 10 Monica Lewinsky. 11 Diego Velázquez. 12 Vivienne Westwood. 13 Reese Witherspoon. 14 Emma Forbes. 15 Both vicars. 16 Tony Blair. 17 Jack Rosenthal. 18 Brian Jones. 19 Ridley Scott. 20 Carol. 21 Football. 22 Hans Holbein. 23 MTV. 24 Gloria Hunniford. 25 Imelda Marcos. 26 Step daughter. 27 Michael. 28 Lord of the Dance. 29 Magic Johnson. 30 Jack Ryder.

Answers – page 317

1 Whose funeral in Milan in 1997 was attended by Elton John and Naomi Campbell?

2 Which Frenchman was the first to launch menswear and ready to wear collections?

3 How was the former Lady Elizabeth Bowes-Lyon better known?

4 What is the first name of Mrs William Hague?

5 Which oil billionaire founded the world's highest-funded art gallery?

6 Which famous American enrolled her baby daughter for Cheltenham Ladies' College in September 1998?

7 What is John and Norma Major's daughter called?

8 Which England cricketer was linked with Liberty X singer Jessica Taylor?

9 Chiang Ching was the third wife of which political leader?

10 Linda Tripp was the confidante of which famous name?

11 Who painted "The Rokeby Venus" in 1647–51?

12 Which fashion designer launched a perfume called Boudoir?

13 Which actress topped Julia Roberts's record fee for a single movie?

14 Who is Nanette Newman's famous TV presenter daughter?

15 What did David Frost's and Virginia Wade's father have in common?

16 Whose first names are Anthony Charles Lynton?

17 Which playwright won a BAFTA award for the "Bar Mitzvah Boy"?

18 Which Rolling Stone bought, and died at AA Milne's house?

19 Which director was knighted in the year his movie "Matchstick Men" came out?

20 What is Margaret Thatcher's journalist daughter called?

21 At which sport did Pope John Paul II excel in his youth?

22 Who painted "The Ambassadors" in 1533?

23 Which TV awards did the Beckams present in late spring 2003?

24 Who married millionaire hairdresser Stephen Way in 1998?

25 Who was the wife of Ferdinand Marcos at the time of his death?

26 What relation was Cherie Blair to Pat Phoenix, who played Elsie Tanner in "Coronation Street"?

27 What was the first famous of Marks of Marks & Spencer?

28 What links Nataraja in Hinduism and performer Michael Flatley?

29 Who was the first basketball player to declare he was HIV positive?

30 Which former "EastEnders" actor did Hear'Say's Kym Marsh marry?

Answers | Pot Luck 35 *(see Quiz 75)*

1 Porcelain. 2 Brian May. 3 Tuscany. 4 pH scale. 5 George W. Bush. 6 Rome. 7 Veins. 8 David Pleat. 9 Janet Jackson. 10 Worzel Gummidge. 11 Thomas Cook. 12 Personal Equity Plan. 13 50 Cent. 14 Theatre. 15 Embroidery. 16 Drachma. 17 Jude Law. 18 19th century. 19 Sainsbury's. 20 Egypt. 21 Terence Conran. 22 Naomi Campbell. 23 Alberta. 24 Pauline Collins. 25 Glair. 26 Pierce Brosnan. 27 Ghana. 28 Estelle Morris. 29 Chelsea Flower Show. 30 Hamburg.

1 Which show provided BBC sales with a third of their 1997 profits?
2 Which woman writer created the character Jane Tennison?
3 Which ex-Tory leader was born the same day as ex-Goodie Bill Oddie?
4 What is Dr Ross's first name in "ER"?
5 In which decade was Parliament first televised?
6 Best known as Kat Slater of "EastEnders", what is actress Jessie Wallace's real name?
7 Which rugby player joined Ulrika Jonsson as a "Gladiators" presenter?
8 Who played Owen Springer in "Reckless"?
9 Which priest replaced Father Peter in "Ballykissangel"?
10 Which ex-"Gladiators" presenter became an "I'm a Celebrity" contestant?
11 On GMTV where did Mark Freden regularly report from?
12 Which superstar did Matthew Corbett abandon finally in 1998?
13 Which role did Denise Robertson have on "This Morning"?
14 Which one-time Spice Girl advertised Walkers crisps with Gary Lineker?
15 Who was the blonde captain on "Shooting Stars"?
16 How is TV presenter Leslie Heseltine better known?
17 How many letters make up the conundrum in "Countdown"?
18 Which night was the dreaded eviction night on "Big Brother Four"?
19 Who contracted amoebic dysentery while making a Holiday show with her daughter?
20 "Frasier" was a spin-off from which series?
21 Who plays Ally McBeal?
22 How many points do you get for a starter in University Challenge?
23 In which soap did Darius from "Pop Idol" make his acting debut?
24 On which show did Tommy Walsh and Charlie Dimmock find fame?
25 For which sport did Frank Bough win an Oxbridge blue?
26 Whom did David Dimbleby replace on "Question Time"?
27 Who wrote the acclaimed series of monologues "Talking Heads"?
28 Who played Darcy in "Pride and Prejudice"?
29 Which fivesome helped launch Channel 5?
30 Jimmy Savile received an honorary doctorate from which university?

Answers	Pot Luck 36 *(see Quiz 78)*

1 Bev. 2 Leprosy. 3 Danny Murphy. 4 Mustard. 5 Tam O'Shanter. 6 On the Moon. 7 Peach & plum. 8 Stereophonics. 9 The bones. 10 An oak tree. 11 Aspirin. 12 Your Eminence. 13 1983. 14 Nelson Mandela. 15 Blackcurrant. 16 Belisha Beacon. 17 Arizona. 18 Daphne du Maurier. 19 Leo Sayer. 20 The Netherlands. 21 1/10th. 22 Aestivation. 23 88. 24 Niamh Kavanagh. 25 A flower. 26 Wakefield. 27 The brain. 28 Cannon. 29 Bathsheba. 30 JB Priestley.

1 Who was Corrie's Fred preparing to marry when he suffered a fatal heart attack?
2 What did Robert the Bruce die of?
3 Who has played for Crewe, Liverpool, Charlton and Spurs?
4 Dijon is famous for which condiment?
5 Which Robbie Burns hero gave his name to a flat cap?
6 Where is the Bay of Rainbows?
7 A nectarine is a cross between which two fruits?
8 Which top-selling band featured Stuart Cable on drums?
9 What is affected by osteomyelitis?
10 What is Charles II said to have hidden in after the Battle of Worcester?
11 What is the common name for the medication acetylsalicylic acid?
12 How is a Cardinal addressed?
13 When was the wearing of seat belts in the front of a car made compulsory?
14 Thabo Mbeki succeeded which President of South Africa?
15 Which fruit is in creme de cassis?
16 Which beacon was named after a 1930s Minister of Transport?
17 The Painted Desert is in which American state?
18 Who wrote "My Cousin Rachel" and "Frenchman's Creek"?
19 Whose hits include "Moonlighting" and "More than I Can Say"?
20 Queen Juliana abdicated from which country's throne in 1980?
21 What fraction is a cable of a nautical mile?
22 What is the opposite of hibernation?
23 How many keys does a normal piano have?
24 Which female Irish singer won the Eurovision Song Contest with "In Your Eyes"?
25 What is a corn-cockle?
26 What town is the "capital" of West Yorkshire's Rhubarb Triangle?
27 Which part of the body uses forty per cent of the oxygen in blood?
28 Which corpulent TV detective was played by William Conrad?
29 Who was the mother of King Solomon?
30 Who wrote "The Good Companions"?

Answers	TV: TV Times 2 *(see Quiz 77)*

1 The Teletubbies. 2 Lynda La Plante. 3 Michael Howard. 4 Doug. 5 1980s. 6 Karen Slater. 7 Jeremy Guscott. 8 Robson Green. 9 Father Aidan. 10 John Fashanu. 11 Hollywood. 12 Sooty. 13 Agony aunt. 14 Victoria Beckham. 15 Ulrika Jonsson. 16 Les Dennis. 17 Nine. 18 Friday. 19 Esther Rantzen. 20 Cheers. 21 Calista Flockhart. 22 10. 23 Hollyoaks. 24 Ground Force. 25 Soccer. 26 Peter Sissons. 27 Alan Bennett. 28 Colin Firth. 29 The Spice Girls. 30 Leeds.

1 In 2004, the Large Binocular Telescope was built on Mt Graham in which US state?
2 Which word describes a body in free fall in space?
3 Which planet has the satellite Europa?
4 Which space station is named after the Russian word for "peace"?
5 Ranger and Surveyor probes preceded exploration of where?
6 What name is given to a site for watching astronomical phenomena?
7 In which decade was Sputnik 1 launched?
8 Saturn rockets were developed for which moon programme?
9 Who was Soyuz TM-12's British passenger in 1991?
10 The first non-stop transatlantic flight was between which two countries?
11 What does a space shuttle land on when it returns to Earth?
12 What is the Oort cloud made out of?
13 Which Space Agency built Ariane?
14 Which communications satellite was the first to relay live TV transmissions?
15 Which rockets shared their name with the giant children of Uranus and Gaia in Greek myth ?
16 Which part of the moon did Armstrong first walk on?
17 Which of our planets is nearest the end of the alphabet?
18 Claudie Andre-Deshays was the first woman in space from which country?
19 Whose spacecraft was Vostok 1?
20 After retiring as an astronaut John Glenn followed a career in what?
21 Which clouds are formed highest above the ground?
22 How was Michael Collins a pioneer of lunar flight?
23 What is the largest planet in the solar system?
24 Phobos is a moon of which planet?
25 What was Skylab?
26 Which pioneering spacecraft was first launched in April 1981?
27 What is Jupiter's red spot made from?
28 Which country launched the first space probe in 1959?
29 Which constellation is known as The Hunter?
30 Which is larger, Mars or Earth?

Answers | Pot Luck 37 *(see Quiz 80)*

1 Cockerel. 2 George V. 3 A Will. 4 Nixon. 5 Daphne du Maurier. 6 Rioja. 7 Clot. 8 1959. 9 Craig David. 10 Steven Spielberg. 11 17th. 12 Shallot. 13 The Grampians. 14 Optician's. 15 Blind. 16 Grounds called The Stadium Of Light. 17 St Mark. 18 The Great Pyramids of Giza. 19 Sausage. 20 Joseph Priestley. 21 Chantelle Houghton. 22 B2. 23 British Prime Ministers. 24 Zacharias. 25 Sunderland. 26 WH Smiths. 27 Sinn Fein. 28 Legs. 29 Danube. 30 Yoghurt.

1 Which creature do French sports fans traditionally let loose before the start of a big match?
2 Which king unveiled the Victoria memorial?
3 What is made by a testator?
4 Who telephoned Neil Armstrong during his first moon walk?
5 Which novelist had three novels adapted by Alfred Hitchcock to films?
6 Which wine-growing region is divided into Baja, Alta and Alavesa?
7 What does fibrin cause to happen to blood?
8 Did Buddy Holly die in 1956, 1959 or 1961?
9 Which top-selling writer/singer was born May 5, 1981, in Southampton?
10 Which director appeared in "The Blues Brothers"?
11 In which century was the Taj Mahal constructed?
12 A Bordelaise sauce is flavoured by which vegetable?
13 Ben Nevis is in which mountain range?
14 Where would you probably be looking at a Snellen Chart?
15 In Bingo, what are numbers ending in zero called?
16 What do Sunderland and Benfica soccer clubs share?
17 Who is the Patron Saint of Venice?
18 What are Mycerinus and Cheprun the second two greatest of?
19 What would you be eating if you ate a Spanish chorizo?
20 Which scientist first discovered the composition of air?
21 Which "Celebrity Big Brother" winner wrote "Living the Dream: My Story"?
22 Which letter and number represent the vitamin riboflavin?
23 Derby, Pelham and Russell have all been what?
24 Who was John the Baptist's father?
25 Alan Stubbs broke his two spells at Everton by playing for which club?
26 Euston became Britain's first railway station to have what in 1848?
27 In 1921 which political party burnt down Dublin's Custom House?
28 Which part of your body is protected by puttees?
29 Which river flows through six different European countries?
30 What is the main ingredient in an Indian raita?

1 Which opera venue is near Lewes?
2 Sir John Barbirolli was conductor of which orchestra at the time of his death?
3 If a sonata is for instruments what is a cantata written for?
4 Which London theatre was the home of Gilbert & Sullivan operas?
5 Sadler's Wells theatre is famous for which performing arts?
6 Equity in the USA deals only with performers where?
7 Wayne Sleep was principal dancer with which ballet company?
8 What do you press with the right hand on an accordion?
9 Which of the Three Tenors played the title role in the film version of "Otello" in 1986?
10 How many strings are there on a double bass?
11 Richard Eyre replaced Peter Hall as artistic director at which London theatre?
12 What were all Joseph Grimaldi's clowns called?
13 What shape is the sound box on a balalaika?
14 Which male voice is between bass and tenor?
15 Where is an annual Fringe Festival held?
16 In which US city was the Actors Studio founded?
17 What is the official name of London's Drury Lane theatre?
18 Miles Davis is famous for playing which musical instrument?
19 Which king did Handel write The Water Music for?
20 Whose 1986 recording of Vivaldi's "The Four Seasons" sold over a million copies?
21 What was Paul McCartney's first classical oratorio?
22 An anthem is usually accompanied by which musical instrument?
23 Which mime artist created the clown-harlequin Bip?
24 In 2004 the Webber Douglas Academy formed a partnership with which drama school?
25 Which theatre near Blackfriars was London's first new theatre in 300 years when opened in 1959?
26 What was the slogan of London's Windmill Theatre?
27 Which musical instruments did Leo Fender create?
28 What was the first black-owned record company in the USA?
29 Who has written more plays, Shakespeare or Ayckbourn?
30 Which Camden theatre re-opened in 2006?

Answers	Pot Luck 38 *(see Quiz 82)*

1 Hertfordshire. 2 A miller. 3 Frank Morgan. 4 Andy. 5 Rome. 6 Canada. 7 Michael Bentine. 8 Nijinsky. 9 Grass. 10 As a tomato. 11 Star fish. 12 Quaver. 13 Vicarage. 14 Southampton. 15 Trollope. 16 Borneo. 17 The Trunk. 18 Maggie Smith. 19 Lactose. 20 Fluke. 21 Vera Lynn. 22 Little Women. 23 Mick Jagger. 24 LA Galaxy. 25 Judaea. 26 Prince Edward. 27 Rowan Williams. 28 Alan Milburn. 29 A barrister. 30 Shell-shaped.

1 Hemel Hempstead and St Albans are in which county?
2 Who would use a quern?
3 Who played the title role in the film "The Wizard of Oz"?
4 Whom did Ricky Gervais play in "Extras"?
5 The Spanish Steps are in which European city?
6 Cars with the international vehicle registration CDN come from where?
7 Which zany comedian devised the TV show "It's a Square World"?
8 Which Russian-sounding horse won the 2000 Guineas, St Leger and the Derby in 1970?
9 What kind of a plant is fescue?
10 When Judi Dench was dressed as a lobster for Film Four, how was Ewan McGregor dressed?
11 What type of sea creature is a brittle star?
12 Musically which note is half the value of a crotchet?
13 "Murder at the..." where was Miss Marple's first appearance?
14 Antmi Niemi joined Fulham from which club?
15 Which writer Anthony created the county of Barsetshire?
16 What is the largest island in Asia?
17 Which part of an elephant has 40,000 muscles?
18 Who played the lead role in the film "The Prime Of Miss Jean Brodie"?
19 Which type of sugar is found in milk?
20 What word can describe a lucky chance and the hook of an anchor?
21 Which female vocalist was known as 'The Forces Sweetheart'?
22 Which novel preceded "Good Wives"?
23 Which pop star married Bianca de Macias in May 1971?
24 Which football team did David Beckham sign for in January 2007?
25 Herod the Great ruled which kingdom?
26 Which Prince's childhood nickname was JAWS?
27 Who succeeded George Carey as Archbishop of Canterbury?
28 Which Blair-ite Alan became Secretary of State for Health?
29 What is the English equivalent of a Scottish Advocate?
30 What shape is a dish called a coquille?

Answers	Performing Arts *(see Quiz 81)*

1 Glyndebourne. 2 Halle. 3 Voices. 4 Savoy. 5 Opera and ballet. 6 Theatre. 7 Royal Ballet. 8 Piano-style keyboard. 9 Placido Domingo. 10 Four. 11 National. 12 Joey. 13 Triangular. 14 Baritone. 15 Edinburgh. 16 New York. 17 Theatre Royal. 18 Trumpet. 19 George I. 20 Nigel Kennedy. 21 Liverpool Oratorio. 22 Organ. 23 Marcel Marceau. 24 Central School of Speech and Drama. 25 Mermaid. 26 We never closed. 27 Electric guitars. 28 Tamla Motown. 29 Ayckbourn. 30 Roundhouse.

1 Who had a hit in 1972 with "A Thing Called Love"?
2 Which hit in letters followed "Stand by Your Man" for Tammy Wynette?
3 Which group had a No. 1 hit in 1976 with "Mississippi"?
4 Which best-selling country and pop star married Mutt Lange?
5 Whose song was a No. 1 for John Denver in 1974?
6 Which Patsy Cline hit was covered by Julio Iglesias in 1994?
7 In which year was "Achey Breaky Heart" a hit for Billy Ray Cyrus?
8 Who had a No. 11 UK hit with "Talking in Your Sleep" in 1978?
9 Hiram Williams is the real name of which singer?
10 Which opera singer joined John Denver to record "Perhaps Love"?
11 Who duetted with Ronan Keating on the chart hit "Last Thing on My Mind"?
12 Which Kris wrote "Help Me Make It Through the Night"?
13 Who had a hit in the summer of 1998 with "How Do I"?
14 Who wrote the autobiography "Coal Miner's Daughter"?
15 Who joined Kenny Rogers on the No. 7 hit "Islands in the Stream"?
16 What is Reba McEntire's real name?
17 Which specialist type of singing links Frank Ifield and Slim Whitman?
18 Who duetted with Mark Knopfler on the album "Neck and Neck"?
19 In the No. 1, which drums were heard by Jim Reeves?
20 Who sang "All I Have to do Is Dream" with Bobbie Gentry in 1969?
21 Who had a backing band called the Waylors?
22 What is the name of the theme park owned by Dolly Parton?
23 George Jones' 1975 hit "The Battle" told of the split from his wife. Who was she?
24 Which Banks were a hit in 1971 for Olivia Newton-John?
25 Which song was a No. 2 UK hit for Tammy Wynette and KLF in 1991?
26 Who wrote the classic song "Crazy"?
27 Who formed the Trio with Dolly Parton and Linda Ronstadt?
28 Who took "Cotton Eye Joe" to No. 1 in 1994?
29 Which No. 9 for Elvis was a No. 10 for Carl Perkins in 1956?
30 Which "modern girl" joined Kenny Rogers on "We've Got Tonight"?

Answers	Pot Luck 39 *(see Quiz 84)*

1 Rose. 2 Tessa Jowell. 3 Westlife. 4 Seaweed. 5 Sweet. 6 Victoria. 7 Oil tanker. 8 Fuller's. 9 Blood poisoning. 10 Leopards. 11 Anthony Eden. 12 Macduff. 13 Friar Tuck. 14 Suffolk. 15 Soles of your feet. 16 Bolero. 17 Racehorses. 18 Passepartout. 19 Pierre Trudeau. 20 Cary Grant. 21 1970s. 22 Portsmouth. 23 Nose. 24 British Grand Prix. 25 Iraq. 26 Enya. 27 William Beveridge. 28 I Just Called to Say I Love You. 29 A horse. 30 Thumb.

1 What was the name of Kate Winslet's character in Titanic?
2 Who was Culture Secretary when the UK won the staging of the 2012 Olympics?
3 Which top-selling band featured Kian Egan on vocals?
4 What is kelp?
5 Who had hits with "Fox on the Run" and "Wig-Wam Bam"?
6 What name is an African lake, a station and a former Queen?
7 What type of vessel was the Torrey Canyon?
8 Which brewing company produces London Pride?
9 What is the more common name for toxaemia?
10 Which members of the big cat family collect in a leap?
11 Who preceded Harold Macmillan as Prime Minister?
12 In the Shakespeare play who killed Macbeth?
13 Which heavy character was missing from the 2006 Robin Hood TV series?
14 Newmarket and Ipswich are both in which county?
15 Reflexology treats your body through what?
16 What can be a short jacket and a dance?
17 What are auctioned at Tattersalls?
18 Who was Phileas Fogg's companion in "Around the World in 80 Days"?
19 Which French-Canadian became Canadian Prime Minister in 1968?
20 Archibald Leach, born in Bristol, became which Hollywood star?
21 In which decade did John Wayne die?
22 Which English club has had Velimir Zajec and Alain Perrin as managers?
23 Which part of your body would interest a rhinologist?
24 In 1926 what was held for the first time at Brooklands?
25 Mesopotamia was the ancient name for which modern-day country?
26 Which female singer made the album "Day without Rain"?
27 Whose report in the 1940s was vital in setting up the welfare state?
28 Which Stevie Wonder No. 1 was in the film "The Woman in Red"?
29 What type of animal is a Lippizaner?
30 Which digit is your pollex?

1 Which Australian was the first to score 60 tries in international rugby?
2 Who was the first Englishman to reach 750 points in major internationals?
3 Who was the first English player to play in 50 internationals?
4 Which country in 1995 asked to increase the number of teams in the Five Nations Cup?
5 Which colours do Bath play in?
6 Which Welsh Union player was a regular captain on "A Question of Sport"?
7 In which part of London did the London Broncos start out?
8 Who won the Man of Steel in 1996 and 2004?
9 For which side did Brian Bevan score 740 tries in 620 matches?
10 What were Bradford before they were Bulls?
11 Who retired as Scottish captain after the 1995 World Cup?
12 Who was Wigan's leading try scorer in the 1994/95 season?
13 Where would you watch Rhinos playing rugby?
14 Paul Sackey was at which club when he first won a cap, aged 27?
15 Which international side has the shortest name?
16 Who are the two sides in the Varsity Match?
17 Which rugby team plays its home games at Welford Road?
18 Who was leading try scorer in the 1995 rugby union World Cup?
19 In 1998 what colour cards were substituted for yellow ones?
20 Who joined Leeds in 1991 after playing on the other side of the Pennines since 1984?
21 What did Bath Football Club change its name to in the mid-90s?
22 Who was the first non-white Springbok, before the end of apartheid?
23 Which rugby side added Warriors to its name?
24 In which decade was Rugby Union last played in the Olympics?
25 How old was Will Carling when he was first made England Captain?
26 Who played a record-breaking 69 times at fly half for England between 1985 and 1995?
27 In 1980 who led England to their first Grand Slam in 23 years?
28 Where is the annual Varsity match played?
29 How many years had Wigan's unbeaten run in the FA Challenge Cup lasted when it ended in 1996?
30 Whom did Martin Offiah play for in his first years as a League player?

Answers	Pot Luck 40 (see Quiz 86)

1 Shoulder blade. 2 Great Stour. 3 Sex Pistols. 4 Falmouth. 5 India. 6 Judo. 7 Henry I. 8 The wind. 9 Maastricht. 10 Young. 11 British Honduras. 12 Don Johnson. 13 Jenkins. 14 River Soar. 15 Francis. 16 My Son, My Son. 17 Anne-Sophie Mutter. 18 Duke of Marlborough. 19 Peter. 20 A knot. 21 Zirconium. 22 London. 23 A ship. 24 Colorado. 25 Likud. 26 Phil Parkinson. 27 London's Burning. 28 The Merry Monarch. 29 Norfolk. 30 Richard Whiteley.

Quiz 86 | Pot Luck 40

Answers – page 327

LEVEL 2

1 Where in your body is your scapula?
2 Canterbury stands on which river?
3 Who had hits with "God Save the Queen" and "C'Mon Everybody"?
4 Sebastian Coe became MP for which constituency in 1992?
5 Which former colony was called the jewel in Queen Victoria's crown?
6 What was the sport of Karen Briggs and Nicola Fairbrother?
7 Which Henry became King of England in 1100?
8 In the film "Mary Poppins", Mary said she would stay until what changed?
9 Which Treaty on European Union was signed in December 1991?
10 Which surname links No. 1 hit singers Jimmy, Paul and Will?
11 What was the former name of Belize?
12 Which actor married Melanie Griffith twice?
13 What was Ffion Hague's maiden name?
14 Which river does Leicester stand on?
15 What is decathlon champion Daley Thompson's first name?
16 Which Vera Lynn song was a No. 1 UK hit in 1954?
17 Which German violinist was married to André Previn?
18 Who was given Blenheim Palace as a reward for his military service?
19 In the Bible, who denied Jesus three times before the cock crowed twice?
20 A Turk's Head is a type of what?
21 Alphabetically which chemical element is the last?
22 Which European capital was considered cleanest in a 1995 survey?
23 What is a frigatoon?
24 "The Garden of the Gods" is in which American state?
25 Ariel Sharon belonged to which political party in Israel?
26 Which manager Phil took Colchester into the Championship for the first time?
27 Which TV series has characters called Gracie, Sicknote and George?
28 What was King Charles II's nickname?
29 Kings Lynn and Norwich are both in which county?
30 Who was the presenter of "Countdown" when it was first televised?

Answers	**Sport: Rugby** *(see Quiz 85)*

1 David Campese. 2 Jonny Wilkinson. 3 Rory Underwood. 4 Italy. 5 Blue, black and white. 6 Gareth Edwards. 7 Fulham. 8 Andy Farrell. 9 Warrington. 10 Northern. 11 Gavin Hastings. 12 Martin Offiah. 13 Leeds. 14 Wasps. 15 Fiji. 16 Oxford University and Cambridge University. 17 Leicester. 18 Jonah Lomu. 19 White. 20 Ellery Hanley. 21 Bath Rugby Club. 22 Errol Tobias. 23 Wigan. 24 1920s. 25 22. 26 Rob Andrew. 27 Bill Beaumont. 28 Twickenham. 29 Eight. 30 Widnes.

1 What was the first film in which Clint Eastwood starred as "The man with no name"?

2 Who played the sadistic sheriff in Eastwood's "Unforgiven"?

3 Which actor's films include "Big Jim McLain", "McLintock" and "McQ"?

4 Which star of "Maverick" played Brett Maverick in the TV series?

5 Which Oscar did Kevin Costner win for "Dances with Wolves"?

6 What is the name of the original tale that the "Magificent Seven" is based on?

7 What weather feature was in the title of the song from Butch Cassidy won an Oscar?

8 Who was the star of "Jeremiah Johnson"?

9 Which comedy actor starred in the comedy western "The Paleface"?

10 Who starred with brother Charlie Sheen in "Young Guns"?

11 Which Oscar winner for "Fargo", married director Joel Coen?

12 Who played the woman poker player in "Maverick"?

13 Which actor was "The Bad"?

14 Which "Back to the Future" film returns to the Wild West?

15 In which musical western does the song "Wandrin' Star" appear?

16 Which Hollywood legend was the narrator in "How the West was Won"?

17 Which film was originally called "Per un Pugno di Dollari"?

18 Which country singer was in "True Grit"?

19 Which son of a "M*A*S*H" star appeared in "Young Guns II"?

20 Whom did John Wayne play in "The Alamo"?

21 Clint Eastwood became mayor of which town?

22 Which 1985 film was a revised remake of the classic "Shane"?

23 Where is the village where the action of "The Magnificent Seven" centres?

24 Where was "The Good, the Bad and the Ugly" made?

25 What was the name of Mel Brooks' spoof western?

26 Which English comic appeared in "Desperado"?

27 Which 80s teenage western starred actors known as the Brat Pack?

28 What was Tonto's horse called?

29 Who was Gene Autry's most famous horse?

30 Traditionally, what colour is the western hero's hat?

---

1 "Men Behaving Badly"'s Leslie Ash was born the same day as which Prince?

2 Who first presented Channel 4's "Fifteen To One"?

3 Alice Beer first found fame on which show?

4 Which show was first broadcast on Friday 9 December 1960?

5 Which "Cardiac Arrest" star also starred in "Friends"?

6 What was the lawyer played by Daniela Nardini in "This Life" called?

7 Which song did Emma Bunton record for the BBC's "Children in Need" 2006?

8 Who was chosen to succeed Des Lynam on "Countdown"?

9 Whose last series was "Paradise Gardens"?

10 In which city did the docu soap "Hotel" take place?

11 Which comedy duo are famous for their head-to-head discussions?

12 In which city did lifeguard Mitch Buchanan work?

13 Who was the female team captain in the 90s "Call My Bluff"?

14 What was the occupation of Linda in "Strictly Confidential"?

15 Who decides who leaves the competition in the "Weakest Link"?

16 Which musician's name completes the title "Later...with..."?

17 Who is the bouncing frog of Fimble Valley?

18 In which show might a contestant ask "Could I have a P please, Bob?"

19 Whom is Robbie Coltrane's son Spencer named after?

20 Which redhead assists Rolf Harris at the "Animal Hospital"?

21 What was the name of the spotty teenager played by Harry Enfield?

22 Presenter Suzanne Dando represented Great Britain at which sport?

23 Which series centred on Skeldale House?

24 Who has hosted "Antiques Roadshow" through most of the 90s?

25 Who tried to emulate Phileas Fogg in a 1989 documentary?

26 Who did Roseanne offer a million dollars to appear on her talk show in October 1998?

27 Gary Lucy came to fame on which show?

28 Which "Ab Fab" star took Caroline Quentin's place as Jonathan Creek's sidekick?

29 Which boy band won the first series of "Popstars: The Rivals"?

30 In which series did mum Joyce have a daughter called Cully?

Answers | Movies: Westerns *(see Quiz 87)*

1 A Fistful of Dollars. 2 Gene Hackman. 3 John Wayne. 4 James Garner. 5 Best Director. 6 The Seven Samurai. 7 Raindrops. 8 Robert Redford. 9 Bob Hope. 10 Emilio Estevez. 11 Frances McDormand. 12 Jodie Foster. 13 Lee van Cleef. 14 No. III. 15 Paint Your Wagon. 16 Spencer Tracy. 17 A Fistful of Dollars. 18 Glen Campbell. 19 Kiefer Sutherland. 20 Davy Crockett. 21 Carmel. 22 Pale Rider. 23 Mexico. 24 Italy. 25 Blazing Saddles. 26 John Cleese. 27 Young Guns. 28 Scout. 29 Champion. 30 White.

1 Which Queen wrote the Casket Letters?
2 Which former Take That star had "Child" at No. 3 in 1996?
3 What can be metric royal, metric demy and metric crown?
4 In which TV series was the character "Boss Hogg"?
5 Who succeeded Charles Clarke as Home Secretary?
6 Which almond cake is traditionally made for Mothering Sunday?
7 Who had hits with "We are Glass" and "Cars"?
8 David Bentley joined Blackburn from which London club?
9 Which actress had lead roles in the films "Out of Africa" and "Silkwood"?
10 Which two European languages are spoken in Madagascar?
11 Which gallery hosted Pet Shop Boys Portraits from Oct. 2006 to Feb. 2007?
12 What were the giant insects in the science fiction film "Them"?
13 Which famous TV cook took his show "Around Britain"?
14 During which war does Norman Mailer's "The Naked and the Dead" take place?
15 Aylesbury and Milton Keynes are both in which county?
16 Which film director based "Tea with Mussolini" on his own experiences in 1930s Florence?
17 Which animal was used by Jenner to develop the vaccine against smallpox?
18 What is a davenport?
19 Which singer starred alongside Kyle McLachlan in "Dune"?
20 Who composed the music for "The Good, the Bad and the Ugly"?
21 Who had hits with "Blue Monday" and "World in Motion"?
22 What kind of musical instrument was a kit?
23 Which country did Charles and Camilla visit in October 2006?
24 Which John Carpenter film set in the Antarctic starred Kurt Russell?
25 Name the first yacht to win the America's Cup?
26 Which singing sisters were called Patti, Laverne and Maxine?
27 In which country are the guerrilla group the Tamil Tigers?
28 What name is given to the principal female singer in an opera?
29 The dish Eggs Florentine contains which vegetable?
30 Which town was Barbara Castle's parliamentary constituency?

Answers	**World Tour** *(see Quiz 90)*

1 Atlantic. 2 Las Vegas. 3 Broadway. 4 Inuit (Eskimos). 5 Cape of Good Hope. 6 Wind. 7 Honshu. 8 Australia. 9 China. 10 K2. 11 Okovango. 12 Indian. 13 Hawaii. 14 China. 15 Namibia. 16 Gobi. 17 Dow Jones. 18 Eskimo. 19 Michigan. 20 Zambia and Zimbabwe. 21 Trinidad. 22 French. 23 Canaries. 24 North coast of Africa. 25 Manhattan. 26 Tip of South America. 27 Greenland. 28 Kilimanjaro. 29 Israel. 30 Pakistan & Afghanistan.

1 The Sargasso Sea is part of which ocean?

2 Which US city's name means "The Fields"?

3 How is New York's "Great White Way" also known?

4 Which Canadians speak Inuktitut?

5 Which Cape was originally called the Cape of Storms?

6 In America what type of natural phenomenon is a Chinook?

7 What is the principal island of Japan?

8 Where is the town of Kurri Kurri?

9 The Guangzhou TV & Sightseeing Tower was constructed in which country?

10 By which abbreviation is the mountain Chogori known?

11 What is the only permanent river in the Kalahari desert?

12 Which Ocean's deepest point is the Java Trench?

13 Where would you be if someone put a lei round your neck?

14 Where is the world's longest canal?

15 Afrikaans is the official language of which country in addition to South Africa?

16 In which desert is the Bactrian camel found?

17 What is the name of the index on the New York Stock Exchange?

18 Which group of people have a name meaning "eater of raw meat"?

19 Which is the only Great Lake wholly in the USA?

20 The Kariba Dam is on the border of which two countries?

21 Calypso is the traditional song form of which Caribbean island?

22 Which European language is spoken in Chad?

23 Las Palmas is in which island group?

24 Approximately where was Carthage to be found?

25 Wall Street and Broadway lie on which island?

26 Where is the Magellan Strait?

27 What is the largest island between the North Atlantic and the Arctic?

28 What is Africa's highest volcano?

29 Where is there a Parliament called the Knesset?

30 Which two countries does the Khyber Pass separate?

1 What is saxifrage?

2 In "EastEnders" which character killed Dirty Den in February 2006?

3 Who hoisted himself on to Sinbad the Sailor's shoulders?

4 How much are you paid if you hold an honorary post?

5 Which UK act first scored the dreaded "nul points" in the Eurovision Song Contest?

6 What can be a five-card game, a smooth, woolly surface or a sleep?

7 Which club did Will Carling play for?

8 Which Australian movie director links "Romeo and Juliet" and "Strictly Ballroom"?

9 Whose music albums have included "An Innocent Man"?

10 'Englander' is an anagram of which country?

11 Which actress played Michael Douglas's wife in "Fatal Attraction"?

12 What is a melodeon?

13 Which animal family are impala, eland and dik-dik all from?

14 Which famous stepson wrote "The Year of Eating Dangerously"?

15 In TV's "Upstairs Downstairs" what was the name of the cook?

16 Whose hits include "Dancin' on the Ceiling" and "Do It to Me"?

17 Which stone is inscribed "Cormac McCarthy fortis me fieri fecit AD 1446"?

18 Which actor played the leading role in the TV drama "Shogun"?

19 What name is given to withered apples used to make rough cider?

20 Who composed the music for the musical "Lady be Good"?

21 What is a grackle?

22 Which building was erected in 1851 for the Great Exhibition?

23 Which children's TV series has included Tucker Jenkins and Zammo?

24 Which "Corrie" character died with Gilbert and Sullivan playing in his car?

25 Which branch would you hold out to seek peace?

26 Arthur Hastings was the sidekick of which fictional sleuth?

27 Whose hits include "Detroit City" and "Love Me Tonight"?

28 The leader of an orchestra plays which instrument?

29 What was Mab's job in fairy folklore?

30 Anderson, Kiely and Myhre played for which Premiership side in 2005–06?

Answers	**Past Times: The 80s** *(see Quiz 92)*

1 UK and Eire. 2 Chernobyl. 3 FW de Klerk. 4 Dubcek. 5 Salman Rushdie. 6 Michael Foot. 7 Mitterrand. 8 Galtieri. 9 Kim Wilde. 10 Jamaica. 11 Greenpeace. 12 Iceland. 13 Twice. 14 Dirty Dancing. 15 Ken Livingstone. 16 Monday. 17 The Labour Party. 18 Grand Hotel. 19 Slobodan Milosevic. 20 Montserrat. 21 Mubarak. 22 Irangate. 23 David Blunkett. 24 Jimmy Carter. 25 Peter Mandelson. 26 Local authority. 27 Benazir Bhutto. 28 Zimbabwe. 29 South Africa. 30 Mikhail Gorbachev.

1 The Hillsborough Agreement was between which two countries?

2 Where was there a major nuclear leak in the USSR in 1986?

3 Who was the last white President of South Africa, elected in 1989?

4 Which former liberal leader was made speaker of the national assembly of Czechoslovakia in 1989?

5 A fatwa calling for the death of which writer was made by Iran in '89?

6 Who succeeded Callaghan as Labour leader?

7 Who became France's first socialist president in 1981?

8 Who was Argentine President during the Falklands Conflict?

9 Which 80s female hit maker is a celebrity gardener this century?

10 Michael Manley became leader of where in 1989?

11 Who owned Rainbow Warrior, sunk by the French in 1985?

12 Vigdis Finnbogadottir became head of state in which country?

13 How many times was Margaret Thatcher elected PM in the 80s?

14 Which film featured "(I've Had) The Time of My Life" in its soundtrack?

15 Who was leader of the GLC from 1981–86?

16 What was the Black day of the week of the 1987 stockmarket crash?

17 Who moved from Transport House to Walworth Road in 1980?

18 In which hotel was the Brighton bomb in 1984?

19 Who became President of Serbia in 1986?

20 Most of which Caribbean island's buildings were destroyed by hurricane Hugo in 1989?

21 Who became Egyptian President after Sadat's assassination?

22 What was the name of the scandal over arms for hostages in which Oliver North was implicated?

23 Which one-time member of Tony Blair's cabinet was leader of Sheffield City Council?

24 Whom did Ronald Reagan defeat to become US President in 1980?

25 Which spin doctor did Neil Kinnock engage to run the 1987 election campaign?

26 In 1989 state schools were allowed to opt out of whose control?

27 Which woman became PM of Pakistan after the death of Zia in a plane crash?

28 Where did the parties of ZANU and ZAPU merge in 1987?

29 In 1986 the pass laws, concerning the carrying of identity documents, were repealed in which country?

30 Which Russian leader introduced the policy of perestroika?

Answers | Pot Luck 42 *(see Quiz 91)*

1 A small rock plant. 2 Chrissie Watts. 3 The Old Man of the Sea. 4 Nothing. 5 Jemini. 6 A nap. 7 Harlequins. 8 Baz Luhrmann. 9 Billy Joel. 10 Greenland. 11 Anne Archer. 12 A musical instrument. 13 Antelope. 14 Tom Parker Bowles. 15 Mrs Bridges. 16 Lionel Richie. 17 The Blarney Stone. 18 Richard Chamberlain. 19 Scrumps. 20 George Gershwin. 21 A bird. 22 Crystal Palace. 23 Grange Hill. 24 Derek Wilton. 25 Olive. 26 Hercule Poirot. 27 Tom Jones. 28 Violin. 29 A midwife. 30 Charlton Athletic.

Quiz 93 Pot Luck 43

Answers – page 336

LEVEL 2

1 What type of animal is a Sooty Mangabey?
2 Which team lost the first FA Cup Final decided on penalties?
3 Whom did William III defeat in 1690 at the Battle of the Boyne?
4 Who won "X Factor 2"?
5 In Old English which word meant a field?
6 What were the eldest sons of French kings called from the 14th century?
7 Ely stands on which river?
8 Which 60s singer married the designer Jeff Banks?
9 In 1945, who became British Prime Minister?
10 In which month in 2006 was "Top of the Pops" aired for the last time?
11 Who had hits with "The Streak" and "Misty" in the 70s?
12 Who was President of the Philippines from 1965 to 1986?
13 Which Gate is a memorial for British Soldiers who fell at Ypres?
14 Who played Fred Kite in the film "I'm Alright, Jack"?
15 In "Bringing Down the House" Steve Martin starred with which rapper?
16 Which complaint was the Jacuzzi originally developed to help?
17 What did Anna Karenina throw herself under in the Tolstoy novel?
18 Who wrote "Dr Zhivago"?
19 In which soap does the Cat & Fiddle rival The Bull?
20 Which comedian was Connie Booth married to?
21 The sons of Max and Mira Weinstein founded which film company?
22 Who preceded Edward VI as Monarch?
23 In the film "The Tommy Steele Story" who played Tommy Steele?
24 Who finished his radio show with "B.F.N. Bye for now"?
25 Who had hits with "The Logical Song" and "Dreamer"?
26 In which year was Lord Mountbatten murdered?
27 What is the start of Psalm 23?
28 Which shaggy horned wild cattle live in the Tibetan mountains?
29 What was a gulag in Russia?
30 In the 1953 film "Houdini" who played the title role?

Answers	Leisure: Books 2 *(see Quiz 94)*

1 Oxford. 2 The Da Vinci Code. 3 Slavery. 4 Dictionary. 5 Jeeves. 6 The Greatest.
7 Lord Peter Wimsey. 8 Black Beauty. 9 Spycatcher. 10 Childcare. 11 Joan Collins.
12 Nigel Lawson. 13 Maeve Binchy. 14 Oranges. 15 Ruth Rendell. 16 Bill Bryson.
17 Agatha Christie. 18 The Godfather. 19 The English Patient. 20 John Le Carré.
21 Schindler's Ark. 22 Marie Stopes. 23 The Odessa File. 24 Alan Titchmarsh. 25
Detective novel. 26 Jeffrey Archer. 27 Wales. 28 A Tale of Two Cities. 29 Exodus. 30
Simenon.

1 In which university city is the Bodleian Library?

2 In which book does Bishop Aringarosa visit Castle Gandolfo?

3 "Uncle Tom's Cabin" was a novel which argued against what?

4 In the US what type of book is Webster famous for?

5 Who is the most famous manservant created by PG Wodehouse?

6 What was Muhammad Ali's autobiography called?

7 Which Dorothy L Sayers' creation was Harriet Vane's husband?

8 Which children's classic was written to encourage adults to be kinder to horses?

9 Which book by ex-intelligence agent Peter Wright, did the British government try to have banned?

10 What was the subject of Benjamin Spock's most famous books?

11 Which soap star wrote "Prime Time"?

12 Which ex-Chancellor of the Exchequer wrote a diet book?

13 Whose first successful novel was "Light a Penny Candle"?

14 What "Are not the Only Fruit" according to Jeanette Winterson?

15 Who wrote the detective novel "Road Rage"?

16 Who wrote "A Walk in the Woods"?

17 "The Murder of Roger Ackroyd" was an early novel by whom?

18 Which is Mario Puzo's most famous novel, first published in 1969?

19 Which Michael Ondaatje book was made into an Oscar-winning film with Ralph Fiennes?

20 Who created George Smiley?

21 Which was the first Thomas Keneally book to win the Booker Prize?

22 Which birth control campaigner wrote the book "Married Love"?

23 What was Frederick Forsyth's follow-up to "The Day of the Jackal"?

24 Which gardening expert wrote "Nobbut a Lad"?

25 "The Woman in White" is the first novel of what type in English?

26 Whose "Not a Penny More, not a Penny Less" was written to clear bankruptcy debts?

27 In Colin Dexter's books where does Lewis come from?

28 Which Dickens novel is about the French Revolution?

29 What is the second book of the Old Testament?

30 Which Georges wrote over a hundred novels featuring Jules Maigret?

1 What did MGM stand for?
2 What colour is puce?
3 Which "Pop Idol" winner appeared on "You are What You Eat"?
4 Who was the first presenter of the TV series "Tomorrow's World"?
5 Which cartoon character was the "fastest mouse in Mexico"?
6 Who had 90s No. 1 hits with "The Power" and "Rhythm is a Dancer"?
7 Which US state is the second smallest?
8 According to the saying, who rush in where angels fear to tread?
9 What is Blue Vinney?
10 Who wrote "Five Children and It" and "Wet Magic"?
11 Which terrier is the largest of the breed?
12 Who was the head of the German SS?
13 What is studied by a haematologist?
14 Which county is Morganwg Ganol in Welsh?
15 What type of creature is a turnstone?
16 Which country from 1867–1914 had a governor called The Khedive?
17 In the film "The Great Escape" which actor played the Forger?
18 Which Egyptian President was assassinated in 1981?
19 In the TV series "To the Manor Born" what was the name of the butler?
20 Which 'N Sync star launched the design label William Rast?
21 Who had hits with "Kiss from a Rose" and "Crazy"?
22 The town of Newcastle is in which Australian state?
23 What was Marc Bolan's real name?
24 What type of food is a bullace?
25 What is a snake's cast-off skin called?
26 The holiday camp Maplins featured in which TV series?
27 Stelios Giannakopoulos joined Bolton from which club?
28 What is mineral water mixed with quinine called?
29 Whose painting was reported to have been sold for $140 million in 2006?
30 What was sought by Jason and the Argonauts?

Answers | **Pop Music: Groups** *(see Quiz 96)*

1 The Blue Flames. 2 Swedish. 3 Red Hot Chilli Peppers. 4 Summer Love. 5 The News. 6 Chairmen of the Board. 7 Our eyes. 8 In Perfect Harmony. 9 Vic Reeves. 10 Def Leppard. 11 Live Forever. 12 Good Vibrations. 13 Simply Red. 14 Three Lions. 15 Cream. 16 1994. 17 California. 18 All Day and All of the Night. 19 Computer Love/The Model. 20 To Trancentral. 21 Bread. 22 Jake. 23 The Bangles. 24 Clannad. 25 Moving On Up. 26 My Perfect Cousin. 27 Elkie Brooks. 28 This millennium. 29 Cosmic Girl. 30 Las Vegas.

1 What was the name of Georgie Fame's backing group?
2 What nationality were "All That She Wants" group Ace of Base?
3 Whose "Live in Hyde Park" album celebrated the success of the 2004 concerts?
4 What "Sensation" were the Bay City Rollers singing about in 1974?
5 Huey Lewis was vocalist for which group?
6 Which Company band had a hit with "Give Me Just a Little More Time"?
7 What did Go West close in their No. 5 from 1985?
8 What followed in brackets on "I'd Like To Teach the World to Sing"?
9 Who did the Wonder Stuff serve as backing group for?
10 Which heavy band took "When Love and Hate Collide" to No. 2?
11 What was Oasis' first UK Top Ten single?
12 What was The Beach Boys' first UK No. 1?
13 Which band made the hit album "Home"?
14 Which Lightning Seeds No. 1 was the official song of the England Football
Team in 1996?
15 Ginger, Jack and Eric formed which trio?
16 In which year did Oasis first have a No. 1-selling album?
17 Which "Hotel" was visited by the Eagles in 1977?
18 What part of the day took the Stranglers to No. 7 in 1988?
19 In 1982, what was the name of the first UK No. 1 by a German group?
20 Which Last Train did KLF catch in their No. 2 UK hit in 1991?
21 Singer/ songwriter David Gates led which group?
22 Who was the brother in the title of a track by Free from 1970?
23 Which girl band had hits with "Manic Monday" and "Walk Like an Egyptian"?
24 Which Irish group had a No. 5 hit with the "Theme from Harry's Game"?
25 What action were M People doing in their No. 2 UK hit from 1993?
26 What relative was "Perfect" according to the hit by the Undertones?
27 Who was the female artist in Vinegar Joe?
28 Have U2 had more No. 1s in the last century or this millennium?
29 What sort of girl took Jamiroquai to No. 6 in 1996?
30 Where was ZZ Top on the No. 10 hit Viva?

Answers	Pot Luck 44 *(see Quiz 95)*

1 Metro Goldwyn Mayer. 2 Purple brown. 3 Michelle McManus. 4 Raymond Baxter.
5 Speedy Gonzales. 6 Snap. 7 Delaware. 8 Fools. 9 Cheese. 10 E. Nesbit. 11
Airedale. 12 Himmler. 13 Blood. 14 Mid Glamorgan. 15 A bird. 16 Egypt. 17
Donald Pleasence. 18 Anwar Sadat. 19 Brabinger. 20 Justin Timberlake. 21 Seal.
22 New South Wales. 23 Mark Field. 24 A fruit (plum). 25 Slough. 26 Hi De Hi. 27
Olympiakos. 28 Tonic water. 29 Jackson Pollock. 30 The Golden Fleece.

1 Who was the first Briton to hold a world javelin record?
2 Hidetoshi Nakata of Japan made his Premiership debut with which club?
3 How many players are there in a Canadian football team?
4 Chester Whites, Durocs and Hampshire are all types of what animal?
5 What is killed by an analgesic?
6 The Dufourspitze is the highest mountain where?
7 When do ducks always lay their eggs?
8 What was the first Top Ten hit for the Sugababes?
9 Who preceded Corazon Aquino as President of the Philippines?
10 Which test would you be taking if you underwent a polygraph test?
11 Which American city's football team is called the Bears?
12 Which vitamin deficiency causes rickets?
13 Which suspension bridge crosses the River Avon?
14 Which volcano erupted in 1883 and lies between Java and Sumatra?
15 What is the vocal tinkling sound made by a deer called?
16 Which sea surrounds Heligoland?
17 Which famous TV duo starred in the sci-fi comedy "Alien Autopsy"?
18 The pituitary gland controls the production of what in the body?
19 Which prefix is a tenth in the metric system?
20 How many pounds does the Olympic hammer weigh?
21 Which museum hosted Kylie: The Exhibition from February to June 2007?
22 What was a Minster originally attached to?
23 What is the popular name for the wood-hyacinth?
24 Where is Britain's National Horseracing Museum?
25 Whom did James Earl Ray assassinate?
26 Which city hosted the final game in the 2006/07 Ashes in Australia?
27 Which fault line is San Francisco on?
28 Who won 100m gold at the 1988 Olympics after Ben Johnson's disqualification?
29 Where was the terrorist group ETA mainly active?
30 Who was called the Father of Medicine?

Answers	**Sport: Who's Who** *(see Quiz 98)*

1 Sonny Liston. 2 Natalie Tauziat. 3 Rocky Marciano. 4 Al Joyner. 5 Joe DiMaggio. 6 Jake La Motta. 7 Silver. 8 Ray Reardon. 9 Raymond van Barnevald. 10 Mary Decker Slaney. 11 Italy. 12 Ernie Els. 13 Nick Faldo. 14 Steve Davis. 15 Cook book. 16 Paul Azinger. 17 Chris Evert. 18 Davis. 19 Squash. 20 Denise Lewis. 21 Graeme Smith. 22 Rocket. 23 John Conteh. 24 Judo. 25 Mike Tyson. 26 Conchita Martinez. 27 Bernard Gallacher. 28 Snooker. 29 Peter Fleming. 30 Nigel Benn.

1 Whom did Muhammad Ali beat when he first became World Champion?
2 Who was runner up to Jana Novotna in the Wimbledon final in 1998?
3 Who was the first heavyweight boxing champion to retire undefeated?
4 Who was the late Flo Jo's husband?
5 Which husband of Marilyn Monroe was elected to the Baseball Hall of Fame?
6 Whose life was recorded on film in "Raging Bull"?
7 What colour individual medal did Sharron Davies win at the Moscow Olympics?
8 Which snooker champion was unkindly nicknamed Dracula?
9 Who beat Phil Taylor in the 2007 World Professional Darts Championship Final?
10 Whom did Zola Budd trip up at the Los Angeles Olympics in 1984?
11 British-born long jumper Fiona May represents which country in international athletics?
12 Which South African golfer's real first name is Theodore?
13 Which golfer split with his coach and his girlfriend in September '98?
14 Whom did Stephen Hendry replace as world No. 1 in the 1989–90 season?
15 Away from cricket, what sort of book did Aussie Matthew Hayden write?
16 Who was appointed USA captain for the 2008 Ryder Cup?
17 Who lost most Ladies Singles finals at Wimbledon in the 80s?
18 Which surname has been shared by three world snooker champions?
19 Peter Nicol won Commonwealth gold for Scotland in which sport?
20 Who successfully defended her heptathlon title at the 1998 Commonwealth Games?
21 Which cricketer with a very English surname was made South Africa captain in 2003?
22 Which Gladiator competed in the heptathlon in the 1998 Commonwealth Games?
23 Which Liverpudlian won the WBC Light Heavyweight Title in 1974?
24 Sharron Davies' one time fiancé Neil Adams was an international in which sport?
25 Who replaced Leon Spinks as Heavyweight Champion in 1987?
26 Who defeated Navratilova in the final at her last Wimbledon?
27 Who captained Europe to Ryder Cup success in 1995?
28 Allison Fisher is a former world champion in which sport?
29 Whom did John McEnroe win five Wimbledon Doubles titles with?
30 Which boxer is nicknamed "The Dark Destroyer"?

1 Which "Game for a Laugh" presenters had the same surname?
2 Who was the subject of "The Naked Civil Servant" with John Hurt?
3 Which sitcom told of Tooting revolutionary Wolfie?
4 Who found fame as "The Saint"?
5 Who played Louie de Palma in "Taxi"?
6 Which spaghetti western star played in "Rawhide" for six years?
7 Who conducted Eric Morecambe playing Grieg's Piano Concerto?
8 Which reporter found fame during her reporting of the Iranian Embassy siege in 1980?
9 In which weekly drama slot was "Cathy Come Home" first shown?
10 Which star of "The Likely Lads" starred in "New Tricks" with Alun Armstrong?
11 Who was the main character on "The Phil Silvers Show"?
12 Who became Mrs Clayton Farlow in "Dallas"?
13 Which series looked back at film clips 25 years old?
14 How were Bruce Wayne and Dick Grayson better known?
15 Which "Carry On" regular was the star of "Bless This House"?
16 Who was "lower class" on "The Frost Report" after John Cleese and Ronnie Barker?
17 Which soap was originally called "The Midland Road"?
18 Which famous singer/actor's daughter shot JR?
19 Which TV veteran narrated "Planet Earth"?
20 What was the surname of Morticia and Gomez?
21 Which area of the country received TV after the area London in 1949?
22 In which sitcom did Richard Beckinsale play Alan Moore?
23 Which series told of the bizarre life of the Clampett family?
24 Which comedian played Colin in "Colin's Sandwich"?
25 Which show has numbered David Jacobs, Noel Edmonds and Rosemarie Ford among its presenters?
26 What was the BBC's first soap of the 60s?
27 Which actor played the part of Uncle Albert in "Only Fools and Horses"?
28 The controversial "Death of a Princess" caused a rift with which country in 1980?
29 Who had a long-running TV show before starring in "Mary Poppins"?
30 Who is the only "Corrie" star remaining from the original cast?

Answers	Pot Luck 46 (see Quiz 100)

1 Dance. 2 Gunpowder. 3 Nebuchadnezzar. 4 Sioux. 5 Golf. 6 James I. 7 Violin.
8 In loco parentis. 9 Dublin. 10 Jersey. 11 Ealing. 12 AE Housman. 13 Harvard.
14 Alessandro Volta. 15 House of Representatives. 16 A race or racial group. 17 The end of the world. 18 Lion. 19 David Dickinson. 20 Hitchcock. 21 Four. 22 Amelia Earhart. 23 Austria. 24 Rubber. 25 The Massacre. 26 Dustin Hoffman. 27 Bay. 28 Hyde Park. 29 Hormone replacement therapy. 30 PSV Eindhoven.

1 In Cuba what is a habanera?
2 Which black powder is the oldest known explosive?
3 Who condemned Shadrach, Meshach and Abednego to the Fiery Furnace?
4 Which tribe did Sitting Bull belong to?
5 Sam Snead found fame in which sport?
6 Who was king at the time of the Gunpowder Plot?
7 Which musical instrument did Jack Benny play?
8 Which Latin phrase means "in place of a parent"?
9 Dun Laoghaire is a port and suburb of where?
10 Gerald Durrell was a director of which zoo?
11 Michael Balcon was head of which influential studios?
12 Who wrote "A Shropshire Lad"?
13 What is the oldest university in the USA?
14 Who was the volt named after?
15 What is the lower house of the US Congress called?
16 Genocide is the destruction of what?
17 In Scandinavian myth what is Gotterdammerung?
18 Which animals' legs did the Griffin have?
19 "The Duke – What a Bobby Dazzler" was the autobiography of which celeb?
20 Which director made "Blackmail", Britain's first successful talkie?
21 How many tournaments make up tennis's Grand Slam?
22 With which woman aviator did Frederick Noonan perish?
23 In which country was Hitler born?
24 What is a puck made from in ice hockey?
25 Which 50 Cent album topped both the UK and US charts in 2005?
26 Which double Oscar winner appeared in the movie "Stranger than Fiction"?
27 What is the Great Australian Bight?
28 Where in London was the Great Exhibition of 1851?
29 What is HRT?
30 Park Ji-Sung joined Man Utd from which club?

Answers	TV: TV Gold *(see Quiz 99)*

1 Matthew & Henry Kelly. 2 Quentin Crisp. 3 Citizen Smith. 4 Roger Moore. 5 Danny De Vito. 6 Clint Eastwood. 7 André Previn. 8 Kate Adie. 9 The Wednesday Play. 10 James Bolam. 11 Bilko. 12 Miss Ellie. 13 All Our Yesterdays. 14 Batman and Robin. 15 Sid James. 16 Ronnie Corbett. 17 Crossroads. 18 Bing Crosby's (Mary). 19 David Attenborough. 20 Addams. 21 Midlands. 22 Rising Damp. 23 The Beverly Hillbillies. 24 Mel Smith. 25 Come Dancing. 26 Compact. 27 Buster Merryfield. 28 Saudi Arabia. 29 Dick Van Dyke. 30 William Roache.

1 Which actor is the son of a Poet Laureate?
2 Which "Chinese Western" actor's real name was Lee Yuen Kam?
3 Which singer and actress was in "Dick Tracy"?
4 Kenneth Branagh cast which toothy comedian as Yorick in "Hamlet"?
5 Who played the adult Damien in "The Omen" films?
6 Which pop wife appeared with Robert Redford, aged four, in "The Great Gatsby"?
7 Which early screen comedian's real name was Louis Cristillo?
8 Who played Cruella de Vil's sidekick Jasper in "101 Dalmatians"?
9 Who beat Meryl Streep for the lead role in "The Horse Whisperer"?
10 Which Glaswegian played a gangster in "Goldeneye"?
11 Which serious actress played comedy opposite Schwarzenegger in "Junior"?
12 Who directed, scripted, composed and starred in "Yentl"?
13 Which ex-child star was US Ambassador to Czechoslovakia in 1989?
14 How were producers Harry, Albert, Sam and Jack known collectively?
15 What was Groucho Marx's real first name?
16 Which Cockney actor married the former Miss Guyana in 1973?
17 Which horror writer directed the film "Maximum Overdrive"?
18 Who played Mary Jane in "Spider-Man 2"?
19 Which star of "Look Who's Talking Too" was a regular on TV's "Cheers"?
20 Which Fonda starred in the remake of "Nikita"?
21 Who is Joely Richardson's famous mother?
22 Which comedies was Michael Balcon responsible for?
23 Which actress wrote "Postcards from the Edge"?
24 Who was the first Bond girl?
25 Which conductor is Woody Allen's father-in-law?
26 Which surname was shared by John, Lionel, Ethel and Drew?
27 "Hitch" was the first romantic comedy lead for which actor?
28 What was Ex-Python Terry Gilliam's futuristic nightmare film, surreally named for a South American country?
29 Who bought the screen rights to "Dick Tracy" and made a film from it?
30 Which blonde actress is Mrs Alec Baldwin?

Answers | Pot Luck 47 *(see Quiz 102)*

1 The Pope. 2 Estate car. 3 The deaf. 4 Dakota. 5 Thomas Sorensen. 6 Tibet. 7 Tax. 8 Munich. 9 Two. 10 SAS. 11 France (de Nimes). 12 Operation Desert Storm. 13 Franz Beckenbauer. 14 Leek. 15 Kite-shaped. 16 Election. 17 Teeth or bone. 18 Variety Club. 19 Friday's Child. 20 Houses of Parliament. 21 Mel Gibson. 22 Hospital. 23 American Revolution. 24 Sleeping policeman. 25 Nurse. 26 Merchant Navy. 27 Third degree. 28 Richard Harris. 29 Lutine Bell. 30 Red.

1 Who would deliver an edict called a bull?
2 What is a shooting brake?
3 Who does the RNID provide help for?
4 What was the first No. 1 single for Stereophonics?
5 Which Danish keeper played for Sunderland and Aston Villa?
6 The Dalai Lama is the spiritual leader of where?
7 In English history what was danegeld?
8 What is the capital of Bavaria?
9 How many days does a decathlon event last?
10 The US Delta Force is based on which British anti-terrorist force?
11 In which country did denim originate?
12 What was the codename for the operation to eject the Iraqis from Kuwait in 1991?
13 Who was the first person to manage and captain a World Cup-winning soccer side?
14 David was responsible for the adoption of what as a Welsh emblem?
15 What shape is the approved mark of the British Standards Institution?
16 At what occasion do you see a returning officer?
17 Caries is the decay and deterioration of what?
18 Which Club's President is the Chief Barker?
19 Which day of the week first appeared in a Will Young title hit?
20 Where in London is the Strangers' Gallery?
21 Which Mel read Helen Hunt's thoughts in the movie "What Women Want"?
22 What sort of institution is UCH?
23 The Battle of Bunker Hill was the first major engagement of what?
24 What name is given to a bump in the road to slow down traffic?
25 What is the profession of an RGN?
26 Whose flag is the red ensign?
27 Which degree of burns is life-threatening?
28 The biography of which late hell-raising actor was called "Behaving Badly"?
29 Which bell is found in the building of Lloyd's of London?
30 What colour is the ceremonial dress of a Yeoman of the Guard?

Answers	**Movies: People** *(see Quiz 101)*

1 Daniel Day-Lewis. 2 Bruce Lee. 3 Madonna. 4 Ken Dodd. 5 Sam Neill. 6 Patsy Kensit. 7 Lou Costello. 8 Hugh Laurie. 9 Kristin Scott Thomas. 10 Robbie Coltrane. 11 Emma Thompson. 12 Barbra Streisand. 13 Shirley Temple. 14 Warner Brothers. 15 Julius. 16 Michael Caine. 17 Stephen King. 18 Kirsten Dunst. 19 Kirstie Alley. 20 Bridget. 21 Vanessa Redgrave. 22 Ealing. 23 Carrie Fisher. 24 Ursula Andress. 25 André Previn. 26 Barrymore. 27 Will Smith. 28 Brazil. 29 Warren Beatty. 30 Kim Basinger.

1 What is Portland Place's most famous House?
2 What does CNN stand for?
3 Which listings magazine celebrated its 75th birthday in 1998?
4 What is Britain's principal world news agency?
5 Which magazine is supposedly edited by Lord Gnome?
6 Where is Grampian TV based?
7 What does the ASA control?
8 What is the magazine of the Consumers' Association?
9 Who is the Daily Mail's most famous cartoon dog?
10 Where is The People's Daily a top-selling papers?
11 Which long-running futuristic comic featured Judge Dredd and Rogue Trooper?
12 Country Life was once edited by which royal photographer?
13 Red and yellow were the colours of which comic strip Rovers?
14 What is the full official title of GQ?
15 Which organisation had a magazine called "Expression!"?
16 Which daily paper founded in 1859 is devoted to horse racing?
17 In which part of the Commonwealth might you tune in to Penguin Radio?
18 Which Times Supplement is aimed at teachers?
19 How is the New Musical Express better known?
20 How does Dennis the Menace's mother always address her husband?
21 Which US-based magazine was the world's best seller until the 80s?
22 How is the journalists' trade union commonly known?
23 Which famous magazine was founded by Hugh Hefner?
24 Where is Yorkshire TV based?
25 In which part of London are Richard Murdoch's newspapers based?
26 Which was the ill-fated satellite TV company that competed with Sky?
27 Which major UK daily newspaper, still in circulation, did Robert Maxwell own?
28 Which left-wing faction had a newspaper called Militant?
29 Which major Murdoch UK paper has the longest name?
30 Which women's magazine did Cherie Blair guest edit?

| **Answers** | **Pot Luck 48** *(see Quiz 104)* |

1 New Kids on the Block. 2 Juliet Bravo. 3 Smallpox. 4 Ben Hur. 5 In space. 6 Chicago. 7 Pat Garrett. 8 American Pie (2003). 9 Milan Baros. 10 Hot and spicy. 11 Petula Clark. 12 Richard III. 13 Anglesey. 14 Bad Manners. 15 Tenerife. 16 Barry McGuigan. 17 Columbia. 18 M4. 19 An Emirate. 20 Dresden. 21 Arkansas. 22 Pacific. 23 The Gridiron. 24 Poetry. 25 Cambridge. 26 Jack Nicholson. 27 The seahorse. 28 Manoeuvres. 29 Leather. 30 Nikita.

1 In the music world what did NKOTB stand for?
2 Hartley was the fictional town setting for which TV police serial?
3 Variola is the proper name for which killer disease?
4 Who competed against Messala in a literary chariot race?
5 Where did Laika, the first dog in space, die?
6 In which musical did "Pop Idol's" Darius Danesh win a coveted role?
7 Which sheriff killed Billy the Kid?
8 What was the first Madonna hit to mention an item of food?
9 Which Liverpool top scorer in 2004–05 was rewarded with a transfer?
10 Is a piri-piri sauce sweet, or hot and spicy?
11 Which Swiss resident won a Grammy for singing "Downtown"?
12 Which Richard died at the Battle of Bosworth Field?
13 Which is larger, the Isle of Wight or Anglesey?
14 Buster Bloodvessel was a member of which Ska-revival band?
15 Which holiday island saw the worst ever air crash with 582 deaths?
16 Which former world boxing champion has the Christian name Finbar?
17 What does the "C" stand for in the musical initials "CBS"?
18 Which motorway joins with the M25 at Heathrow Airport?
19 What is controlled by an Emir?
20 In World War II which German city suffered the most civilian deaths?
21 In which US state did the first Wal-Mart store open?
22 What name is given to the most westerly time zone in America?
23 What is an American football pitch also called?
24 Thomas Hardy wrote what type of material for the last twelve years of his life?
25 Which is further East, Cambridge or Peterborough?
26 Which movie veteran starred with Adam Sandler in "Anger Management"?
27 Which is the slowest-moving fish?
28 What did the "M" stand for in the name of the band OMD?
29 Cordwainers mainly worked with which material?
30 Which Elton John hit was the first name of Russian leader Khrushchev?

Answers	Leisure: Media *(see Quiz 103)*

1 Broadcasting House. 2 Cable News Network. 3 Radio Times. 4 Reuters. 5 Private Eye. 6 Aberdeen. 7 Advertising. 8 Which?. 9 Fred Basset. 10 China. 11 2000 AD. 12 Lord Snowdon. 13 Melchester. 14 Gentlemen's Quarterly. 15 American Express. 16 The Sporting Life. 17 Falkland Islands. 18 Educational. 19 NME. 20 Dad. 21 Reader's Digest. 22 NUJ. 23 Playboy. 24 Leeds. 25 Wapping. 26 BSB. 27 Daily Mirror. 28 Militant Tendency. 29 The News of the World. 30 Prima.

1 Was Freddie born in 1975, 1977 or 1980?
2 He isn't a Freddie, but what's his real name?
3 How many centuries did he make in the 2005 Ashes series?
4 Freddie first captained England in which country?
5 In Jan. 2006 he was awarded the freedom of which city?
6 At which ground did he make his Test debut?
7 Is his first daughter named Carol, Holly or Ivy?
8 Aged 17 he first appeared for which county?
9 What is Freddie's star sign?
10 In the 2005 Ashes did he score just over 400, 450 or 500 runs?
11 Who or what is a Woodworm Flame?
12 Against which country did he make his maiden Test century?
13 What breed were his dogs Red and Arnold?
14 Freddie's a right-handed batsman, but which is his bowling arm?
15 Trying to regain fitness, which major event did he postpone in March 2005?
16 His Test debut was against which country?
17 Who was the scheduled series Test skipper when Freddie took over?
18 In the 2005 Ashes how many wickets did Freddie take?
19 He was in which country when his second child was born in 2006?
20 Who shared the ICC joint player of the year award with Freddie in 2005?
21 Which Test was on his home county ground in the 2005 Ashes?
22 Aged 14, was he playing Northern League for St Annes or St Austel?
23 Against which country did he make his one-day England debut?
24 Which famous Lancashire cricketer Neil became Freddie's agent?
25 What did Freddie wear on his face for the official 2005 Ashes celebrations?
26 In March 2006 Freddie became the England player to hit most what in Tests?
27 Which team won the first Test in the 2005 Ashes?
28 Against which country did he first have a series batting average of 50 plus?
29 In which London square did the main 2005 Ashes celebrations take place?
30 Which Lancashire skipper Michael watched Freddie break into county cricket?

| **Answers** | **Pot Luck 49** *(see Quiz 106)* |

1 Jingles. 2 A stilt. 3 Horse fair. 4 1 October. 5 A mountain. 6 USA. 7 Eddie Izzard. 8 Buddy Holly. 9 Horses. 10 Lethbridge-Stewart. 11 Billy Connolly. 12 French. 13 Barnsdale. 14 Born to Do It. 15 Madrid. 16 Real Madrid. 17 The Times. 18 Demi Moore. 19 Italy. 20 Order of the Garter. 21 Ronnie Corbett. 22 Christopher Robin. 23 Two. 24 Coccyx. 25 Mulder and Scully. 26 Billy Bob Thornton. 27 Bones. 28 Staffordshire. 29 Javelin. 30 Caskets.

1 What are the metal discs in the rim of a tambourine called?
2 Which word can be a pole with a foot rest or a wading bird?
3 What annual event is the Cumbrian town of Appleby noted for?
4 On what date does the pheasant shooting season legally start?
5 Who or what is Cader Idris?
6 Mr Birdseye – of frozen food fame – came from which country?
7 Who was the voice of "It" in the 2004 movie "Five Children and It"?
8 Which 1950s pop star had the first names Charles Hardin?
9 Which animals can be affected by a disease called vlves?
10 Which Brigadier appeared in "Dr Who"?
11 Who played Mr Brown in the film "Mrs Brown"?
12 What is the official language of Haiti?
13 What was the name of Geoff Hamilton's garden?
14 What was Craig David's first album to sell over a million in the UK?
15 Barajas airport is in which city?
16 Ivan Compo joined Bolton from which Spanish side?
17 What is the oldest daily newspaper in England?
18 Demetria Guynes is better known as which actress?
19 Which country surrounds San Marino?
20 Which Order is the highest in the Order of Chivalry in Britain?
21 Who played the leading role in the TV series "Sorry"?
22 What was the name of AA Milne's son?
23 How many hours are there in a dog watch at sea?
24 Which small triangular bone is located at the base of the spinal column in man and some apes?
25 Fox and Dana are the first names of which pair?
26 Who co-starred with Halle Berry in the hit movie "Monster's Ball"?
27 What are osselets and ossicles?
28 Alton Towers Leisure Park is in which county?
29 Steve Backley held the world record in which sports event?
30 In "The Merchant of Venice" the suitors pick one of three what?

Answers	Freddie Flintoff *(see Quiz 105)*

1 1977. 2 Andrew. 3 One. 4 India. 5 Preston. 6 Trent Bridge. 7 Holly. 8 Lancashire. 9 Sagittarius. 10 400 (402). 11 A cricket bat. 12 New Zealand. 13 Boxer. 14 Right. 15 His honeymoon. 16 South Africa. 17 Michael Vaughan. 18 24. 19 India. 20 Jacques Kallis. 21 Third Test. 22 St Annes. 23 Pakistan. 24 Neil Fairbrother. 25 Dark glasses. 26 Sixes. 27 Australia. 28 South Africa. 29 Trafalgar Square. 30 Michael Atherton.

1 What was Diana's official title at the time of her death?
2 Who is the oldest in line to the throne after Prince Charles?
3 Which Prince was a guest on the "Des O'Connor Show" in 1998?
4 On which island was Princess Margaret when she suffered a stroke?
5 Who was older, Princess Diana's mother or her stepmother?
6 In which country did the former Edward VIII marry Mrs Simpson?
7 Albert succeeded Baudouin in which country?
8 In which country did Fergie's mother spend the latter part of her life?
9 What does the Queen's only nephew do for a living?
10 At which sport did Harry excel in his first few weeks at Eton?
11 Who is the only child of the Queen not to have been divorced?
12 Who is third in line to the throne?
13 Who survived the crash in which Princess Diana died?
14 In which London residence did Charles & Camilla live after their marriage?
15 Seven kings of which country have been called Haakon?
16 Which Princess is the mother of Viscount Linley?
17 Which Princess is known by her husband's name?
18 Which former Royal residence was damaged by fire in 1986?
19 "Tiggy" Legge-Bourke was PA to which Prince for three years?
20 Which Princess is the mother of Marina Mowatt?
21 Who was Princess Diana's chauffeur on her final fatal car journey?
22 Which of Prince Charles' sons began his military training first?
23 Which grandchild of the Queen had her tongue pierced?
24 Which Royal in-law was dubbed "Fog" because he was thick and wet?
25 Who took the official engagement photos of Charles and Diana?
26 Who is Lady Sarah Chatto's aunt on her mother's side?
27 Which Princess married the son of a director of Walls sausages?
28 In which royal castle is St George's Chapel?
29 Which musical instrument did the late Princess Margaret play?
30 In 1994 Diana took an advisory role for which organisation?

Answers | **Pot Luck 50** (see Quiz 108)

1 Chester. 2 Tony Christie. 3 Steal. 4 Laughing gas. 5 Florence Nightingale. 6 Liverpool. 7 1977. 8 A pack of tarot cards. 9 December 25. 10 Charlize Theron. 11 M15. 12 Lou Reed. 13 Bailey. 14 Wigan Pier. 15 You have a bite. 16 Manchester. 17 Avalon. 18 Radio. 19 MCC. 20 Steve Davis. 21 Andrew. 22 Beethoven. 23 X rays. 24 Three. 25 Paul Walters. 26 Barbara Cartland. 27 Saddle. 28 Zambia. 29 17th. 30 Four.

1 Deva was a Roman city now known as what?

2 Spanning 30 years on the charts, how is Tony Fitzgerald better known?

3 What does a kleptomaniac do?

4 What is the popular name for the anaesthetic nitrous oxide?

5 Who was the first woman to be awarded the Order of Merit?

6 The doomed ship Titanic was registered in which English city?

7 In which year did Marc Bolan die?

8 What is made up of the minor arcana and the major arcana?

9 The Romanian dictator Ceausescu was executed on which day in 1989?

10 In "The Life and Death of Peter Sellers", who played his wife Britt Ekland?

11 Dame Eliza Manningham Buller was head of which organisation in 2006?

12 Which Lou was vocalist with the Velvet Underground?

13 Which shipping forecast area is due north of Rockall?

14 Which pier featured in a George Orwell book title?

15 If you are an angler why are you pleased if your monkey starts to climb?

16 In which city was painter LS Lowry born?

17 Where was King Arthur taken after his last battle?

18 Did "Dead Ringers" begin on radio or TV?

19 Which all-male bastion allowed women members for the first time in September 1998?

20 Who made the first televised 147 in snooker, in 1982?

21 Which Prince's childhood nickname was "The Sniggerer"?

22 Who wrote the "Emperor Concerto"?

23 For which medical breakthrough did Roentgen win the Nobel Prize in 1901?

24 How many Inns of Court are there in London?

25 Which TV and radio producer was nicknamed Dr Wally by Sir Terry Wogan?

26 Whose codename was "Pink" before she was surprised on "This is Your Life"?

27 What is a pommel a part of?

28 Cars with the international vehicle registration Z come from where?

29 In which century was the Battle of Naseby?

30 How many pecks are there in a bushel?

Answers | The Royals (see Quiz 107)

1 Diana, Princess of Wales. 2 Prince Andrew. 3 Edward. 4 Mustique. 5 Stepmother. 6 France. 7 Belgium. 8 Argentina. 9 Make furniture. 10 Football. 11 Prince Edward. 12 Prince Harry. 13 Trevor Reece Jones. 14 Clarence House. 15 Norway. 16 Margaret. 17 Michael of Kent. 18 Hampton Court. 19 Charles. 20 Alexandra. 21 Henri Paul. 22 Prince Harry. 23 Zara Phillips. 24 Mark Phillips. 25 Lord Snowdon. 26 The Queen. 27 Anne. 28 Windsor. 29 Piano. 30 International Red Cross.

1 Who was Chancellor, Foreign Secretary and PM between 1964 and 1979?
2 Artist Peter Blake found fame designing which world-famous Beatles album sleeve?
3 Which American was known as Ike?
4 Which future President organised the Free French Forces in WWII?
5 What was Indira Gandhi's maiden name?
6 Who became US Vice President in 1993?
7 Which title did Hitler take as Nazi leader?
8 Who was the last Tsarina of Russia?
9 Who was Soviet Foreign Minister from 1957 to 1985?
10 Whose resignation on 1 November 1990 began Thatcher's downfall?
11 Whose 1963 Report led to the closure of many railway stations?
12 Who was famous for his pictures of Campbell's Soup cans?
13 Who was British Prime Minister during the abdication crisis?
14 For how long were Hitler and Eva Braun married?
15 Who was the first singer to record two 007 theme tunes?
16 Which athlete became MP for Falmouth and Cambourne in 1992?
17 Which world leader celebrated his 80th birthday in July 1998?
18 Who was the first Archbishop of Canterbury?
19 Which US President publicly pardoned ex-President Nixon?
20 Who had the title Il Duce?
21 Which US evangelist asked his flock to make a "decision for Christ"?
22 In 1990 which ex-PM went to Iraq to try to secure the release of British hostages?
23 Who was the youngest queen of Henry VIII to be beheaded?
24 Which Prime Minister introduced the Citizens' Charter?
25 Who became Defence Secretary in May 1997?
26 What was the name of Horatio Nelson's daughter by Emma Hamilton?
27 Who said her boss Michael Howard had "something of the night about him"?
28 What was the religion of a French Huguenot?
29 Which Communist leader was named Josip Broz at birth?
30 In which category did Einstein win his Nobel prize in 1921?

Answers	Pop: Who's Who? *(see Quiz 110)*

1 Bay City Rollers. 2 Barbra Streisand. 3 Bill Tarmey. 4 Shakin' Stevens 5 Kate Bush. 6 Chris De Burgh. 7 Bruce Springsteen. 8 The Spice Girls. 9 Bono. 10 Richard Clayderman. 11 George Michael. 12 Emerson, Lake & Palmer. 13 Judith Durham. 14 Meatloaf. 15 Celine Dion. 16 Michael Caine. 17 Bill Medley. 18 Ken Hutchinson – Hutch. 19 Right Said Fred. 20 David Bowie. 21 Lily the Pink. 22 George Michael. 23 Rod Stewart. 24 Shirley Bassey. 25 Morgen. 26 Coco Hernandez. 27 Jarvis Cocker. 28 The Kemp Brothers. 29 Victoria "Posh". 30 Nick Berry.

1 The Longmuir brothers were in which 70s teeny bop group?
2 Who partnered Don Johnson on the Goya theme "Till I Loved You"?
3 Which "Coronation Street" star had a hit in 1994 with "Wind Beneath My Wings"?
4 Which UK male vocalist's real name is Michael Barratt?
5 Who duetted with Peter Gabriel on "Don't Give Up"?
6 Christopher John Davidson is the real name of which Irish vocalist?
7 Who had a No. 1 on both sides of the Atlantic with "Devils & Dust"?
8 Who launched the British Legion Poppy Appeal with Dame Vera Lynn in 1997?
9 Who featured on the 1986 Clannad hit "In a Lifetime"?
10 Which pianist and instrumentalist's real name is Philippe Pages?
11 Who was the younger of the two Wham! members?
12 Keith, Greg and Carl were the Christian names of which 70s trio?
13 Who was lead female singer with 60s group The Seekers?
14 Marvin Lee Aday is better known as which dead ringer vocalist?
15 Who had a No. 5 UK hit with the theme song "Because You Loved Me"?
16 Which actor shares his name with a 1984 hit by Madness?
17 Who sang the theme tune to "Dirty Dancing" with Jennifer Warnes?
18 Which TV detective had a No. 1 hit with "Don't Give Up on Us" in 1976?
19 Which group share their name with a Bernard Cribbins 1962 hit?
20 Who joined with Queen in the 1981 No. 1 hit "Under Pressure"?
21 Who invented Medicinal Compound according to the 1968 No. 1?
22 Which superstar has an autobiography called "Bare"?
23 Which pop legend said, "I really wanted to be a soccer star"?
24 Who partnered Chris Rea on the 1996 hit "Disco La Passione"?
25 Complete the A-ha trio – Pal, Mags and ....?
26 Which character was played by Irene Cara in "Fame"?
27 Who interrupted Michael Jackson's "Earth Song" at the 1996 Brit Awards?
28 Which brothers were members of Spandau Ballet?
29 Who was the first Spice Girl to get engaged?
30 Who links the '86 hit "Every Loser Wins" and the 1992 hit "Heartbeat"?

Answers	**Pot Luck 52** (see Quiz 114)

1 Parrot. 2 Christine Ohuruogu. 3 Monkey. 4 Scottish Nationalists. 5 Doris Lessing. 6 Jon Voight. 7 Sevilla. 8 Best British female solo artist. 9 Kuala Lumpur. 10 Australia. 11 London City. 12 Insects. 13 Flew/Flue. 14 Belfast. 15 Liverpool. 16 Caernarvon Castle. 17 Hummingbird. 18 Two. 19 Trabant. 20 Hats. 21 Death of Diana, Princess of Wales. 22 Bryan Habana. 23 South Korea. 24 Moldova. 25 Minute Waltz. 26 Hatfield. 27 The America's Cup. 28 1 May. 29 Gough Whitlam. 30 Hakuna Matata.

1 Which comedian wrote "Blackadder" with Richard Curtis?
2 Who hosted the talent-spotting show "My Kind of People"?
3 Who hosted the first series of "Guess Who's Coming to Dinner?"?
4 David Dimbleby's first wife wrote what type of books?
5 Which comedian created the character Stavros?
6 Who has the car number plate COM 1C?
7 Which star of "The Grand" is President of the Dyslexia Institute?
8 Which first name is shared by subsequent stars of "Dangerfield"?
9 Which ex-party leader chaired "Have I Got News for You" after Angus Deayton's departure?
10 Which radio name replaced Richard Baker presenting The Proms?
11 Which blonde first presented "Big Breakfast" with Chris Evans?
12 Julie Walters hails from which city?
13 Who replaced Carol Drinkwater as Helen in "All Creatures Great and Small"?
14 Whom did Hillary Clinton give her first ever UK TV interview to?
15 In which docu soap did Jeremy Spake find fame?
16 In "EastEnders" what was Dennis Rickman's relation to Vicki?
17 How is Derrick Evans better known?
18 Who became Jim Davidson's regular assistant on "The Generation Game"?
19 Which ex-Radio 2 presenter moved to "Open House" on Channel 5?
20 Whom could you regularly have Breakfast With... on Sunday mornings?
21 Who replaced Vanessa on ITV's morning talk show?
22 What did Trude Mostue train to be on TV?
23 Who first presented "Changing Rooms"?
24 In which drama series did the character Dr Beth Glover appear?
25 Who was the first woman tennis player to be BBC Sports Personality of the Year?
26 Who was the interviewer on C4's "The Last Resort"?
27 Who presented this century's revived "Treasure Hunt" with Dermot Murnaghan?
28 Whom did Fergie play in "Friends"?
29 Which Major seemed to be influenced by coughing on "Who Wants to be a Millionaire?"?
30 Who moved from "Newsnight" to "Tomorrow's World"?

1 Who won the Best British Group award at the 2007 Brits?
2 Where did golfer Padraig Harrington win his first major, the Open Championship?
3 To which mammal family does the dingo belong?
4 Who preceded David Cameron as leader of the Conservative Party
5 Which tobacco company sponsored the "Football Yearbook" from 1970 to 2001?
6 What is the study of rocks and rock formations?
7 Who was short-listed for the Turner Prize for "Shark in Formaldehyde"?
8 Is the penguin native to the North Pole or the South Pole?
9 Which building, built on an island in San Francisco Bay, is now a tourist attraction?
10 On which two countries' borders is Mount Everest?
11 What is the world's largest mammal by weight?
12 Which former South African President was too ill to attend the 2007 Rugby World Cup final?
13 Which former comedy partner of Stephen Fry stars in the American hospital drama "House"?
14 Which Hungarian Communist politician proclaimed his country to be Soviet Republic in 1919?
15 In which city is the synthetic-turfed Luzhniki Stadium?
16 What is name of the world's largest ocean liner, which entered service in 2004?
17 Which East London station will be the arrival point for international rail-users during the 2012 Olympics?
18 Which British decathlete won gold medals in both 1980 and 1984?
19 What was the name of the family that ran the Fiat motor company until the 1990s?
20 Where was Gianni Versace murdered in 1997?
21 Who did Forest Whitaker play in his Oscar-winning role in "The Last King of Scotland"?
22 Which of Tony Blair's children was born while he was Prime Minister?
23 What is the main currency of Malaysia?
24 What is the capital of Macedonia?
25 Which British musician and poet wrote the opera Peter Grimes?
26 What tourist attraction commemorates the Great Fire of London in 1666?
27 What was the name of the Duke of York's (Prince Andrew) father-in-law?
28 Which country toured England to play rugby league in both 1907 and 2007?
29 Which homonyms could be a primary colour or slang for wasted as in a chance?
30 Who was England cricket captain when they toured Australia in 2006–07?

Answers | TV: Who's Who (see Quiz 111)

1 Ben Elton. 2 Michael Barrymore. 3 Anne Robinson. 4 Cookery books. 5 Harry Enfield. 6 Jimmy Tarbuck. 7 Susan Hampshire. 8 Nigel. 9 William Hague. 10 James Naughtie. 11 Gaby Roslin. 12 Birmingham. 13 Lynda Bellingham. 14 Trevor McDonald. 15 Airport. 16 Half-brother. 17 Mr Motivator. 18 Melanie Stace. 19 Gloria Hunniford. 20 Frost. 21 Trisha Goddard. 22 Vet. 23 Carol Smillie. 24 Peak Practice. 25 Ann Jones. 26 Jonathan Ross. 27 Suzi Perry. 28 Herself. 29 Charles Ingram. 30 Peter Snow.

1 What was film producer Ismail Merchant's final film?
2 Which two actors rejected "Bridge on the River Kwai" before Alec Guinness got the lead role?
3 How is actor/director Nobby Clarke better known?
4 Who played the first cinema vampire in "Nosferatu"?
5 Who was Daniel Day-Lewis' actress mother?
6 Who has a production company called Edited?
7 Which TV hero played a movie villain in "Beethoven"?
8 Who walked off the set of "10" and gave Dudley Moore a movie break?
9 Who did Schwarzenegger's love interest in "Twins" marry after the movie was made?
10 Who links TV's "Yes Minister" and the film "Nuns on the Run"?
11 Who was the voice of Zazu in "The Lion King"?
12 Whose legs were insured for more – Fred Astaire's or Betty Grable's?
13 Whom did Val Kilmer replace as "Batman"?
14 Who had the title role in the remake of "The Absent Minded Professor"?
15 What was the name of the Bond girl in Pierce Brosnan's first outing as 007?
16 In which film did Bing Crosby first play Father O'Malley?
17 Who adapted the play "Cyrano de Bergerac" into the movie "Roxanne"?
18 Who appeared in her father's "Godfather Part III"?
19 Who directed the first two films in which Dianne Wiest won Oscars?
20 The movie "A Good Year" was based on whose novel?
21 Which American soul singer played a black lesbian assassin in her film debut, "Smokin' Aces"?
22 Who adapted Agatha Christie's "Evil Under the Sun" for the big screen?
23 Which production company was set up by Hugh Grant and Elizabeth Hurley?
24 Who is the president played by Anthony Hopkins in "Amistad"?
25 Who played Prinny in "The Madness of King George"?
26 Which were the first two films for which Brenda Blethyn was Oscar-nominated?
27 Which 1966 World Cup star shares his name with the writer of "American Beauty"?
28 Who played Streisand's son in "Prince of Tides"?
29 Who won supporting actor Oscar for "Jerry Maguire"?
30 Who directed "Mrs Doubtfire"?

Answers | Newsworthy (see Quiz 115)

1 Cystic Fibrosis Fund. 2 Electric kettle. 3 Arizona. 4 Theatre Royal Drury Lane. 5 Jack Straw. 6 Jeff Bezos. 7 High tech light bulb. 8 Helmut Kohl. 9 1970. 10 CQD. 11 Halls Creek. 12 Turkey. 13 192. 14 Oxford Light Infantry. 15 World Wildlife Fund. 16 Breitling Orbiter. 17 Yuri Andropov. 18 30th July. 19 Josef Goebbels. 20 1944. 21 Gallstones. 22 Gordon Brown. 23 Pelican Hill. 24 David Ervine. 25 John Glenn. 26 Cyprus (Amoco Cadiz). 27 Seattle. 28 Return him safely to Earth. 29 Raul Alfonsin. 30 Captain Kenneth Cummins.

1 What family of birds do cockatoos belong to?
2 Who won Britain's only gold medal at the 2007 World Athletic Championships?
3 To which family of mammals does the marmoset belong?
4 Which party won most seats in the Scottish Assembly at the May 2007 election?
5 Which British authoress won the 2007 Nobel Prize for Literature?
6 Which actor co-starred with his daughter Angelina Jolie in the "Lara Croft" movies?
7 Which club retained the UEFA Cup in 2007?
8 What award did Amy Winehouse collect at the 2007 Brits?
9 In which city are the 452-metre high Petronas Twin Towers?
10 Where is the world's largest island?
11 Which London airport does not allow inter-continental planes to land there?
12 Entomology is the study of what?
13 Which homonyms could be took to the air or a ventilation shaft?
14 Casement Park is the main Gaelic Athletics Association stadium in which British capital city?
15 Which city was chosen as the European Capital of Culture for 2008?
16 Where was Prince Charles's investiture when he became Prince of Wales in 1969?
17 What is the world's smallest species of bird?
18 How many Olympic gold medals did Lord Sebastian Coe win as an athlete?
19 Which car is synonymous with the East German motor industry?
20 What item of clothing was Gertrude Shilling famous for wearing at Royal Ascot in the late 20th century?
21 What event is at the centre of the Helen Mirren movie "The Queen"?
22 Which player was top try-scorer in the Rugby World Cup 2007?
23 Where is the Baht the main unit of currency?
24 Chisinau is the capital of which country?
25 How is the "Waltz in D Flat Major" composed by Frédéric Chopin better known?
26 The rail crash near which English station in 2000 led to a major overhaul of track maintenance?
27 Which international match-race yachting competition dates back to the 19th century?
28 On which day was the General Election which saw New Labour elected for its first term as government?
29 Who did the Governor-General of Australia, Sir John Kerr, dismiss as the nation's Prime Minister in 1975?
30 What is Timon and Pumbaa's catchy refrain in "The Lion King"?

Answers	**Famous Names** *(see Quiz 118)*

1 Barnardo. 2 Cardiff. 3 Sculpture. 4 Grantham. 5 Katie Holmes. 6 George Carey. 7 Elstree. 8 Peter Hall. 9 Tea merchant/grocer. 10 Norman Hartnell. 11 Gardens. 12 Ted Hughes. 13 Photographer. 14 Mountaineer. 15 Goran Ivanisevic. 16 1970s. 17 Rebecca. 18 Dance. 19 Hairdressing. 20 McDonalds. 21 Glenn Miller. 22 Monopoly. 23 Circus. 24 Popeye. 25 Ride. 26 Alan Bennett. 27 Fraser. 28 Piano. 29 Tony Banks. 30 Janet.

1 Which charity was given the first shorn fleece of Dolly the cloned sheep?
2 The Prometheus was the first of which type of kitchen equipment?
3 Which US state was acquired from the Badsen Purchase?
4 Where was "God Save the King" first sung in public?
5 Who was the first British Foreign Secretary to visit Iran after the fall of the Shah?
6 Who founded Amazon.com?
7 In 1992 Don Hollister and Don Pelazzo were responsible for developing what?
8 Who was Germany's longest-serving post-war Chancellor?
9 When did the first Page Three girl appear in the "The Sun"?
10 Which distress signal did SOS replace?
11 Where was the first gold rush in Western Australia in 1885?
12 In which country was Hrant Dink murdered?
13 In 2000 how many sovereign countries were there in the world?
14 Which was the first regiment to wear khaki?
15 What is the world's largest conservation charity?
16 How was the first balloon to circumnavigate the globe non-stop named?
17 Who became chairman of the KGB in 1967?
18 What date was the first Penguin book published – the same date that England won the World Cup 31 years later?
19 Who was Hitler's propaganda chief?
20 When was PAYE Income Tax introduced?
21 What did laser surgery, pioneered by Ludwig Demling, first destroy?
22 Which politician was accused of possessing "Stalinist ruthlessness" by a former top civil servant in March 2007?
23 At which golf club was the Jack Nicklaus Online Golf Championship played in December 1999?
24 Which leader of the Progressive Unionist Party died in January 2007?
25 Who took part in the USA's first manned orbital flight?
26 Where was the tanker registered, which spilt millions of gallons of oil off the French coast in March 1978?
27 Where was the on-line bookstore Amazon first based?
28 John F Kennedy said the Apollo programme would land a man on the Moon and what else?
29 Who was the first elected President of Argentina after the Falklands War?
30 Dying in December 2006, who was the last surviving Briton to see active service in the First and Second World Wars?

Answers	TV: Famous Faces *(see Quiz 117)*

1 Interiors. 2 Sir Alan Sugar. 3 Ainsley Harriott. 4 Nick. 5 Chris. 6 Francesca Annis. 7 Leslie Ash. 8 Oxo. 9 Sam Ryan. 10 The weather. 11 Christopher Eccleston. 12 Sue Johnston. 13 Mariette. 14 Wheel of Fortune. 15 Kathy Staff. 16 Ashley Jensen. 17 Glenda Jackson. 18 Ainsley Harriott. 19 Daniela Nardini. 20 Ronni Ancona. 21 Nesbitt. 22 I'm A Celebrity...Get Me Out Of Here!. 23 Gary Lineker. 24 Christopher Timothy. 25 Bill Oddie. 26 Steve Coogan. 27 Robson Green. 28 Teri Hatcher. 29 Melvyn Bragg. 30 Baxendale.

1 What was the Black day of the week when the stockmarket crashed in 1987?
2 Who was the first England soccer boss to win his first five games?
3 Where in London was the first Virgin record shop?
4 Which E is the driest inhabited country in the world?
5 What is a pachyderm – a briefcase, a thick-skinned animal or a tree?
6 How many teeth does an anteater have?
7 What is the second largest dwarf planet in our Solar System?
8 Which Pope travelled to more countries than any other?
9 The game of mahjong originated in which country?
10 Which former singer with The Mamas and the Papas died in January 2007?
11 Which first name comes from a Latin word that means small?
12 Who was 50 first – Jim Davidson, Angus Deayton or Les Dennis?
13 The city of Salonika is in which country?
14 Tom Rowlands and Ed Simons became which Brothers?
15 In which fictional village was TV drama "Heartbeat" set?
16 A manifest is a detailed list of a ship's what?
17 In which country was the organisation Greenpeace founded?
18 Whom did Tessa Jowell separate from in 2006?
19 What was Billie's follow-up to "Because We Want To"?
20 The Oxford vs Cambridge Boat Race is staged between Putney and where?
21 What does C stand for in the award CBE?
22 Elk, Fox and Wolf can all have which other animal added to their names?
23 Who had his statue removed from Russia's Red Square in 1991?
24 Who featured as the Prince from "Sleeping Beauty" in a 2007 Disneyland campaign?
25 What do frogs and toads not have which other amphibians have?
26 Who is inaugurated on Inauguration Day, 20th January?
27 Bonny Lad, Express and White Windsor are varieties of which vegetable?
28 Which TV detective was based at Denton police station?
29 Which famous clown shares his name with the Royal Family of Monaco?
30 Which co-star also became Brad Pitt's off-screen partner while making the movie "Se7en"?

Answers	**Whose Movies?** *(see Quiz 113)*

1 The White Countess. 2 Charles Laughton & Noel Coward. 3 Bryan Forbes. 4 Max Shreck. 5 Jill Balcon. 6 Jack Lemmon. 7 David Duchovny. 8 George Segal. 9 John Travolta. 10 Writer Jonathan Lynn. 11 Rowan Atkinson. 12 Betty Grable's. 13 Michael Keaton. 14 Robin Williams (Flubber). 15 Xenia Onatopp. 16 Going My Way. 17 Steve Martin. 18 Sofia Coppola. 19 Woody Allen. 20 Peter Mayle's. 21 Alicia Keys. 22 Anthony Shaffer. 23 Simian Films. 24 John Quincy Adams. 25 Rupert Everett. 26 Little Voice, Secrets & Lies. 27 Alan Ball. 28 Jason Gould. 29 Cuba Gooding Jr. 30 Chris Columbus.

1 What would Linda Barker design on TV?
2 Who grills the hopeful applicants in "The Apprentice?
3 Who replaced Fern Britton as presenter of "Ready Steady Cook"?
4 Who is Dot's villainous son in "EastEnders"?
5 Which Tate has Peter Amory played in Emmerdale since 1989?
6 Which actress has played opposite Trevor Eve and Robson Green on TV and Ralph Fiennes in real life?
7 Who left "Men Behaving Badly" and moved on to "Where the Heart is"?
8 Lynda Bellingham is famous for which ad?
9 What was the name of Amanda Burton's character in "Silent Witness"?
10 What would Martyn Davies talk about on TV?
11 US drama "Heroes" featured which former Doctor Who?
12 Which actress has had major roles in "Brookside" and "The Royle Family"?
13 Which role did the second Mrs Michael Douglas play in "The Darling Buds of May"?
14 Which TV quiz show did Carol Smillie appear on in the early part of her TV career?
15 Who left "Last of the Summer Wine" to rejoin the new-look "Crossroads"?
16 Which English Ashley featured in US's "Ugly Betty"?
17 Which future MP famously appeared on "The Morecambe & Wise Show"?
18 Which chef presented a series of "Gourmet Express" programmes?
19 Which actress starred in "This Life" and "Undercover Cop"?
20 Who starred with Alistair McGowan and is famed for her impression of Victoria Beckham?
21 Which James played Adam in "Cold Feet"?
22 Tony Blackburn was the first winner of which celebrity reality programme?
23 Which former footballer became presenter of "Match of the Day" in 1999?
24 Which former TV vet plays Dr Mac McGuire in "Doctors"?
25 Which ex-Goodie presented "Springwatch"?
26 Who created the character Pauline Calf?
27 Who starred in "Reckless", "Grafters" and "Touching Evil"?
28 Which former Bond girl starred in "Desperate Housewives"?
29 Who presents "The South Bank Show"?
30 Which Helen starred in "Cold Feet"?

Answers | Pot Luck 51 *(see Quiz 112)*

1 Arctic Monkeys. 2 Carnoustie. 3 Dog. 4 Michael Howard. 5 Rothmans. 6 Geology. 7 Damien Hirst. 8 South Pole. 9 Alcatraz Prison. 10 Tibet and Nepal. 11 The blue whale. 12 Nelson Mandela. 13 Hugh Laurie. 14 Béla Kun. 15 Moscow. 16 Queen Mary 2. 17 Stratford. 18 Daley Thompson. 19 Agnelli. 20 Miami Beach. 21 Idi Amin. 22 Leo. 23 Ringgit. 24 Skopje. 25 Benjamin Britten. 26 The Monument. 27 Ronald Ferguson. 28 New Zealand. 29 Blue/Blew. 30 Andrew (Freddie) Flintoff.

1 Which Irish-born Thomas founded his East End Mission for destitute children in 1867?
2 In which Welsh city did Gene Pitney die in 2006?
3 Dame Elisabeth Frink found fame in which field?
4 Where was Margaret Thatcher born?
5 Who is mum to Suri Cruise?
6 Who became Archbishop of Canterbury in 1991?
7 Lew Grade became Baron of which venue associated with the film industry?
8 Who founded the Royal Shakespeare Company?
9 What was the trade of George Harrod who founded the famous London store?
10 Who designed Queen Elizabeth II's coronation gown?
11 What did Gertrude Jekyll design?
12 Which Poet Laureate preceded Andrew Motion?
13 Cecil Beaton was famous for working on "Vogue" magazine in what capacity?
14 How has Chris Bonington found fame?
15 Which Wimbledon champion was called up for military service in 2001?
16 In which decade did Bruce Oldfield display his first collection?
17 What name was Pocahontas given when she was brought to Britain?
18 George Balanchine is a famous name in which branch of the arts?
19 Toni & Guy is what type of famous business?
20 Which famous name in the food world opened in Russia in 1990?
21 Which band leader won the first gold disc?
22 Clarence Darrow modified a board game called The Landlord's Game and renamed it what?
23 Barnum and Bailey together founded what type of entertainment?
24 Who was the first cartoon character to have a statue erected in his honour in the US?
25 Which Sally was the first US woman in space?
26 Who wrote the "Talking Heads" series of monologues?
27 What is the name of the second son of Gordon Brown and wife Sarah?
28 Which musical instrument did Art Tatum play?
29 Which former Labour sports minister died in 2006 aged 62?
30 What is the first name of the opera singer – who became a Dame – Baker?

Answers	Pot Luck 53 *(see Quiz 116)*

1 Monday. 2 Sven Goran Eriksson. 3 Oxford Street. 4 Egypt. 5 Thick-skinned animal. 6 None. 7 Pluto. 8 John Paul II. 9 China. 10 Dennis (Denny) Doherty. 11 Paul. 12 Jim Davidson (2003). 13 Greece. 14 Chemical Brothers. 15 Aidensfield. 16 Cargo. 17 Canada. 18 David Mills. 19 Girlfriend. 20 Mortlake. 21 Commander. 22 Hound. 23 Lenin. 24 David Beckham. 25 Tails. 26 US President. 27 Broad bean. 28 Jack Frost. 29 Grimaldi. 30 Gwyneth Paltrow.

Quiz 119 | Pot Luck 54

Answers – page 363

1 Dermatology is concerned with the study of human what?
2 Alistair Cooke became famous for broadcasting his "Letter from" which country?
3 Which country does Nelly Furtado come from?
4 Disney's feature-length cartoon "Pinocchio" was released in which decade?
5 Whose debut album was "Northern Soul" in 1992?
6 Which game was Abner Doubleday credited with inventing?
7 Which of the Kennedy family was involved in the Chappaquiddick incident in the 1960s?
8 Which name was shared by Charlie Chaplin and Diana Princess of Wales?
9 In Hollywood, which Jean was dubbed the first "Blonde Bombshell"?
10 Which describes Rubik's cube – two-dimensional, three-dimensional or four-dimensional?
11 Which stewed item goes into a compote?
12 In which TV series could a patient have been treated by Dr Jack Kerruish?
13 In which country are the Altamira cave paintings?
14 In batik what is painted on to fabric along with dye?
15 "Monty Python's Flying Circus" used which "Bell" as its theme music?
16 What is contained or held in a creel?
17 Dolores O'Riordan fronted which band in the 1990s?
18 Which Alexander discovered penicillin?
19 Who hosted the 1990s revival of TV's "Going for a Song"?
20 Which children's rhyme is linked to the Black Death?
21 What does tempus fugit mean?
22 What do the letters PB indicate by a sporting competitor's name?
23 A pipistrelle is what kind of creature?
24 Which female gymnast won Britain's first gold medal at a World Championship in 2006?
25 In which country could you watch Alaves play a home soccer match?
26 Which Saint is commemorated at Lourdes?
27 What is the compass point name of the Colonel who was the centre of the US Irangate affair?
28 From which city was the first of TV's "Songs of Praise" broadcast?
29 Who did Caroline Quentin play in TV's "Jonathan Creek"?
30 Who was England's main wicket taker in the 2006–07 Ashes?

| **Answers** | **Pot Luck 55** *(see Quiz 121)* |

1 Blackburn Rovers. 2 Mullet. 3 Samuel. 4 Chelsy Davy. 5 Frisbee. 6 Electrician. 7 Paul Hogan. 8 William Hague. 9 Related. 10 India. 11 Boston. 12 Reading. 13 Iraq. 14 Nicky Campbell. 15 H. 16 Mississippi. 17 Angola. 18 Jester. 19 1930s. 20 A capo. 21 Argentina. 22 Tammy Wynette. 23 Atonement. 24 Mule. 25 Lightning war. 26 Denzel Washington. 27 Jacob. 28 Lembit Opik. 29 Take That. 30 1974.

1 In London, which famous cathedral is near to the Barbican?
2 Where is the National Exhibition Centre?
3 Which Cross is at the west end of The Strand?
4 Cheddar is in which hills?
5 In which Essex town was Anglia University established?
6 Which area of London is famous for its Dogs' Home?
7 The Bristol Channel is an extension of which river?
8 Where is the University of Kent's main campus?
9 In which season would you see Blackpool's famous illuminations?
10 What is the name of Chesterfield's church with the famous twisted spire?
11 The Cheviot Hills run into which countries?
12 Barrow-in-Furness is on which county's coast?
13 In which county is the Prime Minister's country home?
14 What was Cleveland's county town?
15 On which island is Fingal's Cave?
16 The National Motor Museum is near which stately home?
17 Clydebank was famous for which industry?
18 In which county is the Forest of Dean?
19 What is Antony Gormley's famous sculpture near Gateshead?
20 What is London's second airport?
21 Which racecourse exclusively for flat racing is near Chichester?
22 Which city of south-west England was known to the Romans as Aqua Sulis?
23 In which part of London is the Natural History Museum?
24 Where did the Yvonne Arnaud theatre open in 1965?
25 Where in England is the Scott Polar Research Institute?
26 What is Hull's full name?
27 Which town of north-east Scotland is a terminus of the Caledonian Canal?
28 In which London borough is the National Maritime Museum?
29 What is the UK's electronic surveillance service at Cheltenham called?
30 In which London street are the offices of the Bank of England?

Answers	Sporting Action Replay *(see Quiz 122)*

1 1900. 2 Desert Orchid. 3 Mexico City. 4 Gloucestershire. 5 Worcestershire. 6 35.
7 Mile. 8 Montreal. 9 French. 10 Smith. 11 Joe Davis. 12 Four. 13 Chris Evert.
14 Nick Faldo. 15 Jim Clark. 16 Graf. 17 Florence Griffith Joyner. 18 Gavin Hastings.
19 Evander Holyfield. 20 Dream Team. 21 Bobby Jones. 22 Peter Fleming. 23 US boycott. 24 12. 25 US. 26 Atlanta. 27 Shoemaker. 28 Seven. 29 Gareth Edwards.
30 Australia.

1 Ray Harford and Roy Hodgson have both managed which soccer club?
2 The name of which fish means a star in heraldry?
3 What was the first name of Mr Ryder of Ryder Cup fame?
4 Which Ms Davy was linked with Prince Harry?
5 The Pluto Platter had changed its name to what when it started to sell to the public?
6 What was the day job of Lech Walesa before he became a Polish leader?
7 Who created the character Mick "Crocodile" Dundee?
8 "No ideas, no experience, no hope" was how Edward Heath spoke of which political person?
9 In finance, what does the letter R in SERPS stand for?
10 Rudyard Kipling was born in which country?
11 In the US, New York and which other north-eastern city stage major marathons?
12 In 2006 who won promotion to the Premiership for the first time in 135 years?
13 Where were thousands of Kurds killed in the 1980s?
14 Who was the first UK presenter of TV's "Wheel of Fortune"?
15 In music, which of the following is not a note, F, G, H?
16 Which major river flows through New Orleans?
17 Which country was formerly known as Portuguese West Africa?
18 In the comic opera "The Yeoman of the Guard", what is the job that Jack Point carries out?
19 She's still going strong but in which decade was Tina Turner born?
20 What is used to raise the natural pitch of a guitar?
21 Aconcagua is the highest peak in which country?
22 Under which name did singer Virginia Pugh find fame?
23 The special Jewish day Yom Kippur is also known as the Day of what?
24 Which animal shares its name with Samuel Crompton's spinning machine?
25 What does Blitzkrieg mean, from which the word Blitz originated?
26 Who was first to a first Best Actor Oscar – Russell Crowe or Denzel Washington?
27 Which J was George Gershwin's original first name?
28 Which Liberal Democrat MP was once engaged to weather presenter Sian Lloyd?
29 Which pop band featured Gary Barlow and Jason Orange?
30 1966 saw Sir Alf Ramsey's finest hour as England manager, but in which year was he sacked?

| **Answers** | **Pot Luck 54** *(see Quiz 119)* |

1 Skin. 2 America. 3 Canada. 4 1940s. 5 M People. 6 Baseball. 7 Edward. 8 Spencer. 9 Jean Harlow. 10 Three-dimensional. 11 Stewed fruit. 12 Peak Practice. 13 Spain. 14 Wax. 15 The Liberty Bell. 16 Fish. 17 Cranberries. 18 Fleming. 19 Michael Parkinson. 20 Ring-a-ring-a-roses. 21 Time flies. 22 Personal best. 23 Bat. 24 Beth Tweddle. 25 Spain. 26 Bernadette. 27 North. 28 Cardiff. 29 Maddy Magellan. 30 Matthew Hoggard.

1 In which year were women first allowed to compete at the Olympic Games?
2 Which former four times winner of the King George VI Chase died in 2006?
3 Where did Bob Beamon make his record-breaking long jump?
4 Allan Border played county cricket for Essex and which other county?
5 Ian Botham played cricket for Somerset, Durham and which other county?
6 Sergei Bubka has broken in excess of how many world records, 35, 65, 95?
7 In 1981 Sebastian Coe broke the world record in the 800m., 1500m. and what?
8 Where in 1976 did Nadia Comaneci win her perfect 10 in Olympic gymnastics?
9 Which tennis Grand Slam did Jimmy Connors never win?
10 What was Margaret Court's name when she became the first Australian woman to win Wimbledon?
11 Who made the maximum snooker break of 147 in 1955, later acknowledged as a then world record?
12 How many Prix de L'Arc de Triomphe wins did Pat Eddery have in the 1980s?
13 Which American tennis player was undefeated on clay between 1973 and 1979 and had 18 Grand Slam titles?
14 Which Briton first played in the Ryder Cup in 1977 aged 20?
15 Which Scottish driver broke Juan Fangio's record 24 F1 Grand Prix wins?
16 Monica Seles was stabbed on a tennis court because of a supporter's fanatical devotion to which player?
17 Who won the Jesse Owens Award as the outstanding athlete of 1988, the year she broke world records in Seoul?
18 Who captained the British Lions tour of New Zealand in 1993?
19 Out of whose ear did Mike Tyson take a bite during a boxing match in 1997?
20 What was the 1992 US basketball team dubbed?
21 Which golfer was responsible for founding the US Masters in Augusta?
22 Whom did John McEnroe win seven of his eight Grand Slam doubles titles with?
23 What stopped Ed Moses getting a third Olympic gold in 1980?
24 How old was Lester Piggott when he had his first winner?
25 Which Open was Jack Nicklaus' first win?
26 Where did Steve Redgrave win the fourth of his five Olympic gold medals?
27 Which Willie was the first jockey to ride more than 8,000 winners?
28 When Mark Spitz won seven Olympic golds how many world records did he break?
29 Who became Wales's then youngest ever Rugby captain in 1968?
30 Which country was the first to win the ICC Cricket World Cup three times?

Answers	The UK (see Quiz 120)

1 St Paul's. 2 (near) Birmingham. 3 Charing Cross. 4 Mendips. 5 Chelmsford. 6 Battersea. 7 Severn. 8 Canterbury. 9 Autumn. 10 All Saints. 11 England/Scotland. 12 Cumbria. 13 Buckinghamshire. 14 Middlesbrough. 15 Staffa. 16 Beaulieu. 17 Shipping. 18 Gloucestershire. 19 Angel of the North. 20 Gatwick. 21 Goodwood. 22 Bath. 23 South Kensington. 24 Guildford. 25 Cambridge. 26 Kingston Upon Hull. 27 Inverness. 28 Greenwich. 29 GCHQ. 30 Threadneedle Street.

1 Who lost in the final of the women's Australian Open tennis championships in 2007?

2 What type of puzzle requires a grid to be filled in so that each run through of squares adds up to the total in the box above or to the left?

3 Doctors Guy Secretan and Cardine Todd featured in which TV series?

4 What does the term largo mean in music?

5 In cricket, how many bails are on the two sets of wickets?

6 Dying in 2006, who created the famous fictional shark "Jaws"?

7 Who was the first person to have been soccer coach of England and Australia?

8 What did Ben Travers specialise in writing?

9 Joaquin Rodrigo wrote a concerto in the 1930s for which solo instrument?

10 Which movie sequel had the subtitle "Judgment Day"?

11 The composer Sibelius is associated with which country?

12 In Shakespeare's play which king does Macbeth murder?

13 Which P was a country that Paddington bear came from?

14 What did the J stand for in the name of rugby legend JPR Williams?

15 The Golan Heights are on the border of Israel and which other country?

16 Which subject was George Stubbs famous for painting?

17 In the ballroom dancing world, who is married to Darren Bennett?

18 Who goes with Bess in the title of George Gershwin's opera?

19 Which book includes extracts from Jonathan Harker's diary?

20 Which country does snooker's Mark Williams come from?

21 What was Count Basie's actual first name?

22 How many shots does each player get at the target in curling?

23 Susanna Hoffs fronted which band?

24 Where is the Sea of Showers?

25 In which decade did Jesse Owens set a long jump record that would remain unbroken for 25 years?

26 Which musical instrument is Vladimir Ashkenazy famous for playing?

27 The city of Alexandria is in which country?

28 Which Stephen wrote the song "Send in the Clowns"?

29 Ron Atkinson and Danny Wilson have both managed which soccer club?

30 Kayak, rotor and noon are all examples of what type of words?

| **Answers** | **Pot Luck 57** *(see Quiz 125)* |

1 Ridley. 2 Back to basics. 3 Iceland. 4 The Scarlet Pimpernel. 5 France. 6 All About Eve. 7 Emile Heskey. 8 Die. 9 Kingsley. 10 Judge John Deed. 11 1940s. 12 Birmingham. 13 Martin Scorsese. 14 Ackroyd. 15 Southampton. 16 Conciliation. 17 Greek. 18 Rhapsody. 19 Gary Barlow (2001). 20 Spinach. 21 Whooping cough. 22 Seinfeld. 23 Chile. 24 Jean Alexander. 25 Manchester. 26 Simon Le Bon. 27 Celtic. 28 Parallel Lines. 29 George Gillett and Tom Hicks. 30 Warriors.

1 Who voiced King Harold in "Shrek 2"?
2 "The Libertine" starred which actor as John Wilmot, Earl of Rochester?
3 Who was Meg Ryan's husband in real life when she made "Sleepless in Seattle"?
4 "Just My Luck" and "Mean Girls" starred which actress?
5 Which French actress made her debut in "And God Created Woman"?
6 What was the original nationality of director Milos Forman?
7 Which Oscar-winning actress founded the production company Egg Pictures?
8 Who was Clark Gable's leading lady in his final movie?
9 Who is Kate Hudson's famous actress mother?
10 What are Nick Park's most famous movie characters made from?
11 Which movie shot Quentin Tarantino to prominence?
12 Who played Jack Ryan in "Patriot Games"?
13 Which English playwright scripted "The French Lieutenant's Woman"?
14 In which country was actress Neve Campbell born?
15 Which Steven directed "Sex, Lies and Videotape"?
16 Which star of "Dead Man Walking" was the voice of Ivy in "Cats and Dogs"?
17 Which star of "Batman Returns" and "A View to a Kill" danced on Fatboy Slim's "Weapon of Choice"?
18 Darryl Hannah passed on the role of Shelby in "Steel Magnolias" to whom?
19 Who played the title role in the movie about the US president who resigned in office?
20 What is Penelope Cruz's occupation in "Woman on Top"?
21 Who is the voice of the princess in "Shrek"?
22 Who played the title role in "Miss Congeniality"?
23 Who played Mrs Jack Stanton, wife of the Governor, in "Primary Colors"?
24 Who starred in the original "Thomas Crown Affair" and the 1999 remake?
25 Who played the fitness teacher in "Perfect"?
26 Who was Robin Williams' wife in "Mrs Doubtfire"?
27 In 1999 which Shakespeare play did Kenneth Branagh bring to the big screen in the style of an MGM musical?
28 Who won Best Supporting Actress Oscar for "LA Confidential"?
29 How did Christopher Reeve receive his tragic injuries causing almost total immobility?
30 Which late actor starred with Keanu Reeves in "My Own Private Idaho"?

Answers	**Music: Bands** *(see Quiz 126)*

1 Bon Jovi. 2 The Rolling Stones. 3 En Vogue. 4 Ace of Base. 5 Appleton. 6 Beatles.
7 Bohemian Rhapsody. 8 I Want to Hold Your Hand. 9 Lordi. 10 Two. 11 Country
House. 12 Words. 13 Tsunami. 14 Patience. 15 Prodigy. 16 Def Leppard. 17 Guns
N' Roses. 18 U2. 19 Chemical Brothers. 20 REM. 21 The Bangles. 22 Newcastle.
23 Doctor Jones. 24 Mulder & Scully. 25 Northern Ireland. 26 The Great Escape. 27
Creation. 28 Boyzone. 29 Sheffield. 30 Boyzone.

1 In "Coronation Street" what goes with Newton to make the beer for the Rovers' Return?
2 Which John Major campaign urged a return to traditional values?
3 The Althing is the parliament of which country?
4 In fiction, Percy Blakeney was the alias of which hero?
5 In which country was cubism founded?
6 Before "Titanic" what was the last film to win 14 Oscar nominations?
7 Which Emile scored in Sven Goran Eriksson's first game in charge for England?
8 Lester Piggott's first Derby winner was called Never Say what?
9 Which Mr Amis wrote "Lucky Jim"?
10 Martin Shaw played which eponymous TV judge?
11 Still looking Ab Fab, in which decade was Joanna Lumley born?
12 The M1 was originally constructed to link London to where?
13 Harvey Keitel is particularly known for his work with which movie director?
14 Agatha Christie wrote about "The Murder of Roger" who?
15 What was Alan Shearer's first league club?
16 What does the C stand for in ACAS?
17 What was the nationality of fable writer Aesop?
18 What did George Gershwin write "in Blue"?
19 Who was 30 first – Emma Bunton, Gary Barlow or Victoria Beckham?
20 What S is added to pasta to make it green?
21 The illness pertussis is more commonly known as what?
22 Which US sitcom ran to 180 episodes, before finishing in 1998?
23 The southernmost part of South America is owned by which country?
24 Which former soap star became Auntie Wainwright in "Last of the Summer Wine"?
25 The Halle Orchestra is based in which English city?
26 Which pop personality married Yasmin Parvaneh in 1986?
27 Which club did Jock Stein lead to European success?
28 "Sunday Girl" featured on which Blondie album?
29 Who bought Liverpool FC from the Moores family in 2007?
30 In rugby, what was added to Wigan's name in 1997?

Answers | **Pot Luck 56** *(see Quiz 123)*

1 Maria Sharapova. 2 Kakuro. 3 Green Wing. 4 Slowly. 5 Four. 6 Peter Benchley. 7 Terry Venables. 8 Theatrical farce. 9 Guitar. 10 Terminator II. 11 Finland. 12 Duncan. 13 Peru. 14 John. 15 Syria. 16 Horses. 17 Lilia Kopylova. 18 Porgy. 19 Dracula. 20 Wales. 21 William. 22 Two. 23 The Bangles. 24 The moon. 25 1930s. 26 Piano. 27 Egypt. 28 Sondheim. 29 Sheffield Wednesday. 30 Palindromes.

1 Whose Best of 1990s album was "Cross Road"?
2 Who embarked on their "Bigger Bang" tour in 2006?
3 Who had a hit with "Don't Let Go"?
4 "Happy Nation" was the debut album of which Scandinavian band?
5 What was the surname of the sisters in All Saints?
6 Which band had 18 consecutive UK Top Ten hits between July 1964 and March 1976?
7 What was Queen's best-selling single?
8 Which Beatles single was their first No 1 in the US?
9 Which band won the 2006 Eurovision Song Contest?
10 How many albums did the Spice Girls release in the 20th century?
11 What was Blur's first UK No 1?
12 Which 1996 Boyzone hit was a previous hit by the Bee Gees?
13 Which 1999 Manic Street Preachers hit shares its name with a natural disaster?
14 What was Take That's first UK No 1 of the 21st century?
15 Whose album "Fat of the Land" debuted at No 1 on both sides of the Atlantic?
16 Joe Elliot was vocalist with which heavy metal band?
17 Who had an "Appetite for Destruction" in 1987?
18 Whose album had some "Rattle & Hum" in 1988?
19 Who had the award-winning 1999 album "Surrender"?
20 Who were "Out of Time" in 1991?
21 Who had the original hit with Atomic Kitten's "Eternal Flame"?
22 Which city did the 1960s band The Animals come from?
23 What was Aqua's follow-up to "Barbie Girl"?
24 Which Catatonia hit shared its name with a TV duo?
25 Which part of the UK did Ash come from?
26 Which Blur album shared its name with a Steve McQueen film?
27 On which label did Oasis have their first Top Ten Hit?
28 Shane Lynch was a member of which band?
29 Arctic Monkeys hail from which city?
30 Which band had 16 consecutive UK Top Ten hits between December 1994 and December 1999?

---

1 In France all motorways begin with which letter of the alphabet?
2 What does the Blue Cross Charity provide aid to?
3 Which hypnotist wrote "I Can Make You Thin"?
4 In the song "Rule Britannia" what is Britannia told to rule?
5 Which soccer side won four championships in a row with Johan Cruyff as boss?
6 Did Aaron Copland compose music for "Billy Elliot", "Billy the Kid" or "Billy Liar"?
7 In which western classic did John Wayne play the Ringo Kid?
8 What is the qualification to be Father of the House in the House of Commons?
9 In music, which note is written on the bottom line of the treble clef?
10 The Copacabana beach is in which South American city?
11 Whose first No 1 single used the title of a novel by one of the Brontë sisters?
12 Actor John Savident played which character in "Coronation Street"?
13 How many years before "Star Wars" is the action of "The Phantom Menace", 22, 32 or 42?
14 Which band became the most successful 1990s Scandinavian act on the US singles chart?
15 If you were an LLD what subject would you have studied?
16 What was US President Lyndon Johnson's middle name?
17 Joe Royle and Mike Walker have both managed which soccer club?
18 Green Street and Priory Road are near which London soccer club's stadium?
19 Which Napoleonic battle gave its name to a famous chicken dish?
20 In which decade of last century were BBC TV programmes first broadcast?
21 The Beautiful South were formed after the break-up of which group?
22 What was Hetty Wainthropp's young assistant sleuth called?
23 What was the first name of Eva Peron's husband?
24 Who used Marx Brothers film titles as album titles?
25 When was US hospital drama "St Elsewhere" first screened in the UK?
26 Giovanna Gassion sang under which name?
27 How many states were in the original union of the United States?
28 What would a palaeontologist study?
29 R.E.M. sang about "Shiny Happy" what?
30 What do the words post mortem actually mean?

Answers	**Past Times: 1900–1950** *(see Quiz 129)*

1 Manhattan Project. 2 Stanley Baldwin. 3 Brussels. 4 Neville Chamberlain. 5 Austria. 6 First. 7 Gestapo. 8 Cost lives. 9 Alexandra. 10 1916. 11 Morris. 12 Birth control. 13 Lenin. 14 1920s. 15 Munich. 16 Queen Mary. 17 Windsor. 18 Dunkirk. 19 Malta. 20 Dresden. 21 Edinburgh. 22 Round. 23 American. 24 Ethel. 25 Sidney Street. 26 Shilling. 27 David Lloyd George. 28 Lady Elizabeth Bowes Lyon. 29 Sydney. 30 George V.

Quiz 128 Plants

Answers – page 372

1 What is the main characteristic of the wood of the balsa tree?
2 Plantain is a type of which fruit?
3 What is another name for the blackthorn?
4 Which industry's demands meant that rubber production increased in the last century?
5 What does a berry typically contain?
6 In a biennial plant, when do flower and seed production usually occur?
7 What name is given to small hardy plants ideal for rockeries, such as saxifraga?
8 The name tulip is derived from a Turkish word meaning what type of headgear?
9 What type of soil is vital for growing rhododendrons?
10 What is the most common colour of primula vulgaris or common primrose?
11 Clematis is a member of which family of wild flowers?
12 How many petals does an iris usually have?
13 What nationality was the botanist who gave his name to the dahlia?
14 How is the wild Rosa canina better known?
15 What colour is the rose of York?
16 Antirrhinums are also called what?
17 What is gypsophilia mainly grown for?
18 Which Busy plant has the name Impatiens?
19 Forget Me Nots are usually which colour?
20 Which TV cook Ms Lawson shares her name with the Love in a Mist flower?
21 How are the papery daisy-like flowers of helichrysum better known?
22 In which season do Michaelmas daisies flower?
23 Which best describes leaves of a hosta – scalloped, spiky or very large?
24 Which of the following flowers are not grown from bulbs – pansies, snowdrops and tulips?
25 What sort of bell is a campanula?
26 Muscari are what type of hyacinth?
27 What is used to make a mulch – chemicals, organic material or seeds?
28 What makes the seeds of the laburnum potentially dangerous?
29 What colour are the ripe fruits of the mulberry tree?
30 What is the most common colour for alyssum, often used in borders and hanging baskets?

Answers	Pot Luck 59 (see Quiz 130)

1 Coach. 2 Aaron. 3 Camp David. 4 Nicaragua. 5 Backwards and in high heels. 6 Monopoly. 7 Doop. 8 Carter. 9 Catatonia. 10 Falklands War. 11 George Burns. 12 Beverley Craven. 13 Japanese. 14 Branscombe Beach. 15 Ronnie Barker. 16 Jeweller. 17 Foot. 18 Horatio Nelson. 19 The Real Thing. 20 South. 21 Joseph Jr. 22 IS. 23 Australia and Tasmania. 24 Help the Aged. 25 Queen Victoria. 26 Eve Pollard. 27 Dead Man Walking. 28 Archipelago. 29 Edward VII. 30 Louvre.

1 What was the code name of the project to develop the atom bomb?
2 Who was Prime Minister during the Abdication of Edward VIII?
3 In which city did Edith Cavell work in WWI?
4 Which Prime Minister declared war on Germany in 1939?
5 The Anschluss concerned Nazi Germany and which other state?
6 In which decade of the 20th century was the Boy Scout movement founded?
7 How was the Geheime Staatspolizei better known?
8 According to the wartime slogan, careless talk does what?
9 What was Tsar Nicholas II's wife called?
10 In which year was the Easter Rising in Dublin?
11 Lord Nuffield founded which car company which originally bore his name?
12 What type of clinic did Marie Stopes open?
13 Which Russian leader died in 1924?
14 In which decade did the Wall Street Crash take place?
15 In which German city was the Nazi Party founded?
16 Which "Queen" left on her maiden voyage across the Atlantic in 1946?
17 Which Duke and Duchess famously visited Hitler in Berlin in 1937?
18 Which French beaches were evacuated in 1940?
19 Which island received a medal for gallantry after WWII?
20 Which city called the German Florence was heavily bombed in 1945?
21 Which now annual arts Festival opened in for the first time in 1947?
22 What shape was the main part of the first AA badge which appeared in 1906?
23 What nationality was Robert Peary who reached the North Pole in 1909?
24 What was Dr Crippen's mistress's first name, with whom he tried to flee to Canada after murdering his wife?
25 Which East End street was the scene of siege by anarchists in 1911?
26 Taking the King's what meant that volunteers had signed up for the army?
27 Who succeeded Kitchener as War Secretary in 1916?
28 Who did the then Duke of York marry in 1923?
29 Which Bridge had the then longest span when it opened in 1932?
30 Which monarch made the first Christmas radio broadcast?

1 "BBC Sports Personality of the Year" voted Daniel Anderson top what in 2006?
2 What was Elvis Presley's middle name?
3 In the USA, where is the President's official country home?
4 The Sandanista guerrillas overthrew the government of which country in 1979?
5 Talking about Fred Astaire, Ginger Rogers said "I did what he did but I did it …" in which way?
6 Which board game features a racing car, a top hat and a dog?
7 What was the only hit of one-hit wonders Doop?
8 Which President of the USA had Walter Mondale as Vice President?
9 Cerys Matthews became lead singer with which band in the mid-1990s?
10 The "General Belgrano" was sunk in which conflict?
11 Who won an Oscar for "The Sunshine Boys" at the age of 80?
12 Who took "Promise Me" into the charts in the early 1990s?
13 Which country were the aggressors in the Pearl Harbor attack of the 1940s?
14 Where in Devon did a ship's cargo wash up in January 2007?
15 Whose TV roles have included Arkwright and Fletcher?
16 What was the trade of Charles Lewis Tiffany?
17 In which part of the human skeleton are the metatarsels?
18 Whose last words were reputedly, "Thank God I have done my duty"?
19 Which Tony Di Bart No 1 hit from 1994 is the name of a group?
20 Is the Kandahar region in the north or south of Afghanistan?
21 What was the name of John F Kennedy's brother who predeceased him?
22 IC sounds as if it ought to be Iceland's international vehicle registration but isn't – but what is?
23 The Bass Strait lies between which two islands?
24 Which Pulp single title is also the name of a charity?
25 Who opened the Royal Albert Hall?
26 Presenter Claudia Winkleman is the daughter of which former newspaper editor?
27 For which 1990s film with a prison theme did Johnny Cash contribute to the soundtrack?
28 A sea containing many islands is called what?
29 Who succeeded Queen Victoria?
30 Which gallery displays the "Mona Lisa"?

Answers	Plants *(see Quiz 128)*

1 Light. 2 Banana. 3 Sloe. 4 Automobile. 5 Seeds. 6 Second year. 7 Alpines. 8 Turban. 9 Lime free. 10 Yellow. 11 Buttercup. 12 Three. 13 Swedish. 14 Dog rose. 15 White. 16 Snapdragons. 17 Flower arranging. 18 Lizzie. 19 Blue. 20 Nigella. 21 Everlasting flowers. 22 Autumn. 23 Very large. 24 Pansies. 25 Canterbury bell. 26 Grape. 27 Organic material. 28 Poisonous. 29 Dark red. 30 White.

1 What was the name of the 1999 BBC series about prehistoric creatures?
2 Where did Mavis leave for when she left "Coronation Street"?
3 Which Nick Berry series was set in the west country?
4 Which drink did Paul Daniels and Debbie McGee advertise singing off key around a piano?
5 What is Betty's culinary speciality in "Coronation Street"?
6 Who played writer Peter Mayle in the ill-fated series "A Year in Provence"?
7 What was the prize to aim for in Cilla's "Moment of Truth"?
8 Zoe Wanamaker and Robert Lindsay starred in which domestic comedy?
9 In which comedy about relationships did Jack Davenport play Steve while Gina Bellman played Jane?
10 Singer Adam Rickitt found fame in which soap?
11 In "Countdown", how many people occupy Dictionary Corner?
12 How long do the cooks have to cook their team members' ingredients in "Ready Steady Cook"?
13 Which ex-"Coronation Street" actress played 1970s TV star Coral Atkins in "Seeing Red"?
14 In 2001 what momentous new purchase did Deirdre make in "Coronation Street"?
15 In "Bargain Hunt", what sort of bargains are being hunted?
16 Which "The O.C." character, played by Micha Baron, was killed off in series three?
17 What is the postcode of Albert Square, Walford?
18 On which show did Hear'Say shoot to stardom?
19 In "Coronation Street", which character killed Charlie Stubbs?
20 In which series would the Skelthwaite Arms feature?
21 Which Tony played the Sheriff in "Maid Marian and Her Merry Men"?
22 Which comedy show was famous for its "Fork handles" sketch?
23 What was the name of Keith Harris's duck?
24 Which "Rainbow" character was pink?
25 Who first hosted "A Question of TV"?
26 Who was the first presenter of "Changing Rooms"?
27 Which comedy show was famous for its "Dead Parrot" sketch?
28 How many contestants start out on the original, BBC2 version, of "The Weakest Link"?
29 Who won the "Best Actor in a TV Drama" award at the 2007 Golden Globes?
30 Who first presented the interactive travel series "Holiday: You Call the Shots"?

Answers	Celebs *(see Quiz 133)*

1 Priscilla. 2 Chicago. 3 Her dogs. 4 Miss Whiplash. 5 Bruce Forsyth. 6 Eight. 7 Denise Van Outen. 8 Playboy. 9 Edward VIII. 10 Gabriela Sabatini. 11 Mary Quant. 12 Newspapers. 13 Prince Andrew. 14 Gilles. 15 Niece. 16 Cambridge. 17 Natasha. 18 Danielle Lloyd. 19 Catherine. 20 Devonshire. 21 Bernie Ecclestone. 22 Andrew Lloyd Webber. 23 Follett. 24 Norway. 25 Barbara. 26 Harrison Ford. 27 Kathleen Turner. 28 Bristol. 29 Shiloh Nouvel. 30 Meet the Fockers.

1 On which day are US elections for the Senate and Congress always held?
2 Which Harris had a huge hit with "Macarthur Park"?
3 In "Bewitched" what was the name of Samantha's mother?
4 On a Monopoly board what is the first station reached after Go?
5 Which franc is the official currency of Liechtenstein?
6 Howard Wilkinson and George Graham have both managed which soccer club?
7 Who played the man in black in the film "Once Upon a Time in the West"?
8 Which female singer performed with the Miami Sound Machine?
9 In 2006 Simon Shepherd dropped out of which musical, days before its opening?
10 Which bass saxophonist released "The "Impulse Story" album in June 2006?
11 Who quite literally took "Trash" into the charts in the mid-1990s?
12 In which war did the Battle of the Bulge take place?
13 In the past which creatures were used by doctors to drain blood?
14 Which Howard discovered Tutankhamun's tomb in the Valley of the Kings?
15 Who sang about "The Good Ship Lollipop"?
16 What was Southern Rhodesia renamed in the 1980s?
17 Who presented the TV series "Sweet Baby James"?
18 Which US First Lady is credited as being the first to use the name?
19 What was the first movie to play John Wayne opposite Maureen O'Hara?
20 "Oh What a Beautiful Morning" comes from which musical?
21 Which river cuts through the Grand Canyon?
22 Who wrote "Nessun Dorma", now regarded as Pavarotti's theme tune?
23 "And I'll cry if I want to" is the second line of the chorus of which song?
24 Ralph McTell wrote and sang about the "Streets of" where?
25 Who was first to be 50 – John Travolta or Martina Navratilova?
26 On which Sea is the Gaza Strip?
27 Roger Waters and Dave Gilmour were members of which long-lasting group?
28 What has the Nursery End and the Pavilion End?
29 In 2006 the FA announced sponsorship of the FA Cup by which energy supplier?
30 How many members of the Righteous Brothers were actual brothers?

1 Who did Elvis Presley sue for divorce on his 38th birthday?
2 In which city did Hugh Hefner open his first Playboy Club?
3 In 1991 Queen Elizabeth II needed medical treatment after breaking up a fight between whom?
4 How did Lindi St Clair, who battled with the Inland Revenue over the nature of her earnings, style herself?
5 Which TV entertainer has a South American wife called Wilnelia?
6 By the end of the 20th century how many times had Elizabeth Taylor been married?
7 Which blonde TV presenter did Jay Kay split with in the new millennium?
8 Which magazine did Hugh Hefner found?
9 Who was the first English king to travel in an aeroplane?
10 Which Argentine tennis player shares her birthdate – 15 years later – with Olga Korbut?
11 Which designer is most associated with the Sixties and the mini-skirt?
12 Lord Beaverbrook is a famous name in which field?
13 Who was the first Royal to visit New York after September 11th 2001?
14 Who is Jacques Villeneuve's famous father?
15 What relation is Bridget Fonda to Jane Fonda?
16 At which university did Vanessa Feltz study?
17 What is the name of Sir Michael Caine's daughter?
18 Who was stripped of the 2006 Miss Great Britain title?
19 What is Mrs Frankie Dettori called?
20 Chatsworth in Derbyshire is owned by the duke of where?
21 Who owned Formula 1 racing when ITV began in 1996?
22 Whose theatre company did Prince Edward join when he left the Royal Marines?
23 What is the surname of Labour stalwart and author Ken and image consultant Barbara?
24 In which country was Mariella Frostrup born?
25 What is Frank Sinatra's widow's first name?
26 Which actor was married to screenwriter Melissa Mathison?
27 Who was the first US star to play "The Graduate"'s Mrs Robinson on a London stage?
28 Which Marquess is the brother of It Girl Victoria Hervey?
29 Brad Pitt and Angelina Jolie's first child was called what?
30 Which 2005 comedy film starred Barbra Streisand and Dustin Hoffman?

Answers	TV: Trivia (see Quiz 131)

1 Walking with Dinosaurs. 2 Lake District. 3 Harbour Lights. 4 Lager. 5 Hot pot. 6 John Thaw. 7 £20,000. 8 My Family. 9 Coupling. 10 Coronation Street. 11 Two. 12 20 minutes. 13 Sarah Lancashire. 14 Glasses. 15 Antiques. 16 Marissa Cooper. 17 E20. 18 Popstars. 19 Tracy Barlow. 20 Where the Heart is. 21 Robinson. 22 The Two Ronnies. 23 Orville. 24 George. 25 Gaby Roslin. 26 Carol Smillie. 27 Monty Python. 28 Nine. 29 Hugh Laurie. 30 Jamie Theakston.

Euro Tour

Answers – page 374

1 In which county is Bantry Bay in the south of Ireland?
2 What is Italy's Capodimonte famous for?
3 In which city is the Pompidou Centre?
4 Which island is called Kefallinia in Greek?
5 From which resort at the foot of Mont Blanc does the highest cable car in the world rise?
6 What do the British call what the French call Les Iles Normands?
7 Which province of the Irish Republic includes Galway and Sligo?
8 The Amalienborg Palace is the home of which Royal Family?
9 Which Scandinavian country is called Suomi in its own language?
10 The Baltic states are made up of Latvia, Lithuania and where?
11 What is Germany's Schwarzwald?
12 Which monument is at the opposite end of Paris's Champs Elysées from the Place de la Concorde?
13 Where was a refugee camp built for asylum-seekers near the Channel Tunnel?
14 Where is the park called the Bois de Boulogne?
15 What is the capital of the state of the Tyrol?
16 Ithaca is off the west coast of which country?
17 Which Scandinavian strait has a name which means cat's throat?
18 In which Sea are the Balearic Islands?
19 Which breed of dog comes from Kerry in south-west Ireland?
20 In which city is the Prado art gallery?
21 Which town of Lombardy gave its name to a bright reddish mauve dye?
22 What is the Bourse in Paris?
23 On which Sea is Odessa?
24 Which country has the rivers Douro, Tagus and Guadiana?
25 What is the chief city of Catalonia, and Spain's second largest?
26 Which is the farthest north, Belarus, Ukraine or Estonia?
27 What was St Petersburg called for much of the 20th century?
28 Which Sea is to the west of Denmark?
29 Which is the most easterly city, Stuttgart, Munich or Hanover?
30 The Basque country surrounds which mountains?

| **Answers** | **Pot Luck 60** *(see Quiz 132)* |

1 Tuesday. 2 Richard. 3 Endora. 4 Kings Cross. 5 Swiss franc. 6 Leeds. 7 Henry Fonda. 8 Gloria Estefan. 9 The Sound of Music. 10 Charlie Mingus. 11 Suede. 12 World War II. 13 Leeches. 14 Carter. 15 Shirley Temple. 16 Zimbabwe. 17 James Martin. 18 Eleanor Roosevelt. 19 Rio Grande. 20 Oklahoma! 21 Colorado. 22 Puccini. 23 It's My Party. 24 London. 25 John Travolta (2004). 26 Mediterranean. 27 Pink Floyd. 28 Lord's Cricket Ground. 29 e.on. 30 None.

1 In 2006 which cricketer became England's youngest debut centurion?
2 Who became the first Briton to hold a world javelin record?
3 Where in Germany is a passion play staged once every ten years?
4 Which sport can be played under Australian, Association or Gaelic rules?
5 Which country did the Bay City Rollers come from?
6 Which US president had the middle name Milhous?
7 Ellis Island is in which harbour?
8 What was the rank of Georges Simenon's Maigret?
9 Tommy Docherty quipped that he'd had more what than Jack Nicklaus?
10 Which former athlete announced he would leave TV's "Songs of Praise" in 2007?
11 In American Football which creatures are linked to the Chicago team?
12 Artists Manet and Monet both came from which city?
13 Which star of "Strictly Come Dancing" produced an exercise DVD entitled "Latinasize"?
14 Agatha Christie wrote romantic novels under the pseudonym of Mary who?
15 Which country became the first to legalise abortion?
16 Which early pop classic song begins, "I'm so young and you're so old"?
17 In American college football what can go after Cotton, Orange and Sugar?
18 Navan Fort is in which Irish county?
19 In which country is the oldest angling club in the world?
20 Leonardo Da Vinci, Charles de Gaulle, Jan Smuts have all what named after them?
21 What is the next white note on a keyboard below G?
22 Which actor became a human cartoon in the movie "The Mask"?
23 Which city do the Afrikaaners know as Kaapstad?
24 Which motorway links up with the M25 closest to Heathrow Airport?
25 Which Joplin was one of the originators of ragtime?
26 Which actress starred as Princess Leia in the "Star Wars" trilogy?
27 Who joined Rod Stewart and Sting on the 1994 hit "All for Love"?
28 What does Honolulu mean in Hawaiian?
29 What is the traditional colour of an Indian wedding sari?
30 Which pop group had the last word of the Lord's Prayer as the first word of its name?

Answers	Pot Luck 62 *(see Quiz 137)*

1 Jason. **2** John Barnes. **3** The Rockies. **4** Spanish. **5** Baby. **6** As Time Goes By. **7** Smallpox. **8** Jude. **9** Jeremy Vine. **10** Cop. **11** The Little Mermaid. **12** Christopher Biggins. **13** Atlantic. **14** I Believe. **15** Austria. **16** Hormones. **17** Sol Campbell. **18** Latent. **19** Gabrielle. **20** 22. **21** Horse. **22** Thumb. **23** Boombastic. **24** Gianni Versace. **25** Egypt. **26** Colchester. **27** Canterbury. **28** Susan Hampshire. **29** Ealing Comedies. **30** Desert Storm.

1 Which Italian club did Paul Gascoigne play for?
2 Aleksandr Hleb joined Arsenal from which side?
3 Who did Glen Hoddle play for just before he became England manager?
4 Who was Chelsea's top Premiership scorer in the 2005–06 season?
5 In which county was Bobby Charlton born?
6 Which overseas player led Naples to their first ever Italian championship?
7 How old was Stanley Matthews when he made his debut for England?
8 With which club side did Bobby Moore end his career?
9 Whose autobiography was called "My World"?
10 Jaap Stam signed for Manchester United from which club?
11 In the Germany vs England 2001 World Cup qualifier, what was the score at half time?
12 Which club did Chris Sutton join immediately after Blackburn Rovers?
13 Who were the opposition in Gary Lineker's final international when he was taken off by Graham Taylor?
14 Which manager preceded Graeme Souness and Tony Parkes at Blackburn Rovers?
15 In which decade was the European Champions Cup inaugurated?
16 Who won the last FA Cup Final of the 20th century?
17 John Hartson left West Ham for which club in 1999?
18 Who managed Manchester City immediately before Kevin Keegan?
19 The leading goalscorer in the 1998 World Cup finals came from which country?
20 How many goals did Sunderland score in the FA Cup final of 1973?
21 Doyle and Kitson were joint top scorers as which side made the Premiership?
22 Who was the last side to win the old Division 1?
23 Which London side won the European Cup Winners Cup in 1998?
24 In France 98 who was England's top scorer along with Michael Owen?
25 Who beat Manchester United in their first FA Cup campaign of the 21st century?
26 Who did Scotland play the same day that England beat Germany 5–1?
27 Gary McAllister, Peter Reid and Gordon Strachan have managed which side?
28 Which soccer club did Bobby Charlton manage before becoming a Manchester United director?
29 Who has presented the Footballer of the Year award since 1948?
30 Before Michael Owen in Germany, who was the last England player to score a hat trick in international football?

1 What is the real first name of Jay Kay of Jamiroquai?
2 Who became the first person to wear white boots in an FA Cup Final?
3 In which mountain range is Mount Elbert the highest peak?
4 Which nationality goes with the Riding School in Austria?
5 Who or what was swimming on the cover of Nirvana's album "Nevermind"?
6 On TV, which show's theme song begins, "You must remember this"?
7 Variola is the medical name for which disease?
8 Which name appears in a Beatles song title and in a Thomas Hardy novel title?
9 Who presented "Panorama" when it returned to prime-time TV in 2007?
10 What was the profession of Michael Douglas' character in the movie "Basic Instinct"?
11 Hans Christian Andersen's memorial statue in Copenhagen takes the form of which character?
12 Which actor played Lukewarm in "Porridge"?
13 Which is the saltiest of the major oceans of the world?
14 What was coupled with Robson and Jerome's "Up on the Roof"?
15 German leader Adolf Hitler was born in which country?
16 The pituitary gland controls the production of what in the body?
17 Who scored Arsenal's first goal in a Champions League Final?
18 Which word describes hidden or concealed heat?
19 Which female vocalist featured on East 17's mid-1990s hit "If You Ever"?
20 At what age did Will Carling first captain England at rugby?
21 A Lippizaner is what type of animal?
22 A pollex is another name for which part of the body?
23 What was the second No 1 for Shaggy?
24 In 1997, whose funeral in Milan was attended by Elton John and Naomi Campbell?
25 Which country has the car registration code ET?
26 Blur formed in which East Anglian town?
27 In which city was Orlando Bloom born?
28 Which well-respected actress has been President of the Dyslexia Institute?
29 Which comedies was Michael Balcon responsible for?
30 In the 1990s, the operation to eject Iraqis from Kuwait was codenamed which Operation?

Answers	**Pot Luck 61** *(see Quiz 135)*

1 Alastair Cook. 2 Fatima Whitbread. 3 Oberammergau. 4 Football. 5 Scotland. 6 Nixon. 7 New York. 8 Inspector. 9 Clubs. 10 Jonathan Edwards. 11 Bears. 12 Paris. 13 Lilia Kopylova. 14 Westmacott. 15 Iceland. 16 Diana. 17 Bowl. 18 Armagh. 19 Scotland. 20 Airports. 21 F. 22 Jim Carrey. 23 Cape Town. 24 M4. 25 Scott. 26 Carrie Fisher. 27 Bryan Adams. 28 Sheltered bay. 29 Scarlet. 30 Amen Corner.

1 Who is Ethan Coen's director brother?
2 Who directed "Moulin Rouge", starring Nicole Kidman and Ewan McGregor?
3 Who directed the film "Flags of Our Fathers"?
4 What was George Lucas's role in the original "Star Wars"?
5 Who directed the movie about the most disastrous disaster at sea in peace time?
6 Who had the middle name Blount but only used his initial?
7 Which musical duo was the subject of a Mike Leigh movie with Jim Broadbent?
8 Which musical did Alan Parker direct before the drama "Angela's Ashes"?
9 How is Melvin Kaminski of "Young Frankenstein" better known?
10 Which Neil was Oscar-nominated as director and also writer for "The Crying Game"?
11 Who was the director of "When Harry Met Sally"?
12 In which city was Akira Kurosawa born?
13 Which lady was the director of the hit movies "Sleepless in Seattle" and "You Got M@il"?
14 Which father of a musical star directed "An American in Paris"?
15 How is the director of "Wolf" and "The Birdcage" born Michael Igor Peschkowsky better known?
16 Which actor directed "Rocky IV"?
17 Who was Oscar-nominated for "Dead Man Walking"?
18 Ken Russell's "The Music Lovers" was about which Russian composer?
19 For which movie with Robert De Niro did Martin Scorsese receive his first Oscar nomination?
20 Which brothers bought Shepperton Studios in 1994?
21 Which then husband and wife were the stars of Kubrick's "Eyes Wide Shut"?
22 What is the name of Garry Marshall's fellow director sibling, formerly married to the director of "When Harry Met Sally"?
23 Which president was the subject of the 1995 movie written and directed by Oliver Stone?
24 Who was the director of "Gandhi"?
25 Who was the subject of the biography "King Pulp"?
26 Which movie about an Apollo moon mission had Ron Howard as director?
27 Where in New York was Woody Allen born?
28 Terry Gilliam was a member of which comedy team?
29 In which decade did Stanley Kubrick direct "A Clockwork Orange"?
30 Which actor directed "Dances with Wolves" and "The Bodyguard?

Answers	Football *(see Quiz 136)*

1 Lazio. 2 Stuttgart. 3 Chelsea. 4 Frank Lampard. 5 Northumberland. 6 Diego Maradona. 7 20. 8 Fulham. 9 David Beckham. 10 PSV Eindhoven. 11 1–2. 12 Chelsea. 13 Sweden. 14 Brian Kidd. 15 1950s. 16 Manchester United. 17 Wimbledon. 18 Joe Royle. 19 Croatia. 20 One. 21 Reading. 22 Leeds. 23 Chelsea. 24 Alan Shearer. 25 West Ham. 26 Croatia. 27 Coventry. 28 Preston North End. 29 Football Writers' Association. 30 Alan Shearer.

1 Reba McEntire's best-of album was called "Moments" and what else?
2 Scientist Rene Descartes said "I think therefore ..." what?
3 Florentino Perez resigned as president of which major soccer club in February 2006?
4 An ossicle is a small what?
5 In which decade did Einstein die?
6 Which species of trees and shrubs come from the genus Malus?
7 Approximately how many feet are there in a fathom?
8 Which former Conservative Party Chairman wrote "False Impression"?
9 What was the name of the character played by Harry Enfield when he was in "Men Behaving Badly"?
10 Who said, "Honey I forgot to duck" after a failed assassination attempt?
11 In computing, how many bits are there in a byte?
12 What was the last name of chef Gareth in TV's "Chef!"?
13 A snapper is a type of what when it is red, yellowtail or grey?
14 How many seconds are there in a quarter of an hour?
15 In which country were the world's first known theatres built?
16 Which TV series was set at the Globelink News Office?
17 Terry Butcher and Lawrie McMenemy have both managed which soccer club?
18 Who was known in Australia as "The Crocodile Hunter"?
19 Phidippides was the first runner of which epic race?
20 Which novelist created the character George Smiley?
21 What was the first album from Il Divo to top the charts?
22 Which university is the oldest in the USA?
23 Which actor is on the cover of the "Official Dr Who Annual 2007"?
24 Which Thomas introduced the blue and white pottery known as Willow pattern?
25 The Longmuir brothers were in which teen idol band?
26 The Beeching report led to vast cuts in which service?
27 At Royal Ascot which day is Ladies' Day?
28 In which country would you watch Lokeren play a home soccer match?
29 Which singer called his son Otis in tribute to Otis Redding?
30 In which country did the Sharpeville massacre take place?

Answers | Pot Luck 64 *(see Quiz 141)*

1 Shilpa Shetty. 2 Kinetic energy. 3 Los Angeles. 4 Peas. 5 The phoenix. 6 Twopence. 7 REM. 8 Horizontally. 9 The Elephant Man. 10 Sadat. 11 Mike Ruddock. 12 Fireball XL5. 13 Beirut. 14 McPherson. 15 Anfield. 16 Spungeon. 17 Dutch. 18 Bouvier. 19 Jimi Hendrix. 20 Paul Gascoigne. 21 Woodward. 22 Labour. 23 Skiing. 24 Chess. 25 Orenthal. 26 Ainsley Harriott. 27 One. 28 Poisoned himself. 29 Dame Nellie Melba. 30 Los Angeles.

1 What goes with "Inside In" in the title of The Kooks' first album?
2 Which veteran rockers had a 2005 hit with "The Party ain't Over Yet"?
3 Who sang "I'll be Missing You" with Puff Daddy?
4 Which Mariah Carey single was the first to debut at No 1 in the US, in 1995?
5 What was the title of Corinne Bailey Rae's debut album?
6 Who was the first male rapper to have two solo No 1s?
7 S Club 7's "Never Had a Dream Come True" raised money for which charity?
8 Which was the first band to have seven successive No 1s with their first seven releases?
9 Which British band had the first No 1 of the new millennium?
10 Which girl's name featured in a mega hit for Dexy's Midnight Runners?
11 Which was Wham!'s best-selling Christmas single?
12 Which 2000 Spiller song stopped Victoria Beckham from having her first solo No 1?
13 What was the English title of Sarah Brightman's "Con Te Partiro" which she sang with Andrea Bocelli?
14 Who first made the Top Twenty with "Linger"?
15 In 2000 Oxide & Neutrino charted with a reworking of the theme of which hospital series?
16 Who sang "How Do I Live" in 1998?
17 Whose "Killing Me Softly" was a top seller in 1996?
18 Which song from "Bridget Jones's Diary" did Geri Halliwell have a hit with in 2001?
19 What was Britney Spears' second UK No 1?
20 What was Elton John's first solo No 1 in the US?
21 "Three Lions" charted in which World Cup year?
22 Which family charted with "Mmmbop"?
23 Which Oasis member sang on The Chemical Brothers' "Setting Sun"?
24 What was Michael Jackson's last No 1 of the 20th century?
25 In which decade did Japan have their first Top Ten hit?
26 Who hit No 1 with "Deeper Underground" in 1999?
27 Chef's 1998 No 1 came from which cartoon series?
28 Who charted with "All Right Now" in the 1970s and with a 1990s remix?
29 "Vision of Love" was the first Top Ten hit for which singer?
30 In which decade did smooth soul group the Chi-Lites have most hits?

| **Answers** | **Past Times: 1950 on** *(see Quiz 142)* |

1 Kenneth Clarke. **2** Germany. **3** Malawi. **4** Cuba. **5** Palestine. **6** 1940. **7** Chile. **8** Jacques Chirac. **9** Ronald Reagan. **10** 1960s. **11** Barbara. **12** China. **13** Greenham Common. **14** Alexander Gromyko. **15** Salisbury. **16** Erich Honecker. **17** Westminster Abbey. **18** Karadzic. **19** Hampstead & Highgate. **20** Cambodia. **21** Alabama. **22** Charles Manson. **23** Warren. **24** Cricket. **25** Linda Tripp. **26** Humphrey. **27** Chris Evans. **28** Pigs. **29** Althorp. **30** Lisburn.

Quiz 141 | Pot Luck 64

Answers – page 381

1 Which Bollywood actress was at the centre of "Big Brother" controversy in 2007?
2 What name is given to the energy produced when something moves?
3 In movies, E.T. arrived in which city of California?
4 What can be Hurst Beagle or Kelvedon Wonder?
5 In legend which bird rose from its own ashes?
6 In "Mary Poppins" how much does it cost for a bag to "Feed the Birds"?
7 Which three initial letters stand for the speedy reactions of the organ of sight?
8 In a window a transom is a bar situated in which way?
9 What type of man was John Merrick known as?
10 Who became the first Egyptian leader to visit Israel?
11 Which Welsh rugby coach resigned for "family reasons" in 2006?
12 Which craft did Steve Zodiac command?
13 Keanu Reeves was born in which war-torn city?
14 What is the surname of Suggs, singer with Madness?
15 At which ground did Bill Shankly suffer his fatal heart attack?
16 Which Nancy was linked with Sid Vicious?
17 What was the nationality of spy Mata Hari?
18 What was Jacqueline Kennedy's surname before her marriage to the future US President?
19 Which rock musician prophetically said, "Once you're dead you're made for life"?
20 Which controversial footballer briefly was the husband of Sheryl Failes?
21 Which journalist was Bernstein's partner in investigating Watergate?
22 TV chat man Robert Kilroy-Silk was an MP for which party?
23 Which activity was Sonny Bono involved in at the time of his accidental death?
24 Bobby Fischer was the first American world champion in which sport?
25 What does O stand for in OJ Simpson's name?
26 Who produced a "Feel-Good Cookbook"?
27 How many of the Beatles were not known by their real names?
28 What final act did Hermann Goering do some hours before his execution?
29 How was Australian singer Helen Porter Mitchell better known?
30 Marilyn Monroe was born and died in which city?

Answers | Pot Luck 63 (see Quiz 139)

1 Memories. 2 I Am. 3 Real Madrid. 4 Bone. 5 1950s. 6 Apple. 7 Six. 8 Jeffrey Archer. 9 Dermot. 10 Ronald Reagan. 11 Eight. 12 Blackstock. 13 Fish. 14 900. 15 Greece. 16 Drop the Dead Donkey. 17 Sunderland. 18 Steve Irwin. 19 Marathon. 20 John Le Carre. 21 Il Divo. 22 Harvard. 23 David Tennant. 24 Thomas Turner. 25 Bay City Rollers. 26 Railway. 27 Thursday (third day). 28 Belgium. 29 Bryan Ferry. 30 South Africa.

1 Who was the other final contender for the Tory leadership contest in 1997 when William Hague won?
2 In which country were the Baader Meinhof gang based?
3 Hastings Banda became Prime Minister of which country in 1964?
4 The Bay of Pigs near which island was an area which triggered a missile crisis in 1961?
5 Black September were a terrorist group from which country?
6 In which year did the Battle of Britain begin?
7 Pinochet led a military coup in which country?
8 Who succeeded Mitterrand as President of France?
9 Milton Friedman was policy adviser to which US President in the 1980s?
10 In which decade did Colonel Gaddafi seize power in Libya?
11 What was the name of the first First Lady called Bush?
12 Where was there the "Great Leap Forward" in the 1950s?
13 Which site in Berkshire was the scene of anti-nuclear protests, mainly by women, in the 1980s?
14 Who was Soviet Foreign Minister for almost 30 years in the latter half of the 20th century?
15 What was the former name of Harare?
16 Who was East German leader from 1976 to 1989?
17 In which building was Princess Diana's funeral service held?
18 Who became Bosnian president in 1992?
19 In 1992 Glenda Jackson became MP for which constituency?
20 Where did the Khmer Rouge operate?
21 In which state did Martin Luther King lead the famous bus boycott?
22 Who led the sect which killed actress Sharon Tate?
23 Which Commission was set up to investigate the assassination of John F Kennedy?
24 Kerry Packer set up a rebel sports tour in which sport in the 1970s?
25 Who was Monica Lewinsky's confidante?
26 What was the name of the cat "evicted" from Downing Street as the Blairs moved in?
27 Who bought Virgin Radio from Richard Branson in 1997?
28 Who were the Tamworth Two?
29 Where was Princess Diana buried?
30 Near which town was the former Maze Prison sited?

Answers	**Music Charts** *(see Quiz 140)*

1 Inside Out. 2 Status Quo. 3 Faith Evans. 4 Fantasy. 5 Corinne Bailey Rae. 6 Eminem. 7 Children in Need. 8 Westlife. 9 Manic Street Preachers. 10 Eileen. 11 Last Christmas. 12 Groovejet. 13 Time to Say Goodbye. 14 Cranberries. 15 Casualty. 16 LeAnn Rimes. 17 The Fugees. 18 It's Raining Men. 19 Born to Make You Happy. 20 Crocodile Rock. 21 1998. 22 Hanson. 23 Noel Gallagher. 24 Blood on the Dance Floor. 25 1980s. 26 Jamiroquai. 27 South Park. 28 Free. 29 Mariah Carey. 30 1970s.

1 The true-life exploits of Harold Abrahams were told in which movie?
2 Who mysteriously vanished off the yacht Lady Ghislaine?
3 In which street did the infamous Rose and Frederick West live in Gloucester?
4 What is actor Michael Caine's real first name?
5 US President Andrew Jackson was nicknamed Old what?
6 In which country could you watch rugby at Ellis Park?
7 Which saint is on the Pope's signet ring?
8 What colour are the stars on the flag of the European Union?
9 Which country had a President with a spouse named Ladybird?
10 Japp Stam left Manchester United to go to which club?
11 Who won Super Bowl XL in 2006?
12 In which country was the scientist Gabriel Fahrenheit born?
13 Who directs and acts in "The Good Shepherd"?
14 What do Harvard Rules govern?
15 In mathematics, the abbreviation HCF stands for what?
16 How many seconds are there in a single round of championship boxing?
17 Whose songs were featured in the movie "Toy Story"?
18 Which actress, famous as a TV detective, was christened Ilynea Lydia Mironoff?
19 Which was the last host nation to have the Olympic Games opened by the country's king?
20 Which aspect of the weather is brontophobia the fear of?
21 Which of these games has the largest playing area – polo, soccer or tennis?
22 How many ribs has the human body?
23 "Grace and Favour" was a sequel to which sitcom?
24 Which England cricketer returned from India in February, and Australia in December 2006?
25 What nationality was mathematician Sir Isaac Newton?
26 What type of creature is equally at home on land and in water?
27 How many oxygen atoms are contained in a molecule of water?
28 PCs Stamp and Quinnan worked at which police station on TV?
29 What is the study of fluids moving in pipes known as?
30 Which band asked, "What's the Frequency Kenneth?"?

Answers | Pot Luck 66 *(see Quiz 145)*

1 Ag. **2** Taggart. **3** Human glands. **4** The sun. **5** The Calypso. **6** Curling. **7** Three. **8** Good Morning Vietnam. **9** Gerald Ford. **10** Nuremberg. **11** Phillip Pulman. **12** France. **13** Tom Cruise. **14** Weightlifting. **15** Vikings. **16** Gone with the Wind. **17** Battles. **18** Boer War. **19** Leicester. **20** Donald Maclean. **21** Time Team. **22** Archery. **23** M6. **24** A roof. **25** London Marathon. **26** Marion. **27** Piccadilly. **28** Robbie Coltrane (2000). **29** Decathlon. **30** July.

1 Which "Points of View" presenter wrote an autobiography called "Is It Me?"?

2 Which presenter appeared in the comedy "'Orrible"?

3 Who replaced Loyd Grossman as presenter of "Masterchef"?

4 Who presented "Before They were Famous"?

5 Who preceded Michael Aspel on "The Antiques Road Show"?

6 Which David Attenborough series of 2001 was about life in and under the sea?

7 Who presented and co-devised "Art Attack"?

8 Who moved from "Wheel of Fortune" to a daily show on Radio Five Live?

9 Who was the wine buff on "Food & Drink" when Antony Worrall Thompson and Emma Crowhurst became regular food experts?

10 What would Peter Cockcroft talk about on TV?

11 Who replaced Vanessa on ITV's morning chat show?

12 Which Irish presenter introduced "Animal Hospital" with Rolf Harris?

13 Which daytime show does Gloria Hunniford present regularly on Channel 5?

14 Which former "Mastermind" host died in January 2007?

15 In 2003, Vernon Kay married which TV presenter?

16 Alvin Hall presents programmes about looking after your what?

17 Who presented the reality programme "Space Cadets"?

18 Which ex-"Blue Peter" presenter introduced "The Big Breakfast"?

19 Which actress introduced a "Watercolour Challenge" on daytime TV?

20 Which business programme is presented by Adrian Chiles?

21 Who hosted "Fifteen to One"?

22 Who first presented "The National Lottery: Winning Lines"?

23 Who introduces the "Bloomers" series about BBC TV outtakes?

24 Who replaced the late Jill Dando on "Crimewatch"?

25 Which sport does John McCririck present?

26 Which ex-footballer tested the teams on "Friends Like These"?

27 Alphabetically, who comes first in "Countdown" presenters?

28 Who tested contestants on the comedy game show "Oblivious"?

29 Who replaced Paul Daniels on "Wipeout"?

30 Rachel De Thame offers advice on what?

---

1 What is the chemical symbol for silver?
2 Which TV cop show featured DCI Michael Jardine?
3 What are the islets of Langerhans?
4 What does a heliologist study?
5 What was the name of the research ship used by Jacques Cousteau?
6 USA beat Great Britain to a 2006 bronze medal in which Olympic team event?
7 How many pins are there in the front two rows in ten-pin bowling?
8 Which movie gave Robin Williams his first Oscar nomination?
9 Who became US President when Richard Nixon resigned?
10 In which city did trials of major Nazi leaders begin in 1945?
11 Which writer created the character Sally Lockhart?
12 In which country is Satolas international airport?
13 In the movies, who played war veteran Ron Kovic?
14 What are you doing if you carry out a snatch lift and a jerk lift?
15 In American Football which warriors come from Minnesota?
16 In which movie classic was Olivia de Havilland cast as Melanie Wilkes?
17 What do the Sealed Knot Society re-enact?
18 The Siege of Ladysmith took place during which war?
19 Brian Little and Martin O'Neill have both managed which soccer club?
20 Who fled together with Guy Burgess to the USSR in 1951?
21 Tony Robinson presented the long-running history programme "Time" what?
22 In which sport is there a gold-coloured target area worth 10 points?
23 Which motorway takes you south from Carlisle?
24 What is a cupola?
25 Which annual event began in London in 1981?
26 What was John Wayne's less than tough-sounding real first name?
27 Where in London was the first Fortnum & Mason opened?
28 Who was 50 first – Amanda Burton, Keith Chegwin or Robbie Coltrane?
29 In which event did Daley Thompson win Olympic gold?
30 In which month do the French celebrate Bastille Day?

| **Answers** | Pot Luck 65 *(see Quiz 143)* |

1 Chariots of Fire. 2 Robert Maxwell. 3 Cromwell Street. 4 Maurice. 5 Hickory. 6 South Africa. 7 St Peter. 8 Yellow. 9 USA. 10 Lazio. 11 Pittsburgh Steelers. 12 Germany. 13 Robert de Niro. 14 American football. 15 Highest common factor. 16 80. 17 Randy Newman. 18 Helen Mirren. 19 Spain. 20 Thunder. 21 Polo. 22 24. 23 Are You Being Served?. 24 Marcus Trescothick. 25 English. 26 Amphibian. 27 One. 28 Sun Hill. 29 Hydraulics. 30 R.E.M.

1 Baffin Island is between Baffin Bay and which island?
2 Bali is a mountainous island of which country?
3 The Falkland Islands are off which country?
4 Which US state is dubbed the Golden State?
5 Helsinki is on which Gulf?
6 Which city, also the name of a film, has the world's largest mosque?
7 How many islands make up Fiji?
8 Baku is the capital of which country on the Caspian Sea?
9 Where is the Forbidden City?
10 The Barbary Coast is the Mediterranean coast of where?
11 Which Egyptian city is Africa's largest city?
12 Greenwich Village is in which borough of New York City?
13 On which river is Ho Chi Minh City?
14 Where is Waikiki Beach?
15 Baghdad is on which river?
16 In which borough of New York City is Coney island?
17 In which mountains is the volcanic Cotopaxi?
18 Where are the Roaring Forties?
19 Which strait separates Australia from Tasmania?
20 What special sound is made in the language of the Hottentots of south-west Africa?
21 Which country was formerly the Dutch East Indies?
22 Which city gave its name to a type of riding breeches?
23 What is South Africa's largest city?
24 In which ocean are the Bahamas?
25 Which part of New York was named after Jonas Bronck?
26 The holy city of Qom is in which country?
27 Which country is between Nicaragua and Panama?
28 K2 is on the border of Pakistan and which country?
29 In which ocean are the Comoros?
30 Which is the most easterly of the Windward Islands in the Caribbean?

Answers | TV: Presenters *(see Quiz 144)*

1 Terry Wogan. 2 Johnny Vaughan. 3 Gary Rhodes. 4 Angus Deayton. 5 Hugh Scully.
6 The Blue Planet. 7 Neil Buchanan. 8 Nicky Campbell. 9 Oz Clarke. 10 Weather.
11 Trisha. 12 Shauna Lowry. 13 Open House. 14 Magnus Magnusson. 15 Tess
Daly. 16 Money. 17 Johnny Vaughan. 18 Richard Bacon. 19 Hannah Gordon. 20
Working Lunch. 21 William G Stewart. 22 Phillip Schofield. 23 Terry Wogan. 24 Fiona
Bruce. 25 Horse racing. 26 Ian Wright. 27 Des Lynam. 28 Davina McCall. 29 Bob
Monkhouse. 30 Gardening.

Quiz 147 | Pot Luck 67

1 In which country was Amanda Holden's "Wild at Heart" filmed?
2 Which country gave the Statue of Liberty to the USA?
3 Which word went with "Growing" in the title of Billie Piper's autobiography?
4 What was Mel Gibson's first movie where he was actor, director and producer?
5 In motor racing, what colours are on the flag at the end of a race?
6 Which series with Prunella Scales had three years on radio before transferring to TV?
7 Which racecourse is famous for its Royal Enclosure?
8 Where in the UK is the National Motor Museum?
9 What is the maximum number of pieces that can appear on a chessboard?
10 In Gershwin's song, if it's "Summertime," the living is what?
11 Whereabouts in London did Laura Ashley open her first shop?
12 In credit terms, what does A stand for in an APR?
13 What is the world's biggest-selling copyrighted game?
14 What do the Americans call hockey played outside?
15 In which country did karaoke singing originate?
16 What would be your hobby if you used slip?
17 Lennie Lawrence and Colin Todd have both managed which soccer club?
18 Which 1980s band included Cook, Heaton and Hemingway?
19 What was the first capital of the United States?
20 Which TV series has featured the Kings and the Tates?
21 Which Christian name was shared by former British PMs Winston Churchill and James Callaghan?
22 Who was the first Spice Girl to announce her engagement?
23 What is the name of Andy Murray's tennis-playing brother?
24 In which country could you watch Rennes playing Sedan at soccer?
25 What was the middle name of Ronnie Barker's character Norman Fletcher in TV's "Porridge"?
26 What did Jimmy Carter farm before becoming US President?
27 Coal is composed from which element?
28 What was the profession of Georges Auguste Escoffier?
29 President Mobutu fled in 1997 after more than 30 years in office in which country?
30 What year was the "New York Mining Disaster" according to the Bee Gees?

| **Answers** | **Pot Luck 68** *(see Quiz 149)* |

1 Big Bang. 2 Sonny Crockett. 3 Gina G. 4 Lesley Garrett. 5 0.54. 6 The eyes. 7 2004. 8 PE teacher. 9 Michelle Pfeiffer. 10 McLaren. 11 Princess Anne. 12 Beirut. 13 Barbara. 14 Paramount Pictures. 15 Sir Matt Busby. 16 Would I Lie to You? 17 Anatomy. 18 Michael Foot. 19 I. 20 The Bodyguard. 21 17th. 22 Variegated. 23 Holly. 24 Fairground. 25 Raisa. 26 Light years. 27 Devon. 28 Desmond Dekker. 29 Bull. 30 1894.

1 In addition to Leicestershire, which county did David Gower play for?
2 Who was the first cricketer to be awarded a knighthood while still playing Test cricket?
3 In which century was the MCC founded?
4 Which country was readmitted to the Test tour in 1992 along with South Africa?
5 On which ground did Brian Lara hit his record 501 not out?
6 Desmond Hayes earned 116 caps for which side?
7 In which decade did Allan Border make the first of his record-breaking 11,174 runs for Australia?
8 In which Gallery at Lord's are the Ashes kept?
9 What is another name for backward point?
10 What did the first C stand for in TCCB?
11 If an umpire raises his index finger in front of his body, or above his head, what does it mean?
12 Which late South African captain was suspended under suspicion of taking bribes?
13 Which country scored the highest single innings total in a Test, in 1997?
14 Which future cricket knight partnered Peter May to a partnership of 411 in 1957?
15 What was the AXA Life League called between 1969 and 1986?
16 Which Test cricketer has regularly captained a team on "They Think It's All Over"?
17 Against which county did Gary Sobers hit his amazing six sixes in an over?
18 Who topped England's batting averages in the 2006/7 Ashes series?
19 Test matches are the highest standard of what type of cricket?
20 How many Tests did Geoff Boycott play for England?
21 In 1986 which southern African-born player was the youngest to make 2,000 runs in a season?
22 Against which side did Ian Botham make his Test debut?
23 What was Graham Gooch's score on his very first Test match?
24 Which was the first English county side to sign Brian Lara?
25 Glenn McGrath played his final Test match in which city?
26 In the 2006/7 Ashes, which English batsman hit a double century?
27 How long are each of the two pieces of wood which make up the bails?
28 In which decade did Gary Sobers first play for the West Indies?
29 In which century did England play its first Test match?
30 Alphabetically, which is the first of the first-class English county sides?

Answers	Movies: 2000 (see Quiz 150)

1 Ewan McGregor. 2 Spielberg. 3 Penelope Cruz. 4 Helen Hunt. 5 Lara Croft. 6 Egg farm. 7 Ridley Scott. 8 Kathy Burke. 9 Meg Ryan. 10 Erin Brokovich. 11 Pierce Brosnan. 12 Penelope Cruz. 13 Julia Sawalha. 14 Swordfish. 15 Thailand. 16 Pistol. 17 Kate Beckinsale. 18 Cats. 19 Mike Myers. 20 Boxing. 21 Jon Voight. 22 Juliette Binoche. 23 Traffic. 24 Albert Finney. 25 Geoffrey Rush. 26 Jurassic Park III. 27 Nicolas Cage. 28 Gemma Jones. 29 Rachel Weisz. 30 Doctor.

1 Which explosive theory explains the formation of the universe?
2 Who did Don Johnson play in "Miami Vice"?
3 Who sang the British Eurovision Song Contest entry the year before Katrina and the Waves won?
4 Who played the Mother Abbess in the 2006 stage revival of "The Sound of Music"?
5 How would 27% doubled be shown as a decimal?
6 Where in the body are there rods and cones?
7 In which year was the 150th University Boat Race?
8 What was the profession of Zoe in the TV sitcom "May to December"?
9 Who was Oscar-nominated for "Dangerous Liaisons" and "The Fabulous Baker Boys"?
10 Which Malcolm was manager of the punk band The Sex Pistols?
11 Who was the first child of a reigning British monarch to be brought before a criminal court?
12 In which war-torn city was Terry Waite kidnapped?
13 In the White House who went after Nancy and came before Hillary?
14 Which movie company did Tom Cruise part company with in 2006?
15 Who was the first manager to win the European Champions Cup with an English club?
16 Which title links the Eurythmics to a Charles and Eddy No 1?
17 Which branch of biology deals with the structure of animals?
18 Who succeeded James Callaghan as leader of the Labour Party?
19 What is the chemical symbol for iodine?
20 Which film featured the song that gave Whitney Houston her fourth UK No 1?
21 In which century was Blaise Pascal working on his calculating machine?
22 What term describes a leaf with two or more colours?
23 Which species of trees and shrubs come from the genus Ilex?
24 What was Simply Red's first UK No 1?
25 What was Soviet leader Mikael Gorbachev's wife called?
26 Which years measure distance in space?
27 Which English county was part of the name of the horse that collapsed in sight of victory in the Grand National?
28 Dying in 2006, who had had his biggest hit with "Israelites"?
29 Which animal name was given to the wild Bronx boxer Jake La Motta?
30 When was Blackpool Tower built – 1834, 1894 or 1924?

| **Answers** | **Pot Luck 67** (see Quiz 147) |

1 South Africa. 2 France. 3 Pains. 4 Braveheart. 5 Black and white. 6 After Henry. 7 Ascot. 8 Beaulieu. 9 32. 10 Easy. 11 Kensington. 12 Annual. 13 Monopoly. 14 Field hockey. 15 Japan. 16 Pottery. 17 Middlesbrough. 18 Housemartins. 19 New York. 20 Emmerdale. 21 Leonard. 22 Victoria Adams. 23 Jamie. 24 France. 25 Stanley. 26 Peanuts. 27 Carbon. 28 Chef. 29 Zaire. 30 1941.

1 Who was Nicole Kidman's co-star in "Moulin Rouge"?

2 Who directed "AI: Artificial Intelligence"?

3 Who played opposite Nicolas Cage in "Captain Corelli's Mandolin"?

4 Who plays Darcy Maguire in "What Women Want", with Mel Gibson?

5 Who was the star of the computer-animated "Tomb Raider"?

6 What sort of farm features in "Chicken Run"?

7 Who directed "Gladiator"?

8 Who co-starred with Harry Enfield in "Kevin and Perry Go Large"?

9 Who became romantically linked with Russell Crowe during the making of "Proof of Life"?

10 For which movie did Julia Roberts win her first Oscar?

11 Who played the title role in Richard Attenborough's "Grey Owl"?

12 Who plays Johnny Depp's wife in "Blow"?

13 Which "Absolutely Fabulous" star was the voice of Ginger in "Chicken Run"?

14 Which movie starred Hugh Jackman as a computer hacker and John Travolta as a counter-terrorist?

15 In which country was "The Beach" filmed?

16 In "The Mexican", what is the Mexican?

17 Who is the female corner of the love triangle in "Pearl Harbor"?

18 In "Meet the Parents" which animals is Robert De Niro particularly fond of?

19 Who was the voice of Shrek?

20 Which classes should Billy Elliot be going to when he is doing ballet?

21 Who played Lara Croft's father in the "Tomb Raider" film and in real life too?

22 Who plays the single mum in "Chocolat"?

23 Which new millennium movie on the drugs trade starred Michael Douglas?

24 Which English actor played the lawyer in "Erin Brokovich"?

25 Who plays the Marquis de Sade in "Quills"?

26 What was the sequel to "The Lost World" in the "Jurassic Park" films?

27 Who is the star of "The Family Man", a remake of "It's a Wonderful Life"?

28 Who played Bridget's mum in "Bridget Jones's Diary"?

29 Which actress is the object of Jude Law's and Joseph Fiennes' affections in "Enemy at the Gates"?

30 What is John Hurt's profession in "Captain Corelli's Mandolin"?

Answers	Cricket *(see Quiz 148)*

1 Hampshire. 2 Richard Hadlee. 3 18th. 4 Zimbabwe. 5 Edgbaston. 6 West Indies. 7 1970s. 8 Memorial Gallery. 9 Gully. 10 County. 11 The batsman is out. 12 Hansie Cronje. 13 Sri Lanka. 14 Colin Cowdrey. 15 John Player Sunday League. 16 David Gower. 17 Glamorgan. 18 Kevin Pietersen. 19 First class. 20 108. 21 Graeme Hick. 22 Australia. 23 Duck. 24 Warwickshire. 25 Sydney. 26 Paul Collingwood. 27 Just under 5 inches. 28 1950s. 29 19th. 30 Derbyshire.

1 Which character in "The Bill" was played by the late Kevin Lloyd?
2 Which branch of physics deals with motion of objects?
3 Which comedian – voted "wittiest living person" – died in 2006 at the age of 48?
4 Who did Nicole Kidman marry in 2006?
5 Eton school is in which English county?
6 In sport, what word can go after Trent and Stamford?
7 How is Mary O'Brien who died in March 1999 better known?
8 In which country is Malpensa international airport?
9 Which great Test cricketer's forename initials are the same as the abbreviation for Information Technology?
10 What does fibrian cause the blood to do?
11 Which late great duetted with kd lang on his mega-hit "Crying"?
12 How would four-fifths be shown as a decimal?
13 Which sport did Marco Van Basten play?
14 Whose life story was re-created in the biopic "Sweet Dreams"?
15 Which country celebrated its bicentenary in 1988?
16 How many stomachs does a cow have?
17 Which country has the car registration code T?
18 Cu is the chemical symbol for which element?
19 Which country was first to host both the Summer and Winter Olympics in the same year?
20 What was the first name of Stephen Tomkinson's character in "Drop the Dead Donkey"?
21 The late Brian Connolly fronted which glam band?
22 What is the name of the cat in "Sabrina the Teenage Witch"?
23 Pop star Billie married in May 2001 in which US city?
24 Who was the body-snatching partner of Hare?
25 Which entertainer said, "George, don't do that"?
26 Which murder victim was mentioned in the trailers for "Twin Peaks"?
27 In which country would you watch Grasshoppers play a home soccer match?
28 Which soccer club has Worcester Avenue and Paxton Road close to the stadium?
29 Which pop superstar's first wife was Cynthia Powell?
30 Patrick Troughton followed William Hartnell to play which character in a long-running TV series?

Answers	Animals (see Quiz 153)

1 Monkey. 2 Australia. 3 Chick. 4 Marsupial. 5 Umbilical. 6 India. 7 Dodo. 8 African elephant. 9 Cat. 10 Herbivorous. 11 Squirrel. 12 Trees. 13 40%. 14 Smell. 15 Chimpanzee. 16 Alone. 17 Borneo. 18 Reptiles. 19 Hood. 20 Clawed. 21 Border collie. 22 Tapeworm. 23 Whale. 24 Indian cobra. 25 Spawn. 26 Hare. 27 Starfish. 28 Thumb. 29 Cobra. 30 Grizzly bear.

1 What was on the other side of Boney M's "Brown Girl in the Ring"?
2 Which Dawn single was in the charts for 39 weeks in the 1970s?
3 Which film did "You're the One that I Want" come from?
4 Which 1970s hit by Wings was the first UK single to sell two million copies?
5 Who made the album "Don't Shoot Me I'm Only the Piano Player"?
6 Which solo singer who died in 2001 recorded the album "And I Love You So"?
7 Whom did Elton John have a No 1 single with in 1976?
8 Julie Covington had a UK No 1 with a song from which Andrew Lloyd Webber/Tim Rice musical?
9 Who was the most successful solo star from the group which had a No 1 with "Message in a Bottle"?
10 "Matchstalk Men and Matchstalk Cats and Dogs" was about which artist?
11 With which song did Brotherhood of Man win the Eurovision Song Contest?
12 Who had the original hit with "Seasons in the Sun"?
13 Who had "Breakfast In America"?
14 How many times is Annie's name mentioned in John Denver's "Annie's Song"?
15 Who was the first Beatle to have a solo No 1 in the 1970s?
16 Which member of the cast of "Dad's Army" had a No 1 hit record?
17 Who hit No 1 with "Cum on Feel the Noize"?
18 Who declared that he was the Leader of the Gang?
19 Which star of the stage show "Evita" had a hit with "Hold Me Close"?
20 What was the title of the England World Cup squad's anthem of 1970?
21 On which new record label was Mike Oldfield's "Tubular Bells" released?
22 Which Tony featured on Dawn's "Tie a Yellow Ribbon"?
23 Which instrument did Suzi Quatro play on "Can the Can"?
24 Who had a hit with Nilsson's "Without You" 20 years later?
25 Which band made the super selling "Rumours"?
26 Which band did Roy Wood lead in "Angel Fingers"?
27 Whose "Sailing" was describes by its performer as "one for the terraces"?
28 Which band's very first hit was "Debora"?
29 "I'd Like to Teach the World to Sing" was later used to advertised which drink?
30 Who recorded the album "Arrival"?

Answers | **Pot Luck 70 (see Quiz 154)**

1 Leona Lewis. 2 1896. 3 God. 4 Ballykissangel. 5 Aubretia. 6 16. 7 Nile. 8 Francis Ford Coppola. 9 At a walking pace. 10 Nesta. 11 Hooves. 12 Meridiem. 13 Portugal. 14 16th. 15 Wren. 16 Hedgehunter. 17 1960s. 18 Mr Men. 19 Codes. 20 St Denis. 21 Iron. 22 Swedish. 23 Alan Shearer. 24 Grizabella. 25 1920s. 26 Canada. 27 Busy Lizzy. 28 Violet Wilson. 29 The Three Degrees. 30 Rhubarb.

1 What type of creature is a mandrill?
2 The bandicoot is a marsupial from which country?
3 What is a young penguin called?
4 What sort of creature is a Tasmanian devil?
5 Which cord connects the placenta to the embryo in mammals?
6 Which country has the most Asian elephants in their natural habitat?
7 Which extinct flightless bird has the Latin name Didus ineptus?
8 Which weighs the most – African elephant, hippopotamus or white rhinoceros?
9 What can be Persian long hair, British short hair or Oriental short hair?
10 Which word would describe a wombat's diet?
11 The chipmunk is related to which creature?
12 Where do sloths live?
13 What percentage of all living mammals are rodents?
14 Which of the primates' senses is the weakest?
15 Which is the most intelligent – baboon, chimpanzee or gorilla?
16 How does a tiger hunt?
17 The orang utan in the wild is restricted to Sumatra and where?
18 Who has the most teeth, reptiles, fish or mammals?
19 What is the neck region of the cobra called?
20 What sort of feet do tortoises have?
21 Which is the most intelligent breed of dog?
22 Which of the following animals has the greatest length or height – African elephant, giraffe or tapeworm?
23 What can be minke, grey or bowhead?
24 Which snake is traditionally used by snake charmers?
25 What are the fertilised eggs of amphibians called?
26 Which is the fastest – hare, horse or greyhound?
27 Which fish are members of the class Asteroidea?
28 Which is the only "finger" of a bat that is free from the membrane that forms its wing?
29 Which deadly snakes can be Egyptian, Indian or Forest?
30 Which is the heaviest – black bear, grizzly bear or polar bear?

Answers | **Pot Luck 69** *(see Quiz 151)*

1 "Tosh" Lines. 2 Mechanics. 3 Linda Smith. 4 Keith Urban. 5 Berkshire. 6 Bridge. 7 Dusty Springfield. 8 Italy. 9 Botham. 10 Clot. 11 Roy Orbison. 12 0.80. 13 Soccer. 14 Patsy Cline. 15 Australia. 16 Four. 17 Thailand. 18 Copper. 19 France. 20 Damien. 21 Sweet. 22 Salem. 23 Las Vegas. 24 Burke. 25 Joyce Grenfell. 26 Laura Palmer. 27 Switzerland. 28 Spurs. 29 John Lennon. 30 Dr Who.

1 Who was the first female winner of "The X Factor"?
2 When were the first Modern Olympic Games held?
3 What are you afraid of if you suffer from theophobia?
4 Father Peter Clifford appeared in which TV series?
5 Which plant was named after Claude Aubriet?
6 How many pawns start off a chess game?
7 The Aswan Dam was built on which river?
8 Who directed all "The Godfather" series of movies?
9 What does the musical term andante mean?
10 What was Bob Marley's middle name?
11 What does an ungulate animal have?
12 What does the letter m in the time abbreviation p.m. stand for?
13 The Azores belong to which country?
14 In which century was William Shakespeare born?
15 Which bird was on the old coin the farthing?
16 Which 2005 Grand National winner started as favourite for the 2006?
17 In which decade did the Victoria line open on the London Underground?
18 Roger Hargreaves created which Men – "The Flowerpot Men", "The Four Just Men" or "Mr Men"?
19 Cryptography is the study of what?
20 Who is the patron saint of France?
21 What do ferrous metals contain?
22 What nationality was chemist Alfred Nobel?
23 Who was the was the first player to score 100 goals in the Premier League?
24 In the musical "Cats" which cat sings "Memory"?
25 In which decade was the first FA Cup Final played at Wembley?
26 As well as being an animal, the Red Deer is a river in which country?
27 How is the plant Impatiens more usually known?
28 She didn't play a Platt, but which character did actress Jenny Platt play in "Corrie"?
29 How were Ferguson, Thompson and Pickney known collectively?
30 Hawk's Champagne and Prince Albert are types of what?

Answers | **Sounds of the 70s (see Quiz 152)**

1 Rivers of Babylon. 2 Tie a Yellow Ribbon. 3 Grease. 4 Mull of Kintyre. 5 Elton John. 6 Perry Como. 7 Kiki Dee. 8 Evita. 9 Sting. 10 LS Lowry. 11 Save Your Kisses for Me. 12 Terry Jacks. 13 Supertramp. 14 Never. 15 George Harrison. 16 Clive Dunn. 17 Slade. 18 Gary Glitter. 19 David Essex. 20 Back Home. 21 Virgin. 22 Orlando. 23 Bass guitar. 24 Mariah Carey. 25 Fleetwood Mac. 26 Wizzard. 27 Rod Stewart. 28 T. Rex. 29 Coca Cola. 30 Abba.

1 Who defeated Silvio Berlusconi in the 2006 Italian elections?
2 Which country won the 2006 Eurovision Song Contest?
3 Bakelite was the first important what?
4 In which decade did John Logie Baird first demonstrate television?
5 Bangladesh was created from which former territory?
6 Which political leader had a villa retreat at Berchtesgaden?
7 Which Prime Minister suffered the "winter of discontent"?
8 Bill Clinton appointed his wife Hillary to carry out reforms in which social service?
9 What was the Democratic Republic of Congo called between 1971 and 1997?
10 Who did George W Bush defeat to become President in 2000?
11 Inkatha was set up to promote the interests of which South African race?
12 What does the M stand for in IMF?
13 Where in London was a memorial service held three days after the New York and Washington terrorist attacks of September 2001?
14 What does A stand for in IRA?
15 Which Israeli leader was assassinated in 1995?
16 Silvio Berlusconi became which country's Prime Minister in 1994?
17 Who was the first British writer to receive the Nobel Prize for Literature?
18 Who headed the US committee investigating Communist infiltration in public life?
19 Which country has a news agency called TASS?
20 What did Joseph Pulitzer give a Prize for?
21 Who wrote "An Inconvenient Truth" about his concerns about the environment?
22 Which Moors were the scene of the so-called Moors Murders?
23 Where did the Earl and Countess of Wessex marry?
24 Where was the rail crash which caused long delays from 2000 to 2001?
25 In 2001 which country had three kings in as many days when many royals were machine gunned to death?
26 In June 2006 which Oxford college admitted male students for the first time in 113 years?
27 Which Bush family member was Governor of Florida in 2001?
28 Which journalist Diamond, husband of Nigella Lawson, lost his cancer battle in 2001?
29 Peter Mandelson's first Cabinet post was as Secretary for what?
30 What replaced the torch as the Tory party's symbol under David Cameron?

Answers	**Families** *(see Quiz 157)*

1 Phil Vickery. 2 Mary. 3 George Bush. 4 Siamese twins. 5 Les Dennis. 6 Angie. 7 Rosie. 8 Stella. 9 The Archers. 10 Nigel. 11 Emilia Fox. 12 Philip. 13 Jonathan. 14 Jennifer Saunders. 15 Janet Ellis. 16 David Frost. 17 Hardie. 18 Libby Purves. 19 Wendy Turner. 20 Bobby Brown. 21 Fifi Trixibelle. 22 Joe. 23 Jane. 24 Emma Noble. 25 Zoe Ball. 26 Sarah. 27 Dylan. 28 Kent. 29 Arthur Miller. 30 Mel B.

1 What is petrology the study of?
2 In which decade was the record-breaking "Guinness Book of Records" first published?
3 What number of "Doctor Who" was Tom Baker?
4 Which country did Nana Mouskouri come from?
5 Which former England soccer boss passed away at his Suffolk home in February 2006?
6 Quindeca is a prefix indicating which number?
7 What is the chemical symbol for lead?
8 Which garden fruit has poisonous leaves and edible stems?
9 In the song from "The Music Man", 76 of what type of instrument led the big parade?
10 Which lady's Vineyard is an island off Cape Cod?
11 Who was 50 first – Princess Caroline of Monaco, Adrian Edmondson or Rowan Atkinson?
12 What is the scientific study of inheritance called?
13 Which country did the composer Chopin come from?
14 Which reggae artist starred in the film "The Harder They Come"?
15 What percentage is an eighth?
16 According to the words of a Noel Coward song, who "goes out in the midday sun" with "Mad dogs"?
17 In which London Square is the US Embassy?
18 The movie "Saving Private Ryan" dealt with events in which country?
19 In the 1960s, what was the name of Wayne Fontana's backing group?
20 Photosynthesis is the process by which plants use light to make what?
21 The site of ancient Babylon is today in which country?
22 What was the profession of Anna Politkovskaya, who was shot dead in 2006?
23 Who was the first English rugby union player to play in 50 internationals?
24 Which glands produce white blood cells?
25 Juliette Binoche and Kristin Scott Thomas first co-starred in which movie?
26 Which Derbyshire town is famous for its church with a crooked spire?
27 Which Bells helped launch the Virgin label?
28 The Parthenon in Athens was built as a temple to which goddess?
29 Which daytime show brought Noel Edmonds back into the public eye in 2006?
30 The movie "The Last King of Scotland" is a fictionalised story of which dictator?

Answers	TV: Classics *(see Quiz 158)*

1 Vince & Penny. 2 Anthony Andrews. 3 Derek. 4 Jane Marple. 5 Thora Hird. 6 Fforbes Hamilton. 7 Jim Bergerac. 8 South Africa. 9 Come Dancing. 10 Stripes. 11 1950s. 12 Liz. 13 Queen's coronation. 14 Music Hall. 15 Panorama. 16 Robin Hood. 17 Early evening. 18 Hughie Green. 19 Percy Thrower. 20 Keys. 21 The Lone Ranger. 22 Alan Whicker. 23 25. 24 Michael Bentine. 25 77. 26 Eric Morecambe. 27 The Rag Trade. 28 Finlay. 29 Roger Moore. 30 Alma.

Quiz 157 Families

Answers – page 397

1 Which TV chef did Fern Britton marry?
2 What is the first name of Mrs Michael Parkinson?
3 Which US president married Barbara Pierce?
4 Chang and Eng Bunker were famous as what type of siblings?
5 Which TV presenter did Amanda Holden marry?
6 What is the first name of the former Mrs George Best who wrote "George & Me"?
7 What is Lorraine Kelly's young daughter called?
8 Which McCartney became 30 in 2001?
9 On which radio show is Jasper Carrott's daughter a regular voice?
10 Which actor is "This Life"'s Jack Davenport's father?
11 Which actress, who starred in the revival of "Randall & Hopkirk (Deceased)", is the daughter of Joanna David?
12 Which Prince is the grandson of Prince Louis of Battenberg?
13 Which Dimbleby married writer Bel Mooney?
14 Which comedy actress is Mrs Adrian Edmondson?
15 Which former "Blue Peter" presenter is the mother of chart-topping Sophie?
16 Which TV presenter is married to the daughter of the 17th Duke of Norfolk?
17 Which actress Kate is the daughter of Goodie Bill Oddie?
18 Which radio presenter is Mrs Paul Heiney?
19 Which TV presenter with a TV presenter sister married "Minder" actor Gary Webster?
20 Which R & B star married Whitney Houston in 1992?
21 Who is Peaches Geldof's oldest sister?
22 Who is the oldest of the acting McGann brothers?
23 What is Lord Paddy Ashdown's wife called?
24 Which actress/model did ex PM's son James Major marry?
25 Who is Woody Cook's mum?
26 What were Andrew Lloyd Webber's first two wives called?
27 What is the name of the son of Catherine Zeta Jones and Michael Douglas?
28 Lady Helen Taylor is the daughter of which Duchess?
29 Which playwright is Daniel Day Lewis's father-in-law?
30 Which Spice Girl had a daughter called Phoenix Chi?

Answers | **Newsworthy (see Quiz 155)**

1 Romano Prodi. 2 Finland. 3 Plastic. 4 1920s. 5 East Pakistan. 6 Adolf Hitler. 7 James Callaghan. 8 Health. 9 Zaire. 10 Al Gore. 11 Zulus. 12 Monetary. 13 St Paul's. 14 Army. 15 Yitzhak Rabin. 16 Italy. 17 Rudyard Kipling. 18 Senator Joseph McCarthy. 19 Russia. 20 Literature/journalism. 21 Al Gore. 22 Saddleworth. 23 St George's Chapel Windsor. 24 Hatfield. 25 Nepal. 26 St Hilda's. 27 Jeb. 28 John. 29 Trade and Industry. 30 Oak tree.

Quiz 158 TV: Classics

1 Who were "Just Good Friends"?
2 Who shot to stardom with Jeremy Irons in "Brideshead Revisited"?
3 Which "Coronation Street" character died in his car after a road rage attack?
4 Which detective did Joan Hickson play on TV?
5 Which veteran actress presented "Praise Be!" for many years?
6 What was the surname of Audrey in "To the Manor Born"?
7 Which detective did John Nettles play before becoming involved in "The Midsomer Murders"?
8 Where did Kathy leave for when she first left "EastEnders"?
9 Which dance show's presenters have included Terry Wogan, Angela Rippon and Rosemarie Ford?
10 What was the pattern on Andy Pandy's suit?
11 In which decade was TV panel game "What's My Line?" first shown?
12 What was Beverley Callard's character called in "Coronation Street"?
13 For which event were TV cameras first installed in Westminster Abbey?
14 What was the supposed setting for "The Good Old Days"?
15 Which long-running current affairs programme began in 1953?
16 Which legendary hero played by Richard Greene achieved great success on both sides of the Atlantic?
17 At what time of day was "Crackerjack" broadcast?
18 Who hosted "Double Your Money" throughout its 13-year run?
19 Which famous TV gardener started "Gardening Club"?
20 On "Take Your Pick" what did contestants have to win to open boxes?
21 Which children's show had a masked hero seeking justice in America's wild west?
22 Which travelling journalist with trademark glasses and moustache was famous for presenting his "World"?
23 "All Our Yesterdays" showed film footage of events how many years previously?
24 Which member of "The Goons" presented the zany "It's a Square World"?
25 What number preceded "Sunset Strip" in the US private eye series?
26 Whose catchphrases included "You can't see the join," and "Get out of that!"?
27 Which sitcom was set in Fenners Fashions?
28 Which Dr opened his "Casebook" between 1962 and 1971?
29 Which James Bond played the Saint?
30 In "Coronation Street", who was Mike Baldwin's wife immediately before Linda?

Answers | Pot Luck 71 (see Quiz 156)

1 Rocks. 2 1960s. 3 Fourth. 4 Greece. 5 Ron Greenwood. 6 15. 7 Pb. 8 Rhubarb.
9 76 Trombones. 10 Martha's. 11 Rowan Atkinson (2005). 12 Genetics. 13 Poland.
14 Jimmy Cliff. 15 12.5%. 16 Englishmen. 17 Grosvenor. 18 France. 19 The
Mindbenders. 20 Food. 21 Iraq. 22 Journalist. 23 Rory Underwood. 24 Lymph. 25
The English Patient. 26 Chesterfield. 27 Tubular Bells. 28 Athena. 29 Deal or No Deal.
30 Idi Amin.

1 Which worker gave Ken Barrie a hit – Bob the Builder, Postman Pat or the Singing Postman?
2 Who was the President of Argentina during the Falklands conflict?
3 What is the main island of Japan?
4 Saxifrage is a type of what?
5 On the radio, what is the name of the church in "The Archers"?
6 Which animal was used by Jenner when developing a vaccine against smallpox?
7 The song "I Feel Pretty" comes from which musical?
8 A snake's cast-off skin is known as a what?
9 Where is Britain's National Horseracing Museum?
10 Which group thought it was fun to stay at the "YMCA"?
11 What city is the largest in Nevada?
12 Which club did Robert Pires join when he left Arsenal?
13 Whose albums include "Nothing's Gonna Change My World" and "All for a Song"?
14 Which member of Gianni Versace's family took over his fashion empire after his death?
15 In 1998, who married millionaire hairdresser Stephen Way?
16 Which Brothers were Scott, John and Gary?
17 Where did Peter and Annie Mayle spend a year?
18 If New Year's day was a Thursday what day would Valentine's Day be?
19 Who was first to a first Best Actor Oscar – Nicolas Cage or Kevin Spacey?
20 Ruby is linked to which wedding anniversary?
21 In the traditional song, which herb goes with parsley, rosemary and thyme?
22 Who composed the opera "Norma"?
23 Who was the first member of the Royal Family to be interviewed on British TV?
24 A Blue Orpington is a type of what?
25 Which spirit forms the basis for Pimm's No 1?
26 Who left England as fast-bowling coach in 2006 to go to Australia?
27 Which Prime Minister had a wife who wrote a biography of Joan Sutherland?
28 Which store owner first said, "The customer is always right"?
29 Which group had hits with "The Logical Song" and "Dreamer"?
30 The Sargasso Sea forms part of which ocean?

Answers | Pot Luck 73 *(see Quiz 161)*

1 A. 2 Ear. 3 School. 4 Nut. 5 Trombone. 6 Mrs Beeton. 7 Nervous system. 8 Their feet. 9 Forest Whitaker. 10 Lynda LaPlante. 11 Foxglove. 12 Fiddler on the Roof. 13 Miss Marple. 14 Michel Platini. 15 Common. 16 Rugby. 17 None. 18 Helium. 19 Cawley. 20 The Supremes. 21 Friday. 22 Iraq. 23 Left-handed. 24 Bad breath. 25 Starsky & Hutch. 26 Ice hockey. 27 Eclipse. 28 The Grateful Dead. 29 Football (Shrewsbury Town). 30 Shape.

1 If bread is left to "prove" what does it do?
2 Which initials indicate the highest-quality brandy – AC, RSVP or VSOP?
3 What is a chanterelle?
4 What is aioli flavoured with?
5 What type of sauce was named after the Marquis de Bechamel?
6 What would you be eating if you were served calamari?
7 Enchiladas were originally part of which country's cooking?
8 What shape is the pasta called fusilli?
9 Mozzarella was originally made from which type of milk?
10 Which herb is usually used in gremolata?
11 Which pulses are used to make hummus?
12 Other than tomatoes and onions which is the main vegetable used in moussaka?
13 In which country is the famous wine-growing area of the Barossa valley?
14 Chianti comes from which area of Italy?
15 If a dish is cooked en papillote what is it cooked in?
16 Passata is pureed what?
17 A brochette is another word for what?
18 What is prosciutto?
19 What flavour do ratafia biscuits have?
20 What makes a salsa verde green – celery leaves, herbs or spinach?
21 Schnapps is distilled from what?
22 What type of white wine is Barsac famous for?
23 What type of oven is traditionally used for a tandoori?
24 Which Japanese dish is made from rice, seaweed and raw fish?
25 Which herb is usually used in a pesto sauce?
26 What type of dough is calzone made from?
27 What is a bisque?
28 When would antipasto be served?
29 What does baking powder produce when water is added, which makes dough rise?
30 How is something cooked if it is sauté?

1 What is the next white note on a keyboard above G?
2 What is examined with an otoscope?
3 Where does the main action of the TV series "Waterloo Road" take place?
4 What type of food is a macadamia?
5 What was Glenn Miller's main instrument?
6 Isabella Mary Mayson became better known as which cook?
7 Which of our body systems controls sight, hearing and touch?
8 For many years the title sequence of "The Bill" featured which part of the police officer's bodies?
9 Who played Idi Amin in the movie "The Last King of Scotland"?
10 Which writer created TV's Jane Tennison?
11 Which plant produce the drug digitalis?
12 "Sunrise, Sunset" comes from which musical?
13 Who was the sleuth in "The Body in the Library"?
14 Which Frenchman was voted European Footballer of the Year three times in a row?
15 L stands for lowest, M stands for multiple, but what does the C stand for in LCM?
16 What are you watching if William Webb Ellis is credited with founding it?
17 How many sides of a scalene triangle are equal?
18 Which element has the atomic number 2?
19 In tennis Miss Goolagong became which Mrs?
20 The late Florence Ballard was a member of which group?
21 The Norse goddess of love gives her name to which day of the week?
22 In which country was British engineer Kenneth Bigley murdered in 2004?
23 Is golfer Phil Mickelson left-handed or right-handed?
24 What do you suffer from if you have halitosis?
25 Dave & Ken were the first names of which TV duo?
26 The American Buffalo Sabres play which sport?
27 What describes the Earth or moon entering the other's shadow?
28 The late Jerry Garcia was the main guitarist with which band?
29 What sport are you watching if you are at Gay Meadow?
30 What changes when something is metamorphosised?

| **Answers** | **Pot Luck 72** *(see Quiz 159)* |

1 Postman Pat. 2 Galtieri. 3 Hokkaido. 4 Rock plant. 5 St Stephen's. 6 Cow. 7 West Side Story. 8 Slough. 9 Newmarket. 10 Village People. 11 Las Vegas. 12 Villareal. 13 Barbara Dickson. 14 His sister. 15 Gloria Hunniford. 16 The Walker Brothers. 17 Provence. 18 Saturday. 19 Nicolas Cage. 20 Fortieth. 21 Sage. 22 Bellini. 23 Prince Philip. 24 Fowl. 25 Gin. 26 Troy Cooley. 27 Major. 28 Selfridge. 29 Supertramp. 30 Atlantic.

Quiz 162 | Motor Sports

Answers – page 402

1 In which country did Jenson Button have his first Formula One victory?
2 How long is Indianapolis's most famous race?
3 What does the A stand for in FIA?
4 Which European was the second youngest World Champion of all time in 1994?
5 At the beginning of the new millennium which country had the most Grand Prix wins?
6 How many times was a Finn F1 World Champion in the 1990s?
7 Which Grand Prix was held at the Nurburgring in 1998?
8 Who was the head of F1 at the end of the 20th century?
9 How old was James Hunt when he became World Champion – 24, 29 or 33?
10 Where did Damon Hill drive his first F1 race?
11 In which month does the Isle of Man TT race traditionally take place?
12 Whom did Damon Hill race for when he became World Champion in 1996?
13 In which decade was Barry Sheene world 500cc champion twice?
14 During which Grand Prix did Ayrton Senna meet his death?
15 Which race is run on the Circuit de la Sarthe?
16 Which was Mika Hakkinen's team when he announced in 2001 he was going to take a year out of racing?
17 Which motor sport has the governing body the AMA?
18 Kevin Schwartz from which country was a 1991 World Champion on a Suzuki?
19 Which French constructor raced with Williams and Benetton in the 1990s?
20 How many times did Stirling Moss win the World Championship?
21 How many times was Graham Hill World Champion in the 1960s?
22 Which country was Nelson Piquet from?
23 Which driver was the highest-earning sportsman of 1999?
24 What is the first rally of the World Rally Championship?
25 Where is the Francorchamps circuit?
26 In which month does the Indianapolis 500 take place?
27 Which Grand Prix is held at Imola?
28 How many times was a Briton F1 World Champion in the 1990s?
29 In February 2006 it was announced that what would happen to the year's Belgian Grand Prix?
30 Where is the Suzuka circuit?

Answers	Leisure: Food & Drink 3 (see Quiz 160)

1 Rise. 2 VSOP. 3 Mushroom. 4 Garlic. 5 White sauce. 6 Squid. 7 Mexico. 8 Spirals. 9 Buffalo's. 10 Parsley. 11 Chick peas. 12 Aubergine. 13 Australia. 14 Tuscany. 15 Paper. 16 Tomatoes. 17 Kebab. 18 Ham. 19 Almond. 20 Herbs. 21 Potatoes. 22 Sweet. 23 Clay. 24 Sushi. 25 Basil. 26 Pizza. 27 Soup. 28 Before a meal. 29 Carbon dioxide. 30 Fried.

1 What was Radiohead's first top ten single?
2 In America the Stanley Cup is awarded in which sport?
3 There are 6,080 feet in what?
4 Andy Murray parted company from which coach in April 2006?
5 On radio, what did the A stand for in the programme known as ITMA?
6 In snooker how many reds are there on a table when one-third of them have been potted?
7 Which musical instrument did the late Karen Carpenter play?
8 There are 78 cards in what type of pack?
9 Actor Phil Daniels – who plays Kevin Wicks – is a big fan of which Premiership side?
10 How many edges does a cube have?
11 What was the setting for the TV series "Within These Walls"?
12 On a relief map, which lines connect points of the same height?
13 Gossima was a game that developed into which sport?
14 What green-coloured item goes to the winner of the US Masters?
15 What is family name of the main characters in "Sabrina the Teenage Witch"?
16 What type of word reads the same backwards as forwards?
17 Which American gave her name to an item of underwear?
18 Richard Beckinsale played Godber in which classic sitcom?
19 The final of the US Tennis Open is played at which Meadow?
20 David Beckham scored his final goal for Sven's England against which side?
21 How many letters in our alphabet can be written with one straight line?
22 In which decade were satellite pictures first sent across the Atlantic?
23 In 2005 a European space probe landed on Titan – a moon of which planet?
24 On which island was the TV detective series "Bergerac" set?
25 Which is the biggest planet in our Solar System?
26 Whose leaving Genesis led to Phil Collins becoming the main man for vocals?
27 What type of TV programme was broadcast from Barnsdale?
28 Helvetia features on stamps that come from which country?
29 Which Bob first presented "Blockbusters"?
30 In which decade was Amnesty International established?

---

1 How many times in the 20th century did Sean Connery play James Bond?
2 Who played hero Fletcher Reede in "Liar Liar"?
3 Bruno Ganz played Hitler in which 2005 film?
4 Who played the queen to Sid James' King Henry in "Carry On Henry"?
5 In the movie "M*A*S*H" who played the role Alan Alda played on TV?
6 Which Hollywood superstar was the subject of "Mommie Dearest"?
7 In which movie did Tom Hanks play Chuck Noland?
8 Who played Morticia to Raul Julia's Gomez in "The Addams Family"?
9 In what type of place is "The Green Mile" set?
10 Which Tom Cruise movie had the line, "Show me the money!"?
11 Who is Julia Roberts' love rival in "My Best Friend's Wedding"?
12 Jake Gyllenhaal and Jamie Foxx starred in which Gulf War film?
13 Which star of "Singin' in the Rain" appeared with Judy Garland in "Me & My Gal"?
14 Which star of "The Perfect Storm" also starred in "The Thin Red Line"?
15 Which Bridges was "The Big Lebowski"?
16 Who played Estella in the New York-based 1990s version of "Great Expectations"?
17 Which King was played by Leonardo DiCaprio in "The Man in the Iron Mask"?
18 Who plays Annie MacLean in "The Horse Whisperer" with Robert Redford?
19 Who played space hero Harry Stamper in "Armageddon"?
20 Who played Sidney in "Scream" and "Scream 2"?
21 Who plays Gaz in "The Full Monty"?
22 What is Tom Cruise's job in "Mission: Impossible"?
23 Which Redgrave played the astrologer in the life of David Helfgott in "Shine"?
24 Who played airline pilot Steven Hiller in "Independence Day"?
25 Who was the fourth 007?
26 Which historical figure was "Braveheart"?
27 What is the profession of the hero in "The Client", based on John Grisham's novel?
28 What was the name of Andie McDowell's character in "Four Weddings and a Funeral"?
29 In which film did Tom Hanks play a simple hero with a heart of gold?
30 Who played Steve Biko in "Cry Freedom"?

Answers	Science *(see Quiz 166)*

1 Discovery. 2 Detection. 3 Triangle. 4 Greenwich. 5 Alzheimer. 6 Stereo. 7 Cancer. 8 Great Western. 9 The Church. 10 Marie Curie. 11 HMS Beagle. 12 Better microphone. 13 Radioactivity. 14 Stephen Hawking. 15 English Channel. 16 Parkinson. 17 Heating. 18 Earthquakes. 19 Pollution. 20 Wet. 21 Oxygen. 22 Birth. 23 Two. 24 Vitro. 25 Two years. 26 Carbon dioxide. 27 Antibody. 28 Wind. 29 Anaesthetic. 30 Greek.

1 The song "Who Wants to be a Millionaire?" comes from which musical?
2 Which Earl gave his name to a jacket?
3 Andy Warhol thought that everyone would be famous for how long?
4 Which dancer was runner-up in "Just the Two of Us" with Beverley Knight?
5 How is the Jewish Feast Sukkot also known?
6 What sport does Nicole Vaidisova play?
7 What did the Warren Commission investigate in the 1960s?
8 Composer Percy Grainger came from which country?
9 "Love is All Around" was a huge 1990s hit but in which decade was the original released?
10 The My Lai massacre took place during which war?
11 What was discovered in Rabbit Creek, Klondike in 1896?
12 What goes with Liberty and Equality in the motto adopted by the French republic?
13 Farouk was the last King of which country?
14 The 1996 rerelease of "Love is the Drug" was a remix from which band's 1970s hit?
15 What relation was Edward VIII to George VI?
16 Which actress played Mrs Molly Weasley in "Harry Potter and the Prisoner of Azkaban"?
17 Corazon Aquino was President of which country?
18 In which comic did Dan Dare first appear?
19 In England which protesters smashed spinning and weaving machines in factories?
20 Who was first to be 50 – George Best or Carl Lewis?
21 The Ayatollah Khomeini returned home to take power in which country in 1979?
22 What does the letter H stand for in gardening's RHS?
23 Which sport takes its name from the Duke of Beaufort's House?
24 What type of book does Clive Barker write?
25 "Flava" and "I Feel You" were the first two No 1s for which singer?
26 Which fanatical leader was born with the surname Schicklgruber?
27 What does the G stand for in the GM referring to crops?
28 In which decade was the first non-stop transatlantic flight?
29 What has been named after a nickname of US President Theodore Roosevelt?
30 Which acting rugby coach left Wales in 2006 to join Australia's backroom staff?

| **Answers** | **Pot Luck 74** *(see Quiz 163)* |

1 Creep. 2 Ice hockey. 3 A nautical mile. 4 Mark Petchey. 5 Again. 6 10. 7 Drums.
8 Tarot. 9 Chelsea. 10 12. 11 A prison. 12 Contour lines. 13 Table tennis. 14 Jacket. 15 Spellman. 16 Palindrome. 17 Bloomer. 18 Porridge. 19 Flushing Meadow. 20 Ecuador. 21 One. 22 1960s. 23 Around Saturn. 24 Jersey. 25 Jupiter. 26 Peter Gabriel. 27 Gardening. 28 Switzerland. 29 Holness. 30 1960s.

1 Which spacecraft launched the Hubble telescope?
2 What does the letter d stand for in radar?
3 Pythagoras's most famous theorem is about which geometric shape?
4 Which part of London is associated with Mean Time?
5 Which German psychiatrist gave his name to a disease of senile dementia?
6 Famous for demonstrating TV, John Logie Baird also developed what type of sound?
7 The study of oncogenes is crucial in the treatment of which disease?
8 Portsmouth-born Isambard Kingdom Brunel was responsible for the construction of tunnels, bridges and viaducts on which railway's line?
9 Who were the main opponents of Copernicus's assertion that the Sun was at the centre of the Universe?
10 How is the lady born Manya Sklodowska better known?
11 Which dog gave its name to Darwin's explorer ship?
12 What improvement did Edison make to Bell's telephone?
13 What did Geiger's counter measure?
14 Which scientist wrote A Brief History of Time?
15 In 1898 Marconi transmitted radio signals across where – Atlantic, English Channel or the USA?
16 Which physician gave his name to the disease of paralysis agitans?
17 What process is involved in pasteurisation in order to kill bacteria, as researched by Pasteur?
18 Seismologist Charles Richter studied what?
19 What makes acid rain acid – high temperatures, low temperatures or pollution?
20 In what type of atmosphere do algae live – dry, high altitude or wet?
21 Carbohydrates are made up of carbon, hydrogen and what?
22 If a disease is congenital when does it date from?
23 What is the minimum number of species in a hybrid?
24 What does the V stand for in the fertility treatment IVF?
25 A perennial is a plant which lives longer than how long?
26 Dry ice is solid or frozen what?
27 What is a defensive substance produced as a reaction to a foreign body called?
28 Irish naval officer Sir Francis Beaufort gave his name to measurement of what?
29 Sir Humphry Davy discovered that laughing gas has which effect?
30 What was the nationality of Archimedes?

| **Answers** | The Movies: Heroes & Heroines *(see Quiz 164)* |

1 Seven. 2 Jim Carrey. 3 Downfall. 4 Joan Sims. 5 Donald Sutherland. 6 Joan Crawford. 7 Cast Away. 8 Anjelica Houston. 9 Prison. 10 Jerry Maguire. 11 Cameron Diaz. 12 Jarhead. 13 Gene Kelly. 14 George Clooney. 15 Jeff. 16 Gwyneth Paltrow. 17 Louis XIV. 18 Kristin Scott Thomas. 19 Bruce Willis. 20 Neve Campbell. 21 Robert Carlyle. 22 Spy. 23 Lynn. 24 Will Smith. 25 Timothy Dalton. 26 William Wallace. 27 Lawyer. 28 Carrie. 29 Forrest Gump. 30 Denzel Washington.

1 During which part of Handel's "Messiah" does the audience stand?
2 "Morning" comes from which piece of music by Grieg?
3 Which music by Wagner was used as the theme for "Apocalypse Now"?
4 What was the nationality of Bela Bartok who died at the end of WWII?
5 Rachmaninov wrote a "Rhapsody" on whose theme?
6 What type of work is "Pelleas and Melisande" by Debussy?
7 Which religious song about Jerusalem begins "Last night I lay a sleeping"?
8 Dvorak's famous Symphony No 9 is called what?
9 Mendelssohn's "Fingal's Cave" is from which Overture?
10 About which romantic pair did Berlioz write a symphony?
11 "Take a Pair of Sparkling Eyes" comes from which Gilbert & Sullivan opera?
12 Which birthplace of Handel shares its name with a Manchester-based orchestra?
13 Rodrigo's Concerto d'Aranjuez is played on which instrument?
14 Chopin wrote music almost exclusively for which musical instrument?
15 The music "Crimond" is usually sung to which psalm?
16 What range of voice did Kathleen Ferrier have?
17 Which Gilbert & Sullivan opera is set in the Tower of London?
18 Which of Beethoven's Symphonies is the "Choral Symphony"?
19 "One Fine Day" comes from which Puccini opera?
20 Which words were put to Elgar's "Pomp and Circumstance March No 1 in D Major"?
21 What type of work by Beethoven has the title "Moonlight"?
22 "The Dance of the Sugar Plum Fairy" is from which Tchaikovsky ballet?
23 Which Handel composition about anointing Solomon King is sung at English coronations?
24 "Nimrod" is from which Elgar composition?
25 In which English county was Sir Harrison Birtwistle born?
26 Where was Rossini's famous "Barber" from?
27 Which aria can be translated as "None Shall Sleep"?
28 What type of voice normally sings "O for the Wings of a Dove"?
29 How is Bizet's "Les Pecheurs de Perles" also known?
30 What goes with "Peasant" in the Overture by Suppe?

Answers	Headlines (see Quiz 169)

1 Donald Campbell. 2 Kiev. 3 Cuban Missile. 4 Jamaica. 5 Gerald Ford. 6 Anthrax. 7 Pennsylvania. 8 Ayatollah Rafsanjani. 9 Elton John. 10 Lyndon Johnson. 11 Australia. 12 Molly Campbell. 13 November. 14 Oklahoma. 15 Harold. 16 The Philippines. 17 East Sussex. 18 Martin McGuinness. 19 David Cameron. 20 Donald Dewar. 21 The Guardian. 22 President Akihito. 23 Welsh Guards. 24 Tony Banks. 25 Boris Yeltsin. 26 Panorama. 27 Josie. 28 Hyde. 29 Viagra. 30 Battle of Britain.

Answers – page 412

LEVEL 2

1 What was Jamiroquai's first UK Top Ten hit?
2 Which of these is a sport that is very similar to ice hockey – bandy, gandy or handy?
3 What does a barometer measure?
4 What was Frank Spencer's daughter called?
5 Who or what was the dauphin?
6 Who retired injured in 2006 leaving Amelie Mauresmo to claim the Australian Open?
7 Copernicus is often cited as being the father of modern what?
8 Which song gave The Shamen their first No 1?
9 Which Wimbledon singles champion was related by marriage to sports tycoon David Lloyd?
10 Chris Patten was the last British Governor of where?
11 Who played bride-to-be Donna in "Doctor Who"?
12 Which household item was developed by Harry Pickup?
13 Fanny Blankers-Koen was the first woman to win how many Olympic gold medals?
14 What was Cherie Blair's maiden name?
15 Which of Queen Elizabeth II's children was the first to marry?
16 What did Clarice Cliff make?
17 In which month of the year is Mother's Day celebrated in America?
18 Cinnamon comes from which part of a tree?
19 What colour is paprika?
20 Which sought-after clothing items went on sale in the UK for the first time in 1941?
21 Who was "Back in the World" according to the title of a 2003 hit album?
22 The Sierra Nevada mountains are in which American state?
23 Which Joe was a world champion at both snooker and billiards?
24 The letters PL show that a car has come from which country?
25 Which politician said, "All babies look like me" – Iain Duncan Smith, William Hague or Winston Churchill?
26 What does the second s mean in the knitting term psso?
27 Roman Romanov was chairman of which soccer club?
28 Hippophobia is a fear of what?
29 Which actress has played Elizabeth II and George III's wife in movies?
30 What was named after Captain Becher?

Answers | Pot Luck 77 (see Quiz 170)

1 The moon. 2 Carbon. 3 Prisoner Cell Block H. 4 Sydney. 5 Equilibrium. 6 Barbados. 7 Facsimile. 8 Richard Nixon. 9 Waitangi Day. 10 Sex Pistols. 11 Acute. 12 Dr Livesey. 13 Seaside postcard. 14 Lotus. 15 Quakers. 16 Beach Boys. 17 Patrick Swayze (2002). 18 Queen Victoria. 19 Sopwith. 20 Hobby. 21 Milk. 22 Melbourne. 23 Rossini. 24 US Open. 25 Softer. 26 1950s. 27 Albatross. 28 Alicia Keys. 29 Africa. 30 Tottenham Hotspur.

1 In 2001 whose car was found in Lake Coniston, 30 years after an attempt on the water speed record?
2 Which city of the Ukraine was closest to Chernobyl?
3 Which crisis brought about the hot line between the White House and the Kremlin?
4 On which West Indian island did Bob Woolmer meet his death during the 2007 Cricket World Cup?
5 Who replaced President Nixon after Watergate?
6 In October 2001, the US's Senate Majority leader received what in the post?
7 In the Sept 11th 2001 terrorist attacks on the US, in which state did the plane crash which did not crash into a building?
8 Who succeeded Ayatollah Khomeini as president of Iran?
9 In 1979 who was the first western rock star to visit the USSR?
10 Who succeeded JF Kennedy after his assassination?
11 Paul Keating became Prime Minister of where?
12 What is the British name of Misbah Iram Ahmed, the subject of a 2006 custody battle?
13 In which month did JFK die?
14 Which US city was the scene of a terrorist bomb in 1995?
15 What was spy Kim Philby's real first name?
16 Where did Corazon Aquino become president after being widowed?
17 In which county was Piltdown Man discovered in 1912?
18 Who became Minister of Education after the Good Friday agreement?
19 Which British party leader claimed in 2007 that politicians were entitled to a "private past"?
20 Who was the first leader of the Scottish Parliament?
21 Jonathan Aitken was jailed after a libel case against which newspaper?
22 Which Japanese leader visited Britain amid great controversy in 1998?
23 Simon Weston, who was badly burned in the Falklands War served in which regiment?
24 Who was Tony Blair's first Minister for Sport?
25 Who preceded Vladimir Putin as Russian leader?
26 On which programme did ex-nanny Louise Woodward explain her case on British TV?
27 Which member of the Russell family survived a murderous attack where her mother and sister perished?
28 Where in Greater Manchester did Dr Harold Shipman practise?
29 Which drug was launched in the late 1990s as a cure for impotence?
30 In which Battle did Britain use radar for the first time?

Answers	**Music: Classics (see Quiz 167)**

1 Hallelujah Chorus. 2 Peer Gynt. 3 Ride of the Valkyries. 4 Hungarian. 5 Paganini.
6 Opera. 7 The Holy City. 8 From the New World. 9 Hebrides. 10 Romeo & Juliet.
11 The Gondoliers. 12 Halle. 13 Guitar. 14 Piano. 15 23, The Lord's My Shepherd.
16 Contralto. 17 Yeomen of the Guard. 18 Ninth. 19 Madame Butterfly. 20 Land of Hope and Glory. 21 Sonata. 22 Nutcracker. 23 Zadok the Priest. 24 Enigma Variations. 25 Lancashire. 26 Seville. 27 Nessun Dorma. 28 (Boy) Soprano. 29 The Pearl Fishers. 30 Poet.

1 Where does a plaque read: "We came in peace for all mankind. July 1969"?

2 A diamond is made up of which element?

3 Which TV series featured the Wentworth Detention Centre?

4 Michael Hutchence was born in and died in which city?

5 What word describes a state of complete balance?

6 Which West Indian island was host to the 2007 Cricket World Cup final?

7 The word fax is an abbreviation of which word that means a copy?

8 Who was the first US President to resign from office?

9 What is New Zealand's National Day called?

10 Who had a hit with "God Save the Queen" in 1977 and 2002?

11 What name is given to an angle of less than 90 degrees?

12 The adventure yarn "Treasure Island" is narrated by Jim Hawkins and who else?

13 Where would you be most likely to see the artwork of Donald McGill?

14 Which motor racing team has the name of a flower that is sacred in India?

15 Which religious group founded the city of Philadelphia?

16 Carl Wilson of which legendary band died in 1998?

17 Who was 50 first – Tom Hanks, Patrick Swayze or Bruce Willis?

18 Who was the first British monarch to travel by train?

19 Who was the designer of the Sopwith Camel – was it Camel, Sopwith or Sopwith Camel?

20 What can be a small horse or a small falcon?

21 Which everyday food item includes the protein casein?

22 What was Australia's capital before Canberra?

23 Who composed the opera "William Tell"?

24 In which 2006 tournament did Tiger Woods first miss the halfway cut as a professional?

25 If music is diminuendo it gradually becomes what?

26 In which decade were Duke of Edinburgh awards first presented?

27 Which creature provided Fleetwood Mac with a worldwide hit?

28 Who played the character Georgia Sykes in the movie "Smokin' Aces"?

29 Mungo Park is famous for exploration in which part of the world?

30 Gerry Francis and George Graham have both managed which soccer club?

---

1 Chad Varah founded which charity?
2 The Queen's residence of Balmoral is on which river?
3 Which Princess is nearest in line to the throne?
4 Who was the only Irish author to win the Nobel Prize for Literature in the 1990s?
5 Which Richard designed the Thrust, the fastest land vehicle of its day?
6 Millvina Dean was the youngest survivor of which ship?
7 What type of radio did Trevor Bayliss invent?
8 Athina Onassis Roussel will inherit millions due to the fortune her grandfather made in what?
9 Sam Walton founded which US-based chain of stores?
10 Which child of a rock star inherited nearly £80 million – Frances Cobain, Sean Lennon or Lisa Marie Presley?
11 Which "Playboy" magazine Playmate of the Year married an 89-year-old oil billionaire?
12 Which religious figure broadcasts regularly on a radio show called "Decision Hour"?
13 What relation is Jemma Redgrave to Vanessa Redgrave?
14 Gwyneth Paltrow and Chris Martin's second child was called what?
15 How was Lesley Hornby better known?
16 Which of the following is not left-handed – Tim Henman, Brian Lara or Martina Navratilova?
17 Alan Ayckbourn famously stages his plays at which seaside resort?
18 Who succeeded Gaby Roslin on Channel 4's "The Big Breakfast"?
19 Who was Tony Blair's first Press Secretary when he became Prime Minister?
20 Jimmy McGovern and Alan Bleasdale are famous names as what?
21 Which First Lady had the maiden name Roddam?
22 What is the first name of Mrs Gordon Brown?
23 How tall was Prince William when he went to university – 6ft 3", 6ft or 5ft 10"?
24 Who named her baby daughter Bluebell Madonna?
25 What do Victor Edelstein and Catherine Walker design?
26 Who was elected to Alan Clark's constituency after his death?
27 Who was inaugurated as President of the USA exactly 32 years after John F Kennedy?
28 What was Tony Blair's first constituency?
29 The Lauder brothers inherited from their mother Estée who made a fortune in what?
30 Which Princess has middle names Elizabeth Mary?

Answers	TV: Sitcoms *(see Quiz 173)*

1 Chambers. 2 Brabinger. 3 Seattle. 4 Absolutely Fabulous. 5 Victor Meldrew. 6 Tom.
7 Richard Wilson. 8 Sarah Lancashire. 9 Robert Lindsay. 10 Bollinger. 11 Listen very
carefully. 12 Calista Flockhart. 13 Are You Being Served?. 14 White. 15 Julia Roberts.
16 Harold Steptoe. 17 Stephen Tomkinson. 18 Paul Eddington. 19 Samantha. 20
Garth. 21 Nurse. 22 Cheers. 23 Captain Mainwaring. 24 Father Jack. 25 Fawlty
Towers. 26 Ruby Wax. 27 Draughtsman. 28 Richard. 29 Ivy. 30 North east.

1 James Logan gave his name to a type of what – danceband, fruit or road race?
2 Who beat Andre Agassi in his final singles game at Wimbledon?
3 Which Day was inaugurated by Miss Anna Jarvis in Philadelphia in 1907?
4 What was Walt Disney's first TV programme called?
5 What did William Herschel discover?
6 What term describes a plant created from crossing different species?
7 In which decade of last century was Margaret Thatcher born?
8 Which Brontë wrote the novel "Jane Eyre"?
9 Charles Babbage was involved in the early development of what?
10 Which famous oil trouble-shooter passed away in August 2004?
11 What was tennis player Margaret Smith's married name that was linked to her sport?
12 When was the movie "Enigma" set?
13 Steve Bruce and Nigel Spackman have both managed which soccer club?
14 Princess Anne's second marriage took place near which royal residence?
15 Which group had a hit best-of album "Life Story", almost 50 years after their first hit?
16 What sort of car did "Avenger" Emma Peel drive?
17 What was the real first name of Curly Watts in "Coronation Street"?
18 What would you do with a burrito?
19 What is the English name of the lunar sea Lacus Mortis?
20 Which American state is directly below North Carolina?
21 Warrumbungle is found in Australia, but what is it?
22 Which country established a record Test partnership of 624 runs in 2006?
23 What number does Thomas display on his Tank Engine?
24 Who was UN Secretary-General at the time of the Indian Ocean tsunami of 2004?
25 Which Mr Miller married Marilyn Monroe?
26 What did Grover live in Sesame Street?
27 In which branch of mathematics do letters replace unknown quantities?
28 "The Rose" was a Bette Midler movie based on the life of which singer?
29 Which Diane has been Sean Connery's wife?
30 Del Boy Trotter's catchphrase was "Lovely" what?

Answers | Pot Luck 79 *(see Quiz 174)*

1 911. 2 Boy George. 3 Seattle. 4 Alexander the Great. 5 Cate Blanchett. 6 Channel 5. 7 Limestone. 8 Lleyton Hewitt. 9 Neighbours. 10 Scripts. 11 Lower arm. 12 Golf's US Masters. 13 Ceefax. 14 Kamikaze. 15 60 degrees. 16 Surrey. 17 Colony. 18 Toes and fingers. 19 Hungary. 20 297. 21 Nottingham. 22 Steve Delaney. 23 Rita. 24 Wavelengths of light. 25 Ron Atkinson. 26 Swim the English Channel. 27 Three. 28 Des O' Connor. 29 Processing. 30 Sunday.

Answers – page 413 **LEVEL 2**

1 Which series with John Bird was set in a legal practice?
2 In "To the Manor Born" what was the name of Audrey's butler?
3 Where is "Frasier" based?
4 Which show introduced a character called Katy Grin?
5 Whose catchphrase was, "I don't believe it!"?
6 Which character appeared with Linda in "Gimme Gimme Gimme"?
7 Who played opposite Stephanie Cole in "Life as We Know It"?
8 Which ex-"Coronation Street" actress starred in "Blooming Marvellous" with Clive Mantle?
9 Who played Ben to Zoe Wanamaker's Susan in "My Family"?
10 In "Absolutely Fabulous", what was Patsy's favourite champagne?
11 In "Allo Allo", which three words come before "I shall say this only once!"?
12 Who played Ally McBeal?
13 Beane's of Boston was a US version of which UK sitcom set in the retail business?
14 What colour were Seinfeld's shoes?
15 Which 2001 Oscar-winning actress guested on "Friends"?
16 Whose catchphrase was "You dirty old man!"?
17 Which ex "Ballykissangel" star appeared in "Bedtime"?
18 Who found fame as Jerry Leadbetter?
19 Which witch was played by Elizabeth Montgomery in "Bewitched"?
20 Who was Wayne's sidekick in "Wayne's World"?
21 What was Dorothy's profession in "Men Behaving Badly"?
22 Which US programme was the then most watched TV show when it aired for the last time in 1993?
23 Who was in charge of the Walmington on Sea Home Guard?
24 In "Father Ted", which priest was almost permanently drunk?
25 Which sitcom saw Polly, Miss Tibbs and Major Gowen?
26 Which American played the American flatmate in "Girls on Top"?
27 What was Tom Good's job before he gave everything up for "The Good Life"?
28 What was Hyacinth Bucket's husband called?
29 Who was the cafe proprietress in "Last of the Summer Wine"?
30 Where in the UK was "The Likely Lads" set?

Answers	The Famous (see Quiz 171)

1 The Samaritans. 2 Dee. 3 Beatrice. 4 Seamus Heaney. 5 Noble. 6 Titanic. 7 Clockwork. 8 Shipping. 9 Wal-Mart. 10 Lisa Marie Presley. 11 Anna Nicole Smith. 12 Billy Graham. 13 Niece. 14 Moses. 15 Twiggy. 16 Tim Henman. 17 Scarborough. 18 Zoe Ball. 19 Alastair Campbell. 20 Playwrights. 21 Hillary Clinton. 22 Sarah. 23 6ft 3in. 24 Geri Halliwell. 25 Clothes. 26 Michael Portillo. 27 Bill Clinton. 28 Sedgefield. 29 Cosmetics. 30 Beatrice.

1 In the USA which of these numbers do you ring in an emergency, 999, 606, 911?
2 Which singer received a New York community service order for falsely reporting a break-in?
3 The Seahawks from where were runners-up in Super Bowl XL?
4 Which of the following did Shakespeare not write a play about – Alexander the Great, Julius Caesar or Macbeth?
5 Who co-starred with Judi Dench in the movie "Notes on a Scandal"?
6 Which TV launch was connected with the Spice Girls?
7 Which rock is chiefly made from calcium carbonate?
8 Which top tennis player was once engaged to Kim Clijsters?
9 In which TV show did the kids attend Erinsborough High School?
10 What did Ray Galton and Alan Simpson produce – scripts, shoes or songs?
11 Where in the human body is the ulna?
12 Which of these sporting events is held most frequently – golf's US Masters, golf's Ryder Cup or football's World Cup?
13 What was the BBC's first teletext service called?
14 Which Japanese word actually means "divine wind"?
15 In an equilateral triangle, how many degrees does each angle measure?
16 Wentworth golf course is in which English county?
17 What is the collective name for a group of beavers?
18 What are your phalanges?
19 In which country could you watch Ferencvaros playing Vasas at soccer?
20 A4 paper is 210mm by how many mm?
21 In which city is the Goose Fair held?
22 Which actor and comedian created the character Count Arthur Strong?
23 What was Alf Garnett's daughter called?
24 What does the angstrom unit measure?
25 Who did Alex Ferguson replace at Man Utd?
26 Captain Matthew Webb was the first person to do what?
27 When the prefix kilo is used to describe an amount, how many noughts would be written in digits?
28 Who first presented the 1990s revival of the TV game show "Take Your Pick"?
29 In computing, what does the P stand for in CPU?
30 The Prix de l'Arc de Triomphe is run on which day of the week?

---

1 Which novel about Hannibal Lecter sets out to explain "the evolution of his evil"?

2 Who wrote the Young Bond series of books?

3 Who wrote the "Mary Ann" series of romantic novels?

4 What was the surname of Richmal Crompton's most famous schoolboy hero?

5 Who wrote "The Day of the Jackal"?

6 Who wrote the book originally published in the UK as "The Diary of a Young Girl"?

7 Nadine Gordimer hails from which country?

8 Who wrote "The Female Eunuch"?

9 Who is the author of "Riders of the Purple Sage"?

10 Which writer famous for her historical fiction wrote "Regency Buck"?

11 What is Ripley's first name in Patricia Highsmith's "The Talented Mr Ripley" and "Ripley Under Water"?

12 In which language did Czech-born Franz Kafka write?

13 Whose "Guns of Navarone" was made into a film?

14 Whose autobiography was called "Learning to Fly"?

15 Which Josephine wrote "Tonight Josephine"?

16 Which ex-jockey wrote "Shattered"?

17 Which thriller writer penned "The Shape of Snakes"?

18 Which word completes the title of Rick Stein's cookery book, "Rick Stein's Seafood ..."?

19 Whose memoir was called "Bad Blood"?

20 What sort of guide did Leslie Halliwell found?

21 In which city was Barbara Taylor Bradford born?

22 Whose "Death in Holy Orders" was set on the coast of East Anglia?

23 Whose autobiography was called "Himoff!"?

24 Who wrote the novels on which the "Touch of Frost" TV character was based?

25 In which Stephen King novel does the character Annie Wilkes feature?

26 In Ruth Rendell's Wexford novels what is Reg's wife called?

27 Which Alfred wrote many books about walks in his beloved Lake District?

28 Which Ian Rankin novel is set in the backdrop of the 2005 G8 conference?

29 Whose cookery book had a title which began with "Happy Days"?

30 Was Richard Branson's autobiography called "Like a Virgin", "Losing My Virginity" or "The Moon's a Balloon"?

| **Answers** | **Rugby** *(see Quiz 177)* |

1 Australia. 2 Mike Ruddock. 3 Professional. 4 Lebanon. 5 Romania. 6 Prop. 7 Mike Catt. 8 1996. 9 1980s. 10 Lawrence Dallaglio. 11 Paul Newlove. 12 Rugby Union World Cup. 13 Sydney. 14 David Campese. 15 England. 16 Pay (Broken time payments). 17 1920s. 18 South Africa. 19 Pilkington Cup. 20 Llanelli Scarlets. 21 Hunslet. 22 Wales and South Africa. 23 Leeds Rhinos. 24 (Stade de) France. 25 South Africa. 26 Cambridge. 27 Blue Sox. 28 Swalec Cup. 29 Australia. 30 Wigan.

Quiz 176 | Pot Luck 80

Answers – page 420

1 Which word describes the brightness of stars?
2 What did Croft and Perry create between them?
3 Which country was first to win soccer's World Cup four times?
4 In which country is La Coruña international airport?
5 Which are there most of – birds, fish or insects?
6 In MODEM, MO stands for Modulator, what does DEM stand for?
7 The Tour of Spain in cycling takes place how often?
8 Before their 2006 triumph, when did Italy last win the FIFA World Cup?
9 After a drugs test Ben Johnson was stripped of Olympic gold in which race?
10 Carbohydrates consist of carbon, hydrogen and which other element?
11 What is the highest number on the Richter scale?
12 In what type of building did the 2004 hostage crisis take place in Beslan, Russia?
13 What shape is a swallow's tail?
14 The Philippines lie in which ocean?
15 147 is a maximum continuous score in which game?
16 What name describes a component that will transmit electricity or heat?
17 How many legs does a flatworm have?
18 Which instrument did jazzman Charlie "Bird" Parker play?
19 The flower edelweiss is what colour?
20 What does C stand for in the abbreviation VCR?
21 Who had hits with "We Belong Together" and "It's Like That"?
22 "Fidelio" was the only opera of which German composer?
23 What type of leaves does a koala eat?
24 Who had chart success with the album "Fever" in 2001?
25 In which country is Rawalpindi?
26 The clock on Big Ben's tower has how many faces?
27 The Channel Island Sark is noted for its ban on what?
28 Which of the Bee Gees is not a twin?
29 What did Lewis E. Waterman invent?
30 What is the name for a camel with two humps?

Answers	**Pot Luck 81** *(see Quiz 178)*

1 Capability Brown. 2 Cats. 3 F. 4 Vicar. 5 Engineering. 6 Turkey. 7 Never Mind the Buzzcocks. 8 Jacques. 9 Al. 10 Bird. 11 Alicia Keys. 12 Three. 13 Corky. 14 Glasgow. 15 Victoria Wood. 16 Brain. 17 Lower arm. 18 Fool's gold. 19 Newcastle. 20 Two. 21 Wolves. 22 Belgium. 23 Two. 24 Harry. 25 Tuesday. 26 New York. 27 The Royle Family. 28 To the Manor Born. 29 Prime Minister. 30 Lawrence Dallaglio.

1 In which country do Parramatta play?
2 Which Mike managed Wales to their first Grand Slam title in 27 years in 2005?
3 What does the P stand for in RFAPC?
4 Hazen El Masri represented which international side?
5 Which side did Philippe Sella face in his first international?
6 What is the usual position played by England and Bath rugby star Matt Stevens?
7 Who scored all of England's points in their 15–15 draw with Australia in November 1997?
8 In what year was the Regal Trophy discontinued – 1986, 1990 or 1996?
9 In which decade of the 20th century did Ireland last win the Five Nations?
10 Who became England captain for the first time in 1997?
11 Who was the youngest League player in an international in the 20th century?
12 What is another name for the Webb Ellis Trophy?
13 Which city's University had the first Rugby Club in Australia?
14 In 1996 which Australian received a UNESCO award as one of the most outstanding sportsmen of the century?
15 By 2000 which country had won the Rugby International Championships outright most times?
16 Rugby League was formed after a dispute with the Rugby Football Union about what?
17 In which decade was the first Challenge Cup Final at Wembley?
18 Who were the third winners of the Rugby Union World Cup after New Zealand and Australia?
19 Which Cup was called the John Player Cup until 1988?
20 Which rugby club did Gareth Jenkins leave to take over as boss of Wales in 2006?
21 Which side became Hawks in the 1990s?
22 Which sides met in the first game at Cardiff's Millennium Stadium?
23 Who won the last Challenge Cup of the 20th century?
24 Which was the only Five Nations side to have its country's name in its home ground?
25 Who joined Australia and New Zealand in the 1998 Tri Nations series?
26 By the end of the millennium, who had won most Varsity matches?
27 What did Halifax add to their name in the 1990s?
28 Which Cup was previously called the Schweppes Welsh Cup?
29 Which was the first team to win the Rugby World Cup twice?
30 Who were the last winners of the Regal Trophy?

Answers	**Books** *(see Quiz 175)*

1 Hannibal Rising. **2** Charlie Higson. **3** Catherine Cookson. **4** Brown. **5** Frederick Forsyth. **6** Anne Frank. **7** South Africa. **8** Germaine Greer. **9** Zane Grey. **10** Georgette Heyer. **11** Tom. **12** German. **13** Alistair Maclean. **14** Victoria Beckham. **15** Cox. **16** Dick Francis. **17** Minette Walters. **18** Odyssey. **19** Lorna Sage. **20** Film. **21** Leeds. **22** PD James. **23** Richard Whiteley. **24** RD Wingfield. **25** Misery. **26** Dora. **27** Wainwright. **28** The Naming of the Dead. **29** Jamie Oliver. **30** Losing My Virginity.

1 How did Lancelot Brown become better known – Arthur Brown, Capability Brown or James Brown?
2 Allurophobia is a fear of which creature?
3 What is the fourth note in the scale of C?
4 What was the occupation of the sitcom character named Geraldine Grainger?
5 What does Carol Vorderman have a degree in?
6 In which country could you watch Besiktas play a home soccer match?
7 On which TV show did Simon Amstell take over from Mark Lamarr?
8 EC Presidents Delors and Santer both shared which forename?
9 What is the chemical symbol for aluminium?
10 What type of creature is a kookaburra?
11 "Songs in a Minor Key" was the first hit album for which artist?
12 How many different countries did Alfredo di Stefano play international soccer for?
13 Who is Bottle Top Bill's best friend?
14 In which city are you if you walk along Sauchiehall Street?
15 Who wrote the TV sitcom "dinnerladies"?
16 Which part of his body did Einstein leave to Princeton University?
17 Where in the human body is the radius?
18 Iron pyrites are known as what type of gold?
19 Barrack Road goes past the soccer stadium of which club?
20 How many main islands is New Zealand made up of?
21 Graham Taylor and Dave Jones have both managed which soccer club?
22 Waterloo, scene of a famous battle, is in which country?
23 Which number can be typed using only letters on the top row of a keyboard?
24 Which Corbett created Sooty the bear?
25 If the December 1 is a Saturday what day is January 1?
26 Where did the Jumbo jet leave from on its first transatlantic flight?
27 "The Queen of Sheba" was a one-off special of which TV programme?
28 In which sitcom did Richard De Vere marry Audrey?
29 William Pitt became the youngest British what?
30 Which ex-England captain retired from international rugby in 2004 yet came back in 2006?

Answers	Pot Luck 80 (see Quiz 176)

1 Magnitude. 2 TV shows, chiefly sitcoms. 3 Brazil. 4 Spain. 5 Insects. 6 Demodulator. 7 Annually. 8 1982. 9 100m. 10 Oxygen. 11 9. 12 School. 13 Forked. 14 Pacific Ocean. 15 Snooker. 16 A conductor. 17 None. 18 Saxophone. 19 White. 20 Cassette. 21 Mariah Carey. 22 Beethoven. 23 Eucalyptus. 24 Kylie Minogue. 25 Pakistan. 26 Four. 27 Cars. 28 Barry. 29 Fountain pen. 30 Bactrian.

1 Who played Anne Heche's husband in "Donnie Brasco"?

2 Who played Quasimodo in the 1923 version of "The Hunchback of Notre Dame"?

3 How many sound movies did the legendary DW Griffith make?

4 Which category did Disney's "Snow White" have when it first opened?

5 Which wife of Clark Gable was one of Mack Sennett's bathing beauties?

6 Which western with Gary Cooper made Grace Kelly a star?

7 Which 1990s Dreamworks movie is about Moses?

8 What was Quentin Tarantino's first film?

9 Who played Stanley Kowalski in "A Streetcar Named Desire"?

10 What is Nicole Kidman's job in "To Die For"?

11 Who are the musical duo in "Topsy Turvy"?

12 The movie "Thirteen Days" is about which crisis?

13 What was the sequel to "Ace Ventura Pet Detective"?

14 What was the most expensive film of the 20th century?

15 Which sci-fi film of 1999 starred Keanu Reeves?

16 Which of the following movies did not have a dog or dogs as their stars – "Babe", "Beethoven" or "Homeward Bound"?

17 Of the following stars of "Ghostbusters", who did not also write it – Dan Aykroyd, Bill Murray or Harold Ramis?

18 Who plays the widowed hero in "The American President"?

19 Back in the 1960s who was the "Girl on a Motorcycle"?

20 After making "Some Like It Hot", Tony Curtis reputedly said that kissing who was like kissing Hitler?

21 Which Richardson co-starred with Hugh Laurie in "Maybe Baby"?

22 What is Hugh Grant's profession in "Notting Hill"?

23 In which movie did Eddie Murphy play Sherman Klump?

24 How many films did Bogart make with Bacall – was it two, four or six?

25 In which movie did Audrey Hepburn play Holly Golightly?

26 In which city is "Dirty Harry" set?

27 Who does Jack Nicholson play in "The Witches of Eastwick"?

28 In which part of New York is Martin Scorsese's semi-autobiographical movie "Mean Streets" set?

29 What was Wallace & Gromit's first adventure?

30 Which movie classic features Rick and Renault?

Answers	**Natural Phenomena** *(see Quiz 181)*

1 Quicklime. 2 Jupiter. 3 Pluto. 4 Indian. 5 Amazon. 6 Loch Lomond. 7 Canada.
8 North Atlantic (Great Britain). 9 Balmoral. 10 Tornado. 11 Angola. 12 Cornwall.
13 Hydrogen. 14 Plutonium. 15 Ullswater. 16 Calcium carbonate. 17 China clay. 18 500. 19 Mouont McKinley. 20 Russia. 21 Washington. 22 Tungsten. 23 Iceland. 24 Kobe. 25 Emerald. 26 Charles. 27 10%. 28 Yellow. 29 Indonesia. 30 River Ouse.

1 Which of these words is made from letters on the top row of a keyboard – part, pile or pour?

2 The aria "One Fine Day" comes from which opera?

3 Where were satsumas originally grown?

4 Who was famous for his Theory of Evolution?

5 How many faces does a pyramid with a triangular base have?

6 George Ferris gave his name to which fairground attraction?

7 On which group of islands is Mount Fuji?

8 In music how many lines are there for notes to be written on?

9 Which building was constructed on the orders of Shah Jehan?

10 Which US band had hit singles with "Boulevard of Broken Dreams" and "Holiday"?

11 Which was London's first railway station?

12 Which group of people largely shunned the January 2005 democratic elections in Iraq?

13 In blackjack the maximum score is equivalent to potting how many blacks at snooker?

14 Who was the first Scot to be voted European Footballer of the Year?

15 Where would you find your ventricle and atrium?

16 Which creatures live in a formicary?

17 What does the M stand for in the radio abbreviation FM stand for?

18 What was the first name of the commentator who famously said, "They think it's all over"?

19 The Derby at Epsom is run in which month?

20 Which fellow guitarist joined Brian May for a 1990s version of "We are the Champions"?

21 The movie "The China Syndrome" deals with what type of accident?

22 A male fencer needs how many hits for a victory?

23 Who was 50 first – Robin Williams, Kevin Keegan or Princess Anne?

24 Whose 1990s greatest hits album was modestly called "Modern Classics"?

25 How many bytes are there in a kilobyte?

26 In which country did speed skating originate?

27 Which ship sent out the the first S.O.S.?

28 Richie Richardson captained which country at cricket?

29 Which office machine can be flat-bed or hand-held?

30 What was Keane's first album to top the charts?

Answers | Pot Luck 83 *(see Quiz 182)*

1 Head. 2 Silicon Valley. 3 Haiti. 4 Sir Arthur Conan Doyle. 5 Refraction. 6 65. 7 Hearn. 8 St Valentine's Day. 9 St Andrews. 10 A Tolkien novel title. 11 Four. 12 Man in Black. 13 Pink Floyd. 14 Nick Leeson. 15 Eskimo. 16 Marzipan. 17 Snake. 18 Coventry. 19 R Kelly. 20 Leeds United. 21 Sandy Lyle. 22 Simnel cake. 23 Isle of Wight. 24 Live and Let Die. 25 Class. 26 Ken Barlow. 27 Cheese. 28 The bereaved. 29 Talk. 30 Ricky Ponting.

1 What is another name for calcium oxide?

2 What is the next largest body in our solar system after the Sun?

3 What is the only planet to have been discovered by an American – Mars, Pluto or Venus?

4 What is the next deepest ocean after the Pacific?

5 What is the longest river on the American continent?

6 Which is the largest lake on the UK mainland?

7 Which country has the largest area of inland water?

8 In which waters is the EEC's largest island?

9 Which home of the Queen is one of the coldest places in the UK?

10 In December 2006 which natural disaster befell Kensal Rise in North London?

11 The Congo river is in the Democratic Republic of Congo and where else?

12 Which county of mainland England is the warmest?

13 What is the most common element in the universe?

14 Which is the heaviest – plutonium, gold or uranium?

15 What is England's second largest lake?

16 What is the chemical name for chalk?

17 Kaolin is what type of clay?

18 Denmark comprises how many islands – 26, 300 or 500?

19 Which mountain is the highest in the Alaska Range?

20 The Caucasus Mountains divide Georgia and Azerbaijan from where?

21 In which US state is the volcanic mountain of Mount St Helens which erupted in 1980?

22 Which metallic element has its natural occurrence in wolfram?

23 In which country are most of Europe's volcanoes?

24 Where in Japan did a massive earthquake kill over 5,000 people in 1995?

25 What is the most popular form of green beryl called?

26 What was the first name of Richter whose scale measures the intensity of an earthquake?

27 How much of the Earth's area is covered in ice – 5%, 10% or 20%?

28 What colour is the quartz known as citrine?

29 Where is the volcanic island of Sumatra?

30 Which river burst its banks to flood York in 2002?

Answers	Movie Memories (see Quiz 179)

1 Johnny Depp. 2 Lon Chaney. 3 Two. 4 A. 5 Carole Lombard. 6 High Noon. 7 The Prince of Egypt. 8 Reservoir Dogs. 9 Marlon Brando. 10 TV weather presenter. 11 Gilbert & Sullivan. 12 Cuban missile. 13 When Nature Calls. 14 Titanic. 15 The Matrix. 16 Babe. 17 Bill Murray. 18 Michael Douglas. 19 Marianne Faithfull. 20 Marilyn Monroe. 21 Joely. 22 Bookshop owner. 23 The Nutty Professor. 24 Four. 25 Breakfast at Tiffany's. 26 San Francisco. 27 The Devil. 28 Little Italy. 29 A Grand Day Out. 30 Casablanca.

1 What part of the human body is measured using the cephalix index?
2 What nickname is given to the Santa Clara valley in America?
3 In which country did the private security force the Tontons Macoutes operate?
4 Who was the eponymous Arthur in Julian Barnes's novel "Arthur & George"?
5 What word describes the bending of light passing from one medium to another?
6 How old was singer Gene Pitney at the time of his death – 55, 65 or 75?
7 Which Barry managed snooker's Steve Davis through his winning years?
8 On which special day were seven of Bugs Moran's gang murdered in America?
9 Where could Prince William have a round of golf at the local club for his university?
10 What did the group Marillion base their group name on – a Tolkien novel, Marilyn Monroe or a nightclub?
11 What is the minimum number of times the racket must hit the ball in a tennis game?
12 Darts player Alan Glazier and singer Johnny Cash have been both known as what?
13 Who released the classic "Ummagumma" album?
14 Who was responsible for the crime recounted in the film "Rogue Trader"?
15 From which language does the word anorak – a hooded jacket – come?
16 What is on the outside of a Battenburg cake?
17 A taipan is a type of what?
18 Which of these English cities is the furthest south – Birmingham, Coventry or Leicester?
19 Who had American No 1 albums with "TP-2,Com" and "TP.3 Reloaded"?
20 Eric Cantona joined Manchester United from which club?
21 Who was the first Briton to win golf's US Masters?
22 Which cake was originally made for Mothering Sunday?
23 On which Isle was Queen Victoria's residence Osborne House?
24 In which film did Roger Moore first play James Bond?
25 Pulp's debut album was called "Different" what?
26 Mike Baldwin died in the arms of which "Corrie" character?
27 What is the main ingredient in a traditional fondue?
28 The organisation CRUSE was set up to help who?
29 What was "Happy" in the title of Captain Sensible's only No 1 hit?
30 Who hit Australia's highest score in the 2006–07 Ashes series?

1 In which city did Kylie Minogue resume her Showgirl tour in 2006?
2 Which lady sang the soul album "I Never Loved a Man (the Way I Love You)"?
3 Who killed Marvin Gaye?
4 Why was Bob Dylan booed at the Manchester Free Trade Hall in 1966?
5 How many people were on Michael Jackson's "Thriller" album cover?
6 Which Beatle was the first to have a solo No 1 in the US?
7 How old was Elton John when he hit No 1 with the single in memory of Diana Princess of Wales – 46, 51 or 56?
8 Who had a best-selling album "No Jacket Required" in 1985?
9 Which US solo singer had a successful album of "Love Songs" in the 1980s?
10 Which American singer had 35 consecutive UK Top Ten hits.
11 How many years do Cher's No 1 UK hits span – 25, 33 or 39?
12 Which country superstar has had most solo album sales in the USA – Garth Brooks, Dolly Parton or Kenny Rogers?
13 Which superstar band wrote Diana Ross's "Chain Reaction"?
14 In which part of New York was Barry Manilow born?
15 Which superstar played the title role in the 1980s "The Jazz Singer"?
16 Which country singer won a Lifetime Achievement Grammy in 2000?
17 With whom did opera's Monserrat Caballe sing at the Barcelona Olympics?
18 Who recorded "Ten Summoner's Tales" in 1993?
19 Paul McCartney's "Standing Stone" premiered in New York and at which London venue?
20 Who was the first singer to have No 1 hits in five decades?
21 Who wrote the Mariah Carey/Westlife hit "Against All Odds"?
22 Which character in radio's "The Archers" shares her name with a Dolly Parton hit?
23 Which female vocalist duetted with George Michael on "If I Told You That"?
24 Which former Motown star had a new millennium hit with "Not Over Yet"?
25 Which rock star of Scottish parentage was inducted into the Rock and Roll Hall of Fame in 1994?
26 Which James Bond theme did Tina Turner sing?
27 Who is Britain's most successful female chart artist, who became a Dame in 2000?
28 Who sang in a benefit concert following the New York atrocity after suffering her own health problems in 2001?
29 Who was the first major star to make a full album available for downloading?
30 In which year did Cher celebrate her 60th birthday?

| **Answers** | Technology & Industry *(see Quiz 185)* |

1 Myspace. 2 Nintendo. 3 Woolwich. 4 Books. 5 Express. 6 London Underground. 7 Colgate. 8 Red. 9 Railtrack. 10 Marks & Spencer. 11 Disneyland Paris. 12 Tesco. 13 Seattle. 14 Mothercare. 15 Honda. 16 Mobile phones. 17 Benjamin Guinness. 18 Apple. 19 Sony. 20 Charles Rolls. 21 Asda. 22 Ginger Productions. 23 Washing machine. 24 Sugar. 25 Sabena. 26 Germany. 27 Henry Royce. 28 Winfield. 29 Airbus A380. 30 Snooker.

1 Which of the "Monty Python Flying Circus" team was called Michael?
2 Who made the album "Songs from the West Coast"?
3 What did Lord Gyllene win on a Monday in 1997 that would have been on Saturday but for a bomb threat?
4 Robben Island was a prison located near which city?
5 What is the fruit flavour of Cointreau?
6 How old was Billy the Kid when he died?
7 On a computer keyboard where is the letter O in relation to the L – above it, below it or next to it?
8 In rhyme, on what day of the week was Solomon Grundy married?
9 Which "Little" book by Louisa May Alcott became a best seller?
10 Dying in 2006, actress Lynne Perrie had played which TV character for 23 years?
11 Which two colours are most often confused in colour blindness?
12 Which Abba album was No 1 again in 1999 seven years after its release?
13 Who was first to a first Best Actress Oscar – Hilary Swank or Julia Roberts?
14 Which stately home and safari park is owned by the Marquis of Bath?
15 Which ex-Tory MP once said, "Only domestic servants apologise"?
16 Which Spanish club side were the first winners of the European Champions Cup?
17 What type of animal can be Texel and Romney Marsh?
18 The Bee Gees were born on which island?
19 Theatre impresario Bill Kenwright is connected with which soccer club?
20 What was Jemima Khan's maiden name?
21 In the judiciary, what does the D in DPP stand for?
22 Who became the face of Estée Lauder in the mid-1990s?
23 Which is the nearest city to the Tay road bridge?
24 Prime Minister Viktor Yanukovich was defeated in a re-run election in which country?
25 In which decade of last century did Constantinople change its name to Istanbul?
26 In which decade was singer Eva Cassidy born?
27 Which designer was once a partner of Malcolm McLaren?
28 In 2006 it was announced that which country would host cricket's 2019 World Cup?
29 In which century was the last execution at the Tower of London?
30 In which group of islands is Panay?

Answers	**Pot Luck 85** *(see Quiz 186)*

1 Four. 2 Chef. 3 The Torrey Canyon. 4 Mackintosh. 5 Justin Gatlin. 6 1930s. 7 M62. 8 Wall Street. 9 USA. 10 Voodoo Chile. 11 Moscow. 12 France. 13 Toad. 14 And That's the Truth. 15 Della Street. 16 West Ham. 17 Grand Hotel. 18 1861. 19 Once. 20 Elizabeth Taylor. 21 Sale of alcohol. 22 Alaska. 23 Francis. 24 Boston. 25 12. 26 Trevor Eve. 27 NBC. 28 Eddie Fitzgerald. 29 Stansted. 30 Witchcraft.

1 Which website gave the space that helped launch the Arctic Monkeys?
2 Which company launched the DS console and the Wii?
3 Which building society merged with Barclays Bank in 2000?
4 What do Amazon.com chiefly sell?
5 Which newspaper did Lord Beaverbrook take over in the 20th century?
6 Ken Livingstone appointed Bob Kiley to oversee the reform of what?
7 Which brand of toothpaste gave its company a huge boost when George W Bush and Tony Blair both admitted using it?
8 What colour was the Vodafone lettering on England cricket shirts?
9 Which UK transport company went into receivership in October 2001?
10 Which retailer introduced the brand Per Una to boost flagging sales?
11 Where was Yves Gerbeau working when he took over as chief executive of the Millennium Dome?
12 Which was the first UK supermarket to achieve profits of more than £1bn?
13 In which city associated with the technology industry was Bill Gates born?
14 Habitat founder Terence Conran has also been involved in the management of which store catering for young families?
15 Which car and motor cycle manufacturer had the first name Soichiro?
16 What did Virgin trains ban from all but designated carriages from the autumn of 2001?
17 Which industrialist, whose name is known all over the world, was the first Lord Mayor of Dublin?
18 Which company did Steven Jobs leave prior to setting up NeXT Inc?
19 Akio Morita and Masaru Ibuka founded which electronics company?
20 Which motor manufacturer made the first non-stop double crossing of the English Channel by plane?
21 Which supermarket chain introduced the fashion label George?
22 What was the name of Chris Evans' company which bought Virgin radio?
23 What type of motor did Sinclair use in his personal transport C5?
24 The donor of the Tate Gallery made his fortune in which commodity?
25 Which Belgian airline effectively went bust after the World Trade Center atrocity?
26 Energy giants e.on. are based in which European country?
27 Which motor manufacturer designed Spitfire and Hurricane engines in WWII?
28 What was Frank Woolworth's middle name which was used for the store's own brand?
29 What is the world's largest passenger plane?
30 888.com sponsored a World Championship in which sport?

Answers	Music: Superstars *(see Quiz 183)*

1 Melbourne. 2 Aretha Franklin. 3 His father (Marvin Gaye Sr). 4 He played an electric guitar. 5 One. 6 George Harrison. 7 51. 8 Phil Collins. 9 Barbra Streisand. 10 Madonna. 11 33. 12 Garth Brooks. 13 Bee Gees. 14 Brooklyn. 15 Neil Diamond. 16 Willie Nelson. 17 Freddie Mercury. 18 Sting. 19 Albert Hall. 20 Cliff Richard. 21 Phil Collins. 22 Jolene. 23 Whitney Houston. 24 Diana Ross. 25 Rod Stewart. 26 Goldeneye. 27 Shirley Bassey. 28 Mariah Carey. 29 David Bowie. 30 2006.

1 How many members were in the original line-up of Il Divo?
2 In which profession did Marco Pierre White find fame?
3 Which vessel went down on the Seven Stones reef off Land's End?
4 What was the surname of Scot Charles Rennie of the Art Nouveau movement?
5 Which Justin recorded a 9.77 seconds 100 metres at Doha in 2006?
6 Snooker legend John Spencer died in 2006, but in which decade was he born?
7 Hull and Leeds are linked by which motorway?
8 In which film did Michael Douglas live by the maxim that "Greed is good"?
9 In which country is Peterson Field international airport?
10 Which Jimi Hendrix song hit No 1 a few weeks after the singer's death?
11 The news agency TASS is based in which city?
12 In which country was Edith Cresson PM in the 1990s?
13 Which of the following is not a crustacean – crab, lobster or toad?
14 In the 1990s single title what did Meat Loaf add to "I'd Lie for You"?
15 In fiction, what was the name of Perry Mason's secretary?
16 Which soccer team does Russell Brand support?
17 In which Brighton Hotel did an IRA bomb explode in 1984 at the Tory Conference?
18 When did the Pony Express ride into the sunset and close down its service – was it 1791, 1861 or 1921?
19 How many times did Gagarin orbit the Earth on his first journey into space?
20 Who was the first actress to be paid $1 million for a single film?
21 What did the Falstead Act aim to control in the US?
22 The northern terminus of the Pan American highway is in which state?
23 What is Daley Thompson's first name?
24 In which city did Louise Woodward's trial take place after a baby died in her care?
25 How many faces does a dodecahedron have?
26 Which actor played the TV character Detective Superintendent Peter Boyd?
27 What was the USA's first public television service?
28 What was Fitz's full name in "Cracker"?
29 What is Britain's third largest airport?
30 What is the main subject of the play "The Crucible" – chemistry, snooker or witchcraft?

Answers	Pot Luck 84 (see Quiz 184)

1 Palin. 2 Elton John. 3 Grand National. 4 Cape Town. 5 Orange. 6 21. 7 Above it. 8 Wednesday. 9 Little Women. 10 Ivy Tilsley. 11 Green and red. 12 Abba Gold. 13 Hilary Swank. 14 Longleat. 15 Alan Clark. 16 Real Madrid. 17 Sheep. 18 The Isle of Man. 19 Everton. 20 Goldsmith. 21 Director. 22 Elizabeth Hurley. 23 Dundee. 24 Ukraine. 25 1930s. 26 1960s. 27 Vivienne Westwood. 28 England. 29 20th. 30 Philippines.

1 What was Vaclav Havel's profession before he became President of the Czech Republic?
2 In 1985 Oxford University refused to give an honorary degree to which PM?
3 Assassinated Prime Minister Olof Palme led which country?
4 Who called the USSR an "evil empire"?
5 Which Prime Minister of Australia wept on TV when he confessed to marital misdemeanours?
6 Who did John Hinckley Jr shoot?
7 Lord Carrington resigned as Foreign Secretary during which conflict?
8 Which former leader died in jail in March 2006 while on trial for war crimes?
9 Who did Nelson Mandela succeed as head of the ANC?
10 On which day does the US President give his weekly talk to the American people?
11 Who became Secretary of State for Culture Media & Sport after the 2001 election?
12 Betty Boothroyd had which famous position of responsibility?
13 At the turn of the millennium which queen – other than Victoria – had reigned longest?
14 Which of the following Prime Ministers were in their nineties when they died – Clement Attlee, William Gladstone and Harold Macmillan?
15 How many years was Margaret Thatcher British Prime Minister – 9, 11 or 15?
16 Newt Gingrich was a respected politician in which country?
17 Who did Jack Straw replace as Foreign Secretary?
18 In 1999 Ehud Barak became Prime Minister of which country?
19 Who was Bill Clinton's first Vice President?
20 Which former South African prime minister died aged 90 in 2006?
21 Who did Gerhard Schroeder replace as German Chancellor?
22 Who was Mayor of New York at the time of the World Trade Center disaster?
23 Who did Paddy Ashdown replace as Liberal leader?
24 How many leaders did the Conservative Party have in the 1990s?
25 Which British Queen had 17 children?
26 Who did Tony Blair replace as Labour leader?
27 Which monarch succeeded King Hussein of Jordan?
28 Who became French Prime Minister in 1997?
29 Queen Wilhelmina led which country?
30 Who was George W Bush's first Secretary of State?

Answers	TV: Drama *(see Quiz 189)*

1 Detective. 2 WWII. 3 Casualty. 4 Emilia Fox. 5 Goodnight Mister Tom. 6 Colin Firth. 7 Peter. 8 Merseyside. 9 This Life. 10 Miss Marple. 11 Forensic. 12 England & USA. 13 Martin Chuzzlewit. 14 Lindsay Duncan. 15 Cardiac Arrest. 16 Bleak House. 17 Sean Bean. 18 Hearts & Bones. 19 Poirot. 20 Bradford. 21 Bergerac. 22 Ewan McGregor. 23 Cherie Lunghi. 24 Northern Exposure. 25 Philadelphia. 26 Jack Frost. 27 Edward VII. 28 Wednesday. 29 Cracker. 30 Earl of Leicester (Robert Dudley).

1 Who played the title character in the first "Doctor Who" movie?
2 In 2007 the isle of Inis Mor held a festival celebrating which TV show?
3 Which Grand National course fence, other than Becher's, contains the name Brook?
4 Stephen Cameron's 1996 death was a tragic first in which circumstances?
5 Which American was the first to achieve tennis's Men's Singles Grand Slam?
6 In song lyrics, where did Billie Jo Spears want to lay her blanket?
7 Which Roger was drummer with Queen?
8 Along with Doric and Corinthian, what is the third Greek order of architecture?
9 Who was the first British woman to win a world swimming title?
10 Which northern city has the dialling code 0113?
11 What nationality is Salman Rushdie?
12 What was the first hit album by The Killers?
13 Which population was devastated by myxomatosis?
14 Which is the brightest planet as seen from the Earth?
15 What do three horizontal lines represent in mathematics?
16 Which English King was the last to die in battle?
17 In rock opera, Tommy was deaf, dumb and what else?
18 How many times does the letter A appear in the first name of singer/actress Streisand?
19 Sale Sharks won the Guinness Premiership title in 2006, beating which team in the final?
20 What is the next prime number above 100?
21 What is a quadrilateral with one pair of opposite sides parallel called?
22 Which telephone link service was established in July 1937?
23 What is lowered by a beta-blocker?
24 Which country has the greatest number of telephone subscribers?
25 In the song "Country Roads", which place is described as "almost heaven"?
26 Who was the most famous inhabitant of the fictitious village St Mary Mead?
27 Which composer's "6th Symphony" is known as the "Pathétique?
28 Who was 60 first – Gloria Hunniford, Cliff Richard or John Major?
29 Boxer Jack Dempsey was nicknamed which Mauler?
30 Which country suffered most loss of life in the Indian Ocean tsunami of December 2004?

Answers | Pot Luck 87 *(see Quiz 190)*

1 France. 2 William Henry. 3 Christmas Day. 4 Breathing. 5 South. 6 The Number of the Beast. 7 Swedish. 8 Virgin Soldiers. 9 Capri. 10 Syd Little. 11 Sweden. 12 London. 13 None. 14 Dodecanese. 15 September 15th. 16 Tony Hancock. 17 Yellowstone Park. 18 Zip fastener. 19 Wes Craven. 20 Goat. 21 Kathy Bates. 22 Sally Lockhart. 23 Mona Lisa. 24 Parish. 25 K. 26 Lloyds of London. 27 George Michael. 28 Ian Millward. 29 Southampton. 30 Setting Sun.

1 What was the occupation of the person in the title role in "Rebus"?
2 Which War did "Foyle's War" deal with?
3 Ian Kelsey left "Emmerdale" for which hospital drama?
4 Who played Jeannie in the revival of "Randall & Hopkirk (Deceased)"?
5 In which drama did John Thaw play an elderly man who takes in a London evacuee?
6 Who was a memorable and different Mr Darcy on the large and small screen?
7 What was the name of the priest played by Stephen Tompkinson in "Ballykissangel"?
8 Where was the classic "Boys from the Blackstuff" set?
9 Which series featured Miles, Anna and Egg?
10 The late Joan Hickson played which famous sleuth on TV?
11 What type of surgeon was Dangerfield?
12 In which two countries was "The Buccaneers" set?
13 Which 1990s Dickens adaptation had Paul Scofield in the title role?
14 Who played Mrs Peter Mayle in the ill-fated "A Year in Provence"?
15 In which series did Helen Baxendale play Claire Maitland?
16 Anna Maxwell Martin won her first "Best Actress" BAFTA for which drama?
17 Who played Mellors in the 1993 TV adaptation of "Lady Chatterley's Lover"?
18 Which "thirtysomething" drama series starred Amanda Holden and Dervla Kirwan?
19 Which sleuth had a secretary called Miss Lemon?
20 Where was "Band of Gold" set?
21 Which TV detective worked for the Bureau des Etrangers?
22 Which future co-star of Nicole Kidman starred in Dennis Potter's "Lipstick on Your Collar"?
23 Which actress, who made a brief appearance in "EastEnders" in 2001, starred as "The Manageress"?
24 Which series had Dr Joel Fleishmann in the Alaskan town of Cicely?
25 In which state was "Thirtysomething" set?
26 Which TV detective was created in the books of RD Wingfield?
27 Which monarch was on the throne at the time "Upstairs Downstairs" was set?
28 Which day of the week was famous for having a weekly play in the late 1960s?
29 In which series did Robbie Coltrane play Fitz?
30 Jeremy Irons played which Earl in 2005's historical drama "Elizabeth"?

Answers	Leaders *(see Quiz 187)*

1 Dramatist. 2 Margaret Thatcher. 3 Sweden. 4 Ronald Reagan. 5 Bob Hawke. 6 Ronald Reagan. 7 Falklands. 8 Slobodan Milosevic. 9 Oliver Tambo. 10 Saturday. 11 Tessa Jowell. 12 Speaker of the House of Commons. 13 Elizabeth II. 14 Harold Macmillan. 15 11. 16 USA. 17 Robin Cook. 18 Israel. 19 Al Gore. 20 Pieter Botha. 21 Helmut Kohl. 22 Rudolph Giuliani. 23 David Steel. 24 Three. 25 Anne. 26 John Smith. 27 Abdullah. 28 Lionel Jospin. 29 Netherlands. 30 Colin Powell.

1 Which was the world's first country to introduce a driving test?
2 What are Bill Gates's two first names?
3 James Brown, "The Godfather of Soul", died on which special day in 2006?
4 What does the letter B stand for in SCUBA?
5 Is Helmand in the north or south of Afghanistan?
6 Which reissue of a 1982 Iron Maiden hit charted again in 2005?
7 Which language does the word ombudsman derives from?
8 Leslie Thomas wrote a novel about what kind of "Soldiers"?
9 Which island lies in the Bay of Naples?
10 Cyril Mead became known as which half of a comic duo?
11 Which country produced the first Miss World contest winner?
12 Florence Nightingale was given the Freedom of which city?
13 How many top ten hits did Kate Bush have in the last decade of the old millennium?
14 Rhodes is the largest of which group of islands?
15 The Battle of Britain is remembered on which date?
16 Which of these comics died the youngest – Tony Hancock, Eric Morecambe or Peter Sellers?
17 Which US national park has a highway called Alligator Alley?
18 Which invention affecting trousers was patented in Chicago in 1913?
19 Which director started off the "Scream" series of movies?
20 What animal appears on the cover of the Beach Boys' album "Pet Sounds"?
21 Who won the Best Actress Oscar for the movie "Misery"?
22 Which character did Billie Piper play in "The Ruby in the Smoke"?
23 How is the painting La Gioconda also known?
24 In the Church of England what is the smallest administrative unit?
25 Which letter identified Tommy Lee Jones' character in the "Men in Black" movie?
26 In which London building does the Lutine Bell hang?
27 Which male singer called his debut solo album "Faith"?
28 Which rugby head coach Ian suffered a 2006 sacking at Wigan?
29 Which of these is furthest south – Bath, Bristol or Southampton?
30 What was the first top ten hit for the Chemical Brothers?

Answers	Pot Luck 86 (see Quiz 188)

1 Peter Cushing. 2 Father Ted. 3 Valentine's. 4 Road rage attack. 5 Donald Budge. 6 On the ground. 7 Taylor. 8 Ionic. 9 Karen Pickering. 10 Leeds. 11 British. 12 Hot Fuss. 13 Rabbit. 14 Venus. 15 Identically equal to. 16 Richard III. 17 Blind. 18 Twice. 19 Leicester. 20 101. 21 Trapezium. 22 999 service. 23 Heart rate and/ or blood pressure. 24 USA. 25 West Virginia. 26 Miss Marple. 27 Tchaikovsky. 28 Gloria Hunniford (April 2000). 29 Manassa. 30 Indonesia.

1 Which company created the computer game Shenmue?
2 In which decade were books issued as CD Roms?
3 Which comic is older, "Beano" or "Dandy"?
4 Which best-selling toys do Steiff make?
5 Where in the UK is the Kelvingrove art gallery?
6 How many counters does each backgammon player have at the start of play?
7 "Roma" and "Tornado" are types of what?
8 Pokemon Yellow was created by which manufacturer?
9 What is a round of play called in a hand of bridge?
10 In which county is Alton Towers?
11 What is the number to aim for in a game of cribbage?
12 In which decade was the first Home Video System produced?
13 What colour are Scrabble tiles?
14 Which computer games can be Red, Yellow and Pikachu?
15 What type of needlework requires aida fabric?
16 Where was shuffleboard originally played?
17 Which company created the Gran Turismo Real Driving Simulator?
18 Ikebana is the art of what?
19 What are satin, stem and lazy daisy?
20 EasyEverything is the world's biggest what?
21 Which colour do Morris dancers predominantly wear?
22 Where in the UK is the Blackgang Chine Clifftop Theme Park?
23 Which special piece of equipment is needed to do crochet?
24 Who wrote the spy thriller "Without Remorse"?
25 How many dice are used in a craps game?
26 Which company produced the first battery-powered cassette recorder?
27 How many packs of cards are used in a game of canasta?
28 What is the world's most widely played board game?
29 Which company created the MS Flight Simulator?
30 In draughts when can a piece move forwards or backwards?

Answers	**Sporting Legends** *(see Quiz 193)*

1 Severiano Ballesteros. 2 Doctor. 3 Manchester United. 4 1970s. 5 Four. 6 Sydney. 7 1950s. 8 Aberdeen. 9 Chelsea. 10 1970s. 11 400m hurdles. 12 14. 13 Stephen Hendry. 14 Tony Jacklin. 15 Barry John. 16 Michael Johnson. 17 Kapil Dev. 18 Chess. 19 Hamburg. 20 Squash. 21 20. 22 Bjorn Borg. 23 452. 24 Australian. 25 Ravel's Bolero. 26 Ipswich Town. 27 Baseball. 28 Refused to do military service. 29 French. 30 Willie Carson.

1 Usually meaning extra-terrestrial, where is a car from with the registration letters ET?
2 Which football ground has a Matthew Harding Stand?
3 Which method did John Haigh use to dispose of his victims' bodies?
4 Ralph Scheider was an inventor credited with developing which daily used item?
5 What colour were Arsenal's shirts in their first Champions League Final?
6 What does the reference ibid. mean?
7 Which creepy horror movie features the character Jack Torrance?
8 What does the C stand for in COBOL?
9 What is the nationality of Jennifer Lopez's parents?
10 In which city should you "be sure to wear some flowers in your hair"?
11 In which country was the musician Bela Bartok born?
12 In 1918 in Britain women over what age were given the vote?
13 Which Royal first sat in the House of Lords in 1987?
14 Baroness de Laroche was the first woman to be awarded what licence?
15 Leona Lewis was born and bred in which city?
16 In which London street did Selfridge's first open?
17 Michael Steele was in which all-girl group?
18 Which culinary ingredient can be Extra Virgin?
19 On TV, who was the first regular female presenter of "Points Of View"?
20 Who composed the comic opera "The Gondoliers"?
21 Which picnic aid did James Dewar invent?
22 "The Most Beautiful Girl in the World" was the first UK No 1 single for which artist?
23 Which sisters used Bell as a pseudonym?
24 Whose dying words were, "My neck is very slender"?
25 "Goodbye England's Rose" was the first line of which song?
26 Oyster and Morel are both types of which vegetable?
27 Who is the local sporting hero of the city of Oviedo, Spain?
28 What was the title of the first album from the Scissor Sisters?
29 How was designer Laura Mountney better known?
30 ABTA represents which group of people?

Answers | Pot Luck 89 *(see Quiz 194)*

1 Four Tops. 2 Cheltenham. 3 A clove. 4 George VI. 5 Women's Institute. 6 Bikini. 7 Stuart Clark. 8 Colditz. 9 News of the World. 10 Champion Jockey. 11 Michaelmas Day. 12 Beatrix Potter. 13 Axis. 14 1,000 Guineas. 15 Valencia. 16 Push the Button. 17 Peru. 18 Duke of Bedford. 19 Norfolk. 20 Charterhouse. 21 Walt Disney. 22 The Duchess of Windsor. 23 Pankhurst. 24 Brazil. 25 Test tube baby. 26 Belgium. 27 Manchester. 28 Julienne. 29 Greek kilt. 30 South Africa.

1 Which Spaniard became the youngest golfer to win the British Open in the 20th century?

2 What was Roger Bannister's "day job"?

3 Which English club did George Best join immediately after leaving school?

4 In which decade did Ian Botham make his Test debut?

5 How many times did Will Carling lead England to the Five Nations title?

6 In which city did Shane Warne play his last Test match?

7 In which decade did Henry Cooper win his first British heavyweight championship?

8 Which side did Alex Ferguson manage before he went to Manchester United?

9 For which club did Jimmy Greaves make his Football League debut?

10 In which decade did Wayne Gretzky make his professional debut?

11 What was Sally Gunnell's Olympic gold-medal-winning event?

12 Mike Hailwood won how many Isle of Man TT races in the period 1961–1979?

13 Who was the first snooker player to win all nine world ranking tournaments?

14 Who was the European Ryder Cup team's captain from 1983 to 1989?

15 Which Welsh Rugby player scored a record 90 points for his country between 1966 and 1972?

16 Who was the first man to hold the world record at 200m and 400m simultaneously?

17 Who led India to victory in the Cricket World Cup in 1983?

18 Anatoli Karpov was world champion in what?

19 Which team on the European mainland did Kevin Keegan play for?

20 Which sport did Jahangir Khan play?

21 How many Wimbledon titles did Billie Jean King win?

22 Who broke Fred Perry's record of three consecutive Wimbledon titles?

23 To the nearest 50 how many runs did Don Bradman make on his first innings for New South Wales?

24 In 1990 John McEnroe was expelled from which Grand Slam Open for swearing?

25 Which music did Torvill & Dean use when they scored a full hand of perfect scores at the 1984 Olympics?

26 Which team did Alf Ramsey take to the First Division Championship?

27 Which sport did Hank Aaron play?

28 Why was Muhammad Ali stripped of his World Heavyweight tile in 1967?

29 Which was the only Grand Slam title Pete Sampras has not won?

30 Which former Scottish jockey has the first names William Hunter Fisher?

Answers	Hobbies (see Quiz 191)

1 Sega. 2 1990s. 3 Beano. 4 Teddy bears. 5 Glasgow. 6 15. 7 Tomato. 8 Nintendo Game Boy. 9 Trick. 10 Staffordshire. 11 31. 12 1970s. 13 Cream/white. 14 Pokemon. 15 Embroidery. 16 On board ship. 17 Sony Play Station. 18 Flower arranging. 19 Embroidery stitches. 20 Internet cafe. 21 White. 22 Isle of Wight. 23 Hook. 24 Tom Clancy. 25 Two. 26 Philips. 27 Two. 28 Monopoly. 29 Microsoft. 30 When it becomes a king.

1 Levi Stubbs was lead singer with which Tamla Motown group?
2 Which Gloucestershire town had the first public school for girls?
3 What is a small segment of garlic called?
4 Who was the first reigning monarch to visit the USA?
5 Which women's organisation was founded by Mrs Hoodless in 1897?
6 Which fashion statement was created by Louis Reard in 1946?
7 Who topped the Australian bowling averages for the 2006–07 Ashes series?
8 How was the prison camp Oflag IVC better known?
9 Which Queen album had the name of a national newspaper?
10 What did Gordon Richards become a record 26 times between 1925 and 1953?
11 On a calendar, what is the third quarter day in England?
12 Who lived at "Hill Top" near Sawrey, Ambleside?
13 What was the name of the alliance between Germany and Italy in World War II?
14 Which Classic horse race was the first to be run on a Sunday in England?
15 Which club did Fernando Morientes join when he left Liverpool?
16 Which title links a No 1 album by The Chemical Brothers and a Sugababes' No 1 single?
17 In which country does the Amazon begin?
18 Which Duke has an ancestral home at Woburn Abbey?
19 In which county is the Queen's home Sandringham House?
20 All the members of Genesis were ex-pupils of which school?
21 Who said, "I love Mickey Mouse more than any woman I've ever known"?
22 Who said, "No woman can be too rich or too thin"?
23 What was Emmeline Goulden's married name?
24 Which country does supermodel Gisele Bundchen come from?
25 Why was Louise Joy Brown's birth a first in 1978?
26 In which country was the first beauty contest held?
27 In which city did the first Marks & Spencer store open?
28 What term describes thinly cut vegetables slowly cooked in butter?
29 What sort of garment is a fustanella?
30 In which country is the Humewood Golf Club?

Answers | **Pot Luck 88** *(see Quiz 192)*

1 Egypt. 2 Stamford Bridge. 3 Acid bath. 4 Credit card. 5 Yellow. 6 In the same place. 7 The Shining. 8 Common. 9 Puerto Rican. 10 San Francisco. 11 Hungary. 12 30. 13 Prince Andrew. 14 Pilot's licence. 15 London. 16 Oxford Street. 17 The Bangles. 18 Olive oil. 19 Anne Robinson. 20 Gilbert & Sullivan. 21 Thermos flask. 22 Prince. 23 Brontë Sisters. 24 Anne Boleyn. 25 Candle in the Wind 97. 26 Mushroom. 27 Fernando Alonso. 28 Scissor Sisters. 29 Laura Ashley. 30 Travel agents.

1 What are the initials for the human form of BSE?
2 Which letter is used to denote the bird flu virus?
3 A hysterectomy involves removal of what?
4 Osteoporosis is a weakness and brittleness of what?
5 In which decade did a report first appear in the US saying smoking could damage health?
6 What was the nationality of the founder of the Red Cross?
7 Penicillin was the first what?
8 Ebola is also known as which disease?
9 What does S stand for in AIDS?
10 Appendicitis causes pain where?
11 Which insects cause bubonic plague?
12 Which disease – more common in children – is also called varicella?
13 What causes cholera – contaminated water, insects or malnutrition?
14 Which part of the body is affected by conjunctivitis?
15 The infection of wounds by what can bring on tetanus?
16 Which of the following is not a blood group – AB, O or T?
17 What sort of flies transmit sleeping sickness?
18 Cranial osteopathy involves the manipulation of which bones?
19 Reflexologists massage which part of the body?
20 Shiatsu is a massage technique from which country?
21 Anabolic steroids are used to repair or build what?
22 What does an analgesic drug do?
23 What does the H stand for in HIV?
24 In which part of the body is the human's longest bone?
25 Hypertension is another name for what?
26 What is the most common element in the human body?
27 After the skin, what is the next largest human organ?
28 What is another name for the sternum?
29 Which impotence drug was used to strengthen a premature baby in 2006?
30 Where was the first ambulance used?

Answers	The Oscars *(see Quiz 197)*

1 Rachel Weisz. 2 Seven. 3 Gwyneth Paltrow. 4 Charlize Theron. 5 American Beauty. 6 Boys Don't Cry. 7 Tommy Lee Jones. 8 The Cider House Rules. 9 The Piano. 10 March. 11 James Whale. 12 Julia Roberts. 13 Ang Lee. 14 Creature Comforts. 15 John Williams. 16 The Madness of King George. 17 As Good As It Gets. 18 Tom Hanks. 19 Sally Field. 20 Moonstruck. 21 Shirley MacLaine. 22 American Civil War. 23 Oliver Reed. 24 Jane Fonda. 25 Jon Voight. 26 Hayley Mills. 27 Geoffrey Rush. 28 Jeremy Irons. 29 New York. 30 Sam Mendes.

1 In which country did the Women's Institute begin?
2 On TV who became a "hunter gatherer" searching out food from the wild?
3 The French President occupies which official residence?
4 In which country is Archangel international airport?
5 Which Lawrence and Jacqueline wrote the guide to being civilised called "A Pinch of Posh"?
6 Who was backed by The Dakotas?
7 In which ocean is the Sargasso Sea – Atlantic, Indian or Pacific?
8 French designer Christian Dior created what kind of Look in the late 1940s?
9 Which band have had hits with "Getaway" and "Inner Smile"?
10 The Fosse Way links which two English cities?
11 In which capital city was jazz's Hot Club?
12 Prince Edward resigned from which branch of the services in 1987?
13 Who is the oldest of The Three Tenors?
14 In which song were "them good old boys drinkin' whisky & rye"?
15 How is Formosa now known?
16 Who introduced the very first edition of "Countdown" on TV?
17 Lowfields Road goes past which famous soccer stadium?
18 In what year did "Blue Peter" first set sail on the airwaves of TV?
19 Viscount Linley was the first British Royal to be banned from doing what?
20 Peter Sutcliffe became better known under which graphic name?
21 Which month was in hit titles by Pilot and Barbara Dixon?
22 In which mountain range is the Simplon Pass?
23 Marie Curie was the first woman to win which notable prize?
24 Who had an instrumental hit with "Don't Cry for Me Argentina"?
25 In which year did Queen Elizabeth and the Duke of Edinburgh celebrate their Golden Wedding?
26 What is the chief shopping street in Edinburgh?
27 In 2006, who clocked up 20 years as editor of "Private Eye"?
28 René Lalique used which material when making ornaments?
29 Which city is named after US frontiersman Kit Carson?
30 Kurt Cobain's farewell note in 1995 read, "It's better to burn out than" do what?

Answers | Pot Luck 91 *(see Quiz 198)*

1 Ellis. 2 Chile & Argentina. 3 10th. 4 Hat. 5 Pile it high, sell it cheap. 6 Hannah Waterman. 7 Jimmy Carter. 8 Stevens. 9 Queensland. 10 Bradford. 11 Victoria. 12 Glenys. 13 The Cheeky Girls. 14 Chicago. 15 Safety pin. 16 Clooney. 17 Cream. 18 Jack. 19 And now. 20 Grease. 21 Whole Again. 22 Skull. 23 Albert. 24 Woolworth's. 25 Ulrike Meinhof. 26 Kenya. 27 Banana and toffee. 28 Victoria. 29 Leeds United. 30 Simon Jordan.

1 Who won the only Oscar for "The Constant Gardener"?
2 How many Oscars did "Schindler's List" win?
3 Who played Viola in "Shakespeare in Love"?
4 Who won an Oscar for her role in "Monster"?
5 Which movie was the last Best Picture winner of the 1990s?
6 For which movie did Hilary Swank win her first Oscar?
7 Who played the marshal in an Oscar-winning performance in "The Fugitive"?
8 For which movie did Michael Caine win his second Oscar?
9 For which movie did the 11-year-old Anna Paquin win an Oscar in 1993?
10 In which month does the Oscars ceremony usually take place?
11 Which director is the subject of "Gods and Monsters"?
12 Who won the Best Actress Oscar in 2001?
13 Who directed "Crouching Tiger Hidden Dragon"?
14 For which movie did Nick Park win his first Oscar?
15 Who wrote the music for "Jaws"?
16 Which Nicholas Hytner movie had Nigel Hawthorne in the title role?
17 Which 1997 movie with Oscar-winning performances had the ad line, "Brace yourself for Melvin!"?
18 Who "outed" his drama teacher at an Oscars ceremony where he won for the AIDS issue movie "Philadelphia"?
19 Who played Oscar-nominated Julia Roberts' mother in "Steel Magnolias"?
20 For which movie did Cher receive her Oscar in a dress which caused more uproar than the film?
21 Which actress, who had her 67th birthday in 2001, said "I deserve this" on receiving her Oscar in 1983?
22 Against which conflict is "Dances with Wolves" set?
23 Which actor died during the making of the Oscar-winning "Gladiator"?
24 Between Glenda Jackson's two Best Actress Oscars, Liza Minnelli and who else won?
25 Which father of Angelina Jolie won an Oscar for "Coming Home"?
26 Which English actress won an Oscar as a child in 1960?
27 Which star of "Quills" won an Oscar for "Shine"?
28 Who was the only English Best Actor of the 1990s?
29 Where did Woody Allen set "Hannah and Her Sisters"?
30 Which British director directed "American Beauty"?

Answers	Medicine & Health (see Quiz 195)

1 CJD. 2 H. 3 Womb. 4 Bones. 5 1960s. 6 Swiss. 7 Antibiotic. 8 Legionnaire's. 9 Syndrome. 10 Abdomen. 11 Fleas. 12 Chicken pox. 13 Contaminated water. 14 Eyes. 15 Soil. 16 T. 17 Tsetse flies. 18 Skull. 19 Feet. 20 Japan. 21 Muscles. 22 Alleviate pain. 23 Human. 24 Thigh. 25 High blood pressure. 26 Oxygen. 27 Liver. 28 Breastbone. 29 Viagara. 30 France.

1 Which Ruth was the last woman to be hanged in British history?
2 The Transandine railway tunnel links which two countries?
3 Which wedding anniversary is linked to tin?
4 Who or what was Dolly Varden?
5 What was the motto of Tesco founder Sir Jack Cohen?
6 Which actress won "Just the Two of Us" with Marti Pellow?
7 Which US President was married to Rosalynn Smith?
8 Which Cat sang that he loved his dog?
9 The Great Barrier Reef is off which Australian state?
10 Heroic PC Sharon Beshenivsky was murdered in which city in 2005?
11 Which British monarch's name does Princess Eugenie have?
12 What is the first name of MEP Mrs Kinnock?
13 Gabriela Irimia was a member of which group?
14 Ruthie Henshall and Ute Lemper were the first West End stars of which musical?
15 Which Walter Hunt invention of 1849 has Liz Hurley used as a fashion statement?
16 Which 1950s singer Rosemary is aunt of a popular actor George with the same surname?
17 Baker, Bruce and Clapton made up which group?
18 What was the most popular baby boy name in England and Wales from 2000 to 2006?
19 What are the first two words of "My Way"?
20 "Hopelessly Devoted to You" comes from which musical?
21 What was the first UK No 1 for Atomic Kitten?
22 Which part of the body is studied by a phrenologist?
23 What was Frank Sinatra's middle name?
24 Which shopping chain advertised "nothing over sixpence"?
25 Who was the female leader of the Baader Meinhof terrorist group?
26 Where is the Masai Mara game reserve?
27 What are a banoffee pie's main two ingredients?
28 Who was the first British monarch seen on a moving picture?
29 Jack Charlton played all his League football with which club side?
30 Who was Crystal Palace chairman when manager Iain Dowie left "by mutual consent"?

Answers	**Pot Luck 90** *(see Quiz 196)*

1 Canada. 2 Ray Mears. 3 Elysee Palace. 4 Russia. 5 Llewelyn Bowen. 6 Billy J Kramer. 7 Atlantic. 8 New Look. 9 Texas. 10 Lincoln & Exeter. 11 Paris. 12 Royal Marines. 13 Luciano Pavarotti. 14 American Pie. 15 Taiwan. 16 Richard Whiteley. 17 Elland Road (Leeds). 18 1958. 19 Driving. 20 The Yorkshire Ripper. 21 January. 22 Alps. 23 Nobel Prize. 24 The Shadows. 25 1997. 26 Princes Street. 27 Ian Hislop. 28 Glass. 29 Carson City. 30 Fade away.

1 Which female band had a No 1 with "Independent Women Part 1"?

2 Who wrote the "Liverpool Oratorio" with Paul McCartney?

3 Whose album had the invitation "Come On Over" in 1998?

4 Who sang "I Walk the Line" and "A Boy Named Sue"?

5 What did Leo Fender make?

6 Which Australian had 13 consecutive UK Top Ten hits between January 1988 and June 1991?

7 Which duo had a multi-million seller with "Unchained Melody" in 1995?

8 Whose best-selling posthumous album was called "Legend"?

9 Who made the solo albums "Watermark" and "Shepherd Moons"?

10 How were John McDermott, Anthony Kearns and Ronan Tynan styled?

11 Whose albums include "Sogno", "Romanza" and "Sueno"?

12 What type of musician was conductor Daniel Barenboim's wife Jacqueline?

13 How was Nathaniel Adams Coles better known?

14 Which Harry won a Lifetime Achievement Grammy in 2000?

15 Which "title" did bandleader Basie have?

16 Which Harry made the albums "We are in Love" and "Blue Light, Red Light"?

17 With which orchestra did Simon Rattle make his name?

18 Which veteran country singer had two best-selling albums recorded in prisons?

19 Who featured in the movie "Purple Rain"?

20 Who sang the theme song from the Bond movie "Tomorrow Never Dies"?

21 Who won a Grammy in 1992 for "Tears in Heaven"?

22 Who wrote the musical "Oliver!"?

23 Which instrument did Stan Getz play?

24 How many members of boy band A1 are there?

25 Which country do the band Modjo come from?

26 Which English city does Craig David come from?

27 Who recorded the song which the Labour Party used in their 1997 campaign?

28 Who played keyboards with the Strawbs and Yes?

29 Selling well in 2006, who recorded the "The Love Album"?

30 Who made the 2006 debut album "Alright, Still"?

Answers | Folk Music *(see Quiz 201)*

1 Liege & Life (Fairport Convention). 2 Modern Times. 3 Renbourn. 4 Village Green Preservation Society. 5 Norma Waterstone. 6 Thyme. 7 Folk Britannia. 8 Derbyshire. 9 Tom Paxton. 10 Northumberland. 11 Bob Dylan. 12 Drum. 13 Wilson. 14 Kate Rusby. 15 Judy Dyble. 16 Bagpipes. 17 Steeleye Span. 18 Pentangle. 19 Tony Allen. 20 Streets of London. 21 Guitar. 22 Jim Moray. 23 Martin Carthy. 24 Strings. 25 Strawbs. 26 Johnny Cash. 27 Clancy. 28 Kate Rusby. 29 Kathryn Tickell Band. 30 2007.

1 Which European city has the same name as an archer in mythology?
2 Which month comes after the month containing Saint Andrew's Day?
3 Which fruit includes the variety Ellison's Orange?
4 Tyskie is a brand of beer from which country?
5 Aduki, borlotti and cannellini are all types of what?
6 Where would a Spanish lady wear her mantilla?
7 Who was 50 first – Geena Davis, Nigel Kennedy or Annie Lennox?
8 Who was the first woman General of the Salvation Army?
9 Who was the first singer to have seven consecutive singles reach No 1 in the US?
10 Which English cricket captain had a bust-up with umpire Shakoor Rana in Faisalabad?
11 "Rhythm of Life" comes from which musical?
12 Svetlana Savitskaya was the first woman to walk where?
13 Who had UK hits with "Down 4 U" and "Only U"?
14 The frittata is an Italian version of what popular egg dish?
15 What was the highest-ranking job that the fictitious Jim Hacker achieved?
16 How many beats to the bar does a traditional waltz have?
17 Which sweet delicacies have a name meaning "little ovens"?
18 Which title did Hillary Clinton prefer to First Lady?
19 In France what would you buy if you asked for pamplemousses?
20 Which Royal's motto is "Ich dien" or "I serve"?
21 Which flavouring used in tonic water is taken from a cinchona tree?
22 Why might you be embarrassed by your lentigines?
23 Which jazz singer is Mrs Johnny Dankworth?
24 What colour is the background of the flag of the European Union?
25 Kim Carnes sang about which film star's eyes?
26 Who was Fred Elliott about to marry when he died in "Coronation Street"?
27 How many sharps and flats are there in the key of C major?
28 Sven Goran Eriksson first won the Italian Cup as boss of which side?
29 How is the volcanic Mongibello also known?
30 At which English club did Ian Wright end his soccer playing career?

Answers	**21st Century FIFA World Cup** *(see Quiz 202)*

1 1-1. 2 Right foot. 3 Marco Materazzi. 4 Costa Rica. 5 Group B. 6 Michael Owen (Two). 7 Tim Cahill. 8 Fabio Cannavaro. 9 Ukraine. 10 Robert Green. 11 Trinidad & Tobago. 12 David Beckham. 13 Nine men. 14 Angola. 15 S. Korea. 16 Sweden. 17 White. 18 Germany. 19 David Trezeguet. 20 France (v. Brazil). 21 Gelsenkirchen. 22 Portugal v. Holland. 23 Marcello Lippi. 24 Miroslav Klose (5 goals). 25 No 9. 26 Fabio Grosso. 27 Switzerland. 28 Guus Hiddink. 29 Cristiano Ronaldo. 30 Six.

1 What was voted most influential folk album of all time in a 2006 BBC ballot?
2 Which Bob Dylan album namechecks Alicia Keys?
3 Which guitarist John of Pentangle in the 1960s, reached his 60s in 2004?
4 TV's "Jam & Jerusalem" had Kate Rusby singing which song by The Kinks?
5 Who is Eliza Carthy's famous folk-singing mum?
6 In song, what goes with parsley, sage and rosemary?
7 Which 2006 Barbican concert series was covered by the BBC?
8 Which county does singer John Tams come from?
9 Who wrote the folk club favourite "The Last Thing on My Mind"?
10 Kathryn Tickell comes from which English county?
11 Which Minnesota-born star was inducted into the UK Music Hall of Fame in 2005?
12 A bodhran is what type of instrument?
13 What was the middle name of folk pioneer Woody Guthrie?
14 Who charted in 2006 with "All Over Again", a duet with Ronan Keating?
15 Who was Fairport Convention's first female singer?
16 Uillean pipes are a type of what?
17 Womble producer Mike Batt took which folk band into the pop charts?
18 Which five-piece group recorded the influential "Light Flight"?
19 Who forms a duo with accordionist Mike Foster?
20 "In our winter city the rain cries a little pity" is in which Ralph McTell song?
21 Which instrument is associated with Bert Jansch?
22 Which Jim made the album "Sweet England"?
23 Which folk veteran Martin was BBC 2's Folk Singer of the Year in 2005?
24 What produces the sound in an Irish bouzouki?
25 Which band featured singer/songwriter Dave Cousins?
26 Which country star featured with Bob Dylan on "Nashville Skyline"?
27 Tommy Makem featured with which Brothers in the 1960s?
28 Who recorded the album "The Girl Who Couldn't Fly"?
29 Which female's folk band featured in "Last Night of the Proms" in 2001?
30 Which year marks Fairport Convention's fortieth anniversary?

Answers	**Music: Who's Who?** *(see Quiz 199)*

1 Destiny's Child. 2 Carl Davis. 3 Shania Twain. 4 Johnny Cash. 5 Guitars. 6 Kylie Minogue. 7 Robson & Jerome. 8 Bob Marley. 9 Enya. 10 The Irish Tenors. 11 Andrea Bocelli. 12 Cellist. 13 Nat King Cole. 14 Belafonte. 15 Count. 16 Harry Connick Jr. 17 Birmingham. 18 Johnny Cash. 19 Prince. 20 Sheryl Crow. 21 Eric Clapton. 22 Lionel Bart. 23 Saxophone. 24 Four. 25 France. 26 Southampton. 27 D Ream. 28 Rick Wakeman. 29 Westlife. 30 Lily Allen.

1 What was the 90-minute score in the 2006 World Cup Final?
2 Ahead of Germany 2006, Wayne Rooney fractured metatarsals in which foot?
3 Which Italian was involved in the sending-off incident with Zinedine Zidane in 2006?
4 Who did Germany play in the opening game in 2006?
5 Which Group were England in for Germany 2006?
6 Who was England's top scorer in the 2002 finals?
7 Who scored two goals as Australia beat Japan in 2006?
8 Who was the Italian captain in Germany 2006?
9 Which team lost their opener 4–0 yet still made the last eight of Germany 2006?
10 Which keeper missed Germany after a groin injury while playing for England B?
11 Against which opponents did Wayne Rooney first play in Germany 2006?
12 Which English player scored in both 2002 and 2006 World Cup tournaments?
13 In 2006, how many players did USA have at the end of the 1–1 with Italy?
14 Which A claimed their first point in a final tournament in Germany 2006?
15 Which team finished fourth in the 2002 tournament?
16 Against which team did Michael Owen damage his knee in Germany 2006?
17 What colour shirts did the French wear in the 2006 Final?
18 Which team was the first to progress to the quarter finals in 2006?
19 Who missed a penalty in the 2006 Final shoot-out?
20 Which country knocked out the defending champions in 2006?
21 Where was England's 2006 quarter final staged?
22 Which game in Germany 2006 saw 16 yellow cards and four reds?
23 Who was coach of the 2006 FIFA World Cup winners?
24 Who was top scorer in Germany 2006?
25 What number was Wayne Rooney wearing when red carded v. Portugal?
26 Who scored the final penalty in the 2006 Final shoot-out?
27 Which side became the first to be eliminated in a finals without letting in a goal?
28 Who managed South Korea to their success in 2002?
29 Who hit the shoot-out penalty to send England packing in 2006?
30 Excluding shoot-outs, how many goals did England score in Germany 2006?

Answers	Pot Luck 92 *(see Quiz 200)*

1 Paris. 2 December. 3 Apple. 4 Poland. 5 Beans. 6 Head/shoulder. 7 Annie Lennox (2004). 8 Evangeline Booth. 9 Whitney Houston. 10 Mike Gatting. 11 Sweet Charity. 12 Space. 13 Ashanti. 14 Omelette. 15 British Prime Minister. 16 Three. 17 Petits Fours. 18 Presidential Partner. 19 Grapefruit. 20 Prince of Wales. 21 Quinine. 22 Freckles. 23 Cleo Laine. 24 Blue. 25 Bette Davis. 26 Beverley Unwin. 27 None. 28 Roma. 29 Etna. 30 Burnley.

1 Which airport had a major luggage delivery backlog over Xmas 2006?
2 Where in Europe are Partu and Tartu airports to be found?
3 Hopkins Airport is in which US state?
4 Which is further east – Gatwick or Heathrow?
5 Which US president gives his name to an airport in La Paz, Bolivia?
6 The planes hitting the World Trade Center on 9/11 were scheduled to fly to which city?
7 In which country is Yellowknife airport?
8 Which city in Austria is near the Blue Danube airport?
9 Which B is an airport situated in the Hebrides?
10 Santa Ana airport in the US takes the name of which legendary movie hero?
11 Willie Walsh was chief executive of which airline?
12 Which is further north – Aberdeen or Glasgow airport?
13 The plane involved in the Lockerbie bombing was travelling to which US city?
14 Which of Aarborg, Aarhous and Amborovy airports is not in Denmark?
15 In which country is Fornebu airport?
16 The Ben Apps airport in the US has the name of which European city?
17 Liverpool airport was renamed after which pop celebrity?
18 In which country is Linate airport?
19 The Concorde crashing in 2000 in France had taken off from which airport?
20 Which is further south – Bristol or Norwich airport?
21 In which country is Santander airport?
22 In which English county is Stanstead airport?
23 The Robert Bradshaw airport is located on which group of islands?
24 Which explorer gives his name to an airport in Venice?
25 On 9/11 2001, the ill-fated Flight 93 took off from which Washington airport?
26 In which US city is Tacoma airport?
27 Is Peretol airport in Argentina, Italy or Paraguay?
28 The regally named Prince George and Prince Rupert airports are in which country?
29 What was the main cause of the many cancellations from Heathrow, December 2006?
30 In which country is Vaasa airport?

Answers	Andrew Lloyd-Webber *(see Quiz 205)*

1 1940s. 2 How Do You Solve a Problem Like Maria?. 3 Cello. 4 Sarah. 5 Jesus Christ Superstar 6 Evita. 7 Ayckbourn. 8 Dr Barnardo. 9 Mary Magdalen. 10 Christine. 11 Prince Edward. 12 Boyzone. 13 Sunset Boulevard. 14 Tell Me on a Sunday. 15 Joseph and the Amazing Technicolor Dreamcoat. 16 Michael Crawford. 17 Phantom of the Opera. 18 Jeeves. 19 Bombay Dreams. 20 Ball. 21 Phantom of the Opera. 22 Evita. 23 Barbara Dickson. 24 Northern Ireland. 25 Lesley Garrett. 26 Palace. 27 Cats. 28 Roger Moore. 29 1990s. 30 Any Dream Will Do.

1 David Marks and Julia Barfield designed which modern London landmark?
2 In what year was AIDS officially recognised?
3 In which country did Sven Goran Eriksson first coach outside Sweden?
4 Which character did Meryl Streep play in the movie "The Devil Wears Prada"?
5 What is the first name of George Harrison's widow?
6 Who told Tony Blair in the Commons in 2005, "You were the future once"?
7 What was the first independent trade union in the former Eastern bloc?
8 After ten years of hits, who had an album called "Never Gone"?
9 Which club returned to the Football League this century, 44 years after resigning?
10 Which Michael became head of Ryanair?
11 The 2003 album "Final Straw" proved to be anything but for which band?
12 When did Vodafone start to sponsor the England cricket team – 1997, 2000 or 2004?
13 In Spain, who or what is El Gordo?
14 Who chose the celestial objects for the set of six stamps issued in February 2007?
15 In what year were the first Olympics held behind the Iron Curtain opened?
16 "Endless Wire" was the first studio album in 24 years made by which band?
17 Who became the first woman speaker of the USA's House of Representatives?
18 "Dreamgirls" actress Jennifer Hudson was discovered on which US talent show?
19 Which 60-plus singer Tom was knighted in 2006?
20 How many Von Trapp children are there in "The Sound of Music"?
21 The death of which musician moved Don McLean to write "American Pie"?
22 Which actress played the character Nana in "The Royle Family"?
23 Which celebrity chef appeared in "Rachel's Favourite Food"?
24 Which country hosted the first Eurovision Song Contest?
25 Did the national daily paper "Today" cease publication in 1985, 1995 or 2005?
26 Which Ethan starred in "Explorer" before his 20th birthday?
27 Who was the first King of the Belgians?
28 Which comedian wrote "Tim the Tiny Horse"?
29 Shane Filan was a member of which chart-busting boy band?
30 Darfur is a province of which country?

Answers	**Pot Luck 94** (see Quiz 206)

1 Pakistan. 2 Vogue. 3 Stereophonics. 4 Drugs. 5 Witney. 6 New York. 7 Celebrity Big Brother. 8 Darling. 9 RSPB. 10 Damien Martyn. 11 MSC Napoli. 12 James Morrison. 13 Dog. 14 Costello Music. 15 Panama. 16 Dido. 17 Bruce Willis. 18 Rosamunde Pilcher. 19 Feyenoord. 20 Il Divo. 21 Def Leppard. 22 Jimmy Carter. 23 Harrison Ford. 24 Piano. 25 Publishing. 26 Pink. 27 Long playing records. 28 Juliette Binoche. 29 Chris Cornell. 30 Little Chef.

1 In which decade was Lloyd-Webber born?
2 In which 2006 talent show was he an adjudicator?
3 Which musical instrument does his brother Julian play?
4 Which first name is shared by two of his wives?
5 Which musical based on a Bible story followed "Joseph"?
6 Which of his musicals saw Elaine Paige shoot to stardom?
7 With which playwright Alan did he collaborate on the flop "Jeeves"?
8 His musical "The Likes of Us" was based on which children's benefactor?
9 In "Superstar" which character sings "I Don't Know How to Love Him"?
10 Who did the then Mrs Lloyd-Webber play in "The Phantom of the Opera"?
11 Which Royal once worked for his Really Useful Company?
12 Which boy band recorded "No Matter What" from "Whistle Down the Wind"?
13 Which musical was about Norma Desmond?
14 Which1980s song cycle was subtitled "An English Girl in America"?
15 Which of his musicals first opened at the Colet Court School in 1968?
16 Who was the original but short-lived Fosco in "The Woman in White"?
17 Which of his musicals was based on Gaston Leroux's gothic novel?
18 What was his shortest-lived musical of the 20th century?
19 Which Bollywood musical did he present in 2002?
20 Which future superstar Michael starred as Alex in "Aspects of Love"?
21 Which of his musicals was made into a movie in 2004?
22 For which movie did he win his first Oscar?
23 Which Barbara sang on the original recording of "Evita"?
24 "The Beautiful Game" was about sectarian conflict where?
25 Which opera star played the Mother Abbess in his 2006 revival of "The Sound of Music"?
26 Which theatre with a "royal" link was the first which he bought?
27 In which musical did "Memory" feature?
28 Which former 007 dropped out of "Aspects of Love" a month before opening night?
29 In which decade was he knighted and made a life peer?
30 What was the title of the talent show when it was announced it would find the stars of Joseph?

Answers	Airports *(see Quiz 203)*

1 Heathrow. 2 Estonia. 3 Ohio. 4 Gatwick. 5 JF Kennedy. 6 Los Angeles. 7 Canada. 8 Linz. 9 Benbecula. 10 John Wayne. 11 British Airways. 12 Aberdeen. 13 New York. 14 Amborovy. 15 Norway. 16 Athens. 17 John Lennon. 18 Italy. 19 Charles de Gaulle. 20 Bristol. 21 Spain. 22 Essex. 23 West Indies (St Kitts). 24 Marco Polo. 25 Dulles International. 26 Seattle. 27 Italy. 28 Canada. 29 Fog. 30 Finland.

1 Angelina Jolie's movie "A Mighty Heart" was set in which country?
2 Which glossy magazine celebrated its 90th anniversary with the December 2006 edition?
3 Which top-selling band featured Kelly Jones on vocals?
4 Shire is one of Britain's leading makers of what?
5 Was David Cameron returned as MP for Windsor, Witney or Woking?
6 Michael Bloomberg was mayor of which famous city?
7 In January 2007 Carphone Warehouse withdrew sponsorship for which reality TV show?
8 What was the name of Kylie's perfume launched in London, January 2007?
9 Which organisation launched Operation Lapwing in 2007?
10 Who retired from international cricket with Australia 2-0 up in the 2006–07 Ashes?
11 Items from which container ship were washed up in Cornwall in January 2007?
12 Who made the 2006 hit album "Undiscovered"?
13 In a New Year tragedy, what killed young Ellie Lawrence?
14 Fratellis featured what sort of music in the title of the 2006 hit album?
15 Which country has the international car registration code PA?
16 Florian Cloud de Bounevialle Armstrong is better known under which name?
17 Which actor played the psychiatrist in the movie "The Sixth Sense"?
18 Which Rosamunde wrote the novel "The Shell Seekers"?
19 Which Dutch club was disqualified from the 2006–07 Uefa Cup following crowd trouble?
20 Who took "Ancora" to the top of the album charts?
21 Joe Elliot was vocalist with which heavy metal band?
22 Which US President announced that the USA would not take part in the Moscow Olympics?
23 In the 1980s, who starred in three "Indiana Jones" and two "Star Wars" movies?
24 Which instrument is associated with musician Stephen Hough?
25 John Wiley is a US company dealing in which market?
26 Who declared "I'm Not Dead" in the title of her 2006 hit album?
27 What used to go round at 33 and a third r.p.m.?
28 Which French actress and artist was Oscar nominated for "Chocolat"?
29 Who was a singer with Soundgarden and Audioslave?
30 Which chain of roadside restaurants was in danger of closure in 2006?

Answers | Pot Luck 93 (see Quiz 204)

1 London Eye. 2 1981. 3 Portugal. 4 Miranda Priestly. 5 Olivia. 6 David Cameron. 7 Solidarity. 8 Backstreet Boys. 9 Accrington Stanley. 10 Michael O'Leary. 11 Snow Patrol. 12 1997. 13 Spanish lottery. 14 Sir Patrick Moore. 15 1980. 16 The Who. 17 Nancy Pelosi. 18 American Idol. 19 Tom Jones. 20 Seven. 21 Buddy Holly. 22 Liz Smith. 23 Rachel Allen. 24 Switzerland. 25 1995. 26 Hawke. 27 Leopold I. 28 Harry Hill. 29 Westlife. 30 Sudan.

Answers – page 451

1 Which imprint was behind the JK Rowling series of books?
2 Which Patricia wrote the 2006 novel "Predator"?
3 What is the last name of "Unfortunate Events" writer Lemony?
4 Which Fortress featured in the title of a Dan Brown book?
5 Who died aged 44 leaving his novel "The Last Tycoon" unfinished?
6 Who created the character of diary-writing Bridget Jones?
7 Who wrote about the Spanish Civil War in "For Whom the Bell Tolls"?
8 Which pop celebrity from the 1960s wrote "Be My Baby"?
9 Which character appeared in all of Raymond Chandler's novels?
10 Who penned the classic sci-fi story "I Robot"?
11 How did the barrister Rumpole refer to his wife Hilda?
12 In the Morse books as opposed to the TV series, where did Lewis come from?
13 Who won a Booker Prize for "Midnight's Children"?
14 In which decade of the 20th century did HG Wells die?
15 Under which name did American author Samuel Langhorne Clemens write?
16 Who created the most filmed horror character of the 20th C?
17 Whose sports-based novels of the 90s include "Comeback" and "To the Hilt"?
18 Aunt Agatha and Bingo Little feature in the escapades of which man about town?
19 Which writer Stephen was a pioneer in pay as you read on the Internet?
20 In which decade was "The Lord of the Rings" first published?
21 Who is Frank Richards' most famous creation?
22 Who penned the airport lounge best seller titled "Airport"?
23 Which writer wrote about his rural upbringing in Slad, Gloucestershire?
24 In 1917 which Joseph endowed an annual literary prize in America?
25 David John Cornwell wrote spy stories under which name?
26 Which fictional detective refers to using the little grey cells?
27 Georges Simenon created which character known by one name?
28 What was the first name of New Zealand novelist Ms Marsh?
29 Which American novelist with an English place surname wrote "White Fang"?
30 Who wrote the children's classic "Swallows and Amazons"?

Answers	Pop Places *(see Quiz 209)*

1 The River Thames. 2 Cambodia. 3 California. 4 San Francisco. 5 Amsterdam. 6 Japan. 7 Dionne Warwick. 8 New York. 9 Toto. 10 Tina Turner. 11 Roger Whittaker. 12 Glen Campbell. 13 American Idiot. 14 Moscow. 15 Caribbean. 16 Bon Jovi. 17 Philadelphia. 18 Tahiti. 19 Mississippi. 20 Mott the Hoople. 21 The Clash. 22 Twenty-four. 23 Tony Christie. 24 Dakota. 25 Barbados. 26 Liverpool. 27 Madonna. 28 Elton John. 29 Georgia. 30 Bruce Springsteen.

1 What did the Kyoto Protocol intend to curb the emission of?
2 The London NYC Hotel, Manhattan, was the first US restaurant of which UK chef?
3 Who did Condoleezza Rice replace as US Secretary of State?
4 What was Craig David's second UK No 1 single?
5 What does the letter C stand for in the acronym NICE?
6 Who is the record-producing son of SIr George Martin?
7 Nicole Kidman and Brittany Murphy did voices for which animated Antarctic film?
8 Which make of watch sponsored the "Unstoppable" Kevin Pietersen?
9 Justin Timberlake featured on which Snoop Dogg hit of 2005?
10 Which city has the constituencies of Blackley and Gorton?
11 Who replaced Antony Worrall Thompson on "Saturday Kitchen"?
12 Kelly Holmes, Helen Mirren and Anita Roddick have all been named as what?
13 Who voiced the eponymous character in Tim Burton's "Corpse Bride"?
14 Who made "Eyes Open", the best-selling album of 2006?
15 In which city was the BBC drama series "Lilies" set?
16 In which animals was foot and mouth first discovered in the 2001 epidemic?
17 In which decade was composer Hans Zimmer born?
18 Who hosted the talent show "When Will I be Famous?" in 2007?
19 Which instrument has 46 or 47 strings?
20 Duncan Bannatyne and Peter Jones were on the panel of which TV show?
21 In which controversial play did Daniel Radcliffe appear in the West End in 2007?
22 Who or what was the Berliner Mauer?
23 "Goldmember" was the third movie romp for Mike Myers as which spy?
24 Which international keeper moved from Sunderland to Arsenal in 2006?
25 Which event caused Lord Nicholas Windsor to renounce his rights to the throne?
26 Which Tim has represented South Suffolk in parliament this century?
27 In which city renowned for its music was "Dreamgirls" set?
28 Who is the mother of James Kerr and Lennon Gallagher?
29 The movie "Jerry Maguire" was about which American sport?
30 "My Dear Country" first featured on which album by Norah Jones?

Answers	**Pot Luck 96** *(see Quiz 210)*

1 Le Chiffre. 2 26 tracks. 3 George Carey. 4 Sugababes. 5 King Xerxes. 6 South.
7 Jamie Oliver. 8 Michael Jackson. 9 Will Smith. 10 20. 11 Ricky Gervais. 12
Beatrix Potter. 13 Oil. 14 Elstree. 15 Frank McCourt. 16 Kazakhstan. 17 Attack of
the Clones. 18 Respiratory. 19 Naomi Watts. 20 Official census. 21 Dr John Reid.
22 Marquis de Sade. 23 Life Goes On. 24 Fulham. 25 Food. 26 EastEnders. 27
Curriculum. 28 Chelsea. 29 Manchester. 30 Sonia Gandhi.

1 Where is Sixties rock venue Eel Pie Island located?
2 Which Asian country provided Kim Wilde with a 1980s hit?
3 Which US state links with "Dreamin'" and "Girls" in song titles?
4 Which city did Scott McKenzie sing about in the 1967 summer of love?
5 Which city was the title of a Simple Minds EP in 1989?
6 Which geographical group had China, Tokyo and Cantonese in chart titles?
7 Who had a 1960s hit with "Do You Know the Way to San Jose?"?
8 Which city has given hit songs to Frank Sinatra, Gerard Kenny and Sting?
9 Who was in "Africa" in 1983?
10 Which female pop superstar sang about "Nutbush"?
11 Which Roger was "Leavin' Durham Town" in the 1960s?
12 "Wichita Lineman" and "Galveston" provided hits for which Glen?
13 Green Day made the top-selling 2004 album about what kind of "Idiot"?
14 In which Russian city was Michael Jackson a "Stranger" in 1996?
15 Which Queen was a hit for Billy Ocean?
16 Which popular New Jersey band made the popular album "New Jersey"?
17 Which US city links Elton John and Bruce Springsteen in song?
18 Which tropical paradise was the subject of a David Essex hit?
19 Which US state and river was a 1970s hit for Pussycat?
20 Who were "All the Way from Memphis" in 1973?
21 "London Calling" was a hit for which group?
22 How many hours was Gene Pitney away from Tulsa?
23 Which singer did Peter Kay aid on his way to "Amarillo"?
24 Which US state was the title of a Stereophonics 2005 No 1?
25 One-hit wonders Typically Tropical were going to which island?
26 In which city is "Penny Lane"?
27 Who had the 1990s hit version of "Don't Cry for Me Argentina"?
28 Which superstar declared he was "Made in England"?
29 Which G was the state on the mind of the late, great Ray Charles?
30 Who made the mega-selling "Born in the USA"?

---

1 Mads Mikkelsen played which character in the 2006 movie "Casino Royale"?
2 How many Beatles tracks feature on the "Love" album of 2006?
3 Who was Archbishop of Canterbury when it was decided to ordain women as priests?
4 In which girl group did Heidi Range replace Siobhan Donaghy?
5 The invasion force of which Persian ruler was repulsed by 300 Spartan warriors in 480 BC?
6 Central, East and South – which isn't the name of a parliamentary constituency in Leeds?
7 Which chef was on the first "Top Gear" after Richard Hammond returned after his crash?
8 Which Michael made a first UK stage appearance in nine years in 2006's World Music Awards?
9 Which actor starred with his son in "The Pursuit of Happyness"?
10 How many operas did Mozart write?
11 Who toured with the live stand-up show "Fame"?
12 Which female, featured in a film, married solicitor William Heelis in 1913?
13 Which commodity is exported via the Druzhba, or Friendship, pipeline?
14 The "Big Brother" house is in which Borehamwood studios?
15 Who wrote the novel on which "Angela's Ashes" was based?
16 Alma Ata is the capital of which former Soviet state?
17 What was Star Wars Episode II called?
18 What does R stand for in the medical condition SARS?
19 Which actress starred in the creepy movie "The Ring"?
20 Which ten-yearly event was taken on 29th April 2001 in the UK?
21 The constituency of Airdrie & Shotts returned which MP who became Home Secretary?
22 Which Marquis did Geoffrey Rush play in "Quills"?
23 In song, which line follows "Ob-Lad-Di, Ob-Lad-Da"?
24 Which soccer club has a Hammersmith End and a Putney End?
25 Gael Green is a celebrated US critic of what?
26 In 2007 actor Robert Kazinsky was suspended from which soap?
27 In education, what does C stand for in QCA?
28 Which soccer club launched a Chinese-language website in Beijing in January 2007?
29 What is the home city of boxer Ricky Hatton?
30 In 2004 who won the Indian election but declined to become Prime Minister?

Answers	**Pot Luck 95** *(see Quiz 208)*

1 Greenhouse gases. 2 Gordon Ramsay. 3 Colin Powell. 4 7 Days. 5 Clinical. 6 Giles Martin. 7 Happy Feet. 8 Citizen. 9 Signs. 10 Manchester. 11 James Martin. 12 Dames. 13 Helena Bonham Carter. 14 Snow Patrol. 15 Liverpool. 16 Pigs. 17 1950s. 18 Graham Norton. 19 Harp. 20 Dragon's Den. 21 Equus. 22 Berlin Wall. 23 Austin Powers. 24 Mart Poom. 25 Conversion to Roman Catholicism. 26 Tim Yeo. 27 Detroit. 28 Patsy Kensit. 29 American football. 30 Not Too Late.

Answers – page 455

1 In which direction does the Queen face on a UK coin?
2 What was the value of a US "greenback"?
3 What is the Australian currency – dollars, pounds or roos?
4 Which group sang "Money, Money, Money"?
5 What is the top source of UK government income?
6 Which soccer club is the world's richest?
7 Which country was the top gold producer of last century?
8 What is the name of Bill Gates' wife?
9 Sir Edward Elgar appeared on which value of banknote?
10 How is Ralph Lifshitz better known?
11 What does GDP stand for?
12 Which country uses shekels as its currency?
13 What was Judas paid with for betraying Jesus?
14 Which country first used paper money?
15 In proverb, the love of money is the root of all what?
16 Were Bank of England pound notes last issued in 1974, 1984 or 1994?
17 In which industry did Rockefeller make his money?
18 Who recorded the album "Money for Nothing"?
19 In which European country could you spend a forint?
20 Charles Darwin's portrait appeared on banknotes of what value?
21 Which country has the world's richest royal family?
22 In which century was the Bank of England founded?
23 In which US state did the first Wal-Mart store open?
24 Which late rock star is the highest-earning celebrity no longer alive?
25 The portrait of which famous architect featured on £50 banknotes?
26 In the US, Diners Club issued the first what?
27 In which decade did both J Paul Getty and Howard Hughes die?
28 Who is the highest-earning British author?
29 In Iran, what do 100 dinars equal?
30 Who appeared on a banknote of higher value – Florence Nightingale or William Shakespeare?

Answers	Schumacher's Circuit (see Quiz 213)

1 1960s. 2 Ayrton Senna. 3 Belgium. 4 Seven times. 5 Finland. 6 Corinna. 7 Brazilian. 8 Monaco. 9 Alain Prost. 10 1994. 11 Belgian. 12 No. 13 Benetton. 14 Fourth. 15 French. 16 Damon Hill. 17 Bricklayer. 18 Ross Brawn. 19 Damon Hill. 20 Belgian. 21 Rubens Barrichello. 22 Runner-up. 23 Felipe Massa. 24 Juan Manuel Fangio. 25 Nigel Mansell. 26 Benetton. 27 San Marino. 28 1979. 29 91. 30 121.

1 What is his real surname?
2 What was Bowie's first Top Twenty hit of this century?
3 In which decade was he born?
4 Which word complete the song title ""Rebel Never Gets ___"?
5 Which song contains, "And the papers want to know whose shirts you wear"?
6 In which year did Bowie receive a Lifetime Achievement Grammy?
7 Which album was released first – "Stage" or "Tonight"?
8 Whom did he duet with on "Dancing in the Street"?
9 With which band did he record "Under Pressure"?
10 Whose puppet creations featured in the movie "Labyrinth"?
11 Which planet is named in both an album and single title?
12 What was Bowie's first No 1 album?
13 What name did Bowie's son originally have which rhymed with his surname?
14 What were the first three words of the title of his single with Bing Crosby?
15 What or who was Laughing in an early novelty number?
16 Which hit was the first ever to get to No 1 as a reissue?
17 Bowie wrote "All the Young Dudes" for which act?
18 In 1984 what was his Greatest Hits album called?
19 What followed Black Tie in the title of a 1990s album?
20 Which supermodel did Bowie marry in 1992?
21 Which major space event was "Space Oddity" timed to coincide with in 1969?
22 What was Bowie's first top ten hit of the 1990s?
23 What sort of Dogs featured in the title of a 1970s album?
24 Which album came out first – "Heathen" or "Hours"?
25 Which Rick, now a "Grumpy Old Man" played synthesiser on "Space Oddity"?
26 Who recorded the album "Transformer" which was co-produced by Bowie?
27 In which play did he play John Merrick on Broadway?
28 Which school once attended by Prince Charles did Bowie send his son to?
29 Which Tom co-starred with him in "Merry Christmas Mr Lawrence"?
30 Which song was a sequel to the exploits of Major Tom?

1 Was Michael born in the 1960s or the 1970s?
2 Who held the record for pole positions before Schumacher?
3 In which country did he make his first Grand Prix start?
4 How many times was Michael F1 champion?
5 Michael's great rival Mika Hakinnen came from which country?
6 What is the name of Michael's wife?
7 Which 2006 Grand Prix was Schumacher's last?
8 In May 2006 Schumacher was stripped of pole position in which Grand Prix?
9 Who held the record for most victories before Michael?
10 Was Michael first world champion driver in 1992, 1994 or 1996?
11 At which Grand Prix in 1998 was there a collision with David Coulthard?
12 Was Michael ever the youngest F1 world champion?
13 Whom was he driving for when he first became world champion driver?
14 What position did Michael finish in his final race in October 2006?
15 Which Grand Prix did he win for a record eight times?
16 Who was runner-up in Michael's first two seasons as world champion?
17 What was the trade of his father Rolf?
18 Who was Schumacher's technical director at Benetton and at Ferrari?
19 Which Brit was involved in the collision with Michael at Australia in 1994?
20 In which Grand Prix of 2001 did Michael set a new record for victories?
21 Which Brazilian driver and Ferrari team mate was runner-up to Michael in 2002?
22 Where did he finish in the drivers' championship in 2006?
23 Who finished first in Michael's final race in October 2006?
24 Who held the record for winning the drivers' title most times before Michael?
25 In 2002 he broke whose record for winning races in a season?
26 He first won a Grand Prix with which team?
27 In 2006, what was his first victory in his last season?
28 Before Michael, when did Ferrari last claim the drivers' title – 1979, 1989 or 1999?
29 How many career F1 wins did Michael gain?
30 How many points did he gain in his final season of F1 racing in 2006?

Answers	**Money Matters** *(see Quiz 211)*

1 To her right. 2 Dollar. 3 Dollars. 4 Abba. 5 Income tax. 6 Man Utd. 7 South Africa. 8 Melinda. 9 £20. 10 Ralph Lauren. 11 Gross Domestic Product. 12 Israel. 13 Silver. 14 China. 15 Evil. 16 1984. 17 Oil. 18 Dire Straits. 19 Hungary. 20 £5. 21 Saudi Arabia. 22 17thC. 23 Arkansas. 24 Elvis Presley. 25 Sir Christopher Wren. 26 Credit card. 27 1970s. 28 JK Rowling. 29 Rial. 30 William Shakespeare.

1 Who were the opponents in Andy Robinson's last game as England rugby coach?
2 HITA stands for which Industry Trade Association?
3 The Brady Act in the USA imposed some control of what?
4 In which year did Take That have a No 1 single before their 2006 comeback?
5 Which English city was named Capital of Culture for 2008?
6 What was the previous name of Belarus?
7 What was the title of McFly's first No 1 album?
8 Which star of "Iris" played Arabella in "Tea with Mussolini"?
9 Which marketing guru Steve became one of David Cameron's closest advisers?
10 "Employee of the Month" and "Dukes of Hazzard" starred which singer/actress?
11 Who left "Corrie" after 30 years and got an MBE in the 2007 New Year's honours list?
12 What does the RBS logo on Andy Murray's right sleeve stand for?
13 Which country has the most internet users in the world?
14 Which pop magazine closed in 2006 after 30 years of publishing?
15 Which sport does Barry Zito play?
16 Nadine Coyle found fame with which group?
17 Which Phillip presented TV's "Dancing on Ice"?
18 Jake Gyllenhaal and Jamie Foxx starred in which Gulf War film?
19 What was the cause of the fire at Windsor Castle in 1992?
20 How is Beethoven's piano sonata No 14 usually known?
21 Which Luton manager spoke out in 2006 about problems caused by "bungs"?
22 What horror is sold in the shop in the musical "Little Shop of Horrors"?
23 In which country was the drama series "Rough Diamond" set?
24 "You Raise Me Up" was the best-of album from which singer?
25 Andy Coulson stepped down in 2007 from which newspaper?
26 Which famous Helen advertised Virgin Atlantic?
27 Who became BBC sports news editor in 2007, aged 60?
28 Who got married first – Ant or Dec?
29 Who was Burton's manager when they held Man Utd in a 2006 FA Cup tie?
30 Which new version of Windows did Bill Gates launch in 2007?

Answers	Bowie (see Quiz 212)

1 Jones. 2 Everyone Says Hi. 3 1940s. 4 Old. 5 Space Oddity. 6 2006. 7 Tonight.
8 Mick Jagger. 9 Queen. 10 Jim Henson. 11 Mars. 12 Aladdin Sane. 13 Zowie.
14 Peace on Earth. 15 Gnome. 16 Space Oddity. 17 Mott the Hoople. 18 Fame
and Fashion. 19 White Noise. 20 Iman. 21 Moon landing. 22 Jump They Say. 23
Diamond Dogs. 24 Hours. 25 Wakeman. 26 Lou Reed. 27 The Elephant Man. 28
Gordonstoun. 29 Conti. 30 Ashes to Ashes.

Quiz 215 | Famous Movie Firsts | Answers – page 459 | LEVEL 2

1 Which Bond film was released on the same day as The Beatles' first single?
2 In the first "Toy Story", which child owns the toys?
3 Which film company opened the first ever theme park?
4 Where in Italy did the first film festival take place?
5 Which monster lizard first seen in 1955 was in a 1997 blockbuster?
6 What was the first movie in which Eastwood was Harry Callahan?
7 Which Fay was the first scream queen, in "King Kong"?
8 What was Disney's first feature film – with eight people in the title?
9 Which oriental detective Charlie first appeared on screen in 1926?
10 Where were India's first studios, giving rise to the name Bollywood?
11 What was the first two-colour system used in movie-making?
12 "The Robe" was the first movie with what type of screen?
13 "The Scent of Mystery" was the first movie with sight, sound and what?
14 Which 1995 Story was the first computer-animated film?
15 What was the first major movie about the Vietnam War?
16 Which Dickens' film gave Alec Guinness his major movie debut?
17 Which movie with an all-child cast was Alan Parker's directorial debut?
18 Which Ralph played Steed in the first "Avengers" big-screen movie?
19 In which decade were the Oscars first presented?
20 Which Christmas classic was first heard in "Holiday Inn"?
21 Who was Oscar-nominated for his director debut for "Ordinary People"?
22 Which Brothers made the first talkie?
23 In which movie did Al Jolson say, "You ain't heard nothin' yet"?
24 Which Katharine won the first BAFTA Best Actress award?
25 In which French city was the first movie in Europe shown?
26 Mike Nichols won the first director's BAFTA for which Dustin Hoffman classic?
27 In which movie did Elizabeth Taylor first act with Richard Burton?
28 Glenn Close made her film debut in "The World According to ____"?
29 What was Michael Jackson's first movie?
30 What was Tatum O'Neal's first movie which won her an Oscar?

Answers | **Roger Federer** *(see Quiz 217)*

1 Switzerland. 2 2004. 3 USA. 4 Right. 5 South African. 6 1980s. 7 Serena. 8 Sydney. 9 Wimbledon. 10 Tony Roche. 11 Mark Philippoussis. 12 Nadal. 13 Andre Agassi. 14 Three. 15 Cyprus. 16 Switzerland. 17 Maria Sharapova. 18 German. 19 Spain. 20 Andy Roddick. 21 None. 22 Marat Safin. 23 Andy Murray. 24 Pete Sampras. 25 rogerfederer.com. 26 Tsunami. 27 French. 28 Hewitt. 29 Nadal & Murray. 30 Bjorn Borg.

1 Auctioned in 2007, who produced the painting "St James, the Greater"?
2 Which ex-US President died the same month as Ray Charles?
3 Released in 2003, which Sugababes album peaked at 3 in the charts?
4 In which square does the famous department store Macy's stand?
5 Who was the first person to beat Roger Federer in a Grand Slam final?
6 What is the last name of US singer Ashanti?
7 Which England soccer midfielder won an MBE in the 2007 New Year's honours list?
8 Which company bought YouTube in 2006?
9 Did the Lib Dems or Tories have more women MPs after 2005's general election?
10 To the nearest year, how long was Diana divorced from Charles before her death?
11 Which Spielberg movie had the ad line, "Whoever saves one life, saves the world entire"?
12 "Billie Jean" was the only No 1 single from which Michael Jackson album?
13 What was the first Grand Slam claimed by Amelie Mauresmo?
14 Which two ex-Prime Ministers were backbenchers between 1990 and 1992?
15 ir. is the internet code for which country?
16 By what method was Timothy McVeigh executed for the Oklahoma City bombing?
17 Which Premiership side signed Greg Halford from Colchester?
18 How many bicycles did Katie Melua sing about?
19 Which constituency returned Jack Straw to parliament?
20 What was responsible for over 19,000 deaths in Gujurat, India in 2001?
21 What goes with "Demons" in the title of a Dan Brown novel?
22 In which country did Berlusconi follow on from Amato as Prime Minister?
23 Who had No 1 singles with "Ignition" and "Wonderful"?
24 Which team were beaten 9-7 by Europe in golf's inaugural Royal Trophy of 2006?
25 In 2001 Barry George was found guilty of the murder of which favourite TV presenter?
26 Which "Syriana" Oscar winner of 2006 played a doctor in "ER" for five years?
27 Who was the first rock superstar to become chairman of a major soccer club?
28 Which US politician was born Madeleine Korbel in 1937 in Czechoslovakia?
29 In which city did Brazil win the 2002 World Cup?
30 Which rock star Rod became a CBE in the 2007 New Year's honours list?

Answers | **Pioneers (see Quiz 218)**

1 Louise. 2 Netherlands. 3 Nestle. 4 Clockwork radio. 5 Colour blindness. 6 Gillette. 7 Thames. 8 C5. 9 The South Pole. 10 Italian. 11 Concorde. 12 Mars. 13 Ceylon. 14 Frying pan. 15 Earl of Sandwich. 16 Shakespeare's Globe. 17 Moon. 18 Television. 19 1980s. 20 Rollerblades. 21 Sony. 22 Sally Ride. 23 Desmond Tutu. 24 Mexican wave. 25 Sweden. 26 Edward Jenner. 27 Boxing . 28 Shorthand. 29 Cambridgeshire. 30 Saxophone.

1 In which country was he born?
2 In which year did he first became World No 1?
3 Between 2004–06 he won Wimbledon and which other Grand Slam three times?
4 Is he right- or left-handed?
5 What nationality is his mother?
6 In which decade was he born?
7 Which Williams sister was Ladies' Champion when he won his first Wimbledon?
8 In which Olympics was he fourth in 2000?
9 Which was his first Grand Slam title?
10 Which Australian former champion became his coach in 2005?
11 Which Australian did he defeat in his first Wimbledon final?
12 Who beat him in the 2005 French semis and went on to win the title?
13 Which US veteran did he beat in his second US Open Final?
14 In 2004 he became the first since Mats Wilander to win how many Grand Slams in a year?
15 In the 06 Australian Open he beat Marcos Baghdatis who came from where?
16 He is a member of which Davis Cup team?
17 Which Russian lady won Wimbledon when he won his second title there?
18 What is his first language?
19 Which country does his arch-rival Nadal come from?
20 Which American did he beat in the final in his first defence of the Wimbledon title?
21 How many Swiss men had won Wimbledon before him?
22 Whom did he beat in his first Australian final?
23 In 2006 which Brit beat Federer in his only straight-sets loss of that year?
24 Which American's 31-match unbeaten Wimbledon run did he end in 2001?
25 What is his official website called?
26 His first visit as a UNICEF Ambassador was to victims of which 2004 disaster?
27 In 2006 which was the only Grand Slam he did not win?
28 Which Australian did he beat to win his first US Open?
29 In 2006 who were the only two players to beat Federer?
30 Whose record of five consecutive Wimbledon championships did he match in 2007?

Answers	**Famous Movie Firsts** *(see Quiz 215)*

1 Dr No. 2 Andy. 3 Disney. 4 Venice. 5 Godzilla. 6 Dirty Harry. 7 Wray. 8 Snow White & the Seven Dwarfs. 9 Chan. 10 Bombay. 11 Technicolor. 12 Widescreen (Cinemascope). 13 Smell. 14 Toy Story. 15 The Deer Hunter. 16 Great Expectations. 17 Bugsy Malone. 18 Fiennes. 19 1920s. 20 White Christmas. 21 Robert Redford. 22 Warner. 23 The Jazz Singer. 24 Hepburn. 25 Paris. 26 The Graduate. 27 Cleopatra. 28 Garp. 29 The Wiz. 30 Paper Moon.

1 What was the first name of the world's first test tube baby?

2 Which country was the first to legalise voluntary euthanasia?

3 Which Swiss-based company made the first widely used instant coffee?

4 What sort of radio was designed by British inventor Trevor Baylis?

5 The Ishihara Test is a test for what?

6 Which pioneer in men's appearance had the first names King Camp?

7 Air flight pioneer Amy Johnson vanished over which river?

8 What was the name of Clive Sinclair's electric trike?

9 Reaching which place led to the quote, "Great God, this is an awful place"?

10 What was the nationality of Galileo?

11 In 1993 Barbara Harmer became the first woman pilot of which aircraft?

12 Viking was the first probe to send back pictures from which planet?

13 Which country was the first in the world to have a woman Prime Minister?

14 What was the first item of non-stick cookware marketed by Teflon?

15 Which Earl developed a snack where meat was placed between bread slices?

16 Sam Wanamaker was the driving force behind which London theatre?

17 David Scott and James Irwin were the first people to drive where?

18 What had 405 or 625 lines in its early forms?

19 In which decade were camcorders introduced?

20 What was developed by US ice hockey players Scott and Brennan Olson?

21 Which company introduced the first personal stereo?

22 Which Sally was the USA's first spacewoman?

23 Who was the first black archbishop of Cape Town?

24 What sort of wave was seen for the first time at a sporting fixture in 1986?

25 Which Scandinavian country was the first to ban aerosol sprays?

26 Which Edward was a pioneer of vaccination?

27 Jane Couch was the first woman with a professional licence for which sport?

28 Which method of fast writing was developed by Pitman?

29 Specialising in heart surgery, Papworth hospital is in which county?

30 What did the Belgian Adolphe Sax develop?

---

1 What did the Wind cry according to Jimi Hendrix?
2 Which word completes the Yardbirds hit, "Over Under Sideways ____"?
3 Who went "Downtown"?
4 Which song started, "Dirty old river must you keep rolling, Rolling in to the night"?
5 Who first hit the top ten with "Wild Thing"?
6 Which word was the whole of a Mary Hopkin hit and half a Beatles hit?
7 Which group became known as the ones with the girl drummer?
8 Who had a huge hit with "In the Ghetto"?
9 Bob Dylan had what type of "Homesick Blues"?
10 Who sang about a "Swiss Maid"?
11 Which Move hit "sampled" a phrase from the 1812 Overture?
12 Paradoxically, who sang "I Love My Dog"?
13 What other words described Tom Jones' "Funny Forgotten Feelings"?
14 Who were in "Bits and Pieces"?
15 What was the first UK hit for The Supremes?
16 Where did you have to go to find the House of The Rising Sun?
17 "Do You Want to Know a Secret" was a first chart hit for which singer?
18 To whom did the Hollies say Sorry in a 1969 hit?
19 Which Legend gave Dave Dee and the boys a No 1?
20 In a song title what "Has a Thousand Eyes"?
21 Which group invited you all to "F-F-Fade Away"?
22 Who was the biggest-selling artist in the 1967 Summer of Love?
23 What goes before "Yester-You Yesterday"?
24 Which group made a visit to "Atlantis"?
25 What was the name of Manfred Mann's Semi-Detached Suburban character?
26 Which title contained in brackets "Be Sure to Wear Some Flowers in Your Hair"?
27 Who took "Dizzy" to the top?
28 Which vocalist sang "Let the Heartaches Begin"?
29 In song, who took medicinal compounds?
30 Who duetted with Nancy Sinatra on "Something Stupid"?

1 In what year was the slave trade abolished in the British Empire?
2 At what number did the Fowler family once live in "EastEnders"?
3 The title of Madonna's 2003 No 1 US and UK album mentioned "American" what?
4 Sonya Thomas was a champion in which American sport?
5 In 2006, Steve Samson of Essex shot himself while cleaning what?
6 Xue Fei Yang is a classical musician specialising in which instrument?
7 Which TV series featured the characters DS Simms and DI Traynor?
8 Which jockey did Catherine Allen marry in the late 1990s?
9 Rafale is the name of a combat aircraft from which country?
10 Which Royal died in the same month as actor John Thaw?
11 Who won the Best Actress Oscar for "Shakespeare in Love"?
12 Which Italian, once soccer's most expensive player, managed Watford?
13 Which Home Secretary in Tony Blair's cabinet was elected by Norwich South?
14 In the Six Nations Rugby tournament which team is first alphabetically?
15 Who wrote the "Little Book of Big Treats" for Comic Relief 2007?
16 Forget Glenbogle but what animal is in the painting "The Monarch of the Glen"?
17 Who was the second American, after Greg LeMond, to win the Tour de France?
18 Where would you find the sequence E, A, D, G, B, E?
19 Who won a Best Song Oscar for "Into the West" as featured in "The Return of the King"?
20 Did Daley Thompson win Olympic gold in the 1970s, 1980s or 1990s?
21 Which theatre director won an Oscar nomination for the movie "Billy Elliot"?
22 Who wrote "Below the Parapet" about her father?
23 Who played opposite Diane Keaton in the movie "Something's Gotta Give"?
24 Which is higher in a standing human frame, the fibula or the patella?
25 The annual Stirling prize is awarded to which professional group of people?
26 Who provided the score for the movie "Notes on a Scandal"?
27 Which group has had an album titled "Chemistry" and a hit single titled "Biology"?
28 In which sport was Blanche Bingley famous?
29 Which son of a famous playwright played Tchaikovsky in the 2007 BBC drama series?
30 Who was Arsenal's top scorer in their final season at Highbury?

Answers | Pot Luck 100 *(see Quiz 222)*

1 Patsy Kensit. 2 Potatoes. 3 Polonium-210. 4 Iris Murdoch (Iris). 5 118 118. 6 Eddie Murphy. 7 Philippines. 8 Outbreak of foot & mouth. 9 Enron. 10 Craig David. 11 James Joyce. 12 Alec Douglas-Home. 13 Kylie Minogue. 14 Wales. 15 John Major. 16 Evelyn Glennie. 17 Val McDermid. 18 None. 19 Dalziel & Pascoe. 20 Monday. 21 Tony Blair. 22 Sir Thomas More. 23 Who Wants to be a Millionaire? 24 Sugarland Express. 25 Ted Hughes. 26 Scolari. 27 Black. 28 BG. 29 Margaret Beckett. 30 Ian Hislop.

1 What is Macaulay Culkin's brother called who starred in "Father of the Bride"?
2 Which former child star became Mrs Andre Agassi?
3 Who played the Artful Dodger in the 1960s version of "Oliver!"
4 In which movie, remade in 1998, did Hayley Mills sing "Let's Get Together"?
5 Whose autobiography was called "Little Girl Lost"?
6 Who played the possessed child in "The Exorcist"?
7 Which Oscar winner from "As Good as It Gets" was a US TV child star?
8 In which Bruce Willis movie did Haley Joe Osment star?
9 Mark Lester played the title role in which 60s musical?
10 How many movies had Macaulay Culkin made before "Home Alone"?
11 Was Judy Garland 13, 15 or 17 when she starred in "The Wizard of Oz"?
12 In which 1993 dinosaur film did Joseph Mazello star?
13 Lisa Jakub ended up having her father disguised as nanny in which movie?
14 Rumer Willis appeared with Mum in "Striptease"; who is she?
15 Who appeared in "Mermaids", aged 10, and moved on to "The Ice Storm"?
16 Was Jodie Foster 12, 14 or 16 when she starred in "Taxi Driver"?
17 Who was Macaulay Culkin's first wife?
18 Who said, "I was a 16-year-old boy for 30 years"?
19 Former child star Richard Beymer starred in which 60s musical opposite Natalie Wood?
20 In which country was Deanna Durbin born?
21 Which star of "Chasing Amy" started acting at the age of eight?
22 What was Hayley Mills' first film, in 1959?
23 How many times did Judy Garland marry?
24 Who played two parts in "The Prince and the Pauper" in 1977?
25 Which Mary was the "world's sweetheart" and made her first movie aged 16 in 1909?
26 Young Justin Henry was in which divorce movie with Streep and Hoffman?
27 Which Jackie was immortalised in Chaplin's "The Kid"?
28 Who was the gangster's moll in "Bugsy Malone" and later won Oscars?
29 In which movie did Drew Barrymore find fame as Gertie?
30 Who was asked to "Come Home" in Elizabeth Taylor's 1943 movie?

Answers | **Pop Music: The 60s** *(see Quiz 219)*

1 Mary. 2 Down. 3 Petula Clark. 4 Waterloo Sunset. 5 The Troggs. 6 Goodbye. 7 Honeycombs. 8 Elvis Presley. 9 Subterranean. 10 Del Shannon. 11 Night of Fear. 12 Cat Stevens. 13 Familiar. 14 The Dave Clark Five. 15 Where Did Our Love Go?. 16 New Orleans. 17 Billy J Kramer. 18 Suzanne. 19 Xanadu. 20 The Night. 21 The Who. 22 Engelbert Humperdinck. 23 Yester-Me. 24 The Shadows. 25 Mr James. 26 San Francisco. 27 Tommy Roe. 28 Long John Baldry. 29 Lily the Pink. 30 Frank Sinatra.

1 Who took on the role of Faye Morton in "Holby City" in 2007?
2 In December 2006 the government approved plans for trials of which GM crop in Britain?
3 What was the radioactive isotope identified in the death of Alexander Litvinenko?
4 In 2002 Judi Dench won a BAFTA for playing which real person?
5 Which company were the largest provider of telephone directory inquiries in 2005?
6 Who won a Best Supporting Actor Golden Globe for "Dreamgirls"?
7 President Joseph Estrada was forced to resign after protests in which country?
8 What was the cause of widespread closure of rural footpaths in 2001?
9 Which energy-trading conglomerate went bankrupt in December 2001?
10 Who had a big-selling album with "Slicker Than Your Average"?
11 Which Irish novelist opened Dublin's first cinema?
12 Which modern-day PM became Foreign Secretary after he resigned as Premier?
13 Who announced a split from French partner Olivier Martinez in February 2007?
14 In the Six Nations Rugby tournament which team is last alphabetically?
15 Who began his first PM Cabinet meeting with the words, "Well, who'd have thought it?"?
16 Which percussionist was made a Dame in the 2007 New Years Honours list?
17 Which crime writer wrote "The Mermaids Singing"?
18 In 2007 "Casino Royale" was nominated for nine BAFTAS, but how many did it win?
19 Which cop duo were played by Colin Buchanan and Warren Clarke on TV?
20 On which day of the week did England clinch the 2005 Ashes series?
21 Which famous person includes Anthony Charles Lynton in his name?
22 Back in the West End in 2005, a "Man for All Seasons" is about which Thomas?
23 Judith Keppel was the first top prize winner of which TV quiz?
24 Which "Express" was Spielberg's debut as a feature film director?
25 Which Ted was a 1990s Poet Laureate?
26 Which Luis Felipe was the manager of the 2002 World Cup winners Brazil?
27 What was the main colour of the comic character Biffo the Bear?
28 What is the registration for Bulgaria – BA, BG or BUG?
29 Which member of Tony Blair's cabinet represented Derby South?
30 Who was Paul Merton's guest on his final stint on "Room 101"?

| **Answers** | Pot Luck 99 *(see Quiz 220)* |

1 1807. 2 No 45. 3 American Life. 4 Competitive eating. 5 A crossbow. 6 Guitarist. 7 Prime Suspect. 8 Frankie Dettori. 9 France. 10 Princess Margaret. 11 Gwyneth Paltrow. 12 Gianlucca Vialli. 13 Charles Clarke. 14 England. 15 Jamie Oliver. 16 A red deer stag. 17 Lance Armstrong. 18 Guitar (six open strings). 19 Annie Lennox. 20 1980s. 21 Stephen Daldry. 22 Carol Thatcher. 23 Jack Nicholson. 24 Patella. 25 Architects. 26 Philip Glass. 27 Girls Aloud. 28 Tennis. 29 Ed Stoppard. 30 Thierry Henry.

1 How many band members were there in the original line-up?
2 What was the first No 1 single?
3 What was the not very original title of their first album?
4 Which band member plays a musical instrument on stage?
5 What was their second album called?
6 Who was the band's first manager?
7 What is Nicky's surname?
8 Who duetted with Westlife on "Against All Odds"?
9 Where do the band hail from in Ireland?
10 "An empty street" is the first line of which of their songs?
11 Including their debut disc, how many consecutive No 1 singles did the boys have?
12 What is Kian's surname?
13 Which Girl was the subject of their March 2001 charity single?
14 Which single was their first not to reach No 1?
15 Bryan McFadden became engaged to which member of Atomic Kitten?
16 Who has a distinctive scar on his right cheek?
17 Which superstar featured on "When You Tell Me that You Love Me"?
18 What was the title of their Greatest Hits Vol 1 collection of 2002?
19 What is Nicky's birth sign – Leo or Libra?
20 What was the first single to have a one-word title?
21 Who left the band in 2004?
22 Which supermodel appeared in the video of "Uptown Girl"?
23 What is the first name of Mr Feehily?
24 Which N was the first English venue for Westlife on their first UK tour?
25 Which album came out first – "Face to Face" or "Turnaround"?
26 The 2003 "Miss You Nights" was originally a 1976 hit for which singer?
27 What is Shane's surname?
28 What was Bryan McFadden's first solo No 1?
29 At Christmas 2006, TV technology allowed Westlife to duet with which late singer?
30 What were the band originally to have been called?

Answers	Codes & Spies *(see Quiz 225)*

1 40s. 2 Copyright. 3 Hieroglyphics. 4 Enigma. 5 Mole. 6 Tumble drier. 7 Morse. 8 Ring. 9 Ian Fleming. 10 Julius Caesar. 11 8. 12 Stella Rimington. 13 XXV. 14 George. 15 German. 16 Latin. 17 Oddjob. 18 1980s. 19 Red and yellow. 20 Square. 21 Two. 22 Diamonds. 23 Peter Wright. 24 Cold. 25 Semaphore. 26 Black circle. 27 Pig Pen. 28 Anthony Blunt. 29 H. 30 MI5.

1 Who was the third actor to play the Doctor on TV?
2 In which month of the year was "Doctor Who" shown for the very first time?
3 Which planet does the Doctor come from?
4 What is the name of Captain Jack's tiny robots that can treat wounds?
5 What was the name of Rose's mother?
6 Which three words are on the bottom line of the poster on the door of the TARDIS?
7 Daleks were inhabitants of which planet?
8 Who is the creator of Doctor Who?
9 Which MP helped Rose and the Doctor with the Slitheen in control of Downing Street?
10 Which warriors were first seen in the series "The Tenth Planet"?
11 What colour is the Moxx of Balhoon?
12 Which ex-Dr Who is the father of actress Georgia Moffett?
13 Which race used high-tech broadcasting in the year 200,000 to brainwash humans?
14 What does the letter R stand for in TARDIS?
15 Which actor played travelling companion Steven Taylor?
16 In which city did the Doctor find Charles Dickens under threat from the walking dead?
17 Which planet did the Ice Warriors come from?
18 The Doctor challenged the Sycorax leader to what sort of fight?
19 Which surname has been shared by two actors to portray the Doctor?
20 Who was the billionaire collector who held a Dalek in his vault at Utah?
21 What was the registration of the Doctor's car as owned by Jon Pertwee?
22 In which year did Rose's father die?
23 What had been Sarah Jane Smith's job before time travelling?
24 In which year was the Earth destroyed?
25 John Leeson and David Brierly have both supplied the voice to which character?
26 Which real-life historical figure was involved with a werewolf and Warrior Monks?
27 What was the surname of Jamie as portrayed by Fraser Hines?
28 In 18th-century France, where did the court come under attack from the clockwork killers?
29 Which sport did the Doctor like, as portrayed by Peter Davison?
30 Which year will mark the 50th anniversary of the first programme?

Answers	Pot Luck 101 *(see Quiz 226)*

1 Scotland. 2 Kensal Green. 3 Cliff Richard. 4 ITV. 5 QI. 6 Congo. 7 Gareth Gates. 8 Trevor Francis. 9 New Zealand. 10 Kofi Annan. 11 Variety Club of Great Britain. 12 Harriet Harman. 13 All You Need is Love. 14 Korea. 15 Lost in Translation. 16 Sheffield. 17 Jeremy Clarkson. 18 Joyce Smith. 19 King Albert II. 20 Chelsea. 21 Smoking. 22 Roald Dahl. 23 Ronald Reagan. 24 The Goblet of Fire. 25 James Dyson. 26 Graham Rix. 27 History. 28 Confetti. 29 Snooker. 30 Postal charges.

Quiz 225 | Codes & Spies

1 Was Alexander Litvinenko in his 30s, 40s or 50s when he was poisoned?
2 What does a letter c enclosed in a circle stand for?
3 What was the picture language of Ancient Egypt know as?
4 What word links an Elgar work and a movie about code cracking in the war?
5 A spy in a position of trust with the enemy is known as a what?
6 On clothing labels, what does a circle inside a square stand for?
7 Which code is based on dots and dashes?
8 What term links a mobile phone tone and a network of spies?
9 Who created the most famous double agent of them all – James Bond?
10 Who devised an alphabet code – Julius Caesar or Richard the Lionheart?
11 On a standard keyboard the star sign shares a key with which number?
12 Which Stella became head of MI5?
13 How is the number 25 written in Roman numerals?
14 What was the first name of Smiley created by John Le Carré?
15 Runes developed from which language?
16 The English word code derives from the word codex from which language?
17 Which villain did Bond face in "Goldfinger"?
18 In which decade did the double agent Kim Philby die in Russia?
19 What are the normal colours on a semaphore flag?
20 In Ancient Greece, Polybius made a letter cipher that took which shape?
21 How many dots show on an iron to indicate warm?
22 In playing cards, which suit symbol contains four angles?
23 Who wrote "Spycatcher" the controversial 1980s book about the workings of M15?
24 In meteorology what front is shown by triangles pointing up?
25 Depillon, Popham and Paisley all developed which system?
26 In astronomy what is the sign for a new moon?
27 In the 16thC the Freemasons used a diagram code known as which "Pen"?
28 In 1979 which Anthony was revealed as a spy and stripped of his knighthood?
29 In Morse Code which letter is represented by four dots?
30 In which organisation did Martin Furnival Jones replace Roger Hollis?

Answers	**Westlife (see Quiz 223)**

1 Five. 2 Swear It Again. 3 Westlife. 4 None of them does. 5 Coast to Coast. 6 Ronan Keating. 7 Byrne. 8 Mariah Carey. 9 Sligo. 10 My Love. 11 Seven. 12 Egan. 13 Uptown Girl. 14 What Makes a Man. 15 Kerry Katona. 16 Kian. 17 Diana Ross. 18 Unbreakable. 19 Libra. 20 Mandy. 21 Bryan McFadden. 22 Claudia Schiffer. 23 Mark. 24 Newcastle. 25 Turnaround. 26 Cliff Richard. 27 Filan. 28 Real to Me. 29 Roy Orbison. 30 Westside.

1 After 2003, Jonny Wilkinson's next international was in 2007 against which side?
2 Near which London tube station was Tom ap Rhys Pryce murdered?
3 Whose 100th single was called "The Best of Me"?
4 Charles Allen was the chief executive who left which media group in August 2006?
5 "The Book of General Ignorance" was linked to which TV quiz show?
6 What was Zaire renamed in 1997?
7 Whose second album was "Go Your Own Way"?
8 Steve Bruce took over from which soccer manager at Birmingham?
9 In which Southern Hemisphere country was "Lord of the Rings" partly made?
10 Who succeeded Boutros Boutros Ghali as UN Secretary General?
11 Which club has members called Barkers?
12 Which lady became Solicitor General in Tony Blair's government in 2001?
13 In the days before sampling, which No 1 began with the French National anthem?
14 In 2005, which North & South countries agreed on a joint team for Olympics 2008?
15 Scarlett Johansson starred in which Tokyo-set film of 2004?
16 Which city has the constituencies of Hallam and Heeley?
17 Which Jeremy wrote the big-selling book "I Know You Got Soul"?
18 Which lady from the UK won the first two London Marathons?
19 Who was the King of the Belgians at the start of the 21st century?
20 Damian Duff first played in a Premiership-winning side at which club?
21 What became illegal in 1984 on the London Underground?
22 Which children's author wrote the screenplay for "You Only Live Twice"?
23 Who was the first US President to have been divorced?
24 What was the first "Harry Potter" film in which Katie Leung appeared?
25 Which English inventor James created the bagless cyclone vacuum cleaner?
26 Which Graham got the sack as head coach of Hearts in 2006?
27 Bob Geldof was a spearhead of the campaign to Make Poverty what?
28 Which 2006 movie followed three couples trying to hold unusual weddings?
29 Shaun Murphy has won a World Championship in which sport?
30 Which everyday charges were changed to be based on size and shape from September 2006?

Answers	George W Bush *(see Quiz 229)*

1 Walker. 2 Al Gore. 3 Jeb. 4 John Kerry. 5 Yo, Blair! 6 Iran, Iraq & North Korea. 7 Colin Powell. 8 Florida. 9 Condoleezza Rice. 10 Texas. 11 Dick Cheney. 12 Afghanistan. 13 Jenna & Barbara. 14 9/11. 15 Dubya. 16 Donald Rumsfeld. 17 Marathon. 18 43rd. 19 Katrina. 20 Fahrenheit 9/11. 21 St Petersburg. 22 60th. 23 March. 24 Connecticut. 25 One. 26 Yale. 27 Baseball. 28 George & Barbara. 29 Robert Gates. 30 Oil.

1 What was Slade's first No 1 single?
2 Which group went on a "Teenage Rampage"?
3 Who had a 1970s No 1 with "Oh Boy"?
4 Which Barry was "(Dancin') on a Saturday Night"?
5 What was Alvin Stardust's name when he charted in the 60s?
6 Which Gary Glitter song was in Parts 1 & 2?
7 Who penned the T.Rex hits?
8 Who came alive down in "Devilgate Drive?"
9 Who was the leader of Wizzard?
10 Which group had a Noddy as singer?
11 Who was Chapman's song-writing partner?
12 Which Bowie No 1 was a reissue of his song that charted in 1969?
13 Which group had a hit with "Angel Face"?
14 Which song has the chorus line "Bang a gong"?
15 Brian Connolly was lead singer with which group?
16 Who played bass guitar in Suzi Quatro's group?
17 Mott the Hoople recorded Bowie's "All the Young" what?
18 Who recorded "Children of the Revolution"?
19 What was Mud's first top ten hit?
20 Which Micky was producer for the Suzi Quatro hits?
21 Who wished that it could be Christmas everyday?
22 And who was "Lonely This Christmas"?
23 Who was born Mark Feld?
24 Which Midlands town did Slade come from?
25 Which Alvin Stardust hit was one word repeated three times?
26 According to Sweet, "It's, it's a ballroom" what?
27 What words in brackets complete the title of "I'm the Leader of the Gang"?
28 What dance was Wizzard's baby doing in the title of a No 1 hit?
29 Which song features the words, "Do the fairies keep him sober for a day"?
30 Who was the lead singer with the original Mud?

---

1 Who launched the classically trained singers known as Il Divo?
2 Who cited press intrusion for his pulling out as a potential England soccer boss in 2006?
3 Who directed the 2006 movie "Casino Royale"?
4 In 2006, Mario Scaramella met up with which ex-spy shortly before his death?
5 What was the BT directory enquiry service number prior to deregulation?
6 Where were the Centennial Modern Olympics held?
7 In 1996 which Royals were divorced first, the Yorks or the Waleses?
8 Which crisis led to Tony Blair postponing the 20001 General Election?
9 What was the first UK No 1 for the Backstreet Boys?
10 Which veteran off-spinner Shaun made England's tour of India in 2006?
11 Which city has the constituencies of Garston and Walton?
12 What do the letters R and A stand for in DEFRA?
13 What was the title of Amy Winehouse's debut album?
14 On which Isle was Jeremy Irons born?
15 Who links music from the "Da Vinci Code" and "Pirates of the Caribbean: Dead Man's Chest"?
16 Which Spanish side did Arsenal beat to reach their first Championship League Final?
17 Which actor played Antony Royle in "The Royle Family"?
18 Who was Real Madrid coach when Beckham announced his move to the USA?
19 Richard Farleigh of "Dragon's Den" fame comes from which country?
20 The massage technique shiatsu developed in which country?
21 What do you fear if you suffer from photophobia?
22 Which country has the alphabet's first letter as its international vehicle registration code?
23 Which soccer club has Witton Road and Trinity Road around the stadium?
24 Which film won eleven awards at the 2004 Academy Awards?
25 In which month did Thatcher leave Downing Street for the last time as PM?
26 Which celebrity chef wrote "Great British Winter?
27 Which sport is associated with Graeme Dott?
28 What was McFly's second No 1 album called?
29 Johnny Depp played which writer in "Finding Neverland"?
30 What was the first Grand Slam that Roger Federer won without dropping a set?

Answers	Movie Remakes *(see Quiz 230)*

1 Alfie. 2 Gore Verbinski. 3 Gérard Dépardieu. 4 Jack Black. 5 Ocean's Eleven. 6 Denzel Washington. 7 The Talented Mr Ripley. 8 High Society. 9 Mary Shelley's Frankenstein. 10 Evergreen. 11 The Look of Love. 12 Mark Wahlberg. 13 Peter Sellers. 14 Eddie Murphy. 15 King Kong. 16 1966 (Alfie). 17 Laurence Olivier. 18 Alan Menken. 19 Four. 20 Arnold Schwarzenegger (California). 21 Kieran Culkin. 22 Graham Greene. 23 Malkovich. 24 Bram Stoker's Dracula. 25 Kenneth Branagh. 26 Psychiatrist. 27 Spencer Tracy. 28 Lewis Milestone. 29 Telly Savalas. 30 Jack Nicholson.

1 What does the W stand for in Bush's middle name?
2 Who did Bush defeat to become President for the first time?
3 How is Bush's brother, who was Governor of Florida commonly called?
4 Who did Bush beat to be President in 2004?
5 How did George W Bush say he greeted Tony Blair when they met in private?
6 Which countries did he call the "axis of evil"?
7 Who was Bush's first Secretary of State?
8 In which state was Bush at the time of the first 9/11 attack?
9 Who replaced Colin Powell as Secretary of State?
10 Where was Bush Governor before he became President?
11 Who was his first Vice President?
12 Bush ordered the invasion of which country in October 2001?
13 What are his twin daughters called?
14 "The Pearl Harbor of the 21st century took place today", related to which event?
15 Which of his nicknames is based on the pronunciation of his middle initial?
16 Who was his first Secretary of Defense?
17 Which sporting race did he run in 1993, the first US President to do so?
18 Bush became what number of President of the USA?
19 Which major hurricane hit the US shortly into Bush's second term?
20 Which 2004 Michael Moore movie was critical of Bush?
21 Where was the G8 summit when Bush said "Yo Blair"?
22 Which milestone birthday did he celebrate in 2006?
23 In which month of 2003 did he order the invasion of Iraq?
24 Brought up in Texas, in which state was he born?
25 How many sisters does he have?
26 He graduated with a history degree from which university in 1968?
27 What game do the Texas Rangers play, a team Bush had a share in?
28 What are the name of his parents?
29 Who replaced Rumsfeld as Secretary of Defense?
30 He worked for Spectrum 7 and Arbusto Energy which dealt in what?

Answers	**The Last Round** *(see Quiz 231)*

1 Paul McCartney. 2 Leeds Rhinos. 3 Cat. 4 Charles Kennedy. 5 His father, Stuart Imlach. 6 Trussed/Trust. 7 Tracey Emin. 8 Adam Gilchrist. 9 The Millennium Dome. 10 Chesterfield. 11 California and Oregon. 12 Kevin Federline. 13 Des Lynam. 14 Glasgow. 15 Germany. 16 Cunard. 17 Waterloo International. 18 Women's curling team. 19 Volkswagen. 20 Wellington boots. 21 Always Look On The Bright Side of Life. 22 Coombe Hill, Bucks. 23 1971. 24 Tirana. 25. Wagner. 26 1986. 27 Princess Anne. 28 Australia. 29 Gerald R Ford. 30 Pele.

1 Susan Sarandon and Sienna Miller feature in which remake of a 60s movie?
2 Who directed the remake of horror film "The Ring"?
3 Who was the star of the fifth version of "The Count of Monte Cristo"?
4 Who played the character Carl Denham in the 21st-century "King Kong"?
5 George Clooney and Brad Pitt were cast together in which 60s remake?
6 Who was cast as Ben Morro in 2004's "Manchurian Candidate"?
7 What was the 2000 remake of "Purple Moon" called?
8 What was "The Philadelphia Story" called when it was remade into a musical?
9 What was the 1994 Frankenstein movie called, starring Kenneth Branagh?
10 Which song won an Oscar in the 1976 remake of "A Star is Born"?
11 Which song was Oscar-nominated in the pre-Daniel Craig "Casino Royale"?
12 Who played the Michael Caine role in the remake of "The Italian Job"?
13 Which Goon was in the 1979 remake of "The Prisoner of Zenda"?
14 Who played the title role in the remake of "The Nutty Professor"?
15 Fay Wray in the 30s and Jessica Lange in the 70s were in which movie?
16 In which year was the Michael Caine original of a film remade starring Jude Law?
17 Which English Lord was in the remake of the legendary "The Jazz Singer"?
18 Who wrote the music for the animation remake of "The Hunchback of Notre Dame"?
19 How many versions of "Phantom of the Opera" were there in the 20th century?
20 Which actor said "I love doing sequels" when re-elected as Governor on the US?
21 Which brother of the "Home Alone" star was in the remake of "Father of the Bride"?
22 Who wrote "The End of the Affair" remade in 1999?
23 Which John was in the 1990s remake of "Of Mice and Men"?
24 What was the Dracula movie with Gary Oldman and Winona Ryder called?
25 Who directed himself as well as acting in the 1989 remake of "Henry V"?
26 Which profession did Faye Dunaway play in the remake of "The Thomas Crown Affair"?
27 Who starred in the second remake of "Dr Jekyll & Mr Hyde" in 1941?
28 Who directed the 1960 original "Ocean's Eleven"?
29 Which famous TV detective starred in the 1966 remake of "Beau Geste"?
30 Who played the Joker in the second remake of the movie "Batman"?

Answers	Dr Who *(see Quiz 224)*

1 Jon Pertwee. 2 November. 3 Gallifrey. 4 Nanogenes. 5 Jackie. 6 Pull to Open.
7 Skaro. 8 Sydney Newman. 9 Harriet Jones. 10 Cybermen. 11 Blue. 12 Peter
Davison. 13 Jagrafess. 14 Relative. 15 Peter Purves. 16 Cardiff. 17 Mars. 18
Swordfight. 19 Baker. 20 Henry Van Statten. 21 WHO 1. 22 1987. 23 Journalist.
24 5.5/Apple/26. 25 K9. 26 Queen Victoria. 27 McCrimmon. 28 Versailles. 29
Cricket. 30 2013.

Quiz 231 | The Last Round

LEVEL 1

1 Which pop legend was involved in a multi-million pound divorce case with Heather Mills?
2 Which team was crowned the 2007 Super League champions?
3 To which mammal family does the ocelot belong?
4 Who preceded Menzies Campbell as leader of the Liberal Democratic Party?
5 Whose biography earned Gary Imlach the 2005 William Hill Sports Book of the Year?
6 Which homonyms could be tied up or to believe in?
7 Who was nominated for a Turner Prize for her unmade bed?
8 Who scored a century in the 2007 Cricket World Cup Final?
9 What controversial exhibit was transformed into the O2 Arena in 2007?
10 Which Derbyshire town has a church spire that is notoriously crooked?
11 In which two American states can the world's tallest tree, the sequoia, be found?
12 Who engaged in a September 2007 custody battle with Britney Spears for their children?
13 Who came between Richard Whiteley and Des O'Connor as presenter of "Countdown"?
14 Which British airport had a car bomb raid repelled by staff in June 2007?
15 Lukas Podolski and Miroslav Klose are strikers for which European nation?
16 Which shipping line operated the "Queen Elizabeth II" when she first entered service?
17 Which London rail station closed in November 2007?
18 Which was the last British team to win a Winter Olympics gold medal?
19 Which motor manufacturer produced literally "the people's wagon".
20 What would you be wearing if you had a pair of Hunters on?
21 Which song from Monty Python's "The Life of Brian" became a No. 1 chart hit?
22 What is the highest point in The Chilterns?
23 In which year did Britain turn to the decimal money system?
24 What is the capital of Albania?
25 Who composed the Ring Cycle?
26 In what year did the seven-person crew on the US Shuttle "Challenger" perish?
27 Who was the first of the Queen's four children to be married?
28 Which was the first country to win the Rugby Union World Cup twice?
29 Who, taking over in 1974, was the last unelected President of the United States?
30 Who was named Athlete of the Century by the International Olympic Committee in 1999?

The Hard Questions

If you thought that this section of this book would prove to be little or no problem, or that the majority of the questions could be answered and a scant few would test you then you are sorely mistaken. These questions are the *hardest* questions *ever*! So difficult are they that any attempt to answer them all in one sitting will addle your mind and mess with your senses. You'll end up leaving the pub via the window while ordering a pint from the horse brasses on the wall. Don't do It! For a kick off there are almost 6,500 of them, so at 20 seconds a question it will take you close on a day and a half, and that's just the time it takes to read them. What you should do instead is set them for others – addle your friends' minds.

Note the dangerous nature of these questions though. These are you secret weapons use them accordingly unless, of course, someone or some team is getting your back up. In which case you should hit them hard and only let up when you have them cowering under the bench whimpering "Uncle".

These questions work best against league teams, they are genuinely tough and should be used against those people who take their pub quizzes seriously. NEVER use these questions against your inlaws.

1 Asuncion is the capital of which country?
2 Which "Pop Idol" star was born Jan 20, 1979, in Berkshire?
3 Who had hits with "Take Your Time" and "Got to Have Your Love"?
4 What is a paravane used for?
5 Dr James Naismith devised which game?
6 In which decade was Jeremy Paxman born?
7 Which worldwide magazine was conceived by DeWitt Wallace?
8 To within two years, when were postcodes introduced to the UK?
9 Waterways Airways operates from which country?
10 Who is the elder – Rowan Atkinson or Clive Anderson?
11 What is prase?
12 Who, in 1890, composed the music for the opera "Ivanhoe"?
13 A poniard is a type of what?
14 Who led the Expedition of the Thousand in 1860?
15 Which 1960s No. 1 was written by Madden and Morse in 1903?
16 Which part of the body is affected by thlipsis?
17 Who was found dead in the first episode of "EastEnders"?
18 Which Mel Brooks film was a spoof of Hitchcock movies?
19 Which TV cookery series set out to create a menu for the Queen's 80th birthday?
20 Gabriel Heinze joined Man Utd from which club?
21 Antonio Salazar was dictator for many years in which country?
22 Which US anti-terrorist force is based at Fort Bragg?
23 William Benting was an English pioneer of what?
24 By volume, what makes up about 21% of our atmosphere?
25 Who starred with his wife in the film "Mr and Mrs Bridge"?
26 Whose one and only hit was "I've Never Been to Me" in 1982?
27 Which two political parties aligned to form the Ministry of All-the-Talents in 1806?
28 To which Court are US Ambassadors to Britain officially credited?
29 Which US poet had the middle names Weston Loomir?
30 Which was the first African team to compete in the Cricket World Cup?

Answers	TV: Detectives *(see Quiz 2)*

1 Tom Barnaby (Midsomer Murders). **2** Prime Suspect – The Final Act. **3** Liverpool One. **4** Adrian Kershaw. **5** Reginald Hill. **6** Eddie Shoestring. **7** Charlie's Angels. **8** RD Wingfield. **9** CIB. **10** The Remorseful Day. **11** Rupert Davies. **12** Reilly – Ace of Spies. **13** The Rockford Files. **14** Crime Traveller. **15** Denise Welch. **16** Cadfael. **17** Imogen Stubbs. **18** Barbara Havers. **19** Taggart. **20** Stanton. **21** Van der Valk. **22** Sexton Blake. **23** Gideon's Way. **24** Cordelia Gray. **25** Chief Inspector Haskins. **26** Hercule Poirot. **27** The Body in the Library. **28** Reginald Hill (Dalziel & Pascoe).. **29** Henry Crabbe. **30** Simon Templar.

Quiz 2 TV: Detectives Answers – page 475

1 Which DCI was first seen in episodes called "The Killings at Badger's Drift" and "Written in Blood"?

2 What was the final drama featuring Det. Supt Jane Tennison called?

3 In which series was Samantha Janus transferred from the Met to Merseyside?

4 Who was Morse's sidekick in "The Wench is Dead"?

5 Which novelist created the characters of Dalziel and Pascoe?

6 Which detective worked for Radio West?

7 Which series centred on Townsend Investigations?

8 Which novelist created Jack Frost?

9 Which acronymic part of the Met did Tony Clark work for in "Between the Lines"?

10 What was the episode called in which Inspector Morse died?

11 Who introduced the very first series of "Detective"?

12 In which series did Inspector Tsientsin appear?

13 Which famous series was introduced with a message on an answering machine?

14 In which series was Slade assisted by Holly?

15 Who played Frances Spender in the Jimmy Nail series?

16 Whose investigations are based in Shrewsbury but often filmed in central Europe?

17 Who played mini-skirted detective Anna Lee?

18 In the 2003 series, who was Inspector Lynley's Detective Sergeant?

19 Which long running series began with a pilot called "Killer" in 1983?

20 Where did "The Cops" take place?

21 What was the full name of TV's most famous Dutch detective?

22 Who had a Rolls Royce called "The Grey Panther"?

23 Which 60s series had Chief Inspector Keen aiding his Commander?

24 Who is the detective in "An Unsuitable Job for a Woman"?

25 Who was Regan's boss in "The Sweeney"?

26 Which detective lived at Whitehaven Mansions?

27 Which was the first Miss Marple adaptation to star Joan Hickson on TV?

28 Who created the detectives played on TV by actors Clarke and Buchanan?

29 Who had retired from Barstock CID?

30 Claude Eustace Teal was invariably beaten in his dealings with whom?

Answers | Pot Luck 1 *(see Quiz 1)*

1 Paraguay. 2 Will Young. 3 Mantronix. 4 Mine-sweeping. 5 Basketball. 6 1950s. 7 Reader's Digest. 8 1968. 9 New Zealand. 10 Clive Anderson. 11 A type of quartz. 12 Sir Arthur Sullivan. 13 Dagger. 14 Garibaldi. 15 Two Little Boys. 16 The blood vessels. 17 Reg Cox. 18 High Anxiety. 19 Great British Menu. 20 Paris St Germain. 21 Portugal. 22 Delta Force. 23 Slimming diet. 24 Oxygen. 25 Paul Newman. 26 Charlene. 27 Whigs and Tories. 28 St James. 29 Ezra Pound. 30 East Africa (in 1975).

Quiz 3

1 Phil Read won several World Championships in which sport?
2 What did an alchemist use an alembic for?
3 What was Eternal's first UK Top Ten hit?
4 In Hindu mythology who was goddess of destruction and death?
5 In which country is the Mackenzie River?
6 Which instrument did Lionel Hampton play?
7 How many Top Five hits did Elvis Presley have in 2005?
8 What was President Carter's wife's first name?
9 Who won the first squash World Open Championship?
10 Where is England's national hockey stadium?
11 Where was the constituency of former Home Secretary Charles Clarke?
12 Who wrote the novel "Rodney Stone"?
13 How many times is Annie mentioned in the lyrics of "Annie's Song"?
14 In Swift's novel what was Gulliver's first name?
15 To which part of the body does the adjective "cutaneous" refer?
16 In which sport were Hildon and Black Bears British Champions?
17 Whose first Top Ten hit was "What a Waste" in 1978?
18 Who was James I of England's father?
19 Which record label did Geri Halliwell sign up with when she left the Spice Girls?
20 What was the old name for stamp collecting?
21 Which "Countdown" regular wrote "The Language Report"?
22 Alfredo di Stefano of Real Madrid fame was born in which country?
23 What is the name of the police officer in "West Side Story"?
24 Which language's name means "one who hopes"?
25 Which public figure resigned over dealings concerning prostitute Monica Coghlan?
26 In the Old Testament which two books are named after women?
27 The Prix Goncourt is awarded for what?
28 Who joined Patrick Macnee on the 1990 No. 5 UK hit "Kinky Boots"?
29 Who or what is a dourousouli?
30 What was Steve McClaren's best finishing position as a club manager?

Answers	Books 1 *(see Quiz 4)*

1 John Cleese. 2 Full Disclosure. 3 Diana Rigg. 4 Martin Amis. 5 Dame Barbara Cartland. 6 Ronnie Spector. 7 Six. 8 Pat Conroy. 9 Clare Francis. 10 Madonna. 11 Isaac Asimov. 12 Darren Gough. 13 Pig. 14 Sussex. 15 Richard Noble. 16 Torvill & Dean. 17 South Africa. 18 Her Majesty's Stationery Office. 19 Stephen Hawking. 20 A Boy from Bolton. 21 Octaves. 22 Noah Webster. 23 Styles. 24 The Rainbow. 25 The Highway Code. 26 John Humphrys. 27 Bertie Ahern, father of Cecelia. 28 Guinness Book of Records. 29 Bridget Jones's. 30 Agatha Christie.

1 Which comedian wrote "Families and How to Survive Them" with psychiatrist Robin Skynner?

2 What was Andrew Neil's autobiography called?

3 Who wrote an anthology of critics' anecdotes called "No Turn Unstoned"?

4 Whose first novel was "The Rachel Papers" in 1974?

5 Which novelist recorded an "Album of Love Songs" in 1978?

6 Which pop celebrity wrote "Be My Baby"?

7 How many Barchester Chronicles are there?

8 Who wrote the novel on which the movie "Prince of Tides" was based?

9 Who went from "Deceit and Betrayal" to "A Dark Devotion"?

10 Whose book "Sex", coincided with a dance album "Erotica"?

11 Which science fiction writer wrote the Foundation Trilogy?

12 Which cricketer wrote "Dazzler on the Dance Floor"?

13 Who or what was PG Wodehouse's Empress of Blandings?

14 The founder of Wisden played for which English county?

15 Whose quest for speed is recorded in his book "Thrust"?

16 Which sports stars' autobiography was called "Facing the Music?"

17 Rider Haggard's colonial service where influenced his books?

18 Who publishes Hansard?

19 Whose 1998 best seller argued that our universe is a part of a super universe?

20 What was boxer Amir Khan's autobiography called?

21 What did Compton Mackenzie refer to each individual volume of his autobiography as?

22 Whose 19th-century dictionary standardised US English?

23 Where was the Mysterious Affair in the first Agatha Christie in Penguin paperback?

24 Which colourful DH Lawrence book was banned because of its sexual content along with "Lady Chatterley" and "Women in Love"?

25 First appearing in 1931, what sold out of its new edition in three months in 1996?

26 Which journalist wrote "Beyond Words"?

27 Who is the father of the author of "A Place Called Here"?

28 What is the best-selling copyright book of all time?

29 Whose Diary was written by Helen Fielding?

30 Who wrote romantic novels as Mary Westmacott?

Answers | Pot Luck 2 *(see Quiz 3)*

1 Motor Cycling. 2 To distil liquids. 3 Stay. 4 Kali. 5 Canada. 6 Vibraphone. 7 17. 8 Rosalyn. 9 Geoff Hunt. 10 Milton Keynes. 11 Norwich South. 12 Sir Arthur Conan Doyle. 13 Never. 14 Lemuel. 15 Skin. 16 Polo. 17 Ian Dury & The Blockheads. 18 Lord Darnley. 19 Chrysalis. 20 Timbrology. 21 Susie Dent. 22 Argentina. 23 Officer Krupke. 24 Esperanto. 25 Jeffrey Archer. 26 Ruth and Esther. 27 Literature (in France). 28 Honor Blackman. 29 A monkey. 30 Seventh (Premiership).

Quiz 5

Pot Luck 3

Answers – page 480

LEVEL 3

1 Who designed the tapestry behind the altar in Coventry Cathedral?
2 An odalisque is a female what?
3 Who founded the record label Maverick Records?
4 Both Clive Woodward and Andy Robinson are linked with which university?
5 Which English poet had the middle name Chawner?
6 The Russian Revolution began in which year?
7 Which notorious serial killer was found hanged in prison in January 2004?
8 Who is the elder – Zoe Ball or Gary Barlow?
9 In the 1980s Greg Lemond became the first American to do what?
10 Whose one and only hit was "Little Things Mean a Lot"?
11 Who created the Statue of Zeus about 430 BC?
12 Which Jackson Pollock painting reputedly sold for $140 million in 2006?
13 What was film star Edward G. Robinson's real name?
14 Who was the husband of cellist Jacqueline du Pre?
15 What is the drink kumiss made from?
16 Who came up with "The Book of Heroic Failures"?
17 What was discovered in 1930 by Clyde Tombaugh?
18 In the Bible, who was King David's father?
19 In 1865, where did the Confederates surrender?
20 Wellesley is the family name of which Dukes?
21 What is a dhole?
22 Norman Parkinson made his name in which field of art?
23 How many times did Steve Donoghue win the Derby?
24 Who created the Detective Inspector Anna Travis?
25 Lynn Ripley shone under which name as a pop singer?
26 Which theory was formulated by the German physicist Max Planck?
27 Which poet wrote, "She was a phantom of delight"?
28 Which England soccer manager was born in Burnley, Lancashire?
29 The Haber Process manufactures which gas?
30 Who was Banquo's son in Macbeth?

Answers	**Albums** *(see Quiz 6)*

1 Simon & Garfunkel. 2 If U Can't Dance. 3 Mystery Girl. 4 Vertigo. 5 Innuendo.
6 Alison Moyet (Essex). 7 American Pie. 8 Frank Sinatra. 9 All Things Must Pass.
10 Help! – The Beatles. 11 Sheer Heart Attack. 12 A black dog. 13 Face Value.
14 Tony Christie. 15 Blue. 16 Mark Coyle. 17 The Police. 18 The Sound of Music.
19 Goodbye Yellow Brick Road. 20 As a soloist, with Style Council and the Jam. 21
Chris De Burgh. 22 Fleetwood Mac. 23 Saturday Night Fever. 24 A postal strike. 25
Postcard. 26 On. 27 WEA. 28 Transformer. 29 Never for Ever. 30 Queen.

1 Who released the biggest-selling album in Britain in the 70s?
2 What was the final track on "Spice"?
3 Which 1988 album confirmed a comeback by Roy Orbison?
4 Dire Straits first albums came out on which label?
5 Which 6.5-minute hit was the title track of Queen's 7th No. 1 album?
6 Who charted with an album named after an English county?
7 Don McLean's "Vincent" came from which album?
8 Which superstar first charted with "Come Fly with Me"?
9 What was George Harrison's first solo album after the Beatles?
10 What was the first album to make its debut into the UK chart at No. 1?
11 Which album contains the line, "My kingdom for a horse"?
12 Who is not on the front cover of "Urban Hymns", but features on an inside cover shot?
13 What was Phil Collins' first solo No. 1 album?
14 Who had a No. 1 album in 2005, nearly 30 years after his previous album success?
15 What was the main colour on the cover of Enya's "Shepherd Moons"?
16 Who along with Oasis gets production credits on "Definitely Maybe"?
17 Which group had five consecutive No. 1 albums from 1979 to 1986?
18 Which original film soundtrack was on the charts for a staggering 382 weeks?
19 Which album first featured "Candle in the Wind"?
20 Paul Weller has topped the charts in which three guises?
21 Who was the first artist to enter the Swiss album charts at No. 1?
22 What was the last Fleetwood Mac album released before the world smash "Rumours"?
23 Which double-album film soundtrack was a 30 million seller in 1978?
24 Why weren't the album charts published in 1971 for eight weeks?
25 What was the name of Mary Hopkin's debut album?
26 Which word appeared in the titles of Will Young's first and third albums?
27 Tubular Bells launched the Virgin label, but which label put out Tubular Bells II?
28 Which album originally featured "Perfect Day"?
29 Which Kate Bush album featured a song about Delius?
30 In 2005 which group took over as having most weeks on the UK album charts?

Answers | Pot Luck 3 *(see Quiz 5)*

1 Graham Sutherland. 2 Slave. 3 Madonna. 4 Loughborough. 5 Rupert Brooke. 6 1917. 7 Dr Harold Shipman. 8 Zoe Ball. 9 Win the Tour de France. 10 Kitty Kallen. 11 Phidias. 12 Number 5, 1948. 13 Emmanuel Goldenberg. 14 Daniel Barenboim. 15 Milk. 16 Stephen Pile. 17 Pluto. 18 Jesse. 19 Appomattox. 20 Wellington. 21 An Asian wild dog. 22 Photography. 23 Six. 24 Lynda La Plante. 25 Twinkle. 26 Quantum theory. 27 Wordsworth. 28 Ron Greenwood. 29 Ammonia. 30 Fleance.

1 Who were the first group since The Beatles to have 14 consecutive Top Five singles?

2 What was Golden Earring's first UK Top Ten hit?

3 Started in 1850, what were Children's Temperance Societies called?

4 How long had David Cameron been an MP when he became Tory leader?

5 Gravure is a term connected with which industry?

6 What did Thomas Wheildon make?

7 To the nearest hundred how many islands make up the Maldives?

8 Who was Prime Minister during the General Strike?

9 Once of Newcastle, which country did Hugo Viana play for?

10 Mycology is the study of what?

11 What was the Carla Rosa, existing from 1875 to 1958?

12 Who was the last King of Troy according to legend?

13 What was George Burns' real name?

14 The word Ombudsman comes from which language?

15 Who played the barrel organ in "The Magic Roundabout"?

16 Who wrote the play "The Homecoming"?

17 Who was writer and producer for New Kids on the Block?

18 In which American state were Bonnie and Clyde killed in an ambush?

19 The Statue of Liberty's 100th birthday was celebrated in which year?

20 Which Christmas fruits have the Latin name *vaccinium macrocarpon*?

21 What is studied by a pedologist?

22 Spencer Gore was the first winner of what?

23 George Galvin performed in music-hall under what name?

24 Placido Domingo studied music at which National Conservatory?

25 Who was the last Prime Minister during the reign of Queen Victoria?

26 The star Betelgeuse is in which constellation?

27 Which major pop singer/songwriter was born 13 June 1968, in Manchester?

28 Who was the first woman to be Canadian Prime Minister?

29 What do a tinchel of men do?

30 Who is in the portrait auctioned in Nov. 2006, to set a record for an Andy Warhol work?

Answers	Cricket 1 *(see Quiz 8)*

1 Vengsarkar. 2 Mark Taylor. 3 Leeward Islands. 4 Swansea, Glamorgan. 5 Old Trafford. 6 West Indies. 7 Geoff Boycott. 8 Old Trafford. 9 Cigarettes & Alcohol by Oasis. 10 James Andersen. 11 Imperial. 12 Australia. 13 Shell Shield. 14 59. 15 New Zealand & India. 16 Charlton Athletic. 17 Steve Bucknor. 18 Ivon. 19 India v. New Zealand. 20 India & Pakistan. 21 Bob Taylor. 22 Ricky Ponting. 23 Mike Gatting. 24 Wayne Larkins. 25 Mike Atherton. 26 Durham and Lancashire. 27 Alec Stewart. 28 Victoria. 29 Craig McDermott. 30 Surrey.

1 Who was the first overseas batsman to score three Test centuries at Lord's?
2 Which Aussie equalled Don Bradman's batting record in October 1998 but declared rather than beat it?
3 Which West Indian islands did Viv Richards play for?
4 Where did Sobers hit his 36 runs in one over and against whom?
5 Where did Dennis Amiss score the first century in a one-day international?
6 Against whom did Mike Atherton make his first international one-day century?
7 Who deputised for Mike Brearley as England skipper four times in 1977–8?
8 Where did Lance Gibbs take most of his wickets in England?
9 Which song did Phil Tufnell choose to escort him on to the field in the New Zealand test tour?
10 Alphabetically who came first in England's 2006/07 Ashes squad?
11 Until 1965 what did "I" stand for in ICC?
12 Which was the first women's side to win the World Cup in successive occasions?
13 Which competition in the West Indies was replaced by the Red Stripe Cup?
14 How many did Ashley Giles score in his final Ashes 2005 innings?
15 Graham Gooch became the first player to score 1,000 Test runs in an English summer against which sides?
16 Which football team did Alec Stewart's father play for?
17 Who was the first overseas umpire to umpire a Test Match in England?
18 What is David Gower's middle name?
19 Who was playing when the first hat trick by a bowler was scored in a World Cup?
20 Where was the first World Cup outside England played?
21 In 1995 Jack Russell broke whose record for dismissals in a Test match?
22 Who was born in Launceston, Tasmania, Dec. 19, 1974?
23 Whose autobiography was called "Leading from the Front"?
24 Who was the first batsman to score centuries against all the counties?
25 Who was the youngest Lancastrian to score a Test century, in 1990?
26 Which two counties had three players in England's 2006/07 Ashes squad?
27 Who was the first Englishman to score a century in each innings against the West Indies in 1994?
28 Which Australian state did Ben Hollioake's father play for?
29 Who was Australia's leading wicket taker on the 1994–5 Ashes tour?
30 Who won the first ever county championship?

Answers	Pot Luck 4 (see Quiz 7)

1 Steps. 2 Radar Love. 3 Bands of Hope. 4 Four years. 5 Printing (platemaking). 6 Pottery. 7 1200 (1196). 8 Stanley Baldwin. 9 Portugal. 10 Fungi. 11 An Opera Company. 12 Priam. 13 Nathan Birnbaum. 14 Swedish. 15 Mr Rusty. 16 Harold Pinter. 17 Maurice Starr. 18 Louisiana. 19 1986. 20 Cranberries. 21 Soils. 22 Men's singles, Wimbledon. 23 Dan Leno. 24 Mexico. 25 Marquis of Salisbury. 26 Orion. 27 David Gray. 28 Kim Campbell. 29 Hunt. 30 Chairman Mao.

1 Who was the letter which revealed the Gunpowder Plot addressed to?
2 Which lecturer in philosophy wrote "The Second Sex"?
3 Which non-metallic element has the atomic number 6?
4 What was Marc Almond's first solo UK Top Ten hit?
5 Made in 1975 with George Segal, "The Black Bird" was a spoof of which screen classic?
6 In surveying, how long is a Gunter's Chain in feet?
7 Susan Godfrey was the first victim of which atrocity?
8 In which city was the infamous Gatting and Rana Test Match flare up?
9 Who was older when he died, Jimi Hendrix or Marc Bolan?
10 In which film did Chaplin first tackle dialogue?
11 Luke Concannon and John Parker were known as which musical duo?
12 What was a lamia in ancient mythology?
13 What date was the Stock Market's Black Monday of the 1980s?
14 Which saint was shot dead in 288 AD by arrows?
15 Which campaign group flour bombed the House of Commons in May 2004?
16 The European Economic Community was established in which year?
17 In poetry what was hung around the neck of the Ancient Mariner?
18 Turner, Campbell and Chrétien have all held which post?
19 What was the name of the Vicar of Dibley's betrothed?
20 Whose one and only hit was "Turtle Power" in 1990?
21 The sword is the symbol of which of the twelve apostles?
22 Which artist painted "Bubbles" used by Pears to advertise their soap?
23 What can be a unit of length or a small island in Scotland?
24 Who is the elder – Kenneth Branagh or Rory Bremner?
25 What is the name of America's National Cemetery?
26 In which country could you visit Umm?
27 Robert, Grattan and Emmett were which famous Wild West outlaw gang?
28 Who scripted the first series of "Blackadder" with Rowan Atkinson?
29 In 1941 which American defined the Four Freedoms?
30 Which team did England play in Sven-Goran Eriksson's last game as boss?

Answers	**Battle Stations** *(see Quiz 10)*

1 Auchinleck. 2 Panmunjom. 3 Madras. 4 Mohne & Eder. 5 Vidkun Quisling. 6 Right arm. 7 MacArthur. 8 Reims. 9 Richthofen's Flying Circus. 10 Gavrilo Princip. 11 Treaty of Sevres. 12 Switzerland & Luxembourg. 13 Anzio. 14 Second Battle of the Somme. 15 Major Johnny Paul Koroma. 16 29. 17 Contras. 18 Dien Bien Phu. 19 American. 20 Ardennes. 21 Japanese. 22 Tobruk. 23 Near Kiev, Ukraine. 24 Spanish Civil War. 25 Michel Aoun. 26 Boer War. 27 Tutsi v. Hutu. 28 Passchendaele. 29 Von Moltke. 30 Vichy France.

1 Who led the British forces in the First Battle of El Alamein?
2 Where was the peace treaty signed after the Korean War?
3 What was the only place in India attacked by foreign forces in WWI?
4 Which dams were destroyed by bouncing bombs in 1943?
5 Which Norwegian leader aided the 1940 invasion of his country through non-resistance?
6 Which part of his body did Lord Raglan lose at Waterloo?
7 Who was commander of the US forces in the Pacific from March '42?
8 In which city did the German High Command formally surrender to General Eisenhower?
9 What was the German 11th Chasing Squadron known as in WWI?
10 Who assassinated Archduke Franz Ferdinand in 1914 thus precipitating WWI?
11 What was the last of the treaties which ended WWI?
12 Which countries were on either end of the Maginot Line?
13 Which birthplace of Nero was the site of an Allied beachhead invasion in WWII?
14 How is the battle at St Quentin in 1918 also known?
15 Who led the military coup in Sierra Leone's Civil War in 1997?
16 How many countries made up the coalition v. Iraq in the Gulf War?
17 In the Nicaraguan Civil War which faction had US support?
18 Where was France's defeat which brought about the division of Vietnam along the 17th parallel?
19 Hitler's plan "Watch on the Rhine" was aimed at which troops?
20 In which area of Belgium/Luxembourg was the Battle of the Bulge?
21 Which navy was defeated at the Battle of Midway Island in 1942?
22 The retreat by the British from which port brought about the replacement of Auchinleck by Montgomery?
23 Where is Babi Yar, where 100,000 people were slaughtered in 1941?
24 In which war did the Battle of Ebro take place?
25 Which General declared a "war of liberation" against Syrian occupation of Lebanon in 1989?
26 Which war was ended with the Peace of Vereeniging?
27 Who were the two opposing factions in the Rwandan Civil War in the mid-1990s?
28 How is the third battle of Ypres in WWI also known?
29 Who was in charge of the German troops in the First Battle of the Marne?
30 What name was given to that part of France not occupied by the Germans until 1942?

Answers | Pot Luck 5 *(see Quiz 9)*

1 Lord Monteagle. 2 Simone de Beauvoir. 3 Carbon. 4 The Days of Pearly Spencer.
5 The Maltese Falcon. 6 66. 7 Hungerford Massacre. 8 Lahore. 9 Marc Bolan.
10 The Great Dictator. 11 Nizlopi. 12 A snake-bodied female demon. 13 October
19th. 14 Sebastian. 15 Fathers 4 Justice. 16 1957. 17 An albatross. 18 Canadian
PM. 19 Harry Kennedy. 20 Partners in Kryme. 21 St Paul. 22 Millais. 23 Inch. 24
Kenneth Branagh. 25 Arlington. 26 Qatar. 27 The Daltons. 28 Richard Curtis. 29 FD
Roosevelt. 30 Portugal.

1 Which denomination of Ulster banknote featured George Best?
2 What was the middle name of Wallis Simpson, later Duchess of Windsor?
3 Which greedy giant was created by Rabelais?
4 Who is the elder – Tony Blair or Pierce Brosnan?
5 What is sorghum?
6 From what is the writing material true vellum made?
7 What is separated by the oval window and the round window?
8 Whose presidential hopes were ended by model Donna Rice?
9 What fraction of a gold object is a carat as a proportional measure?
10 What is a killick?
11 The Cassini-Huygens probe took pictures of which planet?
12 Which team featured in "Footballers' Wives"?
13 What name is given to an animal that may be slaughtered to provide food under Muslim law?
14 In which county did the Tolpuddle Martyrs form a trade union?
15 What is a bowyang ?
16 Which politician said that northerners die of "ignorance and crisps"?
17 In which decade was actress Kristin Scott Thomas born?
18 In Feb. 2005 a Class 47 diesel locomotive was named after which musician?
19 Which country without a D or a Z in its name has the internet code .dz?
20 What relation was Queen Victoria to George IV?
21 Who won the first WBC cruiserweight title in boxing?
22 Why were the Piccard brothers famous in the 1930s?
23 Which Roman god was the god of beginnings and doors?
24 What is gneiss?
25 What was Florence Nightingale the first woman to receive in 1907?
26 What was a "quod" in old slang?
27 Who preceded David II as King of the Scots?
28 How is Julie Anne Smith better known in movies?
29 "The Purple Rose of Cairo" was written and directed by which actor?
30 Which title did Saddam Hussein take first – President or Prime Minister?

Answers	Quizzes & Games *(see Quiz 12)*

1 Zoe Tyler. 2 The Moment of Truth. 3 Patrick Kielty. 4 Alan Coren. 5 Kenny Everett. 6 David Sneddon. 7 Child's Play. 8 Vincent Price. 9 Countdown (OED). 10 Ally McCoist. 11 Richard Wilson. 12 Blockbusters. 13 Steve Brookstein. 14 Pass the Buck. 15 Max Robertson. 16 John Leslie. 17 Edwina Currie. 18 Newspaper – day of birth. 19 Matthew Kelly. 20 Princess Diana. 21 Blind Date. 22 Max Bygraves. 23 Armand Jammot. 24 Ed Tudor-Pole. 25 Double Your Money. 26 Paul Daniels. 27 British Museum. 28 Leslie Crowther. 29 The Great Garden Game. 30 Anthea Redfern.

1 Who was the voice coach on "How Do You Solve a Problem Like Maria?"?
2 Which show had a "Dream Directory"?
3 Who joined Anthea Turner on "The National Lottery's Big Ticket"?
4 Who opposed Sandi Toksvig in the 90s "Call My Bluff"?
5 Who was the first male team captain in "That's Showbusiness"?
6 Who was the first winner of "Fame Academy"?
7 In which quiz did Ronnie Corbett replace Michael Aspel as host?
8 Which horror movie actor was on the first "Celebrity Squares"?
9 In which show might Mark Nyman adjudicate?
10 Who was the footballing "A Question of Sport" team captain when Sue Barker took over on a regular basis?
11 Who was the Reverend Green in the second series of "Cluedo"?
12 In which show were you pleased to be on the "Hot Spot"?
13 Who was the 2004 winner of "X Factor"?
14 Which weekday elimination quiz was hosted by Fred Dinenage?
15 Who presented the original "Going for a Song"?
16 Which "Blue Peter" presenter took over "Wheel of Fortune"?
17 In "Celebrity Wife Swap" which ex-MP changed places with Mrs John McCririck?
18 What did contestants receive at the end of "Today's the Day"?
19 Who hosted "You Bet" before Darren Day?
20 Who was the subject of an entire show of "100%" in August 1998?
21 Sue Middleton and Alex Tatham famously followed a TV win on which show with marriage?
22 Who presented "Family Fortunes" immediately prior to Les Dennis?
23 Who created Countdown?
24 Who replaced Richard O'Brien on "The Crystal Maze"?
25 "The Sky's the Limit" was a variation of which show?
26 Whom did Bob Monkhouse replace on "Wipeout"?
27 Which building was central to Tony Robinson's "Codex" challenge?
28 Who first asked contestants to "Come on down"?
29 What was Channel 5's first gardening quiz called?
30 Who was the female half of the first husband-and-wife team to present "The Generation Game"?

Answers	Pot Luck 6 *(see Quiz 11)*

1 £5 **2** Warfield. **3** Gargantua. **4** Tony Blair. **5** A cereal crop. **6** Calf skin. **7** Middle ear and inner ear. **8** Gary Hart. **9** 1/24th. **10** A small anchor. **11** Saturn. **12** Earls Park. **13** Halal. **14** Dorset. **15** String tied to the knee to hitch trousers up. **16** Edwina Currie. **17** 1960s. **18** Joe Strummer. **19** Algeria. **20** Niece. **21** Marvin Camel. **22** Balloonists. **23** Janus. **24** A type of rock. **25** The Order of Merit. **26** A prison. **27** Robert the Bruce. **28** Julianne Moore. **29** Woody Allen. **30** President (1979).

Quiz 13 | Pot Luck 7

1 Who led the British force in 1898 at Omdurman?
2 What was Adam Ant's first UK Top Ten hit?
3 How many cubic centimetres in a cubic metre?
4 In which country was Fatos Nano returned to power as PM in 2002?
5 Which real island, famed in fiction, is some 25 miles south of Elba?
6 Who would use a fyke?
7 Who was the first Irish cyclist to win the Tour de France?
8 What first did Bernard Harris achieve when he did his space walk?
9 Who or what is Katherine Gorge?
10 Which two countries are separated by the Kattegat?
11 In which decade did Picasso die?
12 Houses in Sherwood Crescent were destroyed in which disaster?
13 Which classic film was billed as "The Eighth Wonder of the World"?
14 Which Royal House ruled from 1461 to 1485 in England?
15 What is a gribble?
16 How many books are there in the New Testament?
17 How many FA Cup Finals did Roy Keane play in?
18 Which city is the capital of Tibet?
19 "In No Way to Treat a Lady" what did the killer leave on the brow?
20 What is bohea?
21 The Greek goddess Nyx was the personification of what?
22 Ion Iliescu has twice been President of which country?
23 What form did the Yahoos have in Gulliver's Travels ?
24 "I Didn't Get Where I am Today" was which comedy writer's autobiography?
25 In which country is the national drink called pisco?
26 Whose one and only hit was "First Time" in 1988?
27 Which place is in Berkshire in England and Pennsylvania in America?
28 Unlucky for some, what was Westlife's 13th No. 1 single?
29 When George Bush Snr was elected president who was his Democrat opponent?
30 Which rock star has children called Rufus Tiger and Tiger Lily?

| **Answers** | **50s Films** *(see Quiz 14)* |

1 Giant. 2 St Swithin's. 3 Robert Morley. 4 Kim Novak. 5 Darby O'Gill and the Little People. 6 Richard Burton. 7 George Cole. 8 Danny Kaye. 9 Mount Rushmore. 10 Carry On Nurse. 11 Operation Petticoat. 12 Dorothy Dandridge. 13 George Sanders. 14 High Noon. 15 Mike Todd. 16 Viva Zapata!. 17 Jack Lemmon. 18 Anastasia. 19 The Trouble with Harry. 20 The Swan. 21 Yul Brynner. 22 No Way Out. 23 1915. 24 The Long Hot Summer. 25 Bewitched Bothered and Bewildered. 26 Green Grow the Rushes. 27 William Wyler. 28 Yves Montand. 29 Larry Adler. 30 Judy Garland.

1 James Dean died during the filming of which film in 1955?
2 In which hospital would you find Sir Lancelot Spratt?
3 Who played George III in "Beau Brummell"?
4 Who played the blonde that James Stewart was hired to follow in Vertigo?
5 In which 50s film did Sean Connery sing?
6 Which actor wins Christ's robe in a dice game in "The Robe"?
7 Who played the younger Scrooge in the classic with Alistair Sim?
8 Who replaced Astaire for the "Holiday Inn" remake "White Christmas"?
9 Where does the climax of "North by Northwest" take place?
10 What was the second "Carry On" film?
11 What was the only film where Tony Curtis and Cary Grant starred together?
12 Whose voice was dubbed by Marilyn Horne in "Carmen Jones"?
13 Who won Best Supporting Actor for "All About Eve"?
14 Which film was based on "The Tin Star" by John W. Cunningham?
15 Which one-time husband of Elizabeth Taylor produced "Around the World in 80 Days"?
16 What was the second of Brando's four consecutive Oscar nominations for between 1951 and 1954?
17 Who contributed a song for his 1957 film "Fire Down Below"?
18 Ingrid Bergman won a second Oscar for which film, marking her return from Hollywood exile?
19 What was Shirley Maclaine's debut film in 1955?
20 What was the last film Grace Kelly made before becoming a princess?
21 Who played the Pharaoh in "The Ten Commandments"?
22 What was Sidney Poitier's first film, in 1950?
23 "The African Queen", made in 1951, is about events in which year?
24 What was the first film in which Paul Newman and Joanne Woodward appeared together?
25 Which song did Rita Hayworth famously sing in "Pal Joey"?
26 What was Richard Burton's last UK film before turning to Hollywood?
27 Who won his third Best Director for his third Best Picture in 1959?
28 Which French superstar was the husband of the 1959 Oscar-winning Best Supporting Actress?
29 Who composed and played the music for "Genevieve"?
30 Who was replaced by Betty Hutton in "Annie Get Your Gun"?

Answers	**Pot Luck 7** *(see Quiz 13)*

1 Lord Kitchener. 2 Dog Eat Dog. 3 One million. 4 Albania. 5 Monte Cristo. 6 A fisherman. 7 Stephen Roche. 8 First black man to walk in space. 9 National Park in Australia. 10 Denmark and Sweden. 11 1970s. 12 Jumbo jet crash, Lockerbie. 13 King Kong. 14 York. 15 A crustacean. 16 27. 17 Seven. 18 Lhasa. 19 A lipstick kiss. 20 Tea. 21 Night. 22 Romania. 23 Human. 24 David Nobbs. 25 Peru. 26 Robin Beck. 27 Reading. 28 You Raise Me Up. 29 Michael Dukakis. 30 Roger Taylor.

1 The Euroroute E24 is from Birmingham to which county town?

2 Which Scottish university was named after a jeweller and an inventor?

3 Which polo ground is in the park of a burnt-down former country house?

4 What is the smallest theatre at the Barbican in London called?

5 Where is Grimsetter Airport?

6 Which inlet of the Clyde was used as a US submarine base from the early 60s?

7 In which part of London is Kenwood?

8 Which shipping area is due north of Trafalgar?

9 In which county was the Open University founded?

10 John Peel lived in which county for the latter part of his life?

11 How many national parks does the Pennine Way pass through?

12 Which wall runs from the river Forth in the east to Clyde in the west?

13 What is the real name of "Petticoat Lane"?

14 Which county is due north of Buckinghamshire?

15 Where is the Post Office's main sorting office?

16 What name is given to someone born east of the Medway?

17 Which county is due South of Tyne and Wear?

18 Which colloquial name of the main church in Boston serves as a landmark for ships?

19 Who or what was London's Liverpool Street station named after?

20 Where is the official London residence of the Foreign Secretary?

21 What is the administration centre of Wiltshire?

22 How is London's Collegiate Church of St Peter better known?

23 Which House has an Egyptian Hall for banqueting?

24 Which important collection was given to the city of Glasgow in 1944?

25 Which World Heritage Site was built for the Duke of Marlborough?

26 Which house is headquarters and home to the BBC World Service?

27 What is MOMI on London's South Bank?

28 Which famous House is the only surviving part of Whitehall Palace?

29 Where is Scatsa Airport?

30 Which county is due south of Shropshire?

---

1 Where on your body is your philtrum?
2 In which decade was Delia Smith born?
3 Inigo Jones was famous in which profession?
4 Who discovered carbon dioxide in 1754 and called it "fixed air"?
5 Who was the first musician to be made a life peer?
6 Who won golf's World Matchplay Championship in 1987, 1990 and 2001?
7 Who defeated Sweden's forces at Poltava in 1709?
8 What was the last film directed by Alfred Hitchcock?
9 Which country known by two words since 1970 was long ago known as Serendip?
10 Where is the Louis Armstrong Stadium?
11 Who wrote Gary Barlow's second solo No. 1?
12 In "Brideshead Revisited" which actor played the father of Jeremy Irons?
13 What was John Lennon's middle name?
14 Mikel Arteta joined Everton from which club?
15 Whose only UK Top Ten hit from 1971 was called "Rose Garden"?
16 What is the more common name for the flower called the Kingcup?
17 What odds is a horse if it is "Burlington Bertie" in rhyming slang?
18 Who wrote "Tropic of Cancer" and "Tropic of Capricorn"?
19 Which ballet dancer died on the same day as Dizzy Gillespie?
20 What was Chris Rea's first UK Top Ten hit?
21 Amboyna is a richly coloured type of what?
22 What was Sir John Gielgud's first name?
23 Which poet wrote, "I have measured out my life with coffee spoons"?
24 What was Timothy Dalton's last film as James Bond?
25 Plasma in blood consists of platelets and red and white what?
26 Who was the drummer in the group Police?
27 Who invented the Polaroid camera in 1947?
28 "Barefoot in the Park" was written by which US playwright?
29 What is opposed by the John Birch Society in the USA?
30 Which famous inventor had the middle name Alva?

Answers	**Around the UK** (see Quiz 15)

1 Ipswich. 2 Heriot-Watt. 3 Cowdray Park. 4 The Pit. 5 Orkney. 6 Holy Loch. 7 Hampstead. 8 Finisterre. 9 Buckinghamshire. 10 Suffolk. 11 Three. 12 Antonine Wall. 13 Middlesex Street. 14 Northamptonshire. 15 Mount Pleasant. 16 Man of Kent. 17 Durham. 18 The Boston Stump. 19 PM Earl of Liverpool. 20 Carlton House Terrace. 21 Trowbridge. 22 Westminster Abbey. 23 Mansion House. 24 The Burrell Collection. 25 Blenheim Palace. 26 Bush House. 27 Museum of the Moving Image. 28 Banqueting House. 29 Shetlands. 30 Hereford and Worcester.

1 Which TV presenter published his "Unreliable Memoirs" in 1980?
2 Whose novel "A Time to Dance" was adapted into a controversial TV drama?
3 In "From One Charlie to Another", whom did Charlie Watts write about?
4 Which singer wrote the book "Tarantula"?
5 What was the colour of the first Penguin paperback?
6 Which blonde wrote "The Constant Sinner"?
7 Which John Grisham book set a record initial print run of 2.8 million?
8 To be considered for the Booker Prize a book has to be published where first?
9 What according to Dickens was "the best of times, the worst of times"?
10 Whose only novel won the Pullitzer Prize in 1937?
11 Which PM wrote "Sybil"?
12 For which novel did Tom Clancy receive an advance of $14 million?
13 Which joint 1992 Booker Prize winner had his book made into an Oscar-winning film?
14 Which Ian Fleming novel has the shortest title?
15 What was Hercule Poirot's last case called?
16 What did JM Barrie give the royalties from Peter Pan to?
17 Which former "EastEnders" actress wrote "The Other Side of Nowhere"?
18 What was the sequel to DH Lawrence's "The Rainbow"?
19 Who created Pomeroy's wine bar for his hero?
20 Whose early thrillers include "The Eye of the Needle"?
21 Who wrote "The House of Stairs" under a pseudonym?
22 Which detective novelist wrote the screenplay for "Strangers on a Train"?
23 What was Charles Dickens' second novel, after "Pickwick Papers"?
24 Who wrote "The Exorcist" which was made into a successful film?
25 How are Patrick Dannay and Manfred B. Lee better known?
26 Who produced "The Truth That Leads to Eternal Life"?
27 Who wrote the historical romance "Micah Clarke"?
28 Which novelist once owned a Rolls registration number ANY 1?
29 Whose early novels were "Bella", "Harriet" and "Prudence"?
30 Bob Skinner is the creation of which crime/thriller writer?

Answers	Pot Luck 9 *(see Quiz 18)*

1 The Zulus. 2 Phyllis Nelson. 3 Jose Maria Olazabal. 4 Aldeburgh. 5 Tracy-Ann Oberman. 6 Varicella. 7 Stereophonics. 8 Robbie Coltrane. 9 National Theatre. 10 Alan Alda (of M*A*S*H fame). 11 Soot. 12 The tennis Grand Slam. 13 Betty Driver and Elizabeth Dawn. 14 1970. 15 A hangman. 16 Paul Gauguin. 17 Hero. 18 Wear it. 19 Picture Post. 20 The Tube. 21 Jennifer Lopez. 22 Battle of Naseby. 23 1860. 24 New Zealand. 25 A hoofed mammal. 26 Chelsea. 27 Love in Bloom. 28 Kim Appleby. 29 Margaret Atwood. 30 Land's End.

Quiz 18 | Pot Luck 9

1 Cetewayo, Dingaan and Chaka have all led which people?
2 Whose one and only hit was "Move Closer" in 1985?
3 Which injured player did Ian Woosnam replace in the 1995 European Ryder Cup team?
4 Which Suffolk town was the first in Britain to have a woman mayor?
5 Who played Yvonne Hartman, head of the Torchwood Institute in "Doctor Who"?
6 What is the correct name for chickenpox?
7 Which top-selling band featured Richard Jones on bass?
8 Who is the elder – Phil Collins or Robbie Coltrane?
9 In the 80s which building did Prince Charles compare to a "nuclear power station"?
10 Which US actor's autobiography was titled "Never Have Your Dog Stuffed"?
11 The brown pigment bistre is prepared from what?
12 Maureen Connolly was the first female to perform what?
13 Which two "Corrie" actresses were awarded the MBE in millennium year?
14 In which FIFA World Cup were red and yellow cards first used?
15 What did Jack Ketch do for a living?
16 Van Gogh's "Sunflowers" used to hang in the bedroom of which other famous artist?
17 In mythology, whom did Leander swim the Hellespont nightly to see?
18 What would you do with a filibeg?
19 Bert Hardy was a staff photojournalist for which periodical?
20 Madonna's first British TV appearance was on which show?
21 Who was George Clooney's co-star in the movie "Out of Sight"?
22 Which battle was the decisive one in the English Civil War?
23 To ten years, when was the National Rifle Association of Great Britain formed?
24 In which country are the Sutherland Falls?
25 What is an alpaca?
26 Who were Wigan's opponents in their first ever Premiership game?
27 What was American comedian Jack Benny's signature tune?
28 Who had UK Top Ten hits in the 90s with "Don't Worry" and "G.L.A.D."?
29 Who wrote "The Handmaid's Tale"?
30 What did businessman Peter de Savray buy for £6.7 million in 1987?

Answers	Books 2 *(see Quiz 17)*

1 Clive James. 2 Melvyn Bragg. 3 Charlie Parker. 4 Bob Dylan. 5 Blue. 6 Mae West. 7 The Rainmaker. 8 Britain. 9 French Revolution (Tale of Two Cities). 10 Margaret Mitchell. 11 Disraeli. 12 Without Remorse. 13 Michael Ondaatje. 14 Dr No. 15 Curtain. 16 Children's Hospital. 17 Daniella Westbrook. 18 Women in Love. 19 John Mortimer (Rumpole). 20 Ken Follett. 21 Ruth Rendell as Barbara Vine. 22 Raymond Chandler. 23 Oliver Twist. 24 William Blatty. 25 Ellery Queen. 26 Jehovah's Witnesses. 27 Conan Doyle. 28 Jeffrey Archer. 29 Jilly Cooper. 30 Quintin Jardine.

1 Which Pete Ham and Tom Evans song has been at No. 1 with two different artists?

2 The Isley Brothers and which other Motown act recorded "Grapevine" before Marvin Gaye?

3 To the nearest year, how long was there between Sinatra's first and second UK No. 1s?

4 Where is the singer's home in the lyrics of "On the Dock of the Bay"?

5 What was the first song to be Christmas No. 1 in two different versions?

6 Which group wrote the song that was Will Young's second No. 1?

7 Which 1970 seven-week No. 1 was best selling UK single of the year?

8 Whom did Billy Joel dedicate his 1983 version of "Uptown Girl" to?

9 What was Elvis Presley's closing number in his Las Vegas stage act?

10 What was Cliff Richard's first self-produced No. 1?

11 What was the chief of the Diddymen's only UK No. 1?

12 Which standard has the line, "I see friends shaking hands saying how do you do"?

13 Which Beatles hit stayed in the UK Top 50 for 33 weeks in 1963?

14 Who had the first UK No. 1 with "Unchained Melody"?

15 Which film theme was the biggest-selling single of 1979?

16 Who took Led Zeppelin's "Stairway To Heaven" into the singles charts before Rolf Harris?

17 Who wrote "You'll Never Walk Alone"?

18 Which heavenly body is mentioned in the title of the song that gave George Michael his 4th solo and Elton John his 3rd No. 1?

19 Who played Buddy Holly in the 1978 movie "The Buddy Holly Story"?

20 Who wrote Aretha Franklin's first UK hit "Respect"?

21 What was Yusuf Islam's, once known as Cat Stevens, last Top Ten hit before "Father and Son"?

22 Which 1967 No. 1 recorded the longest-ever stay in the UK Top 50?

23 Which 1960s star, who died in 1988, charted with "Love Songs" album in 2001?

24 How many weeks in total did Whitney Houston top the US and UK charts with "I Will Always Love You"?

25 Which hit was the first No. 1 for writers Gerry Goffin and Carole King?

26 Which song includes the line, "nothing to kill or die for"?

27 What was the colour mentioned in the title of Tom Jones' final No. 1 in the 1960s?

28 What is the biggest international hit from Eurovision Song Contest?

29 What was Sam Cooke's real name?

30 What was the Beatles' first No. 1 in America?

Answers	Pot Luck 10 *(see Quiz 20)*

1 Richard. 2 Five. 3 Alexander Selkirk. 4 US President. 5 The Strand Magazine. 6 The Verve. 7 Chamonix, France. 8 Albert Reynolds. 9 A fusil. 10 Once. 11 Have a Go. 12 Room at the Top. 13 Liquids. 14 Shiny Happy People. 15 Gliders. 16 Foot or feet. 17 Royal Flying Corps. 18 Morgan. 19 Grasmere. 20 The skin that separates the nostrils. 21 Sandy Cummings. 22 Ian Woosnam. 23 A seal. 24 Prince Andrew of Greece. 25 Portugal. 26 Debussy. 27 Steps. 28 Paul Channon. 29 Average White Band. 30 St Dominic.

1. Which christian name derives from the Germanic for "strong ruler"?
2. Between 1963 and 2006, how many Bond films featured the Aston Martin DB5?
3. The novel "Robinson Crusoe" was based on whose experiences?
4. What important post did Millard Fillmore hold?
5. Which magazine serialised "The Adventures of Sherlock Holmes" in the 1890s?
6. Which group features Peter Salisbury on drums and Simon Jones on bass?
7. Where were the first Winter Olympics held in 1924?
8. Who preceded John Bruton as Prime Minister of Ireland?
9. What can be a type of musket or a type of rhomboid?
10. How many seasons in the top flight did Alan Curbishley's Charlton win more than they lost?
11. Which long-running radio quiz show was hosted by Wilfred Pickles?
12. In which John Braine book is Joe Lampton the central character ?
13. What does a manometer measure the pressure of?
14. What was R.E.M.'s first UK Top Ten hit?
15. Otto Lilienthal was associated with what form of transport?
16. In furniture, what can be bracket, bun and stile on a chest?
17. What amalgamated in 1918 with the Royal Naval Air Service to form the RAF?
18. What did the M stand for in EM Forster's middle name?
19. Where is the poet Wordsworth buried?
20. What is your columella?
21. In "Big Brother 3" who made a memorable escape by climbing over a roof?
22. Who was the first UK golfer to win the World Match-Play Championship?
23. In folktales a silkie was half man and half what?
24. Who was Prince Philip's father?
25. Jose Barroso took over as Prime Minister of which European country in 2002?
26. Who composed "Clair de Lune"?
27. Which pop quintet announced they were splitting up on Boxing Day 2001?
28. Who was Transport Secretary at the time of the King's Cross tube fire disaster?
29. Whose only UK Top Ten hit was "Pick Up the Pieces" in 1975?
30. Black Friars are members of the religious order established by whom?

Answers | Musical Greats (see Quiz 19)

1 Without You. 2 The Miracles. 3 12 years. 4 Georgia. 5 Mary's Boy Child. 6 The Doors. 7 In the Summertime. 8 Christie Brinkley. 9 Can't Help Falling in Love. 10 Mistletoe and Wine. 11 Tears. 12 What a Wonderful World. 13 She Loves You. 14 Jimmy Young. 15 Bright Eyes. 16 Far Corporation. 17 Rodgers and Hammerstein. 18 Sun. 19 Gary Busey. 20 Otis Redding. 21 Morning Has Broken. 22 Release Me. 23 Roy Orbison. 24 24 weeks. 25 I'm Into Something Good. 26 Imagine. 27 Green. 28 Waterloo by Abba. 29 Cook without an "e". 30 I Wanna Hold Your Hand.

1 Who preceded Frank O'Farrell as Man Utd manager?
2 How did Joan Bazely make history in 1976?
3 Who were the opponents in Peter Shilton's last game for England?
4 Which Premiership side lost nine of its last ten games in 2006 and stayed up?
5 Who offered the England and Scotland squads a week on his Caribbean island if they won the World Cup in 1998?
6 Roy Keane played his last Premiership game for Man Utd against which team?
7 Which club's motto is "Nil Satis Nisi Optimum"?
8 John Benson, Bruce Rioch and Steve Bruce have all managed which club?
9 To three, for how many games was Sven-Goran Eriksson in charge of England?
10 Ray Wilkins was sent off while playing for England against which country?
11 Who did Denis Law play for immediately before Man Utd?
12 Who was the only side to beat England over 90 minutes when Venables was manager?
13 Who appeared in a TV ad for bacon before the 1998 World Cup?
14 Who is Sweden's most capped player of all time?
15 Who led Naples to their first ever Italian championship?
16 Which of the Italian sides David Platt played for had the shortest name?
17 Bolton's Kevin Davies has played over 100 games for three clubs – which was first?
18 Who was fourth in the 1994 World Cup?
19 Roy Hodgson joined Blackburn Rovers from which club?
20 What was Arsenal tube station called before it was called Arsenal?
21 Who was the first Dutchman to play in an FA Cup Final?
22 Whom were Man Utd playing when George Best made his debut?
23 Which sides competed in the first all-British UEFA Cup Final?
24 Who were the first winners of the Inter Toto Cup?
25 How many times did Bobby Moore captain England in 108 internationals?
26 Who was Reading's only ever-present in their 2005–06 Championship win?
27 Where did Paul Ince captain England for the first time?
28 Which club side were the first to win the South American Cup?
29 Which defender scored his only England goal in Sven-Goran Eriksson's first game?
30 Which two Scottish sides did Antti Niemi play for prior to moving to England?

1 What was the first Gareth Gates single not to make No. 1 in the UK?
2 Which creature is represented in the year the Chinese call hou?
3 A fear of cats is known as what?
4 Which country ruled Greece until 1830?
5 Who wrote the line: "The female of the species is more deadly than the male"?
6 How many species of ostrich are there?
7 Dakar is the capital of which country?
8 Which theme gave Clannad their first UK Top Ten hit?
9 Who is the elder – John Prescott or Trevor McDonald?
10 The spice allspice is made from which part of a plant?
11 Which "E" number is used to represent Tartrazine in products?
12 What is the main language of Andorra?
13 Which elderly couple were immortalised in a poem by Henry Woodfall?
14 Where on Dartmoor is Dartmoor prison?
15 Which jazz festival is held annually in Rhode Island?
16 What does the Latin ab initio mean?
17 Which Prime Minister was offered a dukedom when he retired in 1955?
18 The constellation Aquila has which name in English?
19 In which country is the city of Baku?
20 What does the musical term "con fuoco" mean?
21 Which bird appears with two heads on the Albanian flag?
22 Which letter in Braille comprises a single raised dot?
23 Which Noel Edmonds show featured the ill-fated Whirly Wheeler?
24 Subtitled "The Time-Torn Man", Claire Tomalin's book was about which writer?
25 What are separated by the Cook Straits?
26 In which year did the UK become a member of the UN?
27 Which country has the internet code .pi?
28 Which country's team dominated World Fly Fishing at the start of this century?
29 Prime Minister Wilfried Martens was leader of which country?
30 How would the letter E be formed in Morse Code?

Answers | Football 1 (see Quiz 21)

1 Wilf McGuinness. 2 First woman ref of men's soccer. 3 Italy (1990). 4 Man City. 5 Richard Branson. 6 Liverpool. 7 Everton. 8 Wigan Athletic. 9 67 games. 10 Morocco. 11 Torino. 12 Brazil. 13 Peter Schmeichel. 14 Thomas Ravelli. 15 Diego Maradona. 16 Bari. 17 Chesterfield. 18 Bulgaria. 19 Inter Milan. 20 Gillespie Road. 21 Arnold Muhren. 22 West Brom. 23 Spurs v. Wolves. 24 Ajax. 25 90. 26 Ivar Ingimarsson. 27 Boston, USA. 28 Santos. 29 Ugo Ehiogu. 30 Rangers and Hearts.

1 In whose home is "The Green Green Grass" set?
2 "Thirtysomething" was set in which US state?
3 Who did "Casualty's" George play in "May to December"?
4 What were Private Godfrey's sisters called in "Dad's Army"?
5 Which bookie did Vince Pinner work for?
6 Who had a wife, daughter and mother-in-law who were witches?
7 In which real-life town was "Jam and Jerusalem" filmed?
8 Who sang the theme music for "You Rang M'Lord" with Bob Monkhouse?
9 What was Richard's mother called in "To the Manor Born"?
10 Which lead character had the nickname Privet?
11 In which series did George, Kramer and Elaine appear?
12 Which TV husband and wife lived in Lanford Illinois?
13 Who was the first manager of the Bayview Retirement Home?
14 Who in his later years had a black home help called Winston?
15 What was the US series on which "The Upper Hand" was based?
16 Which property was left to Jim Davidson in "Up the Elephant and Round the Castle"?
17 In which hospital did Sheila Sabatini work?
18 Which sitcom was first called "You'll Never Get Rich" in the US?
19 What was Reg Varney's character called in "On the Buses"?
20 What was Thelma's surname before she married Likely Lad Bob?
21 Elaine Nardo was the only female cabbie in which company?
22 What job did Michael Douglas do when he guested on "Will and Grace"?
23 What were Harold Steptoe's middle names?
24 Which character in "Soap" was later given his own series?
25 Who wrote the original series of "Shine on Harvey Moon"?
26 Which sit com star played Vera Hopkins in "Coronation Street"?
27 Who was Roger's wife in "Outside Edge"?
28 Who was the barman of the Nag's Head as frequented by the Trotters?
29 Who created the theme music for "One Foot in the Grave"?
30 Which show centred round the 1-2-1 Club?

Answers | Pot Luck 12 *(see Quiz 24)*

1 Charles Blondin. 2 Vectis. 3 Paul Newman. 4 Fish. 5 Welcome to My World. 6 Emma Thompson. 7 John Williams. 8 Nineveh. 9 July 23rd. 10 The Queen. 11 David Davies. 12 Cyril Fletcher. 13 A ship's timber. 14 Fred Astaire. 15 Pewter. 16 Jazz. 17 August. 18 Arthur. 19 1992. 20 The Greek alphabet. 21 Bend. 22 Ruff. 23 Afghanistan. 24 Westminster Abbey. 25 Fairground Attraction. 26 Architecture. 27 Yellow River. 28 Danny Zuko. 29 Agatha Christie. 30 Frank Capra.

1 Who crossed Niagara Falls in 1859 on a tightrope?
2 What did the Romans call the Isle of Wight?
3 Who is the voice of a 1951 Hudson Hornet in the Pixar movie "Cars"?
4 What are gar, wrasse, alewife and blenny?
5 What was Jim Reeves' first UK Top Ten hit?
6 Who is the actress daughter of actress Phillida Law?
7 Who composed the music for "Jaws" and "Star Wars"?
8 What was the capital of the ancient empire of Assyria?
9 On what date in 1986 did Prince Andrew marry Fergie?
10 Which part did Prunella Scales play in "A Question of Attribution"?
11 Which David was FA executive director during the Faria Alam affair?
12 Which presenter of "That's Life" was famous for his odd odes?
13 What is a futtock?
14 Which film star married Robyn Smith in 1980?
15 Which alloy contains 2% antimony, 8% copper and 90% tin?
16 Liane Carroll is famous for which type of music?
17 In which month did the 2004 Olympics open?
18 Which son of Henry VII married Catherine of Aragon in 1501?
19 In what year did Classic FM begin?
20 What are Lambda, Omicron and Tau all found in?
21 Charing, as in Charing Cross, comes from an Old English word meaning what?
22 What can be a trump at cards or a type of sandpiper?
23 The major town of Herat is in which war-torn country?
24 Where is English actor David Garrick buried?
25 Who followed up a No. 1 with "Find My Love"?
26 Walter Gropius was famous in what field?
27 What is the natural water form which the Chinese call Huang Ho?
28 Famed as Alfie Moon, what part did this actor play in "Grease" in the West End?
29 Which celebrated novelist lived at Greenaway house?
30 Who directed the film "You Can't Take It with You"?

Answers	TV: Sitcoms 1 *(see Quiz 23)*

1 Its star's John Challis (Boycie). 2 Philadelphia. 3 Hilary. 4 Dolly & Cissy. 5 Eddie Brown's. 6 Darrin Stephens (Bewitched). 7 North Tanton. 8 Paul Shane. 9 Mrs Polouvicka. 10 Bernard Hedges. 11 Seinfeld. 12 Roseanne & Dan Conner. 13 Harvey Bains. 14 Alf Garnett. 15 Who's the Boss?. 16 17 Railway Terrace. 17 The Gillies Hospital. 18 The Phil Silvers Show. 19 Stan Butler. 20 Chambers. 21 The Sunshine Cab Company. 22 Police detective. 23 Albert Kitchenere. 24 The butler Benson. 25 Marks & Gran. 26 Kathy Staff. 27 Mim. 28 Mike. 29 Eric Idle. 30 Dear John.

1 What is the only mammal to live as a parasite?

2 How is a Sibbald's rorqual also known?

3 For how many hours in a period of 24 does a giraffe sleep?

4 What is the world's largest rodent?

5 What gives the sloth its greenish appearance?

6 Which mammal lives at the highest altitude?

7 Which animals are famously sold at Bampton Fair?

8 The mammal which can live at the greatest depth is a species of what?

9 From which part of a sperm whale is ambergris obtained?

10 Where does a cane toad squirt poison from?

11 What is the longest type of worm?

12 Where would you find a shark's denticles?

13 What does the male mouse deer have that no other deer has?

14 Where does a browser find food?

15 What is the Latin name for the Blue Whale?

16 A Clydesdale was originally a cross between a Scottish draught horse and a what?

17 What colour is a mandrill's beard?

18 The wisent is native to where?

19 Lemurs are only found in their natural habitat where?

20 What is the oldest indigenous breed of cat in the US?

21 What is a koikoi?

22 What is the average life expectancy of the mayfly?

23 Which protein is cartilage made up of?

24 The term monkey refers to all primates except apes, humans and what?

25 Why were Samoyeds originally bred?

26 Falabellas are native to where?

27 What is another name for the aye-aye?

28 Which animal has the longest tail?

29 What name is given to the smaller of a rhino's horns?

30 What does it mean if an animal is homoiothermic?

Answers | Pot Luck 13 *(see Quiz 26)*

1 Reading (2005–06). 2 Plumber. 3 Vladimir and Estragon. 4 Syphilis. 5 Scotland. 6 1950s. 7 JJ Barrie. 8 Rocks. 9 Mozambique. 10 Comet. 11 The Agricultural Hall. 12 Scottish Euro 96 single. 13 A diesel engine. 14 Goat Island. 15 Richard Bacon. 16 Painting. 17 Mexico. 18 Bronze. 19 Gail Platt. 20 He was a horse. 21 Irving Berlin. 22 Belgium. 23 After childbirth. 24 By Jack Rosenthal. 25 Enemy Coast Ahead. 26 Michael Crawford. 27 James and John. 28 30 million. 29 Sean Kelly. 30 TLC.

1 Which English soccer club were the first to clock up 105 points in a season?

2 What was the trade of John Galliano's dad?

3 In the Beckett play which characters were Waiting for Godot?

4 Which disease is diagnosed by the Wasserman Test?

5 The King of Alba ruled in which country?

6 In which decade was Sting born?

7 Whose one and only hit was "No Charge" in 1976?

8 What does a petrologist study?

9 Which African country lies between the sea and Zimbabwe?

10 What are Temple-Tuttle and Kohoutek both types of?

11 In which London hall was England's first official showjumping event held in 1869?

12 Rod Stewart donated the royalties from which single to the Dunblane fund?

13 The ship Petit Pierre was the first to be driven by what in 1902?

14 Which island is in the middle of Niagara Falls?

15 Who was the first "Blue Peter" presenter to be sacked?

16 For what did John Singer Sargent achieve fame?

17 In which country is the majority of the Yucatan Peninsula?

18 The statue of Albert opposite the Albert Hall is made from what?

19 In "Corrie" who was Leanne Battersby's first mother-in-law?

20 Why was the Roman consul Incitatus unusual?

21 Who composed "God Bless America"?

22 Violinist Arthur Grumiaux came from which country?

23 When can a woman suffer puerperal fever?

24 What was Jack Rosenthal's autobiography called?

25 "The Dambusters" film was based on which book?

26 Who is the elder – Michael Crawford or Eric Clapton?

27 Which of Jesus' disciples were sons of Zebedee?

28 In a 2001 census what was Canada's population to the nearest million?

29 Who won the first cycling World Cup?

30 Rozonda Thomas was part of which top-selling girl group?

Answers	**Animal World** (see Quiz 25)

1 Vampire bat. 2 Blue whale. 3 One. 4 Capybara. 5 Algae which grow on it. 6 Mount Everest pika. 7 Exmoor ponies. 8 Bat. 9 Intestine. 10 Behind its eyes. 11 Bootlace worm. 12 On its skin. 13 Canine teeth. 14 Anywhere above ground. 15 Balaenoptera musculus. 16 Flemish horse. 17 Yellow. 18 Europe (bison). 19 Madagascar. 20 Maine coon. 21 Poisonous frog. 22 Couple of hours. 23 Collagen. 24 Tarsiers. 25 Herd reindeer. 26 Argentina. 27 Lemur. 28 Asian elephant. 29 Forehead horn. 30 Warm-blooded.

1 In which 60s film did Richard Attenborough sing?
2 Who became head of production at EMI in 1969?
3 Between which two cities is "The Great Race" set?
4 Who directed the Civil War sequences of "How the West was Won"?
5 Who was Camembert in "Carry On – Don't Lose Your Head"?
6 Who inspired the David Hemmings role in Antonioni's "Blow Up"?
7 What is unusual about Christopher Lee's terrifying role in "Dracula – Prince of Darkness"?
8 What was the sequel to "A Million Years BC"?
9 Who devised the dance routines in "Half a Sixpence"?
10 Who is the only American in "King Rat"?
11 Who was the Doctor in the big screen "Doctor Who and the Daleks"?
12 Which film classic inspired Billy Wilder to make "The Apartment"?
13 Who played Princess Dala in "The Pink Panther"?
14 Who took over directing "Cleopatra" mid way through production?
15 Who was the singing voice of Tony in "West Side Story"?
16 Who wrote the music for "Lawrence of Arabia"?
17 In which film of her father's did Anjelica Huston make her screen debut?
18 Which golf course featured in "Goldfinger"?
19 What was Tracy and Hepburn's final movie together?
20 Which pop star starred in "Rag Doll" in 1960?
21 Which '62 Best Actor studied medicine at the University of California?
22 Who was Oscar-nominated for Pasha in "Doctor Zhivago"?
23 Which 60s Oscar winner was narrated by Michael MacLiammoir?
24 Who killed Ronald Reagan in his last film "The Killers"?
25 Whom did John Wayne play in "North to Alaska"?
26 For which film did Elizabeth Taylor win her second Oscar?
27 For which role was Dustin Hoffman nominated in 1969?
28 Which of the Redgrave clan appeared in "A Man for All Seasons"?
29 Who played opposite then wife Claire Bloom in "The Illustrated Man"?
30 Who was the older winner of the shared Best Actress Oscar in 1968?

Answers	Food & Drink 1 *(see Quiz 28)*

1 Liebfraumilch. 2 Warm. 3 Bray. 4 Stomach remedy. 5 Ice cream. 6 Tomatoes.
7 Crescent-shaped (roll). 8 Steen. 9 Stum. 10 Browned at the edges due to age.
11 Sicily. 12 Semi-sparkling, fully sparkling. 13 Calzone. 14 Maize. 15 Grapes are partly sun-dried before use. 16 Greenwich. 17 Portugal. 18 Barsac, Bommes, Fargues, Preignac. 19 Britain. 20 Peter Bayless. 21 Canary Islands. 22 Wine and methylated spirits. 23 Salsify. 24 Remuage. 25 Pomerol. 26 Wine award in Germany. 27 Bechamel. 28 Oenology. 29 Escoffier. 30 Mirin.

1 Which wine comes from Worms?
2 How is sake usually drunk?
3 In which Berkshire village is Heston Blumenthal's Fat Duck restaurant to be found?
4 What were angostura bitters originally used for?
5 In the US if a dessert is served "à la mode" what is served with it?
6 Which vegetable is a passata made from?
7 What shape is a rugelach?
8 What is chenin blanc wine known as in South Africa?
9 Which term describes the fermented grape juice added to wine that has lost its strength to perk it up?
10 If a wine is madeirised what has happened to it?
11 Where is Marsala, famed for its fortified wine?
12 In wine terms what is the difference between frizzante and spumante?
13 Which folded pizza dough dish takes its name from the Italian for trouser leg?
14 Which cereal is polenta made from?
15 How does Malaga wine achieve its dark colour?
16 In which London borough did Jamie Oliver's healthy school dinner campaign begin?
17 Where does Dao wine come from?
18 In addition to Sauternes itself which four communes can call their wine Sauternes?
19 Where did balti cooking originate?
20 Who was the winner of "Masterchef Goes Large" in the early part of 2006?
21 Other than Spain and Portugal where does sack come from?
22 What is a red biddy?
23 Which food is also called the vegetable oyster?
24 In wine making which term describes turning the bottles so the sediment collects at the cork end?
25 In which district of Bordeaux is Chateau Petrus produced?
26 What is pradikat?
27 Which classic French sauce was named after a courtier of Louis XIV?
28 What is the study of wine called?
29 Which chef created the Bombe Nero and the peche melba?
30 Which sweet rice wine is used in Japanese cookery?

1 A zinfandel is used for making what?

2 What separates Alaska from the other 48 US states?

3 How many times is "Um" sung in the chorus of 60s hit "Um Um Um Um Um Um"?

4 Who was the conductor of the Berlin Philharmonic at the 2006 Proms?

5 On which island which is also a country is Adam's Peak?

6 In which year did London Underground's Bakerloo Line open?

7 Who won Best Actor Oscar for his part in the musical film "Amadeus"?

8 If you have comedos, what are you suffering from?

9 What is the third largest city in Britain?

10 Who is the elder – David Bowie or Edwina Currie?

11 What is Warwickshire's county motif?

12 Which former PM became President of the Czech Republic in 2003?

13 What kind of weapon was an arbalest?

14 Which Austrian physicist gave his name to perceived frequency variations under certain conditions?

15 Imran Khan played cricket for which two English counties?

16 What is the meaning of the legal expression "caveat emptor"?

17 Which optical aid was invented by Benjamin Franklin?

18 What was the Bay City Rollers' first UK Top Ten hit?

19 Where are the ethmoid, vomer and zygomatic bones in your body?

20 Who was Severus Snape when Robbie Coltrane was Rubeus Hagrid?

21 The capital of Japan is an anagram of which former capital?

22 Who rode both Toulon and Moonax to St Leger triumphs?

23 Who wrote "All Quiet on the Western Front"?

24 Where did John McGregor found the first Canoe Club in 1866?

25 What is the main colour on the cover of Celine Dion's album "Let's Talk About Love"?

26 Michael Jackson, Billie and Alicia Keyes have had different singles with which same title?

27 Which European country lost the battle of Ulm in 1805?

28 On TV, who was the victim in the first series of "The Murder Game"?

29 Which country has Guyana to the east and Colombia to the west?

30 How did Emiliano Zapata, the Mexican revolutionary, die in 1919?

Answers	Kings & Queens *(see Quiz 30)*

1 17 Bruton St, London. 2 King George V and Queen Mary. 3 Edward VII. 4 Adelaide. 5 George I. 6 Hit with a cricket ball. 7 George V. 8 Henry II's wife Eleanor of Aquitaine. 9 Edward I (19). 10 It was his second. 11 The Pope. 12 Dunfermline. 13 Square, she was so obese. 14 Richard II. 15 River Soar. 16 Tax collectors. 17 Charles II. 18 St Stephen's Abbey Caen. 19 Henry I. 20 Edward VIII. 21 George I. 22 William IV. 23 Edward VII. 24 Christian IX of Denmark. 25 William II. 26 Four. 27 Norfolk. 28 Two. 29 Jane Seymour & Catherine Parr. 30 Gloucester Cathedral.

1 At which address was Elizabeth II born?
2 Who were the parents of the subject of "The Lost Prince" by Stephen Poliakoff?
3 Who was the only British monarch from the House of Wettin?
4 Who was William IV's queen?
5 Which monarch's mother was Sophia of Bohemia?
6 How did George II's eldest son die?
7 Who was the first British monarch to make a Christmas Day broadcast?
8 Which English king's wife was a former wife of Louis VII of France?
9 Which British monarch produced the most legitimate children?
10 What was notable about Henry VI's coronation in 1470?
11 Who made Henry VIII Fidei Defensor?
12 Where was Charles I born?
13 What shape was Queen Anne's coffin and why?
14 Which English king is reputed to have invented the handkerchief?
15 Where were Richard III's bones thrown when his grave was desecrated?
16 Why was Henry VIII's execution of Richard Empson and Edmund Dudley a popular move?
17 Who was threatened by the Rye House Plot?
18 Where is William the Conqueror buried?
19 Which king founded the first English zoo?
20 Who was the penultimate Emperor of India?
21 The Duchess of Kendal was mistress of which king?
22 Who was the first monarch born in Buckingham Palace?
23 Who was the first Emperor of India?
24 Who was Edward VII's father-in-law?
25 Which English king was killed by Walter Tyrel?
26 How many English kings reigned in the first half of the twentieth century?
27 In which county did George V die?
28 How many shirts did Charles I wear for his execution?
29 Who were Henry VIII's two oldest wives?
30 Where was Henry III crowned?

| **Answers** | **Pot Luck 14** *(see Quiz 29)* |

1 Wine. 2 British Columbia. 3 24. 4 Simon Rattle. 5 Sri Lanka. 6 1906. 7 F. Murray Abraham. 8 Blackheads. 9 Glasgow. 10 Edwina Currie. 11 A standing bear next to a ragged staff. 12 Vaclav Klaus. 13 A giant crossbow. 14 Christian Doppler. 15 Worcestershire and Sussex. 16 Let the buyer beware. 17 Bifocal lenses. 18 Keep On Dancing. 19 Skull. 20 Alan Rickman. 21 Kyoto. 22 Pat Eddery. 23 Erich Remarque. 24 Richmond, Surrey. 25 Black. 26 Girlfriend. 27 Austria. 28 Catherine Prior. 29 Venezuela. 30 Assassinated.

1 Who directed the1930s film "Mr Deeds Goes to Town"?

2 Who was the first Spaniard to win the French Open in tennis this century?

3 Shogi is a Japanese form of which game?

4 Which ex-"EastEnders" actress tried to revive her career in "Reborn in the USA"?

5 Which bird would you find in a squab pie?

6 Who played the lead character in the film "The Loneliness of the Long Distance Runner"?

7 Whose fourth volume of memoirs was called "North Face of Soho"?

8 What was Rolf Harris' first UK Top Ten hit?

9 Which famous actor played Philo Beddoe in two films?

10 Whom did Australia beat when they first won cricket's World Cup?

11 What is the legendary ship The Flying Dutchman doomed to do?

12 Which queen of England had most fingers?

13 Who wrote the novel "Fair Stood the Wind for France"?

14 Who is the elder – Joan Collins or Michael Caine?

15 Whose one and only hit was "Eye Level" in 1973?

16 To three years, when did the M1 motorway open?

17 What was found in 1939 at Sutton Hoo, in Suffolk?

18 What is of interest to a thanatologist?

19 Where would you find calderas?

20 Who wrote the novel "The Lost World"?

21 If something is napiform which vegetable shape is it?

22 What part of the body is studied by a myologist?

23 Which song features the words, "Here am I floating round my tin can"?

24 What was the Triangular Trade mainly concerned with?

25 What, in America, is a cayuse?

26 How many strokes underwater may a competitive breast-stroke swimmer make at the start and turn?

27 The town of Carrara in Italy is famous for what?

28 Who wrote humour books naming Mussolini and Hitler in the titles?

29 McBride, Pemberton and Radzinski all played for Fulham and which other club?

30 The Battle of Antietam was in which war?

Answers	**Classic No. 1s** *(see Quiz 32)*

1 Wet Wet Wet. 2 Unchained. 3 My Sweet Lord. 4 Wooden Heart. 5 Maggie May. 6 Frankie Laine. 7 Gary Jules (Mad World). 8 Ticket to Ride. 9 Peter Cetera. 10 Herbert Kretzmer. 11 Girls' School. 12 Elton John. 13 The Fly (U2). 14 The Fleet's In. 15 Hole in the Head. 16 I Know Him So Well. 17 Whatever Will be Will be. 18 Mandy 19 Hello Goodbye. 20 Careless Whisper. 21 Bridge Over Troubled Water. 22 Who's Sorry Now? 23 Three Times a Lady. 24 John Travolta. 25 Hung Up. 26 Claudette. 27 Craig David. 28 Stranger on the Shore (Acker Bilk). 29 Bohemian Rhapsody. 30 Living Doll.

Quiz 32 | Classic No. 1s | Answers – page 505 | LEVEL 3

1 Who were the first Scottish group to have three No. 1s?
2 Which 1955 American movie had "Unchained Melody" as theme tune?
3 Which No. 1 was the first solo single by George Harrison?
4 Which Elvis hit made him the first artist with three consecutive British No. 1s?
5 Which Rod Stewart hit was originally the B-side of "Reason to Believe"?
6 Who was on top of the charts the week Everest was first climbed?
7 Who featured on the first No. 1 for Michael Andrews?
8 What was the first No. 1 from the Beatles' second film "Help!"?
9 Who wrote Chicago's No. 1 classic "If You Leave Me Now"?
10 Which lyricist of Aznavour's "She" was a writer on "Les Mis"?
11 What was on the other side of the double A No. 1 "Mull of Kintyre"?
12 Who co-wrote a No. 1 duet song under the pseudonym Ann Orson?
13 What finally knocked "(Everything I Do) I Do It for You" off the No. 1 spot?
14 Which film did Frank Ifield's "I Remember You" originally come from?
15 What was the third UK No. 1 single for the Sugababes?
16 What became the all-time best-UK selling single by a female duo?
17 Which Doris Day Oscar-winning song was from "The Man Who Knew Too Much" in 1956?
18 What was the first Westlife No. 1 single with a one-word title?
19 Which No. 1 hit by the Beatles equalled 7 weeks at the top with "From Me to You"?
20 What is the only George Michael song for which Andrew Ridgeley takes equal writing credit?
21 Which album title track gave Simon and Garfunkel their biggest hit?
22 Which 1920s standard gave Concetta Franconero a 6-week No. 1 hit?
23 Which Commodores classic became Motown's best UK seller?
24 Who is the male half of the duo that have spent most weeks at No. 1?
25 Which single marked Madonna's 20-year span of having UK No. 1s?
26 Apart from "Cathy's Clown", which other No. 1 for the Everly Brothers had a girl's name in the title?
27 In 2000, who became the youngest male to write and perform a UK No. 1 single?
28 Which single was the first by a UK performer to top the US charts in the 1960s?
29 Which 1975 megahit remained at No. 1 for 9 weeks?
30 Which No. 1 hit was Cliff Richard's first million-seller?

Answers | **Pot Luck 15** *(see Quiz 31)*

1 Frank Capra. 2 Juan Carlos Ferrero. 3 Chess. 4 Michelle Gayle. 5 Pigeon. 6 Tom Courtenay. 7 Clive James. 8 Tie Me Kangaroo Down Sport. 9 Clint Eastwood. 10 England. 11 Sail for ever. 12 Anne Boleyn (11). 13 HE Bates. 14 Michael Caine (by 2 months). 15 Simon Park Orchestra. 16 1959. 17 A Saxon ship. 18 Death. 19 Volcanoes (they are craters). 20 Sir Arthur Conan Doyle. 21 Turnip. 22 Muscles. 23 Space Oddity. 24 Slaves. 25 A horse. 26 One. 27 White marble. 28 Spike Milligan. 29 Everton. 30 American Civil War.

1 What is Kyzyl Kum in Russia?
2 Neville Cardus was associated with which sport?
3 Who played Paul Henreid's wife in the film "Casablanca"?
4 Which "Simpsons" catchphrase was first to make the on-line version of Oxford English Dictionary?
5 Where did the Dryad nymphs live in Greek mythology?
6 What sort of creature is a killdeer?
7 What type of music is Ira D. Sankey particularly noted for composing?
8 How old was Louis Braille when he invented his reading system for the blind?
9 Which actor starred in the silent films "Robin Hood", "The Three Musketeers" and "The Black Pirate"?
10 What was Five Star's first UK Top Ten hit?
11 Ficus Elastica is the Latin name for which plant?
12 In which sport is there a bonspiel?
13 Arch, loop and whorl are all parts of what?
14 What is pishogue a form of?
15 Permission was given to whom in 1988 to rebuild London's Globe Theatre?
16 Which country has the internet code .at?
17 A fylfot is better known as a what?
18 Alton Byrd was famous in which sport?
19 Who played the magical Supergran in the 1985 TV series?
20 Which 1990s Oscar Best Film did Colin Firth appear in as well as "Shakespeare in Love"?
21 Which actor was "The Virginian" on TV?
22 Which band's albums include "Load" and "Reload"?
23 Richard Meade won Olympic gold in which sport?
24 What is the main difference between squash and rackets?
25 In which year was the CBI set up?
26 Whose first Top Ten hit was "House of Love"?
27 In what unusual type of location was the late, great Jack Lemmon born?
28 In which country did the UK first score a Eurovision Song Contest no points?
29 Who would use a trochee?
30 Who wrote the play called "A Taste of Honey"?

Answers	Tony Blair *(see Quiz 34)*

1 Lynton. 2 Durham. 3 Barrister. 4 Energy. 5 2005. 6 Thanet North. 7 Taurus. 8 179. 9 The Queen & Prince Philip. 10 On the Record. 11 Deirdre Rachid (Coronation Street). 12 Trade & Industry. 13 European monetary union. 14 30. 15 Lord Liverpool. 16 Respect. 17 Hazel. 18 Derry Irvine. 19 Islington. 20 Home Secretary. 21 1998. 22 Grp Capt. Al Lockwood. 23 Tuesday & Thursday. 24 Alastair Campbell. 25 Michael Sheen. 26 Roy Hattersley. 27 Margaret Beckett. 28 Gerhard Schröder. 29 St John's. 30 10.

1 What is Tony Blair's third Christian name?
2 In which city was he brought up?
3 What was his father's profession?
4 What was his first Shadow Cabinet post?
5 In which year was Tony and Cherie's Silver Wedding anniversary?
6 Which constituency did Cherie contest in 1983?
7 Tony Blair was born under which star sign?
8 To five, how big was his Labour majority in the Commons in 1997?
9 In 1997 Blair hosted a "people's banquet" for which Golden Wedding couple?
10 On which TV programme did he say "I'm a pretty straight sort of guy"?
11 He appealed to the Home Secretary to help which soap character?
12 Which first Cabinet post did he give to Peter Mandelson?
13 In 1998 "The Sun" withdrew its support for Blair over which issue?
14 How old was he when he won his first Parliamentary seat?
15 In 1997 he became the youngest Prime Minister since whom?
16 Which R-word did he say would be an important part of his third term as PM?
17 What was his mother's first name?
18 Who was the head of Chambers where he met his future wife Cherie?
19 Where in London were the Blairs living when Tony became PM?
20 What was Blair's first shadow Cabinet post under John Smith?
21 In which year was the Belfast (or Good Friday) agreement signed?
22 Who finished second at Sedgefield in 2003?
23 When was Prime Minister's Question Time before Blair's changes?
24 Which Blair loyalist resigned in August 2003?
25 Who portrayed Tony Blair in the films "The Deal" and "The Queen"?
26 Who preceded him as Shadow Home Secretary?
27 Who was the leader of the Labour Party immediately before Blair?
28 Who succeeded him after his first term as chair of G8?
29 Which Oxford college did he attend?
30 How many years did Tony Blair serve as Prime Minister?

Answers   **Pot Luck 16** *(see Quiz 33)*

1 A desert. 2 Cricket. 3 Ingrid Bergman. 4 D'oh. 5 In trees. 6 A bird (type of plover). 7 Hymns. 8 15. 9 Douglas Fairbanks. 10 System Addict. 11 Rubber plant. 12 Curling. 13 Fingerprints. 14 Sorcery. 15 Sam Wanamaker. 16 Austria. 17 Swastika. 18 Basketball. 19 Gudrun Ure. 20 The English Patient. 21 James Drury. 22 Metallica. 23 3 Day Eventing. 24 Squash uses a softer ball. 25 1965. 26 East 17. 27 In a lift. 28 Latvia. 29 A poet. 30 Shelagh Delaney.

1 With which police identification system is Francis Galton associated?
2 Which trees mainly produced the fossilised resin which becomes amber?
3 In spring 2003, which actor celebrated 25 years in "Emmerdale"?
4 If a ship is careened, what has happened to it?
5 What did Henry Segrave break at Daytona in 1927 and 1929?
6 What was the Beautiful South's first UK Top Ten hit?
7 Which event is the first in a Decathlon?
8 Which US President died on the same day as Aldous Huxley?
9 When is Haley's Comet predicted to make its next visit in Earth's vicinity?
10 Who wrote the "Gormenghast Trilogy"?
11 In which county is Chequers?
12 The King of which country was the "Prisoner of Zenda"?
13 Who was the first jockey to record three consecutive Derby wins?
14 What relation to King Arthur was Mordred?
15 Who designed the first lightning conductor?
16 Iraq's prime minister Nuri al-Maliki is a member of which party?
17 What is matzo?
18 Which actor played Captain Bligh, Quasimodo and Henry VIII in films?
19 Which Archbishop of Canterbury was burnt at the stake in 1556?
20 Darren Huckerby made his soccer league debut with which club?
21 Which "Men Behaving Badly" star was in the original "Les Mis" chorus in the West End?
22 Who played King Arthur in "First Knight"?
23 Whose one and only hit was "Michelle" in 1966?
24 What can be grapnel, sheet and bower?
25 A trudgen is used in which sport?
26 Which river was first explored by Mungo Park, a Scottish surgeon?
27 To five years, when were Nobel Prizes first awarded?
28 In the poem "Beowulf", what kills Beowulf?
29 What would you do with a gigot?
30 The sitcom in which Warren Mitchell made his name took its title from which book?

Answers | **Golf** *(see Quiz 36)*

1 South Africa. 2 Gene Sarazen. 3 Gentleman Golfers of Edinburgh. 4 1967. 5 1989 PGA. 6 Nick Price. 7 John Jacobs. 8 Nick Faldo. 9 Greg Norman. 10 Japan. 11 Carnoustie. 12 Royal Lytham. 13 John Daly in 1991. 14 Worcester, Massachusetts. 15 Willie Park. 16 Bobby Jones (in perpetuity). 17 David Leadbetter. 18 Mark Calcavecchio. 19 Nick Faldo. 20 Walter Hagen. 21 20. 22 Troon. 23 The Walrus. 24 Seven. 25 British Open. 26 K-Club. 27 Twice. 28 Fred Couples. 29 Two shots. 30 Royal Portrush.

1 Who retained golf's Dunhill Cup in 1998?

2 Who was the first man to win the US PGA and the US Open in the same year?

3 What was the world's first golf club called?

4 In which year was the previous Hoylake Open before 2006?

5 What was Payne Stewart's first victory in a major?

6 In 1986 Greg Norman equalled whose record low score of 63 in the US Masters?

7 Whom did Tony Jacklin replace as Ryder Cup captain?

8 Who was only the second person after Jack Nicklaus to win two successive US Opens?

9 Who did Nick Faldo sensationally beat to win his third US Masters?

10 Padraig Harrington won the 2006 Dunlop Phoenix tournament in which country?

11 In 1968 what became the longest course ever used for the British Open?

12 Where did Tom Lehman win his first major?

13 When Steve Jones first won the US Open he was the first qualifier to win a Major since whom?

14 Where did the very first Ryder Cup take place?

15 Who won the first ever British Open?

16 Who is the President of Augusta National Golf Club?

17 Whom did Nick Faldo sack as his coach at the same time as divorcing wife number two?

18 Who was the last American to win the British Open before John Daly in 1995?

19 Who was the first European to win the US Masters in the 90s?

20 Who was the first US-born winner of the British Open?

21 How old was Nick Faldo when he was first in a Ryder Cup team?

22 Which golf course boasts a Postage Stamp?

23 What was Craig Stadler's nickname?

24 By how many strokes did Tony Jacklin win his first US Open?

25 Gary Player won all the Majors but which did he win first?

26 At which golf course was the 2006 Ryder Cup played?

27 How many times did Jack Nicklaus win the US Amateur title before turning pro?

28 Who was the first American to win the US Masters in the 90s?

29 Chris Di Marco finished how many shots behind the winner of the British Open 2006?

30 What is the only Irish course to have staged the British Open?

Answers	**Pot Luck 17** *(see Quiz 35)*

Quiz 37

1 What was discovered by Garcia Lopez de Cardenas in 1540?
2 Whose first Top Ten hit was titled "September"?
3 In the Seven Years War who were Britain's two allies?
4 On which label did Gorillaz first have a No. 1 album?
5 Who was the first player to score 100 points in a NBA basketball game?
6 Rose Louise Hovick achieved fame under what name?
7 Who is the father of Marsha Hunt's daughter Karis?
8 What is the final line in the film "Gone with the Wind"?
9 Which newspaper was featured in the TV series "Hot Metal"?
10 The gemstone ruby is associated with which month?
11 What is the name of Phil and Jill Archer's farm?
12 In 2003, was Taiwan's population estimated at around 23, 27 or 30 million?
13 Which comic actor's father was the deputy speaker of the Irish Parliament?
14 Where on your body are the Mounts of the Sun, Mercury and Venus?
15 Which fungal disease has the name Ceratostomella Ulmi?
16 Who created the cartoon character Colonel Blimp?
17 Where is the village of Skara Brae?
18 Who won the 1989 Best Actor Oscar for the film "My Left Foot"?
19 Who is the elder – Ian Botham or Jim Davidson?
20 Which actor played the title role in the TV series "Dear John"?
21 Whose theme was a No. 4 UK hit in 1959 for Elmer Bernstein?
22 If you are an encratic person, what do you possess?
23 Who said, "There never was a good war, nor a bad peace"?
24 David Beckham made his league debut on loan at which club?
25 Who wrote "The White Company"?
26 Which general was the youngest in the American Civil War?
27 Who was top scorer for Man Utd in 1997–98 and Man City in 2005–06?
28 With which profession is the organisation RIBA associated?
29 Who founded the record label Respond?
30 Who in 1632 painted "The Anatomy Lesson of Dr Tulip"?

1 Whose first husband was John Dunbar when she was 18?
2 In which year did Freddie Flintoff make his Test debut?
3 Who announced her engagement to Riccardo Mazzucchelli in 1995?
4 What did Tara Palmer Tomkinson use to hide her modesty when posing nude with three friends?
5 What relation is Camilla Parker Bowles to Edward VII's mistress Mrs Keppel?
6 Who was Mandy Smith's second husband?
7 Who owns the private zoos, Howletts and Port Lympne?
8 Which Tory MP did Maria-Bienvenida Perez Blanco marry?
9 Former deb Henrietta Tiarks became which Marchioness?
10 Which restaurant chain did Nigella Lawson's great great grandfather found?
11 Who was Duchess of York before Fergie?
12 Which star actor is dad to Dylan and Paris?
13 Heller Toren is the mother of which blonde celeb?
14 Which title did Raine have before she married the late Earl Spencer?
15 Whose Regency home is Ray Mill House in Wiltshire?
16 In 2001 who refused to take a book to his desert island on "Desert Island Discs"?
17 Who is famous for his "wifelets"?
18 Who is Watford Grammar School's most famous old girl?
19 Who was Mick Jagger's best man when he married Bianca?
20 What is Tiggy Legge-Bourke's real first name?
21 Whose debut album was titled "On the 6"?
22 Who wrote an autobiography entitled "Living the Dream"?
23 Who discovered Jean Shrimpton in the 60s?
24 Queen Noor of Jordan studied for what profession before her marriage?
25 Who was the first wife of the ninth Earl Spencer?
26 Whose husbands were Alexander McCorquodale then his cousin Hugh?
27 Who was the most famous daughter of Major Bruce Shand?
28 Who replaced Claudia Schiffer as the face of Chanel?
29 Who became Dior's chief designer in 1996?
30 Which model Hamilton co-founded the elephant charity Tusk Force?

Answers | Pot Luck 18 *(see Quiz 37)*

1 The Grand Canyon. 2 Earth, Wind & Fire. 3 Hanover and Prussia. 4 Parlophone. 5 Wilt Chamberlain. 6 Gypsy Rose Lee. 7 Mick Jagger. 8 "Tomorrow is another day." 9 Daily Crucible. 10 July. 11 Brookfield. 12 23 million. 13 Ardal O'Hanlon. 14 Your hand. 15 Dutch Elm Disease. 16 David Low. 17 The Orkneys. 18 Daniel Day-Lewis. 19 Jim Davidson. 20 Ralph Bates. 21 Staccato's Theme. 22 Self-control. 23 Benjamin Franklin. 24 Preston. 25 Sir Arthur Conan Doyle. 26 George A. Custer. 27 Andy Cole. 28 Architects. 29 Paul Weller. 30 Rembrandt.

Quiz 39 | Pot Luck 19

Answers – page 514

1 Who died in the avalanche in Klosters in 1988 involving Prince Charles' party?
2 Who was chairman of the Joint Chiefs of Staff during the Gulf War?
3 How many hours are there in a fortnight?
4 Which modern-day explorer has Twisleton-Wykeham as part of his name?
5 What was S Club 7's first hit single with a one-word title?
6 Who was Elizabeth I's State Secretary from 1573 to 1590?
7 Edward Whymper is associated with which leisure activity?
8 What did alchemists call the imaginary object that would turn base metals to gold?
9 Nicanor Duarte Frutos became President of which South American country?
10 Who designed and built the world's first iron bridge?
11 Who took her "Toot Toot" into the pop charts in the 80s?
12 Who is the elder – Sean Bean or Daniel Day-Lewis?
13 What was Michel Platini's club when he was three times European Footballer of the Year?
14 On the Chinese calendar, what is the only bird?
15 Where are the Padang Highlands?
16 What are you if you are described as being an ectomorph?
17 Where did Indian ink originally come from?
18 Which Premiership keeper was ever-present during the period from 2001 to 2004?
19 Who was the first female to present the main news on BBC and ITV?
20 What bird was the symbol of Persia's monarchy from 1739 to 1979?
21 What is the metal zinc extracted from?
22 Which game uses the expression "J'adoube"?
23 In London what was the Tyburn?
24 Who attempted the programme of social reform called Fair Deal?
25 Where in England might you do a Furry Dance?
26 What are measured in hadal, abyssal and bathyl zones?
27 Which country has the internet code .lk?
28 The word Eskimo means the eaters of what?
29 If you were banting, what would you be doing?
30 What was the Michael Bolton's first UK Top Ten hit?

Answers	JK Rowling *(see Quiz 40)*

1 1965. 2 1987. 3 Exeter. 4 French. 5 Christopher Little. 6 Bloomsbury Children's Books. 7 London. 8 Peter Needham. 9 Jessica. 10 Sean Harris. 11 July. 12 On a train (from King's Cross). 13 Of. 14 Amnesty International. 15 The Grey Lady. 16 Chris Columbus. 17 Edinburgh. 18 The Daily Prophet. 19 Philospher. 20 Goblet of Fire. 21 Parselmouth. 22 Hermoine Granger. 23 Gryffindor. 24 Portugal. 25 Year Six. 26 James & Lily. 27 Wydean. 28 Quaffle. 29 Left. 30 Harry Potter and the Deathly Hallows.

1 In which year was JK Rowling born?
2 In which year was the first Harry Potter book published?
3 At which University did she study?
4 Although she wanted to study English what did she study?
5 Who became her literary agent?
6 Which publisher and which division of it published her first book?
7 Both of JK's parents came from which city?
8 Who worked on the Latin translation of "Philosopher's Stone"?
9 What was the name of JK's first daughter?
10 Whom is "Chamber of Secrets" dedicated to?
11 The second, third and fourth Harry Potter books were published in which month?
12 Where did her parents meet?
13 All titles begin "Harry Potter and the" what other word is in titles two to five?
14 JK worked for a while in London for which worldwide organisation?
15 Who is the resident ghost of Ravenclaw House?
16 Who first directed a Harry Potter movie – Chris Columbus or Mike Newell?
17 Which Scottish city did JK Rowling move to when teaching English?
18 Which national wizarding newspaper did JK create in her books?
19 Which word was changed to Sorceror in the title of a US edition?
20 Which novel starts with Harry going to the Quidditch World Cup?
21 What is JK's word for a wizard that can talk to snakes?
22 Which character did JK once think of giving the surname Puckle?
23 Which Hogwarts House did JK say she would like to have been in the most?
24 In which mainland European country did JK teach English?
25 Harry Potter is in which year at Hogwarts for "The Half-Blood Prince"?
26 What were the names of Harry's parents?
27 Which secondary school did JK Rowling attend?
28 What is the name of the red ball used for scoring in quidditch?
29 On the cover of "Order of the Phoenix" does the bird look to its left or right?
30 What was the title of the seventh and final Harry Potter book?

Answers	**Pot Luck 19** *(see Quiz 39)*

1 Major Hugh Lindsay. 2 Colin Powell. 3 336. 4 Sir Ranulph Fiennes. 5 Reach. 6 Sir Francis Walsingham. 7 Mountaineering. 8 Philosopher's Stone. 9 Paraguay. 10 Abraham Darby. 11 Denise La Salle. 12 Daniel Day-Lewis. 13 Juventus. 14 Cockerel. 15 Sumatra. 16 Thin. 17 China. 18 Shay Given (Newcastle). 19 Julia Somerville. 20 Peacock. 21 Sphalerite. 22 Chess. 23 A stream. 24 President Truman. 25 Helston, Cornwall. 26 Ocean depths. 27 Sri Lanka. 28 Raw Meat. 29 Dieting. 30 How am I Supposed to Live without You.

1 What is a line joining any two points on a curve called in geometry?
2 What was Suzi Quatro's first UK Top Ten hit?
3 Which battle is remembered in the USA in April on Patriots' Day?
4 Who directed the films "Marathon Man" and "Billy Liar"?
5 Who was the eldest son of Henry III?
6 Who preceded Douglas Hurd as Foreign Secretary?
7 Which part of the body is affected by chorea?
8 Who was William Shakespeare's mother?
9 Which celeb chef spent nine years as head chef at the Long Room at Lord's?
10 Who founded the Outward Bound Trust?
11 What is Jonny Wilkinson's middle name?
12 How old was Klaus Barbie when he was sentenced to life for wartime atrocities?
13 What would you do with a kaki?
14 What are Purple Laver and Devil's Apron types of?
15 Where would ichor supposedly have flowed?
16 Which singing twins were Hal and Herbert?
17 In the Bible, what did Job suffer with?
18 Which straits separate India from Sri Lanka?
19 Who referred to international financiers as "gnomes of Zurich"?
20 Who was the second oldest Goon?
21 What was author John Buchan's real title?
22 Which country do the Hausa people live in?
23 What was the name of Don Quixote's horse?
24 Who wrote the opera "The Love for Three Oranges"?
25 Christopher Nolan was a Whitbread Book of the Year winner with what?
26 Which fur comes from the coypu?
27 Who wrote the travelogue: "I come from Des Moines. Somebody had to"?
28 Who became Minister of Defence when Churchill became PM in 1940?
29 Which tennis No. 1 in both 2001 and 2002 came from Long Island, USA?
30 In Tarantino's directorial debut, Harvey Keitel was White – who was Orange?

Answers	**Food & Drink** *(see Quiz 42)*

1 Type of grape. 2 Buck's Club in London. 3 Doner kebab. 4 Belgium. 5 The Dorchester. 6 Caraway seeds. 7 Australia. 8 Salt cod. 9 John Tovey. 10 Chocolate. 11 Top (garnish). 12 Chile. 13 Ullage. 14 Madame Harel, a French farmer's wife. 15 Chocolate. 16 Greece. 17 Bucket. 18 VDQS. 19 Cinzano, apricot brandy & angostura bitters. 20 Butter made from coconut. 21 Maths. 22 Biscuit. 23 Asparagus. 24 Tarragon, chervil. 25 Plums. 26 Geese or ducks. 27 Lime juice. 28 Mixed green salad. 29 Kebab. 30 Filled tortilla or pancake.

1 What is hanepoot?
2 Who or what was Buck's Fizz named after?
3 Which snack's name comes from the Turkish for rotating?
4 Where is the yeastless beer faro made?
5 Where was Anton Mosimann's first position as chef in the UK?
6 Kummel is a Russian liqueur extracted from what?
7 The macadamia is native to where?
8 What is the main ingredient of a brandade?
9 Who opened the Miller Howe restaurant in 1971?
10 In his diary what did Pepys call "jucalette"?
11 Where in a dish would you put gremolata?
12 Which country has a wine-growing area called O'Higgins?
13 Which term indicates the amount of wine by which a container falls short of being full?
14 Who is credited with creating camembert cheese in about 1790?
15 What is the base of a florentine biscuit made from?
16 Where did malmsey wine originate?
17 Balti is the Indian word for what?
18 Which abbreviation indicates wine between the qualities of vin de pays and appellation contrôlée?
19 What are the ingredients of a Mr Callaghan?
20 What is cocose?
21 What did TV cook Sophie Grigson study at university?
22 In Swiss cooking what is a leckerli?
23 What is added to an omelette to make an omelette Argenteuil?
24 Which herbs are put in a béarnaise sauce?
25 Which fruit is used to make slivovitz?
26 Foie gras is the liver of which creatures?
27 In ceviche raw fish is marinated in what?
28 What is a mesclun?
29 A brochette is another name for what?
30 In Mexican cookery what is a quesadilla?

Answers | Pot Luck 20 *(see Quiz 41)*

1 Chord. 2 Can The Can. 3 Lexington. 4 John Schlesinger. 5 Edward I. 6 John Major. 7 The central nervous system. 8 Mary Arden. 9 Ainsley Harriott. 10 Kurt Hahn. 11 Peter. 12 73. 13 Eat it. 14 Seaweed. 15 In the veins of Greek gods. 16 Kalin Twins. 17 Boils. 18 Palk Straits. 19 Harold Wilson. 20 Harry Secombe. 21 Lord Tweedsmuir. 22 Nigeria. 23 Rosinante. 24 Prokofiev. 25 Under the Eye of the Clock. 26 Nutria fur. 27 Bill Bryson. 28 Churchill. 29 Jennifer Capriati. 30 Tim Roth.

1 What was Sting's debut movie?

2 What was Justin Henry's surname in a 70s Oscar winner?

3 In which film does railwayman Cleavon Little become sheriff?

4 "That's Entertainment" was a compilation of clips from which studio?

5 Who played Siegfried to Simon Ward's James in "All Creatures Great and Small"?

6 Which music plays in the background in "10"?

7 What was Alan Parker's first feature film?

8 Who starred in and produced "The China Syndrome"?

9 What was Tom Selleck's first film, in 1970?

10 Who played Winston's father in "Young Winston"?

11 Whose was the disembodied voice narrating Agatha Christie's "And Then There were None"?

12 Who wrote the music for "Shaft"?

13 Who was the landlord of "10 Rillington Place"?

14 Who sang the title song in "The Aristocats"?

15 For the trailer of which Hitchcock film was the director seen floating in the Thames?

16 Stacy Keach starred in "Fat City" after who turned it down?

17 Who directed "Death Wish"?

18 Who was the first director to cast Goldie Hawn in a non-comedy film?

19 Whom did Jane Fonda play in "Julia"?

20 Why did Peter Finch not collect his Oscar for "Network"?

21 Whose music did Malcolm McDowell like in "A Clockwork Orange"?

22 Who was the only female Oscar winner for "One Flew Over the Cuckoo's Nest"?

23 Who played the editor of the Washington Post in "All the President's Men"?

24 Which club features in "Cabaret"?

25 Who played the brother in "The Railway Children"?

26 Who was Maid Marian opposite Sean Connery in "Robin and Marian"?

27 What was the first film in which Julie Christie and Warren Beatty starred together?

28 What was Peter Ustinov's first film as Hercule Poirot?

29 What was the sequel to "Love Story"?

30 Which film of a Frederick Forsyth novel starred Jon Voight?

Quiz 44 | Pot Luck 21

Answers – page 517

1 What is eaten by a pantophagist?
2 Who were the Fuggers?
3 What do isohyet lines indicate on a map?
4 What are the dark, lowland plains on the moon known as?
5 Where, in 1855, is ice hockey thought to have originated?
6 What was the only UK Top Ten hit for the group Black Sabbath?
7 In which country was musician Leopold Stokowski born?
8 Saddam's death sentence in Nov. 2006 related to a massacre in which town?
9 What was the name of Fingal's dog in Gaelic legend?
10 The Schich Test can be used to test for which disease?
11 In the Oliver Stone film "Natural Born Killers", who played Mickey?
12 What do you do with a maduro?
13 How many albums had Eva Cassidy made before the top-selling "Songbird"?
14 Which novel starts "The past is a foreign country: they do things differently there"?
15 Which TV celeb advertised pizza with Caprice?
16 What is the main colour on the cover of the album "Spice"?
17 In which decade was Betty Boothroyd born?
18 Coptic Christians are found in Egypt and which one other country?
19 Which 1996 tennis tournament saw the debut of a fluorescent ball?
20 What was Errol Flynn's last film in 1959?
21 In which decade was playwright Sir Alan Ayckbourn born?
22 Which son of English parents was the voice of the Scottish ogre in "Shrek"?
23 Which part did Brian Wilde play in the TV series "Porridge"?
24 Which phobia describes a fear of marriage?
25 What was Bjork's first UK Top Ten hit from 1995?
26 Which female media personality has been President of the Ramblers Association?
27 What was a carrack?
28 What term describes using a gentler expression to soften a hard one?
29 Who is the elder – Lynsey de Paul or Noel Edmonds?
30 How many games had Chelsea won halfway through their 2005–06 season?

Answers | 70s Films (see Quiz 43)

1 Quadrophenia. 2 Kramer. 3 Blazing Saddles. 4 MGM. 5 Anthony Hopkins. 6 Ravel's Bolero. 7 Bugsy Malone. 8 Michael Douglas. 9 Myra Breckinridge. 10 Robert Shaw. 11 Orson Welles. 12 Isaac Hayes. 13 John Reginald Christie. 14 Maurice Chevalier. 15 Frenzy. 16 Marlon Brando. 17 Michael Winner. 18 Spielberg (The Sugarland Express). 19 Lilian Hellman. 20 He died shortly after it was made. 21 Beethoven. 22 Louise Fletcher. 23 Jason Robards. 24 The Kit Kat Club. 25 Gary Warren. 26 Audrey Hepburn. 27 McCabe and Mrs Miller. 28 Death on the Nile. 29 Oliver's Story. 30 The Odessa File.

Quiz 45 | TV Gold | Answers – page 520 | **LEVEL 3**

1 In what year was the first "Monty Python" show broadcast?
2 Who was the female presenter of "Tiswas"?
3 What was the final view at the end of "Blackadder Goes Forth"?
4 Which future Oscar nominee played Samantha Briggs in "Dr Who"?
5 Who was the only female on the first "Top of the Pops"?
6 In which TV pub did Vince Hill find fame?
7 On "The Golden Shot" who famously always got her sums wrong?
8 Who was the housekeeper in "All Creatures Great and Small"?
9 Who was the first presenter of "World of Sport" on ITV?
10 What was the booby prize on "Crackerjack"?
11 Who were the trio in "Take Three Girls"?
12 Who had the role of George Starling written for him in 1963?
13 Who originally shared a flat with Sandra in "The Liver Birds"?
14 Which comedian starred as himself in the Northern town of Woodbridge?
15 Who played the shop treasurer in "The Rag Trade"?
16 The lead singer of Herman's Hermits played whose son on TV?
17 Who was the first Teenage Mutant Hero Turtle alphabetically?
18 Who played Yosser in "Boys from the Blackstuff"?
19 Who was doing the asking in "Ask the Family"?
20 Who frequently appeared as Nymphia in "Up Pompeii"?
21 Who starred as Charley Farley, partner of Piggy Malone?
22 Who was the author played by Elaine Stritch in "Two's Company"?
23 Which sitcom began with a one-off play called "The Offer"?
24 Who played Nancy Astor's husband in the 80s series "Nancy Astor"?
25 As which character did David Cassidy shoot to fame in the 70s?
26 In "My Wife Next Door" which sitcom doyenne played George's mother?
27 Who was the only person the horse Mr Ed would talk to?
28 Which character shot Alan Rickman to fame in "The Barchester Chronicles"?
29 In "Fawlty Towers", what was Polly's surname?
30 Which corporal in "M*A*S*H" took to wearing women's clothes in order to be discharged?

Answers	Pot Luck 22 *(see Quiz 46)*

1 Nicholas Stern. 2 1982. 3 A torture device. 4 Fabrics. 5 Margaret Atwood.
6 Japan. 7 A crash. 8 AJ Cronin. 9 Jude Law. 10 Kenya. 11 Daddy Cool. 12 Conscription. 13 Ernest Hemingway. 14 Dawn French. 15 Blucher. 16 Trial of the Pyx. 17 Jennie Lee. 18 Newcastle-upon-Tyne. 19 Trevor Eve. 20 1868. 21 Princess Yashara. 22 Tiger. 23 £92,000. 24 Veterinary Surgeon. 25 Big Ben. 26 Desmond Llewelyn. 27 Lord Nolan. 28 Groucho Marx. 29 Massaging you. 30 The farthing.

1 Which ex-World Bank chief economist reported about global warming in 2006?

2 In which year did Channel 4 start to broadcast?

3 What was the Scavenger's Daughter used for in the 16th century?

4 What can be sornick, nainsook and samite?

5 Who wrote "Life Before Man" and "The Edible Woman"?

6 Which country launched a strike against Russia's fleet in 1904 at Port Arthur?

7 What is the collective name for a group of rhinoceroses?

8 Who created the character Doctor Finlay?

9 Which British-born Hollywood star has children called Rafferty, Iris and Rudy?

10 "The Flame Trees of Thika" was set in which country?

11 What was Boney M's first UK Top Ten hit from 1976?

12 What was the Derby Scheme of 1915?

13 Who wrote "A Farewell to Arms"?

14 Who is the elder – Dawn French or Jennifer Saunders?

15 What name was given to George Stephenson's first locomotive?

16 At which ceremony are coins of the realm tested?

17 Who was Britain's first Minister for the Arts in 1967?

18 Which Northern city was given the Latin name Pons Aelius?

19 In "The Politician's Wife" who played the adulterer opposite Juliet Stevenson?

20 When was Exchange & Mart first published?

21 Whom did Buddha marry before searching for enlightenment?

22 Alphabetically what is the last of the Chinese Zodiac signs?

23 Did Geoff Hurst's World Cup final shirt fetch around £50,000, £92,000 or £130,000 at auction?

24 What was the profession of the pneumatic tyre patentee John Dunlop?

25 What, on 3 December 1923, gave its first broadcast?

26 Whose final movie as Q was in "The World is not Enough"?

27 Which Lord headed the investigating committee into "sleaze" in public life in 1995?

28 Who said, "Don't point that beard at me: it might go off"?

29 If someone was Rolfing you, what would they be doing?

30 What ceased to be legal at midnight, December 31, 1960?

Answers | TV Gold *(see Quiz 45)*

1 1969. 2 Sally James. 3 A poppy field. 4 Pauline Collins. 5 Dusty Springfield. 6 Stars and Garters. 7 Anne Aston. 8 Mrs Edna Hall. 9 Eamonn Andrews. 10 Cabbage. 11 Kate, Avril & Victoria. 12 Richard Briers. 13 Dawn. 14 Harry Worth. 15 Sheila Hancock. 16 Len Fairclough's son in Corrie. 17 Donatello. 18 Bernard Hill. 19 Robert Robinson. 20 Barbara Windsor. 21 Ronnie Corbett. 22 Dorothy McNab. 23 Steptoe & Son. 24 Pierce Brosnan. 25 Keith Partridge. 26 Mollie Sugden. 27 Wilbur Post. 28 Obadiah Slope. 29 Sherman. 30 Maxwell Klinger.

1 What are Celine Dion's first two words on "My Heart Will Go On"?
2 Which artist became the first to achieve one million paid downloads in the US?
3 What did Geri write by her signature on the cover notes of "Spice"?
4 Which sisters gave Stock/Aitken/Waterman their first No. 1 hit?
5 In which year was Diana Ross's first UK solo Top Ten hit?
6 Which hit made Helen Shapiro the youngest British artist to reach No. 1?
7 Who sang female vocals on the Beautiful South's first No. 1?
8 Belinda Carlisle and Bonnie Tyler both covered which 1970 No. 1?
9 Who partnered Janet Jackson on her UK No. 3 hit "Scream"?
10 Who was the first British female soloist to have three chart No. 1 hits?
11 Whose first UK Top Ten hit as a solo artist was "Light of My Life"?
12 Which character was played by Kylie Minogue in "The Delinquents"?
13 What is Enya's full name?
14 Which Bananarama star went on to join Shakespear's Sister?
15 What was Madonna's first UK No. 1?
16 Whose first UK Top Ten hit was "Love Resurrection"?
17 When did Shirley Bassey first reach the UK Top Ten?
18 Formed in 1981, girl band The Colours charted under which name?
19 What was Dina Carroll's first solo Top Ten hit?
20 Jacqui O'Sullivan left which girl group before a 2005 chart comeback?
21 Which film featured the Eternal hit "Someday" in 1996?
22 Whose first UK Top Ten hit was "My One Temptation"?
23 Which UK No. 3 for Stacy Lattisaw was a No. 8 for Dannii Minogue?
24 Which lady recorded the original "Midnight Train To Georgia"?
25 Which lady was "Rockin' Around the Christmas Tree" in 1987?
26 Lisa Scott-Lee and Faye Tozer were members of which top-selling pop quintet?
27 What was Geri Halliwell's first single with a one-word title?
28 Which star singer was born on 9 August in New Jersey?
29 In which girl group did Heidi Range replace Siobhan Donaghy?
30 Who was the first solo female to enter the UK charts at No. 1?

1 How did Marie Curie's husband Pierre die?
2 Which group of people were once known as Millennial Dawnists?
3 In which decade was musician Mark Knopfler born?
4 What are you like if you are described as being saurian?
5 Who was the father of Enoch in the Bible?
6 Who created the character Tristram Shandy?
7 2004 Olympic medals in 100, 200 and 400m went to men from USA and which country?
8 In which country is there a political party called Likud?
9 What was Tammy Wynette's real first name?
10 Which part did Carl Weathers play in the Rocky movies?
11 Where is a howdah normally found?
12 Which Spaniard painted the picture "The Rokeby Venus"?
13 Which River mouth was discovered by Amerigo Vespucci in 1499?
14 In "Corrie", what was the late Mike Baldwin's middle name?
15 What did PT Barnum allegedly say is born every minute?
16 Richard Kuhn, Jutus Liebig and Harold Urey were famous in which scientific field?
17 Who was the first undisputed heavyweight world champion boxer to be European?
18 Who is the elder – Ben Elton or Harry Enfield?
19 Which Diane featured in the original cult movie "The Wicker Man"?
20 Horace Saussure made the first ascent of where in 1787?
21 Which title is traditionally given to the second son of the monarch?
22 What sort of food is Dunlop?
23 What is a cow's first milk after calving called?
24 Which country celebrates the National holiday, the "Day of the Dead"?
25 Who wrote "A Handful of Dust"?
26 What's Geri Halliwell's middle name?
27 The train the Cornish Riviera ran from where to where?
28 In the Second World War what did the Germans send out in "wolf packs"?
29 What was Bow Wow Wow's first UK Top Ten hit?
30 Who wrote the poems "Maud" and "Locksley Hall"?

| **Answers** | **Girl Power** *(see Quiz 47)* |

1 Every Night. 2 Gwen Stefani. 3 Girl Power. 4 Mel and Kim Appleby. 5 1970. 6 You Don't Know. 7 Briana Corrigan. 8 Freda Payne's Band of Gold. 9 Michael Jackson. 10 Sandie Shaw. 11 Louise. 12 Lola Lovell. 13 Eithne Ni Bhraonain. 14 Siobhan Fahey. 15 Into the Groove. 16 Alison Moyet. 17 1957. 18 The Bangles. 19 Don't be a Stranger. 20 Bananarama. 21 Hunchback of Notre Dame. 22 Mica Paris. 23 Jump to the Beat. 24 Cissy Houston. 25 Kim Wilde. 26 Steps. 27 Desire. 28 Whitney Houston. 29 Sugababes. 30 Mariah Carey.

1 Which Grand National winner was the first to be trained by a woman?
2 David Broome was the first British showjumping champion on which horse?
3 Who had his spot kick saved in the first FA Cup Final decided on penalties?
4 How many deliveries were sent down in the final innings of the 2005 Ashes?
5 Jesse Owens was part of which university team when he set his three world records?
6 Who was the second player to hit a maximum 36 runs off one over?
7 In which road in Oxford did Roger Bannister run his four-minute mile?
8 How many people witnessed Brazil's defeat by Uruguay in the 1950 World Cup Final?
9 Who was the first athlete to break 13 minutes for the 5,000m?
10 Who made Chris Boardman's winning bicycle in Barcelona?
11 Which famous pacemaker founded the London Marathon?
12 Which Grand National horse was the first to cross the line the year the race was abandoned?
13 By what score did Steve Davis lose the World Professional Championship Final in 1985?
14 Who was the first man to break one minute for 100m breaststroke in a 25m pool?
15 With whom did Steve Redgrave take the second of his four Olympic golds?
16 Which British man ran the fastest mile in the 1980s?
17 Why did Susan Brown make history in 1981?
18 Which was the last horse before Lammtarra in 1995 to win the classic triple?
19 How many times did Nadia Comaneci score a perfect 10 at Montreal in 1976?
20 To the nearest 10 minutes, how long did it take Brian Lara to score his record 501 against Durham in 1994?
21 Who caddied for Tiger Woods on his first US Masters victory?
22 How many races out of the 16 did Nigel Mansell win to become World Champion?
23 Who was the first player since WWII to score more than 30 goals in three consecutive seasons?
24 Where was Harvey Smith when he made his infamous V sign?
25 Whom did Virginia Wade beat to win her Wimbledon Singles title?
26 How many League games had Stanley Matthews played before his final match aged 50?
27 Seb Coe simultaneously held three world records, at which distances?
28 To the nearest 100 what were the odds against Frankie Dettorri's seven Ascot wins?
29 Who broke the 1500, 3000 and 5000m records in 1994?
30 Whom did Mike Tyson beat to become the youngest WBC champion?

| **Answers** | **Pot Luck 24** *(see Quiz 50)* |

1 50. 2 Polio. 3 A plant. 4 Ted Haggard. 5 Roads. 6 Hobson – the butler/valet.
7 An ornamental hanging in a church. 8 Norwich. 9 Proof of Life. 10 Chris Evans.
11 Vanessa Redgrave. 12 A small barrel. 13 Eight. 14 Cliff Richard. 15 Insects. 16 Priests. 17 Four. 18 Win golf's British and US Opens. 19 Toni Braxton. 20 Harold Wilson. 21 29 February. 22 Donald Coggan. 23 Usher. 24 Pierce. 25 Parsec. 26 Sir Matt Busby. 27 A silken fabric. 28 Artillery. 29 Athenia. 30 1940s.

1 How many chapters are in the book of Genesis in the Bible?
2 The Salk vaccine was developed against which disease?
3 What is a Venus's Looking Glass?
4 Which White House ally said he had been a "deceiver and a liar" in 2006?
5 What were constructed in the Highlands by General Wade in 1724?
6 What was the name of the John Gielgud character in the film "Arthur"?
7 What is a dossal?
8 At which club did Nigel Worthington replace Bryan Hamilton?
9 What was Meg Ryan filming as her marriage to Dennis Quaid hit the rocks?
10 Who is the elder – Chris Evans or Paul Gascoigne?
11 In the film "Isadora" who played the role of Isadora Duncan?
12 What is a barrico?
13 How many American colleges and universities are in the Ivy League?
14 Who played the lead role in the film "Take Me High"?
15 Cicada are types of what?
16 Who are in charge in a theocracy?
17 How many lines has a clerihew?
18 What was Patty Sheehan the first woman to do in the same year?
19 "Breathe Again" was the first UK Top Ten hit for which female vocalist?
20 Who had been Britain's youngest cabinet member before William Hague?
21 Frederick is born on which date in "The Pirates Of Penzance"?
22 Who was Archbishop of Canterbury from 1974 to 1980?
23 In 2004, who set a new US record 28 weeks on top of the single charts?
24 What was the name of the first baby born to contestants who met on "Big Brother"?
25 Which unit of measurement is equal to 3.2616 light years?
26 Which Man Utd manager appeared in a film called "Cup Fever"?
27 What was sendal?
28 What is a firearm called if it has a calibre over 20mm?
29 Which British liner was the first to be sunk by a U-boat on the first day of the Second World War?
30 In which decade was actor David Jason born?

Answers	Sport Moments (see Quiz 49)

1 Corbiere. 2 Beethoven. 3 Paul Scholes (in 2005). 4 Four. 5 Ohio State University. 6 Ravi Shastri. 7 Iffley Road. 8 200,000. 9 Said Aouita. 10 Lotus. 11 Chris Brasher (pacemaker for Bannister). 12 Esha Ness. 13 18-17. 14 Adrian Moorhouse. 15 Andrew Holmes. 16 Steve Cram. 17 First woman to take part in the boat race. 18 Mill Reef (1971). 19 Seven. 20 7hr 54 mins. 21 Mike "Fluff" Cowan. 22 Nine. 23 Alan Shearer. 24 Hickstead. 25 Betty Stove. 26 700. 27 800m, 1000m, 1500m. 28 25,095-1. 29 Noureddine Morceli. 30 Trevor Berbick.

1 What was the last ruling dynasty of China?
2 Which oil field blow-out caused an 8.2 million gallon spill in April 1977?
3 Who became Europe's youngest head of state at 28 in 1993?
4 Where was Archbishop Makarios exiled by the British in the mid-50s?
5 Which Deputy Ministerial post did Winnie Mandela hold in Nelson Mandela's first government?
6 Which German Chancellor achieved post-war reconciliation with France in the 50s and early 60s?
7 Who became the youngest ever member of the GLC in 1969?
8 Which political parties linked in the UK in the 80s to form the Alliance?
9 Which Middle East leaders were awarded the Nobel Peace Prize in 1994?
10 Which film studio released the first talking film?
11 In the Watergate scandal, who or what was CREEP?
12 Who was the third-longest-serving Pope in history?
13 Wembley Stadium was completed for which event?
14 Harold Wilson became Baron of where on his elevation to the peerage?
15 Which quotation from "Richard III" was used to describe the end of 1978 and beginning of 1979?
16 What was nicknamed 'The Flapper Vote' in 1928?
17 Who succeeded the Ayatollah Khomeini as political leader of Iran?
18 Who was the first president of an independent Mozambique?
19 J. Arthur Rank entered films in the 30s to promote which cause?
20 In 1987, what did the Tower Commission investigate in the US?
21 Where was the Recruit Scandal of 1988?
22 Which minister in Thatcher's government shared his name with Henry VIII's chaplain?
23 What did the initials of film company RKO stand for?
24 Whose gang did Al Capone's men massacre on Valentine's Day 1929?
25 A shortage of which commodity was a major issue in the 1998 Indian election?
26 At what number Cromwell Street did Rose and Fred West live?
27 King Michael abdicated which throne in 1947?
28 Whom did Jacques Santer replace as President of the European Commission?
29 The 1964 Rivonia Trial involved those opposed to what?
30 What was the name of Franco's fascist party in Spain?

Answers | **Pot Luck 25** (see Quiz 52)

1 Josie Jump. **2** Dublin. **3** Bookbinding. **4** Nelson Mandela. **5** James Joyce. **6** New York. **7** The flying shuttle. **8** Ken Boothe. **9** Cultivation of plants without soil. **10** Charles II. **11** A whip. **12** Mark Twain. **13** Handsome. **14** Stalin. **15** The Zaire. **16** Four. **17** Horses. **18** Arizona. **19** 1940s. **20** The Victoria Falls. **21** A pine cone. **22** Troops. **23** Muirfield. **24** King Baudouin (Belgium). **25** Esther. **26** September. **27** Ground-hog Day. **28** End of the Road. **29** Sian Lloyd. **30** Salmon.

1 What is the name of the fitness instructor in "Balamory"?
2 In which city in 1882 were the Phoenix Park murders?
3 What is Roxburghe a style of?
4 Which world leader married Graca Machel in 1998?
5 Which writer died in Zurich after an operation for an ulcer in 1941?
6 Which city's underground has more stations than any other?
7 Which weaving invention was invented by John Kay?
8 Who was first to take "Everything I Own" to No. 1 ?
9 What is hydroponics?
10 The Rye House Plot of 1683 was aiming to assassinate which king?
11 What is a quirt?
12 Who wrote "A Connecticut Yankee in King Arthur's Court"?
13 The Christian name Kenneth derives from the Gaelic for what?
14 Which Soviet dictator died on the same day as composer Prokofiev?
15 What is the unit of currency in The People's Republic of Congo?
16 How many No. 1 albums did Take That have?
17 Which animals can suffer the disease strangles?
18 Janet Leigh's car was registered in which American state in "Psycho"?
19 In which decade was Gloria Hunniford born?
20 What were discovered by David Livingstone in 1855?
21 What is a strobilus another name for?
22 The name Commandos comes from an Afrikaans word for what?
23 Where did Nick Faldo win his first British Open?
24 Which European King died in 1993?
25 Which Biblical woman is the Jewish festival Purim a celebration to?
26 In which month is Prince Harry's birthday?
27 In America what is 2 February called?
28 What was Boyz II Men's first UK Top Ten hit?
29 Which woman had the shortest name in the first two series of "I'm a Celebrity"?
30 Grilse, Alevins and Kelts are all forms of what?

Answers	**20th Century** (see Quiz 51)

1 Manchu or Qing ("Ching"). 2 Ekofisk. 3 Mario Frick of Liechtenstein. 4 Seychelles.
5 Arts & Science. 6 Konrad Adenauer. 7 Jeffrey Archer. 8 Liberals and SDP. 9 Arafat, Rabin, and Peres. 10 Warner Brothers. 11 Committee to RE-Elect the President. 12 Pope John Paul II. 13 British Empire Exhibition 1924. 14 Rievaulx. 15 Winter of discontent. 16 Vote to women over 21. 17 Rafsanjani. 18 Samora Machel. 19 Methodism. 20 Irangate. 21 Japan. 22 Nicholas Ridley. 23 Radio Keith Orpheum. 24 Bugs Moran. 25 Onions. 26 25. 27 Romania. 28 Jacques Delors. 29 Apartheid. 30 Falange.

1 Phi Phi Island is a popular holiday destination in which country?
2 Which eating house did Ruthie Rogers found?
3 Which soccer board game was launched by Terry Venables?
4 For what game is the Camrose Trophy awarded?
5 Who founded the Harlem Globetrotters?
6 How many tiles are there in a game of mah-jong?
7 Who designs clothes for younger people under the Emporio label?
8 What type of art was known as Jugenstil in Germany?
9 How long is the rope in water skiing?
10 In the early days of cinema how long would a "two reeler" last?
11 Serigraphy is also known as what?
12 What name is given to the style of skiing on a single broad ski?
13 Which type of outdoor spectacular was created by Paul Houdin and first shown at the Chateau de Chambord in 1952?
14 Which craft takes its name from the Arabic for "striped cloth"?
15 Where did canasta originate?
16 What are the two winning numbers made with two dice in craps?
17 Who opened Les Quat' Saisons in 1977?
18 If you follow FINA rules which sport do you practise?
19 How many dominoes are there in a double six set?
20 Southampton boast of having the first sports area of what type in the country?
21 Which sport would interest you if you followed the work of the ACS?
22 Ellem in Scotland is the oldest club of what type?
23 In the Role-Playing Game known as D&D, what does the second D stand for?
24 Where do cycle races called criteriums take place?
25 If you spent your leisure time in a sulky where would you be?
26 If you were spelunking in the US what would you be doing?
27 In 1976 the NBA and the ABA merged in which sport?
28 In sepek takrow you can hit the ball with any part of the body except which?
29 General Choi Hong Hi is responsible for the development of which martial art?
30 What position does the canoeist adopt in Canadian canoeing?

| **Answers** | Pot Luck 26 *(see Quiz 54)* |

1 Smetana. 2 Mary Peters. 3 Water skiing. 4 Nine years old. 5 John Wesley. 6 Ballet. 7 Heliopolis. 8 The Mediterranean. 9 T. Rex. 10 Enzio. 11 Second sight. 12 Robin Williams. 13 Robert McClure. 14 Gary Lineker. 15 Nicaragua. 16 Scotland. 17 It is haunted. 18 The Futhark. 19 The eyes. 20 My Prerogative. 21 On the Thames. 22 Ronald Searle. 23 Man City. 24 Horse. 25 1960s. 26 Clergy. 27 Pact of Steel. 28 Rupert Graves. 29 Mary O'Brien. 30 Fox.

Quiz 54

1 Who composed the opera "The Bartered Bride"?
2 Who won the 1972 Olympic pentathlon title?
3 Paul Seaton was the first UK male to be European champion in what?
4 How old was Henry III when he became King?
5 Who said, "I look upon the world as my parish"?
6 In which performing art was Beryl Grey famous?
7 Where in Egypt did Cleopatra's needle originally stand?
8 The Silk Road ancient trade route ran between China and where?
9 Micky Finn played bongos in which pop group?
10 What is Sylvester Stallone's middle name?
11 Deuteroscopy is the common name for what?
12 Which actor links "Awakenings", "Toys" and "Cadillac Man"?
13 Who was the first admiral to pass through the Northwest Passage?
14 Who is the elder – Nicholas Lyndhurst or Gary Lineker?
15 Daniel Ortega was President of which country from 1981–90?
16 Where was the Encyclopaedia Britannica first published?
17 Why is Chinge Hall in Lancashire famous?
18 What name is given to the Runic alphabet?
19 What are affected by nystagmus?
20 What was Bobby Brown's first UK Top Ten hit?
21 Where were Frost Fairs held in London until 1831?
22 Which illustrator created the girls of St Trinians?
23 Which Premiership side featured D. Mills and M. Mills in 2005–06?
24 Which creature is represented in the year the Chinese call "ma"?
25 In which decade was pop superstar Mick Hucknall born?
26 Crockford's is a register of what?
27 Italy and Germany formed a military alliance in 1939 called what?
28 In the 2003 "Forsyte Saga", who played the role made famous by Kenneth More?
29 What is Dusty Springfield's real name?
30 What's the English name of the constellation Vulpecula?

Answers | Hobbies 1 (see Quiz 53)

1 Thailand. 2 River Cafe. 3 The Manager. 4 Bridge. 5 Abraham Saperstein. 6 144. 7 Armani. 8 Art Nouveau. 9 23m or 75 feet. 10 20 minutes. 11 Silk screen printing. 12 Monoboarding. 13 Son et lumière. 14 Macramé. 15 Uruguay. 16 7 & 11. 17 Raymond Blanc. 18 Swimming. 19 28. 20 Bowling green. 21 Cricket. 22 Angling. 23 Dragons. 24 Town or city centres. 25 Small cart in harness racing. 26 Potholing. 27 Basketball. 28 Arms and hands. 29 Taekwondo. 30 Kneeling.

1 In whose stately home was the Tarzan film "Greystoke" filmed?
2 What was Sharon Stone's first film, in 1980?
3 "Uncle Buck" was the debut of which movie star?
4 May Day was the Bond girl in which film?
5 What was the occupation of Madame Sousatzka in the Shirley Maclaine film?
6 Who had a lead role in the movie version of "Rising Damp" who wasn't in the TV sitcom?
7 Whom did Alan Rickman play in "Die Hard"?
8 Who are the two letter writers in "84 Charing Cross Road"?
9 Which son of a pop star appears as Jackson's friend in "Moonwalker"?
10 In which film did Jack Nicholson say the catchphrase "Here's Johnny"?
11 Who played Mrs La Motta in "Raging Bull"?
12 Which film all but bankrupted United Artists in 1980?
13 Which ailing actor's voice was dubbed by Rich Little in "Curse of the Pink Panther"?
14 Who played Meryl Streep's eccentric friend in "Plenty"?
15 Who won an Oscar for his first major role in 1982?
16 Who was Glenn Close's character in "Dangerous Liaisons"?
17 Which film included the song "It Might be You"?
18 Who was the only Cambodian Oscar winner of the 80s?
19 Who was the only winner of an Oscar and a BAFTA for "Platoon"?
20 Who was nominated as Best Supporting Actress for "The Color Purple"?
21 In the film "A Royal Love Story", who played Princess Diana?
22 "The Color of Money" re-created the character from which film?
23 Which father and son appeared in "Wall Street"?
24 Which role did Kevin Kline play in "A Fish Called Wanda"?
25 Which presidential candidate's cousin won an Oscar for "Moonstruck"?
26 Apart from Music and Visual Effects, which other Oscar did "E.T." win?
27 Who directed "Psycho III"?
28 Whose music features on the soundtrack of "When Harry Met Sally"?
29 Whose novel was Warren Beatty's "Reds" based on?
30 Who was the aerobics instructor in "Perfect"?

1 Who set up the production company Ardent?

2 Which duo first presented the breakfast show on GMTV?

3 The characters Colonel Rudd and Franco Franco appeared in which 2006 sketch show?

4 Which legendary writer penned the song that became the "Ab Fab" theme?

5 Which character said, "You might very well think that, but I couldn't possibly comment"?

6 Who originally appeared in cabaret as the Menopause Sisters?

7 Who had a small role in "Bergerac" before starring in "Heat and Dust"?

8 Which play told of Falklands casualty Robert Lawrence?

9 How is comedian Chris Collins better known?

10 Who designed the original "Blue Peter" logo?

11 For which two series did Emma Thompson win best actress BAFTAs two years in succession?

12 Which BBC first will Kenneth Kendall always retain?

13 Which Hollywood actress played Lola Lasagne in "Batman"?

14 Who was Frank Ormand, the Pretzel man in "The Simpsons"?

15 What was the prison chief called in "The Governor"?

16 Which British entrepreneur once guested on "Friends"?

17 Who played Joanna in "Dr Who" and was the wife of a future Doctor?

18 Who said to Lord Archer, "There's no beginning to your talents, Jeffrey"?

19 Which pop band was Dani Behr a member of before her TV career?

20 What was Gladiator Warrior's real name?

21 Who wrote and presented a "History of the Tory Party"?

22 On which show did Caroline Aherne develop her Mrs Merton character?

23 Which brothers were played by the McGanns in "The Hanging Gale"?

24 Which TV company was founded by Peter Cadbury?

25 Who wrote the controversial series "The Lakes"?

26 In which series did Eileen Downey find fame?

27 "Ab Fab"'s Edina was based on which PR lady?

28 Who became narrator for "Thomas the Tank Engine" in the US in 1998?

29 Who played Rhett Butler in the TV sequel to "Gone with the Wind"?

30 A comedy writing award was introduced in 1998 in whose memory?

Answers	80s Films *(see Quiz 55)*

1 Duke of Roxburghe's. 2 Stardust Memories. 3 Macaulay Culkin. 4 A View to a Kill.
5 Piano teacher. 6 Denholm Elliott. 7 Hans Gruber. 8 Helene Hanff & Frank Doel. 9
Sean Lennon. 10 The Shining. 11 Cathy Moriarty. 12 Heaven's Gate. 13 David Niven.
14 Tracey Ullman. 15 Ben Kingsley. 16 Marquise de Merteuil. 17 Tootsie. 18 Haing
S. Ngor. 19 Oliver Stone. 20 Oprah Winfrey. 21 Catherine Oxenberg. 22 The Hustler.
23 Martin & Charlie Sheen. 24 Otto. 25 Olympia Dukakis. 26 Sound. 27 Anthony
Perkins. 28 Harry Connick Jr. 29 John Reed's. 30 Jamie Lee Curtis.

1 In Oct. 2005, which UK politician travelled with Condoleezza Rice to her home state?
2 What was Brotherhood of Man's first UK Top Ten hit?
3 In which county did the battle of Edgehill take place?
4 Which country does chart-topping Eric Prydz come from?
5 In which decade was TV presenter Eamonn Holmes born?
6 Which theatre foundations were discovered in London in 1988?
7 Who was lead in the films "Man of the Moment" and "The Square Peg"?
8 Who became England cricket captain to replace Graham Gooch?
9 Which actor won Best Actor Oscar for "On Golden Pond" aged 76?
10 How many countries surround Botswana?
11 Barbara Trentham was the second wife of which English comic?
12 What is Bordeaux Mixture a blend of?
13 Which Spanish artist painted "The Persistence of Memory"?
14 Which film was remade as "Dirty Rotten Scoundrels"?
15 What is the middle name of knighted cricketer Gary Sobers?
16 What was Greta Garbo's last film?
17 The WWSU is the governing body of which sport?
18 What mass is measured in Criths?
19 In which city is the Verrazano Narrows Bridge?
20 Which profession did George Washington start out in?
21 To five, how many Premiership goals did Ruud van Nistelrooy score for Man, Utd?
22 Which country celebrates the crayfish with a party in August?
23 What was the title of the only UK Top Ten hit for James Brown?
24 Who is the elder – Joanna Lumley or Maureen Lipman?
25 What does the abbreviation 'fz' mean in music?
26 Spaniard Francisco Pizarro founded which city?
27 When was the magazine Cosmopolitan first published?
28 Which city was the first to erect a monument to Lord Nelson in Britain?
29 What was Angel Beast an old type of?
30 What is the county emblem of Lincolnshire?

Answers	Euro Tour *(see Quiz 58)*

1 Brenner's Park Hotel. 2 Romania. 3 Tbilisi. 4 Vienna. 5 Gulf of Riga. 6 Brussels. 7 Austria. 8 Koper. 9 Italy. 10 Baltic. 11 Netherlands. 12 Estonia. 13 Gulf of Finland. 14 Great Britain. 15 Mount Etna and Stromboli. 16 Grande Dizence in Switzerland. 17 Finland. 18 London. 19 Germany. 20 Liechtenstein. 21 Ormeli in Norway. 22 Belarus. 23 Assisi in Central Italy. 24 Germany. 25 Italy. 26 Roman Catholic. 27 Corfu. 28 Tourism and tobacco. 29 Spain. 30 Norway.

1 Which German hotel was home to the England WAGS during the 2006 World Cup?
2 Tarom Airlines are based in which country?
3 What is the capital of Georgia?
4 Which capital is further North – Budapest or Vienna?
5 Which Gulf is to the west of Estonia and Latvia?
6 Where is the news agency Centre d'Information Presse based?
7 In which country is Kranebitten International airport?
8 What is the chief port of Slovenia?
9 The Pelagian islands belong to which European country?
10 Bornholm is an island in which Sea?
11 Hoge Veluwe National Park is in which country?
12 Which European country has the internet code .ee?
13 St Petersburg is at the head of which gulf?
14 What is the largest island in Europe?
15 Which two Italian volcanoes erupted in 1994?
16 What is the world's highest dam?
17 Which country is called Suomen Tasavalta in its own language?
18 Which capital is further North – Berlin or London?
19 Aero Lloyd Airlines are based in which country?
20 Which European country has the highest life expectancy for men and women?
21 What is the highest waterfall in Europe?
22 Brest is a major town in which country other than France?
23 In which town did an earthquake claim nine lives in 1997?
24 In which country is the city of Bochum?
25 To which country do the islands of Stromboli and Vulcano belong?
26 What is the prominent religion of Lithuania?
27 Which is the northernmost and second largest of the Ionian islands?
28 What are Andorra's two main industries?
29 In which country is Sondica International airport?
30 Hardangervidda National Park is in which country?

Answers	Pot Luck 27 *(see Quiz 57)*

1 Jack Straw. 2 United We Stand. 3 Warwickshire. 4 Sweden. 5 1950s. 6 The Rose Theatre. 7 Norman Wisdom. 8 Mike Atherton. 9 Henry Fonda. 10 Five. 11 John Cleese. 12 Insecticide. 13 Dali. 14 Bedtime Story. 15 St Aubrun. 16 Two-Faced Woman. 17 Water skiing. 18 Mass of gases. 19 New York. 20 A surveyor. 21 95 goals. 22 Sweden. 23 Living in America. 24 Joanna Lumley. 25 Accented (Forzato). 26 Lima. 27 1972. 28 Glasgow. 29 A card game. 30 An imp.

1 What is No in Japan?
2 Who is the elder – David Mellor or Andrew Lloyd Webber?
3 What is a tulwar?
4 Who, with Paul McCartney, composed the "Liverpool Oratorio"?
5 What were Charles Dickens' two middle names?
6 Which team was the first to top the 50 points mark in a Super Bowl final?
7 In which city is Fettes College?
8 Where was the cloth used to make duffle coats first made?
9 On May 21, 1927, who landed at Le Bourget airport?
10 Where did Joseph of Arimathea's staff take root and bud, in legend?
11 Which song did Frank Sinatra feature in the film "Robin and the Seven Hoods"?
12 What is a skimmer to an American?
13 What name is given to the Greek letter that is the equivalent of letter O?
14 Which gulf is between the heel and sole of Italy?
15 Which famous leader brought an end to the Pharaohs in Egypt?
16 Which HG Wells novel is the musical "Half a Sixpence" based on?
17 To ten years, when was the magazine The Economist founded?
18 What is the final event in a Decathlon?
19 Which of the Manic Street Preachers was officially declared dead in 2002?
20 What was Mariah Carey's first UK Top Ten hit?
21 Which doctor played by Richard Wilson appeared in "Only When I Laugh"?
22 Who was the first wicket keeper to claim 50 stumping victims in Tests?
23 Which elegant white villa dating from the eighteenth century is situated on Hampstead Heath?
24 On which island is Bungee jumping said to have originated?
25 What were the Christian names of the showman Barnum?
26 To three years, in which year did Audrey Hepburn die?
27 Whose one and only hit was "Little Things Mean a Lot" in 1954?
28 Which monarch introduced the sedan chair into England?
29 What physical property lets a needle float on water?
30 Which country has the internet code .ua?

Answers	**The Royals** (see Quiz 60)

1 Anthropology. 2 Sir Robert Fellowes. 3 Marie Christine von Reibnitz. 4 Victoria Cross Heroes. 5 Viscount Linley. 6 Marina Olgilvy. 7 Geelong Grammar. 8 Sports Science. 9 The Queen Mother. 10 Duke of Roxburghe. 11 Dame Kiri Te Kanawa. 12 Techno. 13 The Duke of Kent. 14 Diana. 15 Princess Margaret. 16 Eight. 17 Diana, Fergie. 18 Young England. 19 His wedding day. 20 Elizabeth Arden. 21 Les Jolies Eaux. 22 Barbara Daly. 23 The Rottweiler. 24 Sir George Pinker. 25 Ludgrove. 26 To ease traffic congestion. 27 Pulled the coach. 28 Martin Bashir. 29 Andrew and Alice. 30 Page boy to Fergie.

1 Along with Archaeology, which subject did Prince Edward read at Cambridge?
2 Who became the Queen's Private Secretary in 1990?
3 What was Princess Michael of Kent's maiden name?
4 In 2006 Prince Charles presented a TV series about what kind of heroes?
5 Which Royal had a financial interest in a chain of hamburger restaurants called Deal?
6 Who was the first unmarried Royal to announce her pregnancy in 1989?
7 Which school was attended by Prince Charles and Kerry Packer?
8 What did Peter Phillips study at Exeter University?
9 Who was portrayed as a school dinner lady on "Spitting Image"?
10 At whose home did Prince Andrew propose to Sarah Ferguson?
11 Who sang a Handel aria at Charles and Diana's wedding?
12 In a 16th birthday interview what type of music did Prince William say he preferred?
13 Who had the car registration plate K7?
14 Who was the first Royal bride to include her own family's coat of arms on her marital coat of arms?
15 Who retained the number plate 3 GXM for a new Rolls in 1972?
16 How many Princesses of Wales were there before Diana?
17 Who turned up with Pamela Stephenson at Annabel's on Prince Andrew's stag night dressed as police officers?
18 At which kindergarten did Diana Spencer work?
19 When did Prince Philip become Duke of Edinburgh?
20 The Duchess of Windsor employed a make-up artist daily from which cosmetics house?
21 What was Princess Margaret's house on Mustique called?
22 Who did Diana's make-up on her wedding day?
23 What was Diana's nickname for Camilla?
24 Who delivered Prince William?
25 What was William and Harry's first boarding school?
26 Why did the Queen change the Birthday Parade from Thursday to Saturday?
27 What part did Lady Penelope and St David play at Charles and Diana's wedding?
28 To which reporter did Diana admit her marriage was "a bit crowded"?
29 What were Prince Philip's parents called?
30 What was Prince William's first public duty?

Answers	**Pot Luck 28** *(see Quiz 59)*

1 A type of theatre. 2 Lord Lloyd Webber. 3 A sword. 4 Carl Davis. 5 John Huffham. 6 San Francisco 49ers. 7 Edinburgh. 8 Duffel in Belgium. 9 Charles Lindbergh. 10 Glastonbury. 11 My Kind Of Town. 12 A straw hat. 13 Omicron. 14 Gulf of Taranto. 15 Alexander the Great. 16 Kipps. 17 1843. 18 1500 metres. 19 Richie Edwards. 20 Vision of Love. 21 Dr Thorpe. 22 Bert Oldfield (Australia). 23 Kenwood House. 24 Pentecost Island. 25 Phileas Taylor. 26 1993. 27 Kitty Kallen. 28 James I. 29 Surface tension. 30 Ukraine.

1 The discovery of which plot led to the death of Mary, Queen of Scots?
2 Who was England captain for Sven-Goran Eriksson's first game?
3 Which Duke commanded the English troops at Culloden?
4 Which letter is one dot and one dash in Morse Code?
5 Which Minister was murdered in 1990 outside his home by an IRA bomb?
6 Which Battle was the first in the Hundred Years War?
7 What is served at a Thyestean feast?
8 Who wrote "Goodbye to All That"?
9 Adam Faith's last TV drama role was in which occasional BBC series?
10 James Last was in the album charts this century playing music by which group?
11 Who is the elder – Desmond Lynam or Sir Paul McCartney?
12 In which year did Francis Drake complete the circumnavigation of the world?
13 How do you travel on the Devizes–Westminster race?
14 How old were both Anne Boleyn and Mrs Beeton when they died?
15 Who composed "Easter Parade"?
16 Which country gained independence in 1908 from Turkey?
17 What is the opening track on the Verve's "Urban Hymns"?
18 Which hymn was written by Augustus Toplady after sheltering from a storm?
19 In which decade was William Hague born?
20 Who wrote Dr Johnson's biography?
21 Who is the only English monarch to have won a flat race as a jockey?
22 Mary II died of which disease at the age of 32?
23 Whose only UK hit was "Patches"?
24 Marlon Brando, Clark Gable and Mel Gibson have all played which role?
25 Which drill gets women and children into lifeboats first?
26 Which greyhound was the first to win the Greyhound Derby twice?
27 The Sea of Marmara lies between the Bosporus and what?
28 Who designed The Monument in London?
29 Which scale other than the Richter scale measures earthquakes?
30 How many singles peaked at No. 2 for Elvis in his "comeback" year 2005?

Answers	Oldies & Goldies *(see Quiz 62)*

1 (How Much is) That Doggie in the Window? 2 Amazing Grace. 3 Oh Pretty Woman. 4 Honky Tonk. 5 I'm not in Love. 6 Rosemary Clooney. 7 If you're going. 8 So Gay. 9 Spirit in the Sky. 10 Little Jimmy Osmond. 11 I Can't Stop Loving You. 12 Terry Jacks. 13 Lily the Pink. 14 Adam Faith. 15 My Ding-a-Ling. 16 1973. 17 Needles and Pins. 18 Tab Hunter. 19 Lee Hazelwood. 20 Johnny Remember Me. 21 Jerry Keller. 22 Roy Wood. 23 Moon River. 24 The Good, the Bad and the Ugly. 25 Sunny Afternoon. 26 The Next Time/Bachelor Boy. 27 What a Wonderful World. 28 Land. 29 Zager & Evans. 30 You're My World.

1 What was the first UK No. 1 in which the title posed a question?
2 Which traditional song provided instrumental and vocal versions that charted for 94 weeks?
3 What was Roy Orbison's final chart topper from 1964?
4 Which "Women" was the longest ever at No. 1 for the Rolling Stones?
5 Graham Gouldman and Eric Stewart wrote which 70s classic No. 1?
6 Which 1950s vocalist began singing with the Tony Pastor band?
7 What are the first three words of "San Francisco"?
8 How were the birds singing in the original title of the No. 1 "Why Do Fools Fall in Love"?
9 Which 1986 No. 1 was a cover of a 1970 No. 1?
10 Which artist took over the title of the youngest No. 1 hitmaker in 1972?
11 What is Ray Charles' only UK No. 1?
12 Which Canadian was next to No. 1 after Paul Anka?
13 Which hit gave producer Norrie Paramour his 27th and final No. 1?
14 Emile Ford shared his first week at No. 1 with which artist?
15 Which Chuck Berry hit was No. 1 at the same time in the UK and US?
16 Steve Miller's "The Joker" hit No. 1 in 1990 but when was it recorded?
17 Which hit gave The Searchers their second No. 1?
18 Who had a No. 1 with the original version of "Young Love"?
19 Who wrote and produced Nancy Sinatra's "These Boots are Made for Walking"?
20 Which John Leyton hit was covered in 1985 by Bronski Beat and Marc Almond?
21 Whose only UK hit was "Here Comes Summer"?
22 Who wrote "See My Baby Jive"?
23 What film theme gave Danny Williams his only No. 1 in 1961?
24 What was the first instrumental No. 1 after the Shadows' "Foot Tapper"?
25 What was the Kinks' third and final No. 1 hit in the summer of 1966?
26 What was the only Cliff Richard & the Shadows No. 1 double-A-side?
27 Which 1968 No. 1 was revived in the film "Good Morning Vietnam"?
28 What was Wonderful in the Shadows hit which stayed longest at No. 1?
29 Which act was the first beginning with a letter Z to have a No. 1 single?
30 What was Cilla Black's only US Top 40 hit?

Answers | **Pot Luck 29** *(see Quiz 61)*

1 Babington Plot. 2 David Beckham. 3 Duke of Cumberland. 4 A. 5 Ian Gow. 6 Sluys. 7 Human flesh. 8 Robert Graves. 9 Murder in Mind. 10 Abba. 11 Sir Paul McCartney. 12 1580. 13 Canoe. 14 29 years. 15 Irving Berlin. 16 Bulgaria. 17 Bitter Sweet Symphony. 18 Rock of Ages. 19 1960s. 20 James Boswell. 21 Charles II. 22 Smallpox. 23 Clarence Carter. 24 Fletcher Christian. 25 Birkenhead Drill. 26 Mick the Miller. 27 The Dardanelles. 28 Christopher Wren. 29 Mercalli Scale. 30 Eight.

1 Which language do the words kiosk, tulip and caviar come from?
2 Whose Drum can be seen at Buckland Abbey in Devon?
3 Whose painting of the Liver Building fetched £1m at auction in June 2006?
4 What do the initials stand for in the name of ghost story writer MR James?
5 Which actor played Major Gowen in "Fawlty Towers"?
6 In which decade was Lloyd Grossman born?
7 Whose hymn book was first published in 1873?
8 A durmast is a variety of what?
9 Whose only UK Top Ten Hit was "Blue is the Colour" from 1972?
10 Which Europeans discovered Lake Tanganyika in 1858?
11 Who said, "I never hated a man enough to give him his diamonds back"?
12 Achulophobia is the fear of what?
13 Which brass instrument is wrapped around the player's body?
14 What colour appears with white and green on the Afghanistan flag?
15 In which US state was there a nuclear accident at Three Mile Island in 1979?
16 Who was the first woman to swim the English Channel in 1926?
17 What is the capital of Angola?
18 Under what pseudonym did Richard Horne write "The Last Polar Bears" and other children's books?
19 What is indium?
20 Who is the elder – Paul Merton or Richard Madeley?
21 Who lived at No. 1, London?
22 Where are the Aventine, Viminal and Quirinal Hills?
23 What nationality was Sir Robert Helpmann?
24 What is a clerihew?
25 In which country can you visit Espoo and Vantaa?
26 In which European country is the province of Brabant?
27 What was the title of Gloria Hunniford's book about her late daughter Caron Keating?
28 What was David Cassidy's first UK Top Ten hit?
29 Where did Kun's Red Terror exist in 1919?
30 Which actor was first to sign a $1 million deal for a single picture?

Answers	Olympics 1 *(see Quiz 64)*

1 Singapore. 2 Ice hockey. 3 Yachting. 4 St Moritz. 5 Bars and beam. 6 Michael Johnson. 7 Long jump. 8 Al Oerter. 9 Five. 10 Two. 11 Retained 10,000m and won 5,000m and marathon. 12 Evander Holyfield. 13 Lake Lanier. 14 Simone Jacobs. 15 Michelle Smith. 16 Izzy. 17 Seoul. 18 Allan Wells. 19 Spain. 20 Soling. 21 Poland's Renata Mauer. 22 Tim Henman & Chris Broad. 23 Jayne Torvill. 24 4 x 400m relay. 25 1900. 26 Quarantine laws. 27 Denise Lewis. 28 Montreal. 29 Robin Cousins. 30 Japan.

1 In which country did the final vote about hosting the 2012 Olympics take place?
2 At which sport did future tennis star Drobny win a medal in 1948?
3 Windsurfing is included in the Olympics as part of which sport's events?
4 Where were the Winter Olympics held in 1928 and 1948?
5 On which apparatus did Nadia Comaneci score perfect tens in 1976?
6 Who was the first man to win Olympic gold at 200m and 400m?
7 In which event did Carl Lewis win his ninth and final gold medal?
8 Who won the first of four discus golds in Melbourne in 1956?
9 How many silver medals did skier Raisa Smetanina win with her four golds and one bronze?
10 How many gold medals did Mark Spitz win in his first Olympics?
11 Which amazing treble did Emil Zatopek achieve at the 1952 Games?
12 Who carried the torch into the stadium at the Atlanta games?
13 On which lake did Steve Redgrave win his record-breaking fourth gold medal?
14 Who was the only British woman sprinter to compete in all Olympics between 1984 and 1996?
15 Under what name did Mrs Erik de Bruin win gold at Atlanta?
16 What was the name of the Olympic mascot in Atlanta?
17 Where did Linford Christie run his first Olympic race?
18 Who was the oldest Olympic 100m champion when he won in 1980?
19 Who won women's gold in hockey in Barcelona?
20 Which is the only Olympic yachting event for three-person crews?
21 Who won the first medal at the Atlanta games?
22 Who won Britain's first tennis medal since 1924 in Atlanta?
23 Who replaced her partner Michael Hutchinson before winning gold in 1984?
24 Other than 400m hurdles for which event did Sally Gunnell win a medal in Barcelona?
25 In which year did women first compete in the Olympics?
26 Why were equestrian events held in Sweden in 1956 when the Games were held in Australia?
27 Who was Britain's only female medallist at the Atlanta games?
28 Where did Daley Thompson compete in his first Olympics?
29 Which son of a former Millwall goalie won gold in the USA in 1980?
30 What was the first Asian country to have staged the Winter Olympics?

Answers	**Pot Luck 30** *(see Quiz 63)*

1 Turkish. 2 Francis Drake's. 3 LS Lowry. 4 Montague Rhodes. 5 Ballard Berkeley. 6 1950s. 7 Sankey and Moody's. 8 An oak tree. 9 Chelsea F.C. 10 Richard Burton and John Speke. 11 Zsa Zsa Gabor. 12 Darkness. 13 Sousaphone. 14 Black. 15 Pennsylvania. 16 Gertrude Ederle. 17 Luanda. 18 Harry Horse. 19 A metallic element. 20 Richard Madeley. 21 Duke of Wellington. 22 Rome. 23 Australian. 24 A poem. 25 Finland. 26 Belgium. 27 Next to You. 28 Could It Be Forever/Cherish. 29 Hungary. 30 Marlon Brando.

1 Whom did the Spice Girls sack as their manager in early 1998?
2 What is a porbeagle?
3 Which bandleader married both Ava Gardner and Lana Turner?
4 What was the family name of artists Jacopo and his sons Gentile and Giovanni?
5 Scottish solicitor William Mitchell drew up the rules for which sport?
6 Which group had a 70s hit with "Kiss You All Over"?
7 What is the first name of John Peel's widow?
8 What two colours go with black and yellow in printing's four-colour process?
9 What did Diana Princess of Wales describe as "a shameful friend"?
10 Who won an Oscar for her first screenplay "Silkwood"?
11 What was Bad Manners' first UK Top Ten hit?
12 What is a belvedere?
13 In which month is the feast day of St Cuthbert?
14 In which country are the mountains called the Stirling Range?
15 Which late politician was the first leader of the Scottish Parliament?
16 Which soccer club has been managed by both Jimmy Armfield and Brian Clough?
17 Whose one and only hit was "Float On" in 1977?
18 Who was the first Prime Minister of Israel?
19 Where is New York's Metropolitan Museum of Art?
20 In what year did the London Stock Exchange go computerised?
21 What is a gibus?
22 Who was the first man to hold the post of Astronomer Royal?
23 Who numbered Helen Menken and Mary Philips among his wives?
24 Who founded the record label Anxious Records?
25 Which Michelangelo statue is in Florence?
26 Vera Caslavska was Olympic and World Champion in which sport?
27 In which year was Wimbledon first televised?
28 Where was the first woman MP to enter the Commons born?
29 Who ceased to be queen when Victoria became queen?
30 What do you do if you siffle?

Answers | Hobbies 2 (see Quiz 66)

1 0 to 36. 2 Finland, playing football. 3 Chess. 4 Mahogany. 5 16lb. 6 Bilbao. 7 Steel links. 8 Tintin. 9 Alton Towers. 10 Giverny. 11 Clarice Cliff. 12 Military combat. 13 10. 14 Baker Street. 15 Caman. 16 Tony Hancock. 17 Curling. 18 Tramp. 19 Aikido. 20 Four (11 and 7 respectively). 21 Stamp collecting. 22 Hang gliding. 23 Harz Mountains (Germany). 24 Mogens Tholstrup. 25 Carry it. 26 Gothenburg, Sweden. 27 Nick Nairn. 28 Bungee jumping. 29 Kung fu. 30 Leiden.

1 What is the range of numbers on a roulette wheel?
2 Where would you watch FC Jazz and what would they be doing?
3 FIDE is the governing body of which game?
4 Which furniture-making wood can be Cuban, Honduras and San Domingan?
5 In athletics how much does a hammer weigh?
6 Where is the Guggenheim Museum in Europe?
7 In abseiling what are karabiners?
8 Who first appeared in a strip cartoon "in the Land of the Soviets"?
9 Which UK tourist attraction is on the site of an 8th-century fortress?
10 Where in Normandy would you visit Monet's garden?
11 If you collected Bizarre pottery whose work would you have?
12 Paintball is a simulation of what?
13 How many zones does an archery target have?
14 In which London street was the first artificial ice rink opened?
15 In shinty what is the curved stick called?
16 Which radio star appeared in films such as "The Wrong Box"?
17 In which sport does a match last for a certain number of heads?
18 John Gold was the owner of which night club for over 30 years?
19 Which activity has two main types, tomiki and uyeshiba?
20 How many more people are there in an outer handball team than there are in an indoor one?
21 John Tomlinson is credited with starting which hobby?
22 Which form of flying was perfected by Francis Rogallo in the 1970s?
23 In which mountains is the Brockenbahn steam railway?
24 Which restaurateur owned Daphne's and founded The Collection?
25 In cyclocross what do you do with your bike when you're not riding it?
26 Where is the Liseberg theme park?
27 Who opened the Braeval restaurant in Scotland in 1986?
28 In which activity do you "dive for the horizon"?
29 Wing Chun is a popular form of which art?
30 In which Botanic Gardens was the tulip first introduced in 1594?

Answers | Pot Luck 31 *(see Quiz 65)*

1 Simon Fuller. 2 A shark. 3 Artie Shaw. 4 Bellini. 5 Bowls. 6 Exile. 7 Sheila. 8 Cyan, magenta. 9 Bulimia. 10 Nora Ephron. 11 Special Brew. 12 A viewing turret. 13 March. 14 Australia. 15 Donald Dewar. 16 Leeds. 17 The Floaters. 18 David Ben-Gurion. 19 Central Park. 20 1986. 21 A top hat. 22 John Flamsteed. 23 Humphrey Bogart. 24 Dave Stewart. 25 David. 26 Gymnastics. 27 1937. 28 America. 29 Adelaide. 30 Whistle.

1 Bernard Webb was a pseudonym used by which famous song writer?
2 In which country is the royal family the House of Bernadotte?
3 Acrophobia is the fear of what?
4 In which country is the city of Abidjan?
5 What was the only No. 1 UK hit for the Clash?
6 What colour is the circle on the Bangladesh flag?
7 A Brazilian Huntsman is a type of what?
8 Who played director Ed Wood in the 1994 film biography?
9 A Nutmegger is an inhabitant of which American state?
10 In which decade did South Africa resign from the Commonwealth?
11 How many locks are there on the Suez Canal?
12 What is Mrs Gordon Brown's first name?
13 Who composed Rhapsody on a Theme of Paganini for Piano?
14 What was the number of the British Armoured Division nicknamed the "Desert Rats"?
15 In which year did James Cook land at Botany Bay, Australia?
16 What is the correct form of address to begin a letter to a Baron?
17 In which country is the town of Nakhon?
18 Who is the elder – Caroline Quentin or Linda Robson?
19 What was Neneh Cherry's first UK Top Ten hit?
20 What was the Christian name of aeroplane manufacturer Mr Boeing?
21 In which European country are the provinces of Sofiya and Burgas?
22 What size is A4 paper in millimetres?
23 Australia hosted the 1956 Olympics but equestrian events were held in which other country?
24 Murderer Dr Harold Shipman worked in which Greater Manchester district?
25 Which artist painted "The Watering Place" in 1777?
26 INXS singer Michael Hutchence was born in and died in which city?
27 Who played Russell Crowe's wife in "Cinderella Man"?
28 Whose first novel was called "Glass Houses"?
29 Clarence House was built for which monarch when he was still Duke of Clarence?
30 What is the capital of Bahrain?

Answers | TV Times 2 (see Quiz 68)

1 Angus Deayton. 2 Po. 3 Andrew Lincoln. 4 Science. 5 Tinky Winky. 6 Ascot. 7 Sara. 8 Lakesiders. 9 Duffy (Cathy Shipton). 10 Papa, Bob. 11 Sorted. 12 Jane Asher. 13 My Kind of People. 14 Dame Thora Hird. 15 Tantrums and Tiaras. 16 Francesca Annis. 17 Widows. 18 Helen Rollason. 19 James Naughtie. 20 Ian Hislop. 21 Carla Lane. 22 Twin Peaks. 23 Bedrock (The Flintstones). 24 Heineken. 25 Warrington. 26 Gomez Addams. 27 Paul McGann. 28 Fiona Phillips. 29 1313 Mockingbird Heights. 30 The Woodentop twins.

1 Who played Mike Channel in "KYTV"?
2 Who is the smallest Teletubby?
3 Who found fame as Egg in "This Life"?
4 "Prove It!" was a CITV series about what?
5 Who is the largest Teletubby?
6 Where did the first outside broadcast on "Grandstand" come from?
7 Who is Postman Pat's wife?
8 In which docu soap did Emma Boundy find fame?
9 Which "Casualty" character played a midwife in "Spice World"?
10 Which two words has Nicole uttered to advertise Renault?
11 Which BBC drama series, first seen in 2006, was about a mailroom?
12 Which TV presenter made the cake when Jemima Goldsmith married Imran Khan?
13 What was Michael Barrymore's talent-spotting TV show called?
14 Which late actress won a BAFTA for "A Cream Cracker Under the Settee"?
15 What was the name of the David Furnish-directed documentary about Elton John?
16 Who played the Englishwoman in "Parnell and the Englishwoman"?
17 In which series did Lynda La Plante introduce Dolly Rawlings?
18 Who was the first woman presenter of "Grandstand"?
19 Who replaced Richard Baker as the presenter of the Proms?
20 Who presented Channel 4's religious series "Canterbury Tales"?
21 How is TV playwright Romana Barrack better known?
22 In which show was Harry S Truman the sheriff?
23 In which town would you read "The Daily Slate"?
24 The music from "Raging Bull" was used to advertise which lager?
25 Where is Chris Evans' home town?
26 Who had a pet octopus called Aristotle?
27 Who played the title role in Alan Bleasdale's "The Monocled Mutineer"?
28 Anthea Turner was replaced at GMTV by whom?
29 Where did the Munsters live?
30 On a Friday, on children's TV who were Jenny & Willy?

---

1 In which decade was actor John Cleese born?
2 After which American General were sideburns named?
3 Freetown is the capital of which country?
4 Villinger and Couchepin have been Presidents of which country this century?
5 Which eating house was founded by Ruth Rogers?
6 What is the main language of Angola?
7 What happened to the Olympic flame during the 1976 games?
8 Hartford is the capital of which American State?
9 Which 18th-century artist painted "Peasant Girl Gathering Sticks"?
10 To five years, when was the News of the World founded?
11 What, other than "Amazing Grace", was a Top Ten hit for Judy Collins?
12 A fear of the cold is known as what?
13 In which county is the Rude Man of Cerne?
14 Which country has the dalasi as its currency?
15 What was done in an apodyterium?
16 Emperor Nero was the adopted son of which other emperor?
17 What is the international car index mark for a car from Libya?
18 The spice annatto is made from which part of a plant?
19 Other than Buckingham Palace, which venue sees the daily Changing of the Guard?
20 Which English county does actor Robert Lindsay come from?
21 What was the Commodores' first UK Top Ten hit?
22 In which movie did Harrison Ford play the character John Book?
23 Painter Georges Seurat was born, died and worked in which city?
24 What name is given to elements with atomic numbers 93 to 112?
25 What two colours appear with yellow on the Cameroon flag?
26 Who was the first woman to qualify for the Indy 500 motor race?
27 Which Latin phrase means, "Let the buyer beware"?
28 In which year did women gain the vote in Switzerland?
29 In which country is the city of Bamako?
30 As a child Jonathan Ross appeared in an ad for which food product?

Answers	**90s Films** *(see Quiz 70)*

1 Wag the Dog. 2 Francis Bacon. 3 Arnold Schwarzenegger. 4 River Phoenix. 5 Spanish Civil War. 6 Jean-Claude Van Damme. 7 That Thing You Do!. 8 Pretty Woman. 9 Seal. 10 Ellen Barkin. 11 Frank Drebin. 12 Banker. 13 Julia Roberts. 14 Kevin Kline. 15 Blue Sky. 16 Kennedy & Nixon. 17 James Earl Jones. 18 Abba. 19 Kirsty Alley. 20 Nine Months. 21 Emma Thompson. 22 Elizabeth Taylor. 23 Kevin McCallister. 24 Jim Carrey , who played The Riddler. 25 Ron Shelton. 26 Jude. 27 Christopher Walken. 28 Gonzo. 29 Nil by Mouth. 30 2000 AD.

1 Which Barry Levinson film was used to satirise the US presidency during the Lewinsky crisis?
2 Who is the subject of "Love is the Devil"?
3 Which tough guy directed "Christmas in Connecticut"?
4 Who died during the filming of "Dark Blood" in 1993?
5 Which war is depicted in "Land and Freedom"?
6 Who was Lyon Gaultier in "AWOL"?
7 In which film did Tom Hanks make his directorial debut?
8 Which film's initial title was "$3,000"?
9 Who or what is Andre in the film of the same name?
10 Who was Leonardo DiCaprio's mother in "This Boy's Life"?
11 Who is Leslie Nielsen in the "Naked Gun" films?
12 What is Jim Carrey's job before he finds the mask in the hit movie?
13 Who was Tinkerbell when Spielberg met JM Barrie?
14 Who was the butler in "Princess Caraboo"?
15 What was director Tony Richardson's final film?
16 Which US presidents does Gump meet in "Forrest Gump"?
17 Who was the voice of Mufasa in "The Lion King"?
18 Muriel is a fan of which band in "Muriel's Wedding"?
19 Whom did Woody Allen cast as his ex-wife in "Deconstructing Harry"?
20 What was Hugh Grant's first Hollywood movie?
21 Who was Oscar winning best screen writer for "Sense and Sensibility"?
22 Who was John Goodman's mother-in-law in "The Flintstones"?
23 What is Macaulay Culkin's full name in the "Home Alone" movies?
24 Who designed The Riddler's costume in "Batman Forever"?
25 Who directed "White Men Can't Jump"?
26 In which film did Kate Winslet have her first nude scene?
27 Who played rat catcher Caesar in "Mousehunt"?
28 Who was the author in "The Muppet Christmas Carol"?
29 Which film was Gary Oldman's directorial debut?
30 In which comic did Sylvester Stallone's '95 futuristic police character appear?

| **Answers** | **Pot Luck 33** *(see Quiz 69)* |

1 1930s. 2 Ambrose Burnside. 3 Sierra Leone. 4 Switzerland. 5 River Cafe. 6 Portuguese. 7 Extinguished by a cloudburst. 8 Connecticut. 9 Thomas Gainsborough. 10 1843. 11 Send in the Clowns. 12 Cheimaphobia. 13 Dorset (figure carved in chalk hillside). 14 Gambia. 15 Clothes were removed before bathing. 16 Claudius. 17 LAR. 18 Seeds. 19 Royal Horse Guards, Whitehall. 20 Derbyshire. 21 Easy. 22 Witness. 23 Paris. 24 Trans-uranic elements. 25 Green and Red. 26 Janet Guthrie. 27 Caveat emptor. 28 1971. 29 Mali. 30 Rice Krispies.

1 What is another name for the North American nightjar?
2 Who was the first woman to have a partial face transplant?
3 How is the disease trypanosomiasis also known?
4 What is meant by a haemorrhage which is "occult"?
5 Which protein is present in a hair?
6 What does it mean if a cell is haploid?
7 In addition to tea and coffee where is caffeine found?
8 Where is the flexor carpi radialis?
9 What is an erythrocyte?
10 How is the sand hopper also known?
11 Guano is used as fertiliser but what is it made from?
12 Cranes are found on all continents except which two?
13 What is an alternative name for leptospirosis?
14 Carragheen is a type of what?
15 Where is a caterpillar's spinneret?
16 Which bird flies highest?
17 What is an insect's Malpighian tubes?
18 How does a mamba differ from a cobra?
19 Which part of the brain controls muscular movements, balance and co-ordination?
20 Which bird can swim as fast as a seal?
21 An urodele is another name for which reptile?
22 Which bird builds the largest nest?
23 The world's largest spider is named after which Biblical character?
24 What is a bird's furcula?
25 Disulfiram is used in the treatment of what?
26 What is a hairstreak?
27 On which island would you find the bee hummingbird?
28 Which bird produces the largest egg in relation to its body size?
29 Why should you avoid a chigger?
30 How many hearts does an earthworm have?

Answers	Pot Luck 34 *(see Quiz 72)*

1 Louis Washkansky. 2 Denmark. 3 Bela Bartok. 4 Cliff Richard. 5 Terrorism. 6 George Bush. 7 Elephant. 8 Second or middle row. 9 Turkey. 10 Mackerel. 11 1985. 12 Blackheath. 13 Wallace & Gromit. 14 1940s. 15 One Day I'll Fly Away. 16 Helena Bonham Carter. 17 43,200. 18 Polish. 19 Sexual health in the Third World. 20 Martin Amis. 21 Dot, dot, dot. 22 Shakespeare. 23 Spencer Perceval (British PM). 24 Trumpet. 25 Edo. 26 Excessive growth. 27 New Zealand. 28 Indiana. 29 Kid Creole and the Coconuts. 30 Touch.

1 Who was the first person to receive a heart transplant?
2 In which European country are the counties of Viborg and Aarhus?
3 Who composed the music for the ballet "The Wooden Prince"?
4 Who played the lead role in the film "Two a Penny"?
5 As PM Tony Blair first lost a Commons vote on which high-profile subject?
6 Who was Vice President when Ronald Reagan was President?
7 Which animal head represents the Hindu god Ganesa?
8 Keying in the word DAMSON which row of letters is used the most?
9 In which country is the city of Adana?
10 Which type of fish gives its name to a particular patterning of the sky?
11 In which year did Roy Plomley last present "Desert Island Discs"?
12 The first men's hockey club in England was founded in which London suburb?
13 Who were the movie stars when Ralph Fiennes voiced Victor Quartermaine?
14 In which decade was Michael Gambon born?
15 What was Randy Crawford's first UK Top Ten hit?
16 Which Oscar and BAFTA nominee was a one-time face of Yardley cosmetics?
17 How many seconds are there in half a day?
18 What was the nationality of the astronomer Nicolaus Copernicus?
19 Geri Halliwell became a UN ambassador specialising in what?
20 Who wrote the novels "London Fields" and "Time's Arrow"?
21 How is the letter S formed in Morse Code?
22 The Globe Theatre's Dominic Dromgoole wrote "Will and Me" about whom?
23 Which public figure was shot dead by John Bellingham?
24 Bandleader Quincy Jones chiefly plays which instrument?
25 Changed in 1868, what was the former name of Tokyo?
26 What do you suffer from if you have acromegaly?
27 The yacht Black Magic won the America's Cup for which country?
28 A Hoosier is an inhabitant in which American state?
29 Who had hits with "Stool Pigeon" and "I'm a Wonderful Thing, Baby"?
30 Haphephobia is the fear of what?

Answers	Living World (see Quiz 71)

1 Whippoorwill. 2 Isabelle Diniore. 3 Sleeping sickness. 4 Internal. 5 Keratin. 6 Single set of chromosomes. 7 Kola nuts. 8 Human's forearm. 9 Red blood cell. 10 Beachflea. 11 Bird droppings. 12 South America & Antarctica. 13 Weil's disease. 14 Seaweed. 15 Head. 16 Ruppell's vulture. 17 Excretory organs. 18 Not hooded. 19 Cerebellum. 20 Penguin. 21 Salamander. 22 Male malle fowl. 23 Goliath. 24 Wishbone. 25 Alcoholism. 26 Butterfly. 27 Cuba. 28 Kiwi. 29 Harvest mite (which bites). 30 Ten.

1 Who was known as the "father of the Soviet H-bomb"?
2 In which shipyards did Lech Walesa work before becoming Polish president?
3 Terry Waite was the envoy of which Archbishop of Canterbury when he was kidnapped?
4 Who founded the Police Memorial Trust after PC Yvonne Fletcher's death?
5 Who was the first US Ambassador in London?
6 Who recorded with the Hot Five and the Hot Seven in the 1920s?
7 Which David wrote "Bringing the House Down" about his father John?
8 Who was the 20th Prince of Wales?
9 Who succeeded Len Murray as TUC general secretary in 1984?
10 Who was the first Archbishop of Canterbury to be appointed by the Church Crown Appointments Commission?
11 Which children's author was Russian correspondent for the Daily News during WWI and the Revolution?
12 Which advocate of black rights left the US to live in England in the late 50s?
13 Who was the last British monarch to refuse royal assent of a Bill through Parliament?
14 Who was UK Deputy PM between 1942 and 1945?
15 Which UK PM was responsible for the purchase of US Polaris missiles?
16 Whom did Douglas Hurd replace as Foreign Secretary in 1989?
17 Who became President of the ANC in 1997?
18 Which Chancellor of the Exchequer introduced old-age pensions?
19 Which Fine Gael candidate did Mary McAleese defeat in the 1997 election for Irish President?
20 Which invention improved on Alexander Cumming's invention a century earlier?
21 What was Mikhail Gorbachev's wife called?
22 Who founded Standard Oil in 1870?
23 How was entrepreneur Roland Fuhrhop better known?
24 Which son of Findlaech was killed at Lumphanan?
25 Who was the first Archbishop of Canterbury?
26 Which former Enfield MP has the middle names Denzil Xavier?
27 The name of which UK PM was Ronald Reagan's middle name?
28 Who was shot at a rally in the US in 1972 while campaigning for the Democrats?
29 Which Baron began a continental pigeon post in 1849?
30 Who was German foreign minister during WWII?

Answers	Pot Luck 35 (see Quiz 74)

1 Fruit pods. 2 Nebraska. 3 Weather with You. 4 His height (world's tallest man). 5 Eight. 6 RB. 7 Paolo Wanchope. 8 Vulcan. 9 Martin Bashir. 10 Arithmetic and logic unit. 11 Edgar Rice Burroughs. 12 Three. 13 Andrew Bonar Law. 14 Paul Cezanne. 15 1642. 16 Warren Beatty. 17 Traffic Wardens. 18 Zambia. 19 When he gives up his seat. 20 If You Let Me Stay. 21 My Lord Duke. 22 1989. 23 Indonesia. 24 David Hockney. 25 Henry VIII. 26 Neil Kinnock. 27 Peacock. 28 148mm x 210 mm. 29 French. 30 168.

1 The spice cayenne is made from which part of a plant?
2 Lincoln is the capital of which US state?
3 What was the only UK Top Ten hit from 1992 for Crowded House?
4 What was special about Robert Pershing Wadlow?
5 How many singles had Take That released before their first No. 1 "Pray"?
6 What is the international car index mark for a car from Botswana?
7 Which Costa Rican soccer player is their all-time top scorer?
8 Who was the Roman God of fire?
9 Which British journalist was involved in the Michael Jackson trial of 2005?
10 Mathematically speaking, what is an ALU?
11 In the 1920s who wrote "The Land that Time Forgot"?
12 How many stripes are on the national flag of Estonia?
13 Who is the only British prime minister to have been born outside the UK?
14 Which artist painted "Le Jardinier" in 1906?
15 In which year was the Battle of Edgehill?
16 Who directed the 1990 film "Dick Tracy"?
17 A Chief Constable is responsible for which uniformed force other than the police?
18 Lusaka is the capital of which country?
19 When does an MP apply for the Chiltern Hundreds?
20 What was Terence Trent D'Arby's first UK Top Ten hit?
21 What is the correct form of address to begin a letter to a Duke?
22 In which year did Frank Bruno first fight with Mike Tyson?
23 In which country is the city of Banjarmasin?
24 Who painted "The Rake's Progress" and "A Bigger Splash" in the 1960s?
25 Saint John Fisher was martyred during the reign of which English king?
26 Which ex-political leader wrote the book "Making Our Way"?
27 What's the English name of the constellation Pavo?
28 What size is A5 paper in millimetres?
29 What is the main language of the Republic of Benin?
30 What is the sum total of the spots on a set of dominoes?

Answers | Who was Who? *(see Quiz 73)*

1 Andrei Sakharov. 2 Gdansk. 3 Robert Runcie. 4 Michael Winner. 5 John Adams. 6 Louis Armstrong. 7 Profumo. 8 The future Edward VIII. 9 Norman Willis. 10 Robert Runcie. 11 Arthur Ransome. 12 Paul Robeson. 13 Queen Anne. 14 Attlee. 15 Macmillan. 16 John Major. 17 Thabo Mbeki. 18 Asquith. 19 Mary Bannotti. 20 Flushing toilet. 21 Raisa. 22 John D. Rockefeller. 23 Tiny Rowland. 24 Macbeth. 25 St Augustine. 26 Michael Portillo. 27 Wilson. 28 George Wallace. 29 Paul Julius Reuter. 30 Joachim von Ribbentrop.

1 What was Eddie Cochrane's next UK single after "Three Steps to Heaven"?

2 Who played Jerry Lee Lewis in the 1989 biopic of his life?

3 How does Roger Peterson figure in rock history?

4 What was Billy Fury's first UK Top Ten hit from 1960?

5 In which city were R.E.M. formed?

6 As a teenager Morrissey ran a fan club for which group?

7 Who wrote the Holly classic "It Doesn't Matter Anymore"?

8 Which Elvis No. 1 is the only one written solely by Leiber and Stoller?

9 Which hard-rock band did the Scottish Young brothers form in Australia?

10 "Rock Around the Clock" came out on which label?

11 Who did Keith Richard work for before coming a full-time Stone?

12 Which Slade hit was No. 1 when US soldiers left Vietnam in 1973?

13 What did Rick Allen of Def Leppard lose in 1984?

14 What did an electrician fitting a burglar alarm find in Seattle in 1984?

15 Who first charted with "Rip It Up"?

16 James Jewel Osterberg took the stage under which name?

17 At which studio did the "Million Dollar Quartet" get together in the 50s?

18 In which month did Jim Morrison die in 1971?

19 Where in London was the Sex Pistols' first concert?

20 Which Dickie Valentine hit replaced "Rock Around the Clock" at No. 1?

21 Which place used to form part of The Stranglers name?

22 Who was Francis Rossi's school mate and long-time bass player in Status Quo?

23 How were the Rolling Stones billed for their first live concert?

24 Which Jerry Lee Lewis hit is the only version of the Ray Charles classic to reach the British charts?

25 Who ran the Clovis, New Mexico studio where Buddy Holly recorded?

26 Who was Phil Lynott's father-in-law?

27 Who recorded the album "Ma Kelly's Greasy Spoon"?

28 Which Led Zeppelin drummer died in 1980?

29 Who ran the Chelsea clothes shop called Let It Rock?

30 Which 1955 Glenn Ford movie featured "Rock Around the Clock"?

---

1 In 2006 rugby union, who was captain for England's seventh defeat in a row?
2 In the 1980s, who wrote the short-story collection "A Twist in the Tale"?
3 What is the Parliament of Sark called?
4 What colour appears with white and red on the Faroe Islands flag?
5 In 1995 Hugh Grant got into trouble for performing a lewd act with whom?
6 What is the capital of Belize?
7 The North American Nebula is a region in which constellation?
8 What was The Damned's one and only UK Top Ten hit?
9 Which Inspector did Johnny Depp play in the movie "From Hell"?
10 What is a golomyanka?
11 Which singer with the Billy Cotton Band passed away in March 2005?
12 Bombay, Chartreux and Japanese bobtail are all types of what?
13 Which war is Stephen Crane's novel "The Red Badge of Courage" set in?
14 In which country is the city of Alma-Ata?
15 The writer Thomas Keneally comes from which country?
16 In which decade was actor Colin Firth born?
17 Prithwi Narayan Shah was the first King of which kingdom?
18 Where were William Hague, Jesse Owens and Pele brought together?
19 Homichlophobia is the fear of what?
20 Who became Chancellor of Hull University in 2006?
21 Who or what was a piggin?
22 In which year was the Women's International Bowling Board formed?
23 Which media presenter left his wife Carol McGiffin in 1993?
24 Which ex-Monkee was in a band called Shoe Suede Blues?
25 Among which hills does Chequers lie?
26 Who composed the opera "Noye's Fludde"?
27 The band Coldplay formed while attending which educational establishment?
28 Under which name did Leslie Charles sail to pop success?
29 Which city has the oldest stock exchange in the USA?
30 What does the musical term "giocoso" mean?

Answers	Rockers *(see Quiz 75)*

1 Sweetie Pie. 2 Dennis Quaid. 3 Pilot in the crash that killed Holly. 4 Colette. 5 Athens, Georgia. 6 The New York Dolls. 7 Paul Anka. 8 Jailhouse Rock. 9 AC/DC. 10 Decca. 11 The Post Office. 12 Cum On Feel the Noize. 13 An arm (in a car crash). 14 Kurt Cobain's body. 15 Little Richard. 16 Iggy Pop. 17 Sun Studio, Memphis. 18 July. 19 St Martin's School of Art. 20 Christmas Alphabet. 21 Guildford. 22 Alan Lancaster. 23 Rollin' Stones. 24 What'd I Say. 25 Norman Petty. 26 Leslie Crowther. 27 Status Quo. 28 John Bonham. 29 Malcolm McLaren. 30 Blackboard Jungle.

1 CIPS regulates which sport?
2 In which city were Haagen-Daz ice creams first sold?
3 Where is Rick Stein's famous seafood restaurant?
4 What is octopush?
5 In embroidery, what is the name for areas of raised decoration?
6 Who jointly opened La Gavroche in 1967?
7 Which venue was designed by George London and Henry Wise?
8 What colour might your balls be in croquet?
9 What is the nearest town to the Lightwater Valley Theme Park?
10 Which game was originally called Lexico?
11 The Toucan Terribles are prolific champions at what?
12 What is the name of England's smallest pub in Bury St Edmunds?
13 What did Andrew Forgan and Hugh Philp make?
14 Where was the Grand National run during WWI?
15 Who founded the London restaurants Quaglino's and Mezzo?
16 In judo which Dan grades are awarded a red belt?
17 How many points is the gold circle on an archery target worth?
18 In 1848 William Mitchell drew up the rules to which modern game?
19 In shinty what is the opponent's goal called?
20 Which musical instrument was the creation of Charles Wheatstone?
21 Which soccer club had a fanzine called Fly Me to the Moon?
22 Who opened his first restaurant Harveys in 1987?
23 In paddle tennis what is the ball made from?
24 Which game was derived from baggataway?
25 What is important dress code at France's Domaine de Lambetran?
26 What is a gricer?
27 Where is the UK's largest amusement park?
28 What name is given to the circular target in curling?
29 What is Denmark's Rutschebahnen?
30 What do you wear on your feet in street hockey?

---

1 Who directed the 1992 film "Bram Stoker's Dracula"?
2 Robert Banks Jenkinson was British PM under which title?
3 Which cemetery is to the south of the Valley of the Kings?
4 What is Nick Faldo's middle name?
5 Which artist painted "The White Horse" in 1819?
6 The Lake Pontchartrain Causeway links Mandeville, Louisiana with where?
7 The spice coriander is made from which part of a plant?
8 When was The Sun newspaper founded?
9 Brown, Cornell and Dartmouth are all members of what?
10 What is the international car index mark for a car from Taiwan?
11 Neil Diamond started to train – but didn't qualify – as what?
12 Who featured on the first Top Ten hit for Destiny's Child?
13 What type of musical instrument is the Japanese koto?
14 Who was Vice President when Jimmy Carter was President of USA?
15 Which British composer died on the island of Ischia in 1983?
16 Who was the last person to be executed by beheading in the UK?
17 In which decade did Agatha Christie die?
18 Nemanja Vidic joined Man Utd from which club?
19 In quoits, what name is given to the target at which the rings are thrown?
20 What was the first movie to make $1,000 million at the box office?
21 In cycling what is the first major classic of the season?
22 Which newspaper in the UK was the first to publish a daily weather chart?
23 In which island group is Guadalcanal?
24 Prince Charles, Prince Edward and Prince Philip were all head boys at which school?
25 What appears in the centre of the national flag of Ghana?
26 How many symphonies did Brahms compose?
27 What was the title of Dr Feelgood's only Top Ten hit?
28 Which South American city has a name meaning "fair winds"?
29 Alexander Gordon 1743–1827 gave his name to what?
30 In which country is the city of Antananarivo?

Answers	**Hobbies 3** *(see Quiz 77)*

1 Angling. **2** New York. **3** Padstow, Cornwall. **4** Underwater hockey. **5** Stumpwork.
6 The Roux Brothers. **7** Hampton Court maze. **8** Blue, red, yellow or black. **9** Ripon.
10 Scrabble. **11** Marbles. **12** The Nutshell. **13** Golf clubs. **14** Gatwick. **15**
Terence Conran. **16** 9th to 11th. **17** 10. **18** Bowls. **19** Hail. **20** Harmonica. **21**
Middlesbrough. **22** Marco Pierre White. **23** Sponge. **24** Lacrosse. **25** None (it's a
naturist site). **26** Trainspotter. **27** Blackpool. **28** House. **29** Roller coaster. **30** Roller
skates.

Quiz 79 | TV Times 3

Answers – page 554

1 Which role does Mrs Trevor Eve play in "Holby City"?
2 Who played the British PM in "Suez" which commemorated the 50th anniversary of the crisis?
3 Who co presented "The Big Breakfast" with Zoe Ball?
4 Who played Kadi Toura in the drama series "Roots"?
5 Who was the antiques dealer in the "Paddington" stories?
6 Who used to say, "The next Tonight will be tomorrow night"?
7 Which was the English port in the "Triangle" drama series?
8 Mrs Robert Powell was a member of which famous dance group?
9 Who was the first Teletubby to have its alter ego sacked?
10 Who was Mrs Simpson when Stephen Campbell Moore played Edward VIII?
11 In which series did Charles Dance play Guy Perron?
12 On Channel 4 when Helen Mirren was Elizabeth I, who was Jeremy Irons?
13 Who directed a documentary called "Genderquake" after leaving a top soap?
14 Who followed Phillip Schofield as link man on Children's BBC?
15 Whose final TV role was as Daniel Reece?
16 In "May to December" what was Zoe's name before she married Alec?
17 Who played Dr David Kelly in "The Government Inspector"?
18 Who are the parents of "Live & Kicking"'s first female presenter?
19 What is the profession of Postman Pat's Mrs Goggins?
20 Which series took place in Lochdubh?
21 Who was Bamm Bamm's dad?
22 What was Alan B'Stard's constituency?
23 Which magazine did Amanda work for in "Girls on Top"?
24 Who were Father Ted's colleagues?
25 Which disgraced ex-MP is the uncle of Jack Davenport from "This Life"?
26 What did Angela Rippon dance to on "The Morecambe and Wise Show"?
27 George Baker aka Inspector Wexford appeared as which special agent in "Up Pompeii"?
28 What were the goldfish on "Playschool" called?
29 Who succeeded Amanda Burton in the lead role, in "Silent Witness"?
30 What did Peter do in "The Peter Principle"?

Answers | Pot Luck 38 *(see Quiz 80)*

1 Shetlands. 2 Signed, Sealed, Delivered, I'm Yours. 3 Plum. 4 Colombia. 5 £5.05. 6 Jill Balcon. 7 My Lord Mayor. 8 Three Coins In The Fountain. 9 Crowds. 10 Dog. 11 Bromley. 12 Piracy. 13 Benjamin Britten. 14 Gin and beer. 15 1880s. 16 Archbishop of Canterbury. 17 Argentina. 18 Rhodes. 19 Chess. 20 Arsenal. 21 Carl Douglas. 22 International Phonetic Alphabet. 23 69 goals. 24 Germany. 25 Melvyn Bragg. 26 Francis Coppola. 27 Peas. 28 Ireland. 29 Barry Sonnenfeld. 30 Blue and White.

1 Where is Baltasound Airport?
2 What was Blue's first single not to make the Top Ten?
3 Grand Duke, Stanley and Lombard are all varieties of which fruit?
4 In which country is the city of Cali?
5 In 2005 the hourly minimum wage for over-21s was fixed at what amount?
6 Who was the actress mother of actor Daniel Day-Lewis?
7 What is the correct form of address to begin a letter to a Lady Lord Mayor?
8 What was Frank Sinatra's first UK No. 1?
9 Demophobia is the fear of what?
10 Which creature is represented in the year the Chinese call gou?
11 What is the most southerly London borough?
12 Anne Bonney and Mary Read famously carried out which trade?
13 Who composed the opera "Death In Venice"?
14 What have you had if you've just had a dog's nose?
15 During which decade did the Orient Express first run?
16 The Court of Arches is the chief court of whom?
17 Which country has the austral as a unit of currency?
18 Which island is the largest of the Dodecanese group?
19 Emanuel Lasker was undisputed world champion for over 26 years at what?
20 Which London football team did the author of "We All Live in a Perry Groves World" play for?
21 Whose one and only UK Top Ten hit was "Kung Fu Fighting"?
22 What are the initials IPA an abbreviation of, as well as being an ale?
23 How many league goals did Jimmy Floyd Hasslebaink score for Chelsea?
24 The landau carriage takes its name from a town in which country?
25 Who wrote the novel "A Time to Dance"?
26 Talia Shire is the sister of which film director?
27 What have you got with a plateful of Pisum satvium?
28 Which country left the Commonwealth in 1949?
29 Who directed the movie "Men in Black"?
30 Which two colours appear on the national flag of Honduras?

Answers | TV Times 3 *(see Quiz 79)*

1 Tricia Williams. 2 James Fox. 3 Mark Little. 4 OJ Simpson. 5 Mr Gruber. 6 Cliff Michelmore. 7 Felixstowe. 8 Pan's People. 9 Tinky Winky. 10 Joely Richardson. 11 Jewel in the Crown. 12 The Earl of Leicester. 13 Susan Tully. 14 Andy Crane. 15 Rock Hudson in Dynasty. 16 Angell. 17 Mark Rylance. 18 Bryan Forbes & Nanette Newman. 19 Postmistress. 20 Hamish Macbeth. 21 Barney Rubble. 22 Haltemprice. 23 Spare Cheeks. 24 Douglas & Jack. 25 Jonathan Aitken. 26 Let's Face the Music and Dance. 27 Jamesus Bondus. 28 Bit & Bot. 29 Emilia Fox. 30 Bank Manager.

1 Who has been an Irish international and the head of HJ Heinz?
2 In which decade of which century did the first league varsity match take place?
3 In which city were Barbarians RFC founded?
4 Which was the first league side to score 1,000 points in a season?
5 In 2006, who skippered Argentina when England lost their seventh game in a row?
6 Rob Andrew is qualified in what profession?
7 Where did Brian Moore begin his career?
8 How old was Will Carling when he played for Terra Nova Under 11s?
9 Against which side did Jeremy Guscott make his international debut?
10 Which league side was the first to win all its league games in a season?
11 In which month and year did Andy Robinson take over as England's head coach?
12 In 1986 St Helens beat Carlisle 112-0 in which competition?
13 Who was the first union player to kick eight penalties in an international?
14 What was Jason Leonard's first club?
15 Who were the beaten finalists in the first league Knockout Trophy?
16 Who captained Ireland in their centenary season?
17 Whom did the All Blacks beat 106-4 in 1987?
18 Where was the first floodlit rugby union match played?
19 What name was given to the breakaway clubs from the Rugby Union in 1895?
20 Which club won the first Middlesex Sevens at Twickenham?
21 What position did JJ Williams play for Llanelli?
22 Who returned to England from the Rugby World Cup in 2003 for the birth of daughter Eva?
23 Who recorded the then highest score draw 46-46 in 1994?
24 Who sponsored the rugby league before Courage?
25 In which country was the first rugby league World Cup held?
26 Who was the first UK rugby league club side to play in Australia?
27 Who played a record 17 appearances on five tours with the British Lions?
28 Which New Zealand fly half scored 26 points against England in Nov. 2006?
29 Who made the lowest score (0-0) in the BBC's Floodlit Rugby League competition?
30 Who were the first Scottish rugby union club champions?

Quiz 82 | Pot Luck 39

1 Which country has the forint as its unit of currency?
2 A fear of dreams is known as what?
3 What was Stephen "Tin Tin" Duffy's only Top Ten hit?
4 How long is the Suez Canal?
5 In the military, what is an AFV?
6 Which UK No. 1 was written by Red Dwarf creators Robert Grant and Doug Naylor?
7 Which letter is two dots in Morse Code?
8 In which decade was Rory Bremner born?
9 Mbabane is the capital of which country?
10 What popular pub name comes from the title held by soldier John Manners?
11 What colour are the stars on the national flag of the Republic of Iraq?
12 What does the Latin deo volente mean?
13 Which high-profile politician won the Dulwich and West Norwood seat in 2005?
14 Raleigh is the capital of which US state?
15 What size is B4 paper in millimetres?
16 Ayegbeni Yakubu joined Middlesbrough from which club?
17 In which of his many movies did Anthony Hopkins play Dr Frederick Treves?
18 What is the administrative centre for the Welsh county of Powys?
19 Stotinki can be spent in which country?
20 Where in Westminster Abbey was the Stone of Scone?
21 What is the international car index mark for a car from Chile?
22 To five years when was the magazine Country Life founded?
23 Which late singer was the lead guitarist with the Grateful Dead?
24 In which country is the city of Dalian?
25 Who was the Roman God of death?
26 Whose top hat sold for £22,000 at Sotheby's in 1988?
27 The spice fenugreek is made from which part of a plant?
28 What was Dollar's first UK Top Ten hit in 1979?
29 In the film "Ace Ventura: Pet Detective" Ace is hired to find what?
30 Who was known as "Joltin Joe" and "the Yankee Clipper"?

Answers | Rugby (see Quiz 81)

1 Tony O'Reilly. 2 1981. 3 Bradford. 4 St Helens. 5 Agustin Pichot. 6 Chartered surveyor. 7 Nottingham. 8 Six. 9 Romania. 10 Hull. 11 Oct, 2004. 12 Lancashire Cup. 13 Canada's Mark Wyatt. 14 Barking. 15 Wakefield Trinity. 16 Willie John McBride. 17 Japan. 18 Rodney Parade, Newport. 19 Northern Union. 20 Harlequins. 21 Right wing. 22 Martin Corry. 23 Sheffield Eagles & Leeds. 24 Slalom lager. 25 France. 26 St Helens. 27 Willie John McBride. 28 Dan Carter. 29 Salford & Warrington. 30 Hawick.

1 What is the currency of Bolivia?
2 Between which two rivers does Manhattan lie?
3 Where in Russia was a school besieged by extremists in September 2004?
4 In which country is the city of Curitiba?
5 What is the capital of Brunei?
6 In which country is the deep-water port of Lobito?
7 The islands of Taipa and Coloane are part of which possession?
8 Pluna Airlines are based in which country?
9 Which capital is further North – Khartoum or Addis Ababa?
10 What is the official language of Bhutan?
11 In which country is Kakadu National Park?
12 Which country is due North of Uruguay?
13 Which two countries border Morocco?
14 Which desert lies between the Kalahari and the Atlantic Ocean?
15 Where is the news agency Colprensa based?
16 What is Madison Square Garden situated over?
17 On which island is Nassau, the capital of the Bahamas?
18 In which US state was the first National Park?
19 How is Denali in Alaska also known?
20 The Negev desert tapers to which port?
21 Who designed New Delhi?
22 What is the third longest river in Africa?
23 Which country has the largest oil resources in Africa?
24 Chandrika Kumaratunga was president of which country hit by the 2004 tsunami?
25 In which country is the city of Medan?
26 What is the capital of Burundi?
27 What is South Africa's judicial capital?
28 What is the most north-eastern US state?
29 SAHSA Airlines are based in which country?
30 Which island is situated between Sumatra and Bali?

Answers	**Blockbusters** *(see Quiz 84)*

1 It Happened One Night. 2 Elwood P. Dowd. 3 Lewis Gilbert. 4 Miracle on 34th Street. 5 Philadelphia Story. 6 A Night at the Opera. 7 Walter Pidgeon. 8 Dodi Fayed. 9 Robert Newton. 10 Dances with Wolves. 11 James Cameron. 12 Busby Berkeley. 13 Waterworld. 14 Gary Oldman. 15 Blenheim. 16 Amon Goeth. 17 Bruce Springsteen & Neil Young. 18 Ben Hur. 19 Gandhi. 20 Ellen Burstyn. 21 King Kong, 1933. 22 Bolivia. 23 Endora in Bewitched. 24 The Shadows. 25 Costume. 26 Liv Ullmann. 27 Cary Grant. 28 Mammy (Gone with the Wind). 29 The Full Monty. 30 How to paint.

1 Which 1930s classic was originally called "Night Bus"?

2 Whom does James Stewart play in "Harvey"?

3 Whom did Carol Reed replace at the last minute on "Oliver!"

4 In which 1940s classic did Edward Gwenn play Kris Kringle?

5 Katharine Hepburn bought the rights to a Philip Barry play to make which movie?

6 What was the Marx Brothers' first film for MGM?

7 Who played Mr Miniver in the Greer Garson Oscar winner?

8 Which film producer who died in 1997 co-produced "Chariots of Fire"?

9 Who played Bill Sikes when Alec Guinness was Fagin?

10 What was the first Western to win a Best Picture Oscar after a 60-year gap?

11 Who directed the first "Terminator" films?

12 Who choreographed "42nd Street"?

13 "Titanic" overtook which movie as the most costly ever made?

14 Which actor kidnapped Harrison Ford in "Air Force One"?

15 Which palace was used for Kenneth Branagh's "Hamlet"?

16 What is the name of Ralph Fiennes' character in "Schindler's List"?

17 Whose songs were on the soundtrack of "Philadelphia"?

18 Which 1950s film cost $4 million, twice the maximum of the time?

19 Which film begins with "No man's life can be encompassed in one telling"?

20 Which star of "The Exorcist" also used the name Edna Rae?

21 Which film has the quote, "It wasn't the airplanes. It was beauty killed the beast"?

22 Where were Butch Cassidy and Sundance finally tracked down?

23 What is the most famous TV role of actress Agnes Moorhead?

24 The composer of the only Oscar-nominated song from "Grease" was from which famous quartet?

25 John Mollo won an Oscar in "Star Wars" for what?

26 Who was the only woman to have top billing in "A Bridge Too Far"?

27 Who was originally sought for the role of Shears in "The Bridge on the River Kwai"?

28 Hattie McDaniel was the first black actress to win an Oscar, but for which role?

29 Which movie did "Titanic" overtake as a record UK earner?

30 The ex-GI is in Paris to learn what in "An American in Paris"?

Answers	**World Tour** *(see Quiz 83)*

1 Boliviano. 2 Hudson & East. 3 Beslan. 4 Brazil. 5 Bandar Seri Begawan. 6 Angola. 7 Macao. 8 Uruguay. 9 Khartoum. 10 Dzongkha. 11 Australia. 12 Brazil. 13 Algeria and Mauritania. 14 Namib desert. 15 Bogota. 16 Pennsylvania Station. 17 New Providence Island. 18 Wyoming. 19 Mount McKinley. 20 Eilat. 21 Edwin Lutyens. 22 Niger. 23 Nigeria. 24 Sri Lanka. 25 Indonesia. 26 Bujumbura. 27 Bloemfontein. 28 Maine. 29 Honduras. 30 Java.

1 Both Emma Bunton's dad and Robert Redford's dad worked as what?

2 London's Royal College of Music is in which regal-sounding road?

3 Which actress starred in "Thelma and Louise" and "Lorenzo's Oil"?

4 In which European country are the regions of Kitaa and Tunu?

5 Which Sale Sharks player fractured his left ankle playing for England in Nov. 2006?

6 What name is given to the Greek letter that is the equivalent of letter M?

7 Sophie Okonedo was Oscar-nominated for which film based on real life?

8 Who joined the European Union in 1995 with Finland and Sweden?

9 Which sea would you cross if you sailed from Corfu to Cephalonia?

10 Who has been married to Catherine Deneuve, Marie Helvin and Catherine Dyer?

11 Under which name did Aliaune Thiam top the single and album charts?

12 What was Celine Dion's first solo UK Top Ten hit?

13 Which US state is called the Bullion State?

14 What name did former Mayfair hairdresser Nigel Davies adopt in the 1960s ?

15 What colours appear with black and red on the Jordanian flag?

16 In which year did Dennis the Menace first appear in the Beano?

17 Which British army officer invented shells containing bullets to inflict more casualties?

18 Who was the longest-serving British PM?

19 What was Donovan's autobiography called?

20 What is the capital of Djibouti?

21 Which English seaside resort is associated with Count Dracula?

22 What was Donny Osmond's last UK No. 1?

23 Who wrote "Chicken Soup with Barley"?

24 Doraphobia is the fear of what?

25 What was the pirate Blackbeard's real name?

26 What is the name Blimp derived from in the character Colonel Blimp?

27 Which fund pays the Queen's private expenses as sovereign?

28 Martin Short played Franck Eggelhoffer in a 1990s remake of which movie?

29 Where was Captain James Cook killed in 1779?

30 Who composed the opera "Billy Budd"?

Answers	**Plant World** *(see Quiz 86)*

1 Ginkgo. 2 Oxalic. 3 Callus. 4 Cherokee leader. 5 It dissolves blood corpuscles. 6 Italy. 7 Rockies. 8 North & South Carolina. 9 Blue. 10 Ferns & mosses. 11 Pacific coast of North America. 12 Stalk. 13 African violet. 14 From insects. 15 It loses its green colour. 16 Matchbox bean. 17 Rose of Jericho. 18 Sloes. 19 Cactus. 20 Poppy. 21 General Sherman. 22 Lettuce. 23 On dung. 24 Sierra Nevada. 25 Belladonna. 26 Stalk. 27 By the sea. 28 Silver Fir. 29 Praslin & Curiense. 30 Giant waterlily.

1 How is the maidenhair tree also known?
2 Which acid makes rhubarb leaves poisonous?
3 What is a tissue which forms on a damaged plant surface called?
4 The Sequoia takes its name from what?
5 What makes the death cap mushroom so toxic?
6 Which European country produces more than half of Europe's rice?
7 Where would you find the home of the bristlecone pine?
8 The Venus flytrap is found naturally in which US states?
9 A meadow clary has flowers of what colour?
10 What sort of plants are cryptogams?
11 The world's tallest tree is native only to where?
12 If a leaf is sessile what is missing?
13 What is another name for the Saintpaulia?
14 How does a bladderwort receive its nourishment?
15 If a plant suffers from chlorosis what happens to it?
16 How is the entada known in Australia?
17 What is the only plant which can change its shape?
18 What is the fruit of the Blackthorn bush?
19 What type of plant is a saguaro?
20 To which family does the greater celandine belong?
21 The largest known giant redwood is named after whom?
22 How is the plant lactuca sativa better known?
23 If something is coprophilous where does it grow?
24 The tree sometimes known as Wellingtonia is native to which mountains?
25 Atropine is derived from which plant?
26 Which part of the flax plant is used to make linen?
27 If a plant is halophytic where does it grow?
28 Which tree is the tallest native to Europe?
29 On which two islands would you find the sea coconut?
30 Which plant has the largest leaves?

---

1 A sentence containing all the alphabet's letters is known as a what?
2 What is the international car index mark for a car from Singapore?
3 Who is the elder – Terry Wogan or Bill Wyman?
4 What was the most common surname of MPs after the 2005 general election?
5 In which decade did Fiji leave the Commonwealth?
6 Who wrote the novel "The Pathfinder"?
7 Columbus is the capital of which US state?
8 Who directed the 1991 film "The Silence of the Lambs"?
9 What was Duran Duran's first UK Top Ten hit?
10 Which post was held by William Gilbert at the courts of Elizabeth I and James I?
11 Which poet was awarded an Order of Merit in 1953, three years before his death?
12 Whose 2004 hit album "His Greatest Love Songs" came 37 years after his first hit?
13 Which river was explored by Scotsman Mungo Park?
14 Bill Robertie became the first person to win which World Championship twice?
15 Mogadishu is the capital of which country?
16 Where did the married Princess Elizabeth live before she came to the throne?
17 In music what does the expression "pesante" mean?
18 Who was the Greek goddess of victory?
19 On the first of which month is Canada Day celebrated?
20 What is the title of the head of the College of Arms?
21 In which movie did Hitchcock first appear in one of his cameo roles?
22 Which TV character drove a yellow car called Bessie?
23 In which country is the city of Douala?
24 Whose only UK Top Ten hit was "Jeans On"?
25 For which film did Geena Davis first win an Oscar?
26 In 1860 Willie Park became the first winner of which sporting trophy?
27 In 2005–06 Chelsea won their first nine Premiership games – who won their last nine?
28 What colour separates the black, red and green bands on the Kenyan flag?
29 What part of your body is initialised as the ANS?
30 Which artist painted "Dancer at the Bar" around 1900?

Answers	**Music Superstars** *(see Quiz 88)*

1 Tina Turner. 2 Tony Bennett. 3 Neil Diamond. 4 Girls! Girls! Girls! 5 Sorry Seems to be the Hardest Word. 6 When I Need You. 7 1960s. 8 Bohemian Rhapsody. 9 Bob Dylan. 10 Eleven. 11 Kate Bush. 12 Dancing Queen. 13 Turandot. 14 Barry, Robin & Maurice Gibb. 15 Let's Dance. 16 Jean Terrell. 17 Mark McGrath. 18 Madonna. 19 Epic. 20 1962. 21 Mick Jagger. 22 Roxy Music. 23 Rod Stewart. 24 Thunderclap Newman. 25 Celine Dion and Peabo Bryson. 26 Love Me for a Reason. 27 Zubin Mehta. 28 Hot Chocolate. 29 Blinded by the Light. 30 Rock On.

1 Which veteran singer's first No. 1 album was "Foreign Affair"?
2 Who included Bono, Paul McCartney and Sting on his 2006 album "Duets"?
3 Who wrote "I'm a Believer" for The Monkees?
4 From which film was Elvis Presley's 2005 hit "Return to Sender"?
5 What was Elton John's first solo hit on his own Rocket label?
6 Which Leo Sayer hit gave the Chrysalis label their first No. 1?
7 In which decade did Barbra Streisand first make the UK charts?
8 Which hit was the first to be No. 1 over two separate Christmases?
9 Which singer/songwriter penned the lines, "The carpet, too, is moving under you"?
10 How many consecutive UK No. 1 hits did the Beatles have?
11 Who duetted with Peter Gabriel on "Games without Frontiers"?
12 What was Abba's only No. 1 in the USA?
13 Which opera does Pavarotti's anthem "Nessun Dorma" come from?
14 Which of the Gibb brothers wrote their first UK No. 1 "Massachusetts"?
15 Which David Bowie hit was his fourth UK and second US No. 1 in 1983?
16 Who replaced Diana Ross when she left The Supremes?
17 Who was the first person to duet on a single with Shania Twain?
18 Stephen Bray and Patrick Leonard have both co-written No. 1s with which singer?
19 Michael Jackson's "Thriller" and "Bad" came out on which label?
20 When did Tony Bennett first record "I Left My Heart in San Francisco"?
21 Which group singer put out a solo album called "Primitive Cool"?
22 A John Lennon song gave which group their only UK No. 1?
23 Which singing superstar once had a trial for Brentford FC?
24 Pete Townshend's first No. 1 as a producer was for which group?
25 Who sang the theme song to the film "Beauty and the Beast"?
26 What was the final No. 1 by any of the Osmond family?
27 Who conducted the Three Tenors for their Italia 90 concert?
28 Who is the only group to appear in the charts in every year of the 1970s?
29 Which Springsteen song was a hit for Manfred Mann's Earth Band?
30 Which David Essex hit was the soundtrack for "That'll be the Day"?

---

1 Which US state is called the Gopher State?
2 From which musical is the song "June is Bustin' Out All Over"?
3 In which decade was Frankie Dettori born?
4 The French physician Laennec invented which medical aid?
5 Nelophobia is the fear of what?
6 Who wrote the novel "Death In The Afternoon"?
7 In which country is the city of Fortaleza?
8 Which ex-Russian spy was in the news with claims of poisoning in Nov. 2006?
9 Which tree appears on the Lebanese flag?
10 What's the English name of the constellation Dorado?
11 Whose only UK Top Ten hit was "The Final Countdown"?
12 Who is the most photographed person to attend Riddlesdown High school, Croydon?
13 In which country are the regions of Liguria and Calabria?
14 Which studio produced the series of "Scream" slasher horror movies?
15 The majority of tourists to the USA are from which country?
16 Who composed the opera "The Golden Cockerel"?
17 Who was the youngest performer last century to win an Oscar open to adults?
18 Which country has the ngultrum as a unit of currency?
19 Who is the elder – Ruby Wax or Victoria Wood?
20 How old was James Herriot when he began writing books?
21 Which King of Spain was known as Charles the Mad?
22 Who joined the European Union in the same year as Portugal?
23 What is the Swedish plattar?
24 Which media celeb founded a magazine called "Passing Wind"?
25 Dying in 2005, Renaldo "Obie" Benson was a former member of which singing group?
26 What was Earth, Wind and Fire's first UK Top Ten hit?
27 The wall, bar and frog are all part of a horse's what?
28 What is the capital of the Dominican Republic?
29 What is Julie Andrews' full real name?
30 In which decade was the first Archery World Championship?

Answers	TV Times 4 *(see Quiz 90)*

1 Colin Firth. 2 AA. 3 Robert Lindsay. 4 Boyzone. 5 Nero. 6 Eric Idle. 7 British Rail. 8 Woodburn & MacKenzie. 9 Bella. 10 TISWAS. 11 Cedric Charlton. 12 Cricket St Thomas. 13 No one, he was never seen. 14 A moose. 15 Play Your Cards Right. 16 Letitia Dean. 17 The Winchester. 18 Michael Cole. 19 Alan Alda. 20 World's biggest one-man band. 21 Fleur. 22 Russell T. Davies. 23 Charlie Gimbert. 24 Seymour Utterthwaite. 25 Bullying. 26 Crimewatch UK. 27 Rathouse International. 28 It Ain't Half Hot Mum. 29 Purple. 30 Glenbogle.

1 Who played John McCarthy in "Hostages"?
2 Which emergency service did Anthea Turner work for before her media career?
3 Who played the scheming city council chief in "GBH"?
4 Whom did Andrew Lloyd Webber appear on "Top of the Pops" with in 1998?
5 What was the caterpillar called in "Dangermouse"?
6 Who founded Rutland Weekend Television?
7 Which company did Colin work for in "Colin's Sandwich"?
8 What are the surnames of Kim & Aggie in "How Clean is Your House?"?
9 In alphabetical order, who is the first of "The Tweenies"?
10 Which show had a punk dog called Spit?
11 In "The Darling Buds of May" what was Charley's real name?
12 "To the Manor Born" was set in which village?
13 Who played Joe Maplin in "Hi De Hi!"?
14 What strolled across the opening title in "Northern Exposure"?
15 How was the US series "Card Sharks" known when it transferred to the UK?
16 Who played Lucinda in "Grange Hill"?
17 What was the name of the pub in "Minder"?
18 Who left the employ of Mohammed Fayed to host a daytime chat show on satellite TV?
19 Who hosted "That was the Week that was" in the US?
20 What record did Roy Castle break on the very first "Record Breakers"?
21 What was Zoe and Alec's baby called in "May to December"?
22 Who wrote the "Doctor Who" spin-off which starred John Barrowman?
23 In "Lovejoy" who bough Felsham Manor after Lady Jane left?
24 Who replaced Foggy Dewhurst when Michael Aldridge joined the "Last of the Summer Wine" cast?
25 "See Something, Say Something" was a Nickleodeon feature about what?
26 Which series was based on Germany's "File XY Unsolved"?
27 Which company did Terence "Twiggy" Rathbone own in "Hot Metal"?
28 In which series were jungle sequences shot in Norfolk and desert scenes in Sussex?
29 What colour hair did Crystal Tipps have?
30 In which fictional place did Hector and Molly live?

| **Answers** | **Pot Luck 42** *(see Quiz 89)* |

1 Minnesota. 2 Carousel. 3 1970s. 4 Stethoscope. 5 Glass. 6 Ernest Hemingway. 7 Brazil. 8 Alexander Litvinenko. 9 Cedar tree. 10 Swordfish. 11 Europe. 12 Kate Moss. 13 Italy. 14 Dimension Films. 15 Canada. 16 Rimsky-Korsakov. 17 Tatum O'Neal. 18 Bhutan. 19 Ruby Wax. 20 50 years old. 21 Charles II. 22 Spain. 23 Pancake. 24 Ian Hislop. 25 The Four Tops. 26 September. 27 Hoof. 28 Santo Domingo. 29 Julia Elizabeth Wells. 30 1930s.

1 In which country is the city of Ibadan?
2 What do the initials for the chemical DDT stand for?
3 Who directed the film trilogy "Lethal Weapon"?
4 Arthur Scargill and the Duchess of York were removed from where in 1996?
5 What was Pigmeat Markham's only UK Top Ten hit?
6 What is the main language of the Republic of Chad?
7 Douroucouli, de Brazza's guenon and red colobus are types of what?
8 Which artist painted Black Paintings in the 1820s?
9 Who invented the word "frabjous"?
10 Salem is the capital of which US state?
11 What is Robson Green's middle name?
12 How old was Anna Paquin when she won her first Oscar?
13 Windhoek is the capital of which country?
14 A fear of fear is known as what?
15 What invaded the town of San Antonio de los Caballeros in June '98?
16 What was Rod Stewart's last UK No. 1?
17 Who was the Roman goddess of horses?
18 What does the green pentacle on the Moroccan flag depict?
19 What is the international car index mark for a car from Burundi?
20 What did the M stand for in JMW Turner's name?
21 Mrs Thatcher became Baroness Thatcher of where?
22 What is the drug thiopental used for?
23 Desmond Tutu's middle name is Mpilo, which means what?
24 Bernard Herrmann finished the score to which Scorsese film just before he died?
25 Who had an 80s hit with "She Means Nothing to Me"?
26 Beatriz Merino became PM of which South American country in this century?
27 In 1998 Tommy Dixon was arrested at home after what was mistaken for a gunshot?
28 In which city is the 305 metre long cable-braced Erskine bridge?
29 The spice sassafras is made from which part of a plant?
30 Who became Trade & Industry Secretary in 2006?

| **Answers** | Performing Arts *(see Quiz 92)* |

1 French & English. 2 Arlene Phillips. 3 English National Ballet. 4 A cappella. 5 Cell Mates. 6 Vanessa Mae. 7 Louis B. Mayer. 8 John Ogdon. 9 Rowan Atkinson. 10 Quintet du Hot Club de France. 11 Dash. 12 Mississippi. 13 Placido Domingo. 14 Phil Collins. 15 Popcorn. 16 Shostakovich. 17 Laurence Olivier. 18 Bournemouth Sinfonietta. 19 Tony Richardson. 20 Jerome Robbins. 21 Alan Ayckbourn. 22 The Who. 23 Jim Steinman. 24 Ronnie Barker. 25 Angela Gheorghiu and Roberto Alagna. 26 Hello Dolly. 27 Arpeggio. 28 Leslie Bricusse. 29 South Pacific. 30 Sir Peter Hall.

1 In which languages did Irishman Samuel Beckett write his plays?
2 Who choreographed the 2006 revival of "The Sound of Music"?
3 Princess Diana was patron of which ballet company?
4 Which type of singing means "in the style of the chapel"?
5 Which play did Stephen Fry walk out of in 1995?
6 Who went on a Red Hot world tour in 1996?
7 Who founded the American Academy of Motion Picture Arts and Sciences?
8 Who won the 1962 Tchaikovsky competition with Ashkenazy?
9 Who, in 1981, became the youngest star of a West End one-man show?
10 Grappelli and Reinhardt were leaders of which Quintet?
11 What was the name of Wayne Sleep's 1980 dance company?
12 Tennessee Williams was born in which US state?
13 Which opera singer sang with Sarah Brightman in "Requiem"?
14 Who played the Artful Dodger in the first stage production of "Oliver!"?
15 Which Ben Elton novel was the first to be adapted into a West End play?
16 2006's Last Night of the Proms had a Russian flavour for whose centenary?
17 Who shared management of the Old Vic between 1944 and 1950 with Ralph Richardson?
18 With which orchestra did Simon Rattle make his professional debut?
19 Who established the English Stage Company with George Devine at the Royal Court in 1955?
20 Who choreographed "West Side Story" and "Fiddler on the Roof"?
21 Who was in the Guinness Book of Records for having five plays running in the West End at one time?
22 Whose mini opera "Wire & Glass" was premièred at the 2006 Electric Prom?
23 Who wrote the lyrics for Lloyd Webber's "Whistle Down the Wind"?
24 Who wrote the radio drama "Mum" for his actress daughter Charlotte?
25 Which husband-and-wife team were in London's 2006 Proms in the Park Last Night?
26 Thornton Wilder's "The Matchmaker" was made into which musical?
27 Which musical term means "like a harp"?
28 Who wrote the songs for "Doctor Dolittle"?
29 Sean Connery's first West End appearance was in which chorus line?
30 Who founded the RSC aged 30?

1 In which Hawaiian island is Pearl Harbor?
2 What was Cliff Richard's first 1980s No. 1?
3 JF Kennedy was one of how many children?
4 Under what name did Helen Porter Mitchell sing her way to success?
5 What was John Schlesinger's first US film?
6 In which month is the US holiday President's Day?
7 In which European country are the areas of Telemark and Troms?
8 Joe Fagin's 1980s hit was a theme tune for which TV series?
9 Which country has the pula as a unit of currency?
10 What is the correct form of address to begin a letter to an Earl?
11 Which US state is called the Bay State?
12 Who were Jessica, Kelli, Kevin, Michelle and Tony collectively?
13 Hypegiaphobia is the fear of what?
14 Whom did Joe Louis beat to first become world heavyweight champ?
15 What was Eva Braun working as when she met Adolf Hitler?
16 Adrian Vowels was the first Man of Steel winner from which rugby club?
17 Which Battle was the last in the Hundred Years War?
18 Who joined the European Union in the same year as UK and Denmark?
19 Who composed the opera "Punch and Judy"?
20 What was American hero Paul Revere's day job?
21 Who founded the Pakistan People's Party?
22 In which country is the city of Guayaquil?
23 What was the name of the Queen's first corgi?
24 Who played Sally Bowles in the 1955 film "I am a Camera"?
25 Which rock star had a major stake in the production company that made "Enigma"?
26 Kurt Weill and Henrik Ibsen were born in which month?
27 Who was the first Austrian to top the UK charts?
28 In which well-known building did the late George Best spend Xmas in 1984?
29 Which Frank L. Baum story provided the inspiration for a 2006 new musical?
30 To five either way, how many weeks did Sinatra's "My Way" spend in the UK charts between 1969 and 1971?

Answers	Tennis *(see Quiz 94)*

1 Borotra, Brugnon, Cochet & Lacoste. **2** Vijay Amritraj. **3** Martina Navratilova. **4** Arthur Ashe. **5** Gabriela Sabatini. **6** Pete Sampras. **7** French Open. **8** Margaret Smith. **9** Plus an Olympic gold medal. **10** Karen Hantze. **11** 1968. **12** Michael Stich. **13** Richard Krajicek. **14** Andy Roddick. **15** Justine Henin Ardenne. **16** Russia. **17** The Queen. **18** Men's doubles. **19** French. **20** French Open. **21** Michael Stich. **22** Lindsay Davenport. **23** Kevin Curren. **24** Tony Pickard. **25** Stefan Edberg. **26** Tim Gullikson. **27** Roger Taylor. **28** Kosice, Slovakia. **29** Sue Barker. **30** Sukova.

1 Who were tennis's "Four Musketeers"?
2 Which tennis player appeared in "Octopussy"?
3 Who had the car number plate X CZECH?
4 Who won the first US Men's Open?
5 Who, in 1986, became the youngest woman semi-finalist at Wimbledon for 99 years?
6 Who won the inaugural Grand Slam Cup in Munich in 1990?
7 What was Monica Seles's first Grand Slam title?
8 Who was the first Australian woman to win the Wimbledon Singles?
9 How does a Golden Grand Slam differ from a Grand Slam?
10 With whom did Billie Jean Moffitt win her first Wimbledon Doubles title?
11 What year was the world's first Open tournament?
12 Who was the first German to win the Wimbledon Men's Singles after reunification?
13 At Wimbledon who won an unseeded men's final in the 90s?
14 Whom did Roger Federer beat to win his third US Open?
15 In 2005, who won the women's German Open for the third time?
16 Who were the winners of the 2006 Davis Cup?
17 Who gave Virginia Wade her trophy when she won Wimbledon?
18 Which new competition was included in the Wimbledon championships in 1884 along with the Women's Singles?
19 Which Grand Slam title has Boris Becker never won?
20 Which Grand Slam title did Roger Federer not win in 2006?
21 In 1992 John McEnroe won the Wimbledon Doubles title with whom?
22 Who replaced Martina Hingis as World No. 1 in October 1998?
23 Whom did Boris Becker beat to become Wimbledon's youngest Men's Singles winner?
24 Whom did Greg Rusedski sack as his coach during Wimbledon 1998?
25 Who won his first Open title in 1985 two years after winning the Junior Grand Slam?
26 Which mentor of Pete Sampras died in May 1996?
27 Who was the last British man before Tim Henman to reach a Wimbledon quarter-final?
28 Where was Martina Hingis born?
29 How is Wimbledon semi-finalist Mrs Lampard better known?
30 Which Helena won two titles in one day at Wimbledon 1996?

Answers	**Pot Luck 44** *(see Quiz 93)*

1 Oahu. 2 Mistletoe and Wine. 3 Nine. 4 Nellie Melba. 5 Midnight Cowboy. 6 February. 7 Norway. 8 Auf Wiedersehen, Pet. 9 Botswana. 10 My Lord. 11 Massachusetts. 12 Liberty X. 13 Responsibility. 14 James Braddock. 15 Photographer's assistant. 16 Castleford. 17 Castillon. 18 Republic of Ireland. 19 Harrison Birtwistle. 20 Silversmith. 21 Zulfikar Ali Bhutto. 22 Ecuador. 23 Susan. 24 Julie Harris. 25 Mick Jagger. 26 March. 27 Falco (Rock Me Amadeus). 28 Pentonville Prison. 29 The Wizard of Oz (Wicked!). 30 122.

1 What was the christian name of chocolate founder Mr Cadbury?
2 In which country is the city of Gwangju?
3 Bill Perks the son of a bricklayer became known as who?
4 What does the Latin mea culpa mean?
5 Which creature is represented in the year the Chinese call "long"?
6 Which country has the rufiyaa as a unit of currency?
7 2000 saw the first "X-Men" film – which decade saw the comic characters first appear?
8 What was Enrique Iglesias's first US No. 1 single?
9 What was Foreigner's first UK Top Ten hit in 1981?
10 Who is the elder – Bob Geldof or Nigel Kennedy?
11 Which Hitchock film title ties in with his father's field of work?
12 Who first appeared for England – Joe Cole or Owen Hargreaves?
13 Whose nickname was "Stormin' Norman"?
14 Who directed the 1987 film "Good Morning Vietnam"?
15 Columbia is the capital of which US state?
16 What is a honey locust?
17 Born Marie Grosholtz, under what name is this French lady remembered?
18 What could be signed by Hardy Bros of Ainwick or Charles Forlan?
19 Which saints share their names with three of the five inhabited Scilly Isles?
20 Maputo is the capital of which country?
21 What does the medical term D & C stand for?
22 Who played Marsellus Wallace in "Pulp Fiction"?
23 Which artist painted "Toledo Landscape" around 1610?
24 How is the letter O formed in Morse Code?
25 How many square chains make one hectare in surveying?
26 In which county was Sir Humphry Davy, inventor of the miner's safety lamp, born?
27 What did Terry Wogan study at Belvedere College, Dublin?
28 Who was the Greek god of vegetation and rebirth?
29 Which seasonal rose is from the genus Helleborus?
30 What is the international car index mark for a car from Lebanon?

Answers | Famous Names *(see Quiz 96)*

1 39. 2 Joan Plowright. 3 Antony Worrall Thompson. 4 George Michael. 5 Helen Mirren. 6 Vic Reeves. 7 His hair was too long. 8 Duchess of Kent. 9 Mountbatten's. 10 Bernard Ingham. 11 David Hasselhoff. 12 Catherine Walker. 13 Marco Pierre White. 14 Malcolm McLaren. 15 Jane and Jonathan Ross. 16 Anne-Sophie Mutter. 17 Samira Khashoggi. 18 Duke of Westminster. 19 Ryan Giggs. 20 Michael Grade. 21 Sir Peregrine Worsthorne. 22 Gary & Michelle Lineker. 23 Sean Bean. 24 Soft drinks. 25 Chloe. 26 First cousin. 27 Her favourite restaurant. 28 Ralph Fiennes. 29 Swansea. 30 Alexander McQueen.

Quiz 96 | Famous Names

Answers – page 569

1 How old was David Cameron when he was elected Tory leader?
2 Who was Sue Lawley's final guest on "Desert Island Discs"?
3 Which celeb chef appeared in "Adrian Mole: The Cappuccino Years" and "Footballers' Wives"?
4 Who is known to his family as "Yog"?
5 Who became Mrs Taylor Hackford in 1997?
6 Who changed his name from Jim Moir so it didn't clash with the BBC's Head of Light Entertainment?
7 Why was Cliff Richard banned from entering Singapore in 1972?
8 How is the former Miss Katharine Worsley better known?
9 In whose family home did Charles and Diana spend the first night of their honeymoon?
10 Who was Margaret Thatcher's Press Secretary when she resigned?
11 Which "Baywatch" star's autobiography was called "Making Waves"?
12 Who founded the Chelsea Design Company in 1976?
13 Which Leeds-born chef won three Michelin stars by his early thirties?
14 Who opened the punk boutique Seditionaries in the 70s with Vivienne Westwood?
15 Who have children called Betty Kitten, Harvey Kirby and Honey Kinny?
16 Who was André Previn's fifth wife?
17 Who was Mohammed Fayed's first wife and Dodi Fayed's mother?
18 Who is London's largest landowner?
19 Who is the son of former rugby league international Danny Wilson?
20 Who was raised by his grandmother Olga Winogradsky?
21 Which former editor is Lady Lucinda Lambton's third husband?
22 Who are the parents of George, Harry, Tobias and Angus?
23 Who has "100% Blades" tattooed on his left arm?
24 William Hague's father's business produced what?
25 In 1998 Stella McCartney designed for which fashion house?
26 What relation is Natasha Richardson to Jemma Redgrave?
27 After who or what did Lady Helen Taylor (née Windsor) name her first son?
28 Which Hamlet ran off with his mother Gertrude in 1995?
29 Where was Michael Heseltine born?
30 Who succeeded John Galliano at Givenchy in 1996?

| **Answers** | **Pot Luck 45** *(see Quiz 95)* |

1 John. 2 South Korea. 3 Bill Wyman (Rolling Stones). 4 Through my fault. 5 Dragon. 6 Maldives. 7 1960s. 8 Bailamos. 9 Waiting for a Girl Like You. 10 Bob Geldof. 11 The Birds (Dad a poultry trader). 12 Joe Cole. 13 US General Norman Schwarzkopf. 14 Barry Levinson. 15 South Carolina. 16 A tree. 17 Madame Tussaud. 18 Fishing reel. 19 Agnes, Mary & Martin. 20 Mozambique. 21 Dilation and Curettage. 22 Ving Rhames. 23 El Greco. 24 Dash, dash, dash. 25 Ten. 26 Cornwall. 27 Philosophy. 28 Adonis. 29 Christmas Rose. 30 RL.

1 Which occupation was shared by the fathers of Roger Moore and Burt Reynolds?

2 What are the two colours of the national flag of Pakistan?

3 Who was the elder – Liam Gallagher or Ryan Giggs?

4 What was Gerald Ford's middle name?

5 What was the profession of escapologist Harry Houdini's father?

6 Over 700 people died in Greece in July 1987 due to what?

7 Who composed the opera "The Rape of Lucretia"?

8 Ian Thorpe announced his retirement from swimming at what age?

9 Which gallery is located at Bankside, London SE1 9TG?

10 Who was the "Big Brother" winner following Craig Phillips?

11 Which prince was born in the year Ted Hughes became Poet Laureate?

12 If a wine is said to be flabby what does it lack?

13 What is the capital of Greenland?

14 In music, what does the expression "strepitoso" mean?

15 For a role in which film did Vanessa Redgrave shave her head?

16 Which country has the lev as a unit of currency?

17 For what offence did Sophia Loren spend 17 days in prison in 1982?

18 In which decade was Richard Branson born?

19 In which European country are the regions of Beja and Guarda?

20 Which playwright was born in Whiston on Merseyside in 1947?

21 Which American state is called the Hawkeye State?

22 Which vitamin is also known as biotin?

23 Which singer played a bouncer in "Wayne's World"?

24 In this millennium, who first won the University Boat Race in successive years?

25 Who played Ron Jenkins in "Coronation Street"?

26 "Lost Souls" was the first chart album for which act?

27 Which hit got to No. 2 simultaneously in November 1995 with two separate groups?

28 On TV, James Bolam's Arthur and Michael French's Tom came from which town?

29 Who in Gilbert and Sullivan is "a dealer in magic and spells"?

30 Alphabetically, what is the first English parliamentary constituency?

Answers	**Screen Greats** *(see Quiz 98)*

1 None. 2 Betty Grable. 3 Peter Lorre. 4 Goldfinger. 5 Errol Flynn. 6 20th Century-Fox. 7 Charles Bronson. 8 Tony Curtis. 9 Barbara Stanwyck's. 10 Bela Lugosi. 11 Gene Kelly. 12 Audrey Hepburn. 13 Marlon Brando. 14 Ingrid Bergman. 15 Rita Hayworth. 16 Rebecca. 17 Sophia Loren. 18 One Night in the Tropics. 19 Dustin Hoffman. 20 George C. Scott. 21 Julie Andrews. 22 Lola-Lola. 23 His wife Carole Lombard. 24 Ginger Rogers. 25 Charlotte Brontë. 26 Twenty. 27 Anchors Aweigh. 28 The Big Broadcast. 29 The Barkleys of Broadway. 30 Making a Living.

1 What is the total number of Oscars won by Errol Flynn, Peter Cushing and Richard Burton?

2 Who once had her name changed to Frances Dean by Goldwyn?

3 Who is mentioned by name in Al Stewart's song "The Year of the Cat"?

4 Which Bond film did Sean Connery make prior to Hitchcock's "Marnie"?

5 Eric Porter played Soames on TV but who played Soames in "That Forsyte Woman"?

6 Which was the first US studio Richard Burton worked for?

7 Who was known in Italy as "Il Brutto"?

8 Who changed Bernie for Tony in his first film "Criss Cross"?

9 Bette Midler re-created whose 1930s role in "Stella"?

10 Which screen great did Martin Landau play in "Ed Wood"?

11 Who was lent to Columbia by MGM for "Cover Girl"?

12 Sean Ferrer was the son of which Hollywood Oscar winner?

13 Whose first Oscar was for playing Terry Malloy in a 1950s classic?

14 Who was the mother of actress Isabella Rossellini?

15 Whose pin-up was pinned to the atomic bomb dropped on Bikini?

16 What was Hitchcock's first Hollywood film?

17 Who was the first performer to win an Oscar for a performance entirely in a foreign language?

18 What was Abbot and Costello's first feature film?

19 Who played Sean Connery's son in "Family Business"?

20 Who was the first actor ever to refuse an Oscar?

21 Who was the first British-born British actress of British parents to win an Oscar?

22 What was the name of Marlene Dietrich in "The Blue Angel"?

23 Whose death in 1942 spurred Clark Gable to join the US Air Corps?

24 Whose first film was "Campus Sweethearts" with Rudy Vallee?

25 Which author did Olivia de Havilland play in "Devotion"?

26 How old was Debbie Reynolds when she made "Singin' in the Rain"?

27 What was the first film which teamed Gene Kelly with Frank Sinatra?

28 In which film did Bob Hope find his theme tune?

29 In which 1949 film were Rogers and Astaire reunited after a 10-year break?

30 In which film did Chaplin make his screen debut, in 1914?

Answers | **Pot Luck 46** *(see Quiz 97)*

1 Police officers. 2 White and green. 3 Liam Gallagher. 4 Rudolph. 5 A Rabbi. 6 Heatwave. 7 Benjamin Britten. 8 24. 9 Tate Modern. 10 Brian Dowling. 11 Prince Harry. 12 Acidity. 13 Godthab. 14 Noisy, boisterous. 15 Playing for Time. 16 Bulgaria. 17 Tax evasion. 18 1950s. 19 Portugal. 20 Willy Russell. 21 Iowa. 22 B6. 23 Meat Loaf. 24 Oxford. 25 Ben Kingsley. 26 Doves. 27 Wonderwall. 28 Ormston (Born & Bred). 29 John Wellington Wells (The Sorcerer). 30 Aldershot.

1 Who was the first post-war German Chancellor to have been brought up in the former DDR?

2 The Isle of Man belonged to which two countries before it came under UK administration in 1765?

3 What name meaning "achievement of universal peace" is given to the reign of Emperor Akihito?

4 How did the former Princess Alix of of Hessen meet her death?

5 Who did not seek re-election as Austrian President in 1991 after revelations about his activities in WWII?

6 Who was the first President of Israel?

7 How many days after Waterloo did Napoleon resign?

8 Which governor of Sumatra was responsible for the founding of Singapore?

9 What did the Rarotonga Treaty secure in 1987?

10 What does Rasputin mean, as a name given to Grigory Efimovich?

11 Where were all but six French kings crowned?

12 Which country had a secret police force called the securitate which was replaced in 1990?

13 Which President Roosevelt was Republican?

14 What name was given to the incorporation of Austria into the Third Reich?

15 What did Haile Selassie's title Ras Tafari mean?

16 Who was Nazi minister of eastern occupied territories from 1941–44?

17 Who was secretary of state to Kennedy and Johnson?

18 Which French Prime Minister asked Anthony Eden to have the Queen as head of state?

19 In which country was the Rosetta Stone found in in 1799?

20 What name was given to the socialist movement which carried out the Nicaraguan Revolution?

21 Which Conference drew up the United Nations Charter?

22 How many German Popes were there before Benedict XVI?

23 In which year did Baroness Elliott become the first woman to address the House of Lords?

24 Who succeeded Ian Smith as Prime Minister of Rhodesia which then became known as Zimbabwe?

25 Where was the first Marxist state in Africa created?

26 Where was the Maoist guerrilla group Sendero Luminoso active in the 1980s?

27 Who became New Zealand PM in December 1997?

28 Who was joint secretary general of the ANC with Mandela in 1964?

29 Who were the first three states to break away from Yugoslavia in 1991?

30 Where did the Hundred Flowers Movement encourage government criticism in the 50s?

Answers	Pot Luck 47 *(see Quiz 100)*

1 U2. 2 Brighton & Hove Albion. 3 South Dakota. 4 Joan Crawford. 5 Edward Heath. 6 Boa snakes. 7 Rosemary Conley. 8 Anita Lonsborough. 9 She fell down a flight of stairs. 10 Ouranophobia. 11 Ben E. King. 12 MC. 13 Henri Matisse. 14 Ronnie Barker. 15 Myalgic Encephalitis. 16 Eltham. 17 Steven Spielberg. 18 Mali. 19 Hugh Grant. 20 Catherine Zeta Jones. 21 Delia Smith. 22 Sunderland. 23 Mauritania. 24 Samuel. 25 Balamory. 26 Lewis Carroll. 27 Taiwan. 28 American. 29 Winifred Holtby. 30 2,197.

1 Some England cricketers went to which band's 2006 Sydney concert?
2 Which football team does Des Lynam support?
3 Pierre is the capital of which American State?
4 Which actress was also known as Lucille Le Sueur?
5 Which ex-PM died on 17 July 2005?
6 Which reptiles come from the family Boidae?
7 Who produced a fitness video called "Ultimate Fat Burner"?
8 Who was the first female winner of the BBC Sports Personality of the Year?
9 How did fashion empress Laura Ashley die?
10 A fear of heaven is known as what?
11 Which singer's real name is Benjamin Earl Nelson?
12 What is the international car index mark for a car from Monaco?
13 Which artist painted "La Desserte" in 1908?
14 Who presented David Jason with his BAFTA Fellowship?
15 What is the full name for the medical condition known as ME?
16 Where in the UK did Bob Hope have a theatre named after him?
17 Who directed the 1992 film "Hook"?
18 Bamako is the capital of which country?
19 Who links the movies "Extreme Measures" and "The Remains of the Day"?
20 Who duetted with David Essex on "True Love Ways" in 1994?
21 Whose first book was "How to Cheat at Cooking"?
22 David Bellion joined Man Utd from which club?
23 Which country has the ouguiya as a unit of currency?
24 What was the christian name of shipowner Cunard?
25 In which town was Edie McCredie the minibus driver?
26 Which children's author appeared on the cover of "Sgt Pepper"?
27 In which country is the city of Kaohsiung?
28 What is the nationality of writer and chef Ken Hom?
29 "Testament of Friendship" is about Vera Brittain's friendship with which author?
30 What is 13 cubed?

Answers	**World History** *(see Quiz 99)*

1 Angela Merkel. 2 Norway & Scotland. 3 Heisei. 4 Shot with her husband Tsar Nicholas II. 5 Kurt Waldheim. 6 Chaim Weizmann. 7 Four. 8 Thomas Stanford Raffles. 9 Nuclear-free South Pacific. 10 Dissolute. 11 Reims. 12 Romania. 13 Theodore. 14 Anschluss. 15 Lion of Judah. 16 Alfred Rosenberg. 17 Dean Rusk. 18 Guy Mollet. 19 Egypt. 20 Sandanista. 21 San Francisco. 22 Seven. 23 1958. 24 Bishop Abel Muzorewa. 25 Mozambique. 26 Peru. 27 Jenny Shipley. 28 Walter Sisulu. 29 Slovenia, Macedonia & Croatia. 30 China.

1 Who starred with Steve Coogan on "The Dead Good Show"?

2 Who was the real-life husband of the first girl in the famous Nescafe commercials?

3 How was comedy writer Gerald Wiley better known?

4 Who found fame with Emma Thompson playing Danny McGlone?

5 Who starred in and produced a mini-series called "Sins"?

6 Who was a regular in "Crown Court" as barrister Jeremy Parsons QC?

7 Who is the mother of the actor who played Mr Rochester in the 2006 "Jane Eyre"?

8 What was presenter Matthew Wright's job before moving to TV in 2000?

9 Whose first pop TV series was called "The Power Station"?

10 Which Moll Flanders lost husband Ralph to Francesca Annis?

11 Who was the first male presenter of "Live & Kicking"?

12 What was Lenny Henry's Rastafarian community police officer called?

13 Who came to fame as "Q" of "The Little Ladies"?

14 Who was Cherie Lunghi's character in "The Manageress"?

15 Who played Fletch's son Raymond in "Going Straight"?

16 Which Andy was the 32nd presenter of "Blue Peter"?

17 Who are the two youngest McGann brothers?

18 Who was the first female presenter of "Top Gear"?

19 Who wrote the "Magic Roundabout" scripts when they were first broadcast in the UK?

20 Which actresses created "The House of Eliot"?

21 Who appeared in "Dixon of Dock Green" aged 10 and found fame as Mrs Theodopolopoudos?

22 Who introduced a famine report with the words, "A biblical famine, now in the twentieth century"?

23 Which "EastEnders" star used to be better known by his catchphrase "Terr-i-fic"?

24 Who played Marjory in "The Outside Dog" in the "Talking Heads" series?

25 Who won "New Faces" and went on to present it?

26 Who is the real-life mum of Grace and Henry Durham?

27 Still popular, who broke into TV with the 1986 series "Pet Watch"?

28 Who adapted his novel of the same name into "Men Behaving Badly"?

29 Who played the seventh Doctor Who?

30 Who was the only female presenter at the Live Aid concert?

Answers	Pot Luck 48 *(see Quiz 102)*

1 Betty Joan Perske. 2 Margaret Thatcher. 3 Tennyson. 4 Jeweller. 5 Spice Up Your Life. 6 Scilly Isles. 7 RM. 8 Iran. 9 Oops Up Side Your Head. 10 Conakry. 11 Karpov. 12 Oriental rug. 13 Liberator. 14 Bolivia & Peru v. Chile. 15 Little Sioux River. 16 Children. 17 Conservatives. 18 Michael Ramsey. 19 Brighton. 20 Jane Seymour. 21 Trans-Canada Highway. 22 Kris Kristofferson & Rita Coolidge. 23 Complete works of Shakespeare. 24 Maine. 25 Phil Collins. 26 Myanmar. 27 Sir Edward Heath. 28 Gannex. 29 Romania. 30 2nd (2001–02).

1 What is Lauren Bacall's full real name?
2 About whom did Cliff Richard say, "She really is a woman just like my Mum"?
3 Who wrote the poem "The Idylls of the King"?
4 What was the profession of fizzy drinks maker Jacob Schweppes?
5 What was the fifth No. 1 single for the fab five Spice Girls?
6 Saint Mary's airport serves which Isles?
7 What is the international car index mark for a car from Madagascar?
8 Which country did Hollywood director Barbet Schroeder come from?
9 What was the Gap Band's first UK Top Ten hit?
10 What is the capital of Guinea?
11 Whom did Kasparov beat to become world chess champion in 1985?
12 What is a kelim?
13 What was the by-name for the B24 bomber?
14 Which countries fought the Pacific War in the 19th century?
15 On which river does the US city of Cherokee lie?
16 What or who does UNICEF benefit?
17 Which political party did Mrs Pankhurst join in 1925?
18 Who was the first Archbishop of Canterbury to meet a Pope since the 16th century?
19 The first Bodyshop opened in which town?
20 Who was Elizabeth I's first stepmother?
21 What runs for 4,860 miles from St John's to Victoria?
22 Which husband-and-wife team had a hit with "A Song I'd Like to Sing"?
23 What was the first text to be 'bowdlerised' by Thomas Bowdler?
24 Which American state is called the Pine Tree State?
25 Who is taller – Mick Jagger or Phil Collins?
26 Which country has the kyat as a unit of currency?
27 Who according to Denis Healey, "represented the sensible wing of the Tory party"?
28 What make of raincoat did Harold Wilson popularise?
29 In which European country are the counties of Arad, Arges and Cluj?
30 What was the highest Premiership position of Gerard Houllier's Liverpool?

Answers | Who's Who *(see Quiz 101)*

1 Caroline Aherne. 2 Trevor Eve. 3 Ronnie Barker. 4 Robbie Coltrane. 5 Joan Collins. 6 Richard Wilson. 7 Maggie Smith. 8 TV editor of The Sun. 9 Chris Evans. 10 Alex Kingston. 11 Andi Peters. 12 PC Ganja. 13 Rula Lenska. 14 Gabriella Benson. 15 Nicholas Lyndhurst. 16 Akinwolere. 17 Mark & Stephen. 18 Angela Rippon. 19 Eric Thompson. 20 Jean Marsh & Eileen Atkins. 21 Pauline Quirke. 22 Michael Buerk (Ethiopia). 23 Mike Reid. 24 Julie Walters. 25 Marti Caine. 26 Victoria Wood. 27 Dale Winton. 28 Simon Nye. 29 Sylvester McCoy. 30 Janice Long.

1 What was Bob Geldof's TV production company called?
2 When were downloads added to physical sales in the UK singles chart?
3 Who led the protest about Murdoch's buying of ITV shares in Nov. 2006?
4 What was the first INR radio station?
5 Kelly's Directories catalogue what?
6 Which female Russian journalist was murdered in a high-profile case in 2006?
7 What was the first magazine in the UK in 1691?
8 In which magazine did the Addams Family first appear?
9 Which American syndicated a newspaper column called "My Day"?
10 Who founded the Daily Mail?
11 Where is the newspaper ABC from?
12 Which two UK national newspapers were founded in 1990?
13 Apart from the Tribune, which other US newspaper has Chicago in its name?
14 Which press agency has the abbreviation IRNA?
15 Which newspaper proprietor was born Jan Ludvik Hoch?
16 In 1989 Richard Murdoch bought a 50% stake in which Hungarian tabloid?
17 Which Sunday Times editor made headline news himself regarding details of his affair with Pamella Bordes?
18 Lloyd Grossman was restaurant critic of which magazine in the 1980s?
19 Who took over The Observer in 1981?
20 Apart from the Guardian, which other newspaper did James Naughtie work for before joining the BBC?
21 What type of correspondent for the BBC was Michael Cole before he went to work for Mohammed Fayed?
22 Who was chairman of Saatchi & Saatchi when they took over the Tory Party account?
23 Which agency did the Saatchi brothers found in 1995?
24 Which famous columnist is married to Lady Camilla Harris?
25 Whose affair with David Mellor brought media man Max Clifford into the public gaze?
26 Which media man's sons all have the middle name Paradine?
27 Which track became the first to achieve one million paid downloads in the US?
28 Which co-founder of TV am was married to a future Leader of the House of Lords?
29 What was Ted Turner's family business before he turned to TV?
30 Which media magnate has owned AC Milan and been his country's PM?

Answers	**Pot Luck 49** *(see Quiz 104)*

1 Blue and white. 2 Maldives. 3 20th. 4 BDS. 5 Rob Reiner. 6 82,000. 7 Paradise. 8 Paramount Studios. 9 Angola. 10 Mona Lisa. 11 Rwanda. 12 Mongolia. 13 Aug. 4, 2005. 14 Prince Edward Island. 15 Jacopo Robusti. 16 Dunfermline Athletic. 17 Arabian Sea. 18 Sierra Leone & Liberia. 19 Iris. 20 British United Provident Association. 21 House painting. 22 David Thewlis. 23 Texas. 24 Securities and Investments Board. 25 Reptiles. 26 Sea. 27 Games without Frontiers. 28 Yeah!. 29 John Osborne. 30 Spanish.

Quiz 104 | Pot Luck 49

Answers – page 577

1 What two colours appear on the flag of San Marino?
2 Male is the capital of which country?
3 In which century was Dame Barbara Cartland born?
4 What is the international car index mark for a car from Barbados?
5 Who directed the 1992 film "A Few Good Men"?
6 What was Twickenham's new record crowd on Nov. 5, 2006?
7 Which Persian word means "pleasure garden"?
8 Which film production company began as the Famous Players Film Company?
9 In which country is the port of Lubango?
10 Which painting did Arthur Scargill choose as his luxury on "Desert Island Discs"?
11 Paul Kagame became President of which country plagued by internal fighting?
12 Which country has the tugrik as a unit of currency?
13 When was the Piccadilly line fully operational after the July 7, 2005 bombing?
14 In which Canadian province is the novel "Anne of Green Gables" set?
15 What was painter Tintoretto's real name?
16 Which 1968 Scottish Cup winners did not make another final until 2004?
17 Which Sea, after the Coral Sea, is the largest in area in the world?
18 From which countries do the Mende people originate?
19 Who was the Greek Goddess of the rainbow?
20 What does BUPA stand for?
21 What trade did playwright Brendan Behan learn on leaving school?
22 Who played Paul Verlaine in the film "Total Eclipse" to Leonardo DiCaprio's Rimbaud?
23 What is the only US state to have been an independent republic?
24 In monetary and banking terms, what do the initials SIB stand for?
25 The Gladys Porter Zoo in Texas is noted for its collection of what?
26 Thalassophobia is a fear of what?
27 What was Peter Gabriel's first UK Top Ten hit?
28 What was Usher's first single to top both the UK and US charts?
29 Who wrote the screenplay for the 1963 film "Tom Jones"?
30 What is the main language of the Dominican Republic?

Answers | The Media (see Quiz 103)

1 Planet 24. 2 April 2005. 3 Richard Branson. 4 Classic FM. 5 Towns and cities. 6 Anna Politkovskaya. 7 Compleat Library. 8 New Yorker. 9 Eleanor Roosevelt. 10 Lord Northcliffe. 11 Madrid. 12 The Independent on Sunday & The European. 13 Chicago Sun-Times. 14 Islamic Republic News Agency. 15 Robert Maxwell. 16 Reform. 17 Andrew Neil. 18 Harpers and Queen. 19 Tiny Rowland. 20 The Scotsman. 21 Royal. 22 Tim Bell. 23 M & C Saatchi. 24 Nigel Dempster. 25 Antonia de Sancha. 26 David Frost. 27 Hollaback Girl. 28 Peter Jay. 29 Advertising. 30 Silvio Berlusconi.

Answers – page 580

1 Who was knocked off No. 1 position by "Wannabe"?

2 Whose record has the longest playing time of any to make No. 1?

3 Howie Dorough was in which best-selling boy band?

4 Whose one-hit wonder replaced "Honky Tonk Women" at No. 1 in US and Britain?

5 Which singer left school in 1961 to appear in the film "It's Trad, Dad"?

6 Which No. 1 singer was born Arnold George Dorsey in Madras?

7 Which top musician produced Shakin' Stevens' "Merry Christmas Everyone"?

8 Who sang lead vocal on the chart topper "Babe"?

9 Who wrote the lines, "All alone, without a telephone"?

10 Who has recorded singles with Paul McCartney, Julio Iglesias and Diana Ross?

11 Who was the first drummer with The Stone Roses?

12 Joyce Vincent and Thelma Hopkins were the girls in which 1970s group?

13 Who joined Wendy Richard in the No. 1 from 1962 "Come Outside"?

14 Craig David's "Woman Trouble" featured Robbie Craig and who else?

15 Which chart topper started life at Leigh, Lancashire as Clive Powell?

16 Who set up the DEP record label?

17 Which 60s artist was the first British-born artist with three No. 1 hits?

18 To two years, when did Tony Christie's "Amarillo" first hit the charts?

19 Who wrote "Chain Reaction" for Diana Ross?

20 Who joined the Beatles on their first hit to enter the charts at No. 1?

21 Who recorded the 1993 No. 1 written and produced by Shaw and Rogers?

22 Which actor was talking to the trees on the B side of "Wand'rin' Star"?

23 Who was No. 1 in the UK and US singles and album charts at the same time in 1971?

24 How many versions of "Spirit in the Sky" had made No. 1 before Gareth Gates did?

25 Which Creation Records boss signed Oasis?

26 Which duo made up the Righteous Brothers?

27 Who joined the Beautiful South after being roadie for The Housemartins?

28 Whose death moved Don McLean to write "American Pie"?

29 The Beatles apart, who first took a Lennon & McCartney song to No. 1, with the Dakotas?

30 In the 1950s who was the first instrumentalist to achieve two No. 1s?

Answers	Pot Luck 50 (see Quiz 106)

1 Liberia. 2 Arnold Wesker. 3 Man City. 4 Five. 5 Gillian Shephard. 6 G8. 7 God.
8 Alaska. 9 John Donne. 10 Dreams. 11 Physics. 12 Spain. 13 An antelope.
14 Colombia. 15 1900. 16 The Red House Mystery. 17 Five. 18 Drowning. 19
Romania. 20 Charles Buchinski. 21 MA. 22 San Quentin prison. 23 Rho. 24
Veterans Day. 25 Great Ultimate Boxing. 26 British Open 2006. 27 Mozambique. 28
Brian Johnston. 29 Michael Tippett. 30 Paul Cattermole.

1 Which country has the ports of Buchanan and Grenville?
2 Who wrote "Chips with Everything"?
3 Who were the first English team outside London to claim the European Cup Winners' Cup?
4 In Scrabble what would the word DOG score without any bonus points?
5 Which politician stood down from the Norfolk South West seat in 2005?
6 Which major conference took place at the Gleneagles Hotel, July 2005?
7 Theophobia is the fear of what?
8 Which American state is called the Last Frontier?
9 "For whom the bell tolls" is a quote from whom?
10 What was Gabrielle's first UK Top Ten hit?
11 What did Olivia Newton-John's grandfather win a Nobel Prize for in 1954?
12 In which European country are the regions of Vigo and Murcia?
13 What type of animal is a kudu?
14 Peter Crouch made his England debut against which country?
15 In which year did Michelin produce the first of its Red Guides?
16 Which detective novel did AA Milne write in 1922?
17 How many stripes are there on the Thai flag?
18 What was the first Backstreet Boys' hit with a one-word title?
19 In which country is the town of Constanta?
20 What was Charles Bronson's full real name?
21 What is the international car index mark for a car from Morocco?
22 Where had Jim Rockford been in the years preceding "The Rockford Files"?
23 What name is given to the Greek letter that is the equivalent of letter R?
24 What is Remembrance Sunday called in the US?
25 What does "tai chi chuan" mean in Chinese?
26 What was the first Major won by Tiger Woods after his father's death?
27 In which country is the city of Maputo?
28 Which cricket commentator was awarded the Military Cross in WWII for his "cheerfulness under fire"?
29 Who wrote the opera "The Knot Garden"?
30 Who was the first person to leave S Club 7?

Answers	**Whose Music?** *(see Quiz 105)*

1 Gary Barlow. 2 Meat Loaf. 3 Backstreet Boys. 4 Zager and Evans – In the Year 2525. 5 Helen Shapiro. 6 Engelbert Humperdinck. 7 Dave Edmunds. 8 Mark Owen. 9 Marc Bolan (Metal Guru). 10 Stevie Wonder. 11 Alan "Remi" Wren. 12 Dawn. 13 Mike Sarne. 14 Artful Dodger. 15 Georgie Fame. 16 UB40. 17 Frank Ifield. 18 1971. 19 The Gibb Brothers. 20 Billy Preston on Get Back. 21 Mr Blobby. 22 Clint Eastwood. 23 Rod Stewart. 24 Two versions. 25 Alan McGhee. 26 Bill Medley and Bobby Hatfield. 27 Dave Stead. 28 Buddy Holly. 29 Billy J. Kramer. 30 Eddie Calvert.

Answers – page 582

LEVEL 3

1 Who beat Jahangir Khan's five-year unbeaten record in 1986?
2 Who had the car number plate 1 CUE?
3 How was Walker Smith better known?
4 Who was Man Utd's only Premiership ever-present in 2005–06, his debut season?
5 Whom did Andy Robinson name as his first captain when appointed head coach?
6 What was the nickname of baseball player Ty Cobb?
7 Which woman was undefeated over 400m between 1977 and 1981?
8 Which horse did Willie Shoemaker ride in his last race?
9 Who was the only person to beat Sugar Ray Leonard in a professional fight?
10 Which athlete was nicknamed "The Flying Finn"?
11 Who beat Babe Ruth's long-standing record of 714 home runs in 1974?
12 Who was the first jockey to saddle more than 8,000 winners?
13 Who was the first skier to overtake Pirmin Zurbriggen's four overall world championship titles?
14 Which American football player was nicknamed "Sweetness"?
15 Who in 1985 was the first man for 30 years to hold the 1500m and 5000m world records at the same time?
16 Whose Triple Jump World Record did Jonathan Edwards break?
17 Who was the first South African to win the Benson & Hedges Masters snooker title?
18 Where did Nelson Piquet win his first Grand Prix?
19 Who were the 2006 European women's doubles champions in badminton?
20 Who won the Moto Cross des Nations for the first time in 1975?
21 Who was dubbed the Louisville Lip?
22 Whose record of 24 Grand Prix wins was broken by Jim Clark?
23 Who was the first non-European to win the Tour de France?
24 Who won the 1988 Jesse Owens Award as the year's most outstanding athlete?
25 Fiona May represents which country at which sport?
26 Who was the British Superbike Champion of 2006?
27 Which French cyclist's nickname means "The Badger"?
28 Gene Tunney was only beaten once, by whom?
29 Who was the first Australian to win the Women's World Open Snooker Championship?
30 Who was the first racing driver to win 500 points in Formula 1?

Answers	Pot Luck 51 *(see Quiz 108)*

1 Five. 2 E101. 3 Richard Attenborough. 4 Venezuela. 5 1920s. 6 George Bernard Shaw. 7 Aquarius. 8 The One I Love. 9 White & yellow. 10 Madison. 11 John of Gaunt. 12 Team sport (like tag). 13 Famke Janssen. 14 Mel B. 15 Easel. 16 Aslan Maskhadow. 17 United Arab Emirates. 18 Milk. 19 EAT. 20 Tennessee. 21 Ken Dodd. 22 Amharic. 23 Richard Roundtree. 24 Peace. 25 Goombay Dance Band. 26 Kate Moss. 27 James Fenimore Cooper. 28 Honduras. 29 Clarence. 30 Oliver Stone.

1 What's the most number of raised dots in a single letter of Braille?
2 Which 'E' number is used to represent riboflavin in products?
3 Who was actress Jane Seymour's first father-in-law?
4 In which country is the city of Maracaibo?
5 In which decade was Mohammed Fayed born?
6 Who, on the cover of "Sgt Pepper", was known by his three names?
7 What is Sven-Goran Eriksson's star sign?
8 What was David Gray's next Top Ten single hit after "Babylon"?
9 Which two colours form the background for the Vatican City flag?
10 What is the capital of the American state of Wisconsin?
11 Who was Henry IV's father?
12 In Bangladesh what is kabaddi?
13 Which actress links "Goldeneye" and "X-Men"?
14 Which Spice Girl once appeared as an extra in "Emmerdale"?
15 What's the English name of the constellation Pictor?
16 Which former Chechen president was killed by Russian troops in 2005?
17 Which country has the dirham as a unit of currency?
18 What is the main food of baby whales?
19 What is the international car index mark for a car from Tanzania?
20 In which US state is a university endowed by Cornelius Vanderbilt?
21 Which comedian played Tollmaster in "Doctor Who" in 1987?
22 What is the main language of Ethiopia?
23 Who played the black film detective Shaft?
24 Which Nobel Prize was won in 1975 by Andrei Sakharov?
25 Who had a No. 1 UK hit with "Seven Tears" in 1982?
26 Who is the elder – Jemima Khan or Kate Moss?
27 Who wrote the "Leatherstocking Tales"?
28 Tegucigalpa is the capital of which country?
29 What was the Christian name of frozen food man Mr Birdseye?
30 Who directed the 1991 film "JFK"?

Answers | **Whose Sport?** (see Quiz 107)

1 Ross Norman. 2 Jimmy White. 3 Sugar Ray Robinson. 4 Edwin van der Sar. 5 Jonny Wilkinson. 6 The Georgia Peach. 7 Marita Koch. 8 Patchy Groundfog. 9 Roberto Duran. 10 Paavo Johannes Nurmi. 11 Hank Aaron. 12 Willie Shoemaker. 13 Marc Girardelli. 14 Walter Paynton. 15 Said Aouita. 16 Willie Banks. 17 Perrie Mans. 18 Long Beach USA. 19 Gail Emms & Donna Kellogg. 20 Czechoslovakia. 21 Muhammad Ali. 22 Juan Manuel Fangio. 23 Greg LeMond. 24 Florence Griffith-Joyner. 25 Italy, long jump. 26 Ryuichi Kiyonari. 27 Bernard Hinault. 28 Harry Greb. 29 Lesley McIlraith. 30 Alain Prost.

1 What is chiefly grown in Alabama's Canebrake country?
2 The Julian and Dinaric Alps extend into which two countries?
3 The Amur river forms much of the boundary between which two countries?
4 What is the Maori name for New Zealand?
5 Which two main metals are found in the Atacama Desert in Chile?
6 What is the currency of Malaysia?
7 Which country has the highest density of sheep in the world?
8 Which African country takes its name from the Shona for "House of Stone"?
9 Which volcanic peak is west of Cook inlet in Alaska?
10 San Miguel is the main island of which group?
11 What is the capital of the Lazio region of Italy?
12 What is the former name of the capital of Dominica?
13 Which Brazilian state is the centre of Amazonian tin and gold mining?
14 Aqaba is which country's only port?
15 On which island of the Philippines is Manila?
16 What is the world's flattest continent?
17 Which former fort in New York State is the home of the US Military Academy?
18 Which US state capital lies on the river Jordan?
19 In which country is Africa's lowest point?
20 What is the largest primeval forest left in Europe?
21 The Red Sea is the submerged section of which valley?
22 Regina in Saskatchewan was originally called what?
23 How many countries do the Andes pass through?
24 In which country do the Makua live?
25 What is the highest peak of the Apennines?
26 Which city south east of St Malo was the old capital of Brittany?
27 Which Alps lie north east of the Sea of Showers?
28 Robben Island is a prison in which Bay?
29 What is Malawi's largest city?
30 Which south American port's name means River of January?

Answers | Pot Luck 52 *(see Quiz 110)*

1 Robert Altman. 2 Wood not metal resonators. 3 Indonesia. 4 Tippett. 5 Dick Tracy. 6 Amy Grant. 7 Tea. 8 Geoffrey Boycott. 9 Argentina. 10 Henry. 11 Crimean. 12 Doris Kappelhoff. 13 Kansas. 14 Z. 15 Jawaharlal (Pandit) Nehru. 16 Man City. 17 Sousaphone. 18 Journalism, literature & music. 19 Turkey. 20 Ghosts. 21 Czech Republic. 22 Light My Fire. 23 Max. 24 Ice cream. 25 Muscat. 26 The Phantom. 27 Laura Moffatt. 28 Puppetry. 29 Kidney. 30 William I.

1 Which famous movie director died in Los Angeles in Nov. 2006?
2 How does a marimba differ from a xylophone?
3 In which country is the city of Surabaya?
4 Who composed the opera "The Ice Break"?
5 Which comic strip character was played by Warren Beatty?
6 Whose first UK Top Ten hit was "Baby Baby"?
7 What would you drink from a cha-no-yu?
8 Who said they'd hang their MBE round their cat's neck when they got back home after the 2006/07 Ashes whitewash?
9 Nestor Kirchner became President of which South American country in 2003?
10 What did the last emperor of China Hsuan Tung ask to be called after he was deposed?
11 In which war was the Battle of Inkerman?
12 What is Doris Day's full real name?
13 Which American state is called the Sunflower State?
14 Which letter is two dashes and two dots in Morse Code?
15 Who preceded Lal Shastri as Prime Minister of India?
16 Which club moved from M14 7WN to M11 3FF?
17 According to the Bonzo Dog Doo-Dah Band's "The Intro and the Outro" what is Princess Anne playing?
18 The Pulitzer Prize is awarded in which three categories?
19 In which European country is the region of Anatolia?
20 Phasmophobia is the fear of what?
21 Which country has the koruna as a unit of currency?
22 Which song links UB40 and Will Young?
23 Who is the male hero of the children's book "Where the Wild Things are"?
24 What is cassata a type of?
25 What is the capital of Oman?
26 In the first "Pink Panther" film what was the professional jewel thief called?
27 Which politician had the smallest majority after the 2005 general election?
28 In Japan what type of entertainment is bunraku?
29 Pyelitis affects which organ of the body?
30 Which king of England was crowned on Christmas Day?

Answers | Exploration *(see Quiz 109)*

1 Cotton. 2 Albania & Yugoslavia. 3 China & Russia. 4 Aotearoa. 5 Silver & copper. 6 Ringgit. 7 Wales. 8 Zimbabwe. 9 Mount Redoubt. 10 Azores. 11 Rome. 12 Charlotte Town. 13 Rondonia. 14 Jordan. 15 Luzon. 16 Australia. 17 West Point. 18 Salt Lake City. 19 Djibouti. 20 Hainburg in Austria. 21 Great Rift Valley. 22 Pile of Bones. 23 Seven. 24 Mozambique. 25 Gran Sasso d'Italia. 26 Rennes. 27 Lunar Alps. 28 Table Bay. 29 Blantyre. 30 Rio de Janeiro.

1 Who were the opposition in Sven's first game?
2 Which secretary of the FA alleged having an affair with Sven?
3 Which player scored the first goal in Sven's reign?
4 Wayne Rooney made his debut against which team?
5 World Cup 2006's first qualifier was a 2-2 against which side?
6 What was the half-time score in Sven's last game?
7 At which ground was the Swede's first game?
8 Who was right-back for 2002's World Cup Final tournament?
9 Which England player touched the ball last in Sven's reign?
10 To three, how many goals did England let in during the Sven years?
11 Which FA director of communications resigned in 2004?
12 Who was the first keeper to feature in Sven's first game?
13 In which German city was his last game?
14 Sven had a good start, winning how many games?
15 Peter Crouch was at which club when he made his England debut?
16 Which caretaker boss did Sven take over from?
17 The Fake Sheikh scam linked Eriksson with moving to which club?
18 Did Frank Lampard appear for England before Sven took over?
19 What was Sven's last club side as boss before joining England?
20 Who won his 51st and last cap in 2002's World Cup game v. Brazil?
21 How many games did England lose under Sven?
22 Which 31-year-old Chris won a cap in Sven's first game?
23 To five, how many goals did England score for Sven?
24 Which team were the first to beat Sven's England?
25 Who scored the last goal in open play in Sven's reign?
26 Did Gareth Southgate win over half his caps with Sven or before him?
27 Who was the last substitute used by Sven?
28 Who acted as Sven's assistant coach during his period in change of England?
29 To three, how many games did Sven's England win?
30 Who was the only player throughout Sven's first and last games?

Answers | TV: Soaps (see Quiz 113)

1 Twice. 2 Hairdresser. 3 Maggie (ER). 4 Sharon Maughan. 5 Luke. 6 Melrose Place. 7 Viv Martell. 8 Five. 9 Dennis. 10 Black Forest Clinic. 11 Ricky Tomlinson. 12 Derek Thompson. 13 Fallon. 14 Julie Goodyear. 15 Meadowcroft. 16 Leonard Swindley. 17 QE2. 18 Conundrum. 19 Tara King. 20 Mal Young. 21 Lucy-Jo Hudson. 22 Dynasty. 23 Carol Boswell. 24 The Brothers. 25 Liam. 26 Hathaway. 27 Thomas. 28 Compact. 29 Dynasty. 30 Debbie Travers-Macy.

1 Who was the first US President to ride in a car?
2 The drink Kir was named after the mayor of which town?
3 Where was the SALT II treaty signed?
4 Who was the leader of the Taliban at the beginning of the raids on Afghanistan in October 2001?
5 In which country was the first double hand transplant carried out?
6 In the US what were "swift walkers"?
7 Where was the first sugar beet extraction factory built?
8 In which city was Britain's Independent Labour Party founded?
9 Which Oscar-winning actor links "Tomb Raider" and "Pearl Harbor"?
10 In what year were dog licences abolished in the UK?
11 Of the three top names in the US's Ivy League which is the middle one alphabetically?
12 On which river is the state capital of Mississippi?
13 Which Pope excommunicated Martin Luther?
14 Who made jasperware?
15 To three, how many games did Sven Goran Eriksson's England draw?
16 Which future party leader was the then youngest-ever government minister when he became Under-Secretary to the Navy on his 30th birthday?
17 During which months did Jack the Ripper kill five prostitutes?
18 Jatakas are stories of the previous lives of whom?
19 Which US President pardoned the first US President to have resigned from office?
20 Which monarch knighted Isaac Newton?
21 Which state is to the south west of Rajashan in India?
22 What colour is the head and neck of the jabiru?
23 Which rock star died two years to the day after the death of Rolling Stone Brian Jones?
24 Where was Europe's oldest university founded?
25 Where were emeralds first mined?
26 Which dams in the Ruhr were hit by the Dam Busters in 1943?
27 In which city was Chop Suey invented?
28 Where was the world's first electric power station?
29 A strophium was an early prototype of which garment?
30 A car from where can display the letters WAG?

Answers	Plants *(see Quiz 114)*

1 Alaska. 2 Chlorophyll. 3 Dead matter. 4 New Zealand. 5 0.9%. 6 Barley. 7 Lamina. 8 Gymnosperm. 9 Hollies. 10 Epiphyte. 11 Cork. 12 Forget Me Not. 13 Small stalk. 14 Myrtle sprig. 15 Honesty. 16 Azalea. 17 Pink. 18 Autumn crocus. 19 Rosa gallica. 20 Carnations. 21 Saffron. 22 Glory of the snow. 23 South Africa. 24 Sap. 25 Boston. 26 Root. 27 Aubretia. 28 Parsley. 29 Daffodil. 30 Flemish.

1 How many times a week was "Coronation Street" originally broadcast?
2 Which profession did Helen Shapiro's character play in "Albion Market"?
3 For which character did Sally Field win an Emmy in 2000?
4 Which ex-"Holby City" star is the mother of actress Alice Eve?
5 What was "Nora Batty's" surname in the revival of "Crossroads"?
6 What was the spin-off of "Beverly Hills 90210"?
7 Which character did the barmaid from "Only Fools and Horses" play in "The Bill"?
8 How many members of the family were there which was created on "Soapstars"?
9 In "Coronation Street" who was Elsie Tanner's son?
10 Which overseas soap had the character Klaus Brinkmann?
11 In "Brookside" which actor who had been a striker in real life played a builder on strike?
12 Which member of the "Casualty" cast played an IRA terrorist in "The Long Good Friday"?
13 In "The Colbys" who shared her name with a youngster in "The Archers"?
14 Which "Coronation Street" barmaid was given an OBE?
15 What was the original title of "Brookside" to have been?
16 "Pardon the Expression" was a spin-off series about which "Coronation Street" character?
17 In "Crossroads", where was Meg when the motel burned down?
18 What was the final episode of "Dallas" called?
19 Which character did "Emmerdale"'s Rosemary King play in "The Avengers"?
20 Which producer of "Brookside" took over the same year that the set expanded to include the shopping centre?
21 Which ex-Corrie star played Hayley Mills' granddaughter in "Wild at Heart"?
22 In which soap did the voice of Charlie in "Charlie's Angels" appear?
23 Which character did "Emmerdale"'s Diane Sugden play in "The Liver Birds"?
24 Which soap/drama centred on Hammond Transport Services?
25 Whom did Bianca leave "EastEnders" with?
26 In "The Archers" what was Siobhan's surname when she lived in Ambridge?
27 What was Sinbad's real name?
28 Which magazine soap had "Crossroads" creators previously created?
29 Which soap boasted appearances by Gerald Ford and Henry Kissinger?
30 Which role did the 2007 Olivier Award Best Actress play in "The Archers"?

Answers	**Sven's England Years** (see Quiz 111)

1 Spain. 2 Faria Alam. 3 Nick Barmby. 4 Australia. 5 Austria. 6 0-0. 7 Villa Park. 8 Danny Mills. 9 Jamie Carragher (missed penalty in shoot-out). 10 61 goals. 11 Colin Gibson. 12 David James. 13 Gelsenkirchen. 14 Five. 15 Southampton. 16 Howard Wilkinson. 17 Aston Villa. 18 Yes (Once). 19 Lazio. 20 Teddy Sheringham. 21 Ten. 22 Chris Powell. 23 128 goals. 24 Holland. 25 David Beckham. 26 Before Sven. 27 Jamie Carragher. 28 Tord Grip. 29 40 wins. 30 Rio Ferdinand.

1 In which US state is the Tongass National Forest?
2 Which of the following do algae have – chlorophyll, roots and stems?
3 What does a saphrophyte feed on?
4 Urtica ferox is a deadly tree nettle native to where?
5 How much chlorophyll does spinach have – 0.9%, 0.12% or 0.17%?
6 Which of the following originated in the Middle East – barley, maize or millet?
7 What is another name for the blade of a plant?
8 What name is given to a plant whose seed is not enclosed In an ovary?
9 Which of the following are in the Aquilfoliacae group – conifers, hollies or ivies?
10 What name is given to a plant which grows on another without damaging it?
11 The Whistler Tree is what type of tree?
12 Myosotis is another name for which flower?
13 What is a funicle?
14 According to legend which plant did Adam take from the Garden of Eden?
15 How is lunaria biennis better known?
16 What type of plant is a Silver Slipper?
17 What colour are the blooms of the Zephirine Drouhin?
18 What is another name for the meadow saffron?
19 What is the rose of Lancaster also called?
20 What are Alice Forbes and Bailey's Delight?
21 What is crocus sativus?
22 How is chionodoxa also known?
23 The agapanthus is native to where?
24 Which part of asafoetida is used?
25 The borlotti bean also takes its name from which city?
26 Which part of a mooli is edible?
27 How is rock cress better known?
28 Which herb reputedly travels seven times to the devil before it will emerge?
29 The amaryllis is related to which popular spring flower?
30 What is the nationality of the man who gave his name to the plant Lobelia?

1 Which John won the Best Director Oscar for the movie "The Informer"?
2 The world's first known drilling for oil took place in which US state?
3 At which London club did Bill Wyman have his 70th birthday bash?
4 The Kate Bush album "Never for Ever" featured a song about which classical composer?
5 On which special day was William the Conqueror crowned King of England?
6 Which day of the week was dubbed the "Black" day of the 1929 Wall Street Crash?
7 The first kindergarten was established in which country?
8 Ingemar Johansson became Sweden's first champion in which sport?
9 Roger Moore played 007 in how many films?
10 Matching the date of the French Revolution, how many steps are there to the top of the Eiffel Tower?
11 In which US state was John Travolta born?
12 Which security item was Joseph Farwell Glidden's patent in 1873?
13 In which city was the first Model T Ford produced in Britain?
14 In which country would you watch Jazz Pori play a home soccer match?
15 Which England cricket captain was born in Italy?
16 King Michael abdicated which European throne in 1947?
17 Which Mr Smith was the main character of the novel "1984"?
18 "A Man for All Seasons" was set in the 16th century but was written in which century?
19 The first prime minister of Australia shared his surname with which fictional detective?
20 Which country did 1990s group Whale come from?
21 Who was the first Scot to appear on an English bank note?
22 If 12 January falls on a Friday, on what day does 12 February fall?
23 John Street and Cherry Street go past the soccer stadium of which club?
24 How many hurdles are there in total in a six-lane 400-metre hurdle race?
25 Which paper did Superman work on?
26 In which year did Shirley Bassey, the Tigress of Tiger Bay, first have a Top Ten single?
27 The first heart transplant patient survived for how long after the operation?
28 Which actor links the movies "Sliding Doors" and "Pandaemonium"?
29 In which country is the city of Londrina?
30 What is the first word of "My Heart Will Go On"?

Answers | Pot Luck 55 (see Quiz 117)

1 Prince Edward. 2 Body Shop. 3 Doug Mountjoy. 4 Friendship 7. 5 Charles Blondin. 6 Painting. 7 Portugal. 8 46 years. 9 Argentine. 10 Sued. 11 Pink. 12 Farce. 13 Fulham. 14 Vanbrugh. 15 Belgium. 16 Henry. 17 The Forfarshire. 18 Tonga. 19 White Town. 20 Pope. 21 Bruton Street. 22 Norway. 23 Soccer club. 24 Paddington. 25 Brazil. 26 Frank Coraci. 27 France. 28 Coca Cola. 29 Brazil. 30 Pointer Sisters.

1 Who was the only American lady to have a million-seller in the UK in the 1980s?

2 Who directed Michael Jackson's best-selling album?

3 Whose album of "Love Songs" was the top-selling album of 1982?

4 Who was the first country artist to have two UK No 1s?

5 What was Blondie's third single from the "Eat to the Beat" album?

6 Who wrote the first double A side of the 1980s to debut at No 1?

7 What were the Detroit Spinners called in the UK before using this name?

8 Which song was at No 1 when Prince Charles & Diana married?

9 The writer of Kelly Marie's "Feels Like I'm in Love" was a member of which 1970s band?

10 Who was the last Australian with a UK No 1 before Men at Work's first No 1?

11 What was the only song from "Thriller" to reach No 1 in the UK?

12 The brother of the writer of "True" starred in which TV soap?

13 Who was Billy Joel's 1983 No 1 dedicated to?

14 Which album did Lionel Richie's first No 1 of 1984 come from?

15 Who co-wrote and produced Blondie's "Call Me"?

16 Who was the only American man to have a million-seller in the UK in the 1980s?

17 Which top-selling hit of 1985 was a hit for a Canadian singer in the 1990s?

18 Which movie gave ELO their only UK No 1?

19 What colour shirt is Michael Jackson wearing on the cover of "Thriller"?

20 Which record of John Lennon's went to No 1 almost immediately after his murder?

21 What was the fourth British Eurovision Song Contest winner, which charted in this decade?

22 Which song did Smokey Robinson release to celebrate his silver anniversary in show business?

23 Under what name did Mary Sandeman have a 1980s No 1?

24 Who was the first white singer to have No 1 on the Motown label?

25 Where did Paul McCartney and Stevie Wonder record their No 1 duet?

26 Which big 1980s band were once called In Praise of Lemmings?

27 What was the first single to be at No 1 in the 80s?

28 Who directed the video for the Pet Shop Boys' second No 1?

29 Which band topped the charts in the 1980s, as well as the 1960s and 1970s?

30 What was the surname of the singer who sang "Orinoco Flow"?

Answers	UK Travel *(see Quiz 118)*

1 Canada. 2 32. 3 Gentlemen's toilet. 4 Aberystwyth. 5 Christchurch. 6 Kessock. 7 Victoria. 8 Caernarvon. 9 Pratt. 10 603. 11 Powys. 12 Widnes. 13 Dorset. 14 Dover. 15 Anne. 16 John Christie. 17 Lincoln Cathedral. 18 Bedford. 19 Llantrisant. 20 220 miles. 21 Angus. 22 1988. 23 Stour. 24 Granta. 25 1940. 26 Book dealer. 27 Berkshire. 28 Caerphilly. 29 Gillespie Road. 30 Brighton.

1 Who was Prince Andrew's best man for his wedding to Sarah Ferguson?
2 What did L'Oréal buy for £652 million in 2006?
3 Who did Steve Davis beat to win his first World Snooker Championship?
4 John Glenn orbited the Earth in 1962 in which craft?
5 How did daredevil stuntman Jean Francois Gravelet become known?
6 John Sell Cotman became famous for doing what?
7 In which country is the Penina golf course?
8 How long was the Nazi Rudolf Hess in prison?
9 What was the nationality of Cuban revolutionary leader Che Guevara?
10 Satirical editor Richard Ingrams suggested his motto should be "Publish and be" what?
11 What colour is the flesh of a dragon fruit?
12 What kind of theatrical play was the speciality of Brian Rix?
13 In his second Anfield spell, Robbie Fowler first scored against which side?
14 Which Sir John was the designer of Castle Howard and Blenheim Palace?
15 Albert became a king of which country in 1993?
16 What is Warren Beatty's other Christian name?
17 The crew of which boat were saved by the heroics of Grace Darling?
18 In which country did Queen Salote Tupou III rule for nearly 50 years?
19 Under which name did producer Jyoti Mishra have a No 1 hit?
20 Nicholas Breakspear was the first British what?
21 In which London Street is the residence where Princess Elizabeth – later Elizabeth II – was born?
22 In which country would you watch Tromso playing Molde at soccer?
23 What was the setting of the 1960s soap "United!"?
24 Michael Hordern provided the voiceover for which TV bear?
25 Djalma Santos played soccer 100 times for which country?
26 Who directed the movie "The Wedding Singer"?
27 After abdicating, in which country did the former Edward VIII marry?
28 Dr John Pemberton invented which world-famous drink?
29 In which country is the city of Recife?
30 How were June, Anita, Ruth and Bonnie known collectively?

Answers | Pot Luck 54 *(see Quiz 115)*

1 John Ford. 2 Pennsylvania. 3 Ronnie Scott's. 4 Delius. 5 Christmas Day. 6 Thursday. 7 Switzerland. 8 Boxing. 9 Seven. 10 1789. 11 New Jersey. 12 Barbed wire. 13 Manchester. 14 Finland. 15 Ted Dexter. 16 Romania. 17 Winston Smith. 18 20th. 19 Barton. 20 Sweden. 21 Adam Smith. 22 Monday. 23 Sheffield Utd. 24 60. 25 Daily Planet. 26 1957. 27 18 days. 28 John Hannah. 29 Brazil. 30 Every.

1 In which Square is the UK's highest building?
2 How many capsules or pods does the London Eye have?
3 What did the Theatre of Small Convenience in Malvern used to be?
4 Where is the National Library of Wales?
5 Where does the Avon flow into what the French call La Manche?
6 Which Bridge spans the Beauly Firth?
7 What was London's first new underground railway line to open in the second half of the 20th century?
8 Which Welsh city is near the old Roman fort of Segontium?
9 What was Lord Camden's name before he became a Lord and before the London borough was named after him?
10 How many miles is it from Land's End to John O'Groats?
11 Which county is to the west of Hereford & Worcester?
12 At which northern railway station did Paul Simon write "Homeward Bound"?
13 In which county is the Cerne Giant?
14 Which of the Cinque Ports is nearest the beginning of the alphabet?
15 One of the founders of Fortnum and Mason was a footman in the service of which monarch?
16 Who inaugurated the Glyndebourne Festival?
17 Which is the UK's tallest structure built before the 20th century?
18 Where is the Cranfield Institute of Technology?
19 Where in Wales is the Royal Mint?
20 How long is Britain's longest river?
21 Which county is the largest to the east of Perth & Kinross?
22 When were the Broads designated a National Park?
23 Constable country is along which river?
24 What is the local name of the river which runs through Cambridge?
25 In what year were marriages at the famous blacksmith's shop in southern Scotland made illegal?
26 The founder of Guy's Hospital followed which profession?
27 Which county is to the south of Oxfordshire?
28 Where is the second largest castle in England and Wales?
29 What was Arsenal tube station called before it was called Arsenal?
30 Where did Britain's first nudist beach open in 1979?

Answers | **Sounds of the 80s (see Quiz 116)**

1 Jennifer Rush. 2 Quincey Jones. 3 Barbra Streisand. 4 Kenny Rogers. 5 Atomic. 6 Paul Weller. 7 Motown Spinners. 8 Ghost Town – The Specials. 9 Mungo Jerry. 10 Rolf Harris. 11 Billie Jean. 12 EastEnders (the Kemps). 13 Christie Brinkley. 14 Can't Slow Down. 15 Giorgio Moroder. 16 Stevie Wonder. 17 The Power of Love. 18 Xanadu. 19 Cream. 20 (Just Like) Starting Over. 21 Making Your Mind Up. 22 Being with you. 23 Aneka. 24 Charlene. 25 Montserrat. 26 Culture Club. 27 Another Brick in the Wall. 28 Derek Jarman. 29 Bee Gees. 30 Brennan.

1 Chester Carlson invented a machine that produces what?
2 Jobs and Wozniak pioneered development in which field?
3 In which country would you watch Karpaty playing Krivbas at soccer?
4 One language is spoken in more countries of the world than any other – which is it?
5 General Choi Hong Hi developed which martial art?
6 What position does the canoeist adopt in Canadian canoeing?
7 What did Wilhelm Rontgen discover to help medical science?
8 Which movement did George Williams found in 1844?
9 How is St Kentigern, patron saint of Glasgow, also known?
10 Brigham Young was a leader of which religious movement?
11 In 2006 how many million people used the internet in China, according to state sources?
12 In 1989, who became the first US male tennis player in over 30 years to win the French Open?
13 Iwao Takamato created the design of which popular cartoon dog?
14 In 1987 Lindy Chamberlain said her baby had been snatched by what?
15 How many track races are included in the decathlon?
16 Who was the last boxer to fight Muhammad Ali?
17 Which film soundtrack topped the first classified UK album chart?
18 Who was convicted of murdering nanny Sandra Rivett?
19 In which country is the city of San Cristobal?
20 Who was the first US President not to be elected into office and who subsequently failed to win a presidential election?
21 Polly Nicholas was the first victim of which killer?
22 2007 marked the 150th anniversary of which British-born classical composer?
23 Who composed the opera "Adelaide di Borgogna"?
24 France, Great Britain and which other country competed in every Winter Olympic Games of the 20th century?
25 William Kemmler was the first man to die in what?
26 What is Japan's highest peak?
27 Who won the Best Actress Oscar for the movie "Blue Sky"?
28 The Galapagos Islands belong to which country?
29 What was the only top ten hit for West End featuring Sybil?
30 What was the name of Franco's fascist party in Spain?

Answers | Pot Luck 57 *(see Quiz 121)*

1 25 March. 2 Dixie Dean. 3 Harold Macmillan. 4 1994. 5 Hi-De-Hi!. 6 Norwegian. 7 1914. 8 Armani. 9 Henry I. 10 Half-marathon. 11 Godzilla. 12 Colchester. 13 John Adams. 14 Bay. 15 Ajax. 16 Normal. 17 Voice over Internet Protocol. 18 144. 19 Unchained. 20 Transformer. 21 Alexander. 22 Swimming. 23 British Empire Exhibition. 24 Rievaulx. 25 21. 26 Julie Walters (2000). 27 Abstract Expressionism. 28 20 mins. 29 Silk screen. 30 Blythe Danner.

1 Who beat Costa Rica in Germany 2006 to make the second round for the first time?
2 In the penultimate World Cup Final of last century, what was the score at 90 minutes?
3 Which of FIFA's original member came nearest the end of the alphabet?
4 Why did India pull out of the fourth World Cup?
5 When did West Germany win their second European Championship ?
6 Which was the most northerly club Peter Shilton played for?
7 In July 2000 which club owned the world's most expensive footballer?
8 Which was the first indoor arena used in a World Cup Final?
9 Liverpool signed defender Daniel Agger from which club?
10 For how much did the first hat trick scorer in a World Cup final sell his shirt in 2000?
11 In which 2001 movie did Pele make an appearance?
12 Whose World Cup medal was sold for almost £125,000 in 2001?
13 For how many years was the League Cup the Rumbelows League Cup?
14 The Football League Cup was a two-legged final until which year?
15 Who won the FA Cup the year Prince William was born?
16 The world's second most expensive goalie at the beginning of 2001 had been transferred from which club?
17 Who won the first post-WWII Scottish FA Cup?
18 In which country did West Germany win their first World Cup?
19 Roy Keane made his Celtic debut in a Scottish Cup game against which team?
20 Who were the first runners-up of the Milk Cup?
21 Which was the first country to have players who scored more than once in a World Cup Final?
22 Who was Tommy Lawton playing for when he scored his first League hat trick?
23 Who was the first man to score twice in a European Championships final?
24 The first Yorkshire side to win the Fairs Cup in the 1960s beat which side in the final?
25 Which was the first side to win the UEFA Cup on penalties?
26 Who were runners-up in the first FA Cup final played at Wembley?
27 Who were the last runners-up of the old First Division?
28 At the end of the millennium who was the world's most expensive goalkeeper?
29 In which stadium was the sixth World Cup final held?
30 In the last World Cup final of the 20th century played outside Europe, what colour shirts did the winners wear?

1 Before the Calendar Act of of 1752 what date was New Year's Day?
2 Which English goal scorer had the first names William Ralph?
3 Who described Margaret Thatcher's privatisation policy as "selling the family silver"?
4 In which year did Ayrton Senna die in a Grand Prix accident?
5 Crimpton-on-Sea was the location for which sitcom?
6 What was the nationality of the first team to reach the South Pole?
7 When was the Panama Canal opened?
8 Which designer made clothes for younger people under the Emporio label?
9 Which monarch was responsible for founding the first English zoo?
10 Haile Gebrselassie set a 2006 sporting world record in which event?
11 In which monster movie film did the character Dr Niko Tatopoulos appear?
12 Which city was known as Camulodunum in Roman times?
13 Who was the first president to live in the White House?
14 What was the official colour of legendary racehorse Arkle?
15 Which soccer team from Holland is named after a mythological Greek figure?
16 Where is the University of Illinois?
17 What does the BT service VoIP stand for?
18 How many tiles are there in a game of mah-jong?
19 Which 1955 movie used "Unchained Melody" as its theme tune?
20 No 1 in the 1990s, "Perfect Day" first appeared on which early 1970s album?
21 What was Cary Grant's middle name?
22 Which sport follows FINA rules?
23 The original Wembley Stadium was costructed for which event?
24 Harold Wilson became Baron of where when he was made a peer?
25 After "The Flapper Vote" in 1928, women over what age could vote in an election?
26 Who was 50 first – Ruby Wax, Julie Walters or Kim Basinger?
27 What school of painting does Mark Rothko belong to?
28 In the silent days of cinema how long would a "two-reeler" last?
29 Serigraphy is also known as what type of printing?
30 Who is Gwyneth Paltrow's mother?

---

1 Who was the last person to be born first in line to the British throne?
2 Whom did the Queen make the first STD call to?
3 Which Royal's wedding saw the first performance of Mendelssohn's Wedding March?
4 How old was Prince Charles on his engagement to Lady Diana Spencer?
5 Who in 1934 said, "I can see no reason why women should not wear shorts"?
6 Who was the first British monarch to eat a hot dog?
7 Who was the last Royal of the 20th century to serve in the armed forces in a war zone?
8 What is Prince William's penultimate Christian name?
9 How many interviews did the Queen Mother give in the 20th century?
10 Which Queen of Jordan succeeded Queen Noor?
11 From where did the Duke & Duchess of York leave for honeymoon by helicopter?
12 Which Royal celebrated her 18th birthday in August 2006?
13 Who was the first royal bride to include her family's motto on her personal coat of arms?
14 Who was Reviewing Officer at Harry's passing out parade at Sandhurst?
15 On which soap did cast members "visit" Duchy Home Farm?
16 In which month did Edward VIII cease to be Edward VIII?
17 Who won the Ladies' Singles at Wimbledon just before Charles and Diana married?
18 Which Prince of Wales considered marrying a Lady Diana Spencer before Prince Charles?
19 Where did the Duke and Duchess of York consider having their daughters educated until there was a scandal about that school's principal?
20 Sir William Worsley was the father of which Duchess?
21 Medically, what did the Queen Mother receive just before her 101st birthday?
22 At which Cambridge college was Prince Charles educated?
23 What was the name of Diana, Princess of Wales' stepfather?
24 Who is the Queen's second oldest granddaughter?
25 In order of succession, who is higher – Eloise Taylor or Estella Taylor?
26 Who attempted to kidnap Princess Anne in 1974?
27 Whose portrait of Lady Diana Spencer was damaged in the National Portrait Gallery shortly after her wedding to Prince Charles?
28 Who was the first Royal bride to omit the word "obey" in her marriage vows?
29 Which royal family is the richest in the world?
30 Where is Queen Mary's Dolls' House on permanent display?

Answers	Football 2 *(see Quiz 120)*

1 Ecudaor. 2 0–0. 3 Switzerland. 4 They had to wear boots. 5 1980. 6 Bolton Wanderers. 7 Real Madrid. 8 Pontiac Silverdome, Detroit. 9 Brondby. 10 £91,750. 11 Mike Bassett: England Manager. 12 Gordon Banks. 13 Two. 14 1966. 15 Tottenham Hotspur. 16 Monaco (Barthez to Manchester United). 17 Aberdeen. 18 Switzerland. 19 Clyde. 20 Tottenham Hotspur. 21 Italy. 22 Burnley. 23 Gerd Müller. 24 Ferencvaros. 25 Tottenham Hotspur. 26 West Ham. 27 Manchester United. 28 Angelo Peruzzi. 29 Rasunda (Stockholm). 30 Yellow.

1 Alex James and Dave Rowntree played in which band?
2 The Olympic Games were first televised by the BBC in which year?
3 Where in suburbia was the sitcom "The Good Life" set?
4 In India what was Suttee?
5 Constantine, Liberius and Sissinius are names of what?
6 What was Abba's only single to make No 1 in the USA?
7 On a keyboard all the letters from F to L are in alphabetical order apart from which one?
8 Who was the Foreign Secretary who lost his seat in the 1997 British General Election?
9 Which retail company was founded by Donald Fisher?
10 Willie Park became the first winner of which sporting trophy?
11 Jane Wyman was the first wife of which famous American?
12 What colour separates the black, red and green bands on the Kenyan flag?
13 If you are misocapnic what do you dislike?
14 Whose first solo album after leaving a chart-topping group was "All Things Must Pass"?
15 Which year marked the 200th anniversary of Hans Christian Andersen's birth?
16 In which year did the first kidney transplant take place?
17 Which first name is derived from Greek for rock or stone?
18 What was Il Divo's third album called?
19 How many episodes of "Fawlty Towers" were made in total?
20 Which country was the first to retain soccer's World Cup?
21 How long does the French presidential term in office last?
22 Bruce Willis was born in which country?
23 What was the number of the Earl of Derby who gave his name to the Classic horse race the Derby?
24 In which country is the city of Panshan?
25 In which century was Robbie Burns born?
26 Who links the groups Slik, Visage and Ultravox?
27 Which element has the atomic number one?
28 Solo round-the-world yachtsman Francis Chichester sailed in which craft?
29 Which famous person was born on Feb 5th, 1948, in Torsby?
30 Esperanto actually means one who does what?

Answers | The 20th Century (1900–1950) *(see Quiz 125)*

1 Humpty Dumpty Store, Oklahoma. 2 Paris Observatory. 3 1946. 4 Pluto. 5 Little Boy. 6 First on National Health. 7 Stockings. 8 July. 9 Folkestone. 10 1900. 11 Popov. 12 Policewomen. 13 Hull. 14 League of German Maidens. 15 13. 16 Japan. 17 Banting & Best. 18 Ernest. 19 Plymouth. 20 Italy. 21 Bao Dai. 22 Bateman. 23 Beaverbrook. 24 Begin. 25 Abercrombie. 26 Balfour. 27 Gertrude Bell. 28 Poland (Ben Gurion). 29 Virginia Woolf. 30 1,100.

1 Which company won a Special Oscar for producing "the pioneer outstanding talking picture"?

2 Which movie classic was remade in the 1950s as "You Can't Run Away from It"?

3 Who won the first ever posthumous Oscar for "Gone with the Wind"?

4 Which studio made the original "King Kong"?

5 Which dance was Fred Astaire and Ginger Rogers' first together on screen?

6 For which movie did James Stewart receive his first Oscar nomination?

7 Which song was Oscar-nominated in the Fred Astaire/Ginger Rogers musical of 1935?

8 Which gossip columnist asked for the withdrawal of the movie "Citizen Kane" because its main character bore a passing resemblance to her boss?

9 Which category of censorship did "The Outlaw" have on its UK release?

10 Who was the prostitute played by Ingrid Bergman in "Dr Jekyll & Mr Hyde"?

11 In which movie did Bogart say, "I'm the only cause I'm interested in"?

12 To which studio did George M Cohan sell the movie rights of his life story?

13 Which piece of music ends the movie "Mrs Miniver"?

14 To the nearest 10 minutes how long did "The Wizard of Oz" last?

15 Which leader banned the Marx Brothers' "Duck Soup"?

16 Who plays Judy Garland's mother in "Meet Me in St Louis"?

17 Where is the setting for Lauren Bacall's screen debut?

18 Whose music accompanied Mickey's broomstick dance in "Fantasia"?

19 Who was the voice of Snow White in Disney's classic?

20 To whom or what did Cary Grant sing "I Can't Give You Anything but Love" in "Bringing Up Baby"?

21 Why does Trevor Howard first assist Celia Johnson in "Brief Encounter"?

22 Where does the climax of the UK's first talkie take place?

23 Who won the only Oscar for "Key Largo"?

24 What was Hitchcock's favourite of his British movies?

25 Which skier was the third screen Tarzan?

26 Who was the fuddy duddy professor in the film which made Dietrich a star?

27 Whose play was the movie "Harvey" based on?

28 Who was Charlie Chaplin's co-star in his last silent movie?

29 Who was Katharine Hepburn's character in "The African Queen"?

30 How old was Elizabeth Taylor when she first kissed Montgomery Clift on screen?

Answers | Pot Luck 59 *(see Quiz 126)*

1 2005. 2 Haltemprice. 3 Pink Floyd. 4 Warner Brothers. 5 59.4. 6 Everton.
7 Freshwater angling. 8 Canada. 9 Scottish. 10 DDT. 11 Crazy. 12 1972.
13 Cabaret. 14 Jim Davidson. 15 Joanna Lumley. 16 Tim Henman. 17 Japan.
18 Grapes. 19 David Dundas. 20 Winston Churchill. 21 23 wickets. 22 Canada/USA. 23 Venus. 24 The Accidental Tourist. 25 Hans Wegner. 26 Jack Nicklaus. 27 Sir Thomas Cullinan, superintendent at Premier Mine. 28 Paris. 29 IMF. 30 Tipp-Ex.

1 Which store inaugurated supermarket trolleys in 1937?

2 Where was the first speaking clock revealed?

3 In which year did the World Bank open?

4 What was discovered by Clyde Tombaugh?

5 What was the codename of the bomb which was dropped on Hiroshima?

6 Why was Jean Murray's birth near Wigan in 1948 memorable?

7 In 1942 women were allowed to enter the Vatican without wearing what?

8 In which month was the "Beano" first published?

9 In which UK resort was the first international beauty contest held?

10 When did Coca Cola go on sale in Britain?

11 What was the name of the first pilot killed in warfare?

12 In 1914 Miss Allen and Miss Harburn became the first what?

13 Where was Britain's first crematorium opened?

14 What was the female equivalent of the Hitler Youth called?

15 Which lifeboat did "Titanic" survivor Millvina Dean take when she escaped from the doomed ship aged nine weeks?

16 Who joined the Axis Powers after signing the Anti Comintern Pact?

17 Who first isolated insulin?

18 What was the first name of the Duchess of Windsor's second husband?

19 Britain's first woman MP represented which constituency?

20 The Hoare Laval pact allowed the annexation of which country?

21 Who abdicated as Vietnamese Emperor at the end of WWII?

22 Who developed the The Man Who ... cartoons?

23 Who was Minister of Aircraft Production in Winston Churchill's wartime Cabinet?

24 Who was the first head of Israel's Herut Party?

25 Which pioneer town planner drew up plans for green belts in the Great London Plan of 1935?

26 Who was Foreign Secretary during WWI?

27 Who in her capacity as Oriental Secretary to the British High Commissioner helped negotiate the independence of Iraq in the early 1920s?

28 Where was Israel's first Prime Minister born?

29 Who was Vanessa Bell's famous younger sister?

30 Dying in 1931, how many inventions had Thomas Edison patented in his lifetime?

Answers	**Pot Luck 58** (see Quiz 123)

1 Blur. 2 1948. 3 Surbiton. 4 Widow sacrifice. 5 Popes. 6 Dancing Queen. 7 I. 8 Malcolm Rifkind. 9 GAP. 10 Golf's British Open. 11 Ronald Reagan. 12 White. 13 Tobacco smoke. 14 George Harrison. 15 2005. 16 1950. 17 Peter. 18 Siempre. 19 12. 20 Italy. 21 Seven years. 22 West Germany. 23 12th. 24 China. 25 18th. 26 Midge Ure. 27 Hydrogen. 28 Gipsy Moth IV. 29 Sven Goran Eriksson. 30 Hopes.

1 YouTube was founded in which year?
2 Which constituency did MP Alan B'Stard's represent in TV's "The New Statesman"?
3 "Atom Heart Mother" was the first album to top the UK charts by which long-lasting group?
4 Which film studio released the first talking film?
5 Roger Bannister's first sub-four-minute mile was recorded at 3 minutes and how many seconds?
6 Which club did Mark Hughes Join when he left Chelsea?
7 In which sport has Bob Nudd been world champion?
8 Which Commonwealth country was the first to issue a special Christmas stamp?
9 What was the nationality of the first manager to win the European Cup with an English club?
10 Which initials are linked to the discovery by Paul Muller?
11 What was the first top ten hit for Seal?
12 When was the last manned moon landing of the last century?
13 Which musical is based on the writing of Christopher Isherwood?
14 TV presenter Alison Holloway became the third wife of which comic?
15 "Stare Back and Smile" was the autobiography of which actress?
16 Who was the first winner on Wimbledon's new No 1 court in the 1990s?
17 In which country is the city of Nara?
18 Concord and Louise Bonne are both types of what?
19 Whose one and only UK top ten hit was "Jeans On"?
20 Who was Queen Elizabeth II's first Prime Minister?
21 How many wickets did Shane Warne take in his final Test series?
22 Which two countries share the world's longest frontier?
23 Which planet's day is actually longer than its year?
24 For which film did Geena Davis first win an Oscar?
25 Which renowned Danish furniture designer engaged in a lifelong quest to design the perfect chair?
26 Which former golfer shares a birthday with opera star Placido Domingo?
27 Who or what was the fabulous Cullinan Diamond named after?
28 The first solo transatlantic flight started in New York but where did it finish?
29 Usually known by its initials, what was set up at the Bretton Wood Agreement of 1944?
30 Which office item was registered by Wolfgang Dabisch in 1962?

Answers	Movie Classics (see Quiz 124)

1 Warner Bros. 2 It Happened One Night. 3 Writer Sidney Howard. 4 RKO. 5 Carioca.
6 Mr Smith Goes to Washington. 7 Cheek to Cheek (Top Hat). 8 Louella Parsons. 9 U.
10 Ivy Patterson. 11 Casablanca. 12 Warner Bros. 13 Land of Hope & Glory. 14 101.
15 Benito Mussolini. 16 Mary Astor. 17 Martinique (To Have & Have Not). 18 Paul
Dukas. 19 Adriana Caselotti. 20 Katharine Hepburn's pet leopard. 21 She has grit in her
eye. 22 British Museum (Blackmail). 23 Claire Trevor. 24 39 Steps. 25 Lex Barker. 26
Emil Jannings. 27 Mary Chase. 28 Paulette Goddard. 29 Rose Sayer. 30 17.

1 What was the last answer Judith Keppel gave to win a million on "Who Wants to be a Millionaire?"?
2 Who was "The Flying Gardener"?
3 What was the name of Amanda Holden's character in "EastEnders"?
4 How many World Cups had there been before the first one was broadcast in colour?
5 Who presented the BBC's "10 O'Clock News" on September 11th 2001?
6 In which series did Tricky Woo appear?
7 In what type of programmes does Charlotte Uhlenbroek mainly appear?
8 What was the first, unsuccessful, spin-off of "Baywatch"?
9 Who was the first woman sports presenter on Independent Television?
10 Who was Channel 4's chief executive during the "Celebrity Big Brother" Shilpa Shetty storm?
11 In 1999 who had a TV special called "Just for You"?
12 Which famous football commentator died the same day that England had their memorable World Cup qualifying win over Germany?
13 At which surgery did Will Preston and Jack Kerruish work?
14 With which celebrity golfer did Tiger Woods appear on US TV aged two?
15 Who was the first US President to be interviewed by Barbara Walters?
16 Which husband and wife presented the Channel 4 programme, "Top Ten TV Lovers"?
17 How long did the Saturday-morning show "Live & Kicking" run?
18 Which Derbyshire Hall became Thornfield in the 2006 BBC "Jane Eyre"?
19 In which year was "Life on Mars" set?
20 Which of Dennis Potter's dramas was the first he directed himself?
21 What was Britain's first daily TV quiz?
22 Who was in Dictionary Corner in Des O'Connor's first week as "Countdown" host?
23 About which series did a cast member say, "When the show got to No 1, I decided it could only be because none of us wears a bra"?
24 Who were the first Dalziel & Pascoe on TV?
25 What was the name of the company in the US comedy "Designing Women"?
26 What did Richard Arnold look at on GMTV?
27 Which show received the first National Television Award for Comedy?
28 Who wrote the novels on which "Lloyd & Hill" was based?
29 Which actress played Annie Blackburn in "Twin Peaks"?
30 Who launched the first Pay TV system?

Answers	Animals *(see Quiz 129)*

1 Basking shark. 2 Monkeys. 3 Koala bear. 4 Thomas Savage. 5 Bison. 6 Turtles. 7 Sailfish. 8 Thailand. 9 Whale shark. 10 Nevada. 11 Vulture. 12 Bandicoot. 13 Flying lemur. 14 400. 15 Lion. 16 Giant squid. 17 Fisher marten. 18 Otter. 19 Rabies. 20 Swan. 21 Sperm whale. 22 Kiwi. 23 Teal. 24 Smell. 25 Voice. 26 Third eye. 27 Marsupial mole. 28 Mexico. 29 Blunt nose lizard. 30 Capybara.

Quiz 128 | Pot Luck 60

1 What is another name for tungsten?
2 In the Watergate scandal, the Republican Committee to Re elect the President was known as what?
3 Which city was capital of Spain before Madrid?
4 What does a herpetologist study?
5 What type of fruit features in the title of a Chekhov play?
6 Coffee is named after the city of Kaffa in which country?
7 Against orders, what is Epimethius supposed to have opened?
8 Which present-day place in the East of England was the centre of the ancient kingdom of Lindsey?
9 Who sailed in "Lively Lady"?
10 What did John Speke and James Grant discover in the 19th century?
11 In Da Vinci's masterpiece the Mona Lisa in which direction is the lady looking?
12 How many titles did Jimmy Connors win in his tennis career?
13 What is the most number of letters in the name of any one calendar month?
14 How many storeys are there in the Empire State Building?
15 Who was the world's richest self-made millionaire at the end of the old millennium?
16 Which country did Scotsman Robert Louis Stevenson die in?
17 In which country would you watch Brann playing Bryne at soccer?
18 In the stage farce, where did Charley's Aunt come from?
19 Which of The Beatles has the same name as the patentor of the dental drill?
20 Who wrote "An Accidental MP"?
21 Which referee sent off Wayne Rooney against Portugal in 2006?
22 In 1984 WPC Yvonne Fletcher was shot outside which London Embassy?
23 Who was the first US President to make a visit to China?
24 The first rugby union player to score 50 international tries played for which country?
25 ANDi was the first genetically modified what?
26 What was the first album to make its debut at No 1 in the UK chart?
27 Who was the last British Royal to visit Hong Kong while it was under British rule?
28 Who did Mehmet Ali Agca try to assassinate in 1981?
29 What was the first top ten hit for Simple Minds?
30 In which city did the original Wallace and Gromit models get mislaid in the 1990s?

Answers	Music Charts (see Quiz 130)

1 The Way I am. 2 Never Had a Dream Come True. 3 Bills, Bills, Bills. 4 Oasis. 5 Written in the Stars. 6 Summertime of Our Lives. 7 Wishing I was Lucky. 8 Arsenal. 9 One week. 10 Deeper Shade of Blue. 11 Bohemian Rhapsody. 12 War of Nerves. 13 Five and Queen. 14 Hercules. 15 Billie. 16 Madison Avenue. 17 Samantha Fox. 18 Gangster Trippin'. 19 E-17. 20 Tsunami. 21 Six. 22 Rolf Harris. 23 Westlife. 24 Des O'Connor. 25 Fairytale of New York. 26 Six. 27 Manchester United. 28 12. 29 Even After All. 30 When Doves Cry.

1 What is the second largest species of fish?
2 What type of animals were space travellers Sam and Miss Sam?
3 Which animals spends the largest amount of time asleep?
4 Who first named the gorilla?
5 Which usually weighs the most – a bison, a moose or a polar bear?
6 What are Pacific leatherbacks and Atlantic leatherbacks?
7 Which of these swims the fastest – marlin, sailfish or swordfish?
8 Kittis's hognosed bat is native to which country?
9 What is Rhincodon typus?
10 The devil's hole pupfish restricts its habitat to an isolated part of which US state?
11 What is a Ruppell's griffon?
12 What has the highest reproductive rate of all marsupials?
13 What is another name for the colugo?
14 Approximately how many domestic breeds of dog are there?
15 What is the most socially organised member of the cat family?
16 Which is the largest – giant African snail, giant clam or giant squid?
17 Which creature is unique in its ability to penetrate the quills of a porcupine?
18 What is the only truly amphibious member of the weasel family?
19 The skunk is a major carrier of which disease?
20 The greatest number of feathers counted on a bird was on a what?
21 Which is the largest of the toothed whales?
22 What is the smallest of the Ratitae order?
23 Which flies the fastest – mallard, pintail or teal?
24 Which sense does the Old World vulture lack?
25 What is the most beautiful part of the bulbul?
26 What does the tuatara have on top of its head?
27 What is the only marsupial which specialises in burrowing?
28 Where is the Bolson tortoise native to?
29 What is the San Joaquin leopard lizard also known as?
30 What is the largest living rodent?

---

1 What was Eminem's chart success between his first two UK No 1s?
2 What was SClub7's second No 1 which went straight to the top spot?
3 What was Beyonce Knowles' band's first US No 1?
4 Which chart-topping band's line-up has included Tony McCarroll and Gem Archer?
5 What was LeAnn Rimes' first UK hit with another artist?
6 What was A1's follow-up to their UK chart debut?
7 Their biggest hit was "Love is All Around" in 1994, what was their first?
8 Which soccer side charted with "Hot Stuff"?
9 For how long was the NME chart a Top 25?
10 What was Steps' first Top Ten hit of the new millennium?
11 Which classic single topped the chart when Mel C was born?
12 What was All Saints' last hit of the 1990s?
13 With whom did "We Will Rock You" first chart?
14 From which movie was Stephen Gately's solo chart debut?
15 Who was the first lady to top the charts three times before being able to vote in the UK?
16 How are chart toppers Andy Van Dorsselaer and Cheyne Coates better known?
17 Who was the only British female to have three US & UK Top Ten singles in the 1980s?
18 What was Fatboy Slim's second single to enter the UK Top Ten?
19 What did Brian Harvey's band change their name to on their return to the charts in 1998?
20 What was the Manic Street Preachers' last hit of the 1990s?
21 What was Mansun's last 1990s hit to have a number in the title?
22 Who had the final chart topper of the 1960s?
23 Which was the first band to have four UK No 1's in a single year?
24 Who had a Top Twenty hit in 1969 with "Dick a Dum Dum"?
25 What was the Pogues' follow-up to their first Top Ten hit?
26 How many Top Ten hits did Ocean Colour Scene have in a row in the 1990s?
27 Whose last hit of the 1990s was "Move Move Move"?
28 How many successive Top Twenty singles did Prodigy have by the end of the millennium?
29 What was Finley Quaye's first Top Ten single?
30 Which single was Prince's most successful before "Purple Rain"?

Answers	Pot Luck 60 *(see Quiz 128)*

1 Wolfram. 2 CREEP. 3 Valladolid. 4 Reptiles. 5 Cherry. 6 Ethiopia. 7 Pandora's box. 8 Lincoln. 9 Alec Rose. 10 Source of the Nile. 11 To her right. 12 109. 13 Nine. 14 102. 15 Bill Gates. 16 Samoa. 17 Norway. 18 Brazil. 19 George Harrison. 20 Martin Bell. 21 Horacio Elizondo. 22 Libyan. 23 Nixon. 24 Australia. 25 Monkey. 26 Help!. 27 Prince Charles. 28 The Pope. 29 Don't You (Forget About Me). 30 New York.

1 What is named after Benjamin Hall?
2 Who wrote "I'm a Believer" for The Monkees?
3 What is the name for a sentence containing all the letters of the alphabet?
4 How many of the first five letters of Singapore appear on the international car index mark for a car from that country?
5 The time it takes a planet to orbit the sun is called what?
6 In 2007 which company unveiled "Plan A", to become carbon neutral in five years?
7 In which decade of last century did Fiji leave the Commonwealth?
8 Which US state has a capital bearing the name of 15th-century explorer Christopher?
9 "Girls on Film" was the first Top Ten hit for which group?
10 A fear of dust is known as what?
11 Which Marc Bolan song features on the soundtrack of "Moulin Rouge"?
12 Who did Justine Henin-Hardenne beat to claim her third French Open title?
13 What does the musical notation "pesante" mean – heavy and ponderous, unaffected or lively?
14 Who was the Greek goddess of victory?
15 In which month is Canada Day celebrated?
16 Which agoraphobic won the Costa prize for "The Tenderness of Wolves"?
17 In which city did the first Cruft's dog show take place?
18 To the nearest ten, how many minutes did the audience have to scream during the first "Scream" movie?
19 What did Melville Bissell patent in 1881?
20 What was the first Tom Cruise/Nicole Kidman film after their marriage?
21 In which decade was the Brazilian Grand Prix first held?
22 Who coined the name vaccination?
23 Which European leader was executed with his wife in December 1989?
24 On which label did Vengaboys first make No 1 – Positiva, Outpost or Skint?
25 The old London Bridge was dismantled, transported and rebuilt in which US state?
26 As a fully grown male which weighs the most – a baboon, a mandrill or a proboscis monkey?
27 Which Elvis Presley movie featured the song "Return to Sender"?
28 What was the occupation of John Dunlop of tyre fame?
29 In song lyrics, what – according to Buggles – "Killed the Radio Star"?
30 The owner of the Cleveland Browns took over which Premiership club?

Answers	**Pot Luck 62** *(see Quiz 133)*

1 Dr Crippen. 2 Google. 3 Henrik Stenson. 4 Norman Tebbit. 5 Simon. 6 Tenerife. 7 Winchester. 8 Blue Peter. 9 Shropshire. 10 200m and 800m. 11 Three. 12 20. 13 Bohemian Rhapsody. 14 Face Value. 15 DeForest. 16 Venezuela. 17 Goodbye Yellow Brick Road. 18 1975. 19 Katharine Hepburn. 20 Simian Films. 21 1666. 22 Kenya. 23 Madonna. 24 Belgium. 25 Nobel prizes. 26 Harry James. 27 Jack Ruby. 28 Italy. 29 1974. 30 Vincent.

1 Which is the largest province of the country which has Madrid as its capital?
2 Which building houses the Bayeux Tapestry?
3 France, Italy, Sweden – which does not have an internet code made up of its first two letters?
4 In which department of Basse Normandie is the village where the famous soft cheese is made?
5 Where are the Bakony Mountains?
6 Where is Switzerland's oldest university?
7 What is Europe's most southerly point?
8 Which country is to the immediate north of the Ukraine?
9 In which Sea are Gotland and Oland?
10 Which language is Euskara?
11 Which city is the burial place of William the Conqueror and Beau Brummel?
12 Which Austrian city was known as Thermae Helveticae to the Romans?
13 Anjou is now part of which French departement?
14 In Austria what is the Fohn?
15 The Campine coalfield is to the east of which country?
16 Which country is to the immediate south of Croatia?
17 Where is the Jotunheimen range of mountains?
18 Which Italian port takes its name from the Greek for elbow?
19 Which language is spoken in Wallonia?
20 What is the capital of Brabant?
21 How many countries border the Federal Republic of Germany?
22 In which country is the city of Esztergom?
23 What is the currency of Slovenia?
24 What is the capital of the German province to the south of Brandenburg?
25 What is the capital of the province to the west of Abruzzio?
26 In which country are the Pripet Marshes?
27 Which river bisects Andorra?
28 Who designed the Finlandia Concert Hall in Helsinki?
29 In which mountain range is Europe's highest peak?
30 Of the ten largest cities in Europe which three were once part of the Soviet Union?

Answers	Unforgettables *(see Quiz 134)*

1 Brian Jones and Jim Morrison. 2 Lake Tanganyika. 3 13 years. 4 331. 5 Somalia. 6 Montserrat Caballe. 7 Hotel de la Reine. 8 Martha Washington. 9 Victor Gollancz. 10 John Reed. 11 Mrs Ronald Reagan. 12 Bernard Herrmann. 13 Dashiel Hammett. 14 Rex Harrison. 15 Alexander Graham Bell. 16 Ian Richardson. 17 19 May. 18 Three. 19 Agatha Christie. 20 Elizabeth Arden. 21 Clement Attlee. 22 Doctor. 23 Giles Gilbert Scott. 24 Leonard. 25 Bertrand Russell. 26 Jennifer Jones. 27 Where's the Bourbon?. 28 John Paul II. 29 Alfred Hitchcock. 30 Frankie Howerd.

1 Which villain had a mistress called Ethel Le Neve?
2 Which company bought YouTube in 2006?
3 Who holed the winning shot in the 2006 Ryder Cup?
4 Which Norman said his father "got on his bike and looked for work"?
5 Who was named as being in The Chipmunks along with Alvin and Theodore?
6 On which island were 583 people killed in a 1970s air disaster?
7 Where is Britain's longest cathedral?
8 Leila Williams was the first female presenter of which long-running TV show?
9 In which English county was the world's first iron bridge built?
10 100m hurdles and which two other track events are included in the World Championship women's heptathlon?
11 How many of Henry VIII's children followed him to the throne?
12 How old was Mike Tyson when he became boxing's youngest ever heavyweight world champion?
13 Which hit was the first single to be No 1 over two separate Christmases?
14 What was the first solo No 1 album for Phil Collins?
15 What was the middle name of Humphrey Bogart?
16 In which country is the city of Maracay?
17 Elton John's original "Candle in the Wind" first featured on which album?
18 In what year did Charlie Chaplin eventually receive a knighthood?
19 Ludlow Ogden married which famous Hollywood actress?
20 Which production company was set up by Hugh Grant and Liz Hurley?
21 In which year was fire insurance first pioneered in London – was it 1666, 1812 or 1914?
22 In which country was Mau Mau a nationalist movement?
23 Stephen Bray and Patrick Leonard have both co-written No 1 singles with which solo singer?
24 In which country did the Battle of Passchendaele take place?
25 Which prizes were first awarded in 1901?
26 Which bandleader did Betty Grable marry in 1943?
27 Involved in a famous 20th-century murder how was Jacob Rubinstein better known?
28 Who held the wooden spoon at the start of the 2007 Six Nations Rugby tournament?
29 In which year was Juan Peron – of "Evita" fame – last in office as President of Argentina?
30 Don McLean's "American Pie" album featured which song that he took to No 1 as a UK single?

1 Which two major rock stars died on 3 July, one in 1969 one in 1971?
2 Where did Henry Stanley say, "Dr Livingstone I presume"?
3 For how long were Napoleon and Josephine married?
4 How many weekly radio addresses did Ronald Reagan make?
5 Which country did Audrey Hepburn visit as a UNICEF Ambassador shortly before her death?
6 Which opera star was born on the late Maria Callas's 10th birthday?
7 In which hotel did John Lennon and Yoko Ono have their famous "bed in"?
8 Who was the first First Lady of the USA – although the actual phrase had yet to be coined?
9 Which publisher founded the charity War on Want?
10 Who was the first American to be buried in the Kremlin?
11 What was the actress born Anne Frances Robbins' most famous married name?
12 To whom did Martin Scorsese dedicate "Taxi Driver"?
13 Which novelist investigated the Fatty Arbuckle assault case when working for the Pinkerton Detective Agency?
14 Who edited the anthology of romantic poems "If Love be Love"?
15 Who said on 10th March 1876, "Come here, Watson, I want you"?
16 Which actor played Sir Epicure Mammon in "The Alchemist" at the National, 2006?
17 On what date did Marilyn Monroe famously sing "Happy Birthday" to John F Kennedy?
18 How many No 1 singles did Roy Orbison achieve in the UK during his lifetime?
19 Mary Westmacott is also known as whom?
20 How is cosmetics queen Florence Nightingale Graham better known?
21 Who was the first Labour PM to have an absolute majority in House of Commons?
22 What was the occupation of the first independent President of Malawi?
23 Who designed Battersea Power Station?
24 What was the first name of Baron Callaghan of Cardiff?
25 Who was the first president of CND?
26 Who was the widow of the producer of "Gone with the Wind"?
27 What was Marilyn Monroe's only line of dialogue in the scene which took 59 takes in "Some Like It Hot"?
28 Who was the youngest Pope of the 20th century?
29 Which film director married Alma Reville?
30 Which late comedian's autobiography was called "On My Way I Lost It"?

1 Who wrote Blondie's 1999 chart topper "Maria"?
2 "Tenko" was a popular TV series but what does Tenko mean?
3 The first ever programme of "Top of the Pops" was broadcast from which city?
4 Ed Koch is a former mayor of which American city?
5 What is the nationality of actor William Shatner famous as Captain Kirk?
6 What's the job of Jack Nicholson's character in the movie "Wolf"?
7 In which country is the city of Sorocaba?
8 What was the first top ten hit for Wilson Phillips?
9 On which special day did Dirty Den serve divorce papers on Angie in "EastEnders"?
10 In which department did TV MP Jim Hacker first become a minister?
11 In 1995 which visiting side became the first team in 22 years to win a Test series in the West Indies?
12 What did the letter K stand for in the film company name RKO?
13 What was the first name of the late classically trained actor John Gielgud?
14 Joseph Merlin invented what kind of sporting footwear?
15 Who as a youngster was brought up in disguise in Smallville, USA?
16 In which county did the Great Train Robbery take place?
17 How many neck bones does a giraffe have?
18 Who presented the Rugby World Cup to Francois Pienaar in 1995?
19 Which religious movement was founded by Mary Baker Eddy?
20 What was singer songwriter Hoagy Carmichael's real first name?
21 Who was head coach of Los Angeles Galaxy when the Beckham deal was announced?
22 What four nationalities make up the members of Il Divo?
23 Kim Campbell was the first woman PM of which country?
24 According to a Henry Kissinger quote what was "the ultimate aphrodisiac"?
25 Elizabeth Garrett Anderson is recognised as being the first British woman to carry out which profession?
26 Which Mike broke Bob Beaman's 23-year long jump record in 1992?
27 Which boxer coached actor Daniel Day-Lewis for his role in "The Boxer"?
28 Which Indian Prime Minister resigned in the same month that Saddam Hussein became president of Iraq?
29 Johann Christophe Denner invented which musical instrument?
30 In which year did Yasser Arafat become PLO chairman?

Answers	Pot Luck 64 *(see Quiz 137)*

1 Dundalk. 2 May. 3 Invincible (adamas). 4 Cello. 5 Root. 6 Isabella Rossellini.
7 Cuban missile. 8 Ibadan. 9 Fidel Castro. 10 Stephen Dorrell. 11 The Blue Room.
12 University College. 13 The Absinthe Fairy. 14 Private Lives. 15 Sweden (5 points).
16 Leprosy. 17 Texas. 18 Iberus (hence Iberia) 19 Capricorn. 20 William Rodgers.
21 New Zealand. 22 His mother (Statue of Liberty). 23 Iraq. 24 Steven Spielberg.
25 Margot. 26 Valerie. 27 What hath God wrought?. 28 Platform shoes. 29 Nancy Griffith. 30 Royal Exchange.

1 To whom did Helen Mirren dedicate her 2007 movie BAFTA?

2 Which wife of Robert De Niro appeared in "New York New York"?

3 What is the real name of the actress who played the title role in "Octopussy"?

4 Which role did Lorraine Bracco play in "Goodfellas"?

5 Which pseudonym did Kim Basinger use when she performed as a solo singer in her early career?

6 For which of his movies did Nicolas Cage reputedly swallow a live cockroach?

7 Who was the fourth movie "Batman"?

8 Who traditionally sings the US National Anthem at each season's first home game of baseball team the New York Mets?

9 Who was Oscar nominated for playing Olive in "Little Miss Sunshine"?

10 Who was the big screen's first nude Lady Macbeth?

11 Who was known in France as "le sacre monstre"?

12 Which character did Hugh Grant play in "Music and Lyrics"?

13 Which actress was president of Actors Equity in the US from 1982 to 1985?

14 What was Disney's last hand-painted movie?

15 Which star of "Drugstore Cowboy" is a grand-nephew of the creator of Flash Gordon?

16 Which profession did the director of "If" play in "Chariots of Fire"?

17 What was Daniel Day Lewis's very first movie at the age of 14?

18 Who set up a production company called Tribeca Films?

19 Whose production company was called Memorial Enterprises?

20 Who was Carrie Fisher's first stepmother?

21 Who directed the second "Bridget Jones" movie?

22 Which leader did Anthony Hopkins play in "Victory at Entebbe"?

23 What was Jodie Foster's second movie as director?

24 Who prefaced his first book with, "This book is for people who like movies"?

25 John Huston died during the making of which film, due to be directed by his son?

26 Who did Kirstie Alley play in her debut movie?

27 Which star of "The Exorcist" competed in equestrian events as Martha McDonald?

28 What was Bob Hoskins' next film after his first Oscar nomination?

29 Joel and Ethan Coen are said to have written "Raising Arizona" with which actress in mind?

30 Famous daughter Anjelica Huston played opposite the son of which General in "A Walk with Love and Death"?

Answers | **Sporting Legends** (see Quiz 138)

1 Seven. 2 Reggie Jackson. 3 24. 4 Arnold Palmer. 5 13. 6 Elizabeth Ryan. 7 1966. 8 Horacio Elizondo. 9 Backstroke. 10 Philippe Sella. 11 112. 12 Tiger Woods. 13 Bruce Sheldon. 14 Gary Player. 15 Natalie Tauziat. 16 Tuberculosis. 17 1959. 18 Brooklyn Dodgers. 19 Merlin Olsen. 20 Tracey Edwards. 21 Wimbledon. 22 Liz McColgan. 23 Seamus McDonagh. 24 Billie Jean King. 25 Marvin Hart. 26 Huddersfield. 27 Sabatini. 28 Jack Brabham. 29 Melbourne. 30 Knocked overboard on his yacht.

1 Which town do The Corrs hail from?
2 In which month was Britain's first official bank holiday?
3 The word diamond comes from a Greek word meaning what?
4 Which musical instrument does Han-Na Chang play?
5 What part of the plant does phylloxera vitifoliae attack?
6 Which actress lost her Lancome contract around her 40th birthday?
7 During which crisis did a US politician comment, "We're eyeball to eyeball and I think the other fellow just blinked"?
8 What is the second largest city of Nigeria?
9 Which world leader was excommunicated in 1962?
10 Who was health secretary when the link between BSE and CJD was first admitted?
11 In which play did Elle Macpherson make her stage debut?
12 What is the oldest Oxford college?
13 Which role did the singer of the No 1 "Can't Get You Out of My Head" play in "Moulin Rouge"?
14 In which play did Noel Coward write, "Very flat, Norfolk"?
15 Which team topped the 2002 World Cup Group stage with fewest points?
16 What is another name for Hansen's disease?
17 Alaska replaced which state as the USA's largest?
18 What was the Roman name for the River Ebro?
19 What is Mel Gibson's star sign?
20 Which male founder of the SDP had the surname nearest the end of the alphabet?
21 Where did Jim Bulger form a coalition government in December 1996?
22 Who did FA-Bartholdi use as a model for his most famous sculpture?
23 The ancient civilisation of Sumeria is now in which country?
24 Who directed the movie about Gigolo Joe, a robot boy and his teddy bear?
25 What was Anne Frank's older sister called?
26 What was the first name of TS Eliot's widow?
27 What was the first message transmitted by telegraph?
28 What were buskins?
29 Who made the album "Clock without Hands"?
30 What was the Stock Exchange called when it was first founded?

Answers	Pot Luck 63 *(see Quiz 135)*

1 Jimmy Destri. 2 Roll call. 3 Manchester. 4 New York. 5 Canadian. 6 Book editor. 7 Brazil. 8 Hold On. 9 Christmas Day. 10 Administrative Affairs. 11 Australia. 12 Keith. 13 Arthur. 14 Roller skate. 15 Superman. 16 Bedfordshire. 17 Seven. 18 Nelson Mandela. 19 Christian Science. 20 Hoagland. 21 Frank Yallop. 22 French, Swiss, Spanish & American. 23 Canada. 24 Power. 25 Doctor. 26 Powell. 27 Barry McGuigan. 28 Morarji Desai. 29 Clarinet. 30 1968.

1 How many times did Jaden Gil Agassi's mum win Wimbledon?
2 Who was the second man, after Babe Ruth, to hit three home runs in one baseball World Series game?
3 For how many years was Matt Busby boss of Manchester United?
4 Who won golf's British Open in its centenary year?
5 How many conversions were among the 35 points Jonny Wilkinson scored at Twickenham in February 2001?
6 Who died on the day that Billie Jean King beat her Wimbledon title record?
7 When did Jack Nicklaus win his third US Masters?
8 Which referee sent off Zinedine Zidane against Italy in the World Cup Final?
9 Which of backstroke, butterfly or freestyle did Mark Spitz not swim at Munich in 1972?
10 Who won a record 111 international caps for Rugby between 1982 and 1995?
11 How many games were played in Wimbledon's longest match?
12 Whom did Nick Faldo hand a green jacket to in April 1997 in Georgia?
13 Whom did Mike Tyson beat to win his third world heavyweight title?
14 Who was the first US Open golf winner to be neither British nor American?
15 Against whom did Jana Novotna play her third Wimbledon Singles Final?
16 Harry Vardon won two British Open golf titles after contracting which illness?
17 Which was Pele's most successful individual year as a goalscorer?
18 Against whom did New York Yankees pitcher Don Larson pitch a World Series perfect game?
19 Who completed the Los Angeles Rams' "Fearsome Foursome" along with Deacon Jones, Lamarr Lundy and Roosevelt Grier?
20 In the Whitbread Round the World Race who skippered "Maiden"?
21 Of her 24 Grand Slam titles which did Margaret Court win the least?
22 Who was the only female BBC Sports Personality of the Year in the 1990s?
23 Who did Evander Holyfield beat in his first win by a knockout in the 1990s?
24 Who was the first president of the WTA?
25 Who won the first 20th-century heavyweight boxing championship to be stopped?
26 For which team did Albert Rosenfield score his record 80 Rugby League tries in 1914?
27 Who did Steffi Graf beat to win her first 1990s Wimbledon Singles title?
28 Who was the first man to win the world F1 championship in his own car?
29 Where did Shane Warne take his 700th Test wicket?
30 How did Eric Tabarly meet his death?

Answers | Movies Who's Who? (see Quiz 136)

1 Ian Richardson. 2 Diahnne Abbott. 3 Maude Wikstrum. 4 Karen Hill. 5 Chelsea. 6 Vampire's Kiss. 7 George Clooney. 8 Glenn Close. 9 Abigail Breslin. 10 Francesca Annis. 11 Charles Bronson. 12 Alex Fletcher. 13 Ellen Burstyn. 14 The Little Mermaid. 15 Matt Dillon. 16 Schoolmaster (Lindsay Anderson). 17 Sunday Bloody Sunday. 18 Robert De Niro. 19 Albert Finney. 20 Elizabeth Taylor. 21 Beeban Kidron. 22 Yitzhak Rabin. 23 Home for the Holidays. 24 Leslie Halliwell. 25 Mr North. 26 Lt Saavik (Star Trek II). 27 Linda Blair. 28 A Prayer for the Dying. 29 Holly Hunter. 30 Dayan.

1 Which film director said, "Not only is there no God, try getting a plumber at weekends"?
2 What was the first building in England to be lit by incandescent light?
3 Who accompanied Dr Michael Stroud on the first unsupported crossing of the Antarctic?
4 Which name is the Hebrew for trickster or supplanter?
5 What was the name of the first nuclear submarine to circumnavigate the world underwater?
6 Who was the first British monarch to visit China?
7 Which were the last two imperial territories in Africa?
8 In which city was the premiere of Orson Welles' first film?
9 In India, which is furthest south, Bombay, Calcutta, or Hyderabad?
10 Who developed the computer language Java?
11 Which magazine did Charles Russell found?
12 The original Globe Theatre burned down during which Shakespeare play?
13 What did the middle initial stand for in the name of the author who wrote "Three Men in a Boat"?
14 In the UK what was the first speed limit for cars in the country as opposed to town?
15 Which 1960s Norman Jewison film won five Oscars?
16 What does the Arabic word jihad mean?
17 Which island did Columbus call St Iago?
18 Which 19th-century Prime Minister was the subject of a biography written by Baron Jenkins of Hillhead after he left Parliament?
19 In Germany 2006, who got a four-game ban for elbowing USA's Brian McBride?
20 Which Henry James novel was the subject of an opera by Benjamin Britten?
21 Who wrote the TV series "Clocking Off" and "Linda Green"?
22 With which architect did Gertrude Jekyll work?
23 Who was the first president of Iran?
24 Which monarch knighted Sir Winston Churchill?
25 In which US state is the George Rogers Clark National Historical Park?
26 Who reputedly said, "Die my dear doctor. That's the last thing I shall do"?
27 Which Pope excommunicated King John and declared the Magna Carta void?
28 In cars, what was the Procon Ten?
29 What did the island of Hispaniola later become?
30 Among his first five consecutive Tour de France wins, in which year did Miguel Indurain set the record for the fastest average speed?

Answers | Pot Luck 66 *(see Quiz 141)*

1 Vermouth (Wermut). 2 Carolyn Murphy. 3 Rachel Portman. 4 Elena Xanthoudakis. 5 Rio Ferdinand. 6 Madonna. 7 Pam Warren. 8 Nevada. 9 Return of Apollo 11 from the Moon. 10 Herbert Marcuse. 11 Jo Moore. 12 Rome. 13 Diamonds are a Girl's Best Friend. 14 Kirov. 15 Terry Venables. 16 Scott Walker. 17 Thomas Gresham. 18 Chris Smith. 19 Wasp. 20 Resolution. 21 Claire Danes. 22 Over the Moon. 23 Noel Coward. 24 Cairo. 25 Martin Campbell. 26 Dith Pran. 27 Billy Crystal. 28 Albert Camus & TS Eliot. 29 The Cochran. 30 Jim Davidson.

1 Whom did Major run against to become Tory Party leader and PM?
2 Who was the first man to be General Secretary and President of the USSR?
3 Who was Chairman of the Republican National Committee during the Watergate scandal?
4 What was Hosni Mubarak's profession before entering politics?
5 Jacques Santer became president of the European Commission after Britain's veto of whom?
6 What was the name of the autobiography of the first woman leader of a British political party?
7 Who succeeded Willy Brandt as Chancellor of West Germany?
8 Which US president won the Pulitzer Prize for "Profiles in Courage"?
9 Who was Albania's second Prime Minister in 1997?
10 Who was the first President of a united post-WWII Germany?
11 Who became Israel's acting PM after the assassination of Rabin?
12 Gro Harlem Brundtland was the first woman PM in which country?
13 Which Conservative Canadian politician served between Pierre Trudeau's two terms of office?
14 Who was the first British President of the EU?
15 Before becoming Pope Karol Jozef Wojtyia was Archbishop of where?
16 At which educational institution did Bill Clinton meet Hillary Rodham?
17 Which then leader won the 1969 Hobart Ocean race?
18 How was Prince Ras Tafari Makonnen better known?
19 Who was the first living ex-PM of Australia not to accept the Companion to the Order of Australia after he left politics?
20 Who was President of Chile during the Falklands conflict?
21 How long after becoming German Chancellor did Hitler assume the title of Führer?
22 Who was the longest-serving US President of the 1970s?
23 Which Austrian president was a former Secretary General to the UN?
24 Winston Churchill became Chancellor of the Exchequer under which PM?
25 Who succeeded Chairman Mao as Chairman of China's ruling Communist Party?
26 What was Tony Blair's first responsibility in Labour's Shadow Cabinet?
27 Who did Ronald Reagan defeat the second time he became US president?
28 Who was the last King of Greece in the 20th century?
29 Who was the second President of France's Fifth Republic?
30 Who was the first and last Executive President of the USSR?

Answers	TV Adverts *(see Quiz 142)*

1 Nationwide. 2 Mir. 3 Labi Siffre. 4 Fly Away. 5 Michael Jackson. 6 Peter O'Toole.
7 The Joker. 8 Schwartz. 9 Frank Muir. 10 Elgar's Cello Concerto in E Minor. 11
Halifax. 12 (Auto) Windscreens. 13 Benylin. 14 Meg Smith. 15 Penelope Keith.
16 Benecol. 17 David Ginola. 18 Paul Dukas. 19 Giuseppe Verdi. 20 Peter Sellers.
21 Optivita. 22 Trevor Eve. 23 Sainsbury's. 24 Lesley Dunlop. 25 Mr Oizo. 26
Specsavers. 27 Pastoral Symphony. 28 Advertising Standards Authority. 29 Junk food
adverts. 30 Gibbs SR.

Quiz 141 | Pot Luck 66

Answers – page 613

LEVEL 3

1 Which wine takes its name from the German for wormwood, an early ingredient?
2 Who replaced Liz Hurley as the face of Estée Lauder?
3 Who won an Oscar for the score of "Emma"?
4 Which soprano won the 2006 International Mozart Competition?
5 Which player played all of Sven's first and last games as England boss?
6 Which superstar had a Max Factor cosmetics contract for just one year?
7 Which co-winner of the Woman of the Year 2001 was a survivor of the Paddington rail crash?
8 Where in the US were atomic bombs first tested?
9 What did Richard Nixon describe as, "The greatest week in the history of the world since the Creation"?
10 Who wrote "One Dimensional Man"?
11 Who sent an e mail saying it would be a good day to bury bad news the day the World Trade Center was hit?
12 Which was the world's largest city at the end of the first millennium?
13 Which song has the line, "We all lose our charms in the end"?
14 Which ballet company was called the Maryinsky until 1935?
15 Which former England football manager shares a birthday with cricketer Kapil Dev?
16 Which 60s/70 star produced Pulp's "We Love Life"?
17 Who founded what was to become the Stock Exchange?
18 Who did Tessa Jowell replace in Tony Blair's Cabinet after the 2001 election?
19 What is an ichneumon fly?
20 What was the name of the first ship to cross the Antarctic Circle?
21 Who was the voice of Princess Mononoke in the "Studio Ghibli" movie?
22 In which play did a 65+ Joan Collins star in skimpy underwear in 2001?
23 Who said, "Work is much more fun than fun"?
24 Where did the last Shah of Iran die?
25 Who directed Pierce Brosnan's first outing as 007?
26 Who is the central character in "The Killing Fields"?
27 Who produced and co-wrote the 2001 movie where Julia Roberts and Catherine Zeta Jones played sisters?
28 Which two winners of a Nobel Prize for Literature both died on 4th January, one in 1960 and one in 1965?
29 What was the name of the first dishwasher?
30 Whose autobiography was called "Close to the Edge"?

Answers	**Pot Luck 65 (see Quiz 139)**

1 Woody Allen. 2 Gateshead Town Hall. 3 Ranulph Fiennes. 4 Jacob. 5 Triton. 6 Elizabeth II. 7 Mozambique & Angola. 8 New York (Citizen Kane). 9 Hyderabad. 10 Sun Microsystems. 11 The Watchtower. 12 Henry VIII. 13 Klapka. 14 4 mph. 15 In the Heat of the Night. 16 Holy War/Struggle. 17 Jamaica. 18 William Gladstone. 19 Daniele de Rossi. 20 The Turn of the Screw. 21 Paul Abbott. 22 Edwin Lutyens. 23 Abolhassan Bani Sadr. 24 Elizabeth II. 25 Indiana. 26 Lord Palmerston. 27 Innocent III. 28 Collapsible steering wheel. 29 Haiti. 30 His second win, 1992.

1 Which Building Society boasts that it is "proud to be different"?
2 Where was the first TV ad filmed in space actually filmed?
3 Who sang the song for the 2001 ad for the Peugeot 307?
4 In 1999 which song was the first advert No 1 for three years?
5 Who was the first artist to appear in a Pepsi ad?
6 Which veteran actor appeared in the ad for Zurich insurance?
7 Which Steve Miller Band song advertised jeans?
8 Who sponsored "Richard & Judy" on their Channel 4 return at the beginning of 2007?
9 Which writer advertised Cadbury's Fruit & Nut accompanied by music by Tchaikovsky?
10 Which music used in "Hilary & Jackie" encouraged the drinking of Buxton Spring Water?
11 Which building society fell foul of Equity for using its own employees in an ad?
12 Which part of a car is connected with the "Toreador's Song" from "Carmen"?
13 Which cough mixture was Pavarotti's "theme song" used to advertise?
14 What was the name of the first woman to appear in a UK TV ad?
15 Which ex-"Good Life" cast member became the voice behind Lurpak butter?
16 "Countdown"'s statistician extolled the virtues of which margarine?
17 Which footballer was "worth it"?
18 Who wrote the "Sorcerer's Apprentice", used in an ad for round tea bags?
19 Whose "Requiem Mass" accompanied the virtues of Irn Bru?
20 Who was the first voice of the PG Tips chimps?
21 Which oat cereal was advertised by Ray Winstone?
22 Which actor's wife was in the famous long-running Gold Blend coffee ad?
23 Which supermarket chain employs the Naked Chef?
24 Which "Where the Heart is" star passed around the Kleenex tissues?
25 Who recorded the seventh No 1 hit to be associated with Levi jeans?
26 Who sponsored "Countdown" at the time Des O'Connor took over?
27 Which Beethoven Symphony advertised Blue Band margarine?
28 Which organisation makes sure that all advertising meets certain codes of practice?
29 In November 2006, Ofcom announced a ban on what during programmes targeted at under-16s?
30 Toothpaste was the first product advertised on UK TV – but which brand?

Answers	**World Leaders** *(see Quiz 140)*

1 Michael Heseltine and Douglas Hurd. 2 Leonid Brezhnev. 3 George Bush Sr. 4 Pilot. 5 Jean Luc Dehaene. 6 Margaret Thatcher: The Downing Street Years. 7 Helmut Schmidt. 8 JF Kennedy. 9 Bashkim Fino. 10 Richard Von Weizsacker. 11 Shimon Peres. 12 Norway. 13 Joseph Clark. 14 Roy Jenkins. 15 Cracow. 15 Yale Law School. 17 Edward Heath. 18 Haile Selassie. 19 Paul Keating. 20 Augusto Pinochet. 21 A year. 22 Richard Nixon. 23 Kurt Waldheim. 24 Stanley Baldwin. 25 Hua Guofeng. 26 Energy. 27 Walter Mondale. 28 Constantine II. 29 Georges Pompidou. 30 Mikael Gorbachev.

1 At which meeting was the establishing of an International Monetary Fund proposed?
2 How is Iran's Dasht e Kavir also known?
3 Which is farthest north – Kerry, Limerick or Munster?
4 Which famous car did Issigonis design as well as the Mini?
5 WG Grace died on which future England captain's 15th birthday?
6 Where was the first permanent English settlement in the New World?
7 The lady born Sheila Gilhooly wrote the second part of whose autobiography?
8 Who described Herbert Von Karajan as "a kind of musical Malcolm Sargent"?
9 What does M stand for in HTML?
10 In 1994 Johannesburg was made capital of which region?
11 Which painter, and sister of a famous painter was the model and mistress of Rodin?
12 What is the southernmost city of New Zealand?
13 Who is the heroine of "Fear of Flying"?
14 Who made his debut in "The Wise Little Hen" in 1934?
15 Which classic did Kylie Minogue sing when she starred in the show which opened the Fox Studios in Sydney in 1999?
16 On which Channel is Alaska's capital?
17 Who broke the solo flight record to Cape Town in 1932?
18 What was the speed limit raised to when it no longer required a person with a red flag to walk in front of a motor vehicle?
19 Where did "The Mousetrap" have its first night in the West End?
20 Which newspaper published the first crossword?
21 Where is Yupik or Yuk spoken?
22 How are the Sandwich Islands now known?
23 Which UN Secretary General negotiated peace in the Iran–Iraq War?
24 Who did Helmut Kohl overtake as Germany's longest serving Chancellor in 1995?
25 What was Prince Philip's military rank when he married Princess Elizabeth?
26 Which Great Britain forward was sacked by Leeds Rhinos in January 2006?
27 What is the English title of the play "La Cantatrice Chauve"?
28 "Whom the Gods Would Destroy" was an episode in a series about which TV detective?
29 In which city did Tchaikovsky die?
30 In which month did Margaret Thatcher announce her resignation as Prime Minister?

Answers	**Pot Luck 68** *(see Quiz 145)*

1 Australian Open (2007). 2 The Colosseum in Rome. 3 David Scarboro. 4 Wrigley's Chewing Gum. 5 Likeness. 6 Rue Cambon. 7 Jordan. 8 Alexander Korda. 9 Michelle. 10 Appendix. 11 Kuwait City. 12 Margarine. 13 WH Auden. 14 Under a Blackpool tram. 15 Cramp. 16 Grover Cleveland. 17 1400. 18 Millais. 19 Thomas Jefferson's. 20 The Catcher in the Rye. 21 US Open. 22 Sweden. 23 Southwark. 24 2 mph. 25 Idaho. 26 Lambeth. 27 Lanzarote. 28 Pall Mall. 29 Hamburg. 30 John F Kennedy.

1 What was the name of the first storm to be given a name?
2 Which volcanic rock is named after a mountain range in South America?
3 What is our Solar System's nearest stellar neighbour?
4 Which Asian country has the greatest area of inland water?
5 What is the highest waterfall in Norway?
6 What is the next largest body in the Solar System after Venus?
7 What is the largest lake in the UK after Neagh?
8 In which US state is the Mammoth cave system?
9 What is V4641 Sgr?
10 What was the first asteroid to be discovered?
11 Where was the meteorite Hoba West found?
12 What is the world's highest island after New Guinea?
13 What is the name of the nearest planetary nebula to the Earth?
14 What percentage of the sky does the smallest constellation take up?
15 Which of the following is the brightest – Rigel, Sirius or Vega?
16 What was the second planet to have been visited by a spacecraft?
17 On which island is the Aceh province that was devastated by the 2004 tsunami?
18 Which state along with Texas and Nebraska is known as Tornado Alley?
19 About how many million years did the longest ice age last?
20 Which planet has the longest day in the solar system?
21 Which element discovered in 1931 is the rarest on Earth?
22 What is the defined visibility of a sea fog?
23 Which nebula is brightest in the night sky?
24 In which constellation is Procyon?
25 In which constellation is the Hyades cluster?
26 At which university is the McDonald Observatory?
27 Where was the meteorite Rowton found?
28 Which Asian Sea is the deepest?
29 From which country was the Andromeda Galaxy first observed?
30 After Pluto which is the next furthest body from the Sun?

1 In which Grand Slam final did a woman first umpire a Men's Final?
2 Which landmark was called the Flavian Amphitheatre when it opened?
3 Who played Mark Fowler in "EastEnders" before Todd Carty?
4 What was the first recorded purchase using a bar code?
5 The word icon comes from a Greek word meaning what?
6 In which street did Coco Chanel found her fashion house?
7 What is pop star Gabrielle's son called?
8 Who founded London Film Productions in 1932?
9 What is Cameron Diaz's middle name?
10 In 1885, Mary Gartside was the first person to have which part of the body successfully removed?
11 The industrial suburb of Shuwaikh is in which city?
12 Which food item was patented by Hippolyte Mege Mouries?
13 Which poet's centenary took place on 21st February 2007?
14 In "Coronation Street", how did Alan Bradley meet his death?
15 What is the result if lactic acid accumulates in the muscles during exercise?
16 Who was the first US President to marry while in office?
17 How many kilometres are there from Great Britain's most south-westerly tip to its northernmost one?
18 Who painted the picture which gave Lillie Langtry her nickname of the Jersey Lily?
19 Which President's grandchild was the first baby to be born in the White House?
20 Which book was John Lennon's murderer carrying when he killed the rock star?
21 What was golfer Geoff Ogilvy's first major?
22 What was the first European country to issue banknotes?
23 In which part of London is the Menier Chocolate Factory theatre?
24 In the UK what was the first speed limit for cars in town?
25 What is the USA's Spud State as it produces over a quarter of the country's potato crop?
26 In which London borough is the cricket ground owned by the Duchy of Cornwall?
27 What is the most easterly of the Canary Islands?
28 What was the first street in the world to be lit by gas lamps?
29 The first hour of "Tomorrow Never Dies" is set in which European city?
30 Who, when asked how he became a war hero said, "they sank my boat"?

1 Which band was formed by Anthony Kiedis and Michael Balzary?
2 Which single gave The Spice Girls their ninth No 1?
3 At which Sheffield pub did the Arctic Monkeys perform their first gig?
4 On which label did Jamiroquai release their first single?
5 Which top-selling performer was born in Louisiana on 2nd December 1981?
6 Who directed the video of Michael Jackson's best-selling album?
7 How is Eileen Edwards better known?
8 For which 1980s movie did the oldest woman to have a UK No 1 win an Oscar?
9 How was Chris Hamill better known?
10 Which actress directed the video of Belinda Carlisle's first No 1?
11 Who was the first band to top both the singles and album charts with their debut releases?
12 Who sang "I Don't Like Mondays" with Bob Geldof in a Wembley Stadium concert in 1995?
13 Who appeared as the character Mimi Clifton in "Midsomer Murders"?
14 Who won the Best New Act Grammy of 1983?
15 How was Hilary Lester known on the single "Save Your Love"?
16 Who was the first British female to top the charts on both sides of the Atlantic with the same single?
17 Which soccer star provided rap contributions to "World in Motion"?
18 Who had the original hit with Bombalurina's biggest 1990 hit?
19 Who sang Bart's lines on The Simpsons' first No 1 hit in the UK?
20 Who was the oldest lady Eric Clapton was singing with on his first No 1?
21 Who was the first non-Briton to represent the UK in the Eurovision Song Contest?
22 Which singer's brother was drummer with Billy J Kramer's backing band?
23 Who released the album "Organic" in 1996?
24 Who had a 1990s No 1 from the West End show in which he was starring?
25 Rozonda Thomas was a member of which trio?
26 Who made the album "Almost Naked", with appropriate sleeve, in 1996?
27 "Still D.R.E." was the first Top Ten hit for which artist?
28 Which late singer wrote the musical "Apples" in 1989?
29 The bands Garden Wall and Anon amalgamated to form who?
30 Who collaborated with Elvis Costello on "Painted from Memory"?

Answers | **Natural Phenomena** *(see Quiz 144)*

1 Carol. 2 Andesite. 3 Proxima centauri. 4 India. 5 Utigard. 6 Mars. 7 Erne. 8 Kentucky. 9 Black hole. 10 Ceres. 11 Namibia. 12 Akutan. 13 Helix. 14 0.16%. 15 Sirius. 16 Venus. 17 Sumatra. 18 Iowa. 19 70. 20 Venus. 21 Astatine. 22 1000 yds. 23 Orion. 24 Canis minor. 25 Taurus. 26 Texas. 27 Shropshire. 28 South China. 29 Germany. 30 Neptune.

Quiz 147 | Pot Luck 69

Answers – page 623

1 The first Top Ten hit for Sash! had a title in which language?
2 In which decade was the Italian Grand Prix first held?
3 How long is the rope at the start of a water-skiing competition?
4 Kate Winslet was nominated for a BAFTA in 2007 for which movie?
5 What contained a poleyn and a pauldron?
6 In which country is the city of Cali?
7 Apart from in America, in which country is the city of Salem found?
8 Which Bananarama star went on to join Shakespear's Sister?
9 In which TV series did Johnny Depp play a character named Tom Hanson?
10 How is TV comic Cyril John Mead better known?
11 In which century was Leonardo da Vinci born?
12 In what type of car did James Dean meet his death?
13 How many rivers are there in the United Arab Emirates?
14 In which avenue is the White House situated?
15 How is French Somaliland now known?
16 What was the first Top Ten hit for Nightcrawlers?
17 Where is Hellgate Bridge?
18 Mt Godwin-Austen is also known by which letter and number?
19 Who was Education Secretary, Home Secretary and Chancellor of the Exchequer in the 1990s?
20 How many James Bond films were released during the lifetime of creator Ian Fleming?
21 In which year will Alcoholics Anonymous celebrate their centenary?
22 In which Chinese Year was Beyonce born?
23 What common factor links children of Cheryl Baker and children of Mollie Sugden?
24 Who played Ron Jenkins in "Coronation Street"?
25 Which hit got to No 2 simultaneously in November 1995 with two separate groups?
26 Who in Gilbert and Sullivan is "a dealer in magic and spells"?
27 Which country do the Aleutian Islands belong to?
28 What does the Arabic word intifada mean?
29 In which ocean are the Maldives?
30 In which London borough was the first cash dispenser installed?

Answers	Celebs (see Quiz 149)

1 Catherine Zeta Jones. 2 Kate Middleton. 3 Nino Cerruti. 4 Richmond upon Thames. 5 Moses & Dylan. 6 Kate Capshaw. 7 Jean Paul Gaultier. 8 Lauren. 9 Miranda Priestly. 10 Elizabeth Taylor. 11 Languages. 12 Burt Reynolds. 13 Transplant patient. 14 Ian Hislop. 15 Neil Cunningham. 16 Politicians' wives. 17 19. 18 Grays, Essex. 19 Custard pie. 20 2006. 21 Robbie Williams. 22 Wilnelia. 23 Lawson. 24 Elton John. 25 Renny Harlin. 26 Meg. 27 18 years. 28 Advertiser's logo. 29 1958. 30 Elton John.

1 Which is further north – St Lucia or St Vincent?
2 Where was the world's largest shopping centre opened in 1985?
3 In 1990, in which country was the world's largest McDonald's?
4 Which Tower in Hong Kong is 100 storeys high?
5 In which country did fashion designer Cabeen launch his men's range of clothes?
6 What is Ecuador's largest Pacific seaport?
7 Where is the Seacon Square shopping centre?
8 Which is further south – Atlanta or Dallas?
9 Which country has the internet code .lk?
10 Where was the first state-subsidised theatre in the English-speaking world opened?
11 Which Canal links the Ebrie Lagoon and the Gulf of Guinea?
12 Which of these islands is the largest – Great Britain, Java or Sumatra?
13 What does the Mississippi-Missouri eventually flow into?
14 Which of these deserts is the smallest – Great Basin, Great Sandy or Great Victoria?
15 Why is Amarillo, Texas, so called?
16 On which river is Jordan's capital?
17 The capital of Maryland is on which river?
18 Which of these Seas is the largest – Arabian, Coral or South China?
19 The Appalachian mountains end in the centre of which state?
20 On which island does the Otira Rail Tunnel run?
21 Which of the following Australian cities is the most southerly – Melbourne, Perth or Sydney?
22 What is the Great Slave?
23 What was Brazil's first planned city?
24 What is the principal language of Andhra Pradesh?
25 Palmerston, Mangaia and Rarotonga are among which islands?
26 In which sea do the so-called ABC islands lie?
27 Which town is closest to the Everest base camp – Kathmandu, Namche or Sagarmatha?
28 In 2000 which was the largest city in the world by population?
29 Where is the "Leap the Dips" roller coaster?
30 The Dogon are inhabitants of where?

Answers	**Pot Luck 70** *(see Quiz 150)*

1 Marie Antoinette. 2 Hamish Macbeth. 3 Anne Reid. 4 Wine. 5 Kandy. 6 Texas. 7 Benjamin Netanyahu. 8 Ruth Ellis (last woman to be hanged in Britain). 9 Sicily. 10 Felix Unger. 11 Sandie Shaw. 12 A Bridge Too Far. 13 Vincent Price. 14 Give It Away. 15 Hattie McDaniel. 16 Hit by a cricket ball. 17 Dr No. 18 Liberia and Ethiopia. 19 Nigeria. 20 Dwight Eisenhower. 21 Austin, Minnesota. 22 England (2 goals). 23 Springfield, Illinois. 24 Comédie Française. 25 Sulby. 26 Busta Rhymes. 27 1988. 28 Momofuku Ando. 29 Grand National. 30 Uranus.

1 Who was the highest-placed mother in "Celebrity Bodies" magazine poll of autumn 2001?
2 In February 2007, who was voted top natural beauty in a poll commissioned by a biscuit company?
3 For which fashion house did Armani first work?
4 The older Attenborough brother is Baron of where?
5 What were the names of Woody Allen's adopted children with Mia Farrow?
6 Who was Mrs Spielberg after Amy Irving?
7 Who designed the dress Nicole Kidman wore when she won her first Oscar?
8 Which designer's real surname is Lifschitz?
9 Which character did Meryl Streep play in "The Devil Wears Prada"?
10 Who hosted "Victoria's Secret Fashion Show" in Cannes in 2000 with Elton John?
11 What did chef Antonio Carluccio study in Vienna?
12 Who was the first male centrefold in "Playgirl" magazine?
13 In 1997 Baebhen Schuttke became Britain's youngest what?
14 Who said, after losing a libel case, "If this is justice, I'm a banana"?
15 Who designed Ffion Hague's wedding dress?
16 Linda McDougal wrote a book about which group of women?
17 How old was Lady Diana Spencer when she became engaged?
18 Which town in which county does Russell Brand hail from?
19 What was Bill Gates hit in the face with on a trip to Belgium in 1998?
20 Which year marked the 50th anniversary of the Prince Rainier/Grace Kelly marriage?
21 Which celeb's parents ran the Red Lion pub in Burslem?
22 What is Mrs Bruce Forsyth called?
23 What was Twiggy's surname when she was a presenter of "This Morning"?
24 Who is the famous partner of David Furnish?
25 Who was Geena Davis's third husband?
26 What was the first name of the first Mrs Noel Gallagher?
27 For how many years did Andrew Lloyd Webber's show on roller skates run in the West End?
28 In 1987 Luis Reina became the first matador in the bull ring to wear what?
29 In which year were Michael Jackson, Madonna and Prince all born?
30 Which pop star received a knighthood in the same honours list as Tom Finney?

| **Answers** | **Pot Luck 69** *(see Quiz 147)* |

1 French. 2 1920s. 3 23m. 4 Little Children. 5 A suit of armour. 6 Colombia. 7 India. 8 Siobhan Fahey. 9 21 Jump Street. 10 Syd Little. 11 15th. 12 Porsche. 13 None. 14 Pennsylvania Avenue. 15 Djibouti. 16 Push the Feeling on. 17 New York. 18 K2. 19 Kenneth Clarke. 20 Two. 21 2035. 22 Year of the Rooster. 23 Twins. 24 Ben Kingsley. 25 Wonderwall. 26 John Wellington Wells. 27 USA. 28 Uprising. 29 Indian. 30 Enfield.

1 Jason Schwarztmann featured in which 2006 film directed by Sofia Coppola?
2 Which series took place in Lochdubh?
3 Which ex-"Corrie" star played Catherine Tate's mother in "The Bad Mother's Handbook"?
4 What would stum be added to, to give it more strength?
5 How is the sacred city of Senkadagala now known?
6 Odessa is found in Washington and which other US state?
7 Who beat Simon Peres in the Israeli elections of 1996?
8 "Dance with the Stranger" was about whom?
9 Marsala wine is produced on which island?
10 Which character did Jack Lemmon play in "The Odd Couple"?
11 Who was the first British female soloist to have a hat trick of chart No 1 hits?
12 In which war film did the character Major General Roy Urquhart appear?
13 Known for his spooky voice, which actor voices over on Michael Jackson's video "Thriller"?
14 What was the first Top Ten hit for Red Hot Chili Peppers?
15 Who was the first black actress to win an Oscar?
16 In what unusual circumstances did George II's eldest son die?
17 Which Bond movie dealing with world-threatening scenarios opened during the Cuban missile crisis?
18 Who were the only independent nations in Africa at the outbreak of WWI?
19 In which country was Lassa fever first identified?
20 Who was the first US President to appear on colour television?
21 Where is there a Spam Museum?
22 Which team qualified from the 2002 World Cup Group stage with fewest goals?
23 Which town in which state was the home of Abraham Lincoln?
24 What was the world's first national theatre?
25 What is the longest river of the island which has a Parliament called Tynwald?
26 Trevor Smith became known as which rapper?
27 In which year did the £1 note cease to be legal tender in England?
28 Which Taiwanese-Japanese entrepreneur is credited with creating the craze for Pot Noodles?
29 Which Grand event was first broadcast live on BBC television in 1960?
30 Which planet was the first to be discovered by use of a telescope?

Answers	**World Travel** *(see Quiz 148)*

1 St Lucia. 2 Alberta, Canada. 3 Russia. 4 Nina. 5 China. 6 Guayaquil. 7 Bangkok.
8 Dallas. 9 Sri Lanka. 10 Dublin. 11 Vridi. 12 Sumatra. 13 Gulf of Mexico. 14 Great Sandy. 15 Yellow colour of a creek bank. 16 Zarqa. 17 Severn. 18 Coral. 19 Alabama. 20 South island, New Zealand. 21 Perth. 22 Lake. 23 Aracaju. 24 Telugu. 25 Cook Islands. 26 Caribbean. 27 Namche. 28 Tokyo. 29 Lakemont Park, Pennsylvania. 30 Mali.

1 Who sang the title song of a movie for which Marvin Hamlisch won two 1974 Oscars?
2 Who did Betty Hutton replace in "Annie Get Your Gun"?
3 "Fiddler on the Roof" and which other big musical did Norman Jewison direct in the 1970s?
4 Who was Gene Kelly's co-star in his Hollywood debut?
5 Which character did Debbie Allen play in the movie and TV show about Manhattan's High School for the Performing Arts?
6 For which song from "Lady be Good" did Oscar Hammerstein II win an Oscar?
7 Which novelist, when a Pinkerton detective in real life, investigated the gambling affairs of the man Barbra Streisand married in "Funny Girl"?
8 What was the Hollywood debut of the man born Harold Leek?
9 Who directed Nicole Kidman's first movie after divorcing Tom Cruise?
10 Whom did Miss Olsen fall in love with in the 1970s movie?
11 Where does Tony Manero do his day job in a big 1970s musical?
12 In which city is the song "Do Re Mi" sung in a musical?
13 Who wrote the music for the last Best Oscar-winning song of the 1990s?
14 Who played the male lead in the musical which included "Let's Hear It for the Boy"?
15 Who said, "I am simple, complex, generous, selfish, unattractive, beautiful, lazy, driven"?
16 In which musical do teenagers tune in to Wolfman Jack's rock 'n' roll show?
17 What is the name of the flower shop owner in "Little Shop of Horrors"?
18 Where is the 1983 musical with Jennifer Beals and Michael Nouri set?
19 Who plays the angry young intellectual in "Fiddler on the Roof"?
20 Who played Janet in the musical movie with the song "Dammit Janet"?
21 Who directed and choreographed the original production of "West Side Story" on stage before being involved in the movie?
22 In which state is the movie based on the life of Loretta Lynn set?
23 Which was the first Disney musical of the 1990s to win Best Song Oscar?
24 Who sang "Honeysuckle Rose" in "New York New York"?
25 What won the Best Song Oscar in Julie Andrews' first Oscar-winning film?
26 For which movie did Howard Ashman win his last Oscar in his own lifetime?
27 Which musical film included a psychopathic agricultural worker called Fry?
28 Who directed "Spiceworld: The Movie"?
29 What was Olivia Newton John's surname in "Grease"?
30 What was Jennifer Beals studying while she was making "Flashdance"?

Answers	Horse Racing *(see Quiz 153)*

1 Limerick, Ireland. 2 Lovely Cottage. 3 Willie Carson. 4 Lammtarra. 5 Vodaphone. 6 Lord Huntingdon. 7 Pat Eddery. 8 Jean Luc Lagardere. 9 Melling Chase. 10 Esha Ness. 11 Eleanor. 12 Durbar II. 13 Cape Verdi. 14 Mr Frisk. 15 Entrepreneur. 16 Gay Trip. 17 Olivier Peslier. 18 Athens Wood. 19 Greville Starkey. 20 Prince Charles. 21 Golden Fleece. 22 Party Politics. 23 Humble Duty. 24 Lester Piggott. 25 1945. 26 Royal Tan. 27 Powerstown Park. 28 Las Meninas. 29 Victory Note. 30 Kahyasi.

1 Mr Ashwell of Herne Hill patented which famous sign?
2 How many of the five 2006–07 Ashes Tests made it to the fifth day?
3 Junta is the Spanish word for what?
4 What was usually the penultimate word in an episode of "The Two Ronnies"?
5 Which world leader was executed on Christmas Day 1989?
6 Which 1960s classic song had the line, "Nobody knows where my Johnny has gone"?
7 "Infamous" starred Toby Jones as which writer?
8 Which favourite sitcom star played Jeremy Parsons QC in Crown Court?
9 What did Radovan Karadzic practise before founding the Serbian Democratic Party?
10 Grace Stafford was the voice of which cartoon character?
11 Which father of an ex-"Coronation Street" star wrote over 100 episodes of the soap including one of Elsie Tanner's weddings?
12 What was the name of the evacuation operation which created the artificial Lake Kariba?
13 To the nearest 20 degrees centigrade what is the melting point of iron?
14 Which Emperor was responsible for building the Great Wall of China?
15 What in London was originally called Nottingham House?
16 Which Florida port and tourist city used to be known as Cayo Hueso or Bone Island?
17 What was the name of the first kibbutz?
18 When did "The Star Spangled Banner" become the US National Anthem?
19 Who wrote the novel on which Quentin Tarantino's follow-up to "Pulp Fiction" was based?
20 With which club did Mike Tindall begin his professional rugby career?
21 The phrase "iron curtain" was first used by Churchill but who is credited with the idea behind it?
22 What is the oldest lead and zinc mining town in Zambia?
23 Elizabeth Taylor's second divorce was from whom?
24 In which game reserve are the Kapachira Falls?
25 What is the Burmese name for the main river of Myanmar?
26 Who wrote a poem about the Tay Bridge Disaster of 1879?
27 Who wrote the book "Palestine: Peace Not Apartheid"?
28 Where was the first purpose-built music hall built?
29 Which was the last navy to scrap the daily rum ration?
30 In which Bond film did Toby Stephens play Gustav Graves?

Answers	21st Century Headlines *(see Quiz 154)*

1 Michel Desjoyeaux. 2 15. 3 New York. 4 I Love You. 5 Brooklands. 6 Dennis Tito.
7 Selby. 8 MacPherson. 9 60%. 10 Douro. 11 Australian. 12 Peter Tachell. 13
Poole. 14 Georgia. 15 Mahzer Mahmood. 16 30th Dec. 17 Refused to use metric
measures. 18 Vandevelde. 19 NBC. 20 Kursk. 21 Chesterfield. 22 Barak. 23 His
TV set. 24 PY Gerbeau. 25 Alun Michael. 26 Chappaqua. 27 Croatia. 28 Australian
Labor Party. 29 Freedom Party. 30 110.

1 In which county was the first steeplechase held?
2 Which horse won the first post-WWII Grand National?
3 Which jockey rode the 2,000 Guineas-winner four times between 1972 and 1989?
4 Which horse ran the fastest Epsom Derby of the 1990s?
5 Who sponsored the Derby at the turn of the century?
6 Who resigned as the Queen's trainer towards the end of the 1990s?
7 Who was the first jockey in the 1990s to ride 200 winners?
8 Who owned Sagamix when he won the Prix de l'Arc de Triomphe in 1998?
9 The steeplechaser One Man had to be put down after being injured in which race?
10 Which horse finished first in the last Grand National of the millennium to be abandoned?
11 What was the first filly to win the Derby?
12 Which horse won the Derby the year WWI began?
13 What was Frankie Dettori's first 1000 Guineas win of the 1990s?
14 Which horse ran the fastest Grand National of the 1990s?
15 What was Mick Kinane's second 2000 Guineas win of the 1990s?
16 Which horse won the Grand National the year that Nijinsky won the Derby?
17 Which jockey won his third successive Prix de l'Arc de Triomphe in 1998?
18 Which horse won the St Leger the year that Mill Reef won the Derby?
19 Who rode the only Derby winner with Shirley in its name?
20 Which member of the Royal family got married the year Aldaniti won the National?
21 Which horse won the Derby the year after the legendary Shergar?
22 Which horse won the Grand National the year of the first 1990s General Election?
23 What was Lester Piggott's first 1000 Guineas winner in the second half of the 20th century?
24 Rodrigo de Triano was which jockey's thirtieth Classic winner?
25 What was the last year before 1993 that the Grand National was not run?
26 Before Royal Athlete what was the last Grand National winner to have Royal in its name?
27 In which park is Ireland's Clonmel Racecourse?
28 What was the first 1000 Guineas winner of the 1990s to have two words in its name?
29 Which was the fastest of the first four British horses in the 1998 French 2000 Guineas?
30 Which horse ran the fastest Epsom Derby of the 1980s?

1 Who beat Ellen MacArthur in the Vendee Globe race 2000–001?
2 How many naval personnel were taken into custody by Iran in March 2007?
3 The plane involved in the first supersonic air crash was heading for where?
4 Which computer virus was first detected in Hong Kong in May 2000?
5 From which airfield did Jennifer Murray begin and end her helicopter circumnavigation of the world solo in 2000?
6 Who was the first private individual to make a journey into space?
7 Where in England was there a major rail crash in March 2001?
8 What was the name of the inquiry into the death of Stephen Lawrence?
9 Around what percentage of the electorate voted in the January 2005 Iraq elections?
10 Over which river did a bridge collapse in 2001 causing the resignation of that country's minister of public works?
11 At which 2001 Grand Prix was a marshal killed after he was struck by a wheel?
12 Who tried to make a citizen's arrest on Robert Mugabe in Brussels in 2001?
13 Which judge presided over the first Lee Bowyer and Jonathan Woodgate trial?
14 Zurab Zhvania who died in 2005 was Prime Minister of which country?
15 Which reporter set up the "Sophiegate" scam?
16 On which date was Sadaam Hussein hanged in 2006?
17 How did Steve Thoburn hit the headlines?
18 What was the name of the Belgian that M & S appointed to turn around the company's ailing fortunes?
19 Which station aired Anne Robinson's ruthless quiz show in the US?
20 Which Russian nuclear submarine sank in 2000?
21 Towards the end of the 2000–01 football season which side was docked three points for financial irregularities?
22 Who did Ariel Sharon replace as Israeli PM in February 2001?
23 Mitch Hallen hit the headlines as he married what?
24 Who succeeded Jennie Page as chief executive of the Millennium Dome?
25 Who did Rhodri Morgan replace as First Secretary of the Welsh Assembly?
26 Where did Hillary Clinton buy a home before announcing she would run for the Senate?
27 Stipe Mesic was elected President of where?
28 In 2005 Mark Latham resigned as leader of which political party?
29 Which political party did Jorg Haider head?
30 How many storeys did the twin towers of the World Trade Center have?

Answers	Pot Luck 71 *(see Quiz 152)*

1 Vacant/Engaged toilet sign. 2 Three. 3 Join. 4 Him. 5 Ceausescu. 6 It's My Party. 7 Truman Capote. 8 Richard Wilson. 9 Psychiatry. 10 Woody Woodpecker. 11 Geoffrey Lancashire (father of Sarah). 12 Noah. 13 1535°. 14 Shih Huang Ti. 15 Kensington Palace. 16 Key West. 17 Deganya. 18 1931. 19 Elmore Leonard (Jackie Brown). 20 Bath. 21 Josef Goebbels, in Das Reich. 22 Kabwe. 23 Michael Wilding. 24 Majete. 25 Ayeyarwady. 26 William McGonagall. 27 Jimmy Carter. 28 Bolton. 29 New Zealand. 30 Die Another Day.

Answers – page 631

1 Which French region incorporates the city of Paris?

2 "Ruby" and "Boxing Champ" featured on which album?

3 Which Betty Marsden character's catchphrase was, "Many many times," in the radio classic "Round the Horne"?

4 What was Kazuo Ishiguro's next novel after "Artist of the Floating World" which won the Booker Prize?

5 Which Beatles song was recorded as "Sie liebt dich" in West Germany?

6 What was the codename of the bomb which was dropped on Nagasaki?

7 Which port is Italy's chief naval station?

8 Who did Robin Givens divorce in 1989?

9 Which DH Lawrence novel was set in Mexico?

10 Who spent more years as Chancellor of the Exchequer in the 1980s than anyone else?

11 On which river is the Yorkshire city which hosts a piano competition every three years?

12 The movie "Starter for Ten" was based on a book by which writer?

13 What do the Greeks call Nicosia?

14 In which church is JS Bach buried?

15 Which was the last European power to have imperial territories in Africa?

16 Who was chief photographer of "Rolling Stone" magazine from 1973 to 1983?

17 In which country is the city of Tetouan?

18 EAT is the tasty sound code for which country?

19 What type of wine is described by the term frizzante?

20 Which country did the group Rednex come from?

21 Which movie great had his final TV role as Daniel Reece in "Dynasty"?

22 In which country is the city of Brasov?

23 Kim Basinger lost a multi-million-pound lawsuit after pulling out of which movie?

24 In which decade was the Mexican Grand Prix first held?

25 Who played Sir Arthur Sullivan in "Topsy Turvy"?

26 In which London borough is Sadlers' Wells Theatre?

27 In which key is Schubert's "Unfinished Symphony"?

28 Which leaders signed the SALT II treaty?

29 The Silk Road ran from Shanghai to which Sea?

30 Which actor manager was born Henry Brodribb?

Answers | Pot Luck 73 *(see Quiz 157)*

1 Cambodia. 2 H. 3 Minder. 4 Kandahar. 5 1920s. 6 Lemur. 7 David Wasco.
8 Ben Hur. 9 Gambia. 10 Goldeneye. 11 The Bangles. 12 Mayor of Casterbridge.
13 Blood Diamond. 14 The Return of the Native. 15 Heart-Shaped Box. 16 Gladys
Aylward. 17 William IV. 18 Cissy Houston. 19 Argentina. 20 Bond movie. 21 Bolivia.
22 The Flintstones. 23 Sherlock Holmes. 24 Barbara Bach. 25 Venezuela. 26 Bryn
Terfel. 27 Ronnie Barker. 28 Tarsiers. 29 Ten players. 30 Angell.

Quiz 156 | TV: Classics

1 In which month in 1966 was "Star Trek" first broadcast?
2 Which Briton won an Emmy as Best Supporting Actress in 1971?
3 Who directed the series "7 Up" and its sequels, about the lives and aspirations of a group of children?
4 Which studio was the first "Blue Peter" filmed from?
5 Whose music was used for the series "Light of Experience"?
6 Who was known as "The Switchboard Girl"?
7 The first TV broadcast of "Alice in Wonderland" was under which banner?
8 What was the name of the very first programme designed for children of school age?
9 Who presented "Cookery Lesson" in the 1950s?
10 In which year was the first General Election results broadcast production?
11 Who was the creator of Mr Pastry?
12 Which town was shown on the first cross-Channel broadcast?
13 Which children's title replaced "Watch with Mother"?
14 Who replaced Eamonn Andrews on "What's My Line"?
15 At what time was the first BBC TV news broadcast put on air?
16 Which Olympics was "Sportsview" the first to cover?
17 Who was the first presenter of "Sunday Night at the London Palladium"?
18 What was the UK version of "Tic Tac Dough"?
19 Which series's spin-off was called "Oxbridge 2000"?
20 How long had "Grandstand" been running before a regular Sunday programme was introduced?
21 On which day of the week did "Juke Box Jury" begin?
22 In which series did Chief Supt Lockhart appear?
23 The Ponderosa Ranch was near which City?
24 Which puppet series featured Tex Tucker?
25 Which "Dad's Army" regular appeared in "It's a Square World"?
26 Ian Hendry played which crime-buster alongside Patrick Macnee in "The Avengers"?
27 Which astronomer created "A for Andromeda"?
28 Which Prime Minister appeared with "Morecambe & Wise"?
29 Who wrote "Brothers in Law"?
30 In what year did "Top of the Pops" celebrate its 2000th show?

Answers | Science (see Quiz 158)

1 Star sailor. 2 Charles Kowal. 3 Mars. 4 Kentucky. 5 Kodak. 6 Czechoslovakia. 7 Humerus. 8 Calcium hydroxide. 9 Tanzania. 10 Orion. 11 Tibia. 12 Vomiting. 13 Titan. 14 Dialysis machine. 15 Five. 16 90+. 17 Neptune. 18 Therapeutics plc. 19 Lungs. 20 Jupiter. 21 1880s. 22 John Russell Hind. 23 iPhone. 24 Carbon. 25 Titan. 26 Benthos. 27 Lakes. 28 13. 29 Triton. 30 Heavy water.

1 Which country has the internet code .kh?
2 On a computer keyboard what letter is below and between Y and U?
3 Which TV series featured a pub called the Winchester?
4 What was the first capital of Afghanistan after it became independent?
5 In which decade was the Monaco Grand Prix first held?
6 Which creature is also known as the aye-aye?
7 Who co-wrote the screenplay of "Pulp Fiction" along with Quentin Tarantino?
8 Which 1950s film cost $4million, double the maximum spend of the time?
9 In which country is the city of Banjul?
10 Xenia Onatopp was the villain in which movie?
11 The girl band once known as The Colours made the charts using which name?
12 In fiction, what position did Michael Henchard rise to?
13 Jennifer Connelly and Djimon Honsou starred in which 2007 film?
14 Which Thomas Hardy novel starts with a brooding description of Egdon Heath?
15 What was the last Top Ten hit for Nirvana?
16 Whose story was told in "Inn of the Sixth Happiness" with Ingrid Bergman?
17 Who was the first British monarch to be born in Buckingham Palace?
18 Who recorded the original "Midnight Train to Georgia" before Gladys Knight had the big international hit?
19 Falabellas are native to which country?
20 Rowan Atkinson made his big-screen debut in a movie in which series of films?
21 In which country were Butch Cassidy and Sundance finally tracked down?
22 On TV which family read "The Daily Slate"?
23 Who in London had 221B as part of his address?
24 Which Bond girl married a Beatle?
25 Barcelona is found in Spain and which other country?
26 Who made the albums "Some Enchanted Evening" and "We'll Keep a Welcome"?
27 Gerald Wiley was an assumed name of which TV comedy writer?
28 The term monkey includes all the primates except man, apes and what else?
29 How many Italian players scored the 12 goals in open play in Germany 2006?
30 What was Zoe's name before her marriage to Alec in "May to December"?

Answers	Pot Luck 72 *(see Quiz 155)*

1 Ile de France. 2 Yours Truly, Angry Mob (Kaiser Chiefs). 3 Lady Beatrice Counterblast.
4 The Remains of the Day. 5 She Loves You. 6 Fat Man. 7 La Spezia. 8 Mike Tyson.
9 The Plumed Serpent. 10 Nigel Lawson. 11 Aire. 12 David Nicholls. 13 Lefkosia.
14 St Thomas's Leipzig. 15 Portugal. 16 Annie Leibovitz. 17 Morocco. 18 Tanzania.
19 Semi-sparkling. 20 Sweden. 21 Rock Hudson. 22 Romania. 23 Boxing Helena.
24 1960s. 25 Allan Corduner. 26 Islington. 27 B Minor. 28 Jimmy Carter and Leonid Brezhnev. 29 Mediterranean. 30 Henry Irving.

1 What did the word astronaut originally mean?
2 Who discovered the mystery object Chiron?
3 What was the third planet to have been visited by a spacecraft?
4 In which US state is the Fisher Ridge cave system?
5 Which company introduced Photo CD?
6 What was the third country to have a man in space?
7 Which is the longest bone in the arm?
8 What is another name for slaked lime?
9 Where was the meteorite Mbosi found?
10 In which constellation is Rigel?
11 Which bone is named after the Italian for flute?
12 What is emetophobia a fear of?
13 What is Saturn's biggest moon?
14 Willem Johan Kolff devised which item of equipment, a pioneer in medicine and health?
15 How much faster does the strongest wind blow on Neptune than on Earth?
16 How many miles below the Earth' surface do diamonds form?
17 What is the next largest body in the Solar System after Uranus?
18 Which company created Dolly the Sheep?
19 What is the next largest human organ after the brain?
20 Asteroids usually appear between the orbits of Mars and which other planet?
21 In which decade were contact lenses first devised?
22 Who discovered the asteroid Flora?
23 Which device did Apple CEO Steve Jobs say would "reinvent" telecommunications in 2007?
24 What is the most common element in the human body after oxygen?
25 Which satellite has the thickest atmosphere?
26 What name is given to the animal and plant life which lives at the bottom of the sea?
27 What does a limnologist study?
28 How many people were in space on 14th March 1995, a then record?
29 What is Neptune's largest moon?
30 What is D2O?

1   "Titanic" overtook which movie as the most costly ever made?
2   Which animal is linked with the US state of Minnesota?
3   In which American city sharing its name with a European city were R.E.M. formed?
4   In which month did the Japanese launch the 1941 attack on Pearl Harbor?
5   Who or what is a merlon?
6   The unlikely-sounding writing duo Ham and Evans penned which song that made No 1 for two different artists?
7   Who wrote the book on which 101 Dalmatians was based?
8   England led Australia by what score at half time in the 2003 rugby World Cup Final?
9   How long was the run of Arthur Miller's first Broadway play?
10 What was the creature-named publishing company set up by Paul Hamlyn?
11 What was the occupation of Louis Washkansky, the first heart transplant recipient?
12 Who played Ava Gardner in the movie "The Aviator"?
13 What was Eternal's first single not to make the Top Ten?
14 Who drew the caricature sequences at the start of TV's "Yes Minister"?
15 Which character did Jim Davidson play in "Up the Elephant and Round the Castle"?
16 In 1824 William Buckland named the first what?
17 What was the middle name of sub-four-minute-miler Roger Bannister?
18 Which creatures were wild in the title of a Jung Chang novel?
19 In which royal residence did Queen Victoria die?
20 To which Olympic thrower was runner Mary Decker married?
21 What was the first – and only – Top Ten hit for Silver Convention?
22 What celestial body is portrayed in the seventh movement of Gustav Holst's "Planet Suite"?
23 From which play was the movie "Casablanca" adapted?
24 "June is Bustin' Out All Over" features in which musical?
25 Which horse was the first ever winner of the Derby?
26 In which country is the city of Kumasi?
27 Which player scored the first penalty in the 2006 FIFA World Cup Final shoot-out?
28 How many Motown acts recorded "I Heard It Through the Grapevine" before Marvin Gaye?
29 Laennec is credited with inventing which medical aid?
30 What percentage of zebras have exactly the same pattern of stripes?

Answers	Pot Luck 75 *(see Quiz 161)*

1 Order of discovery. 2 The Man without a Face. 3 Iran. 4 One by One. 5 Janice Long. 6 Anaemia. 7 Samuels. 8 Giacomo Puccini. 9 Influenza. 10 Benson. 11 2000 Guineas. 12 Zimbabwe. 13 Mariah Carey. 14 Richard III. 15 David Copperfield. 16 Nicholas Lyndhurst. 17 Dulwich College. 18 Peru. 19 Angela Rippon. 20 Snodgrass. 21 Gall bladder. 22 South Africa. 23 Malcolm Bradbury. 24 Sally Phillips. 25 JCB. 26 Nigel West. 27 Nancy Slnatra. 28 1951. 29 Uncle. 30 Alphabetical order.

1 On the soundtrack of "Bridget Jones's Diary" who sang the only song with Miss Jones in the title?
2 "Virtual Insanity" originally appeared on which album?
3 Who sang "I could be violet sky"?
4 Which duo was the duo with the best-selling single of the 1990s in the UK?
5 Whose No 1 had the line, "You're about as easy as a nuclear war"?
6 In which year was the album "1" the best-seller in over six countries despite only being released in the November?
7 What was the second of Motown's first two consecutive No 1s?
8 Who wrote the Spanish lyrics "Volver A Empezar" to a Cole Porter classic?
9 Survivor were commissioned to write which song for the third "Rocky" film?
10 Which famous writing team wrote Phil Collins' first solo No 1?
11 With which single did Whitney Houston's husband top the chart in the 1980s when part of a band?
12 What was the Freddie Mercury song on "Five Live" EP?
13 Who penned Michael Jackson's "You are Not Alone"?
14 Who was Guiot, a provider of words and music on Shakespear's Sister's "Stay"?
15 Which single topped the charts in the US after being used in a movie based on a 1970s TV series?
16 What was the first German Eurovision winner to top the UK charts?
17 What was the name of the third single written to raise funds for Comic Relief?
18 Who wrote Take That's first No 1?
19 Which Motown star co-wrote Paul Young's first No 1?
20 What was The Jam's last single before disbanding?
21 Who was the first person to write five No 1 singles as sole composer?
22 Who joined Skinner & Baddiel as writer of the Euro 96 anthem?
23 From which album was The Fugees' second No 1 single taken?
24 What was the first No 1 of the 21st century to have a boy's name in the title?
25 What was Oasis's first No 1 with Noel Gallagher as writer and lead vocals?
26 How did Bucks Fizz's second No 1 finish?
27 In which song did Terry meet Julie every Friday night?
28 In Nelly Furtado's song which line goes after "Flames to dust"?
29 The Bluebells' 1993 hit was used to advertise what?
30 What was the shortest title on the compilation EP Abba-esque?

Answers	Transport (see Quiz 162)

1 Jahre Viking. 2 Chicago. 3 Farringdon. 4 Volkswagen Beetle. 5 Imperial Airways. 6 General Motors. 7 Little Piece of Coal. 8 Czechoslovakia. 9 District. 10 Maggiore. 11 Helicopter. 12 2003. 13 Jeantaud. 14 Honda. 15 Tractor. 16 Nissan Sunny. 17 Finland. 18 Seven. 19 Ice. 20 Wilbur Wright. 21 Central. 22 Russia. 23 Honda. 24 1948. 25 Jeep. 26 St Petersburg. 27 Buick. 28 Fire engine. 29 Lada Riva. 30 Blackbird.

1 Which order is the system of numbering asteroids?
2 In which 1993 movie did Mel Gibson direct himself?
3 In which country is the city of Qom?
4 What was Cher's last Top Ten hit before the massive No 1 "Believe"?
5 Who was the only female presenter at the Live Aid concert?
6 Which blood disorder is caused by a lack of folic acid?
7 Which surname does Janet Leigh's character use when signing in to the Bates Motel?
8 Who wrote the operatic comedy "Gianni Schicchi"?
9 John Huxham coined the name for which common illness?
10 What was the surname of Cherie Lunghi's character Gabriella in "The Manageress"?
11 In 1998 which race did Aiden O'Brien not win – the Ascot Gold Cup, King George VI and Queen Elizabeth Stakes or the 2000 Guineas?
12 Alphabetically, which team was last in the 2007 Cricket World Cup?
13 Who became the first solo female singer to enter the UK charts at No 1?
14 The bones of which king were thrown in the River Soar after his grave was desecrated?
15 In fiction, whose first wife was called Dora Spenlove?
16 Who played Ronnie Barker's son Raymond in "Going Straight"?
17 PG Wodehouse and Raymond Chandler both went to which English school?
18 In which country is the city of Chiclayo?
19 Who was the first female to present TV's "Top Gear"?
20 Which Carrie featured in Clint Eastwood's "Pale Rider"?
21 Which part of his anatomy did Jim Carrey have removed following the making of the movie "The Mask"?
22 In which country did Harold Macmillan deliver his famous "Wind of Change" speech?
23 Who dramatised Tom Sharpe's "Porterhouse Blue" for television?
24 Who played Shazza in "Bridget Jones's Diary"?
25 What were the initials of Mr Bamford who gave his name to a heavy vehicle?
26 Under what name is one-time MP Rupert Allason known as an author?
27 Which 60-plus performer was featured in a 2005 hit for Audio Bullys?
28 In what year was the first colour TV programme transmitted in America?
29 In motor racing, what relation was Emerson to Christian Fittipaldi?
30 Earth comes first of the planets in order of what?

Answers	Pot Luck 74 *(see Quiz 159)*

1 Waterworld. 2 Gopher. 3 Athens. 4 December. 5 Part of a parapet. 6 Without You.
7 Dodie Smith. 8 14-5. 9 One week. 10 Octopus. 11 Dentist. 12 Kate Beckinsale.
13 So Good. 14 Gerald Scarfe. 15 Jim London. 16 Dinosaur. 17 Gilbert. 18
Swans. 19 Osborne House. 20 Bob Slaney. 21 Get Up and Boogie. 22 Neptune. 23
Everybody Comes to Rick's. 24 Carousel. 25 Diomed. 26 Ghana. 27 Pirlo. 28 Two.
29 Stethoscope. 30 None.

1 In 2000 what was the world's largest ship?
2 Where did the first car hire company start, in 1918?
3 The first Underground railway ran from Paddington to which Street?
4 In the 1970s which vehicle became the most constructed car of all time?
5 Which airline served the first cooked meals on a scheduled flight?
6 Which was the largest Internet advertiser in 2000?
7 What was the meaning of the name of the dog Ugolek who was a space traveller in the 1960s?
8 Which was the first country to make seat belts compulsory?
9 What was London's second underground railway line?
10 On which Lake was the first hydrofoil tested?
11 What is a Mil Mi 26?
12 In which year were Concorde supersonic airlines finally withdrawn?
13 Which car held the first land speed record?
14 Of the following, which make of motor cycle was made first – Honda, Suzuki or Yamaha?
15 What was Henry Ford's Fordson?
16 Which of the following was produced first – Ford Escort, Ford Orion or Nissan Sunny?
17 The cruise ship "Explorer of the Seas" was built in which country?
18 How many people died in the space shuttle tragedy of 2003?
19 On what surface did Henry Ford set a land speed record in 1904?
20 Who piloted the first flight of over one hour with a passenger?
21 Bethnal Green tube station is on which London Underground line?
22 Which country has the most submarines?
23 Which company produced the first zero-level-emission engine?
24 Which year saw the arrival of the Land Rover and the 2CV?
25 Which vehicle was known as the Bantam, the Gnat and the Peep before its final name stuck?
26 Which Russian city has the most comprehensive tramway system?
27 What was the make of the first car to have front and rear flashing indicators?
28 What type of vehicle is a Hawaiian Eagle?
29 Which of the following was produced last – Lada Riva, Nissan Pulsar or Renault 4?
30 Which reconnaissance aircraft is the world's fastest?

Answers	**Words & Music** *(see Quiz 160)*

1 Robbie Williams. 2 Travelling without Moving. 3 Mica (Grace Kelly). 4 Robson and Jerome. 5 Duran Duran. 6 2000. 7 One Day in Your Life. 8 Julio Iglesias. 9 Eye of the Tiger. 10 Holland Dozier Holland. 11 Candy Girl. 12 Somebody to Love. 13 R Kelly. 14 Dave Stewart. 15 Independent Woman (Charlie's Angels). 16 A Little Peace. 17 The Stonk. 18 Gary Barlow. 19 Marvin Gaye. 20 Beat Surrender. 21 Sting. 22 Ian Broudie. 23 The Score. 24 Stan (Eminem). 25 Don't Look Back in Anger. 26 With a poem. 27 Waterloo Sunset. 28 Lovers to friends. 29 Volkswagen. 30 Terence Higgins Trust.

1 Which right-hand man of Slobodan Milosevic was arrested in March 2001?
2 Which country does Osama Bin Laden hail from?
3 In 1998 General Pinochet was arrested in the UK pending extradition to where?
4 What was the job of Anthony Blunt when he was stripped of his knighthood?
5 Michael Barratt was not the last person to be hanged in the UK but why was he a famous "last"?
6 Where was the murderer of 10 Rillington Place executed?
7 Which villain died on the same date as Freddie Mercury but almost 30 years earlier?
8 How many patients was Harold Shipman originally convicted of killing?
9 Which celebrity surname did Barry George use?
10 Timothy McVeigh was executed for which bombing?
11 On what date did Lord Lucan disappear?
12 Which father of a famous novelist played the villain Captain Hook in the first production of Peter Pan?
13 Volkert van der Graaf was sentenced for the murder of which person?
14 What was the nickname of Protestant paramilitary leader Billy Wright?
15 Who was the first woman to be executed in Texas in the 20th century?
16 Ta Mok was a successor to which leader?
17 On TV what was the surname of the Weatherfield One?
18 In 1902 Harry Jackson was the first person convicted on the basis of what evidence?
19 How was Illich Ramirez Sanchez better known?
20 Which Oscar-nominated film of 2007 was about a former dictator of Uganda?
21 What was the name of Jack the Ripper's final victim?
22 The book "Cried Unheard" was about which convicted killer?
23 Which movie was about pardoned murderer Derek Bentley?
24 Who did James Earl Ray shoot?
25 Where did Michael Ryan carry out his murders?
26 How did Great Train Robber Charles Wilson meet his death?
27 Which group captured hostages John McCarthy, Brian Keenan and Frank Reed in Lebanon?
28 Which of the three men in the Guinness scandal received an 18-month jail sentence?
29 Who was the first person to be executed by lethal injection in the USA?
30 How old was Ian Huntley when he was convicted of the Soham murders?

Answers	**Olympics 2** *(see Quiz 165)*

1 Paris. 2 Donovan Bailey. 3 Sinclair. 4 Spiridon Louis. 5 London. 6 Sergey Belov. 7 1916. 8 Averoff. 9 Upton Park FC. 10 John Boland. 11 Luigi Carrozza. 12 80. 13 1 May 2001. 14 Birgit Fischer (nee Schmidt). 15 Gymnastics (Nikolai Andrianov). 16 Norway. 17 Al Oerter. 18 Italy. 19 Miroslav Mecir. 20 Moscow. 21 Ornskoldsvik, Sweden. 22 Equatorial Guinea. 23 Toronto. 24 10. 25 1960s. 26 Millie. 27 1500 metres. 28 Steve Redgrave. 29 Montreal. 30 1940/1944.

1 In which decade did mountain biking become an Olympic event?
2 What was the occupation of the Jack Russell who gave his name to a breed of dog?
3 "The Meltdown" was the sequel to which movie?
4 Which was the first country to give women the vote?
5 On average, how many times does an adult heart beat a minute?
6 Who had a No 1 hit with Bryan Adams and also with Lisa Lopes?
7 Quarter, quell, quote – which of these words is made from letters on the top row of a keyboard?
8 In "Just Good Friends", what were the first names of Vince Pinner's parents?
9 In which country would you watch Polonia play a home soccer match?
10 In the Bible what is the name of John the Baptist's mother?
11 Which country did Martina Hingis represent when she first won Wimbledon?
12 Who directed Jamie Bell's major debut movie?
13 Collectively, who were Bobby Farrell, Marcia Barrett, Liz Mitchell and Maisie Williams?
14 What does the Archbishop of York signs himself as?
15 Burt Reynolds was born in which American state?
16 How is vichyssoise soup usually served?
17 What type of "Schoolboy" appears in the title of a John Le Carre novel?
18 Delft pottery is usually which colours?
19 Which Hill is the highest point in the Cotswolds?
20 Which song begins, "I see trees of green, Red roses too"?
21 Who was 50 first, Carrie Fisher, Mel Gibson or Kevin Costner?
22 In which decade of last century was Andy Warhol born?
23 What was held at Mount Tremblant, Mosport and Montreal at different years in the 1970s?
24 What was the name of Steptoe and Son's horse?
25 In which country did the Russian revolutionary Leon Trotsky die?
26 What was the first Top Ten hit for Go West?
27 In 1919 the Curzon Line divided Poland on what basis?
28 What was founded following the Dumbarton Oaks Conference of the 1940s?
29 Which present-day county goes with White to name the favourite horse of the monarch Richard III?
30 Who did Cassius Clay beat when he first became world heavyweight champion?

Answers	Pot Luck 77 *(see Quiz 166)*

1 Church. 2 10. 3 India. 4 Danish. 5 Glass. 6 The New York Dolls. 7 December. 8 Mary Carillo. 9 Annapurna. 10 British Honduras. 11 28. 12 Harness racing cart. 13 Basketball. 14 Sorry Seems to be the Hardest Word. 15 Polio. 16 When I Need You. 17 Arms and hands. 18 50. 19 Gloucester Cathedral. 20 30. 21 Waterloo Bridge. 22 Blackburn Rovers. 23 Charles the Mad. 24 Portugal. 25 Pointed. 26 Eva Green. 27 Jimmy Young. 28 Elizabeth. 29 1930s. 30 86 minutes.

1 Where did the first man to win five gold medals in one Games win them?
2 Who lowered Carl Lewis's Olympic 100m record in Atlanta?
3 What was the middle name of the athlete disqualified from the 100m in Seoul?
4 Who won the first Marathon of the Modern Olympics?
5 Of the first three Marathons of the Modern Olympics which had the longest course?
6 Who scored the winning basket in the 1972 Olympic basketball final?
7 Which Olympics were cancelled due to WWI?
8 In which stadium were the first Modern Olympics held?
9 Who represented Britain the first time soccer was included in the Olympics?
10 Who won the first men's singles tennis final of the modern Olympics?
11 In 20th-century Olympics, who made the highest batting average in baseball?
12 In the 2000 Olympics how many different countries won medals?
13 On which date was the first Briton to win five consecutive gold medals knighted?
14 Which woman won four gold medals in successive games starting in Seoul?
15 Which discipline was practised by the man who won 15 Olympic medals between 1972 and 1980?
16 In the 20th century which country won most medals at the Winter Olympics?
17 Who first won four consecutive individual titles in the same event?
18 Who were the silver medallists in basketball the year of the US boycott?
19 Who won the first Olympic gold for the men's singles in tennis after it was reinstated after 60 years?
20 In which city was it announced that Beijing would host the 2008 Olympics?
21 Where were the first Winter Paralympics held?
22 From which country does the competitor nicknamed Eric the Eel come from?
23 Which city in the Americas was beaten by Beijing to host the 2008 Olympics?
24 By winning the dressage in Sydney, Germany made it a total of how many team golds in this event?
25 In which decade were the first Summer Paralympics held?
26 Which creature went with Syd and Olly in the Sydney Olympics?
27 In Sydney, which discipline did Dean Macey compete in last?
28 Which Olympic gold medallist was a member of the team which won the British four-man bobsleigh championship in 1989?
29 Where did the first Olympic women's basketball tournament take place?
30 Which Olympics were cancelled due to WWII?

Answers	Villains *(see Quiz 163)*

1 Markovic. 2 Saudi Arabia. 3 Spain. 4 Surveyor of the Queen's Pictures. 5 Last man to be hanged in public. 6 Pentonville. 7 Lee Harvey Oswald. 8 15. 9 Bulsara. 10 Oklahoma. 11 7 November. 12 Gerald Du Maurier. 13 Pim Fortuyn. 14 King Rat. 15 Karla Faye Tucker. 16 Pol Pot. 17 Rachid. 18 Fingerprints. 19 Carlos the Jackal. 20 The Last King of Scotland 21 Marie Kelly. 22 Mary Bell. 23 Let Him Have It. 24 Martin Luther King. 25 Hungerford. 26 Shot in Spain. 27 Hezbollah. 28 Tony Parnes. 29 Charles Brooks. 30 29 years old.

1 In what type of building would a dossal be hung?
2 Shergar won the 1981 Derby by a record how many lengths?
3 In which country is the city of Meerut?
4 What is the nationality of speedway champion Hans Hollen Nielsen?
5 Nelophobia is the fear of what?
6 As a teenager Morrissey ran a fan club for which American band?
7 In which month of 2003 was Saddam Hussein captured?
8 Who was John McEnroe's partner in his first Grand Slam title, a mixed doubles win in the French Open?
9 Maurice Herzog was the first person to conquer which mountain?
10 Belize changed its name from what?
11 How many dominoes are there in a double six set?
12 Who or what is a sulky?
13 In the mid-1970s the NBA and the ABA merged in which sport?
14 What was Elton John's first solo hit on his own Rocket label?
15 The Salk vaccine was developed in the fight against which disease?
16 Which Leo Sayer hit gave the Chrysalis label their first No 1?
17 In sepek takrow you can hit the ball with any part of the body except which?
18 How old was James Herriot when he began writing books?
19 In which cathedral was King Henry III crowned?
20 How old was Eric Cantona when he retired from soccer?
21 What was Vivien Leigh's first movie after Gone with the Wind?
22 Which British club was Sven Goran Eriksson reported to be joining in 1996?
23 How was Charles II King of Spain unkindly known?
24 Which country joined the European Union in the same year as Spain?
25 What shape is the top of a lancet window?
26 "The Dreamers" starred which future Bond girl?
27 Who had the first UK No 1 with "Unchained Melody"?
28 What is Julie Andrews' middle name?
29 In which decade of last century was the first Archery World Championship held?
30 In minutes, how brief was the movie "Brief Encounter"?

Answers	Pot Luck 76 (see Quiz 164)

1 1990s. 2 Clergyman. 3 Ice Age. 4 New Zealand. 5 60–80. 6 Melanie C. 7 Quote. 8 Rita & Les. 9 Poland. 10 Elizabeth. 11 Switzerland. 12 Stephen Daldry. 13 Boney M. 14 Ebor. 15 Georgia. 16 Cold. 17 Honourable. 18 Blue and white. 19 Cleeve Hill. 20 What a Wonderful World. 21 Kevin Costner (2005). 22 1930s. 23 Canadian Grand Prix. 24 Hercules. 25 Mexico. 26 We Close Our Eyes. 27 Language. 28 United Nations. 29 White Surrey. 30 Sonny Liston.

Quiz 167 | Movie Legends

Answers – page 643

1 Who was the male star of the first film to have a Royal Command Performance?
2 Which first name was Harpo Marx born with?
3 What was Woody Allen's first film with Mia Farrow?
4 Which actress wrote an autobiography called "Every Frenchman Has One"?
5 Lauren Bacall was "discovered" when she appeared on the cover of which magazine?
6 What was Ingrid Bergman's final film for the big screen?
7 On which ship was Humphrey Bogart injured in WWI?
8 On which island was Yul Brynner born?
9 Who was the mother of Cary Grant's only child?
10 Which director fired Bette Davis on her very first professional engagement?
11 Ann Margret's screen debut was as which Hollywood legend's daughter?
12 What did Walt Disney do in WWI?
13 What was Robert Donat's last word on screen in the last film before his death?
14 Who played jazz piano in "In the Line of Fire"?
15 Whose debut movie "Every Sunday" also featured the star born Frances Gumm?
16 How was Paulette Goddard billed when she was a Ziegfeld Girl?
17 At the age of 13 Sam Goldwyn was apprenticed as a maker of what?
18 In which movie did the first Mrs Charlie Chaplin play Dorothy?
19 What was the British title of the movie where Alfred Hitchcock made his first cameo appearance?
20 Who played Judy Holliday's tutor in the 1950 film directed by George Cukor?
21 In which year between 1941 and 1953 was Bob Hope not in the Top Ten Hollywood money-making stars?
22 Which Hollywood gossip columnist was born Elda Furry?
23 Who played the title role in the movie about the greatest escapologist of all time?
24 Which movie gave Trevor Howard his first Oscar nomination?
25 What was Rock Hudson's debut movie?
26 Which Howard Hughes movie launched the career of Jean Harlow?
27 Who in the movie industry was knighted by King Olav V in 1979?
28 Who did Susan Hayward play in the penultimate film for which she was Oscar-nominated?
29 Who was introduced to the public in "Orphan's Benefit"?
30 Irving Berlin could only write music in which key?

Answers	Crime (see Quiz 169)

1 Identikit. 2 Louisiana. 3 Argentina. 4 Little war. 5 The Nuremberg Files. 6 Texas. 7 Auburn. 8 Lanarkshire. 9 Washington Sniper. 10 Arkansas. 11 Louise Woodward. 12 Anna Lindh. 13 21st July. 14 Festina. 15 Dar es Salaam. 16 Market Street. 17 Strangeways. 18 Jerusalem. 19 Pickles. 20 Iraq. 21 Thailand. 22 Young offenders. 23 Eastbourne. 24 Luxor. 25 Bit opponent's ear. 26 Selling beef on the bone. 27 Bletchley Park Museum. 28 Norfolk & Norwich. 29 Beverly Hills. 30 Armley.

1 David Bryant became the first world champion in which sport?
2 In which country is the city of Karaj?
3 Which silent movie comic turned director used the pseudonym William Goodrich?
4 In which decade of the last century did women's hockey become an Olympic event?
5 In the 1997 Tory leadership election, who finished third?
6 Who first took Led Zeppelin's "Stairway to Heaven" into the singles charts?
7 A terrorist bomb outside Paddy's Bar took place in 2002 on which holiday island?
8 Which Briton held the record number of Grand Prix victories before Alain Prost set a new record?
9 Which animated film was Walt Disney working on at the time of his death?
10 "GoldenEye" was named after Ian Fleming's home in which country?
11 Who found more success after leaving his band King Crabbs?
12 Which character does James Stewart play in the movie classic Harvey?
13 In which country is the port of Lobito?
14 What was the first Top Ten hit for Morrissey?
15 Which MP's father-in-law was played by Sean Connery in "A Bridge Too Far"?
16 What was the first movie that the Marx Brothers made for MGM?
17 Which English king was nicknamed because of his red face?
18 How many Oscars did composer Tim Rice win during the 1990s?
19 In which movie did the character Kimberly Wells feature?
20 Jim Clark spent all his racing career with which team?
21 Who plays the older detective in TV's Dalziel and Pascoe?
22 Which team did defending champions Brazil play in their Germany 2006 opener?
23 Who was the first PM to move to 10 Downing Street?
24 How many chapters are there in the first book of the Old Testament?
25 Which Dickens novel featured Jerry Cruncher?
26 Which team won the first University Boat Race?
27 Who starred as Isadora Duncan in the movie "Isadora"?
28 A barrico is a type of small what?
29 The 1930s movie classic "It Happened One Night" was originally called what?
30 Which Patty was the first woman to win golf's British and US Opens in the same year?

| **Answers** | **Pot Luck 79** *(see Quiz 170)* |

1 Frederick. 2 Hamburg. 3 Boynton. 4 Brunei. 5 Veronica Guerin. 6 Lord Byron. 7 Parsec. 8 Athenia. 9 Georgia. 10 Gary Busey. 11 151. 12 East. 13 Ten. 14 A library. 15 Wyoming. 16 Alan Lancaster. 17 France. 18 Year of the Dragon. 19 1920s. 20 Wet Wet Wet. 21 Iceland. 22 John Lennon. 23 Luise Rainer. 24 London Stock Exchange. 25 Dinner jacket. 26 John Lewis Partnership. 27 Cecil Beaton. 28 Bon Jovi. 29 Wiseguy. 30 Spain.

1 Guy Trebert was the first person apprehended due to what?
2 In which state were Bonnie & Clyde arrested?
3 In 1960 in which country was Adolf Eichmann apprehended?
4 What does the word guerrilla mean?
5 What was the name of the Internet site used by US anti-abortionists which resulted in a massive fine for them?
6 Where is the USA's Ellis II prison unit?
7 In which prison was the electric chair first used?
8 In which county is Schotts prison?
9 Arrested in October 2002, John Allen Muhammed was known as what?
10 In 1998 two schoolboys were tried in which state for shootings at Westside Middle School?
11 Elaine Whitfield Sharp was a chief defence lawyer in whose trial?
12 Which Swedish Foreign Minister died of stab wounds in September 2003?
13 In 2005, what was the date of the failed terrorist attack on the London transport system?
14 Which team was suspended from the Tour de France over drug allegations in 1998?
15 Other than Nairobi where was a US embassy attacked at the end of the 1990s?
16 In which Street was the Omagh bomb detonated?
17 Which British prison was the scene of a major riot in 1990?
18 In which city was Yitzhak Rabin shot?
19 Which Judge in the early 1990s famously imprisoned a teenage shoplifter and her baby?
20 Farzad Bazoft was convicted and executed for spying where?
21 In which country were Karen Smith and Patricia Cahill accused of smuggling heroin in 1990?
22 What type of institution is Glenochil – remand centre, women's prison or young offenders?
23 Ian Gow was MP for where when he was killed by an IRA bomb?
24 Where in Egypt was there a massacre of tourists in 1997?
25 Why was Kevin Yates given a six-month suspension by the rugby union in 1998?
26 Jim Sutherland was the first man to be convicted of which crime?
27 Where was the Enigma coding machine stolen from in 2000?
28 In which hospital did Reggie Kray receive his final treatment before his death?
29 Where in America was George Michael arrested in 1998?
30 What is the name of the famous prison in Yorkshire's major city?

---

1 In "The Pirates of Penzance" who was born on the 29th of February?
2 Where was Monica Seles playing when she was stabbed during a tennis match in 1993?
3 What does the B stand for in JB Priestley's name?
4 Bandar Seri Begawan is the capital of where?
5 Which Irish journalist inspired the story of the movie "When the Sky Falls"?
6 Who said,"I awoke one morning and found myself famous"?
7 Which unit of measurement equals 3.2616 light years?
8 Which British liner was the first to be sunk by a U-boat on the first day of the Second World War?
9 Which state is Otis Redding's home in the lyrics of "On the Dock of the Bay"?
10 Who played Buddy in the 1970s movie "The Buddy Holly Story"?
11 What is the next prime number after 149?
12 Manhattan lies between the Hudson and which river?
13 To the nearest million, what is the population of Portugal?
14 Where do tragic lovers Jenny and Oliver meet for the first time in "Love Story"?
15 In which US state was the first National Park established?
16 Who was Francis Rossi's school mate and long-time bass player in Status Quo?
17 Which was the first country in the world to introduce national conscription?
18 In which Chinese Year was Sharon Osbourne born?
19 In which decade was the surgeon Christiaan Barnard born?
20 Who were the first Scottish group to have three No 1 singles?
21 USA's Reagan and Russia's Gorbachev first met in which country?
22 Which prominent figure did Mark Chapman murder?
23 Who was the first winner of consecutive best actress Oscars?
24 In 1973 Susan Shaw became the first woman to work on the floor where?
25 Which item of evening wear for men was created by Griswold Louillard?
26 "Never knowingly undersold" was the slogan of which chain store?
27 Which designer created the Ascot scene costumes for the film "My Fair Lady"?
28 Tico Torres was drummer with which globally successful band?
29 The movie "Goodfellas" was based on which novel?
30 In which country is the city of Murcia?

Answers	**Pot Luck 78** *(see Quiz 168)*

1 Bowls. 2 Iran. 3 Fatty Arbuckle. 4 1980s. 5 John Redwood. 6 Far Corporation. 7 Bali. 8 Jackie Stewart. 9 The Jungle Book. 10 Jamaica. 11 Jimmy Nail. 12 Elwood P Dowd. 13 Angola. 14 Suedehead. 15 Menzies Campbell. 16 A Night at the Opera. 17 William II, Rufus. 18 Three. 19 The China Syndrome. 20 Lotus. 21 Warren Clarke. 22 Croatia. 23 Hugh Walpole. 24 50. 25 A Tale of Two Cities. 26 Oxford. 27 Vanessa Redgrave. 28 Barrel. 29 Night Bus. 30 Sheehan.

1 Which star of a classic sitcom is the son of the actor born Alphonso Giuseppe Giovanni Roberto d'Abruzzo?

2 In which show did "Star Wars" Luke Skywalker make his professional debut?

3 Which series did "The Offer" become?

4 Who played Hamish the restaurant critic in "Absolutely Fabulous"?

5 How many couples were "Coupling"?

6 What make of car was Bo & Luke Hazzard's "General Lee"?

7 In what type of establishment was "Desmonds" set?

8 Who said, "I have been complimented on my gestures by the chief psychiatrist of Broadmoor"?

9 In which month and year was the last episode of "Seinfeld" first broadcast in the US?

10 Which sitcom started life as "The Bishop Rides Again"?

11 Who was married to Ben in "My Family"?

12 Which actress/dancer is the elder sister of "The Cosby Show" regular Phylicia Rashad?

13 What was the last screen work of the actor who played Mainwaring in "Dad's Army"?

14 Which gay German officer in "Allo Allo" spent an episode disguised as a flamenco dancer?

15 Who were initially called Bobby and Billy?

16 For which firm did Samantha's husband work in "Bewitched"?

17 Which writer on "Birds of a Feather" also played Tracey's husband on the show?

18 Which "Blackadder" series covered the Regency period?

19 For which character did Kirstie Alley win an Emmy in 1991?

20 Whom did the creator of "Ally McBeal" model his main character on?

21 In "Bread" what was the name of the vicar Aveline married?

22 Who sang the theme song to "Brush Strokes"?

23 What type of coat did Wolfie Smith wear?

24 Which character in "Cheers" was the sister in real life of the show's early producer?

25 What was the address of the Huxtables?

26 Which "Dad's Army" regular had written almost 40 plays?

27 In "The Day Today" who appeared under his own name?

28 Who played the Devil in the 2001 "Absolutely Fabulous"?

29 Where was the US version of "Till Death Us Do Part" set?

30 What is the real name of the actor who played George Constanza in "Seinfeld"?

Answers	**Music Legends** *(see Quiz 173)*

1 Satisfaction. 2 Stephen King. 3 John Lennon's. 4 Five. 5 Barbra Streisand. 6 Liberace. 7 Malcolm Arnold. 8 1971. 9 Patsy Cline. 11 Kay Starr. 10 Elvis Presley (Surrender). 12 Cathy's Clown. 13 The Searchers. 14 1990s. 15 Lennon & McCartney. 16 Shirley Bassey. 17 Jerry Lee Lewis. 18 Frankie Laine. 19 Bee Gees. 20 Dreamboat (Alma Cogan). 21 Tony Bennett. 22 Ray Charles. 23 Doris Day. 24 Berwick Street (London). 25 Connie Francis. 26 Mantovani (Moulin Rouge). 27 Status Quo. 28 Dusty Springfield. 29 Winifred Atwell. 30 Reg Presley.

1 Holly Hunter and Craig T Nelson provided voices for which animated family?
2 Which TV Mr was Richard Hearne?
3 In which country would you watch Boavista play a home soccer match?
4 Which herb goes into a bearnaise sauce along with tarragon?
5 What was the first Top Ten hit for 911?
6 What was the surname of the first Peter to be a presenter on "Blue Peter"?
7 Which singer with No 1's in his own right wrote the Buddy Holly classic "It Doesn't Matter Anymore?
8 Who was murdered in the first ever episode of "EastEnders"?
9 Which black and white cat was for many years on the cover of the "Dandy" comic?
10 Who was the longest reigning British King?
11 Mesclun is a type of what?
12 Made back in 1950, what was Marlon Brando's first film?
13 Who was the first Prime Minister to use Chequers?
14 What is a Dorset Blue Vinney?
15 Which character did Drew Barrymore play in "Music and Lyrics"?
16 What is the name of the alter ego of Turner Prize-winning potter Grayson Perry?
17 How many different Olympic Games did Tessa Sanderson compete in?
18 Who visited Kirrin Island?
19 What does a palmiped possess?
20 Chronos was the Greek god of what?
21 Which original Rolling Stone was eligible for a bus pass in October 2001?
22 What is Ted's middle name in the movie "Bill & Ted's Excellent Adventure"?
23 A natatorium is another name for a what?
24 How is comedian Robert Harper better known?
25 In which city were Haagen-Dazs ice creams first sold?
26 Sue Barker and Penelope Keith both married husbands following which career?
27 What is the collective noun for a flock of larks?
28 What was the first Top Ten hit for 2 Unlimited?
29 In Mexican cookery what is a quesadilla?
30 How old was Prince Charles when he was invested as Prince of Wales?

Answers | **Pot Luck 81** *(see Quiz 174)*

1 Dolly Parton. 2 The English Channel. 3 K7. 4 Bastian Schweinsteiger. 5 £20 note. 6 Fletcher Christian. 7 Egypt. 8 H5N1. 9 Otis Redding. 10 George V. 11 Release Me. 12 Ice cream. 13 Original. 14 Pakistan. 15 50 pence. 16 Mr Loud. 17 A wind which blows from Morocco to Spain. 18 Go. 19 Paris. 20 Delia Smith. 21 Italy. 22 Sunday in the Park with George. 23 The Beagle. 24 Rio Lobos. 25 Windsurfing. 26 Emma Bunton. 27 Iggy Pop. 28 Big Jazza. 29 Rob Bowman. 30 Apiphobia.

1 Which single did The Rolling Stones release on the day The Beatles received their MBEs?
2 Michael Jackson's longest music video was the concept of whom?
3 Whose piano was bought by George Michael for £1.45 million in London in 2000?
4 What was the highest UK chart position of "My Way"?
5 Who released the album "Timeless – Live in Concert" in 2000?
6 Which pianist had the real first names Wladziu Valentino?
7 Who wrote the music for the classic movie "Bridge on the River Kwai"?
8 Before "Supernatural" in 1999 in which year did Santana last have a US No 1 album?
9 Who died in the same crash as Hawkshaw Hawkins and Cowboy Copas?
10 Which 1950s chart topper was born Katherine Starks?
11 Who recorded the English lyrics version of "Torna A Sorrento" in 1961?
12 What was the Everly Brothers' first hit on both sides of the Atlantic?
13 Which Mersey band was the first to top the charts not managed by Brian Epstein?
14 In which decade has Tom Jones had least Top Ten hits?
15 Which songwriters gave The Overlanders their only hit?
16 Who made a "Diamond Tour" in 1998?
17 Whose autobiography was entitled "Killer"?
18 Who was No 1 when Queen Elizabeth II was crowned?
19 Which trio were the subject of "The South Bank Show" in March 1997?
20 What was the only No 1 for the girl with "the giggle in her voice"?
21 Who won a Grammy for "For the Ladies"?
22 Who sang "Ol' Man River" at Frank Sinatra's 80th birthday party?
23 Who won the Best Song Oscar in 1953, in a movie she starred in?
24 Which street features on the cover of Oasis's "(What's the Story) Morning Glory"?
25 Who recorded "Something Stupid" with the lead singer of Culture Club?
26 Which orchestra leader had a hit from a film with the same title as a 2001 blockbuster?
27 Who celebrated their 30th anniversary in the music business with the album "Don't Stop"?
28 Who sang the theme song about the movie on the Profumo Affair?
29 Which 1954 chart topper was, according to the man himself, a huge influence on Elton John?
30 Which composer of Wet Wet Wet's biggest hit is an expert on crop circles?

1 Which singer/actress was Mrs Carl Dean?
2 Harriet Quimby was the first woman to fly over what?
3 The 1990s hit "Come Baby Come" was the first Top Ten appearance for which act?
4 Who scored twice for Germany as they finished 2006's third-place match?
5 Scientist Michael Faraday died in 1867 but where was his face much seen late in the 20th century?
6 Clark Gable, Marlon Brando and Mel Gibson have all played which screen role?
7 In which country is the city of Tanta?
8 Which strain of bird flu was involved in the outbreak in Suffolk in February 2007?
9 Who wrote Aretha Franklin's first UK hit "Respect"?
10 Who became the first British monarch to make a broadcast on Christmas Day?
11 Which 1967 No 1 recorded the longest-ever stay in the UK Top 50?
12 A dessert served "a la mode" in America would include what?
13 Under what name did Everett Bradley and Walter Taieb make the charts in the 1990s?
14 Who won the first ever World Cup in hockey?
15 What was Britain's first issued decimal coin?
16 Who – aptly enough – patented the first upright piano?
17 What is leveche, and where does it come from?
18 What was the first Top Ten hit for Moby?
19 The world's first speaking clock service started in which city?
20 Whom is editor and publisher Michael Wynn-Jones married to?
21 Umberto II was the last king of which country?
22 Which musical won five awards at the 2007 Olivier Awards?
23 What was the animal name of Charles Darwin's survey ship?
24 Which movie was John Wayne making when he won his Oscar for "True Grit"?
25 Stephan van den Berg was the first Olympic gold winner in which water sport?
26 Which ex-Spice Girl shares a birthday with actor Martin Shaw?
27 James Jewel Osterberg became better known under which name?
28 Which role did Robbie Coltrane play in "Tutti Frutti"?
29 Who directed the movie "The X Files"?
30 What is a phobia about bees known as?

Answers	**Pot Luck 80** *(see Quiz 172)*

1 The Incredibles. 2 Pastry. 3 Portugal. 4 Chervil. 5 Don't Make Me Wait. 6 Purves. 7 Paul Anka. 8 Reg Cox. 9 Korky. 10 George III. 11 Mixed green salad. 12 The Men. 13 Lloyd George. 14 A cheese. 15 Sophie Fisher. 16 Claire. 17 Six. 18 The Famous Five. 19 Webbed feet. 20 Time. 21 Bill Wyman. 22 Theodore. 23 Swimming pool. 24 Bobby Ball. 25 New York. 26 Policemen. 27 Exultation. 28 Get Ready for This. 29 Filled tortilla. 30 20.

1 Which book received the greatest publisher's advance in the 20th century?
2 Whose "Decline and Fall" is described in Evelyn Waugh's first novel?
3 Who won the Booker Prize the year after Paddy Clarke first won in the 1990s?
4 Who provided the "Four Words" at the start of "The Book of General Ignorance"?
5 Which zoo was founded by the author of "The Overloaded Ark"?
6 Who are the two sisters in the novel subtitled "The Sacred and Profane Memories of Captain Charles Ryder"?
7 Where is Michael Ondaatje's "In the Skin of a Lion" set?
8 Which book has the cover line "Three Secrets, Two Women, One Grail"?
9 In which village does the hero of George Eliot's first full-length novel live?
10 Whose diary opens Bram Stoker's most famous novel?
11 Who wrote the novel about the WWII drama brought to the small screen by Steven Spielberg and Tom Hanks?
12 "One Flew Over the Cuckoo's Nest" is told from whose standpoint?
13 What is Charles Dickens' only other work of historical fiction along with "A Tale of Two Cities"?
14 In "Animal Farm" what is the name of the animal seen as Trotsky?
15 Which painting did Donald Sassoon write about?
16 What is the title of journalist John Simpson's "Tales from a Traveller's Life"?
17 What was the first novel in which PD James' Cordelia Gray appeared?
18 Which poet is the official biographer of Philip Larkin?
19 Which sportsman's autobiography was called "A Season in Paradise"?
20 Which Award did "A Stitch in Time" win?
21 Who was the youngest of the "Little Women"?
22 Who is the subject of "Dear Tom"?
23 Approximately how many books per year did Barbara Cartland write during the last 20 years of her life?
24 From which Shakespeare play does the title of "Brave New World" come?
25 Which novel by "The Snowman"'s author was about a nuclear attack?
26 Which novel did the author of "Akenfield" write in 1960?
27 What is "Barchester Towers" the sequel to?
28 What was the title of the 2001 bestseller by the writer who had achieved 20th-century success with "The Day of the Jackal" and "The Odessa File"?
29 What was the first novel in which Hercule Poirot appeared?
30 "Killing Dragons" is about the conquering of what?

Answers – page 652

1 In motor racing, who was the first driver to be sacked twice by Benetton?
2 Who was the first "Coronation Street" actress to be awarded an OBE?
3 A brochette is another name for what type of food?
4 Who adapted "The Cider House Rules" into a movie?
5 In which country is the city of Makeyevka?
6 What does a lapidary deal in?
7 On 19th February 2007, Notting Hill, Kensington, Westminster became subjected to what?
8 Which group had 1970 top ten hits with "Sunny", "Belfast" and "Painter Man"?
9 What did D stand for in Franklin D Roosevelt's name?
10 In which 1980s movie did Mr & Mrs Harvey Keitel star?
11 Victor Emmanuel was the first King of which European country?
12 Leander is the oldest club in the world in which sport?
13 In 2007 who won the Orange Rising Star Award at the BAFTAS?
14 What is Sebastian Coe's middle name?
15 Which 1990s English soccer champions have a ground with the Darwen End?
16 Where in the US was the first artificial turf soccer pitch?
17 What was the first Top Ten single for Iron Maiden?
18 Which city hosts the oldest modern-day marathon race?
19 Whose wives included Helen Menken and Mary Philips?
20 On TV for many years Michael Miles invited contestants to do what?
21 Paris and which other capital city were the first to be linked by telephone?
22 What was Gary Cooper's job before he became an actor?
23 The Strathcona Cup is competed for in which sport?
24 What was the first Top Ten single for James?
25 Which folk singer and writer who inspired Dylan, passed away in February 2007?
26 Who dropped out of "The Godfather, Part III", allowing Sofia Coppola to play the role?
27 Michael Fagan made the headlines when he broke into where?
28 In which film did a pilot named Klaatu appear?
29 How does Roger Peterson fit into the history of pop music?
30 Geraldine Rees was the first woman jockey to finish which race?

Answers | Pot Luck 83 *(see Quiz 178)*

1 Long jump and high jump. 2 Max Bygraves. 3 The Queen. 4 Mark Lawson. 5 Stuart Gray. 6 Tony McCoy. 7 Tom Stoppard. 8 One. 9 Kate Long. 10 Boat Race. 11 200m. 12 Irvin Kershner. 13 Mexico. 14 Colin Clive. 15 Jersey Joe Walcott. 16 Greece. 17 Lincoln. 18 The Old Bailey. 19 Germany. 20 Two. 21 Drowned. 22 Shoes. 23 Charly. 24 Place it was first detected. 25 Pilot's licence. 26 Algeria. 27 Germany & Japan. 28 Global Challenger. 29 May. 30 Mats Wilander.

Quiz 177 | Famous Names

Answers – page 649

1 Which two Beatles children had the same birthday?
2 Who invented the Barbie doll?
3 Which fictional Dan first put in an appearance in 1937?
4 Who was the first person to hit a golf ball on the Moon?
5 How was Ferdinand Joseph Lamothe better known?
6 Who created Popeye?
7 Which famous names expressed they used the same toothpaste in 2001?
8 Which member of a famous film and writing family owned Sam's Restaurant in Manhattan?
9 Which film director is the son of a former first flute of the New York Symphony Orchestra under Toscanini?
10 Who wrote an autobiography called "Open Secret"?
11 Who are Kate Hudson's parents?
12 Which university awarded the Prize named after publisher Pulitzer?
13 How is Patricia Plangman better known?
14 Who invented Scrabble?
15 Which late comedian's autobiography was called "Still on My Way to Hollywood"?
16 Who was the first movie child to earn a million dollars?
17 The rebuilding of the Globe Theatre on the south bank of the Thames was the brainchild of whom?
18 Which two Goons had the same birthday?
19 Which member of the Monty Python team wrote "The Rutland Dirty Weekend Book"?
20 Liliane Bettencourt is heiress to which company's fortune?
21 What type of sports person tested the first Rolex Oyster watch?
22 Which father of a future President was executive producer on many Gloria Swanson movies?
23 Who was the first African-American to be featured on the cover of "Sports Illustrated"'s swimsuit issue?
24 Dr Lawrence Summers stood down in 2005 as president of which university?
25 Which author has a prize for children's book illustration named after her?
26 Who owned the original yacht after whom the Americas Cup was named?
27 What did Giorgio Armani study at university?
28 What was the first name of "Mr Laura Ashley"?
29 Which position was held by Sir Martin Rees at the turn of the century?
30 Jesse Boot, of Boots fame, was which Lord when he died in 1931?

Answers	Books 3 *(see Quiz 175)*

1 Without Remorse. 2 Paul Pennyfeather. 3 James Kelman. 4 Alan Davies. 5 Jersey. 6 Julia and Cordelia. 7 Toronto. 8 Labyrinth. 9 Hayslope. 10 Jonathan Harker. 11 Stephen Ambrose. 12 Bromden. 13 Barnaby Rudge. 14 Snowball. 15 Mona Lisa. 16 A Mad World, My Masters. 17 An Unsuitable Job for a Woman. 18 Andrew Motion. 19 Henrik Larsson. 20 Whitbread. 21 Amy. 22 Tom Courtenay. 23 23. 24 The Tempest. 25 When the Wind Blows. 26 A Treasonable Growth. 27 The Warden. 28 The Veteran. 29 The Mysterious Affair at Styles. 30 The Alps.

1 At the 1948 Olympics in which two events did Fanny Blankers Koen choose not to compete despite holding the world record in both?
2 Who was the only British male to feature in the first ever UK album chart?
3 For which movie did Helen Mirren win her first movie BAFTA?
4 Which former politician's son became a regular presenter of Radio 4's "Front Row"?
5 Who was Southampton manager for 113 days in 2001?
6 In 2001 which jockey was the fastest to ride 100 winners in a season?
7 Which well-known literary figure wrote the screenplay for the movie "Billy Bathgate"?
8 How many women had been a Prime Minister before Indira Gandhi took office?
9 Catherine Tate played Karen Cooper in a TV series based on whose novel?
10 Susan Brown was the first woman to compete in which race?
11 What was Carl Lewis's third Olympic gold among the four he won in Los Angeles?
12 Who directed the movie "The Empire Strikes Back"?
13 In which country is the city of Culiacan?
14 Who played the part of Frankenstein in the 1930s classic movie?
15 Before losing to Rocky Marciano who said, "If I can't beat this bum take my name off the record books"?
16 In which country did malmsey wine originate?
17 Which US President patented a type of lifebelt?
18 In London what was built on the site of Newgate prison?
19 In which country were post codes first introduced?
20 How many "Die Hard" movies were made before Samuel L Jackson was introduced as Bruce Willis's sidekick?
21 Australian prime minister Harold Holt died in what circumstances?
22 Imelda Marcos had hundreds of pairs of what?
23 What was the first Top Ten hit for Prodigy?
24 Lassa Fever was named after whom or what?
25 Lord Brabazon was the first Briton to receive which type of licence?
26 In which country was the first HQ of the French Foreign Legion?
27 Which two countries concluded the Anti-Comintern Pact in 1936?
28 What was Tony Bullimore's craft when he capsized in the 1996 Vendee Globe?
29 Which month of the year was part of the name of a Bond girl?
30 Who did Yannick Noah beat to become the first Frenchman to win the French Open tennis champion for 37 years?

Answers | Pot Luck 82 *(see Quiz 176)*

1 Johnny Herbert. 2 Violet Carson. 3 Kebab. 4 John Irving. 5 Ukraine. 6 Gemstones. 7 Congestion charge. 8 Boney M. 9 Delano. 10 The Naples Connection. 11 Italy. 12 Rowing. 13 Eva Green. 14 Newbold. 15 Blackburn Rovers. 16 Houston. 17 Run to the Hills. 18 Boston. 19 Humphrey Bogart. 20 Take Your Pick. 21 Brussels. 22 Cartoonist/illustrator. 23 Curling. 24 Sit Down. 25 Eric von Schmidt. 26 Winona Ryder. 27 Buckingham Palace. 28 The Day the Earth Stood Still. 29 In charge of the flight that claimed the life of Buddy Holly. 30 Grand National.

1 Who took 107 international wickets in 1998?
2 How many different countries had won the ICC World Cup before 2007?
3 Who won the County Championship in 1966?
4 By how many wickets did Middlesex win the last Gillette Cup?
5 In the 1970s which NatWest Trophy winner had the shortest name?
6 Which humorous writer said October was a strange month for the real cricket fan as it was then he discovered his wife had left him in May?
7 Which was the more northerly County to share the title in 1977?
8 Who captained the first South African side after the fall of apartheid?
9 Against whom did Sachin Tendulkar score his 18th ODI century?
10 Against which country did Trevor Chappell bowl an underarm delivery?
11 Who took eight wickets for England in the first ever Test match?
12 Where did Brian Lara score 390 runs in one day in June 1994?
13 Who was man of the match after taking a Test hat-trick against the West Indies in 1995?
14 How was Mansur Ali Khan better known?
15 Who was the first Pakistan cricketer to score 1000 runs and take 100 wickets in a year twice?
16 Which captain won every toss against South Africa in 1960?
17 Who was the first player to score 2000 first-class runs in a season without scoring a century?
18 Who played for Australia in the 1980s and for South Africa in 1991?
19 Which then Lancashire soccer club did EH "Patsy" Hendren play for?
20 Where was the first Oxford and Cambridge match played?
21 How many balls did Adam Gilchrist need to reach an 2006–07 Ashes ton at Perth?
22 Who took all 10 wickets against Pakistan in February 1999?
23 Which football club employed ex-England captain Rachael Heyhoe Flint?
24 Which Englishman overtook the Englishman who overtook Geoff Boycott's record of runs scored in Test cricket?
25 Why was Geoff Boycott banned from Test cricket in 1982?
26 To the nearest 20, how many record-breaking Test runs did Viv Richards make in one calendar year in 1976?
27 Which was the first city to have four Test grounds?
28 How many runs did Jim Laker concede in his 19-wicket haul in a 1956 Test?
29 Who won the County Championship for seven consecutive years in the 1950s?
30 Where did Brian Lara score 375 runs against England in April 1994?

Answers | Hollywood *(see Quiz 181)*

1 Mrs Deisda Wilcox. 2 Ordinary People (Tim Hutton). 3 Peggy Sue Got Married. 4 Apollo 13. 5 Fatty Arbuckle. 6 The Harder They Fall. 7 Main Street to Broadway. 8 Warner Bros. 9 Wired. 10 Jason Robards Jr. 11 He Knows You're Alone. 12 Cat. 13 Pentimento. 14 Cosmopolitan. 15 Woman of the Year. 16 Stardust Memories. 17 William Holden. 18 Invitation to the Dance. 19 Joaquin Phoenix. 20 Godzilla. 21 DW Griffith. 22 Elaine May. 23 Waiting to Exhale. 24 Elliott Gould. 25 Amy Irving & Priscilla Pointer. 26 Julianne Moore. 27 A Bronx Tale. 28 Three. 29 Dr Cameron. 30 M Night Shyamalan.

1 Which Saw movie was released in 2006?
2 Who scored the injury-time penalty by which Italy beat Australia in Germany 2006?
3 At which university did Anthony Minghella teach before becoming an Oscar winner?
4 Balti is the Indian word for what?
5 Who won an Oscar for the song "Three Coins in the Fountain"?
6 Frank McCourt's memoirs were set in which Irish county?
7 Which Elvis single made him the first artist to have three consecutive British No 1s?
8 Hanepoot is a type of what?
9 What was named after Buck's Club in London?
10 Which food item comes from the Turkish for rotating?
11 Kummel is a Russian liqueur extracted from what?
12 Which country has a wine-growing area called O'Higgins?
13 Which rays did Ernest Rutherford discover?
14 What subject did TV cook Sophie Grigson study at university?
15 What is added to an omelette to make an Omelette Argenteuil?
16 After winning the world title, who was Jack Dempsey's first opponent where the fight went to the full distance?
17 Who did Tottenham Hotspur beat in the final to become FA Cup and League Champions for the first time?
18 Which No 1 single mentions Jackie – Madame – Onassis?
19 Who was the first professional to captain England at cricket?
20 In 1952 at the Chateau de Chambord what type of display was first shown?
21 In which country did the card game canasta originate?
22 What did the Tower Commission investigate in the US in the 1980s?
23 Which band's vocalists have included Blaze Bayley and Bruce Dickinson?
24 On TV, who had a house featuring a dog, cat and a frog?
25 In which city did Kurt Cobain die?
26 How is writer Salvatore Lombino better known?
27 Radium has the atomic number of which bingo call?
28 How is comedian Edward McGinnis better known?
29 Cocose is a butter made from what?
30 Which was the first US state to abolish slavery?

Answers	**Pot Luck 85** *(see Quiz 182)*

1 Savage Garden. 2 Gary Oldman. 3 Have a heart transplant. 4 Bertie Mee. 5 Giles Foden. 6 Angling. 7 Texas. 8 Hampton Court maze. 9 Harmonica. 10 Do They Know It's Christmas?. 11 Lacrosse. 12 Peru. 13 Boxing. 14 House. 15 Rudolph. 16 Degerfos. 17 Boisterous. 18 Irene Nemirosvsky. 19 Elizabeth Taylor. 20 Iowa. 21 Kenya. 22 Gandhi. 23 Roper. 24 Handkerchief. 25 Wilhelm. 26 Pack horse. 27 Germany. 28 Jack Ryan. 29 Symptoms of disease. 30 Connie Francis.

Answers – page 653

1 Who named Hollywood?

2 What was the first film of the actor married to Debra Winger from 1986 to 1990?

3 Helen Hunt's fourth movie shares its name with which later musical?

4 What was music composer James Horner's first Oscar nomination of the 1990s?

5 Who used the pseudonym William Goodrich when Hollywood turned his back on him after a scandal?

6 Humphrey Bogart underwent surgery for cancer of the oesophagus after making which film?

7 In which 1953 film did Oscar Hammerstein II appear as himself?

8 Which studio gave Lauren Bacall her film debut?

9 Which movie was based on the life of John Belushi?

10 Who portrayed the author of "The Maltese Falcon" in "Julia"?

11 His directorial debut was "That Thing You Do", but what was his first movie as an actor?

12 What type of screen animal was Rhubarb?

13 Which Lillian Hellman novel became the movie "Julia", starring Jane Fonda?

14 Which company did William Randolph Hearst found with the express purpose of making his mistress Marion Davies a star?

15 Which MGM movie did Katharine Hepburn make directly after "The Philadelphia Story"?

16 What was Woody Allen's last film with United Artists?

17 Which Hollywood star was co-owner of the Mount Kenya Safari Club?

18 What was Gene Kelly's solo directing debut?

19 Who played Commodus in Russell Crowe's Oscar-winning movie?

20 "Deeper Underground" was written for which Hollywood movie?

21 Which Hollywood legend did Charles Dance play in "Good Morning Babylon"?

22 Who co-wrote "Heaven Can Wait" with Warren Beatty?

23 What was Whitney Houston's follow-up to her on-screen debut?

24 Who was the first non-Swede to star in an Ingmar Bergman movie?

25 Which mother and daughter appeared in "Carrie"?

26 Who played opposite Anthony Hopkins in the follow-up to "Silence of the Lambs"?

27 What was Robert De Niro's directorial debut?

28 How many Golden Globes did "Dreamgirls" win?

29 Which role did Spottiswoode Aitken play in "Birth of a Nation"?

30 Who wrote and directed "The Sixth Sense"?

Quiz 182 Pot Luck 85

1 Daniel Jones and Darren Hayes made the pop charts under what name?
2 To whom was Uma Thurman married before Ethan Hawke?
3 Philip Blaiberg was the second person to do what?
4 Which double-winning soccer manager died in October 2001?
5 On whose book was the movie "The Last King of Scotland" based?
6 CIPS is the body which regulates which sport?
7 The gigantic nightclub Gilley's Club is in which US state?
8 London and Wise designed which famous much-visited feature?
9 Charles Wheatstone is the creator of what?
10 Which debut single became the first to enter the charts straight at No 1?
11 Baggataway developed into which game?
12 In which country is the city of Callao?
13 What was the first sport screened on ITV?
14 What name is given to the circular target in curling?
15 What is the middle name of former US President Gerald Ford?
16 Sven Goran Eriksson first coached at which club in the late 1970s?
17 What does the musical term strepitoso mean – boisterous, in military style or in strict tempo?
18 Who wrote the besteller "Suite Française"?
19 Who has been married to Larry Fortensky, John Warner and Nicky Hilton?
20 Which state in America is known as the Hawkeye State?
21 Princess Elizabeth was visiting which country at the time that she become Queen Elizabeth II?
22 "No man's life can be encompassed in one telling" are the opening words of which epic movie?
23 What was the surname of sitcom marrieds George and Mildred?
24 Richard II is said to have popularised the use of which everyday item?
25 What is Leonardo Di Caprio's middle name?
26 Who or what is a sumpter?
27 In which country is the city of Wuppertal?
28 Who was Zsa Zsa Gabor's sixth husband?
29 What is semeiology the study of?
30 Concetta Franconero took old standard songs back into the pop charts under which name?

1 In which US state is the Jewel cave system?
2 The largest man-made excavation in the world mines which element?
3 Which animal weighs the most – grizzly bear, polar bear or a walrus?
4 What is Europe's largest island which is not a country in its own right?
5 Which desert is on the US–Mexico border?
6 What is the most common element in the earth's crust after oxygen?
7 Which planet orbits the Sun fastest?
8 Acid rain results due to a pollution of the atmosphere with oxides of nitrogen and what?
9 What is another name for a tsunami?
10 What colour is apatite?
11 Where was the meteorite High Possil found?
12 Where is the highest waterfall outside South America?
13 What is the world's highest island?
14 How many states does Lake Michigan cover?
15 Which planet has the hottest surface?
16 Orogenesis is concerned with the formation of what?
17 Which unit measures distances beyond the solar system?
18 Where was the meteorite Armanty found on Earth?
19 Actinobiology studies the effect of what on living organisms?
20 Cryogenics studies materials under what conditions?
21 Of the five largest glaciers in the world which is the only one not in Antarctica?
22 Which part of planet Earth would a pedologist observe?
23 The Appleton layer plays a role in what – heat control, sifting of toxic gases or radio communication?
24 It isn't a sea, but what is the Afsluidijk Sea?
25 How many countries does the Mekong river flow through?
26 What is the most common element in the universe after hydrogen?
27 Which planet is the lightest?
28 Which scale measures the hardness of substances?
29 How many light years is Alpha Centauri from the Earth?
30 What substance is around 90% of the Earth's core made from?

Answers | TV: Drama *(see Quiz 185)*

1 Hearts & Bones. 2 DCI Tom Barnaby. 3 William Boyd. 4 Ian Rankin. 5 Mersey Beat. 6 Sherlock Holmes. 7 Ken Loach. 8 Band of Brothers. 9 Arthur Parker. 10 Holding On. 11 Victoria & Albert. 12 Peak Practice. 13 Hamish Macbeth. 14 James Nesbitt. 15 Sabbach. 16 Chicago. 17 The Final Cut. 18 The Way We Live Now. 19 Warren Clarke. 20 Hamble. 21 John Sullivan. 22 Masterpiece Theater. 23 Anthony Minghella. 24 Colin Bateman. 25 Alan Davies. 26 Jewel in the Crown. 27 Chris Kelly. 28 Pharmaceutical. 29 Sir Godber Evans. 30 Telly Savalas (Kojak).

1 Which country is directly south of the southern area of Morocco?
2 Which band has had Briana Corrigan and Jacqui Abbot among its vocalists?
3 To the nearest ten, how many minutes did the original "Planet of the Apes" movie last?
4 Which Elton John song mentions a "man who sells potions"?
5 Who wrote the screenplay for the phenomenally successful movie "The Bodyguard"?
6 In which country is the city of Chiba?
7 The song "Secret Love" came from which movie?
8 In which country is the city of Constanta?
9 Which Offenbach composition was used to advertise Bailey's Irish Cream?
10 TV's popular sitcom "To the Manor Born" was set in which village?
11 Who is Postman Pat's wife?
12 Pete Townshend's first No 1 as a producer was for which group?
13 Who was the first non-African to win the Olympic 5000m after Lasse Viren in Canada?
14 How did James Wight become better known to the reading world?
15 Dao wine comes from which country?
16 Who received an Oscar nomination for the original score for "The Talented Mr Ripley"?
17 What is the name of the state-of-the-art, super-bright light generator located in south Oxfordshire?
18 Sibbald's rorqual is also known as what?
19 A passata is made from which vegetable?
20 Who got the fastest individual goal of Japan and South Korea's 2002 tournament?
21 Who won the Best Director Oscar for the movie "Cavalcade"?
22 Which country borders Argentina, Brazil and Bolivia?
23 Who conducted the Three Tenors in their Italia 90 concert?
24 Which Springsteen song was a hit for Manfred Mann's Earth Band?
25 Who directed the first "Terminator" film?
26 In which country is the city of Campos?
27 Which poet wrote "Sea Fever"?
28 Who became Sudanese president in 1993?
29 What was the third line on the London Underground?
30 A maxwell unit is a measure of what?

| **Answers** | Pot Luck 87 *(see Quiz 186)* |

1 17th October. 2 Spit. 3 Space Shuttle launch. 4 Angus Deayton. 5 Ticket to Ride. 6 Oenology. 7 Valentino Rossi. 8 Roberta Flack. 9 Jean Terrell. 10 Jürgen Hingsen. 11 Private Godfrey. 12 Michinomiya. 13 Crescent-shaped. 14 Princess. 15 William. 16 Azerbaijan. 17 Bryan Robson. 18 Poles. 19 Daniel Day-Lewis. 20 James Naughtie. 21 Bernard Herrmann. 22 Sandwich. 23 Multiplex. 24 India. 25 Twin Peaks. 26 2061. 27 Three. 28 Maurice Jarre. 29 Betty Stove. 30 The Phil Silvers Show.

Quiz 185 | TV: Drama

Answers – page 657

1 In which drama did Rich, Emma, Annie and Sam share a surname?
2 Who was Sgt Gavin Troy's boss?
3 Who wrote the novel on which "Armadillo" was based?
4 Whose novels were used as the basis for the drama series "Rebus"?
5 In which series did Supt Susan Blake take charge?
6 "Murder Rooms" was a drama series about which detective?
7 Which veteran film maker wrote "Navigators" about the break-up of the rail network?
8 Which series was about Easy Company, a unit of paratroopers?
9 What was the name of the songsheet salesman in "Pennies from Heaven"?
10 Which 1990s Tony Marchant series about life in London starred Phil Daniels?
11 Which famous couple were portrayed by Jonathan Firth and Victoria Hamilton in a 2001 drama?
12 In which series did character Erica Matthews replace Beth Glover?
13 Which detective was played on TV by the star of "The Full Monty" and "Angela's Ashes"?
14 Who played Adam in "Cold Feet"?
15 Where was the German-made series "Heimat" based?
16 The outside scenes for "Hill Street Blues" were filmed in which city?
17 What was the last part of the trilogy which began with "House of Cards"?
18 In which series was Auguste Melmotte a central character?
19 Who played Faith's husband in "Down to Earth"?
20 Alongside which river was "Howard's Way" set?
21 Who wrote the David Jason series based on an infamous Dickens character?
22 Under what label was "I Claudius" broadcast in the USA?
23 Which early writer of "Morse" went on to write the movie "Truly Madly Deeply"?
24 Who wrote "Murphy's Law" for James Nesbitt?
25 If Lesley Sharp played Rose, who played Bob in 2001?
26 Which epic won the 1984 International Emmy for Best Drama?
27 Which one-time food show presenter produced "Kavanagh QC"?
28 Swallow was about which industry?
29 Who did Ian Richardson play in "Porterhouse Blue"?
30 Which actor who played a TV cop won a Purple Heart in Korea in real life?

Answers	Planet Earth (see Quiz 183)

1 South Dakota. 2 Copper. 3 Walrus. 4 West Spitsbergen. 5 Sonoran. 6 Silicon. 7 Mercury. 8 Sulphur. 9 Seismic wave. 10 Green. 11 Strathclyde. 12 South Africa. 13 New Guinea. 14 Four. 15 Venus. 16 Mountain chains. 17 Parsec. 18 Western Mongolia. 19 Radiation. 20 Low temperatures. 21 Novaya Zemlya. 22 Soil. 23 Radio communication. 24 Dam. 25 Six. 26 Helium. 27 Saturn. 28 Moh. 29 4.35. 30 Iron.

1 In 2006, what was the date of the One Day in History project?
2 Which dog did Chris Tarrant have to contend with on "TISWAS"?
3 John Young was the commander on which notable flight?
4 Who played Mike Channel in "KYTV"?
5 What was the first No 1 single from The Beatles' film "Help!"?
6 What is the study of wine known as?
7 Which motor cyclist took his 10th win of the 2001 season in the Malaysian Grand Prix?
8 Who sang the title song in "Someone to Watch Over Me" with Sting and Gene Ammons?
9 Who replaced Diana Ross when she left The Supremes?
10 Who was world record holder when Daley Thompson won Olympic gold in 1984?
11 In sitcom, which character had sisters called Dolly & Cissy?
12 What was the first name of Japan's Emperor Hirohito?
13 What shape is a roll if it is rugelach?
14 "Say I'm Your Number One" was the only Top Ten hit for which act?
15 What was Clark Gable's real first name?
16 In which country is the city of Baku?
17 Who else hit a hat-trick for England during the time that Gary Lineker was notching his five hat-tricks?
18 What did the initial P stand for in the name of writer LP Hartley?
19 Julia Roberts turned down "Shakespeare in Love" because which actor of her choice did not get to play Shakespeare?
20 Which newsman replaced Richard Baker as the presenter of the Proms on BBC?
21 Who scored the music for the famous shower scene in "Psycho"?
22 Which food item was linked to Colin in the title of a Mel Smith sitcom series?
23 Who were the building firm working on the new Wembley Stadium?
24 In which country is the city of Guntur?
25 As well as being an ex-US President, Harry S Truman was a sheriff in which TV series?
26 When is Halley's Comet predicted to make its next visit in Earth's vicinity?
27 How many books were there in Mervyn Peake's "Gormenghast" series?
28 Who produced the stirring movie music for "Lawrence of Arabia"?
29 Who won the first set in the last Wimbledon Ladies' Singles final to have a British competitor?
30 Which sitcom was first called "You'll Never Get Rich" in the US?

Answers | **Pot Luck 86 (see Quiz 184)**

1 Mauritania. 2 Beautiful South. 3 120. 4 Your Song. 5 Lawrence Kasdan. 6 Japan. 7 Calamity Jane. 8 Romania. 9 Barcarolle. 10 Cricket St Thomas. 11 Sarah. 12 Thunderclap Newman. 13 Dieter Baumann. 14 James Herriot. 15 Portugal. 16 Gabriel Yared. 17 Diamond Synchotron. 18 Blue whale. 19 Tomatoes. 20 Hakan Sukur. 21 Frank Lloyd. 22 Paraguay. 23 Zubin Mehta. 24 Blinded by the Light. 25 James Cameron. 26 Brazil. 27 John Masefield. 28 Omar al-Bashir. 29 Piccadilly line. 30 Magnetic flux.

1 Which tribe did Rwanda's majority tribe try to wipe out in the 1990s?
2 On which day of the week in 1953 was Everest conquered?
3 Which Apollo mission saw the fastest human speed record?
4 In 1990 who was granted a US patent for an energy-saving double filament light bulb?
5 The Clean Air Act was introduced after which year when 4,000 people died in London's worst recorded smog?
6 Where did Francisco Bahamonde rule?
7 Radio Caroline first began broadcasting five miles off which port?
8 Who commanded the first nuclear submarine under the North Pole?
9 On which day of the week was the Channel Tunnel opened?
10 How old was Spain's General Franco when he died?
11 Which country first had a postcode made up of letters and numbers?
12 What was the "Queen Elizabeth" being used as when sabotaged in Hong Kong harbour?
13 Which US President during the height of the Cold War, said there would be no Soviet domination of Eastern Europe?
14 In which city was the first Cadillac made?
15 In 1951's general election where was Margaret Roberts (later Thatcher) defeated?
16 For how many years in World War II were the lights in Piccadilly Circus blacked out?
17 Who was the first centre spread in "Playboy"?
18 Jacqueline Cochrane was the first woman to break what?
19 Who was the first cartoon character to appear on a US postage stamp?
20 Who or what were Able and Baker, the first pair of their kind to return from space?
21 Who devised transparent solar panels which can be used as windows and as a means of producing solar power?
22 Che Guevara was killed while training guerrillas against which government?
23 In which hospital was the world's first test tube baby born?
24 Who was the youngest winner of the Nobel Peace Prize in 1964?
25 Which charity began as a newspaper appeal "The Forgotten Prisoners"?
26 In what year was the first phone card issued in Japan?
27 Which play first won five of the awards named after Antoinette Perry?
28 In 1997 which country saw the largest and most numerous forest fires?
29 Which company's pesticide plant in Bhopal had a tragic chemical leak?
30 In which game did Nintendo's Mario character first appear?

Answers	Music: Solo Performers *(see Quiz 189)*

1 Microsoft Network. 2 Marian Anderson. 3 Feels Like Home. 4 Tears on My Pillow. 5 Anita Harris. 6 Mary Hopkin. 7 Jilted John. 8 Courtney Love. 9 Barry Gibb. 10 Frozen. 11 Liza Minnelli. 12 Kylie Minogue. 13 Prince. 14 Suzi Quatro. 15 Greetings From Asbury Park. 16 Alvin Stardust. 17 Brentford. 18 Evergreen. 19 Smokey Robinson. 20 Barry Manilow. 21 Apple. 22 Marty Wilde. 23 Paul Simon. 24 58. 25 Jewel of the Nile. 26 Peter Asher. 27 Sinead O'Connor. 28 Don McLean. 29 Eartha Kitt. 30 Carole King.

1 Who broke the world 200m record at the Atlanta Olympics?
2 Who composed the musical score for "On the Town"?
3 What was Orlando Bloom's occupation in "Elizabethtown"?
4 Dzongkha is the official language of which monarchy?
5 Which Spice Girl wrote "Girl Power" by her signature on the cover notes of the album "Spice"?
6 What's the number of HAL the computer in Kubrick's movie "2001"?
7 Which capital is furthest north – Addis Ababa, Kampala, Khartoum or Nairobi?
8 Which Premiership club was helped out by Russian businessman Alexandre Gaydamak?
9 What was the final Bond film in which Lois Maxwell played Miss Moneypenny?
10 In which country is the city of Las?
11 Nice ads, but which make of car were Papa and Nicole advertising?
12 Who was the first female presenter of TV's "Grandstand"?
13 Which Rod Stewart No 1 was originally the flip side of "Reason to Believe"?
14 The man who broke Sebastian Coe's 800m world record was running for which country?
15 Who was the first jockey to win the Derby in three consecutive races?
16 Mungo Park, the explorer of the River Niger, came from which country?
17 In sitcom, which vehicle was connected with Stan Butler?
18 Ambergris obtained from which sea creature?
19 "You'll Never Find Another Love Like Mine" was the only Top Ten hit for which singer?
20 Which screen tough guy made his debut as a mugger in Woody Allen's "Bananas"?
21 On a computer keyboard where is the letter B in relation to V?
22 Which group still meeting up for reunions included Peter Tork and Michael Nesmith?
23 In round figures, what was Irving Berlin's output of writing popular songs?
24 In which decade was the Argentinian Grand Prix first held?
25 Who gave Stock/Aitken/Waterman their first No1 hit?
26 On which atoll was the US's first hydrogen bomb detonated?
27 In fiction which detective married Harriet Vane?
28 Which country can have the letters NO added to its name to name its currency?
29 Which cereal is polenta made from?
30 Who was the first woman to lecture at the Sorbonne?

Quiz 189 | Music: Solo Performers | Answers – page 661 | LEVEL 3

1 Which on-line company broadcast Madonna's Brixton Academy concert live on the Internet?
2 Who was the first black performer to sing at the New York Metropolitan Opera?
3 What was the title of the second No 1 album for Norah Jones?
4 What was Kylie Minogue's last No 1 produced by Stock, Aitken and Waterman?
5 Which solo performer promoted Slendertone keep fit equipment in 1997?
6 Which solo singer married record producer Tony Visconti?
7 How did Graham Fellows aka John Shuttleworth appear in the UK charts in 1978?
8 Which singer's daughter by a controversial performer was called Frances Bean?
9 Who produced Lulu's album which included the tracks "Every Woman Knows" and "How 'Bout Us"?
10 What did Madonna sing on her first live UK TV show for 15 years in 1998?
11 Which music and musical star deputised for Julie Andrews on Broadway in Victor/Victoria in the mid-1990s?
12 Who was about to release an album called "Impossible Princess" in 1997 but changed the title after the death of Princess Diana?
13 Who married Mayte Garcia in 1996?
14 Which singer appeared as Leather Tuscadero in "Happy Days"?
15 What was "The Boss's" debut album?
16 Which singer has appeared in "Hollyoaks" and was Gaston in "Beauty & The Beast" in the West End?
17 Which club gave a teenage Roderick David Stewart a soccer trial?
18 For what did Barbra Streisand win an Oscar for Best Song?
19 Which singer had children called Berry and Tamla?
20 Whose musical Harmony opened on Broadway in 1998?
21 Which company released James Taylor's debut album?
22 Which 1950s star wrote Status Quo's "Ice in the Sun"?
23 Which singer wrote the then biggest musical flop in New York history in 1998?
24 How many albums had Cliff Richard made by his 40th year in show business?
25 From which movie soundtrack was Billy Ocean's biggest hit?
26 Which 1964 chart topper won the Producer of the Year Grammy in 1977?
27 Whose debut album was "The Lion and the Cobra"?
28 Who was the subject of the song "Killing Me Softly"?
29 Which vocalist who recorded with Bronski Beat in the the late 1980s was described by Orson Welles as "the most exciting woman in the world"?
30 To which singer was the album "Tapestry Revisited" dedicated?

1 Who designed the first lightning conductor?
2 The soundtrack of the movie "Philadelphia" featured songs by Bruce Springsteen and who else?
3 Which sitcom introduced viewers to the 1-2-1 Club?
4 The trudgen is a movement in which sport?
5 Where are denticles found on a shark?
6 Where in Illinois in 2007 did Barack Obama announce he was running for the Presidency?
7 Which country is home to the airline Pluna?
8 Who was the first actor ever to refuse an Oscar?
9 Who lived at Cemetery Ridge?
10 Under which name did Orson Whipple Hungerford III become an actor riding across our screens?
11 Who described himself as "an average guy who could carry a tune"?
12 Who is the smallest Teletubby?
13 What was Jude Law's first film?
14 Which movie great set up the American Foundation for AIDS Research?
15 The Kakadu National Park is located in which country?
16 What could Sean Connery's character change in "The Avengers"?
17 Who wrote "Menopause the Musical"?
18 Which TV star is mum to Robert, Ben and Jack Willis?
19 Charles Townes pioneered what?
20 Where in America was Alcoholics Anonymous founded?
21 In the Elvis song, which two words follow "Return to sender"?
22 Kalium is an alternative name for which element?
23 What was the title of Whitney Houston's first album?
24 Which musical work for the stage is set in the town of Titipu?
25 Which Count is the villain in "The Woman in White" by Wilkie Collins?
26 John Potter became the most capped English player in which sport?
27 What is the unique about the flight of a hummingbird?
28 Which film comedy was "Trois Hommes et Un Couffin" in French?
29 Calzone, a folded pizza dough dish, takes its name from what in Italian?
30 What was the first Top Ten hit for Sheryl Crow?

Answers | Pot Luck 88 (see Quiz 188)

1 Michael Johnson. 2 Leonard Bernstein. 3 Shoe designer. 4 Bhutan. 5 Geri. 6 9000. 7 Khartoum. 8 Portsmouth. 9 A View To A Kill. 10 Romania. 11 Renault. 12 Helen Rollason. 13 Maggie May. 14 Denmark (Wilson Kipketer). 15 Steve Donoghue. 16 Scotland. 17 Bus. 18 Sperm whale. 19 Lou Rawls. 20 Sylvester Stallone. 21 Right. 22 The Monkees. 23 900. 24 1940s. 25 Mel and Kim. 26 Eniwetok. 27 Lord Peter Wimsey. 28 Bolivia. 29 Maize. 30 Marie Curie.

1 What culinary item is produced by Filippo Berio?
2 What type of milk was first processed in 1899?
3 In which year did Bird's Eye Fish Fingers first go on sale in the UK?
4 Which drink had the first registered British trademark?
5 Which French city is famous for Cointreau?
6 Which author of "La Bonne Chère" ran the French Pavilion at Disneyworld, Orlando?
7 Which type of pasta lends it name to a type of chocolate decoration?
8 Who created vichysoisse?
9 Who founded the restaurant with Rose Gray where Jamie Oliver was "discovered"?
10 Which area is the only one not to grow a Muscat which is sweet?
11 The Chardonnay grape is a native of where?
12 Which food or drink was named after American John McAdam?
13 Where did Balti cooking originate?
14 In wine making what is another name for tartrate?
15 What are the most common herbs in a bearnaise sauce?
16 Which herb is used in gremolata?
17 When were pressure cookers invented – 1891, 1905 or1933?
18 Where was Anton Mosimann's first post as chef in the UK?
19 Which size of wine bottle is the equivalent of 12 standard bottles?
20 Which monk was responsible for putting the liqueur Chartreuse on sale?
21 Which nuts are usually used in a pesto sauce?
22 Which food item comes form the Hindi meaning pounded meat?
23 Pyrex was made originally to be used where?
24 What is arborio?
25 Auslese is usually made from which grape?
26 Which food comes from the Tamil word meaning pepper water?
27 Dom Bernardo Vincelli devised which drink?
28 Who opened the Miller Howe restaurant in 1971?
29 Fitou is made from which grape?
30 What is unusual about the harvesting of Spätlese grapes?

Answers	The Oscars *(see Quiz 193)*

1 The Piano. 2 Four. 3 Carole Bayer Sager. 4 This Sporting Life. 5 Driving Miss Daisy. 6 Russell Crowe. 7 Sgt Elias. 8 Gwyneth Paltrow. 9 58. 10 Places in the Heart. 11 Driving Miss Daisy. 12 Marvin Hamlisch. 13 Best Screenplay. 14 Cleopatra. 15 None. 16 Writer. 17 Barbra Streisand. 18 The People vs Larry Flint. 19 With a Song in My Heart. 20 Gregory Peck. 21 Justin Henry (Kramer vs Kramer). 22 17. 23 Bernard Hill. 24 Cary Grant. 25 Bob Hope. 26 Carnal Knowledge. 27 Separate Tables. 28 Chariots of Fire (Ian Holm). 29 Five. 30 Lenny.

1 Kubrick's movie "Eyes Wide Shut" used the music of Jazz Suite No 2 by which composer?
2 In which country is the city of Joao Pessoa?
3 On a computer keyboard what letter is below and between G and H?
4 Which English palace was used for the Kenneth Branagh's movie version of "Hamlet"?
5 What was the first name of owner Mr Maplin in the sitcom "Hi De Hi!"?
6 "Cathy" and "Claudette" appear in No 1's for which artists?
7 What is the opponent's goal called in shinty?
8 Whose Divenire Tour took place in 2007?
9 On a computer keyboard what letter is below and between J and K?
10 Which agony aunt shares a birthday with actor John Hurt?
11 Which warrior ruler had a horse called Bucephalus?
12 What species of sea creature is a "Mesonychotenthis hamiltoni"?
13 Eric Oliver was the first world champion in what?
14 What did the second A stand for in ANZAC?
15 What was Cliff Richard's first million seller?
16 Which term indicates the amount of wine by which a container falls short of being full?
17 King Edward VII's father in law was king of which country?
18 In which country is the city of Hermosilla?
19 In the Bond movie what was Goldfinger's first name?
20 When was "The Highway Code" first published?
21 On which horse did Gordon Richards have his only Derby triumph?
22 Which cards were not included in a pack of cards until 1857?
23 Which number followed NCC on the side of the "Starship Enterprise"?
24 What did Harry Brearley invent in 1913 to revolutionise kitchens?
25 In movies, what is the first name of Ralph Fiennes' character in "Schindler's List"?
26 What is Madame Harel credited with creating around 1790?
27 Whose play was turned into the movie "Shadowlands"?
28 Romana Barrack is better known as a TV playwright under which name?
29 Which English club had most players represented in Germany 2006?
30 With which record label did Norah Jones sign in 2002?

---

1 Which movie shared the Palme d'Or with "Farewell My Concubine"?
2 How many Oscar nominations did "Little Miss Sunshine" receive?
3 Who was Burt Bacharach's lyricist on the song which won an Oscar for "Arthur"?
4 For which film did Richard Harris receive his first nomination?
5 In which movie did Dan Aykroyd play Jessica Tandy's son?
6 Which future Oscar-winner won the Australian Film Institute Award as Best Supporting Actor for "Proof"?
7 Which character did Willem Dafoe play in "Platoon"?
8 Which Oscar-winning actress is the daughter of stage actress Blythe Danner?
9 How many years did Robert Donat age in his 1939 Oscar-winning movie?
10 Which movie led to Sally Field's "You like me. You really like me," speech?
11 What was Morgan Freeman's second Oscar nomination?
12 Who was the first person to win three Oscars in one night?
13 Which Oscar did Woody Allen win when Michael Caine also won for the same movie?
14 For which movie was Rex Harrison nominated a year before his first win?
15 How many films had Goldie Hawn made before she had her first nomination for Best Supporting Actress?
16 In which category did "The Piano"'s director win an Oscar?
17 Lauren Bacall won her first Oscar nomination playing whose mother?
18 For which movie did "Cheers" Woody receive his first nomination?
19 Susan Hayward received five nominations; which movie was her third?
20 Audrey Hepburn won her first nomination for a role opposite whom?
21 Who was the youngest performer ever to be nominated for an Oscar?
22 How many years were there between Julie Andrews' second and third nominations?
23 Who played the husband in the movie for which Pauline Collins was nominated?
24 Who played opposite Joan Fontaine when she won her Oscar for a Hitchcock movie?
25 Who first hosted the Oscar ceremony in 1940?
26 For which Mike Nichols' film was Ann Margret nominated for an Oscar?
27 For which movie did Wendy Hiller win between her nominations for "Pygmalion" and "A Man for All Seasons"?
28 For which 1981 film was the husband of Penelope Wilton nominated?
29 How many Special Academy Awards did Bob Hope win?
30 For which film did Dustin Hoffman have his third nomination?

Answers	**Food & Drink** (see Quiz 191)

1 Olive oil. 2 Evaporated milk. 3 1955. 4 Bass Pale Ale. 5 Angers. 6 Paul Bocuse. 7 Vermicelli. 8 Louis Diat. 9 Ruth Rogers. 10 Alsace. 11 Burgundy. 12 Macadamia nuts. 13 Britain. 14 Argol. 15 Tarragon & chervil. 16 Parsley. 17 1905. 18 Dorchester. 19 Salmanazar. 20 Jerome Maubee. 21 Pine nuts. 22 Kofta. 23 Railroad kitchens. 24 Rice. 25 Riesling. 26 Mulligatawny. 27 Benedictine. 28 John Tovey. 29 Carignan. 30 Harvested late.

1 To ten years when was the Rotary Club founded?
2 Which horse with a John Wayne link won the first Grand National?
3 What does the second R stand for in the acronym RADAR?
4 Which monarch attended the very first Royal Ascot?
5 Which country was the first to introduce vehicle registration plates?
6 Jo-Raquel Tejad become known as which movie actress?
7 What is the largest castle in England?
8 Who scored the quickest ever FA Cup Final goal?
9 What was George II supposedly sitting on at the time of his death?
10 EOKA was an active terrorist organisation on which island?
11 Who wrote the novel "The Ordeal of Gilbert Pinfold"?
12 A cross between a Scottish draught horse and a Flemish horse produced which breed?
13 Under what name did Paul and Phil Hartnoll have hit records?
14 What is the name of the Royal Hong Kong Jockey Club's racecourse?
15 How is Denali in Alaska also known?
16 Which place used to form part of The Stranglers' name?
17 In which year did Bernhard Langer first play in a Ryder Cup?
18 What is the usual general temperature requirements for serving sake?
19 Who combined with Leiber to write the rock classic "Jailhouse Rock"?
20 Which food additive prevents fat and water separating out?
21 Who was Republic of Ireland boss when Sven was appointed?
22 What was the only Top Ten hit for US female group First Choice?
23 At which track did Michael Schumacher achieve his record-breaking 52nd career win?
24 Dyce Airport serves which city?
25 Who was born first, Albert Einstein or Charles Darwin?
26 In "Penny Lane", what is the occupation of the person selling poppies from a tray?
27 Alan Shearer scored his only England hat trick against which team?
28 In which country is the city of Tabris?
29 Which former member of Steps featured in "Celebrity Big Brother" in 2007?
30 What was the directorial debut of the screenwriter of "Gosford Park"?

Answers   Pot Luck 90 *(see Quiz 192)*

1 Shostakovich. 2 Brazil. 3 B. 4 Blenheim. 5 Joe. 6 Everly Brothers. 7 Hail. 8 Ludovico Einaudi. 9 M. 10 Claire Rayner. 11 Alexander the Great. 12 Squid. 13 Sidecar. 14 Army. 15 Living Doll. 16 Ullage. 17 Denmark. 18 Mexico. 19 Auric. 20 1931. 21 Pinza. 22 Jokers. 23 1701. 24 Stainless steel. 25 Amon. 26 Camembert cheese. 27 William Nicholson. 28 Carla Lane. 29 Arsenal (15 players). 30 Blue Note.

1 Who were the first fully professional team of baseball players?
2 Who was runner-up when a Dutchman won Wimbledon's Men's Singles in the 1990s?
3 Which actress named her son after baseball pitcher Satchel Paige?
4 Which country won the baseball silver medal at the 2000 Olympic Games?
5 The last time they won Olympic gold in ice hockey in the 20th century the USSR team was known by what name?
6 How old was Jack Nicklaus when he became the oldest US Masters winner?
7 Who won the longest match in a Grand Slam in the 1990s?
8 Which motor sport team did the then record holder for Grand Prix victories buy in 1997 before giving it his own name a year later?
9 Who were the second winners of the NBA in the US?
10 Which side did Martin Corry play for when he made his England debut?
11 Which English-born footballer was picked to play for Scotland during the time his father managed for Wales?
12 When did Karine Ruby's sport become an Olympic event?
13 Who did the older Williams sister beat in her second Wimbledon final?
14 Where did Linford Christie win his fastest 100m?
15 In the 1990s who was the fastest winner of the New York City Marathon?
16 Who was the oldest winner of the singles at the French Open Tennis?
17 Who was the first non-European to run a mile in under four minutes?
18 Where did Carl Lewis set his personal best in the long jump?
19 In 1998 which team's player set a new baseball record for most home runs in a season?
20 What nationality was the youngest Wimbledon Men's Singles winner?
21 How many gold medals did Carl Lewis win at his second Olympics?
22 Who won the first London Marathon of the new millennium?
23 Which country was the second to play Test cricket against England?
24 Who holds the record as the biggest money earner between 1993 and 2001 in women's golf?
25 How many world records did Sergey Bubka break before the end of 1999?
26 Who, in December 1993, was the fastest European woman in the world?
27 On which make of motor cycle was the fastest world championship of the 1970s raced?
28 Who became the youngest man to end the year as World No 1 in 2001?
29 Which European won most US Open Men's Singles titles in the 1990s?
30 Which name was added in the 1990s to the side which has won the Challenge Cup most times in Rugby League?

Answers	**Movie Firsts** *(see Quiz 197)*

1 Otto Preminger's The Moon is Blue. 2 A Matter of Life and Death. 3 Imperial Airways. 4 40. 5 Fury. 6 Schumann's Scenes from Childhood. 7 Point Blank. 8 Marlon Brando. 9 White Christmas. 10 Behind the Great Wall. 11 Taking Off. 12 Nosferatu. 13 Earthquake. 14 The Replacement Killers. 15 Cimarron. 16 Love Finds Andy Hardy. 17 Little Lord Fauntleroy. 18 Richard Gere. 19 The Last Emperor. 20 Trouble with Harry. 21 Rope. 22 Al Jolson. 23 The Lost World. 24 The Robe. 25 Photoplay. 26 Blackmail. 27 Birth of a Nation. 28 Mike Nichols. 29 DW Griffith. 30 Hayley Mills.

1 Matthew Fisher won a 2006 court case for part copyright of which 1960s song?
2 Which Dutch-based broadcaster agreed to buy worldwide rights to "Who Wants to be a Millionaire?"?
3 "Tory Idol" was first staged to select a candidate in which constituency?
4 How many points did England score in Andy Robinson's last game as rugby coach?
5 Nick Carter was in which best-selling boy band?
6 Which programme won a BAFTA in 2006 for best "situation comedy"?
7 In which US state did "Enron: The Musical" open in 2006?
8 What was the name of the first daughter of Katie Holmes and Tom Cruise?
9 Which club side did the late Ferenc Puskas take to a European Cup Final?
10 Which 1970's T. Rex drummer was still playing in a Christian band 30 years on?
11 Who did Martina Hingis beat to claim her first WTA Tour title in her 2006 comeback?
12 At the time of his death Ian Richardson was due to play in which TV series?
13 What was the name of Martin Luther King's widow who died in 2006?
14 Justin King became chief executive of which supermarket group in 2004?
15 Veronica Donovan and Fernando Sucre featured in which US drama series?
16 Who became Andy Roddick's tennis coach in 2006?
17 Who quit Motherwell to move to warmer climes as Sydney FC soccer boss in 2006?
18 Roman Abramovich was governor of which region in north-east Russia?
19 In which year was Shirley Bassey 70?
20 What type of entertainment was George M Cohan famous for?
21 In January 2007 who became the youngest person to sail across the Atlantic single-handed?
22 In which city did Tony Blair deliver his final conference speech to the Labour Party?
23 Clinton Woods was an IBF world title holder at which weight?
24 Which "Sunday Mirror" columnist appeared in "Celebrity Big Brother" in 2007?
25 Steve Culp played which character in "Desperate Housewives"?
26 Which soccer club has Cattell Road and Tilton Road around the stadium?
27 Who was born John Beverley and would have celebrated his 50th birthday in 2007?
28 Where is the volcanic Mount Metrap?
29 The right-wing political action group the Moral Majority was founded where?
30 Who wrote the play "Bent" revived with Alan Cumming in 2006?

Answers | 80s Pop *(see Quiz 198)*

1 Soft Cell. 2 Joe Jackson. 3 Virgin. 4 Madonna. 5 New Edition. 6 Birmingham. 7 Steve Winwood. 8 Respect Yourself. 9 Coco Hernandez. 10 Red Red Wine. 11 Nothing Has Been Proved. 12 David Bowie. 13 Scotland. 14 Mad World. 15 OMD. 16 1988. 17 Zenyatta Mondatta. 18 Giorgio Moroder. 19 Santa Claus. 20 Ultravox. 21 I Want to Know What Love is. 22 Germany. 23 Odyssey. 24 Eye of the Tiger. 25 Living in a Box. 26 Karma Chameleon. 27 Super Trouper. 28 Joe Dolce. 29 Two Tribes. 30 Kelly Marie.

1 What was the first mainstream film to use the word "virgin"?
2 What was the first Royal Command Performance film?
3 Which airline showed the first in flight movie?
4 How old was Mae West when she made her movie debut?
5 What was Fritz Lang's first Hollywood film?
6 What did Kevin Kline play on the piano in his first movie "Sophie's Choice"?
7 What was John Boorman's US directing debut?
8 Who was the first actor to receive $1 million for a single picture?
9 VistaVision was first used in which classic movie?
10 What was the first movie shown in Aromarama?
11 What was Milos Forman's first US movie?
12 What was the first movie to feature Dracula?
13 Which movie was the first to have Sensurround?
14 In which movie did Chow Yun-Fat make his US debut?
15 What was the first western to win an Oscar for best film?
16 What was the first movie which teamed Mickey Rooney and Judy Garland?
17 What was Selznick's first movie from his own independent company?
18 Who was the first American to join the Young Vic company on an American tour?
19 What was the first production from the west allowed in Bejing's Forbidden City?
20 What was Shirley MacLaine's first movie?
21 What was Hitchcock's first film for an independent producer?
22 Who was the first US singer/actor to entertain the troops in Korea?
23 What was the first in-flight movie?
24 What was the first movie shown in Cinemascope?
25 "Motion Picture Story Magazine" and which other title were the US's first film magazines?
26 What was Hitchcock's first talkie?
27 What was the first movie shown at the White House?
28 "Who's Afraid of Virginia Woolf" was the movie debut of which director?
29 Which movie pioneer said, "I moved the whole world on to a 20 foot screen"?
30 Whose screen debut was aged 13 with father John in "Tiger Bay"?

Answers	**Sporting Who's Who?** *(see Quiz 195)*

1 Cincinnati Red Stockings. 2 Malavai Washington. 3 Mia Farrow. 4 Cuba. 5 Unified Team. 6 46. 7 Alex Corretja. 8 Ligier (Alain Prost). 9 Baltimore Bullets. 10 Bristol. 11 Jonathan Gould. 12 1998 (Snowboarding). 13 Justine Henin. 14 Stuttgart. 15 John Kagwe. 16 Andres Gimeno. 17 John Landy. 18 Tokyo. 19 St Louis Cardinals. 20 West German (Boris Becker). 21 Two. 22 Antonio Pinto. 23 South Africa. 24 Annika Sorenstam. 25 35. 26 Christine Arron. 27 Suzuki (Barry Sheene). 28 Lleyton Hewitt. 29 Stefan Edberg. 30 Warriors.

1 Dave Ball was part of which hit-making combination?
2 Who had 80s hits with "It's Different for Girls" and "Steppin' Out"?
3 Which label did Culture Club record on?
4 Patrick Leonard co-wrote and produced No 1 hits for which artist?
5 Which group met at school at Roxbury, Massachusetts?
6 Duran Duran got together in which city?
7 "Roll with It" and "Higher Love" were US No 1s for which British artist?
8 What was the first top ten hit for Bruce Willis?
9 What was the name of the Irene Cara character in Alan Parker's "Fame"?
10 What was the first No 1 single for UB40?
11 What gave Dusty Springfield a solo Top Twenty hit after a twenty-year gap?
12 Who went on a Serious Moonlight Tour?
13 Which country did Aneka, the singer of "Japanese Boy", come from?
14 What was the first Top Ten hit for Tears for Fears?
15 Andy McCluskey provided vocals and synthesiser for which outfit?
16 In which year did U2 first make it to No 1?
17 The Police's "Don't Stand so Close to Me" was from which album?
18 Who wrote and produced Berlin's "Take My Breath Away"?
19 Who was "On the Dole" in a song from the Spitting Image team?
20 Warren Cann and Chris Cross were part of which group?
21 The New Jersey Mass Choir appear on which 80s No 1?
22 Nicole's No 1 won the Eurovision Song Contest for which country?
23 Who were Tony Reynolds and Louise and Lillian Lopez?
24 Which No 1 was linked to the movie "Rocky III"?
25 Who had hits with "Blow the House Down" and "Room in Your Heart"?
26 Which was the first 80s No 1 to be top for six weeks?
27 Abba's "The Winner Takes It All" track came from which album?
28 Who followed up a No 1 with the unsuccessful "Reggae Matilda"?
29 Which single spent most weeks at No 1 in the 80s?
30 Under what name did Jacqueline McKinnon make No 1?

1 Who first popularised the expression "Iron Curtain"?
2 Which newspaper used "Iron Curtain" earlier in the sense of protection?
3 What was the official name of the Soviet Union?
4 What name, meaning speaking aloud, was given to Gorbachev's new approach?
5 What was the communist economic association called?
6 Which Treaty Organisation was set up as a communist counterpart to NATO?
7 Which Eastern European country was the only one to maintain close relations with China?
8 What was East Germany's official name?
9 Which communist country remained outside the military alliance of Eastern Bloc countries in 1955?
10 In which country were the AVF the security police?
11 Who succeeded Stalin as Communist Party leader?
12 What was the period of liberalisation in Czechoslovakia in 1968 called?
13 Which General introduced martial law in Poland in 1981?
14 What was the Czech Charter 77 protesting about in 1977?
15 In which year was the Berlin Wall built?
16 What name was given to the state of tension between the communist states and the west after World War II?
17 What name was given to the reconstruction of Soviet society through Gorbachev's reforms?
18 Who was East Germany's last Chairman of the Council of State?
19 Where in Gdansk was Solidarity founded?
20 What were the KGB in the Soviet Union?
21 Which former head of the KGB became General Party Secretary in 1982?
22 Who was the first Russian to be General Secretary and President simultaneously?
23 What does the T stand for in the acronym SALT?
24 Astana replaced Almaty as the capital city of which former Soviet state?
25 Which communist state was ruled by the Volkskammer?
26 Who was the leading architect of East Germany in the 50s and 60s?
27 Who was the East German leader tried for high treason in 1993?
28 Which Hungarian army major fled his homeland after the Soviet invasion and died a world-revered sportsman in 2006?
29 Which Soviet foreign minister formulated the Sinatra doctrine?
30 Why was the Sinatra doctrine so called?

---

1 What did Rachel Lowe try and market to the "Dragon's Den" team?
2 Where in London did ex-Russian spy Alexander Litvinenko live prior to his murder?
3 Which Prime Minister was dubbed Finland's sexiest man in 2006 tabloids?
4 Barry George was convicted of the murder of which TV presenter?
5 Sherron Watkins was vice president of which famous company?
6 Eto'o and Belletti scored Champions League Final goals for which club?
7 Sarah Alexander, Jack Davenport and Ben Miles starred in which TV comedy?
8 Stuart Rose took over as chief executive of which major company in 2004?
9 The debut album from The Arctic Monkeys appeared on which record label?
10 In 2007, Dr Drew Faust became first female president of which institution?
11 Which England player bowled just one over in the 2006–07 Ashes series?
12 Which famous economist, a former adviser to JF Kennedy, died in 2006, aged 97?
13 Who wrote the novel "Melted into Air"?
14 Hans Horrevoets was swept overboard and died in which 2006 sporting event?
15 The track "Chasing Cars" appeared on which top-selling album?
16 Which book beat the "Beano" to be top-selling annual around Xmas 2006?
17 Which year marks the 100th anniversary of the Ryder Cup?
18 Which much-used item was invented by Douglas Engelbardt?
19 Which single gave Geri Halliwell her third No 1 solo hit?
20 Michael Sinnott made movies in the USA under which name?
21 Who left Leeds to become director of rugby at Llanelli in 2006?
22 In which month of the year did Britain have its first woman Prime Minister?
23 Where was author Jean Rhys born?
24 Emily Blunt and Bill Nighy won Golden Globes for their roles in which drama?
25 Aged 16, David Howell, of Sussex, became the UK's youngest what?
26 Billie Joe Armstrong was vocalist for which top-selling band?
27 Who played "Leatherface" in the film "The Texas Chain Saw Massacre"?
28 Who were the opponents as Ronaldo set a new individual World Cup finals tally?
29 In 2006, Steve McClaren became England coach on a contract for how many years?
30 American journalist Daniel Pearl was kidnapped and killed in which country in 2002?

1 Who played most games for Birmingham as they went down in 2006?
2 Who started the 2004–05 season as Southampton boss?
3 Colin Todd and John Gregory managed which team on the way down?
4 In 2006, who replaced Mick McCarthy as interim manager at Sunderland?
5 Going down in 2003 – did West Ham have 33, 37 or 42 points?
6 Which Jamie suffered relegation with Ipswich and Birmingham?
7 Which team set the record of 29 Premiership defeats in 42 games?
8 Which team did boss Danny Wilson take into and out of the Premiership?
9 Who was boss of the Baggies when they went down in 2003?
10 In 2003 Sunderland set a fewest goals in a season record of how many?
11 Did Alan Shearer ever play for a team in a relegation season?
12 Who was Palace's regular keeper in the 2005 relegation season?
13 At which club did Craig Bellamy first experience Premiership relegation?
14 Craig Fleming played every game as which team went down?
15 Which manager Dave got Sheff Utd into and out of the the top flight in the 90s?
16 Nathan Ellington and who else were WBA's 2006 joint top scorers with 5 goals?
17 Which team ended the season with an unlucky for some 13 straight defeats?
18 Which Chris played for Blackburn and Birmingham in relegation seasons?
19 Who was top scorer when Southampton left the top flight in 2005?
20 Which club were the last side to be relegated from the Premiership last century?
21 Ashton, Francis and McKenzie were joint top scorers as which team went down?
22 Who played most games in goal in Coventry's 2001 relegation season?
23 Who was boss as Bradford City left the Premiership in 2001?
24 How many goals did Andy Johnson hit as Palace went down in 2005?
25 Veterans Barton and Lee left Newcastle for which club that went down in 2002?
26 Ashley Ward was relegated with which three B teams?
27 Which defender went down with Wimbledon in 2000 and Ipswich in 2002?
28 In 2006, Sunderland were relegated after holding which title chasers to a 0-0 draw?
29 Who won the Premiership with Blackburn and went down with West Ham in 2003?
30 Per Frandsen was an ever present in the season which northern club went down?

Answers	**Iron Curtain** *(see Quiz 199)*

1 Churchill. 2 Pravda. 3 Union of Soviet Socialist Republics. 4 Glasnost. 5 COMECON (Council for Mutual Economic Assistance). 6 Warsaw Pact. 7 Albania. 8 German Democratic Republic. 9 Yugoslavia. 10 Hungary. 11 Khrushchev. 12 Prague Spring. 13 Jaruzelski. 14 Human rights. 15 1961. 16 Cold War. 17 Perestroika. 18 Erich Honecker. 19 Shipyards. 20 Committee for State Security. 21 Andropov. 22 Brezhnev. 23 Talks. 24 Kazakhstan. 25 East Germany. 26 Walter Ulbricht. 27 Erich Honecker. 28 Ferenc Puskas. 29 Shevardnaze. 30 It ran on a My Way basis.

1 In 2006 ScottishPower agreed a takeover by a company from which country?
2 Peter Crouch's first Liverpool Premiership goal was against which team?
3 In SIGIR, the second I stands for Iraq – what does the R stand for?
4 Which pop quintet featured Claire Richards and Lee Latchford-Evans?
5 Which LS Lowry painting did Bury Council auction for over £1 million in November 2006?
6 Sir Roy Meadow gave evidence in court cases in what expert capacity?
7 Who wrote the theme music that has been used for "The Sky at Night"?
8 Theo Walcott made his international debut against which country?
9 Felipe Calderon became President of which country in 2006?
10 Who in "The Simpsons" owned an iguana named Jub-Jub?
11 Who was 50 first – Jimmy Nail, Jeremy Paxman or Victoria Wood?
12 What was the third UK No 1 for Atomic Kitten?
13 Who photographed the cover of Renee Fleming's CD "Homage"?
14 Which year celebrates 50 years of parking meters in London?
15 In which country was a killer brown bear known as JJ put down in 2006?
16 In 2006, David Davies became Commonwealth Games swimming champ in which event?
17 Who produced the creepy movie "Poltergeist"?
18 Which creamy cheese comes from the Haute Savoie?
19 Which Saint has 15th July as his Feast Day?
20 Diane Abbot became Britain's first black woman to serve as what?
21 Carmine Galante was reputedly the boss of what when he was shot in New York in 1979?
22 Which male voice choir had classical success with "Voices of the Valley"?
23 Which ex-England soccer manager died in the same month as Spike Milligan?
24 Which Dutch politician was assassinated by an animal rights campaigner in 2002?
25 What was the third film to win 11 Oscars?
26 Which sponsor's name was on Alan Shearer's shirt in his final Premiership game?
27 What was the autobiography of Mike Oldfield called?
28 What did Sergey Brin and Larry Page launch in 1998?
29 Rafik Hariri was killed in a bomb attack in which city?
30 Nathan Robertson and Gail Emms formed a winning partnership in which sport?

1 "Santa Claus is Comin' to Town" was on the other side of "My Hometown" in 1985 for whom?

2 Which residents of Home Hill had a Xmastime No 1 in 1997?

3 Which Welsh performer topped the charts in 1985 with "Merry Christmas Everyone"?

4 Who duetted with Cliff Richard on "Whenever God Shines His Light" in December 1989?

5 Which Mel was "Rockin Around the Christmas Tree" with Kim Wilde?

6 Who sang "All I Want for Christmas is You" in 1994?

7 Which song of the 1980s featured boy soprano Peter Auty?

8 Which weatherman was in the title of a song during the Xmas period in 1988?

9 What was Wham!'s classic Christmas hit?

10 Which duo's song was knocked off the top spot by Michael Jackson's "Earth Song" in 1995?

11 Which group featured Bono, Katie Melua and Snow Patrol?

12 Who was the first non-human Xmas No 1?

13 Who pleaded "Please Come Home for Christmas" in 1994?

14 Which pop classic has the line, "Well here it is, Merry Christmas"?

15 Which ex-Beatle had an Xmas hit with "Wonderful Christmas Time"?

16 Which female took "Christmas Through Your Eyes" to No 8 in 1992?

17 Which much-played hit has the words, "When the snowman brings the snow"?

18 Who had three consecutive Xmas No 1s in the later half of the 90s?

19 Which David duetted with Bing Crosby in 1982?

20 Which Jive Bunny single was a Xmas No 1 in 1989?

21 Which minor hit was a Xmas follow-up to the Xmas No 1 "Mr Blobby"?

22 Which George Michael hit replaced "Earth Song" after Xmas 1995?

23 Who had a Xmas No 1 with "Saviour's Day" in 1990?

24 Which Chris's classic is "Driving Home for Christmas"?

25 Which duo had "Merry Christmas Darling" in the 1990 charts?

26 In which year did John and Yoko's "Happy Xmas (War is Over)" first hit the charts?

27 The voice of Gary Jules featured on which Xmas No 1?

28 What was the first Xmas No 1 for Girls Aloud?

29 Who had the last Xmas No 1 of last century?

30 Which actress had a hit with Ewan McGregor before an Xmas No 1 duet?

Answers	US Presidents *(see Quiz 205)*

1 Roosevelt. 2 Hubert Humphrey. 3 60%. 4 Warren Harding. 5 Friday. 6 Truman. 7 William Taft. 8 2001. 9 Leon Czolgosz. 10 Jimmy Carter. 11 Kennedy. 12 USA. 13 Roosevelt. 14 Jack Kemp. 15 Florida. 16 George Bush (Snr). 17 Lincoln. 18 Earl. 19 Tennessee. 20 24 years old. 21 FD Roosevelt. 22 Richard the Lionheart. 23 Woodrow Wilson. 24 Jackie Oh!. 25 Jimmy Carter. 26 George W Bush (Jnr). 27 Harry S Truman. 28 Ronald Reagan. 29 Adams. 30 Andrew Jackson.

1 On which day of the week was Prince Harry born?
2 What is William's second Christian name?
3 In 2006 the princes announced which date for a "Concert for Diana"?
4 In which subject did William get his highest A-level grade?
5 What is the name of their stepbrother?
6 How tall is William?
7 Where were the princes staying when they heard of their mother's death?
8 On which Royal's birthday was William christened?
9 What is their stepsister's married name?
10 In which country did William carry out his first official duties representing the Queen?
11 Whom did William succeed as President of the FA?
12 Which surname did William use when he was at university?
13 Where was Harry baptised?
14 Which portrait painter was one of Harry's godfathers?
15 In which subject did Harry achieve his higher A-level result?
16 Where in Africa did Harry spend part of his gap year?
17 What is the meaning of "Sentebale", the charity Harry set up in Lesotho?
18 It was announced in 2006 that Harry would join which Household Cavalry regiment?
19 In a 18th-birthday interview William said he would miss which Eton house master?
20 When William gave his 18th-birthday interview, who or what was Widgeon?
21 How old was William when his father remarried?
22 What was the first name of their maternal grandfather?
23 Which Archbishop of Canterbury christened both princes?
24 As a child William expressed support for which football club?
25 Which two Berkshire schools did both princes attend?
26 In autumn 2005 William took a work placement with which bank?
27 William became Vice Royal Patron of which Union from February 2007?
28 Which high-profile event did Kate Middleton first attend as William's guest?
29 If William used his first name when king what would his title be?
30 Which was the first charity William became patron of?

Answers	**Pot Luck 95** *(see Quiz 206)*

1 Highland Spring. 2 Turkey. 3 Newcastle. 4 £12,100. 5 Bobby Robson. 6 Durian. 7 Danny Grewcock. 8 Nottm Forest. 9 Michael Johnson. 10 Clouds. 11 Horatio Nelson. 12 Forth & Clyde canal. 13 Les Misérables. 14 Dundrum Castle. 15 Look at Me. 16 St Petersburg. 17 Transformer. 18 27 points. 19 Houses of Parliament. 20 2012. 21 Swimming. 22 1994. 23 The Final Act. 24 118 minutes. 25 Crosswords. 26 141. 27 Films. 28 If Tomorrow Never Comes. 29 Teague Sparrow. 30 John Tusa.

Quiz 205 | US Presidents

Answers – page 677

1 Which US President did Guiseppe Zangara attempt to assassinate?
2 Who was vice president directly before Spiro Agnew?
3 What percentage of voters turned out when George W Bush was re-elected in 2004?
4 Which US President had the middle name Gamaliel?
5 On which day of the week was Kennedy assassinated?
6 Dean Acheson was US Secretary of State under which President?
7 Which US President was the heaviest?
8 In which year was George Bush Jnr first inaugurated as US President?
9 Who was the first assassin of a US President last century?
10 Who was the first US President to have been born in a hospital?
11 Which President conferred honorary US citizenship on Winston Churchill?
12 What did Ronald Reagan describe as a shining city on a hill?
13 Who said, "A radical is a man with both feet planted firmly in the air"?
14 In 1996 who was Bob Dole's Vice Presidential candidate?
15 Which state was crucial to the outcome of the 2000 election?
16 Who described Ronald Reagan's policies as "Voodoo economics"?
17 What type of car was Kennedy travelling in when he was shot?
18 Which aristocratic title is one of Jimmy Carter's Christian names?
19 Al Gore was Senator of which state before becoming Bill Clinton's Vice President in 1992?
20 How old was John F Kennedy's assassin?
21 Who was the Democrat before Clinton to be elected for a second term?
22 Whom was Richard Nixon named after?
23 Which 20th century US President shared his surname with a 20th century British PM?
24 What was the name of Kitty Kelley's biography of Jackie Kennedy Onassis?
25 Which president's campaign slogan was "Why not the best"?
26 Who became the 43rd US President?
27 Who is credited with the quote, "If you can't stand the heat get out of the kitchen"?
28 Who used the line "Randy, where's the rest of me?" as the title of an early autobiography?
29 The second and sixth President were father and son called what?
30 Which President came first – Andrew Jackson or Abraham Lincoln?

Answers	**Xmas Singles** *(see Quiz 203)*

1 Bruce Springsteen. **2** Teletubbies. **3** Shakin' Stevens. **4** Van Morrison. **5** Smith. **6** Mariah Carey. **7** Walking in the Air. **8** John Kettley. **9** Last Christmas. **10** Robson & Jerome. **11** Band Aid 20. **12** Mr Blobby. **13** Jon Bon Jovi. **14** Merry Xmas Everybody. **15** Paul McCartney. **16** Gloria Estefan. **17** I Wish It Could be Christmas Every Day. **18** The Spice Girls. **19** Bowie. **20** Let's Party. **21** Xmas in Blobbyland. **22** Jesus to a Child. **23** Cliff Richard. **24** Chris Rea. **25** Carpenters. **26** 1972. **27** Mad World. **28** Sounds of the Underground. **29** Westlife. **30** Nicole Kidman.

1 Which company producing bottled water set up a £1 million sponsorship deal with Andy Murray?
2 Where did Pope Benedict visit on his first trip to a mainly Muslim nation?
3 In January 2007 Bob Geldof received an honorary degree from which university?
4 To £500, how much did a "Beano" first edition fetch in a new auction record price in 2004?
5 Who was the last previous manager who was boss of England longer than Sven?
6 What was the name of the December 2006 typhoon that devastated central Philippines?
7 Who was sent off for punching Lawrence Dallaglio in a European Challenge Cup final?
8 Colwick Road goes past the soccer stadium of which soccer club?
9 Which man first simultaneously held world records at 200m and 400m?
10 Nephology is the scientific study of what?
11 Whose last words were reputed to be, "Thank God I have done my duty"?
12 On which Scottish waterway is the Falkirk Wheel?
13 Which musical was voted Britain's favourite in a 2005 Radio 2 poll?
14 What is the name of the 12th-century fortress built by John de Courcy in County Down?
15 What was "Ginger" Spice's first solo single after she left The Spice Girls?
16 In 1991 Vladimir Putin became Deputy Mayor of which city?
17 No 1 in the 1990s, "Perfect Day" first appeared on which early 1970s album?
18 How many points did Jonny Wilkinson score on his 2007 England comeback?
19 Brian Haw staged a long-running anti-war protest outside which building?
20 Which year marks the centenary of the death of polar explorer Capt. Scott?
21 Gregor Tait won Commonwealth medal in which sport?
22 In which year was the British National Lottery started?
23 What was the final instalment of "Prime Suspect" called?
24 How many minutes did Michael Owen play in Germany 2006?
25 What did Margery Ruth Crisp produce for many years?
26 How many countries ratified the Kyoto protocol?
27 Awarded a CBE in the 2007 honours, what does Peter Greenaway make?
28 What was the third solo No 1 for Ronan Keating?
29 Which pirate did Keith Richards play in a major movie?
30 Who was managing director of London's Barbican Centre from 1995 to 2007?

Answers	Princes William & Harry *(see Quiz 204)*

1 Saturday. 2 Arthur. 3 1st July 2007. 4 Geography. 5 Tom Parker Bowles. 6 6ft 3 inches. 7 Balmoral. 8 Queen Mother's. 9 Laura Lopes. 10 New Zealand. 11 Duke of Kent. 12 Wales. 13 St George's Chapel, Windsor. 14 Bryan Organ. 15 Art. 16 Lesotho. 17 Forget-Me-Not. 18 Blues and Royals. 19 Dr Gailey. 20 His dog. 21 22 years. 22 John. 23 Robert Runcie. 24 Aston Villa. 25 Ludgrove School and Eton College. 26 HSBC. 27 Welsh Rugby Union. 28 Sandhurst passing out parade. 29 William V. 30 Centrepoint.

Quiz 207 Mrs Thatcher

Answers – page 683

1 What was Margaret Thatcher's maiden name?
2 As a barrister what did she specialise in?
3 Harold Macmillan described Thatcher's privatisation policy as "selling the family" what?
4 What is the date of Margaret Thatcher's birthday?
5 Which Oxford college did she attend?
6 In which department was Thatcher's first shadow ministerial job?
7 The scrapping of which free school item brought controversy in June 1971?
8 Who was second to Thatcher in the Tory leadership battle in 1975?
9 Which Thatcher aide was killed in 1979 by a bomb in the House of Commons car park?
10 Whom did Thatcher quote on the steps of No 10 on becoming PM?
11 Whom did Thatcher describe as "A man we can do business with"?
12 Over what did she say, "Failure? The possibility does not exist"?
13 Mrs Thatcher was at which Brighton hotel that was bombed in October 1984?
14 Who signed the Anglo-Irish Agreement with Thatcher in 1985?
15 Which major transport project did she give the go-ahead to in January 1986?
16 Michael Heseltine and which other Cabinet member resigned over Westland?
17 How many different Labour leaders did Thatcher beat in General Elections?
18 What did Sir Alan Walters advise Thatcher on?
19 Who was her most famous Press Secretary?
20 Why could Mrs Thatcher have been called Lady Thatcher from 1990?
21 Who replaced Nigel Lawson as Chancellor?
22 Who first challenged Thatcher as party leader when she was PM?
23 What was Geoffrey Howe's Cabinet position when he resigned in 1990?
24 In which town was Margaret Thatcher born?
25 During which rally was Mark Thatcher lost in 1982?
26 In which metal was the Iron Lady's statue cast that was erected in the Houses of Parliament in February 2007?
27 Who did Geoffrey Howe back in the Heseltine/Hurd/Major contest?
28 For her life peerage she became Baroness Thatcher of where?
29 Which sportsman described Thatcher as "nice and cuddly" when he met her?
30 Which seat did Thatcher fight before fighting, and winning Finchley?

Answers	**UK Politics** *(see Quiz 209)*

1 Thomas Clarke. 2 2005. 3 Dennis Skinner. 4 1983. 5 One (Margaret Thatcher).
6 Crawley. 7 Livingston. 8 Green Party. 9 Asquith. 10 Tyneside North. 11
Normanton. 12 Harold Wilson. 13 Cheadle. 14 28%. 15 Below the Parapet. 16
John Bercow (Buckingham). 17 Brighton. 18 90 years. 19 59%. 20 Cecil Parkinson.
21 Francis Elliott & James Hanning. 22 Elspeth. 23 Tatton. 24 John Major. 25
Harold Wilson's. 26 Aldershot. 27 1992. 28 13,517,911 voters. 29 Seven. 30
David Trimble.

1 Who described James Bond as "a blunt instrument wielded by a government department"?

2 How many official Bond films had been made before Daniel Craig took over?

3 Which Bond film did Deborah Kerr appear in?

4 Who played Pussy Galore in "Goldfinger"?

5 What was the given first name of Bond producer Cubby Broccoli?

6 Which movie's villain was Xenia Onatopp?

7 Which movie first had the toothpaste with plastic explosives?

8 Which was the first Bond movie not to have an action sequence before the credits?

9 In which movie did Rowan Atkinson make his big-screen debut?

10 On which island does Dr No hold Bond and Honeychile Rider?

11 Which 007 backed the restaurant chain the Spy House?

12 Which movie had the electro-magnetic watch with the spinning blade?

13 To fifteen minutes, how long does "You Only Live Twice" last?

14 Which golf course featured in "Goldfinger"?

15 What was the most successful Bond film of the 70s and 80s in terms of cinema admissions?

16 Which character was played by Harold Sakata?

17 May Day was the Bond girl in which film?

18 In the films what replaced the Soviet organisation Smersh which existed in the books?

19 What was Goldfinger's first name?

20 In which movie did Blofeld kidnap US and USSR spaceships to try and gain planetary control?

21 Which quinine-flavoured aperitif did James Bond advocate for a Martini?

22 What is the name of the villain in the movie that preceded "The World is Not Enough"?

23 What was "GoldenEye" named after?

24 What is the motto of the villain in "Tomorrow Never Dies"?

25 What was the last film where Lois Maxwell played Miss Moneypenny?

26 Which film was Roger Moore's last as Bond?

27 Which artists were first to have a US No 1 with a Bond theme?

28 What was the first Bond book that Fleming wrote?

29 In which movie did the silver Aston Martin DB5 appear?

30 Employed by Hugo Drax, who was Dr Holly Goodhead actually working for?

Answers | **Pot Luck 96** *(see Quiz 210)*

1 12. 2 Late blight (potato crops). 3 16. 4 University College hospital. 5 Computer graphics. 6 Back to Black. 7 Willie Pep. 8 2010. 9 Million Dollar Baby. 10 38%. 11 I'll Stand by You. 12 116-year-old. 13 Matt Lucas. 14 Speed skating. 15 Italy. 16 John Malkovich. 17 The Mighty Quinn. 18 Nick Barmby. 19 Diner's Club. 20 Quinten Hann. 21 Sir Nicholas Stern. 22 Gary Barlow. 23 Bill Haley. 24 Five. 25 Stern. 26 Claire Connor. 27 2015. 28 Three. 29 Watford. 30 Peter Phillips.

1 Which Labour MP had the largest majority after 2005's election?
2 In which year did John Major become Sir John Major?
3 Who had a larger majority in 2005 – Gordon Brown or Dennis Skinner?
4 In which year did Tony Blair first become an MP?
5 How many PMs were in office for an entire decade in the last century?
6 Which constituency recorded the smallest majority for an MP in 2005?
7 Which constituency did the late Robin Cook represent?
8 Which political party has had its offices situated at 1a Waterloo Road, London?
9 Alphabetically speaking which PM came first in the 20th century?
10 Which constituency returned Steven Byers to parliament?
11 Ed Balls won which seat to enter parliament?
12 Which ex-PM became Baron of Rievaulx when he was made a peer?
13 Which constituency held the first by-election after the 2005 UK general election?
14 To five, what percentage of Labour MPs were women after 2005's election?
15 What was the name of the book Carol Thatcher wrote about her father?
16 Which Tory MP had the greatest majority at the 2005 general election?
17 Which English place has the constituencies Kemptown and Pavilion?
18 How old was Robert Leakey, the oldest candidate in 2005's election?
19 What percentage of the electorate turned out for the 2001 general election?
20 Who was Tory Party Chairman when Mrs Thatcher won her second term in office?
21 Who wrote "Cameron, the Rise of the New Conservative"?
22 What is the first name of the wife of the Lib Dem leader who succeeded Charles Kennedy?
23 Which seat did former news reader Martin Bell win from Neil Hamilton?
24 Arabella Warburton was PA to which Prime Minister?
25 Whose resignation Honours List was known as the Lavender List?
26 Alphabetically, which constituency comes first in England?
27 In which year did Margaret Thatcher leave parliament as an MP?
28 To half a million, how many people voted Labour as the party took power in 1997?
29 Without hyphenated names, how many Smiths were MPs after the 2005 election?
30 Which well-known political figure lost his seat at Upper Bann in 2005?

Answers	Mrs Thatcher (see Quiz 197)

1 Roberts. 2 Taxation law. 3 Silver. 4 13th October. 5 Somerville. 6 Transport. 7 Milk. 8 William Whitelaw. 9 Airey Neave. 10 St Francis of Assisi. 11 Gorbachev. 12 Falklands invasion. 13 Grand Hotel. 14 Dr Garret FitzGerald. 15 Channel Tunnel. 16 Leon Brittan. 17 Three. 18 Economic affairs. 19 Bernard Ingham. 20 Denis Thatcher was knighted. 21 John Major. 22 Sir Anthony Mayer. 23 Deputy Prime Minister. 24 Grantham. 25 Paris Dakar. 26 Bronze. 27 Heseltine. 28 Kesteven. 29 Paul Gascoigne. 30 Dartford.

1 The Rugby World Cup of 2007 was based in how many cities?
2 Phytophthora infestans is reckoned to cost farming some £50m a year – what is it?
3 How many teams played in the 2007 Cricket World Cup finals?
4 At which London hospital did Alexander Litvinenko die in November 2006?
5 Ivan Sutherland is associated with the development of what?
6 "Rehab" and "Just Friends" appeared on which Amy Winehouse album?
7 Which six-times-married featherweight champion boxer died in November 2006, aged 84?
8 Which year marks the 150th anniversary of golf's Open?
9 Which 2004 movie was adapted from "Rope Burns", a book by FX Toole?
10 Library book borrowing fell by how many per cent from 1995 to 2004?
11 What was the second No 1 single for Girls Aloud?
12 How old was the world's oldest woman Elizabeth Bolden when she died in 2006?
13 Kevin McGee shared a civil partnership ceremony with which celeb in December 2006?
14 Enrico Fabris won gold in which Olympic event in February 2006?
15 King Juan Carlos of Spain was born in which country?
16 Who has the double role in "Mary Reilly", based on "Dr Jekyll & Mr Hyde"?
17 Which No 1 has the lines, "Come all without, Come all within"?
18 Which Nick scored in Sven Goran Eriksson's first game in charge for England?
19 Which credit card – first used in restaurants – did Frank McNamara create?
20 Which Australian snooker player was found guilty of match fixing in February 2006?
21 Which ex-World Bank chief economist produced a 2006 report on climate change?
22 Which Take That singer shares a birthday with astronaut Buzz Aldrin?
23 Which major US rock singer died the month before the first London Marathon?
24 How many vessels did the Royal Navy lose in the Falklands War?
25 In which magazine were the fictitious Hitler Diaries published in the 1980s?
26 Who captained English ladies to their cricket series triumph over Australia in 2005?
27 Which year celebrates 50 years since Radio Caroline was established?
28 How many of Joseph Kennedy's sons became Senators?
29 Henrik Larsson first scored in the Premiership against which team?
30 In order of succession, who is nearer to the throne – Peter Phillips or Viscount Linley?

Answers | **James Bond** (see Quiz 208)

1 Ian Fleming. 2 20. 3 Casino Royale. 4 Honor Blackman. 5 Albert. 6 Goldeneye. 7 Licence to Kill. 8 Dr No. 9 Never Say Never Again. 10 Crab Key Island. 11 George Lazenby. 12 Live and Let Die. 13 117 minutes. 14 Stoke Poges. 15 Thunderball. 16 Oddjob. 17 A View to a Kill. 18 Spectre. 19 Auric. 20 You Only Live Twice. 21 Kina Lillet. 22 Carver. 23 Ian Fleming's home in Jamaica. 24 No news is bad news. 25 A View to a Kill. 26 A View to a Kill. 27 Duran Duran. 28 Casino Royale. 29 Goldfinger. 30 CIA.

1 Which great rock guitarist had a daughter named Dandelion?
2 In which London street is there a blue plaque denoting where Jimi Hendrix lived?
3 Peter Buck is in which mega rock band?
4 What did Brian May study at university?
5 Who inspired Eric Clapton to write "Layla"?
6 Which Roy guested on Pink Floyd's "Wish You were Here"?
7 Who made the 60s album "The Twang's the Thang"?
8 Carlos Santa was born in which country?
9 Who made the album "Outrider" in 1988?
10 What was the name of BB King's beloved Gibson guitar?
11 Who awarded Mark Knopfler an honorary music doctorate in 1993?
12 Which heavy metal guitarist said "if it's too loud you're too old"?
13 Which city did the blues guitarist Gary Moore come from?
14 What was Eric Clapton's No 1 album of 1994?
15 Which guitarist's first two names were Brian Robson?
16 Which album did Mark Knopfler release with Chet Atkins in 1990?
17 Which guitarist did Ron Wood replace in The Rolling Stones?
18 Who duetted on "Wonderful Land" on the 1993 "Heart Beat" album?
19 Which British guitarist was instrumental in reuniting the Everly Brothers in the 80s?
20 "Guitar Boogie Shuffle" in 1959 was the only Top Ten hit for which guitarist?
21 Which group included guitarists John Williams and Kevin Peek?
22 What did Brian May reputedly make his first guitar from?
23 What type of guitar did Jimi Hendrix use on the "Are You Experienced?" album?
24 Which two acts took "Cavatina" the theme from "The Deer Hunter" into the Top Ten?
25 Where did Jimi Hendrix take part in a fund-raising "Guitar In" in 1967?
26 Whose career history album was called "Crossroads"?
27 What did Brian May play at the end of the "Concert for Life" at Wembley in 1992?
28 What was Jeff Beck's debut solo album called?
29 What honour did Eric Clapton receive in January 1995?
30 What was the debut album by the Brian May Band?

Answers	**The Last Round** *(see Quiz 215)*

1 Japan. 2 Arsenal. 3 22 months. 4 David Owen. 5 Casino Royale. 6 Handwriting.
7 Christian Furr. 8 Albatross. 9 Post Office Tower. 10 Africa. 11 Lake Baikal. 12 18
miles. 13 Strait/Straight. 14 Lake Windermere. 15 Ernst Happel Stadion, Vienna. 16 960.
17 William Huskisson. 18 Neil Broad. 19 Gothenburg. 20 1991. 21 Peter Sallis. 22
James Callaghan. 23 Shivnarine Chanderpaul. 24 Conakry. 25 Zubin Mehta. 26 1989.
27 101. 28 (London) Wasps. 29 1979. 30 North Antrim.

1 Who said he would pursue, "the ultimate goal of ending tyranny in our world"?
2 Who was the first Football Writers' Association player of the year for three times?
3 Keeper Ben Foster made his England debut against which side?
4 In which horror movie did Johnny Depp make his debut?
5 Anna Wintour had been in charge of US and UK editions of which glossy mag?
6 "Harry Potter and the Prisoner of Azkaban" featured which comedian as a shrunken head?
7 English-born Pamela Harriman became US Ambassador to where?
8 Which TV programme was recorded at "Farthings" a cottage in Selsey, Sussex?
9 In which year did a Scot first appear on an English bank note?
10 Hamid Karzai became president in the first free elections in which country?
11 How many England players turned out for all five Tests in Australia 2006–07?
12 Who directed "Miss Potter"?
13 Which cartoonist produced the book "My Vision for a New You"?
14 Tom Koenigs was the diplomat heading a UN mission in which country?
15 Which Beatles No 1 contains the line, "let it out and let it in"?
16 In which state is "Halloween" set?
17 Who played King Theoden of Rohan in the last two parts of the "Lord of the Rings" trilogy?
18 Who was Man Utd's captain in the 1999 European Champions Cup Final?
19 Who was the first black American to win the Nobel Peace prize?
20 England's Peter Nicol won three successive Commonwealth Games golds in which sport?
21 Who wrote the book on which Hitchcock's first Oscar-winning Hollywood film was based?
22 Which British Royals married the year that Spain legalised divorce?
23 When President, Ronald Reagan was shot outside which hotel?
24 Zamora, Konchesky and who else had West Ham penalties saved in 2006's FA Cup Final?
25 Who wrote the novel "Second Honeymoon"?
26 Owen Arthur has been Prime Minister of which Comonwealth country?
27 In which European city did Hannibal Lecter live with his uncle?
28 Who was born first – David Cassidy or Eva Cassidy?
29 Sajid Mahmood made his Test debut in 2006 against which country?
30 Charles Duelfer's report of October 2004 dealt with affairs in which country?

Answers | **Pot Luck 98** *(see Quiz 214)*

1 George Best. 2 Bracciano. 3 December 2002. 4 150,000. 5 White Hart Lane (vs. Holland). 6 Backstreet Boys. 7 Mitrokhin commission. 8 Maryland. 9 His Latest Flame. 10 17 years. 11 Australia. 12 Ipswich. 13 12 players. 14 Mervyn King. 15 Swimming (freestyle). 16 Mead Publications. 17 Dirk Benedict. 18 Germany. 19 The Ballad of John & Yoko. 20 Nostromo. 21 2009. 22 The Palace. 23 Joseph. 24 Damien Hirst. 25 John Hume. 26 The Shining. 27 John Kettley (2002). 28 Jamaica. 29 Geri Halliwell. 30 Birmingham.

1 His verse autobiography was called "Summoned by" what?
2 The poems "Croydon" and "Westgate on Sea" were in which anthology?
3 John Betjeman succeeded which Poet Laureate?
4 Which poem starts, "She died in the upstairs bedroom"?
5 What was the occupation of Betjeman's father?
6 In which decade was "A Nip in the Air" published?
7 Which Oxford University college did he attend?
8 Where does Betjeman urge the "friendly bombs" to fall?
9 Which popular guide book series did he work on?
10 "I made hay" begins which poem?
11 In which year was Betjeman knighted?
12 Which poem with the name of a county, starts, "How did the Devil come?"?
13 What did he lose from the family name during the First World War?
14 In which year did John Betjeman become Poet Laureate?
15 Whom did Betjeman marry?
16 In which decade did "A Few Late Flowering Chrysanthemums" appear?
17 Which London Underground line featured in a programme made for the BBC?
18 Which poem is "To Randolph Churchill, but not about him"?
19 Who was the longest-serving Poet Laureate of the last century?
20 Which place name ends the line, "Dear, Mary Wilson, this is ____"?
21 In which year did Betjeman die?
22 Which anthology was published in the swinging 60s?
23 What was the name of his daughter born in the 1940s?
24 Who was "burnished by Aldershot sun"?
25 He wrote and did editorial work for which magazine concerned with architecture?
26 "The Costa Blanca" and "Aldershot Crematorium" appear in which collection?
27 Who followed John Betjeman as Poet Laureate?
28 What kind of marmalade is named in "Myfanwy"?
29 Betjeman died in which place?
30 Which poem has the line, "He such a thumping crook"?

1 A limited edition bank note issued in November 2006 featured which person?
2 Katie Holmes and Tom Cruise married in which castle in Italy?
3 When was the BT monopoly of directory enquiry service calls deregulated?
4 Around how many customers did Farepak have at the time of its 2006 collapse?
5 At which ground did Sven Goran Eriksson's England first lose a game?
6 Brian Littrell was in which best-selling boy band?
7 Which commission investigated KGB infiltration in the Italian government?
8 In which state does the action of "The Blair Witch Project" take place?
9 What was on the other side of Elvis' original release of "Little Sister"?
10 Mirza Tahir Hussain spent how many years on death row before his November 2006 pardon?
11 Which country were chosen to host cricket's 2015 World Cup?
12 Gemma Adams and Tania Nicol were victims murdered near which town?
13 How many players did Australia use in the 2006–07 Ashes series?
14 Which Mervyn was Governor of the Bank of England in 2007?
15 Caitlin McClatchey won Commonwealth Gold in which sport?
16 What is the name of the magazine company featured in TV's "Ugly Betty"?
17 Which former "A-Team" actor featured in "Celebrity Big Brother" in 2007?
18 Henrik Larsson missed a penalty against which team in Germany 2006?
19 Which No 1 contained the line, "They're going to crucify me"?
20 What name links a Joseph Conrad novel and the craft in the movie "Alien"?
21 Which year will be the centenary of when Joan of Arc became a Saint?
22 At which West End theatre did "The Woman In White" open?
23 Which middle name is shared by David Beckham and Kevin Keegan?
24 Whose artistic works include "Away from the Flock"?
25 Who shared the 1998 Nobel Peace Prize with David Trimble?
26 In which Jack Nicholson movie did Danny have an imaginary friend called Tony?
27 Who was 50 first – John Kettley, Tony Blair or Richard Madeley?
28 Which country did Asafa Powell run for?
29 Who was the first UK female to have four solo No 1 hit singles?
30 The Rt Rev. David Urquhart became Bishop of where in November 2006?

1 What country does the "no-brand" fashion label Uniqlo come from?
2 Which is the only English football club to have lost European Cup, European Cup-Winners' Cup and UEFA Cup finals?
3 How long is the average gestation period of a cow elephant?
4 Who joined Roy Jenkins, Bill Rodgers and Shirley Williams as the Social Democrats' "Gang of Four"?
5 Which was the first James Bond novel by Ian Fleming to be published (in 1953)?
6 Graphology is the study of what?
7 Which artist did Queen Elizabeth choose to paint her official portrait in 2004?
8 Which bird is killed in Samuel Taylor Coleridge's poem "The Rime of the Ancient Mariner"?
9 What was London's Telecom Tower known as when it opened in the 1960s?
10 The Cape of Good Hope is off which continent's southern tip?
11 Which is the world's deepest lake?
12 How far did Jade Goody run in the 2006 London Marathon despite not training?
13 Which homonyms could be a narrow sea lane or direct?
14 Which is England's largest and deepest lake?
15 Which stadium was chosen to host the final of the Euro 2008 tournament?
16 How many farthings were there in £1?
17 Which politician was the first rail fatality, killed under the wheels of Stephenson's "Rocket" in 1830?
18 Who partnered Tim Henman to win the silver medal in the 1996 Olympic tennis men's doubles?
19 Near which Swedish city were did Volvo open its first production line?
20 When did Nicky Clarke open his first hairdressing salon in London?
21 Who was the voice of Wallace in Nick Park's "Wallace & Gromit" series?
22 Who was the last Labour Prime Minister to lose a 20th century General Election?
23 Who was the highest scorer in the 2007 England v West Indies Test series?
24 What is the capital of Guinea?
25 Who conducted the Three Tenors at their first concert together at Rome in July 1990?
26 In what year did "The Marchioness" sink, killing 51 people, in the River Thames?
27 How old was Queen Elizabeth the Queen Mother when she died?
28 Which rugby union club won its second Heineken European Cup in 2007?
29 In what year was former President of Pakistan Zulfiqar Ali Bhutto executed?
30 Which parliamentary constituency has Revd Ian Paisley represented since 1970?

Answers	John Betjeman *(see Quiz 213)*

1 Bells. 2 Mount Zion. 3 Cecil Day-Lewis. 4 Death in Leamington. 5 Cabinet maker. 6 1970s. 7 Magdalen College. 8 On Slough. 9 Shell Guides. 10 The Last Laugh. 11 1969. 12 Norfolk. 13 Letter n (was Betjemann). 14 1972. 15 Penelope Chetwode. 16 1950s. 17 Metropolitan. 18 The Wykehamist. 19 John Masefield. 20 Diss. 21 1984. 22 High and Low. 23 Candida. 24 Joan Hunter Dunn. 25 Architectural Review. 26 A Nip in the Air. 27 Ted Hughes. 28 Robertson's. 29 Trebetherick. 30 In a Bath Teashop.

How to Set Up Your Own
Pub Quiz

It isn't easy, get that right from the start. This isn't going to be easy. Think instead of words like "difficult", "taxing", "infuriating". Consider yourself with damp palms and a dry throat and then, when you have concentrated on that, put it out of your mind and think of the recognition you will receive down the local, imagine all the regulars lifting you high upon their shoulders dancing and weaving their way around the pub. It won't help but it's good to dream every once in a while.

What you will need:

- A good selection of Biros (never be tempted to give your own pen up, not even to family members)
- A copy of *The Biggest Pub Quiz Book Ever! 2*
- A set of answer sheets photocopied from the back of the book
- A good speaking voice and possibly a microphone and an amp
- A pub
- At least one pint inside you
- At least one more on your table
- A table

What to do:

Choose your local to start with; there is no need to get halfway through your first quiz and decide you weren't cut out for all this and then find yourself in the roughest pub in Christendom 30 miles and a long run from home.

Chat it through with the landlord and agree on whether you will be charging or not; if you don't then there is little chance of a prize for the winners other than a free pint each and this is obviously at the landlord's discretion – if you pack his pub to bursting then five free pints won't worry him, but if it's only you and a couple of others then he may be less than unwilling, as publicans tend to be. If you decide on an entry payment keep it reasonable; you don't want to take the fun out of the quiz; some people will be well aware that they have very little hope of winning and will be reluctant to celebrate the fact by mortgaging their house.

Once location and prize are all sorted then advertising the event is paramount. Get people's attention, sell, sell, sell or, alternatively, stick up a gaudy-looking poster on the door of the bogs. Be sure to specify all the details, time, prize and so on – remember you are selling to people whose tiny attention span is being whittled down to nothing by alcohol.

After this it is time for the big night. If you are holding the event in the "snug" which seats ten or so you can rely on your voice, if not you should get hold of a good microphone and an amplifier so that you can boom out your questions and enunciate the length and breadth of the pub (once again, clear this with the landlord and don't let liquid anywhere near the electrical equipment). Make sure to practise, and get comfortable with the sound of your own voice and relax as much as possible, try not to rely on alcohol too much or "round one" will be followed by "rown' too" which will eventually give way to "runfree". Relax your voice so that you can handle any queries from the teams, and any venomous abuse from the "lively" bar area.

When you enter the pub make sure you take everything listed above. Also, make sure you have a set of tie-break questions and that you instruct everybody who is taking part as to the rules – and be firm. It will only upset people if you start handing out impromptu solutions, and let's face it the wisdom of Solomon is not needed when you are talking pub quiz rules; "no cheating" is a perfectly healthy stance to start with.

Finally, keep the teams to a maximum of five members, hand out your answer papers and pens and, when everybody is good and settled, start the quiz. It might not be easy and it might not propel you to international stardom or pay for a life of luxury but you will enjoy yourself. No, really.

1 _____

2 _____

3 _____

4 _____

5 _____

6 _____

7 _____

8 _____

9 _____

10 _____

11 _____

12 _____

13 _____

14 _____

15 _____

16 _____

17 _____

18 _____

19 _____

20 _____

21 _____

22 _____

23 _____

24 _____

25 _____

26 _____

27 _____

28 _____

29 _____

30 _____

ANSWERS

1 _____

2 _____

3 _____

4 _____

5 _____

6 _____

7 _____

8 _____

9 _____

10 _____

11 _____

12 _____

13 _____

14 _____

15 _____

16 _____

17 _____

18 _____

19 _____

20 _____

21 _____

22 _____

23 _____

24 _____

25 _____

26 _____

27 _____

28 _____

29 _____

30 _____

ANSWERS

1 _____	16 _____
2 _____	17 _____
3 _____	18 _____
4 _____	19 _____
5 _____	20 _____
6 _____	21 _____
7 _____	22 _____
8 _____	23 _____
9 _____	24 _____
10 _____	25 _____
11 _____	26 _____
12 _____	27 _____
13 _____	28 _____
14 _____	29 _____
15 _____	30 _____

ANSWERS

1 _____		16 _____	
2 _____		17 _____	
3 _____		18 _____	
4 _____		19 _____	
5 _____		20 _____	
6 _____		21 _____	
7 _____		22 _____	
8 _____		23 _____	
9 _____		24 _____	
10 _____		25 _____	
11 _____		26 _____	
12 _____		27 _____	
13 _____		28 _____	
14 _____		29 _____	
15 _____		30 _____	

ANSWERS

1 _____

2 _____

3 _____

4 _____

5 _____

6 _____

7 _____

8 _____

9 _____

10 _____

11 _____

12 _____

13 _____

14 _____

15 _____

16 _____

17 _____

18 _____

19 _____

20 _____

21 _____

22 _____

23 _____

24 _____

25 _____

26 _____

27 _____

28 _____

29 _____

30 _____

ANSWERS

Level 2

1 _____	16 _____
2 _____	17 _____
3 _____	18 _____
4 _____	19 _____
5 _____	20 _____
6 _____	21 _____
7 _____	22 _____
8 _____	23 _____
9 _____	24 _____
10 _____	25 _____
11 _____	26 _____
12 _____	27 _____
13 _____	28 _____
14 _____	29 _____
15 _____	30 _____

ANSWERS

1 _____

2 _____

3 _____

4 _____

5 _____

6 _____

7 _____

8 _____

9 _____

10 _____

11 _____

12 _____

13 _____

14 _____

15 _____

16 _____

17 _____

18 _____

19 _____

20 _____

21 _____

22 _____

23 _____

24 _____

25 _____

26 _____

27 _____

28 _____

29 _____

30 _____

ANSWERS

Level 2

1 _____

2 _____

3 _____

4 _____

5 _____

6 _____

7 _____

8 _____

9 _____

10 _____

11 _____

12 _____

13 _____

14 _____

15 _____

16 _____

17 _____

18 _____

19 _____

20 _____

21 _____

22 _____

23 _____

24 _____

25 _____

26 _____

27 _____

28 _____

29 _____

30 _____

ANSWERS

1 _____   16 _____

2 _____   17 _____

3 _____   18 _____

4 _____   19 _____

5 _____   20 _____

6 _____   21 _____

7 _____   22 _____

8 _____   23 _____

9 _____   24 _____

10 _____   25 _____

11 _____   26 _____

12 _____   27 _____

13 _____   28 _____

14 _____   29 _____

15 _____   30 _____

ANSWERS

1 _____

2 _____

3 _____

4 _____

5 _____

6 _____

7 _____

8 _____

9 _____

10 _____

11 _____

12 _____

13 _____

14 _____

15 _____

16 _____

17 _____

18 _____

19 _____

20 _____

21 _____

22 _____

23 _____

24 _____

25 _____

26 _____

27 _____

28 _____

29 _____

30 _____

ANSWERS

1 _____

2 _____

3 _____

4 _____

5 _____

6 _____

7 _____

8 _____

9 _____

10 _____

11 _____

12 _____

13 _____

14 _____

15 _____

16 _____

17 _____

18 _____

19 _____

20 _____

21 _____

22 _____

23 _____

24 _____

25 _____

26 _____

27 _____

28 _____

29 _____

30 _____